Historical Dictionary
of the
Modern Olympic
Movement

Historical Dictionary
of the
Modern
Olympic Movement

EDITED BY
John E. Findling
and Kimberly D. Pelle

GREENWOOD PRESS
WESTPORT, CONNECTICUT • LONDON

Library of Congress Cataloging-in-Publication Data

Historical dictionary of the modern Olympic movement / edited by John
    E. Findling and Kimberly D. Pelle.
        p.   cm.
    Includes bibliographical references and index.
    ISBN 0–313–28477–6 (alk. paper)
      1. Olympics—History—Encyclopedias.   I. Findling, John E.
    II. Pelle, Kimberly D.
    GV721.5.H546   1996
    796.48—dc20   95–569

British Library Cataloguing in Publication Data is available.

Copyright © 1996 by John E. Findling and Kimberly D. Pelle

All rights reserved. No portion of this book may be
reproduced, by any process or technique, without the
express written consent of the publisher.

Library of Congress Catalog Card Number: 95–569
ISBN: 0–313–28477–6

First published in 1996

Greenwood Press, 88 Post Road West, Westport, CT 06881
An imprint of Greenwood Publishing Group, Inc.

Printed in the United States of America

The paper used in this book complies with the
Permanent Paper Standard issued by the National
Information Standards Organization (Z39.48–1984).

10 9 8 7 6 5 4 3 2 1

FOR
Barbara and Art
Janet and Fred

CONTENTS

Part II   The Winter Games

PREFACE

This book originated with a suggestion from our editor, Cynthia Harris, at Greenwood Publishing, who sought a reference book on the Olympics that was similar in format and style to our *Historical Dictionary of World's Fairs and Expositions, 1851–1988* (Greenwood Press, 1990). There have been many reference books published about the Olympic Games, but virtually all of them emphasize the athletic achievements of top performers at the Games: the medal winners; the world record times, distances, and weights; and the nations whose athletes have performed the best.

This book deals instead with the historical context in which the modern Olympic Games have taken place. We asked the contributing authors to emphasize such matters as site selection and development, political questions or controversies, collateral events, programmatic changes, and political and economic consequences, while keeping their discussion of winners and losers to a minimum. Each author has also written a substantial bibliographical essay to guide interested readers to the best primary and secondary sources on each Games, and the book concludes with an extensive general bibliography that covers works of a topical or biographical nature, or works that touch on several different Games. Other scholars have contributed the appendixes, which cover the International Olympic Committee and its seven presidents, the U.S. Olympic Committee, and Olympic documentary and feature films.

Many people have helped us in the preparation of this book. Bob Barney and Bob Barnett gave us some valuable suggestions as we began the project, and Bob and Ashleigh Barney were genial hosts on a trip to the Centre for Olympic Studies in London, Ontario. The library staff at Indiana University Southeast (IUS) was, as always, very helpful in facilitating interlibrary loan requests and helping us in many other ways. The office staff of the Division of Social Sciences at IUS, especially Brigette Colligan, assisted with word processing and other clerical chores, often on short notice, and we thank them. Brook Dutko handled some important word processing duties, and Lee Bruce dug out some elusive bibliographical information. The computer wizards at IUS, notably Kevin Hostetler, saved us much grief with their ability to turn disks full of mysterious symbols into readable Wordperfect.

We are also grateful to many individuals who helped us find much of the information contained in this book. Maynard Brichford and his staff at the University of Illinois Archives facilitated our trip into the massive Avery Brundage Collection. Gisela Terrell introduced us to the Olympic material at the National Track and Field Hall of Fame Historical Research Library at Butler University in Indianapolis. Cindy Slater of the U.S. Olympic Committee provided a careful description of that organization's archival holdings, as did Wayne Wilson of the Amateur Athletic Foundation in Los Angeles. Max Howell of the University of Queensland put us in touch with various Australian sport history archives and libraries, and Greg Blood and Melissa Petherbridge graciously responded to our requests for information. We are grateful to the staffs of the Centre for Olympic Studies and the main library at the University of Western Ontario in London for making sure we saw all of their holdings.

We also thank Karel Wendl of the International Olympic Committee's research center for making it possible to examine the many materials kept at its library and archives in Lausanne. Thanks to Michele Veillard, the archivist; Denis Echard and Laura Davies, the editor and assistant editor, respectively, of *Olympic Review;* Jean-François Pahud, the curator of the Olympic Museum; Alexandra Leclef Mandl, director of the photographic department; and Fekrou Kidane, *chef du cabinet* of the IOC. They all shared their time and knowledge with us. We thank as well Swantje Scharenberg at the Institut fur Sport-Wissenschaften, Georg-August-Universität, Göttingen; Karl Lennartz, Carl-Diem-Institut, Cologne; and Ulrike Merke, Sportbibliothek, Technische Universitat, Munich, for their assistance.

Finally, Joe Arbena, Bruce Kidd, Nancy Bouchier, Douglas Brown, Gordon MacDonald, Scott Martyn, Norm Baker, James Riordan, Yvonne Condon, and Allen Guttmann provided various kinds of help or encouragement along the way, and we thank them. Our spouses, Carol Findling and Jay Pelle, and our children bore our joys and frustrations willingly; their part in bringing this project to completion was, as always, very important.

John E. Findling
Kimberly D. Pelle

INTRODUCTION

Within the Olympic idea there inevitably develops [a] . . . conflict of the past with the future and of reality with the ideal

—Carl Diem

The Olympic Games are the foremost sporting event in the world, attracting young men and women to compete together in a spirit of honor and fellowship. Athletes consider the Games to be special because of the idealism attached to them and the moral code that is demanded of them as competitors. These qualities make them different from world championships, though both events seek to discover and acclaim the best in their field of endeavor. The claim of Pierre de Coubertin, the creator of the modern Olympic Games, that it is as important to take part as it is to win and that the athletes should compete in an honorable gathering respecting the rules of sport and the efforts of others, is more than a popular cliché; it is a heroic ideal accepted by most Olympians. Indeed it is this specialness of the event that provides much of its public appeal and has guaranteed its growth from a quaint idea of the 1890s to a major world event every four years. John MacAloon, writing of Coubertin and the origins of the modern Olympic Games, suggested that the Games "have grown from a fin-de-siècle curiosity of regional interest to an international cultural [and sporting] performance of global proportion."

The first "Games of the modern era," those held in Athens in 1896, were contested by only 300 athletes from eleven countries. In contrast, the Olympic Games in Sydney in the year 2000 will attract 10,000 athletes from nearly 200 countries. There will be 15,000 media representatives in Australia to cover the Games, which will be viewed on television by half the world's population.

Television rights to the Olympics will cost nearly $700 million, and the estimated cost of the Games will be $3 billion. The Olympic Games have become, in a century, "the Mount Everest of sport," as John Lucas describes them.

THE IDEAL VERSUS THE REALITY

Coubertin believed that the Games would encourage a community among athletes that would overshadow their national differences:

To ask the peoples of the world to love one another . . . is childishness. [But] to ask them to respect one another is not in the least utopian. [However] in order to respect one another it is first necessary to know one another . . . through sport.

The Games, he argued, would also be a display of physical and moral excellence that would be an inspiration to the young and aspiring. The fact that the Olympic Games are of such importance would indicate that Coubertin was successful.

The twentieth-century growth and conduct of the Olympic Games, however, has not been without criticism. Indeed the Games have been criticized from the very beginning. A colleague (but later antagonist) of Coubertin, Georges Herbert, suggested in a letter in 1911 to the *renovateur* of the Games that he was "deluding" himself "as to their importance." They are, he asserted, "exclusively . . . [an] exhibition of international athletes"—nothing more, that is, than another international contest. Herbert argued that there was nothing educational about them, nothing of a higher moral order that would appeal to the general populace, as Coubertin had claimed. Olympic historian John Lucas quite rightly adjudges that by 1911, the Games had "ceased to be 'games' or an ideal place in which to 'play.' " Nevertheless, they were seen still as "arenas of honor"; Herbert was incorrect in his assessment that they would not appeal to the general public. His letter to Coubertin was written on the eve of the 1912 Games in Stockholm, where more than 2,500 athletes representing twenty-eight countries competed. If any further evidence of their appeal was needed, the resumption of the Olympics after the Great War (1914–1918) attested to their resilience and perceived significance.

Their significance, of course, was viewed differently depending on whether one was an athlete or a politician. The 1936 Games in Berlin confirmed the political value of the Olympics, but they were not the first to be used in this way. Excellence in both organization and athletic performance had become a measure of national status in the Olympic Games conducted in Amsterdam (1928) and Los Angeles (1932), as well as Berlin. R. M. Goodhue is correct in his assertion that "one cannot detach 1936 from the previous Olympic Games. [These Games] were not an aberration. The conditions that made 1936 possible were apparent in the development of the Games from 1900 to 1932."

Despite the significance of the Games, however, to those who would use them to confirm their identity or indicate their development, athletes have persisted in viewing them in the idealistic light of their founder. They were arenas of honor, contests with dignity. Without really being aware of it, the athletes of the twentieth century endorse the values of the classical era. The Greeks called their games *agones,* from which our word *agony* stems. It is the anguish of the struggle that reveals the essence of the person in the sporting contest.

Still, despite the value of the Games to contemporary athletes and their appeal to those who would witness the human struggle in the world's greatest arena, criticism of the Games continues, especially when an incident creates controversy and calls into question the idealism that is meant to suffuse the Olympic contests. This is the contradiction of the Games—their agony and ecstasy. The popularity and growth of the modern Olympic Games, with their espoused idealism, have been both their strength and their weakness. There is no doubting the appeal of the Games and the words of Coubertin. The language of the Olympic philosophy grips the heart and stirs the soul—certainly of those who believe in the heroic nature of sport. Olympic words and phrases suggest a value for sport contests beyond simple exercise, and this sentiment is the source of the power of the idealistic Olympic message. Coubertin explained Olympism thus:

The Olympic idea . . . is a strong physical culture based in part on the spirit of chivalry . . . [which we call] ''fair play'' . . . a love of sport for itself, for its high educative value, for the pursuit of human perfection.

The problem for the Olympic movement has been that any controversial incidents that occur during them are counterpoised against the idealistic words of Coubertin and the keepers of the flame who followed him. Ideological difference, racism, gender issues, illicit behavior including the use of drugs, commercial and political exploitation: at various times, all of those have focused attention on the relevance of the heroic ideals in the face of apparent discountenance. Indeed, when the incidents are significant enough to cause general unease, the question of continuing the Games is raised. Coubertin was aware of the problems and the criticism. He knew that his ''Olympic idea'' was considered ''utopian and impractical.'' In a letter, in 1931, to Liselott Diem, who was the wife of Carl Diem, and a longtime German Olympic leader, he declared that ''at every Olympiad I have read that it was going to be the last.'' It has been so since his death in 1937 despite the incredible growth of his idea.

CONTINUE THE GAMES?

The continuance of the Games is still questioned. ''The Games must end!'' was the headline in a world press appalled at the use of a sporting arena for political terrorism when eleven Israeli athletes were murdered at the athletes' living quarters in Munich in 1972. A cynic was reported in *Time* magazine as saying ''The only time people get into uniform is for war of the Olympics.'' A

"Five Ring Circus" was the phrase used to describe the Olympics and the political boycott of the Moscow Games in 1980. Retaliation by the Eastern bloc countries four years later in 1984 and the unease felt by many about the commercialization of the Games in Los Angeles did little to stem the tide of criticism. British journalist Ian Wooldridge declared in a radio interview in 1984 that the International Olympic Committee had "all but handed over the games to Walt Disney" and commercial interests. They were called the "MacDonald Games" or the "Coca Cola games" depending on where the television images were coming from—the swimming pool or the athletic arena.

At least those games made a profit. In 1976, Montreal went into long-term debt to pay for sporting facilities. It is no wonder that the first arrivals to the Olympic city were treated to the disconcerting spectacle of local citizens' driving in a motorcade around the fence of the village urging, "Olympians, go home! We don't want you here!"

In Seoul in 1988, the poor and their shantytown were displaced to make way for the Olympic facilities on the Han River. Where were they to go? Critics of the Games vehemently argue that the Olympic flame is kept alight often at the expense of pressing social issues that should take precedence in host cities. Jean-Marie Brohm criticizes the modern Olympics for being a gross commercial spectacle and asserts:

If a balance sheet is drawn up of the last four or five Olympic Games the sorry conclusion must be that they form part of an economic system of waste, uncontrolled affluence and the large display of luxury, while the rest of the planet is sunk in famine and ignorance.

The debate about whether to hold the Games while there is social unrest or spend valuable resources on sport where there are blatant inequities still to be addressed causes much heart searching during an Olympic festival by both critics and supporters of Coubertin's idea. It is inappropriate to discuss it here but it must be acknowledged as a cause of concern and disquiet as the Games grow in size and presentation.

The idea that the growth of the modern Games into a Hollywood spectacle would please their founder is at odds with a plea that Coubertin made in the 1930s: "My friends, I have not laboured to restore the Olympic Games for you to make a spectacle of them . . . to use them for business or political ends." He was quite clear about their moral and educational value and is on record as saying, "Sport must decide whether it is to be a market or a temple!"

In some circumstances there is no division between those who admire the Olympic philosophy and the critics—for example, no disagreement between antagonists or protagonists about condemning the use of ergogenic aids in a "chivalrous" Olympian contest that advocates "a freely exercised morality" as an inspiration to the young. The incidence of drug taking to boost athletic performance is deplored by both Olympic proponents and critics alike. The fact that the Olympic ideals stress fair play and promote the contest as an illustration of ''an ever more highly aspiring, bolder and purer humanity'' means that whenever there is a breach of Olympic morality, there is appropriate condemnation of the athlete (Carl Diem, *The Olympic Idea: Discourses and Essays,* 1970, p. 22). When the incidence of drug taking seems to be widespread, then cynicism about the honesty of all Olympic athletes is openly expressed, along with justifiable concern that if the high ideals expected of Olympians cannot be ensured, then the Games themselves lose the special moral value that sets them apart from other sporting events. Carl Diem, de Coubertin's German disciple, argued that ''the true sportsman finds his standard of behavior within himself . . . and the Games are a reminder of sporting ideals'' to be honored. This is one of the appealing aspects of the Games for athlete and spectator alike, the quality that sets the Games apart—that makes them special.

When the Canadian sprinter Ben Johnson was disqualified for drug use after winning the 100-meter event in Seoul in 1988 and his coach, Charlie Francis, declared at the inquiry in Canada that ''as many as 80 per cent of the world's leading athletes may be using steroids to improve their . . . performances,'' many expressed the opinion that the Olympic Games could no longer be considered a special illustration of human excellence in honorable competition. Kevin Doyle, editor of *Maclean's,* Canada's weekly news magazine, writing of the ''national disgrace,'' concluded, ''And the Olympics, once the grandest spectacle in international sports, have now been reduced to the status of mud-wrestling.''

Supporters of the Olympic philosophy share the concern of the critics about the apparent decline in sporting morality and the suggestions of widespread drug use. They feel let down by athletes like Johnson, but not enough to give in to the cry to abolish the Games. They argue that because a few athletes cannot uphold the ideals of fair competition in an Olympic arena, others should not suffer the implied assertions of imorality and lose their opportunity for ''noble competition.'' They should not be denied their quest for excellence in the world's greatest sporting event. Indeed, fellow athletes in Seoul felt so enraged and betrayed by Johnson and his apparent cheating that they affixed a notice to the door of his room in the Olympic Village that declared he had gone from ''Hero to Zero!''

Carl Diem was right when he suggested that the morality inherent in Olympic competition ''finds a deep place in the soul'' of the genuine Olympian. He was also astute enough though to observe that ''within the Olympic idea there inevitably develops . . . a conflict . . . between reality and the ideal.''

The attachment to the philosophy of Olympism and the effort to preserve what are thought to be worthwhile sporting ideals are the reasons that supporters of the Games refuse to be swayed by the social arguments of the critics of the modern Olympic athlete and sports administrator. It is an example of those who, aware of the problems of contemporary Games, still advocate their continuance, and indeed believe that the Games are ''one of the greatest leavening forces for good'' in an imperfect world. As Roger Bannister, the British Olympic athlete put it:

It may seem paradoxical that, despite all the problems, I believe in the Olympic Games . . . as one of the great causes in the world which are capable of engaging the most serious determination of our young people and harnessing much of that . . . idealism which is latent in human beings. . . . We should not give up an ideal because it has not been attained. (J. Segrave and D. Chu, *Olympism,* 1981, p. 145)

No doubt the Games and their professed philosophy and idealism are seriously questioned and sometimes threatened (some would argue compromised) by the contemporary realities of commercialism, technology, and political events that seem to affect them. But the threats to the Olympic ideals are in no way due to the differences in time between Coubertin's era and the present. Sport philosopher Robert Osterhoudt reminds us that

Coubertin was by inclination and by influence very much more fully swayed by the idealistic optimism and purposive certainty of the nineteenth century than he was by the contrary sentiment that governs the current epoch. . . . Olympism is trapped in the conjunction between the 19th and 20th centuries.

This is not to suggest though that the idealistic philosophy of Coubertin and the Olympic movement have no contemporary relevance. They do. Despite those who would argue the irrelevance of the Olympic Games and erosion of Coubertin's ideals or suggest that these nineteenth-century ideals have been overtaken by and are at odds with modern values and attitudes, countless others point to the Games as a constant reminder of the heroic possibilities of sport. The fact that the Olympic ideals appear to conflict with reality does not negate the ideals themselves.

Robert Osterhoudt contends that Olympism embodies the highest principles of sport's promised odyssey and as such is unique among modern sporting institutions. No other institution has ''stood so steadfastly'' against the dehumanizing abuses of contemporary elite competition or been so insistent on combining sporting excellence with ''good and virtuous conduct.'' He concludes that because ''Olympism has brought sport nearer its fully human possibilities than any other modern event,'' the Games should, indeed must, be preserved.

The Olympic ideal encourages chivalrous contest. Humanity needs such heroic illustrations in the education of its youth as a counterpoint to the negative and sometimes degenerative effects of contemporary sport spectacles. Olympic contests with their Coubertin philosophy present a heroic view of humanity that our young and aspiring can identify with. Heroes and heroines renew the faith of these youngsters in the quality of the human spirit. American poet Wallace Stevens warned that:

> Unless we believe in the hero,
> What is there to believe?
> Indecisive what, the fellow
> of what good?

Carl Diem, explaining the apparent disparity between Olympic ideals and contemporary reality, suggested that the Olympic Games were ''a regulative force in sport. Like a gyroscope they keep it pointing towards its true [humanizing] goal. This gyroscope, too, may be buffeted by the gale . . . but there is the test. . . . Sport teaches us that no victory can be won without a battle and the Olympic idea will have to go on battling'' to combat the critics—those who would discontinue the Olympic Games because the sporting ideals inherent in the philosophy are too difficult to live (or play) by or are sometimes broken in a world that seems to be less concerned with honor (Diem, *Olympic Idea*, p.22).

The fact that the Olympics move into another century after the year 2000 Games in Sydney bears eloquent testimony to their resilience and ability to counter contemporary criticism. They are valued for their idealism and for the moral code they demonstrate in heroic sporting contests.

John A. Daly

PROLOGUE: THE ANCIENT GAMES

Throughout the modern world, sport is a cultural value etched indelibly into the lives of most people. Concern for personal health and fitness, dispositions toward particular sports, participation in international competitions, and collective pride in athletic accomplishment all speak to this fact. Deeply ingrained into this worldwide fascination with sports is an intense interest in the modern Olympic Games, whether witnessing them as spectators in Olympic venues or from thousands of miles away as television viewers. Of the world's approximately 5 billion people, well over half were touched in some way by the Games of the XXVth Olympiad in Barcelona in 1992. And, of some 200 countries in the world today, 170 of them were represented in Barcelona.

The beginning of the historical explanation of this global cultural phenomenon evolves from the experience of the ancient Greek world, the birthplace of much of Western culture. None of the great civilizations that preceded Greece in chronological time served as a model for its development. With the Greeks, something new evolved in the world: an evolution of spirit and initiative that the modern world has come to recognize and respect as having had no equal in the long path of human progress. History has yet to find a greater historian than Thucydides, greater philosophers than Plato and Aristotle, or greater poets than Homer and Pindar. Greece promoted a new world from one that issued dark confusions. The Greece of antiquity, of course, is assigned its place in the ancient world by chronology. In truth, though, it was modern—different from any of its contemporaries. No other culture in its time placed so much value on sport and glorification of the human body, a place and glorification that has taken over two thousand years for contemporary humans to approach once again. The record demonstrates that the Greeks enjoyed sport on a grand scale. They played with a sense of joy, commitment, and, above all, a feeling of celebration. And nowhere else in antiquity was such celebration more evident than at Olympia.

Crucial toward an understanding of sport and the Olympic Games in antiquity is the ancient Greek context in which they evolved. Early Greek culture was markedly military in character. Keen rivalries and competition for commercial dominance and protection of self-interests often led to confrontation between various factions, with war not uncommonly the final arbiter of disputes. Beyond doubt, there was a striking connection between military training and sporting competition. The description of one such connection has provided the Western world with two of its earliest and most enduring sport literature commentaries— passages from Homer's *Iliad* and *Odyssey*. Homer's works, particularly his descriptions of funeral contests, give us a good idea of sport festival preludes leading to the establishment of the Olympic Games.

According to Greek tradition, sometime near the middle of the thirteenth century B.C. a major military episode occurred. Events leading to the war between a confederation of Achaean states and Troy, episodes surrounding the war's ten-year struggle, its final outcome, and adventures encountered by warriors returning to their homelands afterwards provided grist for enduring oral legend. For some five centuries, the tales of the war were transmitted orally. Then, somewhere around the middle of the eighth century B.C., the Greek poet Homer set the tales to recited verse. Homer's grand epic, probably recorded in written form after 700 B.C., is read today in the form of two poems: the *Iliad*, which focuses on the war itself—its causes, preparations, battles, sieges, and conclusion—and the *Odyssey*, which narrates a great warrior's ten-year, adventure-laden return journey to his island home of Ithaca in the Ionian Sea. In antiquity, the *Iliad* and *Odyssey* became the reading and recitation standard for every Greek lad. Almost three thousand years after their composition, they are still read in various languages by millions of people the world over. They provide the basis for our understanding how athletic competition in great festival context rose in the ancient world.

The events Homer described probably occurred somewhere around 1250 B.C. Since Homer composed the poems some five hundred years after the fact, the modern world regarded them as pure fiction, unsupported as his descriptions were by corroborating archaeological evidence. In the latter part of the nineteenth century, however, the dilettante German archaeologist Heinrich Schliemann carried out extensive excavations in Anatolian Turkey near the south shore of the Dardanelles. Not only did he locate and uncover ruins and priceless artifacts dated to Troy's time but he also found ample evidence of cultures existing on the site well before and after the demise of Troy itself. The scientific and literary world greeted his finds with elaborate acclaim. Thus, the historical value of Homer's epic poems gained some veracity, enhanced by later archaeological discoveries at other early Greek sites.

The twenty-third book of the *Iliad* provides a glorious example of military physical skills transferred to competitive sport. What we really have with Homer is the first description of what can be termed a type of sport tournament, a precursor to the Olympic Games, in which athletes competed for prestige and prizes, rules governed various events, competitive strategies were pondered, exhortations and argument among spectators noted, the aid of divine spirits cultivated, and both sportsmanlike and unsportsmanlike conduct witnessed. These qualities are all facets of modern sport competition and yet were all present some three thousand years ago. Homer verifies the latter stages of the Achaean siege of Troy. The Achaean prince, Patroclus, is slain in battle by the Trojan warrior Hector. Patroclus's friend and military comrade, the renowned Achilles, seeks revenge against Hector. After slaying Hector, Patroclus's funeral celebration is organized. One dimension of the funeral celebration is a series of sporting contests. Achilles does not compete; instead, he is the organizer of the contests as well as their patron, and he provides valuable prizes to the victors. Most competitors are of noble birth—the sons of kings. They are well trained in military skills and transfer that skill to the various athletic events. We are told of a chariot race (in great detail), contests in boxing, archery, weight throwing (discus), javelin, wrestling, running, and, most dangerous of all, a fight in full armor with spears.

In the *Iliad* Homer tells us that a great crowd of spectators gathers on a plain near the sea to witness the funeral games. Diomedes wins the two-horse chariot race, besting four other competitors. Each gains a prize for his efforts with Diomedes winning the most coveted: a young maiden and an ornate tripod, spoils of war from Achaean victories over Trojan forces. Homer's account of the chariot race suggests all sorts of modern sporting parallels. Before the race gets underway, Antilochus of Pylos receives sage strategy and counsel from his father, King Nestor, once a great athlete himself at funeral games held many years earlier. We are also told of an official stationed at the race course's turning post to report any attempts at turning short of the mark. Angry verbal confrontations, nearly resulting in blows, occur among the spectators. King Idomeneus of Crete and Aias of Locris are such spectatorial antagonists. Nor were the athletes above devious attempts to achieve victory. Antilochus, displaying rough and unsportsmanlike tactics, forces Menelaus's chariot off the course near the turning point.

The drama and excitement generated by the chariot race extended to the other events. A brash young prince, Epeios, won at boxing, making good his threat to all rivals ''that he would tear their bodies into pieces and break their bones.'' Epeios decisively whipped the only individual who dared to oppose him: Euryalus of Thebes. In the wrestling match, Odysseus drew with Aias of Salamis. They agreed to share the prize, a large tripod cauldron and a girl skilled in handicraft. Aias of Locris, the bellicose spectator previously noted, joined Odysseus and Antilochus in the running race. Aias looked like a sure winner, but he slipped in oxen dung short of the finish post. He recovered to finish second, gaining the runner-up prize: a large bull. Odysseus, the winner, won a much-coveted silver bowl from Phoenicia. Antilochus, earlier berated for his unsportsmanlike conduct in the chariot race, finished third and last. This time, he was a model of decorum, complimenting Odysseus on his victory and at the same time pocketing a half-talent of gold as a reward for his conduct. The weight-throwing contest (it has been called a discus throw by many interpreters) resulted in Polypoites' besting Aias of Salamis with a throw of such distance that onlookers were held in a spell of amazement. The iron ingot thrown by Polypoites was given to him as his victory prize. It was touted by Achilles as sufficient enough to provide its owner with enough first-class iron for five years.

For the archery contest, Achilles ordered a ship's mast planted in the sandy soil with a pigeon tied to its upright end by one of its feet. For sheer drama, the ensuing contest surpassed all. There were two entrants: Teucrus and Meriones. Teucrus shot first. His arrow was near the mark; in fact, it severed the cord that secured the pigeon. As the freed pigeon flew away, Meriones snatched the bow from his fellow competitor, hastily strung an arrow, and shot the flying target through the chest. The mortally wounded bird landed at the slayer's feet.

In the javelin, or spear-throwing, contest, Agamemnon, king of Mycenae and commander in chief of the Achaean forces, was matched against Meriones of Crete. Fresh from his dramatic victory in the archery contest, Meriones was clearly keen for still another triumph. However, Achilles cancelled the contest and accorded the first prize of a flower-decorated cauldron to Agamemmon, it being well known to all that he had no equal in the skill. The disappointed Meriones received a bronze lance. Aias and Diomedes squared off against each other in the armed-spear duel, the aim being to penetrate the opponent's defense and draw blood from a lance touch. Each attacked three times, Aias jabbing at his opponent's shield and Diomedes trying to get above the shield to Aias's throat. Not wishing to see a warrior's death as the outcome of the contest, the onlookers requested Achilles to end the event. Achilles agreed, dividing the prizes between Aias and Diomedes, but Diomedes gained the most cherished article: a large silver-adorned sword of Thracian origin.

Aside from the *Iliad*'s description of athletic sport in Achaean times, Homer's second poem, the *Odyssey,* also contributes insights. In essence, the *Odyssey* is a tale of Odysseus's adventures on the long journey home to his island of Ithaca. Near the end of the ordeal, Odysseus is shipwrecked and cast up on the shores of a land called Phaeacia. No one is certain exactly where Phaeacia was in the greater Greek world or even if it was a real place. Odysseus was taken in by the Phaeacians and treated like an honored guest, being provided with food and accommodation. At a banquet in his honor Odysseus's host arranged for entertainment featuring music, dance, and athletic activities, including throwing the discus. The Phaeacians perceived that Odysseus had an athletic body despite the privations encountered at sea for a lengthy period of time. He was invited to try his hand at besting the Phaeacian locals in throwing the weight (discus). Odysseus, having witnessed the Phaeacians throwing and knowing that they were far inferior to his own skill, politely refused the invitation, claiming that his long sea voyage home had robbed him of any chance to train. Heckled and ridiculed by one Phaeacian athlete in particular, he took up a discus heavier than any other yet thrown in the contest and proceeded to heave it farther than all other marks. His startling athletic achievement established his noble status among the Phaeacians. Such is the prestige that attends athletic achievement, then and now.

Homer's descriptions of early Greek sport deserve further commentary and analysis. How much may the status and context of sport during Homer's actual lifetime have influenced his verse? We shall probably never know the definitive answer to this question so we can base our judgment only on that evidence before us: Greek archaeological recovery wedded to Homer's literary works based on several centuries-old oral tradition. During Homer's lifetime in Greek history, however, sport and athletics were in their infancy when compared to a century or two later. The record of what in time became known as the ancient Olympic festival had barely evolved by Homer's time. Thus, perhaps oral tradition was of greater consequence in shaping Homer's narrative than was the actual world in the eighth century B.C. Most certainly we know that a Greek world existed during the time about which Homer wrote, a world in which people were bonded by strong cultural commonalities. Among the most evident of these were a common religious worship of anthropomorphic gods and goddesses, an early Greek language, and an appreciation for and practice of sport in ceremonial, celebration, recreation, and competition context. Competitive sporting activities were largely associated with contests featuring basic military expertise of the times: running, throwing, hand-to-hand combat, chariot driving, and archery.

We shall probably never know whether the common Greek man sported. Homer's tales involve mostly aristocratic warriors: kings and the sons of kings. Such a privileged individual was described in the Greek language as *agathos,* a man trained for war and therefore brave. *Agathos* contrasted to *kakos,* an ordinary man, untrained and therefore cowardly and bad. A stronger derivative of the term *agathos* was *agathos ex agathon,* brave among the brave. A further extension was *aristos,* high born. The qualities of *agathos* and *aristos* can be summed up in the word *arete,* a term Homer used for qualities inherent in a warrior: strength, skill, bravery, and heroism. It was the responsibility of a father to see to it that his sons developed in such a way as to strive for *arete,* to become heroic and godlike and, in time, to assume a leadership role in society. Although we have no exact counterpart of the word *arete,* we can be satisfied with "excellence." Thus, a quest for excellence in ancient times was the responsibility of all leaders in society. Several of Homer's warriors—Achilles and Odysseus, for example—were personifications. Many fell far short of the ideal. But it is the pursuit of ideal that translates into progress and achievement, not particularly attainment of the goal. The quest for excellence in all things military overlapped into other areas of human endeavor: wisdom, intelligence, and eloquence. The quest for athletic excellence in competition against others is seeded in the ideology of *arete.*

THE ANCIENT OLYMPIC GAMES

A legitimate place from which to begin an investigation of Greek athletics and the evolution of the ancient Olympic Games is the religious sanctuary Olympia. The ancient site of Olympia was located in the northwest Peloponnese in the district presided over by the town of Elis. Archaeological evidence demonstrates that Olympia was inhabited during Achaean times. Achaean cult objects devoted to nature, fertility, and vegetation gods have been found there. When the Achaeans' successors (later Greeks, sometimes called Dorians) settled on the Peloponnese, the site of Olympia claimed their attention as a religious sanctuary where both old Achaean gods and new Dorian deities were worshipped. In time, with the ascendance of the Olympian family in Greek religion, Zeus became the chief figure worshipped at Olympia.

We will never know for sure what type of athletic activities, if any, might have been celebrated at Olympia as part of early Dorian religious sacrifice and ceremony. History, however, has assigned the date 776 B.C. as the first record of athletic activity at Olympia. The date is etched into the record because the ancient Olympic victor list commences from that year. Surely athletic activities in keeping with older traditions were carried out at the site long before 776, just as archaeological evidence tells us that religious activity definitely occurred at Olympia well before 776. Based on ancient theories, various points of view exist that attempt to explain the rejuvenation of athletics as part of the religious festival at Olympia. In consistent fashion, they point to athletics being closely connected with religious events. For instance, Pindar stated that the Olympic Games originated during the late Achaean period to honor the victory of the god Heracles over King Augeas of Elis. Thus, the sanctuary of Olympia originally may have been a celebration site for Heracles, with Zeus later evolving in influence following the rise of Dorian prominence. Pindar's view was supported in later times by the noted Greek scholars Lysias and Aristotle. The Roman poet Strabo stated that the original Olympic religious festival evolved from the initiative of the Elean citizen, Oxylus, in celebration of his people's return to Elis after being forced by severe drought conditions to move westward to Aetolia for a period. Strabo's notation gives an 1104 B.C. date. An explanation rendered by the historian Phlegon of Tralles, writing in 138 A.D., recounts that Iphitus of Elis, Lycurgus of Sparta, and Cleisthenes of Pisa, all Dorians, visited the great oracle at Delphi to gain an answer for purging their lands of famine and pestilence. The word conveyed to them was that Zeus was angry because the onetime athletic dimension of the religious celebrations at Olympia had ceased. A revival of athletics was said to have taken place in order to please Zeus and restore good times.

Two anecdotal tales are perhaps of less consequence in explaining the origin of athletics at Olympia but nevertheless form an interesting aside. One points to the establishment of athletic and religious festivals at Olympia in commemoration of the Olympian victory over the rival Titans. The supreme Olympian

God, Zeus, vied with his father, Cronus, sovereign leader of the Titans. When the Olympians triumphed, Zeus bade that the citizens of the Elean district establish a religious festival in his honour. Zeus is said to have commemorated his father's memory by naming a small mountain near the sanctuary site after him. The Hill of Kronus today, abuts the northeast boundary of the sanctuary's archaeological remains. The other anecdotal story etched in mythology alludes to an earlier time, two or three generations before the Achaean siege of Troy. King Oenomaus of Pisa was the proud father of a lovely daughter whose hand he offered in marriage to the first suitor to escape with her in his chariot. The story goes that various young men accepted the challenge, but all were pursued and killed by Oenomaus and his men—that is, until the hero Pelops (after whom the Peloponnese is named) secretly tampered with his prospective father-in-law's chariot, causing a wheel to come off during the chase. The mishap resulted in the king's death and his daughter, Hippodamia, was claimed by Pelops as his bride. Pelops, the myth tells us, celebrated his victory and marriage with a festival, of which a chariot race was one celebratory function. Some ancient interpreters of the myth have changed the story to relate that a festival with chariot racing was established upon Pelops' death, thus making such an occasion a funeral event, akin to that for Patroclus described by Homer in the *Iliad.*

Regardless of which version is closest to the mark, we know that a quadrennial religious celebration (perhaps originally celebrated every eight years) and attendant competitive sporting events evolved at Olympia. The festival at Olympia, called the Olympic Games, was the oldest, most enduring athletic festival in the ancient Greek world. It was also the most conservative and resistant to change. As an athletic festival it was by far the most prestigious. Finally, the athletic affairs at Olympia became models for the rise of other athletic festivals.

The first recorded victor at the ancient Olympic Games was apparently a simple cook, an Elean by the name of Koroebus. The event, a one-length sprint of the race course, which in earlier times may have been laid out between two altars, became known as the stadium run (*stade*). For over fifty years (twelve succeeding Olympiads) the *stade* was the sole athletic event. By 676 B.C., a set program of events at Olympia had evolved. Besides the *stade,* it included the *diaulos* (two lengths of the running course), *dolichos* (multiple lengths of the running course), wrestling, boxing, pankration, pentathlon, and chariot racing. Athletic events for boys were introduced in 632. At various times experimentation with other forms of events occurred, including a race in armor and equestrian contests for foals (colts) and mule carts. For almost a thousand years, Olympia's athletic program stood in place, the supreme model for others to emulate.

In its early years the Olympic festival was attended by athletes residing solely on the Peloponnese, attesting to the festival's local character. Indeed, we do not learn of an Olympic victor from outside the Peloponnese until 720, when Orsippos of Megara won the *stade.* In 696 an Athenian was the victor in the stadium run, the first in a long list of Olympic victors from Greece's most glorious city. By the early part of the sixth century the Olympic victor list abounds with winners from Greek colony city-states located across the entire Mediterranean basin. Joining the perennial Peloponnesian athletic powers, Sparta, Elis, and Messene, are Thessaly and Larisa in the north, Kroton and Syracuse in Italy and Sicily, Rhodes, Crete, and Mytilene in the Aegean, Miletos, Ephesus, Pergamon, and Halicarnassus in Anatolia, and Alexandria in Egypt.

Other religious sanctuaries and city-states copied Olympia's athletics program, modifying the slate of events to suit their needs and desires. Delphi, home of Apollo, the virtuous son of Zeus, had long been a religious sanctuary of unrivaled importance in the Greek world. It commenced an athletic program in about 586 B.C. Delphi's Pythian Festival, named after Apollo's feat of killing a menacing python during mythological times, occurred once every four years, two years before and two years after each Olympic festival. The Isthmian Games, celebrating Poseidon (Zeus's brother, and god of the sea), evolved in 582. A festival at Nemea, a few kilometers from the ancient Achaean city of Mycenae, was still another athletic-religious event of importance. Originated in 573, the Nemean Festival honored Zeus, though its earliest lineage as a religious site can be traced to another of Heracles' victories in Greek myth, this time over a livestock-ravaging lion. Both the Nemean and Isthmian festivals were held every other year—the Nemean in the odd-numbered years and the Isthmian in the even. The four great festivals—Olympian, Pythian, Nemean, and Isthmian—formed what became known as the Pan-Hellenic Crown Games. To all Greeks they were the most important festivals. To win at any was a cause for great celebration by an athlete's city-state, as well as by the athlete himself, for he most certainly could look forward to commensurate enrichment for his efforts. And to win at Olympia was the most rewarding of all.

The Pan-Hellenic Crown Games were certainly not the only athletic meetings in the Greek world. Athens organized one of the most flamboyant civic athletic festivals in ancient Greece. Aside from religious sacrifice surrounding the celebration of her patron goddess, Athena, the Pan-Athenaic Festival featured religious pomp and pageantry as well as spirited athletic competition. There were various categories of athletic events: for non-Athenian athletes, for Athenian male adults, for military cadets, and for boys. Prizes at the games were of significant value. By the middle of the fifth century B.C., other athletic festivals of note had evolved in Greece proper. On the Peloponnese alone, athletic meetings were organized at Tegea, Argos, Corinth, Epidauraus, Sicyon, Pellene, Pheneus, Clitor, and Parrhesia, and in central Greece at Plataea, Eleusis, and Megara. In Africa, Cyrene hosted games, and in Italy, Kroton. On the Aegean islands of Delos and Rhodes, prestigious festivals were held regularly. Later, under Alexander's influence, the penchant for organizing and staging athletic festivals was multiplied in Greek communities located in Asia Minor.

Greek athletes were not unlike their modern counterparts. They trained arduously, benefited from sports trainers and coaches, were adored by an admiring public, and more often than not were rewarded handsomely for their efforts. Olympic athletes had to be citizens of pure Greek parentage, although this restriction may have been relaxed in later times when the Greek world spread to include a conglomerate of ethnic strains. A participant at Olympia must have trained under local supervision for a period of almost a year. One month before the Olympic festival commenced, prospective competitors presented themselves to a council of judges (*Hellanodicae*), who judged and supervised their final preparations. Any found to be unworthy of the Olympic tradition of athletic excellence were sent away. Only the most deserving vied at Olympia.

An athlete's training was carried out in a *gymnasium,* or, if he specialized in combat events, in a *palaestra,* a public training place for athletes. He was supervised by a cadre of overseers including a coach (*gymnastes*), anointers, masseurs, and other support staff. Runners ran and practiced starts and turns around a post. Wrestlers, boxers, and pankratiasts drilled on various techniques of offensive and defensive maneuvers and engaged in weight training to build strength and body mass. Pentathletes practiced the subdisciplines of their event: sprinting, jumping, throwing the discus and javelin, and wrestling. Equestrian activities were not seen in the *gymnasium.* Such events, especially chariot racing, remained the province of the wealthy until well after athletics in ancient Greece had become democratized to include participants from all strata of life. The training was intensive, prolonged, and specialized. In this regard, as well as in the matters of prize consideration and social prestige, there is little to distinguish the ancient Greek athlete from today's professional or quasi-professional athlete.

Most athletic-religious festivals were carried out over a period of several days. We know that at Olympia the events were held over five days, with the first day and a portion of the last given over to religious sacrifice and ceremony. The remaining time focused on athletic competition and celebration of individual sporting achievement.

The remains of ancient Greek athletic stadiums tell us that spectators by the thousands viewed the agonistic struggles of ancient athletes. At Olympia some 40,000 may have gathered to worship and spectate. Olympia featured one of the simplest, most unadorned stadiums in the Greek world; individuals simply arranged themselves on the grassy slopes of artificially constructed embankments. At Delphi the onlookers at the athletic events were about 7,000 in number. Unlike at Olympia, however, they sat on beautifully constructed tiers of stone seats built in Roman times. The grandest stadium in the ancient Greek world is at Aphrodisias, high in the mountains of Anatolian Turkey. That magnificent stadium accommodated over 80,000. Following their conquest of Greece, the Romans used one end of the Aphrodisias stadium as an amphitheater in which to stage activities much more violent than Greek athletics.

Spectators journeying to Olympia to pay homage to Zeus and to witness supreme athletic endeavor were protected by a so-called Olympic truce, which guaranteed their passage against harm from warring Greek factions and other types of harassment, including bandits. Violators of the truce, if apprehended, were fined heavily.

There was more to the festival than religious and sporting activity. The assembly of large numbers of Greeks, many of them powerful and influential, provided opportunities for all sorts of sociopolitical action. Military and commercial agreements might be struck, one's political and philosophical views on a number of subjects voiced, and proficiency displayed in Greek cultural endeavors—art, public speaking, and music. Indeed, the greatest festivals in antiquity were places where people came not only to see but also to be seen, with Olympia the most important forum for these kinds of activities.

The spectator's lot was not always comfortable. Spectators most often had to sleep in rustic bivouac fashion, subsisting on supplies they brought with them or purchased from nearby vendors. They sat for hours under the hot sun, slapping and fanning at innumerable insects, and listening to or being involved in the types of arguments and confrontations that invariably arise among zealous sports fans. We note one such incident in Homer's account. To watch competitions between local athletes at local festivals was one thing; to watch confrontations among the best athletes drawn from all over the Greek world was quite another experience. Olympia held the greatest attraction for both athletes and spectators.

Homer's description of the prizes bestowed on athletes at the funeral games tells us that they were of significant utilitarian value. Without exception, Achilles' prizes prompted intense competition. There is enough evidence to suggest that the value of competitive prizes grew as sport in ancient Greek society became more institutionalized. True, we hear of the simple olive wreath being given to the victor of events held at Olympia, a laurel wreath at Delphi, pine at Isthmia, and celery at Nemea, but these were merely symbolic awards. What might be bestowed on the victorious athlete when he returned home was certainly more than the term *symbolic* connotes. In fact, the result was most often a grand expansion of the tradition related by Homer. We have many examples to guide our understanding on this point. Early in the sixth century B.C., the Athenian lawmaker Solon decreed that Athenian victors at the Isthmian games receive 100 drachmas from the public treasury. More grandly compensated, a victory at Olympia was worth 500 drachmas. In comparison, the annual wage of an ordinary seaman in the employ of the Athenian merchant fleet was 100 drachmas. We hear also of such gratuities to the victorious athlete as immunity from paying taxes, honored seats at civic and religious functions, free repasts at the civic messes, glorious statues struck in his honor, poetry composed and orations delivered on his behalf. At Aphrodisias, in the first century A.D., a prize money list for specific athletic events has survived. The inscription tells us that the winner of the pentathlon garnered a prize of 500 dinar, 750 dinar for the *dolichos*, 1,000 for the *diaulos*, 1,250 for the *stade*, 2,000 each for boxing and wrestling, and 3,000 for the brutal pankration. As the wage of a common laborer at the time was approximately 1 dinar per day, one can readily see the wisdom

		PRIZE IN AMPHORAS OF OIL	DRACHMA VALUE (12 drachmas per amphora)	NUMBER OF DAYS WAGES at 1.417 DRACHMA PER DAY (skilled)	NUMBER OF YEARS FULL EMPLOYMENT (at 300 days)
STADE					
men	first	100	1,200	847	2.82
	second	20	240	169	.56
youths	first	60	720	508	1.69
	second	12	144	102	.34
boys	first	50	600	423	1.41
	second	10	120	85	.28
PENTATHLON					
men	first	60	720	508	1.69
	second	12	144	102	.34
youths	first	40	480	339	1.13
	second	8	96	68	.23
boys	first	30	360	254	.85
	second	6	72	51	.17
WRESTLING					
men	first	60	720	508	1.69
	second	12	144	102	.34
youths	first	40	480	339	1.13
	second	8	96	68	.23
boys	first	30	360	254	.85
	second	6	72	51	.17
BOXING					
men	first	60	720	508	1.69
	second	12	144	102	.34
youths	first	40	480	339	1.13
	second	8	96	68	.23
boys	first	30	360	254	.85
	second	6	72	51	.17
PANKRATION					
men	first	80	960	678	2.26
	second	16	192	136	.45
youths	first	50	600	423	1.41
	second	10	120	85	.28
boys	first	40	480	339	1.13
	second	8	96	68	.26
EQUESTRIAN EVENTS Chariot race					
	first	140	1,680	1,186	3.95
	second	40	480	339	1.13

of pursuing athletics as a profession. The inscription tells us something else also: the tamer, less violent events were the least rewarded; the more violent ones commanded huge purses. This phenomenon was probably a reflection of Roman influence in Greek culture.

On the subject of athletic prizes in ancient Greece, no other record is perhaps as graphic as that rendered by an Athenian inscription from the first half of the fourth century B.C. First-place winners in various athletic events of the great Athenian civic festival, the Pan-Athenaea, were awarded amphoras of olive oil, both of significant value in the Athenian economy. The amphoras were large, beautifully executed, and exquisitely painted with sporting motifs. The table above underscores the attractiveness of pursuing athletics as a profession in one's physically active years. (The equivalencies in earning power have been suggested by David Young.)

It appears that remuneration for victories at athletic festivals increased commensurately with the increase of wealth across the wide sphere of Greek influence in the Mediterranean area. Compensation for athletic success some two thousand years ago and earlier, and that noted today, together with the translation of such earnings to buying power then and now, appears to reflect little difference. This has not, in general, been the message passed on by the earliest scholars of sport in Greek antiquity. There is much to be admired and thankful for in the writings of E. N. Gardiner, H. A. Harris, and other post-Victorian British investigators, but their consensus that Greek athletes in antiquity were the counterpart of virtuous English amateurs of the late nineteenth and early twentieth centuries is off target. Ancient Greek athletes were motivated by the same forces that stimulate gifted, higher-level athletes of today: recognition, prestige, status, and, above all, the chance for a big payday.

Although Homer described wrestlers in the *Iliad* as athletes wearing loincloth girdles, a startling characteristic of later Greek culture was that athletic exercise was carried out in the nude. One theory is that this phenomenon evolved from attempts by early Greek artists to reflect legendary tales in graphic perspective; heroic subjects were often presented in naked form. The mythological personality most favored for nude presentation was Heracles. In mythology, Heracles alone was allowed to appear before Zeus and the other gods in nude fashion. Because of his image as a warrior-athlete, Heracles had an early association with Olympia. He became a cult symbol for athletes and physical exercisers alike, all of whom trained and competed in the nude, just as they envisioned their patron had.

The events that formed the core of the athletic competitions were different in many ways from what we know of the same types of exercises in modern context. On the other hand, there are innumerable similarities as well. Modern Greeks in the late nineteenth century in part used knowledge of ancient competitions to select and frame rules for some of the contests in the first modern Olympics held in Athens in 1896.

The *stade* run in ancient times, a length of the stadium sprint, needs little description. Competitors, crouched slightly at the start with toes of each foot resting in starting grooves cut in stone sills arranged across the race course, ran in a straight line to the end of the stadium (usually about 200 yards). The *diaulos* (the equivalent of the modern 400 meters) was a bit different. A turn had to be made at the far end of the stadium, necessitating a return to the starting line. The start was the same as in the *stade*. Our best evidence for the turn maneuver suggests that all runners turned around a central turning post in a counterclockwise direction. Negotiation of the turn made for some tricky navigation. The *dolichos* was a long-distance running event, perhaps a race of between 1,500 and 3,000 meters. Runners turned around central turning posts situated at each end of the stadium. The *dolichos'* greater distance probably made for a more strung-out field of competitors; thus, excitement at the turns was probably diminished as the race progressed because of less crowded conditions. From time to time other types of running races occurred also, including the race in armor and torch races. In the race in armor, a competitor wore a helmet and carried a shield; at times he wore *greaves* (leg guards). The length of the race was most often a *diaulos,* but at Nemea it was a double *diaulos.* At Plataea, in commemoration of the Greek victory over the Persians at Marathon, a battle in which Plataeans were participants, the race in armor was 15 *stades* in length, well over 1½ miles. The torch races, when held, were probably associated with religious ritual. We observe sixth- and fifth-century vase paintings displaying youthful runners' passing the torch to a teammate, perhaps an ancient forerunner of the relay race.

The combative events had particular appeal to most spectators; tests of strength and fortitude under trying circumstances usually do. Wrestling involved trying to throw one's opponent to the ground. It appears to have been a grappling exercise, carried on in upright fashion, similar to modern Greco-Roman wrestling. Interpreters have suggested that a three-out-of-five fall format comprised a match. Vase painting wrestling scenes attest that the ancients employed most of the maneuvers seen in modern forms of wrestling. The pankration was an event often misinterpreted by contemporary writers to be wrestling or boxing. It was a particularly brutal exercise, exhibiting elements of both boxing and wrestling. Unlike boxers, however, pankratiasts did not wear boxing thongs on their fists. Much of the match featured grappling on the ground, such as in modern freestyle wrestling. The brutal aspects of the pankration related to the fact that the rules permitted such violent tactics as throat holds and kicking actions and the bending of fingers, arms, and legs until they were broken or badly injured. The aim of the pankratiast was to render his opponent unconscious or reduce him to such a state that he voluntarily gave up. The submissive signal of the defeated individual was an upheld arm with extended index finger. Only gouging of the eyes and biting appeared to be prohibited by the referee, who supervised the event from close perspective. Violators of the rules were at times flogged by the official to encourage a halt to such conduct. Boxing was simpler. Pugilists wore leather thongs to protect their hands. Over the centuries, the ''glove'' became more sophisticated in form, finally covering the hand completely. The gloves' later character resulted in a potentially lethal, punishment-inflicting item rather than one used solely for protection. There were neither rounds nor weight classifications. Opponents fought until one was knocked out, rendered incapable of continuing, or voluntarily gave up. Competitors in wrestling, pankration, and boxing progressed through a series of elimination bouts until two athletes remained, each then vying in a final match for the symbolic victory wreath and the rewards, which were conferred on him later.

The pentathlon event consisted of five components, three of which occurred only in the pentathlon. Called the triad disciplines, they were the jump, hurling the discus, and the javelin throw. The other two events were the *stade* run and wrestling. Greeks were of different opinions on the stature of the pentathlon. One school of thought, represented by Aristotle's opinion, looked upon the pentathlon as the supreme example of athletic ability in that it displayed versatility and harmony. On the other hand, Plato and those who agreed with him thought the event to be one for "second raters"—athletes who were not good enough to win in any of the other events. The evidence clearly supports Plato's contention. In the almost one thousand years of recorded ancient Olympic Games history, not once is it noted that a Greek won both the pentathlon and another event as well in the same festival. In fact, the pentathlon event itself was conspicuously absent from the Olympic victor lists as early as the late Hellenistic period. Each competitor in the discus and javelin threw from a *balbis,* an open-ended rectangular area similar to the modern javelin throwing area. Throws were measured for distance. We do not know how many tries athletes were allowed. The javelin was thrown with the aid of an *ankule,* a thong looped around the shaft near the center of gravity, which added a slinging action to the spear. The pentathlon jump has prompted argument among scholars of Greek athletic events, but the thesis that appears best to satisfy the ancient evidence supports a multiple jumping exercise of five successive leaps along the jumping pit (*skamma*). We know that small weights (between 3 and 10 pounds), called *halteres,* were gripped in both hands of the jumper throughout the exercise. Scholars believe that the swinging action of the *halteres* added distance to the jump over what might be accomplished if they were not used. We do not know how many tries a pentathlete jumper received or what was actually required to win the overall event. The best analysis appears to support a notion that an athlete had to win three of the subdisciplines in order to be declared the champion. The triad events (discus, jump and javelin) were first, followed by the *stade.* Wrestling, if necessary, was last. If one competitor won all of the triad events, the pentathlon was ended, he having won the necessary three subevents. If the results of the triad event competitions produced two or three different winners then those competitors proceeded to run and wrestle in order to determine a pentathlon champion.

The remaining events of the athletic festival's program were equestrian in nature; of these, chariot racing was by far the most important. Chariot racing was usually the province of the aristocratic faction of Greek society. They alone owned the means to support the breeding, care, and training of animals, as well as maintenance of drivers. At times a consortium of less wealthy individuals sponsored chariot teams. Most teams had four horses. The prize and distinction for winning always went to the owner, never the driver, who was usually a simple domestic groomsman serving in the aristocrat's stable. Kings and tyrants were known to celebrate chariot victories by striking coins with racing scenes stamped on them. Chariot racing occurred over a course laid out across level ground, with turning barriers installed at each end of the racing venue. At Olympia the race course was situated on the floodplain of the Alpheus River.

Of absorbing interest to contemporary sports fans are the exploits of famous

Olympic athletes: Jim Thorpe, Paavo Nurmi, Jesse Owens, Wilma Rudolph, and Carl Lewis, among others. Many of the most notable are etched in modern history as sport heroes, celebrated in literature, sports halls of fame, indeed, in oral tradition. Ancient Greece was no different; there, too, sport heroes abounded. We have noted those about whom Homer wrote, but there were many others of later Greek times too. The greatest in legend and deed was Milon of Kroton. Kroton, located in southern Italy, became noted in the late sixth and early fifth centuries for the Olympic achievements of its athletes. Milon was a wrestler. As a boy in 540 B.C., he won at Olympia; as an adult he captured five Olympic wrestling crowns (532, 528, 524, 520, and 516). He was denied a seventh Olympic crown in 512, being defeated by his disciple, the Kroton wrestler, Timasitheos, a youth of twenty-eight. Added to Milon's wrestling feats at Olympia were his seven titles won at Delphi, nine at Nemea, and ten at Isthmia. Six times Milon was *periodonikes,* winner of crowns at Olympia, Delphi, Nemea, and Isthmia in the period of one Olympiad (four years). Leonidas of Rhodes was antiquity's most renowned sprinter and middle-distance runner. In the Olympic Games of 164, he won three crowns: *stade, diaulos,* and race in armor. In 160 and 156 he duplicated the feat. In 152, at age 36, Leonidas was accorded heroic status in Rhodes for once again capturing his favorite triple. Leonidas finished his career with twelve Olympic crowns, the most in history, ancient or modern.

Of a host of other noted athletes and their achievements in ancient Greek sport, Theagenes of Thasos deserves mention. He first triumphed in boxing at Olympia in 480; then he turned his attention to the pankration, which he won at the Games of 476. These two feats in themselves do not tell the whole story about Theagenes, who became what modern history would call the consummate professional athlete, touring the Greek world for years to participate in the sporting festivals of various cities. When he finally retired, he had won some thirteen hundred victories, nine of them the coveted crown at Nemea, ten at Isthmia, and several more at Delphi. All except one, were gained in the pankration or boxing events. Competing at games held in Phthia, the home of Homer's Achilles, he entered the *dolichos,* motivated by a desire to gain victory in a foot race held in the homeland of the swiftest of the most ancient of athletic heroes. His quest was achieved. After Theagenes' death, Thasos erected a huge statue in his honor; he became embossed in Thacian legend.

Finally, we should note perhaps the noblest athletic hero in ancient history: Diagoras, the Rhodian boxer. Diagoras was descended from royal lineage. His great grandfather was Damagetos, king of Ialysos. A huge man for his time (well over 6 feet), he owned ''a fine face, proud step, and statuesque stance.'' Diagoras was called *euthymaches* (fair fighter) because he never stepped aside, stooped, or shied away from an opponent. He fought with dignity, pride, and sportsmanlike bearing, qualities that ancient Greeks appreciated then as we revere them now. Diagoras won the boxing at Olympia in 464, gained two Nemean and four Isthmian crowns, and won competitions several times at games held on the Greek mainland and on various Aegean islands. His eldest son, Damagetos, won the Olympic pankration in 452 and 448; his second eldest son, Akousilaos, the boxing in 448. One can imagine Diagoras' joy and pride at witnessing both his sons' being crowned victors at Olympia in 448. Legend has it that his sons presented their father with their crowns and carried him on their shoulders out from among the spectators onto the running course. An ovation of recognition and adoration erupted. Issuing from the spectators came the shouted voice of a Spartan: "Die now, Diagoras, there is nothing left for you but to ascend to Olympos." We are told that Diagoras heard the voice and, from the shoulders of his sons, bent his wreath-crowned head and breathed his last. If this legend is true, then he was deprived of perhaps even greater joy: living to witness three consecutive Olympic pankration titles won by his youngest son, Doreius, in 432, 428 and 424. Diagoras' sports achievement record and those of his sons are authenticated; the particulars of his death may or may not have occurred. Nevertheless, sport legends in ancient Greece were embellished with as many glorifying twists as locker room tales are today. A large bronze statue of Diagoras borne aloft on the shoulders of his two sons still stands on the grounds of the International Olympic Academy adjacent to the ancient stadium of Olympia where the legendary occurrence was supposedly witnessed.

To this point, the narrative has been void of remarks about women in the sphere of sport, exercise, and the body in ancient Greece. In our modern world, of course, vigorous participation in all types of sport at all levels by women is natural and expected; female competitions at the modern Olympic Games form one of the most interesting and exciting dimensions of the festival. This was certainly not the case in antiquity. Aside from Spartan society, women were excluded from the sporting and body exercise venues of males. In general, women did not exercise or train for athletics; neither were they spectators. During the great religious and athletic celebrations for Zeus, women were not permitted in the vicinity of Olympia.

A possible reason that women were not allowed to participate in male athletic festivals was that many such festivals, particularly at Olympia, were traditionally linked to a celebration of Heracles, who was associated with war and sporting vigor. Female presence at an athletic site was felt to diminish the power and strength necessary to triumph. The evidence of antiquity emphatically supports this view. Women attended various religious festivals with men but not those associated with Heracles and sport performance. One religious festival reserved exclusively for girls was the Heraia, which celebrated the goddess Hera, sister and wife of Zeus. The Heraia festival was held at the same Olympia sanctuary site where men celebrated games for Zeus. The temple of Hera within the sanctuary has been dated an earlier structure than the more massive and dominating Temple of Zeus. At the Heraia there was one exhibition of athleticism, a single running race for unmarried girls. Instead of glory and wealth from war and sport, women pursued *arete*. A woman's prescription for *arete* involved domestic affairs: how well children were raised, how well household staff was managed, how well a husband was cared for—in effect, the maintenance of the home and family environment. We today are not too far removed from a time when a woman's role in life was primarily the same as in antiquity. Many moderns, men and women alike, might wince at this observation, but women in antiquity would not do so. The female role was well defined, as was the male's. Women pursued their goals with as much zeal, determination, and quest for excellence as did men.

EPILOGUE

Sport, indeed the Olympic Games, continued to be present throughout the Greek world until the time of Christ and much later. Although we have noted that Homer and Pindar were outstanding examples of Greeks who glorified sport in the 300-year period between 750 and 450 B.C., Greek writers of later periods, although favorably disposed to the value of physical education and physical exercise, often rendered severe criticisms against the specialization and brutality of athletes, as well as the status they were accorded in society. Euripides, noted as an eternal pessimist, viewed athletes as "a worthless race." Xenophanes not only railed against the athlete's lofty social position but stated that the recompense he received was out of keeping with his accomplishments. The noted sixth-century Ionian philosopher also enunciated that "wisdom is better than the strength of men and horses." Aesop stated that there was "no glory in defeating a weaker opponent, skill is the real measurement." Plato and Aristotle were also vigorous critics of the specialization of athletes, a phenomenon that went hand in hand with a noted rise in professionalism. Plato scorned athletics as producing "hardness and savagery, violence and disharmony." In the same vein Aristotle decried the one-sidedness of the overtrained and specialized, a characteristic in opposition to pursuing a versatile, liberally oriented life.

Despite growing criticism of athletics and athletes emanating from the fourth century on, sport festivals continued to have wide popular appeal throughout the Greek world. Sport tournaments and festivals proliferated, finding new glorification in the magnified Greek empire in the Middle East established by Alexander in the second half of the fourth century B.C.

By the time of Christ, several factors had become apparent in the slow erosion of Greek athletics and the ancient Olympic Games. Prominent among them was the influence of Rome, which had reduced Greece to an occupied province by the middle of the second century. The Roman penchant for cruel and barbarous dimensions of sport, reflected in wild-beast fights and human gladiatorial combat, began to filter into the Greek consciousness. Track and field activities, the foundation of ancient Greek festivals, declined in favor of violent, combative events of Roman character.

In general the portrait of Greece during the Roman era of influence was one that exhibited a greater spectatorial phenomenon and less energetic physical exercise. The hardy physical exercises of the *gymnasium* were replaced at times by the rise of still another Roman institution: luxurious and lengthy bathing. In effect, a sweeping sedentarianism developed, weakening a human race that was once the epitome of physical action.

By far the most damaging factor in the decline of sport in ancient Greece was the rise of Christianity. Christianity offered hope and dreams for something better than the degradation characteristic of later Roman civilization. Actions by some Christian leaders were initiatives aimed at reducing the trappings of Greek and Roman paganism. In time, Greek and Roman temples were razed. Cathedrals and places of Christian worship rose on the foundations of the ancient temples of Zeus, Apollo, Poseidon, and the other gods and goddesses of antiquity. Sport, associated from its very beginning with the gods of antiquity, was one such pagan trapping that received its share of scrutiny and derision from early Christians. Over a period of some four hundred years after the birth of Christ, the growth and influence of Christianity took its toll. What once had been a vast Greek domain in the Mediterranean and Middle East, succeeded in time by Roman conquest and cultural influence, slowly became Christianized. By the late fourth century A.D., the Christian envelopment was complete. The ancient festival at Olympia had also ceased. Although the last recorded event at Olympia occurred in A.D. 369, the victory lists are silent of any activity from A.D. 281 to A.D. 365. The Christian emperor Theodosius I issued a decree in A.D. 393 abolishing in word what had in fact disappeared in deed over a century before: the ancient Olympic Games, supreme emblem of ancient paganism.

From time to time athletic games continued to be held in Greek cities in the eastern Mediterranean world, faint reminders of once-glorious times for sport. By using increasingly severe measures, Christian emperors sought to eradicate them from cultural memory. The attempts of the new religion to disassociate itself completely from most pagan reminders were largely successful.

Five hundred years after Christ, sport in the ancient Greek world had reached the end of a life cycle. The life cycle's birth and infant stage can be seen in the sporting culture of the Achaeans, about which Homer rhapsodized. The formative teenage, maturing, and productive years were reflected in the glory of Greece's Classical and Hellenistic ages. Finally, sport reached its twilight years, a withering period featured by erosion of interest, participation, and celebration. Yet sport in ancient Greece never experienced mortal death. Like our own genealogical process, which sees the essence of us passed on to our children and grandchildren, so too was the cultural legacy of sport and the Olympic Games in ancient Greece passed to future generations. Inspiration from that legacy provided much of the initiative that brought about the modern Olympic movement. It gave rise to a thriving, contemporary fitness ethic and germinated body concepts that today have important overtones for healthy lifestyles geared to movement rather than sedentarianism. This cultural phenomenon began with the ancient Greeks. Perhaps by studying their history with dedication and appreciation, we will become more in tune with the message inscribed above the entrance to the ancient temple of Apollo at Delphi, which all Greeks noted as they entered to worship: "Know thyself."

BIBLIOGRAPHICAL ESSAY

A study of sport and the Olympic Games in antiquity has to begin with an examination of the literary comment made by the ancient Greeks themselves. In this regard, Homer's *Iliad* and *Odyssey* are fundamental. The works of Herodotus, Philostratus, Thucydides, and Plutarch, among others, provide important commentary from the context of being viewed as original sources. For the best of modern surveys of ancient sources on the history of Greek athletics and the ancient Olympic Games, consult the following: Nigel B. Crowther, "Studies in Greek Athletics," *Classical World* 78, 79 (1985); Stephen G. Miller, *Arete: Ancient Writers, Papyri, and Inscriptions on the History and Ideals of Greek Athletics and Games* (Chicago, 1979); and Rachel Sargent Robinson, *Sources for the History of Greek Athletics* (Cincinnati, 1955). For the best scholarly surveys of sport and physical education in Greek antiquity, see Clarence A. Forbes, *Greek Physical Education* (New York, 1929); E. Norman Gardiner, *Greek Athletic Sports and Festivals* (London, 1910); Harold A. Harris, *Greek Athletes and Athletics* (London, 1964); Donald G. Kyle, "Directions in Ancient Sport History," *Journal of Sport History* 10 (Spring 1983): 7–52; Vera Olivova, *Sports and Games in the Ancient World* (London, 1984); Thomas F. Scanlon, "The Ecumenical Olympics: The Games in the Roman Era," in *The Olympic Games in Transition* (Champaign, Ill., 1988); Waldo Sweet, *Sport and Recreation in Ancient Greece* (New York, 1987); Nicholaos Yalouris, *The Eternal Olympics* (New York, 1976); W. Rushke, ed., *Archaeology of the Olympics* (Madison, Wis., 1988); and M. I. Finley and H. W. Pleket, *The Olympic Games: The First Thousand Years* (London, 1976).

There are scores of scholarly treatments on specific aspects of the world of ancient Greek athletics. On the subject of prizes and awards, see H. W. Pleket, "Games, Prizes, Athletes and Ideology," in *Stadion* 1 (1975): 49–89; and David C. Young, *The Olympic Myth of Greek Amateur Athletics* (Chicago, 1984). On nudity, see John Mouratidis, "The Origin of Nudity in Greek Athletics," *Journal of Sport History* 12 (1985): 213–32. On combat sports, consult Nigel B. Crowther, "Rounds and Byes in Greek Athletics," *Stadion* 18 (1992): 68–74; Michael Poliakoff, *Combat Sports in the Ancient Greek World: Competition, Violence and Culture* (New Haven, 1987); and Thomas F. Scanlon, "Greek Boxing Gloves: Terminology and Evolution," *Stadion* 8–9 (1982–1983): 31–46. On the pentathlon and its sub-events, see Robert Knight Barney, "The Ancient Greek Pentathlon Jump: A Preliminary Reinterpretive Examination," in Fernand Landry and W.A.R. Orban, eds., *Philosophy, Theology and History of Sport and Physical Activity* (Miami, 1978); Joachim Ebert, *Zum Pentathlon der Antike* (Berlin, 1963); and Harald Schmid and Norbert Muller, "New Recognition of Theories of the Long Jump in Ancient Greece," in *Proceedings: 1988 Seoul Olympic Scientific Congress* (Seoul, 1988). On running competition, see Stephen G. Miller, "Turns and Lanes in the Ancient Stadium," *American Journal of Archaeology* 84 (1980): 161–66. For information on the Pan-Athenaean Games in Athens, a civic festival rivaling the quadrennial Olympic Games, see Donald G. Kyle, *Athletics in Ancient Athens* (Leiden, 1987).

Finally, for general treatments of Greek cultural dispositions on the subject of sport, consult Edith Hamilton, *The Greek Way* (New York, 1963); Michael Poliakoff, "Stadium and Arena: Reflections on Greek, Roman, and Contemporary Social History,'' *Olympika: The International Journal of Olympic Studies* 2 (1993): 67–78; David Sansone, *Greek Athletics and the Genesis of Sport* (Berkeley, 1988); and James G. Thompson, ''Ancient Greek Attitudes on Athletics,'' *Canadian Journal of History of Sport* (December 1974): 159–66.

Robert K. Barney

Historical Dictionary
of the
Modern Olympic
Movement

PART I

THE SUMMER GAMES

ATHENS 1896

THE GAMES OF THE 1st OLYMPIAD

On Easter Sunday, April 6, 1896, the modern Olympic Games were inaugurated in Athens, Greece. It was a momentous occasion, due mainly to the enthusiasm and vision of a French nobleman, Baron Pierre de Coubertin. Coubertin had conceived the idea of reviving the Olympic Games and devoted his life to developing and spreading the word about Olympism. He published numerous articles and spoke to many groups about the possibility of reviving the ancient Olympic Games, abolished by official decree in A.D. 329. In addition to the lofty ideals of peace and brotherhood that the baron felt would be engendered by the Games, he was deeply moved by the excavations in Greece at Olympia, home of the ancient Olympics. These diggings, which began between 1875 and 1881, had unearthed numerous sites and treasures associated with the ancient Games. In 1908 Coubertin wrote that nothing in the history of the ancient world had made more of an impression on him than Olympia:

Long before I thought about reviving the Games, I had built up in my mind the contours of Olympia. Germany had excavated the ruins of ancient Olympia. . . . It was . . . [a] practical idea to renew the Games, especially as it seemed that international sport should play a new role in the world. (Graham and Ueberhorst, *The Modern Olympics,* p. 17)

In the early 1890s there was a growing concern with the rising popularity of athletics about the commercialism in sport. Due to this concern, it was proposed that the French host an international congress, ''Study of the Question of Amateurism.'' Coubertin enthusiastically made preparations for the meeting with the backing of many organizations and influential people. To give the congress an international flavor, he selected Charles Herbert, secretary of the Amateur Athletes Association in Great Britain, and William M. Sloane, professor at Princeton University in the United States, to assist him in planning the program.

Many other prominent people, such as the duke of Sparta, the king of Belgium, the prince of Wales, and the crown prince of Sweden, accepted honorary memberships to the congress. The main topics to be discussed involved the problem of amateurism and the possibility of the revival of the Olympic Games. Christopher Hill, in *Olympic Politics* (1992), points out Coubertin's political skill in using the subject of amateurism at the congress as a ruse to have the delegates discuss his main interest, the revival of the Olympic Games. Regardless of whether Coubertin misled the delegates, the seventy-nine people representing twelve countries in attendance at this historic congress at the Sorbonne in June 1894 were enthusiastic about the baron's idea and voted unanimously to revive the Games. Coubertin, pleased at this vote of confidence, envisioned that the first modern Games would be in Paris in 1900, the same year France would hold an international exposition. But the delegates thought 1900 was too long to wait and proposed the Games be started in 1896. The Greek delegate, Demetrios Vikelas, suggested that in the light of the history of the ancient Games, the first modern Games should be held in Athens, with Paris hosting the 1900 Games. All agreed, and thus in 1894, Athens, and Greece, had two years to prepare for this new international athletic event. The delegates also voted that the Games were to be held at four-year intervals and were not to imitate the ancient Games but be exclusively modern in character. Coubertin would choose an international committee, soon to be known as the International Olympic Committee (IOC). And, perhaps to justify the purpose of the congress, it was ruled that only amateurs would be allowed in these new Games.

With the same enthusiasm and dedication Coubertin directed toward the 1894 congress, he now devoted to the plans for the 1896 Games. He first chose his international committee, fourteen affluent men who could afford not only to pay their own travel expenses to meetings but also could contribute substantially to the activities of the IOC. He selected as president Vikelas, the delegate from Athens. Among the other members were his friends from the congress organizing committee, Herbert of Great Britain and Sloane of the United States. Some of the members were wealthy men who did not contribute much to the IOC, and later Coubertin called them *"une façade."*

After the initial excitement of Greece's being awarded the first modern Olympic Games, it soon became apparent that the government, on the verge of bankruptcy, would not commit to their support. The most ardent and powerful foe was Prime Minister Charilaos Tricoupis. Coubertin, fearing his dream would not come to fruition, rushed to Athens to give speeches, meet with sport officials, and do everything he could to generate enthusiasm and national pride for the Games. Crown Prince Constantine agreed to head an organizational committee with Vikelas, although it was evident that Coubertin was in charge. Coubertin's efforts were well received by the press, and soon the general public became enthusiastic about hosting the Olympic Games. To secure funds, the committee used several approaches. The government issued a set of commemorative stamps, which brought in 400,000 drachmas, and promised not to collect taxes from the gate receipts. Next, the committee appealed to citizens, especially the wealthy ones, residing in the country as well as those living abroad, for contributions. One of the most generous of these gifts was from George Averoff, who lived in Alexandria. He pledged to pay for the restoration of the stadium, originally constructed in 330 B.C. The total cost of the reconstruction was approximately 1 million drachmas. Because of Averoff's generosity, there was sufficient money to construct a shooting gallery, a velodrome, and a pier for the spectators at the swimming events.

While the Greek organizing committee was occupied with its fund raising and preparations, Coubertin was back in Paris attending to all the other details about these first modern Games. There were many problems to be solved in the overall organization of this international athletic contest. Bill Henry, Olympic historian, noted some of the questions Coubertin had to answer: "Who should invite the nations to the games? Who should write the invitations? What events should be held? How is a bicycle track constructed? Under what rules should athletes compete? What should they be given for prizes?" (Henry, *An Approved History of the Olympic Games*, 1981: 42).

There were many more questions and details. Coubertin was concerned about the symbolism of the Games and made plans for the opening and closing ceremonies that would suggest a theme of "peaceful internationalism." Coubertin's personal attention to detail was remarkable: he sent the invitations to the countries urging them to send athletes to the Games; planned the program, eliminating sports that seemed inadequate; selected the Thomas Cook Travel Agency to arrange for foreigners to travel to Greece; and chose the design and texture of the medals and diplomas to be awarded as prizes.

Meanwhile, preparations continued in Athens. The stadium reconstruction, a remarkable feat accomplished in a short time, was the work of well-known architect Anastas Metaxas. To preserve the antiquity but at the same time incorporate newer building methods, Metaxas consulted with archeologists from Germany and France. Hundreds of laborers, working around the clock, cleared the site and installed new blocks of white marble. By the beginning of the Games, all the marble was in place in the lower tier. The upper tier was built with temporary wooden seats; marble replaced this wood after the Games were over. Reports differ, but the seating capacity was between 50,000 and 70,000. The cinder track was constructed with the help of a groundskeeper from London. This constant work in the heart of the city did much to excite the citizens about the forthcoming Olympic Games.

For these first modern Olympic Games, only the first- and second-place winners received prizes, although each competitor was awarded a commemorative medal. In fact, there were no gold medals. The winner received a silver medal, a diploma, and a crown of olive branches, and the second-place finisher a bronze medal, a diploma, and a crown of laurel. Jules Chaplain, a distinguished French sculptor, designed the medals. All the prizes were awarded on the last day of the Games by George I.

There were 311 male athletes from thirteen countries present (no consideration of women participants was ever mentioned regarding these first Games), of whom all but 81 were from Greece. Among other nations, France and Germany each sent teams of 19 athletes, the United States had 13, and Great Britain sent 8. No other country had more than 4 athletes on its team. Most came at their own expense for an Olympic program that had nine sports and forty-three events. Many of these so-called national teams were not the best athletes from their respective country but came to the Games under unusual conditions. Since the idea was so new, most nations did not have an Olympic selection committee, and each team organized itself. For example, the U.S. team consisted of ten track and field athletes, one swimmer, and two pistol experts (brothers who were army captains). The team leader was Sloane from Princeton, who, since the congress of 1894, had been not only an ardent supporter of the Olympic Games but also a member of the new IOC. Although the New York Athletic Club had the most national track and field champions, it was not interested in sending any to these first Olympic Games. Sloane persuaded four Princeton track athletes to attend the Games. The captain, Robert Garrett, came from a wealthy family and probably paid his own expenses as well as those of his three Princeton teammates. The Boston Athletic Association encouraged five of its track and field competitors to join the team; along with them came a Harvard undergraduate, James B. Connolly. In addition to the 13 athletes, the team had a manager, John Graham, from the Boston Athletic Association, and a trainer, Scotty McMasters, from Princeton. The Boston group was financed by a wealthy stockbroker, Arthur Burnham, and the governor of Massachusetts, Oliver Ames. Thus, although the team was not composed of the strongest athletes in the United States, it consisted of enthusiastic and dedicated men who were champions in many ways at these first modern Olympic Games.

On Easter, April 6, 1896, Athens was a picture of colorful displays and celebratory banners. All the buildings were draped in bunting with multicolored streamers and green wreaths. Banners and other symbols bore the letters "O.A.," the Greek initials of the Olympic Games, and the two dates, 776 B.C. and A.D. 1896, linking the past to the present. The official report of the Games indicates the festive mood that day:

The day of the national celebration, which probably since it had been adopted as the national day, had not been celebrated with such great resplendence. The movements of the crowds were indescribable, from the early hours, in Stadium and Hermes Streets and in Constitution Square, all of them festively decorated. At every moment the cheerful bands from (different cities) echoed everywhere. (Coubertin, "The Logical Culmination of a Great Moment," p. 243)

The Games did not officially open until the afternoon of this Easter, and a momentous ceremony held in the morning is often omitted in descriptions of the Games. To honor George Averoff, who provided the money for the stadium, officials unveiled a statue of him near the stadium entrance. The life-sized study in white marble was the work of a Greek sculptor, Georgeos Vroutos. As Crown Prince Constantine removed the drape, there were shouts of "Long live Averoff!" and "Long live the nation!" The shy and modest Averoff was not present at this ceremony nor did he attend the Games, though he had been personally invited by the king. As the ceremonies were going on, the crowd was surging toward the stadium to buy tickets. There had been no advance sales, so more than 40,000 people were trying to buy tickets for the opening ceremony at 3:00. The tickets cost only 1 drachma for the upper tier and 2 for the lower seats (about 12 and 24 cents, respectively), but the demand was so great that shrewd speculators were buying up whole blocks of tickets and reselling them for a profit. In other words, there was scalping at these first modern Games.

The gates opened at noon, and by 2:00 P.M. all seats were occupied. It is estimated that in addition to the spectators in the stadium, another 50,000 sat on a nearby hillside, which afforded a view of the stadium. The royal family arrived and, with other noteworthy officials surrounding them, took their special seats adorned with red velvet cushions. King George was in his military dress uniform and the queen was in a white dress. The athletes assembled in double rows in the infield to witness the ceremonies, which began with a speech by Crown Prince Constantine that few could hear in these days before loudspeakers and radio. After Constantine's speech, the king rose and said, "I hereby proclaim the opening of the first International Olympic Games at Athens." As cannons roared, hundreds of pigeons were released. This proclamation was followed by the singing of the Olympic hymn written by the national poet, Costis Palamas, with music composed by Spyros Samaros. It so moved the audience that they demanded and received an encore. Then trumpets sounded the beginning of competition.

The program for the Games included track and field, fencing, weight lifting, rifle and pistol shooting, tennis, cycling, swimming, gymnastics, and wrestling. The U.S. team dominated the track and field competition, winning first place in nine of the twelve events, including all of the field events. The highlight of the track and field competition, however, was the marathon.

At the 1894 congress, where the delegates enthusiastically voted to reestablish the Olympic Games, Professor Michel Bréal, a distinguished French classical scholar and friend of Coubertin, suggested that there be a symbolic race in the first Olympics and offered a trophy to be awarded to the winner. It was agreed to commemorate the battle of Marathon, 490 B.C., when the Athenian messenger, Phiedippides, ran from Marathon to Athens, announced, "Rejoice, we have won," and promptly fell dead. The distance from Marathon to Athens (and therefore of the race) has been variously estimated from 22 to nearly 26 miles.

By Friday, April 11, the day of the race, public interest and anticipation was extremely high. The crowd in the stadium was even larger than that on opening day. Including the people outside the stadium, some 120,000 viewed the race. Because of the historical connection, the Greeks viewed the marathon as the principal event of the Games. Advance publicity stirred nationalist sentiments, and numerous gifts, including free haircuts, groceries, and clothes, were promised if a Greek won the race.

The night before the race, the twenty-five entrants were taken to Marathon, where the contest was started by a pistol shot from the army officer who had persuaded Spiridon Loues, a soldier in his regiment, to enter. The marathon was a new experience for most of the participants, who had never run or trained for such a distance. Many dropped out along the way due to exhaustion and their lack of knowledge about pacing.

As the runners approached the stadium, the word spread that the Greek runner, Spiridon Loues, was in the lead. The crowd roared in anticipation as they watched the entrance to the stadium. Loues entered, and as he covered the last

200 meters, he was accompanied on each side by the royal princes, Constantine and George. According to the official report:

Nothing could describe what happened in the stadium at that hour. . . . The Greek flag [was raised]. A storm of excitement was brought forth. The air vibrated with victory cries; handkerchiefs were waved as were small Greek flags, which until this moment had been hidden. The spectators were beside themselves with joy and the thrill of victory. (Graham and Ueberhorst, *The Modern Olympics*, p. 23)

Among other events, tennis and swimming were perhaps the most unusual. Tennis best exemplifies the novelty of the Games and the lack of rules regarding eligibility requirements. The sixteen entrants used the Athens Tennis Club courts in single elimination tournaments for both singles and doubles competition. The winner of both was John Boland of Ireland, who just happened to be visiting Athens at the time and read about the Games. He bought a racquet, entered, and was victorious. His doubles partner was Fritz Traun of Germany, whose original partner had become ill. Their victory was the only time in the Olympics with an international competitive unit.

Swimming was contested in the Bay of Phaleron near Piraeus, the seaport serving Athens. The starting line was marked by floating pumpkins, and the finish line was indicated by a red flag on the shore. A ferry took the swimmers to the starting line, where they bobbed in the water until a pistol shot started the race. Cold and breezy weather had lowered the water temperature to an estimated 13 degrees Celsius (55°F), cold enough to induce Gardner Williams, the only American competitor, to announce that he was freezing and withdraw from the 100-meter race. Both swimming events were won by a Hungarian, Alfred Hajos, who contended best with the cold water and 12-foot waves. A special Olympic event was a 100-meter swimming race for sailors from the Greek navy.

The final events of the first modern Olympic Games were the king's breakfast and the awards ceremony. A festive banquet for athletes, officials, and journalists, later known as the king's breakfast, was held at the royal palace for some 260 people. Much attention was focused on Spiridon Loues, not only for winning the marathon and bringing glory to Greece but also for his splendid appearance; he was attired in the national uniform of Greece, with a narrow jacket, flaring fustanella (or short skirt), and tights. The festivities began with an orchestra's playing the national anthem and the Olympic hymn, followed by speeches and toasts. When the meal was completed, more speeches followed. In his speech, quoted in the official report of the games, the king revealed the new spirit of his countrymen:

Greece, the mother and nursery of athletic contests in Pan Hellenic Antiquity, in undertaking and carrying out these today with courage under the eyes of Europe and of the New World, can, now that the general success has been acknowledged, hope that the foreigners who honored it will appoint our lead as a peaceful meeting place of the nations, as a continuous and permanent field for the Olympic Games. (Quoted in "The Olympic Games—Athens 1896," *Olympic Review*, p. 174)

Although the speech was greeted by great applause, it was noteworthy that Coubertin was never acknowledged formally as the instigator of the Games nor was it mentioned that he was the new IOC president for the 1900 Games, to be held in Paris. Later Coubertin commented about the slight: "The care that the Greeks took to 'suppress' me on every occasion pained but did not astonish me."

All the Olympic awards were distributed at a ceremony that concluded the Games. After a day's postponement due to bad weather, the ceremony took place on April 15. After the arrival of the royal party, those without tickets were admitted free to ensure the stadium was full. Again, hundreds of other spectators sat or stood on the hill nearby. Before awarding the prizes, the king heard a special classical Greek ode written for the occasion. Then each athlete was summoned to the platform by the herald's trumpet to receive his prize.

In addition to the usual awards, certain extra prizes were awarded to the winners and contestants. Each athlete received a commemorative medal. Robert Garrett, winner of the discus and shot put, was not only given the discus he used to win that event but also a silver vase from the crown princess and a marble bust of the goddess Athena. Loues received an antique amphora over 2,000 years old, as well as a silver urn Bréal had donated.

The highlight of the ceremonies was the parade of athletes. Organized by nation, they paraded around the track led by Loues, again dressed in his colorful national garb. At the close of this march, they reassembled in front of the king, who ended the Games with the statement, "I proclaim the ending of the first Olympic Games."

After the Games, Coubertin had to counteract the nationalistic fervor spreading among a number of officials that Greece be selected as the permanent site for future Olympic Games. He felt strongly that if Greece ever succeeded with this lofty ambition, it would be the end of his dream and the modern Olympic Games. He was determined that the Games be rotated to different sites in order to spread the word and increase the internationalism of the event. In "The Olympic Games of 1896," which he wrote for the November 1896 *Century* magazine, he emphasized that this report was "by Their Founder, Baron Pierre de Coubertin, now President of The International Committee," and he included important information about the rotation of the Games.

In Congress at Paris in 1894, it was agreed that every country should celebrate the Olympic Games in turn. . . . The presidency of this [IOC] Committee falls to the country in which the next games are to be held. A Greek, M. Bikelas, has presided for the last two years. A Frenchman now presides and will do so until 1900, since the next games are to take place at Paris during the Exposition. (p. 3a)

He reinforced the importance of different sites for the Games by rhetorically asking, "Where will those of 1904 take place? Perhaps at New York, perhaps at Berlin, or at Stockholm. The question is soon to be decided."

Shortly after the end of the Games Coubertin offered a compromise to Crown Prince Constantine regarding Greece's proposal to be the permanent site of the Olympic Games. He suggested that the original plan of rotating the Games should be kept in force and that Greece, in the non-Olympic years, could hold Pan Hellenic Games, the first of which could be in 1898. Within a year, however, Greece was at war with Turkey. Although the war lasted only a month, it left Greece defeated and bankrupt, thus unable to host Games in either 1898 or 1900.

The final move to end any idea of Greece's hosting the Games on a permanent basis took place at an IOC meeting in July 1897, at the French seaport city of Le Havre. John Lucas states that it "was Coubertin's way of turning his back on the Greek-Turkish war, of dismissing any possibility of Athens as the next Olympic site. No Greeks showed up at Le Havre and thus, Coubertin was left unencumbered by their brand of Olympic loyalty" (Lucas, *The Modern Olympic Games,* p. 49).

No longer was there a threat to the baron's dream of different Olympic sites to spread the word of Olympism. There have been many changes since 1896, some of which the baron looked upon with disfavor, but today the Olympic Games is the major sporting spectacle in the world, with thousands of athletes from over 180 countries participating—an enormous change from the approximately 300 athletes and the 13 countries represented in 1896.

BIBLIOGRAPHICAL ESSAY

The official report for the Athens Games is *The Olympic Games B.C. 776–A.D. 1896*; Published with the Sanction and under the Patronage of the Central Committee in Athens, published first in Athens in 1896 and subsequently in several different editions, many of them multilingual, including text in English. The report was published in two parts: the first, *The Olympic Games in Ancient Times,* edited by Spiridon P. Lambros and Nikolaos G. Politis, includes the history of the ancient Games, as well as information on the background and facilities for the 1896 Games. The second part, *The Olympic Games of 1896,* edited by Pierre de Coubertin, Timoleon Philemon, Nikolaos G. Politis, and Charalambos Anninos, covers the Games themselves. There were no national Olympic committees formed in 1896; hence, there are no national reports. Karl Lennartz, *Kenntwisse und Vorstellung von Olympia und der Olympische Spielen in der Zeit von 393–1896* (Schorndorf, 1974), is a collection of historical documents from the time after the end of the ancient Games to the beginning of the modern era.

Major secondary sources of information include John MacAloon, *The Great Symbol: Pierre de Coubertin and the Origins of the Modern Olympic Games* (Chicago, 1981), an intellectual biography of Coubertin that provides many details about the events leading up to the Games, the Games themselves, and incidents after the Games. The book contains a thorough bibliography. Richard Mandell, *The First Modern Olympics* (Berkeley,

Calif., 1976), is a general history of the Games, with many significant descriptions of the various venues, the background, and the accomplishments of the athletes. Ath. Tarasoulleas, *Olympic Games in Athens, 1896–1906* (Vironas, Greece, 1988), is a day-by-day account of the Games, illustrated with period postcards and containing summaries and winners of each event. Karl Lennartz and Walter Teutenberg, *Die deutsche Olympia-Mannschaft von 1896* (Kassel, 1992), offers profiles of the members of the German Olympic team that was sent to Athens. See also David C. Young, "The Origins of the Modern Olympics: A New Version," *International Journal of the History of Sport* 4, 3 (1987): 271–300, which discusses a series of national games held in Greece between 1859 and 1889.

A number of general Olympic histories pay particular attention to the Athens Games. See, for example, Peter J. Graham and Horst Ueberhorst, eds., *The Modern Olympics* (West Point, N.Y., 1976); Christopher Hill, *Olympic Politics* (Manchester, 1992); Bill Henry, *An Approved History of the Olympic Games* (Los Angeles, 1984); and John Lucas, *The Modern Olympic Games* (Cranbury, N.J., 1980).

Among contemporary articles regarding the Games, consult Pierre de Coubertin, "The Olympic Games of 1896," *Century Magazine* 53 (1896): 39–53 and "The Logical Culmination of a Great Moment," reprinted in *Olympic Review* 161 (1981): 243, for his views on the Games, and Rufus Richardson, "The Revival of the Olympic Games," *Scribner's Magazine* 19 (April 1896): 452–59. Other contemporary accounts include James B. Connolly, *Olympic Victor: A Story of the Modern Games* (New York, 1908); James S. Murray, *Souvenir of the Olympic Games at Athens* (Boston, 1896); Ellery H. Clark, *Reminiscences of an Athlete: Twenty Years on Track and Field* (Boston, 1911); and Burton Holmes, *The Olympian Games in Athens, 1896: The First Modern Olympics* (New York, 1984), a book originally published as a travelogue in 1901.

Joanna Davenport

PARIS 1900

THE GAMES OF THE IID OLYMPIAD

The discord and criticism that surrounded the 1900 Games were the reverse of the general euphoria that characterized the Athens Games in 1896. In Athens, the ancient tradition of athleticism was successfully revived, and the king of Greece, among others, prevailed on Baron Pierre de Coubertin and the International Olympic Committee (IOC) to declare that city the permanent home of the Olympic Games. Their resistance inflamed the Greeks, and editorials and letters complained that the baron was "a thief, trying to strip Greece of one of the historic jewels of her raiment" (MacAloon, *This Great Symbol,* p. 272).

The 33-year-old baron and his wife retreated to Corfu to escape the widespread criticism, its tranquility erasing any doubts about the rigidity of his stance that the Games were for the world and that venues for its display should be variable. Moreover, the birth of the Games and his son, Jacques, in the same year reinforced Coubertin's own sense of destiny and belief in his life's mission. He believed that the Paris Games would place him on the world's pedestal and convince the world that he was the sole founder of the modern Olympic movement.

The first Olympic congress at Le Havre in 1897 was an attempt to bring together the various European sporting authorities. This was successful in that the congress affirmed that the 1900 Games should not go to Athens. However, the question of where they should go was not as clear-cut as Coubertin might have envisaged. When he suggested Paris as the host city, the Union des Sociétés françaises de sports athlétiques (USFSA), of which he was secretary-general, opposed the idea. The French government was also unenthusiastic, but Coubertin finally persuaded government officials to sponsor the next Olympic Games in conjunction with the *exposition universelle* already scheduled for 1900.

Coubertin's dream was to reconstruct the ancient site of Olympia at the exposition—its temples, stadia, gymnasia, and statues. He thought that such a glorification of sport would focus attention on the Olympic movement and promote internationalism through athletic competition.

Many factors, however, mitigated against Coubertin's dreams. First, he had personal problems. In 1898, his first-born son, Jacques, was left too long in the sun and had a stroke, which left him severely retarded. The resultant grief and trauma not only affected Coubertin's marriage but also could have affected his judgment during the crucial period from 1898 to 1900. Second, the appointment of the engineer and bachelor, Alfred Picard, as commissioner general of the exposition sealed Coubertin's doom. It was not long before plans to build elaborate athletic facilities for the Games were scrapped in order to showcase other aspects of the exposition that might better display French culture and civilization and at the same time be more profitable. Picard did agree, however, that various exhibitions of physical exercise and sports could be scattered among the various sections of the exposition. The organization was, to say the least, bizarre: skating and fencing were part of the cutlery section; rowing fell under lifesaving; and track and field were categorized with provident societies.

Coubertin established an organizing committee of elite aristocrats under the chairmanship of vicomte de la Rochefoucauld, which outlined a program on May 29, 1898, that basically followed the successful 1896 program, adding boxing, soccer, and polo and replacing shooting with archery. There was criticism of the aristocratic makeup of the committee, but more important, internal political difficulties within the USFSA led to the decision on November 9, 1898, that it should disavow any relationship with the Olympic Games and instead organize its own Games. The municipal council of Paris supported this decision, which led to Coubertin's resignation from the USFSA and the dissolution of Rochefoucauld's committee.

On February 19, 1899, Picard named Daniel Merillon, a USFSA member, as director-general of the athletic contests of the exposition. Merillon was at the time president of the French Shooting Federation, and his plans for the athletic contests were approved in early June 1899. Under Merillon's plans, the track and field events were held on the grounds of the Racing Club of France, at Croix-Catelan in the Bois de Boulogne; the swimming at Aenieres in the polluted waters of the Seine River; the yachting at Meulan; the fencing at Tuileries in the Palais des Expositions; the lawn tennis at the Ile de Puteaux; the gymnastics at Vincennes; the equestrian events at the Avenue de Breteuil; the cycling at the Parc des Princes; and the shooting at various venues.

The term "Olympic Games" was discarded and replaced with "Concours internationaux d'exercices physiques et de sport." In the press, the competitions were hailed variously as "International Games," "International Championships," "Paris Championships," and "World Championships." Occasionally in the foreign press one read of the "Olympian Games" or, rarely, "Olympic Games." The Games lasted from May 20 to October 28, with no official opening or closing ceremonies. There were also world amateur and professional championships held in this period of complete disarray, and Coubertin's name was not mentioned in magazines or newspapers.

Indeed, with Coubertin's resignation, the lack of IOC involvement, and the USFSA takeover, an interesting thesis could be advanced that the Olympic Games were not held in 1900, that they had been abandoned, that the movement had failed. This, of course, is not the official stance of the IOC, though it is certain that most competitors had no idea that they were competing in the IId Olympic Games. In 1912, the IOC attempted to sort out from the muddle which of the events and contests could be designated as "Olympic" sports and which winners would be placed on the Olympic roll.

By putting Merillon in charge of the sports, Picard ensured that nothing interfered with or detracted from the main attraction, which was the exposition. This allowed the French to ignore the IOC, determining the events to be held and establishing their own rules. The Merillon program was divided into ten sections: Athletic Sports and Games; Gymnastics; Fencing; Marksmanship; Horsemanship; Cycling; Automobilism; Nautical Sports; Life-Saving (Fireman's Drill); and Air Sports (Ballooning).

The choices of ballooning, automobile racing, and fireman's drill seem incongruous by today's Olympic standards, and even in 1900 their suitability was questioned. Coubertin flatly declared that although "interesting," they were "not pure sport." Perhaps even more at variance with Olympic ideals, however, was the decision to include events for professionals. Coubertin, an avowed apostle of amateurism, had to compromise his principles, but he managed to rationalize his position by pointing out the uniqueness of the exposition being held at the turn of the century and the opportunity it provided for bringing together people of all classes and from all nations. Competition for professionals would be allowed on this one occasion because of its special character, but Coubertin vowed to prevent it from happening again.

Coubertin's opinion was of little consequence in the Paris Games of 1900 because he and the IOC were engaged in a sporting festival completely and absolutely out of their control. Officially the IOC has in later years accepted events in archery, soccer, track and field, cycling, equestrian sports, fencing, golf, gymnastics, lawn tennis, rowing, rugby, shooting, swimming, water polo, and yachting as part of the 1900 Olympic Games, while not sanctioning cricket, croquet, polo, ballooning, pelota, automobile racing, military exercises, firefighting competitions, and angling for live fish in the Seine. Even then, many oddities by modern standards were accorded Olympic status: the standing high jump; the standing long jump; the standing hop, step, and jump; the tug-of-war; the equestrian high jump; the equestrian long jump; the 200-meter obstacle swim; the 60-meter underwater swim; and live pigeon shooting.

Official records give the number of competitors as 1,319, which included eleven females, and the number of nations competing as twenty-two. There were no national teams and no Olympic Village to house the athletes, who stayed in Paris hotels and at Versailles.

Track and field events were held in the beautiful Bois du Boulogne, the private property of the wealthy Racing Club of France, which did not want the splendor of its surroundings spoiled. Because the club refused to allow any trees to be cut down, discus and javelin throws often landed in wooded areas. Robert Garrett, a member of the American team, was exasperated as he attempted to throw the discus straight down a line of trees and failed to repeat his gold medal win of 1896. The French considered it impractical to lay a cinder track and settled for an undulating grass track, which had a gradient of 60 centimeters in 100 meters. For hurdles, old and rigid telephone poles were used. A grandstand was hastily constructed, but a row of trees separated the track from the spectators.

The Courses à pied et concours athlétiques opened without fanfare or ceremony on Saturday, July 14, the revered national holiday of Bastille Day. Several events, including all the finals, were therefore scheduled for Sunday, in spite of the fact that the organizers had previously agreed there would be no Sunday competition. The U.S. athletes, easily the largest foreign contingent, protested vigorously at being asked to compete on the Lord's Day. Students from Yale, Princeton, Syracuse, Chicago, and Michigan universities were forbidden to take part, but those from the New York Athletic Club and the University of Pennsylvania were allowed to decide for themselves. In the long jump, Alvin Kraenzlein won; Myer Prinstein, the U.S. intercollegiate champion and world record holder, watched from the sidelines. The United States did not compete in Sunday's cross-country team event, which the British, with Australian Stanley Rowley as fifth man, won.

Despite their absence on Sunday, the Americans reigned supreme, taking seventeen of the twenty-three titles. Together, four men—Ray Ewry, Alvin Kraenzlein, Irving Baxter, and John Tewksbury—won eleven first, five second, and one third place. Kraenzlein's four victories—in the 60-meter dash, the 110-meter hurdles, the 200-meter hurdles, and the running long jump—remain a record in individual track victories. Regulations now prevent an athlete from entering more than three individual events. Apart from his record-setting performance, Kraenzlein revolutionized hurdling technique by clearing the hurdles with the forward leg straight and the trailing leg bent behind him.

Ray Ewry distinguished himself by winning three events: the standing long jump, the standing high jump, and the standing hop, step, and jump. He had suffered from polio as a child but through exercise developed unusual strength in his legs. Ewry competed in five Olympic Games, including those of 1906, winning a total of ten first places, a record that has not been broken in track and field competition.

The marathon, which had been the highlight of 1896, was run in confusion and uncertainty. The competitors ran four laps around the track, then through the Bois du Boulogne before circling Paris, following the old Parisian city fortifications. On the streets, they were obstructed by spectators and cyclists, there being no officials to protect them. Fewer than half the runners finished. The first to finish, A. L. Newton of the United States, who took the lead halfway through the race and claimed he was never passed, nevertheless lost the race to Michael Theato of France, a local baker who was thoroughly familiar with the course and its shortcuts.

As far as world records were concerned, the Games were a success. Six world records were broken, and all previous Olympic track and field times or distances were improved upon, except in the marathon, which was won in 2 hours, 59 minutes, 45 seconds.

Although the track and field competitions were considered to be the main Olympic championships, there were other events. The French dominated fencing, gymnastics, archery, and rowing. Great Britain defeated France, 4–0, in soccer, and France won over Germany, 25–16, in rugby. The United States won the golf events, and the British took the tennis titles. The swimming, held outside

Paris on the Seine, drew competitors from numerous European countries, but the Americans were conspicuously absent. The sole Australian entrant, Freddie Lane, won the 200-meter freestyle and the 200-meter obstacle races.

One positive feature of the 1900 Games was the entry of women into Olympic competition, mainly because Coubertin, who adamantly opposed their participation, was not in control of the program. Coubertin saw the Olympic Games as exalting male athleticism and abhorred the thought of women making fools of themselves by sweating in public. Until his death, he tenaciously attacked the "regrettable impurity" that had infiltrated the Games with women's participation. In 1900, the French included women's golf and tennis in the athletic sports and games section, and at least five countries sent competitors: the United States, Great Britain, France, Bohemia (Czechoslovakia), and Switzerland.

The honor of being the first female Olympic champion went to Charlotte Cooper of Great Britain, who defeated Helene Prevost of France, 6–4, 6–2, in tennis. Cooper won the mixed doubles on the same day, teaming with Reginald Doherty of Great Britain to defeat the French pair of Prevost and Henri Mahoney, 6–4, 7–5.

Golf was an Olympic sport only in 1900 and 1904, but only in 1900 could women compete. Nine women from four countries entered a nine-hole stroke play event at the Compiègne Club just north of Paris. Margaret Abbott, who was born in Calcutta but learned to play golf in Chicago, shot a 47 to win the event. She was one of Chicago's top women golfers and had won many local tournaments. She was studying art and music in Paris when she heard about the Olympic golf tournament and decided to enter. Her mother also played in the event, finishing eighth. Pauline Whittier won second place with a 49. She had been living in Switzerland and played golf at St. Moritz. Third place was won by Dana Pankhurst Wright Pratt with a 53.

The 1900 Games were conducted despite the overriding scandal of the blatantly racist, anti-Jewish Dreyfus Affair and the financial debacle of the Panama Canal, as French nationalism seemed to require such displays to reinforce their feelings of cultural and artistic superiority. The rise of Germany's economic power and the decline of France reawakened anti-German feelings within France that made the organizers of the exposition determined to show the best of French wares.

But the exposition did not succeed in its goal of establishing French economic and cultural superiority. Germany put on a fine display of its latest inventions, and many German tourists flocked to Paris to see the exposition. In comparison, the French exhibits looked second rate, and the French people were only too aware of that fact.

The exposition was a failure in the sporting sense as well. The athletic contests were poorly organized, the events were held in dismal facilities, and both professionals and amateurs competed. An Australian competitor, Stan Rowley, summed up the feelings of many for his country's national press:

To treat these events as world's championships would be really an insult to the important events they are supposed to be. They are treated by most of the competitors as—A HUGE JOKE—and when it comes to that one has come all this way from Australia to compete in them, it really seems ridiculous. (*The Referee,* 1900)

These Games were certainly not worthy to be considered an Olympic Games, and with the lack of involvement of Coubertin and the IOC, it can successfully be argued that no Olympics were held in Paris in 1900. The movement that showed so much promise in 1896 seemed to have collapsed by 1900.

BIBLIOGRAPHICAL ESSAY

There is generally considered to be no official report of the 1900 Paris Games. Two reports related to the exposition, however, may serve as virtual official reports. *Exposition universelle internationale de 1900 à Paris. Concours internationaux d'exercices physiques et de sports. Rapports* (Paris, 1901), contains a summary of the results of the athletic competition and includes photographs and tables. A second exposition document, *Exposition universelle internationale de 1900. Direction générale de l'exploitation. Réglaments et programmes des concours nationaux et internationaux d'exercices physiques et de sports* (Paris, 1901), contains information on the rules and schedules of the various events and discusses some of the events, such as ballooning, which were not subsequently sanctioned by the IOC. For a similar program description in English, see Ferdinand Peck, *Programme of the International Contests of Physical Exercises and Sports* (New York, 1900).

A Paris magazine, *La Vie au grand air 1900,* published interesting summaries and photographs of sport at the exposition, including photographs of Coubertin's friend Father Didion, who gave the movement its "Citius, Altius, Fortius" (Faster, Higher, Stronger) slogan; the professional athletes; the cycling championships; and much more. Coubertin's view of the Games is contained in his article, "The Mystery of the Olympian Games," *North American Review* (June 1900): 806–9.

Various secondary works shed light on the history of these Games. John J. MacAloon, *This Great Symbol* (Chicago, 1981), describes Coubertin's personal life during this time, including his family tragedy and psychological turmoil. Richard Mandell, *Paris 1900: The Great World's Fair* (Toronto, 1967), is a good history of the exposition but includes little about the Olympics. A more succinct history of the exposition is Robert W. Brown, "Paris 1900," in John E. Findling and Kimberly D. Pelle, eds., *Historical Dictionary of World's Fairs and Expositions, 1851–1988* (Westport, Conn., 1990), pp. 155–64. Reet Howell and Max Howell, *Aussie Gold: The Story of Australia at the Olympics* (Albion, Queensland, 1986), uses correspondence and interviews of competitors and their descendants to describe the Games from an Australian perspective.

Reet Ann Howell and Max L. Howell

ST. LOUIS 1904
THE GAMES OF THE IIID OLYMPICS

Historians consider the third Olympic Games, held in St. Louis, to have been the worst in the history of the Olympic movement. Originally awarded to Chicago, the Games were moved to St. Louis, where the events were caught up in the promotional hoopla of a world's fair. The St. Louis Olympic Games were bathed in nationalism, ethnocentrism, controversy, confusion, booterism, and bad taste. They were, in short, a clear reflection of American sport, if not America itself, shortly after the turn of the century.

From the very beginning of the Olympic movement, Chicago was a prime candidate to be the first American city to host the Olympic Games. The fiasco that was the Paris Games influenced Baron Pierre de Coubertin's ideas about where the next Olympic Games should be held and sparked the interest of two prominent figures in American sport who had observed the 1900 Games. James E. Sullivan, the secretary of the powerful Amateur Athletic Union (AAU), was an influential figure in American amateur sport. A meticulous organizer, record keeper, and somewhat skilled public relations man, Sullivan had been appalled by the disorganized state of the Paris Games. Amos Alonzo Stagg was the well-known football and track coach at the University of Chicago. He had taken the University of Chicago track and field team to Paris to participate in the Games and later used his experiences there to help promote the Chicago Olympic effort.

A May 1901 article in the *Chicago Tribune* about the 1904 Olympic Games stirred an interest in bringing the competition to Chicago. University of Chicago president William Rainey Harper formed a committee of eight, chaired by prominent attorney Henry J. Furber and including Stagg, to study the question of bidding for the 1904 Games. With encouragement from Coubertin and promises for funding from Chicago merchants, the committee decided to bid for the Games.

When the International Olympic Committee (IOC) met in Paris in May 1901 to select the site for the 1904 Games, the only two cities to put forward serious bids were St. Louis and Chicago. The St. Louis bid had problems. The plan was to tie the Games into the scheduled 1903 world's fair. Coubertin adamantly opposed both: linking the Games with another world's fair and moving them forward to 1903.

The Chicago bid held much more appeal for Coubertin. He had been extremely impressed with the city during his visit to the 1893 World's Columbian Exposition and liked the idea that the Games would be associated with the University of Chicago. The city's main selling point, however, was that local merchants had promised $200,000 to support the event. With Coubertin's enthusiasm for Chicago and the promise of financial support, a favorable vote from the IOC members was a forgone conclusion. On May 21, 1901, the Chicago Olympic Committee received a telegram from Coubertin: "Chicago Wins."

Over the next two years, a series of circumstances occurred that allowed St. Louis to steal the Olympic Games. On March 3, 1901, Congress passed the Louisiana Purchase Exposition bill, which authorized funding for the St. Louis fair. The exposition company then had little more than two years to organize the fair before the proposed opening date of May 1, 1903. When construction delays and the likelihood of only a small number of exhibits threatened financial disaster, the Louisiana Purchase Exposition Company received congressional authority to postpone the opening of the fair for one year. The one-year extension and the redoubling of the efforts of the exposition company to secure exhibits and attractions put the world's fair and the Chicago Olympic Games on a collision course.

Meanwhile, the Chicago Olympic Committee continued to promote the Games. In August 1902, it released a letter of support from President Theodore Roosevelt. At the same time, the organizers of the Louisiana Purchase Exposition began serious consideration of ways to acquire the Olympic Games as an added attraction for the exposition. In early October, exposition officials requested a preliminary meeting with Furber concerning the Games; two weeks later exposition president David Francis traveled to Chicago to talk with the members of Chicago Olympic Committee.

After the meeting, Furber informed Coubertin that the St. Louis exposition organizers felt that the Olympic Games in Chicago would threaten their enterprise, and if the Olympics were not switched to St. Louis, they would put on their own athletic events. This, wrote Furber, could damage the Games seriously. Furber concluded that if Coubertin wished to change the site, the Chicago committee would raise no objection.

The controversy placed Coubertin and the IOC in a difficult dilemma. If Coubertin forced Chicago to live up to its commitment to hold the Games in 1904, they might be so overshadowed by the St. Louis events that they would attract few athletes and little public attention. Worse, Chicago could back out of its agreement at the last minute, and the Games would have to be canceled. Equally distasteful to Coubertin was the transfer of the Games to St. Louis, where they would be only a sideshow attraction to the much larger international exposition.

Apparently Coubertin decided that St. Louis was the less harmful choice, for when the IOC met in Paris on December 23, 1903, it voted to transfer the 1904 Games to St. Louis. Shortly afterward, Coubertin wrote to Walter Liginger, president of the AAU, asking that he and James E. Sullivan take charge of the events. Liginger quickly accepted.

St. Louis, Missouri, sits on the floodplain of the great curve in the Mississippi River and in 1900 was the fourth largest city in the United States, with a population of 575,238. St. Louis was a midwestern city with a foreign-born population of 19.4 percent. About 10 percent of the residents had been born in Germany, and many more were first-generation German-Americans.

In 1901 the Louisiana Purchase Exposition Company had been incorporated to produce a world's fair that would bring prestige to and focus on St. Louis. David R. Francis, the former mayor of St. Louis and governor of Missouri, was elected president of the company, which decided to locate the exposition in Forest Park, a wooded park on the western side of the city. The groundbreaking ceremony was held on December 20, 1901.

On Saturday, April 20, 1904, a beautiful sunny day, the Louisiana Purchase Exposition opened. The crowd of 187,793 was treated to a parade of hundreds of dignitaries from the U.S. and foreign governments, military units, and bands. Promptly at 1:06 P.M., President Roosevelt in Washington, D.C., pressed a gold telegraph key that "unfurled the flags and put in motion all of the tremendous engines of the Exposition."

The Louisiana Purchase Exposition had three major objectives, as did most other world's fairs of that period: to promote St. Louis and to demonstrate the city's ability to establish and administer a first-class expedition; to provide an attractive spectacle to draw enough people to break even financially, a difficult task with $19.6 million at stake; and to demonstrate progress, a term many felt was synonymous with civilization as represented by the industrialized, Western nations. Consequently the exposition devoted much of the exposition space to industrial and commercial exhibits, particularly those demonstrating modern technology.

The exposition was massive, covering 2 square miles and including more than 200 buildings, virtually a city unto itself. It had its own railway, bank, post office, electrical generators, hotel, and restaurants and could accommodate daytime crowds of more than 100,000. The Renaissance-style architecture, the grand water basin, and the many lagoons were reminiscent of the 1893 Chicago fair, but it was twice as large and cost twice as much to build as the earlier fair.

Organizationally, the fair was divided into sixteen departments. One of them, the Department of Physical Culture, was both cultural and reinforced the belief of the superiority of Western industrial society. In general, the Physical Culture Department exhibits demonstrated the progress made by modern people in attaining better health. The exhibits, including athletic events by various clubs and educational institutions, fulfilled educational objectives, and the department was used to attract professional meetings to the fair.

Moreover, exposition organizers used athletic events as inexpensive attractions, and the free publicity that these events received on sports pages, both locally and nationally, was invaluable in promoting the fair. As plans for the fair became more grandiose, so did the scope of the Physical Culture exhibit. The most important boost to the exhibit occurred when the opening of the fair was postponed from 1903 to 1904, enabling the Louisiana Purchase Exposition to steal the Olympic Games from Chicago.

The securing of the Olympic Games necessitated the hiring of James E. Sullivan as chief of the Department of Physical Culture. Sullivan's wide-ranging background made him an ideal choice for the job. He had worked at the U.S. pavilion at the Paris exposition in 1900 and had been director of athletics at the Pan-American Exposition at Buffalo in 1901. At the time of his appointment as chief, Sullivan was the secretary of the AAU and president of its Metropolitan Athletic Association (New York City). He had owned and published *Sporting Times* and in 1904 was the owner of the American Sports Publishing Company, which published the *Spalding Athletic Guide Series* and many other books about physical education and athletics.

The Department of Physical Culture was housed in a permanent, three-story building later used as a gymnasium by Washington University. The department was also responsible for the Olympic stadium, which held 10,000 spectators and had a one-third-mile track rather than the standard one-quarter-mile track. All of the athletic events, including the Olympic events were held out-of-doors, in the infield of the stadium, with the exception of two basketball games, which were played in the gymnasium because of rain.

Sullivan used his numerous contacts to promote the Physical Culture exhibit by attracting professional meetings, scheduling championship athletic events, and recruiting participants for the Olympic Games.

Sullivan staged more than forty different athletic events, which by his own estimate drew an astonishing 9,576 participants. At that time the IOC did not have an established program of Olympic events. The selection of events was left to the organizers of the Games, and Sullivan at one time or another referred to every one of the events he scheduled as Olympic, creating tremendous confusion. The Physical Culture Department events began on May 14 with a track meet for Missouri high schools and dragged on for six months before concluding on November 26 with an "Olympic College Football" game in which Carlisle beat Haskell 34–4 in a game between the two Indian schools.

The most popular events were the gymnastics exhibitions and competitions held by the German Turner Clubs. A mass exhibition on June 23 drew 3,500 participants, and a July event drew 140 competitors, many of whom traveled from Germany to participate. Other successful events were the public school basketball and track championships, the YMCA championships, and a demonstration of Bohemian gymnastics by 1,000 American Sokol Club members. The least successful events were the Olympic roque tournament (a croquet-like game), with just three participants, and the abbreviated Olympic water polo, soccer, and lacrosse tournaments, each of which drew three teams.

The 1904 Olympic Games was an athletic sideshow to the world's fair in much the same way as the 1900 Olympic Games in Paris had been. Coubertin had suspected as much and did not even make the trip to St. Louis to attend the Games.

Sullivan organized about sixteen different athletic events that could be considered Olympic because they were open to all competitors, had foreign entries, or are current Olympic events. The program was spread out over five months, beginning on July 4. On that day, a ten-event AAU track and field competition was held, and the winner, Thomas Kiely, is listed in most sources as the Olympic decathlon champion. The events continued through mid-November, concluding with a three-team soccer tournament that was won easily by the Galt (Canada) Football Club over two hastily organized, inept St. Louis teams.

Few European athletes bothered to travel to St. Louis to compete. Americans were virtually the only competitors in many events, including boxing, wrestling, roque, tennis, tug-of-war, gymnastics, and archery (the only event for women). In fact, athletes from the United States swept every medal in every event in those sports, most of which also served as U.S. championship events. All the athletes wore the uniforms of their athletic club rather than that of their country. The most spirited competition in the Games was between the New York and Chicago athletic clubs.

Two events drew some foreign athletes: golf and fencing. The golf tournament attracted a handful of Canadians among the eighty-five entrants (one-third of whom were from local St. Louis clubs), and George Lyon, the 1903 Canadian champion, beat H. Chandler Egan, the defending U.S. champion, 3–2, in the final round of match play. The fencing competition, which drew only nine participants (one German, two Cubans, and six Americans), was dominated by Ramón Fonst and Manuel Díaz, both Cubans.

The swimming events were the most internationally competitive, with good swimmers from Hungary and Germany as well from both the Chicago and New York athletic clubs. The outstanding swimmers were Zolton Holomay of Hungary, Charles Daniels of the New York Athletic Club, and Emil Rausch of Germany, each of whom won two gold medals.

The 1904 Olympic Games represented the best showing ever by the United States, which won 81 of the 94 gold medals contested and captured 242 of the 269 medals awarded. Germany, Canada, Hungary, and Cuba were the only other countries to claim medal winners.

The 1904 Olympic Games are noted for two bizarre events, the marathon race and a set of events for primitive people known as "Anthropology Days," that have helped mark the 1904 Games as possibly the worst-ever Olympic Games.

The marathon was run under horrible conditions, with the apparent winner having ridden in an automobile and the actual winner openly given stimulants during the race. The race started in mid-afternoon in 90-degree August heat over rutted, dusty, dirt roads with only one water stop. Only fourteen of the thirty-one starters were able to complete the race, which Thomas Hicks won in a time of 3 hours, 28 minutes, 53 seconds, the worst winning time ever in Olympic marathon history. During the race, Hicks was openly given strychnine (which in large doses is lethal but in small doses is a stimulant), the first known example of drug-enhanced performance used in the Olympic Games. Hicks's victory was not immediately apparent, however, because of a hoax pulled by Fred Lorz. Lorz, an experienced marathoner, dropped out of the race at the 13-mile mark because of cramps and was picked up by an official's car. After several miles, the car in which Lorz was riding ran off the road and into a tree. Unhurt, Lorz decided to run on to the stadium. As he did, he passed the leader, entered the stadium, circled the track, and broke the tape as the apparent winner. Just as he was about to be presented the silver cup as the marathon winner, Lorz admitted that he had ridden part of the way in a car and had broken the tape as a joke. The AAU had no sense of humor and suspended him for life for his prank. He was later reinstated, however, and won the 1905 Boston Marathon.

Comic relief abounded in the marathon, in part provided by Felix Carvajal, a Cuban mail carrier, who ran in street clothing, stole fruit from a farmer's orchard, lay down to rest for part of the race, and still finished fourth.

Anthropology Days, or primitive peoples' Olympic Games, was a two-day series of athletic events cosponsored by the Physical Culture and Anthropology departments at the fair. The event was a scientific attempt to prove the theory that primitive people had extraordinary physical ability because they led a life that demanded a high level of physical performance. Actually the event was a bizarre exhibition in which Sullivan took untrained, unmotivated people who had been sedentary for four or five months and ran them through a series of athletic events. When their performances did not measure up to those of modern athletes, Sullivan made disparaging remarks about the participants.

The Anthropology Days were consistent with the fair's goals of drawing spectators and proving the supremacy of Anglo-Saxon civilization. One of the ways the fair attempted to demonstrate that supremacy was to juxtapose exhibits of modern technology with those of primitive people, and there were many primitive people in their natural setting: Cocopa Indians from Mexico; Kwakiutl Indians from Vancouver Island, Canada; Ainu from Japan; Patagonians from Argentina; pygmies from Africa; various Philippine tribes; "American" Indians; South Africans; Asians; and Turks.

The first day's events were mostly standard track and field events, including the 100-yard dash, shot put, running broad jump, baseball throw, and 56-pound weight throw. None of the performances by the participants was particularly good. The second day's activities included events supposedly geared to primitive sports. The day began with a telegraph pole climbing contest and included a javelin throwing (for accuracy) contest, tug-of-war, a 1-mile run, and archery. The pygmies concluded the day's activities with a demonstration of their version of "shinny" and then divided up for a "mud fight."

At the end of this "scientific" demonstration, Sullivan concluded that primitive people had neither good natural athletic skills nor the intelligence to make team sports work. However, W. J. McGee, the head of the fair's Anthropology Department, believed that the primitive people would become proficient in a short time if they were properly trained and instructed. In the end, the event proved nothing and was at best only a bizarre sideshow of the fair.

In retrospect, Pierre de Coubertin made the prophetic statement of the time concerning Anthropology Days: "As for that outrageous charade, it will of course lose its appeal when black men, red men and yellow men learn to run, jump, and throw and leave the white man far behind them.''

BIBLIOGRAPHICAL ESSAY

The 1904 Olympic Games, despite being held in the United States, present considerable confusion for researchers. Part of the problem is due to the fact that there was no set program, and James E. Sullivan, the Games director, referred to every event as Olympian. Moreover, the results of the Games do not fit well into the modern record summaries, nor do they mesh with modern conceptions of what the Games should include. Most modern popular accounts tend to repeat the lowlights and myths of the Games, such as the marathon, the involvement of President Roosevelt, and Anthropology Days with journalistic enthusiasm but varying degrees of accuracy. Bill Mallon, however, has sorted out much of the confusion over the results of the Games events in *A Statistical Summary of the 1904 Olympic Games* (Durham, N.C., 1981).

The Missouri Historical Society (MHS) in St. Louis has the best collection of primary source material on the 1904 Olympic Games. It holds the official records of the Louisiana Purchase Exposition Company, including the records of the Department of Physical Culture, complete with a finding aid. Excellent sources in this collection are Mark Bennitt, ed., *History of the Louisiana Purchase Exposition* (St. Louis, 1905); David R. Francis, *The Universal Exposition of 1904* (St. Louis, 1913); and various fair bulletins and programs. The MHS Department of Prints and Photographs archives has a number of photographs of the Olympic Games. The University of Chicago Archives holds the papers of William Rainey Harper and Amos Alonzo Stagg, both of whom were on the Chicago Olympic committee. The U.S. Olympic Committee archives in Colorado Springs, Colorado, has scrapbooks of clippings on the Games from a variety of newspapers.

A short history of the exposition is Yvonne Condon, "St. Louis 1904," in John E. Findling and Kimberly D. Pelle, eds., *Historical Dictionary of World's Fairs and Expositions, 1851–1988* (Westport, Conn., 1990). See also the chapter on the exposition in Robert Rydell, *All the World's a Fair* (Chicago, 1984), which has an excellent description and analysis of Anthropology Days.

The Games committee did not prepare an official report for the IOC, but James E. Sullivan, ed., *Spalding's Official Athletic Almanac for 1905: Special Olympic Number, Containing the Official Report of the Olympic Games of 1904* (New York, 1905), constitutes the "official" account of the Games. This work contains the results of all of the athletic events staged in the Olympic stadium, a narrative description of Anthropology Days, and more than 100 photographs.

Another contemporary account of the Games is Charles J. P. Lucas, *The Olympic Games 1904* (St. Louis, 1905), an eyewitness description of the track and field events, with a chapter devoted to the marathon, in which Lucas served as a trainer for the winner and observed the entire race from an automobile following the lead runner. A German account is Theodor Lewald, *Denkschrift uber Deutschlands Beteiligung an der Weltausstellung von St. Louis 1904* (Berlin, 1905). The *St. Louis Globe-Democrat* and *St. Louis Dispatch* covered almost every event at the fairgrounds in some detail, while the *New York Times* and *Chicago Tribune* presented extensive though uneven coverage of the site controversy and athletic competition.

Modern accounts of the Games include Mark Dyreson, "The Playing Fields of Progress,'' *Gateway Heritage* (Fall 1993): 5–23, and John E. Findling, ''World's Fairs and the Olympic Games,'' *World's Fair* 11 (October–December 1990): 13–15. See also Robert K. Barney, ''Born from Dilemma: America Awakens to the Modern Olympic Games, 1901–1903,'' *Olympika* 1 (1992): 92–135, and John A. Lucas, ''Early Antagonists: Pierre de Coubertin versus James E. Sullivan,'' *Stadion* 3 (1977): 264–66, on the struggle between Chicago and St. Louis to host the Games. Frank Cosentino and Glynn Leshon, *Olympic Gold: Canada's Winners in the Summer Games* (Toronto, 1975), provides information about the Canadian gold medal–winning lacrosse and soccer teams and biographical data on Etienne Desmarteam and George Lyon, Canada's individual gold medal winners.

C. Robert Barnett

ATHENS 1906

THE INTERCALATED GAMES

The success of the 1896 Games encouraged the Greek organizers to claim the Olympics for Athens on a permanent basis. Many of the earlier participants, King George I of Greece, and the Greek cabinet all supported these plans. Had this come to pass, however, the International Olympic Committee's (IOC) reason for existence would have been lost. Pierre de Coubertin therefore suggested to the king and the crown prince the title, ''Panhellenic Games.'' A few IOC members put forth a compromise: Olympic Games in Athens and in other cities, alternating every two years.

This matter was to have been decided at the IOC session in Berlin planned for fall 1896, but Coubertin canceled this meeting. The 1896 revolt of the Christian population against the Ottoman troops in Crete and the war with Turkey for control of this island in 1897, a war that ended with the defeat of Greece, forced the country to concentrate on matters other than the Olympic Games. But at the IOC session of 1901, there was again talk of these Greek plans. A proposal of the German IOC members stated:

In the year 1902 a session of our committee is to take place in Athens, at which an exact schedule and program for future Olympic Games is to be established—with special consideration for those to be held in the future in Athens. The international competitions will take place every two years, alternating between Athens and other large cities of the cultured states, such that every 4 years these Olympic Games will be celebrated in the Greek capital. In the year 1906 the second Olympic Games will take place in Athens, the third in 1910, etc. (*Dokumente*, p. 20)

But in the *Revue Olympique*'s report on the meeting, this part of the proposal was shortened and reproduced in a slightly distorted way. Thus, the parts were missing that specified that the schedule should be tailored for Athens and that games in Athens were planned for 1906 and 1910. From the way in which Coubertin reported the discussion, it is clear how little this proposal suited him. Such plans had already been proposed five years earlier, he wrote. The objections to it in 1896 were still present, although he did not say what they were. The mere fact that the plans had not been able to be realized for five years showed that it was dangerous for the IOC to take this initiative. Games in Athens would have a national character and therefore would not fall under the IOC's jurisdiction. Instead, Coubertin revived the suggestion of panhellenic games. Prince Alexander Merkati, the Greek IOC member, was of the opinion that Games in Athens had to be welcomed and supported by the IOC. But Coubertin clothed the words of Merkati in many ''ifs'' and ''buts'': ''in case the plan should be realized,'' ''in case they should succeed in being accomplished.''

Then came the sentence: "All these decisions were received unanimously." The impartial reader relates this at first to Merkati's appeals. In fact, the part of the proposal about Athens made by the German IOC members must have been voted on at this point. There was no talk of a change in the proposal. Knowing the original of the proposal, the report of the discussion and vote following this, and in addition a statement in *21 Jahre,* "then in 1901 the German members . . . presented an identical proposal . . . , and we accepted this proposal," one must come to the following conclusion: At the 1901 session in Paris the IOC resolved that the Olympic Games would take place every two years, alternating between Athens and other cities.

Coubertin succeeded in putting off the question of the Athens games until the Brussels IOC session in 1905. There, however, his position in the IOC was so weakened due to the problems associated with the St. Louis Games that he had to concede. The IOC now supported holding Olympic Games in Athens in 1906.

In the spring of 1905, the stadium's marble construction was fully completed, and as a dress rehearsal, the 1905 "Panhellenic Games" took place there. In accordance with the IOC decision of 1901, Olympic Games were offered to Greece for 1906. The Greek committee had decided on this year at the suggestion of the crown prince. And even before the IOC session in Brussels, invitations to other nations were sent. Thus, on May 5, 1905, the Greek ambassador Kleon Rangabe delivered "the official invitation of the Comité des Jeux Olympiques à Athènes" to Germany. Coubertin's comment on the Brussels session, "With great perseverance and flexibility, Prince Merkati had prepared the reconciliation—without a single misstep," was only a thin veiling of the fact that in Brussels Coubertin could do nothing more than recognize that in 1906 there would be Olympic Games in Athens.

The preparations of the Greeks were made more difficult by the burning of the Melas-House, the office of the organizing committee, which destroyed most of the records from 1896. Nevertheless, in 1905 preparatory work was begun, with information sent to the foreign nations. Spyridon Lambros, the general secretary of the committee, announced that the Games would occur in the spring of 1906. In the fall, the president of the Greek Gymnastics Instructors Association, Ioannis Chryssafis, traveled to Stockholm, Copenhagen, Paris, and Berlin in order to learn about the competition rules of the most important sports. In December 1905 the Greeks sent out the official program with dates, regulations regarding amateurs, and registration deadlines. The program was published in four pamphlets.

The Games opened on Sunday, April 22, 1906. By the early afternoon, the stadium was filled with 50,000 spectators, many of whom had to stand. Just after 3:00 P.M., King George, with his sister, Queen Alexandra of Great Britain, Edward VII of Great Britain, and his sister-in-law, the Greek queen Olga, followed by the prince of Wales with his wife, Princess Mary, and the Greek court, entered the stadium. Next, the competitors marched into the stadium in rows of four, grouped according to nation, each with its flag at the front, and took up places across from the royal box. Thus, as early as 1906, there was an "entrance march of the nations." (In the literature, the origin of this part of the opening ceremony has always been attributed to the 1908 London Games.)

In Athens the German team came into the stadium first, followed by the Americans, English, Swedes, French, Italians, Belgians, Danes, Norwegians, Austrians, Hungarians, Finns, Egyptians, Swiss, and the Greeks. As hosts, the Greeks entered in last place, a custom that has been maintained to the present day. It is not known why Germany entered at the head or how the order of the nations was determined. There was even some question as to how many nations participated. The German sport authority, Carl Diem, reported fifteen nations, while the official report listed twenty nations, including Australia, Bohemia, Holland, Canada, and Smyrna, which were not listed by Diem. Perhaps Diem counted Bohemia with Austria and both Australia and Canada with Great Britain. Had he forgotten the Dutch and the Russians, or did they arrive too late for the ceremony? Were the Russians counted with the Finns, and with which flag did the Finns enter? Flags were a problem. The Bohemians demanded that their flag be raised rather than the Austrian flag, the Hungarians that the Hungarian, and the Cypriots the flag of Cyprus. But in 1906 the committee could still reject these demands relatively easily. After the completion of an event, the flags of the nations of the athletes placing first, second, and third were raised, along with the numbers of the victors and their achievements.

According to the official report, some 893 athletes took part in the Games (Egypt 1, Australia 4, Belgium 15, Denmark 65, Germany 47, Finland 4, France 58, Greece 338, Great Britain 47, Holland 16, Italy 82, Canada 3, Norway 32, Austria 31, Sweden 66, Switzerland 8, Smyrna 1, Bohemia 3, Hungary 35, United States 37).

After the athletes had taken their places, Crown Prince Constantine stepped forward as chairman of the organizing committee and gave a short address, in which he referred to the ancient tradition of the Games and to the Greek law that prescribed regular Games in Athens. The king declared the Games open, and the Samara hymns were played, as they had been in 1896. This portion of the opening ceremony remains customary to this day. The athletes then left the field, and the events began with three gymnastics teams performing exhibitions prior to the actual competition: the Greeks, the Swedes, and the Danish women's team.

The formal competition began with the Danes. They performed Swedish free exercises, vaults, parallel bar gymnastics, and floor exercises with handstands, flips, and many jumps. From the astounded commentary of the German gymnastics people present, one can see that these exercises were still unknown in Germany. Altogether the exercises of the Danes were viewed as the best up to that time.

The German gymnasts under Fritz Hofmann competed as the fifth team and were greeted with loud applause. Their successes of 1896 were still remembered. Considered the favorites, they performed free exercises, vaults, collective exercises on six parallel bars and six horizontal bars, and free gymnastics on horizontal and parallel bars. The effort of the Germans, however, was disappointing. The next afternoon the Hungarians performed with little success. The Norwegian squad followed, twenty-one men strong, and gave a similar program to those of the Swedes and Danes, only more precise and more difficult. Finally came two Italian squads, Rome and Pistoja. Their program was simple but extraordinarily precise. Their collective gymnastics on the apparatuses was also well done. Interestingly, the team captain of "Rome" was injured and unable to walk, and so followed his team from apparatus to apparatus on bicycle. The decision of the judges was as follows:

1. Norway, 19.00 points.
2. Denmark, 18.00 points.
3. Italy (Pistoja), 16.71 points.
4. Italy (Rome), 16.60 points.
5. Germany, 16.25 points.
6. Hungary, 14.25 points.

According to the regulations, teams that received 18 to 20 points were awarded first place and teams that had scored 16 to 18 points second place. Thus, Norway and Denmark won first place, and both Italian teams and Germany won second places.

The next day of the Games featured the gymnastics five-event combined (horizontal bars, parallel bars, long horse, rings, and jumps) and six-event combined (the jump on the side horse constituted the sixth event). Harsh criticism arose over the fact that 3 full minutes were given to the gymnasts for each exercise on an apparatus. In the five-event combined, twelve Germans, five Frenchmen, seven Hungarians, eight Greeks, three Italians, two Englishmen, one Norwegian, and one Bohemian competed. The absence of the Scandinavians, who had focused on the squad competition, was striking. If one examines the list of results closely, the superiority of the French (first, third, and sixth place in the five-event combined; first, third, and sixth place in the sixth-event combined) and the Italians (second and fifth in both disciplines) is clear.

In the tug-of-war, the German gymnasts, joining with the track and field athletes, were able to win a first place over the Austrians and the Greeks. On the trip from Trieste to Athens, a team for this event was chosen from the strongest German competitors in other sports.

Although the other mixed discipline, the pentathlon, had been actively practiced for over twenty-five years in the German-speaking countries, German participants did not distinguish themselves. At these Games, the pentathlon consisted of the standing long jump, discus throw, javelin throw, 200-yard dash, and boxing. Contestants were allowed to continue according to the order of their placement in earlier events. For the fourth event, the dash, only the athletes in eighth place or better could compete, and in boxing, the final event, the top six remaining athletes competed. The Swedes were best prepared and won first, third, and sixth place.

On the second day of the Games, while the gymnasts were finishing the team gymnastics in the stadium, the fencing tournament began in Zappeion, and cycling and the soccer tournament began in New Phaleron. The fencing tournament lasted from April 23 to 28. Athletically, it was a contest between the French and Italian schools, but because the Greek judges tended more toward the French fencing method, there were several disputes over rule interpretations, complicated by the lack of a written set of rules. The French won the greatest number of first places, with Georges Dillon-Kavanagh capturing first in foil, Count Georges de la Falaise winning the sword fencing, and the sword team prevailing in its event. The German foil competitor, Gustav Casmir, was also successful; he was first in two events and second in the individual foil. In that event, a controversy developed. After the first and second rounds, six participants qualified for the final round. In this round, Casmir and Dillon-Kavanagh were tied. The Italian Frederico Cesarano withdrew from the final round, since he could not finish better than sixth, and his marks were scratched. Casmir, who had beaten him, lost a point and fell to second place. A protest by the German team was rejected.

The cycling racetrack in New Phaleron was 333.3 meters long but had curves that were scarcely banked, and this gave rise to a number of complaints. In cycling the Italian Francesco Verri won the 333.3-meter, the 1,000-meter, and the 5,000-meter races. The marathon road race in cycling took place on the same day as the marathon run, May 1. About 1:00 P.M., twenty-four riders left the Olympia stadium along the marathon route, but the layout of the course was poor, and many had accidents. The German riders were among those affected by this; Eric Dannenberg seriously injured himself and gave up, and Adolf Bohm also fell but still finished fifth, covered with blood and dust, behind three Frenchmen and a Belgian. A total of thirteen riders were able to finish the race. The German stunt cyclists received big applause when they gave a demonstration on April 30 on a wooden podium constructed in the stadium especially for them.

The water events of swimming, diving, and rowing took place in the Bay of Phaleron. The organization of these events was poor. The judges had trouble, for example, keeping the swimming lanes free of private boats. In swimming the Germans could not do justice to their status as favorites, partly because the Greek committee was not ready to admit the breaststroke and backstroke, the strength of the German swimmers, into the program. On the third day of the Games, April 24, the swimming competition began with the 1-mile swim, won by the Englishman Henry Taylor in 28 minutes, 28 seconds. The German Emil Rausch, who in St. Louis had won at this distance with a much faster time, could not, as a sidestroke swimmer, handle the high waves. In fact, swimming and rowing had to be postponed on April 26 due to rough water. The weather improved in the following days, and the German swimmers performed better.

In diving, the Germans proved their superiority. After dives from 4, 8, and 12 meters, Gottlob Walz won with 156.0 points over Georg Hoffmann's 150.2.

Track and field, the "real Olympic games," according to Diem, began on April 25 with gorgeous weather and a sold-out stadium; 302 athletes from nineteen countries took part. The first event in the morning was the discus throw, which the American Martin Sheridan won with a throw of 41.46 meters. These Games also featured the Greek-style discus event, in which the competitors threw the discus from a forward-sloping pedestal. Most believed that the Greeks would win, but Finland's Werner Järvinen beat Nicolaos Georgantas, as reporters criticized the style of throwing the discus.

The ten trial heats for the 100-meter dash began in the afternoon of April 25. The final race two days later was won by the American Archie Hahn in 11.2 seconds. The 800-meter race, which followed, was won by Paul Pilgrim of the United States, amid complaints about the wide track and narrow curves and the fact that the race had to be run clockwise, which was new for the foreign participants.

On Thursday, April 26, there was a scandal when in the two-armed weight lifting event, the Greek judges counted a faulty try of 142.5 kilograms by the Greek Dimitrios Tofalos. His competitor, Josef Steinbach of Austria, was continually disturbed by the public during his tries and was not able to match this weight.

One of several events on April 27 was the long jump. Carl Diem was disappointed at the lack of good jumping on the part of many athletes. According to him, the reason lay in the approach: "With our athletes one sees at the approach first a couple of hops, then a few powerful leaps, then at the end a couple of triple steps, and 5 meters are reached." With the Americans he observed a smooth approach in which the jumper increased his speed as he approached the takeoff line. The *Deutsche Turn-Zeitung* noted the differences in jumping technique during the jump itself. The Europeans jumped with the upper body bent forward and the legs curled under. The Americans swung their legs far ahead in flight, as did the winner, Myer Prinstein, with a jump of 7.20 meters.

The shot put approach also captured the attention of the German commentators. Diem was surprised that the athletes were allowed to step over the line after the throw. But according to the rule, they had to have already thrown at that point. The Germans and Austrians took this rule too literally, stopping abruptly, and therefore did not qualify for the final round.

On May 1, the marathon was held. It started in Marathon, as it had ten years before, but at 42 kilometers, the route was 2,000 meters longer this time. Again the Greeks hoped for a victory, again the stadium was full to the last seat, and again the start took place at 2:00 P.M. on a hot day. One new feature was the automobiles that were in place along the route. To the great disappointment of the Greeks, no Hellene won, but rather a Canadian, William John Sherring, who ran into the stadium with a lead of nearly 7 minutes and finished in the record time of 2 hours, 51 minutes, 23.6 seconds, still appearing quite fresh. For the last 100 hundred meters in the stadium, he was accompanied by Prince George.

On Wednesday morning, May 2, one additional event, a 3,000-meter walk, was conducted in order to give the walkers who had been disqualified in the 1,500-meter walk because of faulty walking style an additional chance. Hermann Muller of Germany, who had not competed in the 1,500-meter event, won second place just 15 hours after competing in the marathon.

During the afternoon, the closing ceremony took place in the stadium. After gymnastics exercises by Athens schoolchildren, the king and crown prince distributed the prizes to the winners. There were winners' awards and an olive wreath for the first three in each event. Each participant received a souvenir medal. In the evening there was a reception given by the Greek Committee in Zappeion.

These Olympic Games were, in contrast to Paris and St. Louis, a success; they earned the name Olympic Games and can be compared with the first Games in Athens. There was a stadium with spectators, Games that were conducted for their own sake, and a city that for the time of the Games had an Olympic heritage. That had all been true in 1896 as well, but this time the Games were truly international, with many foreign teams and many of the top athletes in the world.

Two shortcomings must nonetheless be noted: the lack of rules for the individual Olympic sports and the lack of impartiality on the part of many judges. The IOC can be blamed for the first failure. The German committee had called for an international judging system, and the Greeks had agreed. The German team furnished judges for some types of sports, but how responsibly these were used is impossible to know. The Austrians almost left the Games because of the injustices. The German cycling and motorist newspaper reported that the German cyclists were restrained from refreshing themselves at a spring during the marathon bicycle race.

If one evaluated the results based on today's criteria, the ranking of the nations would look as follows:

	Gold	Silver	Bronze	Total
France	15	9	16	40
United States	12	6	6	24
Greece	8	13	12	33
Great Britain	8	11	5	24
Italy	7	6	3	16
Germany	4	6	5	15
Switzerland	4	3	1	8
Austria	3	3	3	9

Although the impartiality of the judges and the local patriotism of the spectators were criticized, everyone praised the hospitality of the Greek people and the enthusiastic participation of the royal family, several members of whom were present at almost every event.

The German doctor August Smith and his two assistants examined almost all the athletes in Athens. Smith had already conducted observations of Berlin athletes during four years of training and competition. He had concentrated on measuring the heart size of athletes with the help of so-called orthodiagraphic x-ray radioscopy. Smith determined that athletes who performed for short periods had small hearts, and that endurance performers had larger hearts, and he concluded that heart size increases through endurance training. With the knowledge of pathological hypertrophy, he proclaimed that the heart enlarged through training was harmful. In addition, he cited immoderate food and alcohol consumption as another cause of a harmful enlargement of the heart. For Smith and his coworkers, the American sprinters and jumpers were the healthiest athletes, for they had the smallest, and therefore "healthiest," hearts. The positive factors of thickened heart muscle through endurance training (lower pulse rate, larger pulse volume, better use of oxygen, increased capillarization) were not recognized. The publication of the results of these experiments in Germany led to great reservations about intensive athletic training, which persisted for a long time.

It was announced on a number of occasions that in 1910 and 1914 the Olympic Games would again be held in Athens, but because of the many political crises in the Balkans, these plans could not be carried out. After World War I, this was no longer a topic of interest. Later the Olympic Games of 1906 were denigrated to "interim games."

BIBLIOGRAPHICAL ESSAY

The official report for these "unofficial Games" is Pan. S. Savvidis, ed., *Leukoma ton en Athenais B' Diethnon Olympiakon Agonon 1906/Jeux olympiques internationaux 1906. Album. Athenes.* (Athens, 1907), published in Greek. The Greek organizing committee also published general programs and the official results: *Ordre des concours et des fêtes* (Athens, 1906), *Programme général* (Athens, 1906), and *Diethnais Olympiakoi Agones 1906. Episema Apotolesmata/Jeux olympiques internationaux 1906. Resultats officiels* (n.p., 1906) (the last in both Greek and French).

The most comprehensive modern history of the Games is Karl Lennartz and Walter Teutenberg, *Die Olympischen Spiele 1906 in Athen* (Kassel, 1992), which includes a number of documents and photographs from the Games, as well as a summary of the results and a list of participants with some biographical information on each. Another useful work in German is *Dokumente zur Frühgeschichte der Olympischen Spiele* (Cologne, 1971), a compilation of key documents from a number of early Games. Carl Diem, the German sport leader, attended the Games and wrote *Die Olympischen Spiele 1906* (Berlin, 1907), which is reproduced in the Lennartz and Teutenberg history.

The best account in English is James E. Sullivan, ed., *The Olympic Games at Athens 1906* (New York, 1906), part of the Spalding Athletic Library. Sullivan was the head of the Amateur Athletic Union at this time. See also John A. Lucas, "American Involvement in the Athens Olympian Games of 1906: Bridge between Failure and Success,'' *Stadion* 6 (1980): 217–28, which also includes a bibliography of other works in English on the Games.

Karl Lennartz
Translated by Stephanie L. Peters and Curtis H. Peters

LONDON 1908

THE GAMES OF THE IVTH OLYMPIAD

As the Games of the 1908 Olympiad approached, the host country, England, steeped in sporting tradition and one of the most economically powerful nations in the world, was beset with problems of funding, politics, partisanship, competition, and weather. The 1908 Olympic Games had originally been awarded to Rome, Italy. This was to be an opportunity for the Italian government to show that it was truly one of the world's great powers, but when Mt. Vesuvius erupted in 1906, the government found that it did not have the resources to bring about recovery and finance the Olympic Games. In order to prevent the Italian economy from collapsing, the government relinquished the right to host the 1908 Games, which were then awarded to London.

In the face of England's problems, the British Olympic Organizing Council prepared for the staging of the games of the fourth modern Olympiad. With or without sufficient funding, the London organizers were set to host teams from Australia, Austria, Belgium, the Bahamas, Canada, Denmark, France, Germany, Greece, Holland, Hungary, Italy, Norway, Russia, Sweden, South Africa, Switzerland, and the United States.

As late as July 1, 1908, Lord Desborough, president of the organizing council, issued a call to British citizens to contribute additional funds to ensure that the Games maintained their ''high standards.'' With the start of the Games scheduled for July 13, the council had only £15,000 of the £65,000 Desborough indicated it needed. In an effort to solicit funds from all possible sources, Desborough chided government officials by revealing that for the 1896 Games, Greece, the host country, had appropriated £125,000 and pointing to the lack of funding from the British government for the 1908 Games. In the end, the only revenue the British Olympic Council was assured of was a one-fourth share of the gross gate receipts. The remainder was to go to the Franco-British Exhibition, on whose grounds the Games were being held.

Lacking financial support, Desborough and his council members were forced to abandon several activities slated for the athletes, among them a reception and excursions to a few of the historical sites and cities of Great Britain. Without the generosity of the general public, explained Desborough, the hospitality afforded the British at previous Olympic Games would not be able to be returned in England.

Despite the lack of financial support, organizers of the London Games openly welcomed British royalty and many other heads of state attending the opening ceremonies on July 13. Included among this cast of dignitaries were Edward VII of Great Britain, who officially opened the Games, accompanied by Queen Alexandra; King George of Greece; King Haakon of Norway; Crown Prince Gustav Adolf of Sweden; and officials from all nineteen participating countries.

Leaving Buckingham Palace just a little after 3:00 P.M., King Edward arrived at the stadium for the opening ceremonies at 3:30. Upon his arrival, the king was officially greeted by Lord Desborough; Baron Pierre de Coubertin, founder of the modern Olympic Games; the members of the International Olympic Committee; and three members of the British Olympic Association, Lord Selby, Lord Blythe, and M. Imre Kiralfy.

The king remained at the opening activities for almost 2 hours. His interest in the Games was no surprise, given that he was a prolific sportsman. The British press assured readers that King Edward was the most appropriate person to open the Games and that England, with its fine tradition in field sports, was the right country to host the event known for bringing peace to nations of the world rather than war.

Although the government's financial support for the Games was weak, receptions for the foreign leaders and international Olympic officials were hosted by prominent citizens on behalf of the British government. The hospitality and flowery speeches at these events mitigated somewhat the lack of financial support on the part of the government.

Taking center stage at these 1908 Games, along with a lack of funding, was the weather and attendance. Throughout the Games, the weather ranged from fair to poor, and although no one can control the weather, criticism of weather conditions was constant. *The Times* (London) noted that at its best in mid-July, the British weather is not very good. From the opening day of the Games, it was frequently rainy and chilly. On only a few occasions was the weather excellent. For example, on the day of the marathon, the crowd enjoyed the best weather of the Games and turned out in record numbers. The large crowds on the last two days of the Games were a blessed sight for Olympic officials. The early attendance of the Games had been so poor that organizers reduced the price of admission into the stadium.

Although the weather cleared for the marathon, it magnified another of the major flaws of the London Games: rule disputes. During the marathon, one of the many controversies occurred. After entering the stadium well ahead of his closest competitor, Pietri Dorando of Italy, struggling and in pain, more than likely unable to finish the race, was aided by British officials, a clear violation of the rules concerning attendants on the course. Dorando's condition was so bad that rumors that he had died persisted after the day's events were completed.

The next runner entering the stadium after Dorando was an American, John J. Hayes. As the rules required, Hayes completed the race on his own power, and then, under instructions from U.S. officials and coaches, filed a protest against the actions of the British officials. The governing body ruled in favor of the American runner and disqualified Dorando, enabling the United States to capture three of the first four places in the race. The officials running the Games believed that Italy's Dorando should have been declared the marathon winner and that the Americans were being poor sportsmen. With Lord Desborough, recognized as a fair and honest person, firmly concurring that officials had been wrong to aid Dorando, the hearing committee had little choice but to allow Hayes's protest.

Controversy was a constant companion of the London Olympic Games, and the marathon affair only served to confirm the belief of many Americans that the British officials were willing to go to almost any lengths to prevent a U.S. victory. Anglo-American friction had begun with the opening day ceremonies, when the American, Swedish, and Finnish flags were not displayed. In protest, some Swedes left the games. Finland, under Russian domination, could not afford to do much in protest. When Ralph Rose, a shot-putter and flag bearer, refused, as a customary courtesy, to dip the American flag when passing before King Edward, the remaining activities were held with open animosity. The marathon was no exception.

The marathon protest was just one of several launched by the Americans; others were made in the tug-of-war, the 400-meter run, and the pole vault. In addition, several nations were concerned with the scoring system being utilized.

The tug-of-war rules used at the Games, written by the British Olympic Association, prohibited participants from wearing specially prepared boots or shoes or boots or shoes with any projecting nails, tips, springs, or points. According to the Americans, not all the competing teams were made to comply with these rules. Of the nineteen countries competing, only two entered teams in the tug-of-war: the host country, England, with three teams, and the Americans, with one team. The American team first competed against a team from Liverpool, wearing heavy boots with steel rims around the heels, a clear violation of the stated rules. The Americans, in regular street shoes, protested but were told that the shoes were acceptable because they were the type normally worn by the Liverpool policemen comprising the team.

Despite believing that they were being unfairly treated, the Americans decided to compete against the Liverpool team, but they made no effort to win, to show that the use of the boots against street shoes was unsportsmanlike and gave the Liverpool team an unfair advantage.

The Liverpool team easily defeated the Americans. Matthew Halpin, the American team manager, told event officials that if the rules were not adhered to, his team would not continue. The officials ignored this protest, and the American team left the field. After hearing of the incident, James E. Sullivan, commissioner of the American contingent, formally protested to the British Olympic Association. The British association referred the case to the Amateur Athletic Association, which ruled that the decision was fair.

During the second week of the Games, another of the many Anglo-American disputes arose. While running the 400-meter race, John C. Carpenter of the American team was accused of fouling another runner and was disqualified. The disqualification came despite a rule providing that in the case of any boring (fouling), the race would be rerun a half-hour later. Running in the finals of this race were three Americans—Carpenter; John B. Taylor, a black from the University of Pennsylvania; and William C. Robbins of Cambridge, Massachusetts—and one British runner, Lieutenant Wyndham Halswelle, the British champion.

The controversy began when Carpenter was called for fouling Halswelle. The two men had traded the lead back and forth during the latter stage of the race, but British officials came on to the track and declared the race over before the runners reached the finish line. All the runners continued, except Taylor who stopped when informed by the officials. Spectators argued whether a foul had been committed. The Amateur Athletic Association held a hearing on the situation, taking testimony from the British officials and Halswelle. Not one American official or runner was asked to testify before the association. After Carpenter's disqualification, the race was rerun two days later, but Carpenter's American teammates refused to compete, allowing Halswelle to win in a walkover. The hostility between the British officials and the American contingent intensified.

In part because of the many controversies that plagued the London Games, Olympic officials declined to present an overall team championship trophy to any nation. The chief concern was the scoring system used for the Games. Another concern was the inclusion of events in which few, if any, countries other than Great Britain participated. These issues combined with the disputes over questionable officiating led the Games committee to declare that an overall championship trophy would not be given. Only individual event winners were recognized.

Even the closing ceremonies caused concern. As Queen Alexandra was presenting the awards, she paid special attention to Italy's Dorando, giving him a personal gift, a cup, as well as an Olympic wreath. Considering that he was not a winner, some of the Americans felt that this was a slight to Johnny Hayes and the United States.

Hayes, as well as the rest of the American team, heard from President Theodore Roosevelt. Upon the team's arrival back in the United States, they were received by the president at his home in Oyster Bay, New York. He congratulated the team for their victory on behalf of the nation.

Officials and athletes from many of the nineteen participating countries complained of the handling of the fourth modern Olympic Games. Prior to these Games, each nation understood that the management of each event would be handled by the association governing that sport in Great Britain. That association would be responsible both for providing all officials and for the conduct of the athletes. Foreign representatives taking part in the Games had no part in their management.

Having local associations with sole responsibility over their respective events caused much of the confusion over the conduct of the Games. The scoring system also caused much confusion. British officials scored the contests by awarding 1 point to each victory and nothing to second- and third-place finishers. Events both inside and outside the stadium were scored. The contests inside the stadium included track and field events. Events outside the stadium included regatta, lacrosse, and tennis. This system placed Great Britain well ahead of all other nations, since very few of them participated in activities outside the stadium.

The U.S. scoring system, used in previous Games, was to award five points for first place, three points for second place, and one point for third place. The Americans calculated their scores only for the stadium events. Like most other teams, the United States sent athletes to participate mainly in stadium events, while Great Britain, not having to travel, had athletes in all events.

What each of these nations and their athletes recognized, however, was that the host city and country, London, England, made certain that the Games themselves were the feature attraction. This had not been the case with either the 1900 Games in Paris or the 1904 Games in St. Louis, where a world's fair had been the main event and the Olympic Games just a minor sideshow.

Organizers of the Franco-British Exhibition were strong advocates of the Olympic movement and sought to make the Games the featured attraction in 1908. The track and field stadium seated 68,000 people and had been paid for by the Franco-British Exhibition organizers. As a consequence, the economic success of the 1908 London Olympics was of little concern for the Games organizers. Regardless of the attendance or sponsorships, they did not have to worry about their largest capital expenditure.

Attendance at most of the Games was poor. For only a few events did the crowds meet or exceed expectations. In addition to the poor weather, the cost of admission was a major contributor to the poor attendance. Ticket prices ranged from 70 cents to $5. Although the organizers intended to double these prices on the day of the marathon, the poor attendance forced them to reduce prices.

Despite the controversial nature of the 1908 London Olympics, most observers and participants agreed that the Games were helpful for the future of the Olympics. They served as a vehicle for ways in which future Games could be structured. No longer would local officials and host countries have sole responsibility for scoring, officiating, or judging the events. No longer would the Games take a subordinate status to other events. The London Games aided the Olympic movement in becoming a worldwide spectacle with international cooperation on all issues of concern.

BIBLIOGRAPHICAL ESSAY

Some archival records of the 1908 London Olympics are housed at the International Olympic Academy in Athens and at the International Olympic Committee archives in Lausanne. The official report is Theodore A. Cook, ed., *The Fourth Olympiad: Being the Official Report of the Olympic Games of 1908 Celebrated in London under the Patronage of His Most Gracious King Edward VII and By the Sanction of the International Olympic Committee* (London, 1909). The rules and regulations governing the competition are spelled out in *The Rules of Sport: Being the International Code for All*

Competitions in the Olympic Games (London, 1908). See also Max Howell and Reet Howell, *The Olympic Movement Restored: The 1908 Games* (Quebec, 1976), and Ossi Brucker, "Die Tragoedie den Marathonlaufers Dorando Pietri," *Olympische Feuer* 33 (1983): 46–58.

Other books that may be helpful for the history of the 1908 Games are: David Chester, *The Olympic Games Handbook: An Authentic History of Both the Ancient and Modern Olympic Games* (New York, 1975), and Endre Kahlich, *Olympic Games, 1896–1972* (Budapest, 1972). For a comparison of the way the Games were viewed on both sides of the Atlantic, see George R. Matthews, "The Controversial Olympic Games of 1908 As Viewed by the *New York Times* and the *Times* of London," *Journal of Sport History* 7, 2 (Summer 1980): 40–53. Bruce Kidd, *Tom Longboat* (Don Mills, Ontario, 1980), is a biography of the great Canadian Indian long-distance runner who competed in the controversial marathon at the 1908 Games.

The Theodore Roosevelt Papers at the Library of Congress, Washington, D.C., contain some references to the 1908 Games. The primary newspaper source is the *Times* (London), especially July 11–28, although the *New York Times,* the *Los Angeles Times,* and the *Washington Post* also contain articles of interest.

James R. Coates, Jr.

STOCKHOLM 1912

THE GAMES OF THE VTH OLYMPIAD

Although the Games at London in 1908 were truly international in character and well organized, the most successful competitions in the period prior to World War I were the Stockholm Olympics in 1912. The Vth Olympiad proved to be the greatest festival of sport the world has ever witnessed: outstanding facilities, large and enthusiastic crowds and participants, a new stadium, northern in its character, exciting competitions and great achievements, and new events such as horse riding and the modern pentathlon. In addition, the first Olympic art competitions were carried out in five categories: architecture, literature, music, painting, and sculpture. Japan became the first Asian state to participate in the Games. All told, fairness and an impressive demonstration of the Olympic ideal characterized the Stockholm Olympics.

At the Berlin International Olympic Committee (IOC) meeting in 1909, Sweden was chosen to host the Vth Olympic Games, chiefly due to the efforts of Colonel Victor Balck, an IOC member since its foundation in Paris in 1894. Balck became chairman of the Swedish organizing committee, divided into twenty-two subcommittees, which worked continuously to prepare the Stockholm Olympics. In his diary, Carl Diem, the German Olympic leader, mentioned that Germany withdrew its candidacy in favor of Sweden at the Berlin congress, enabling Stockholm to be elected unanimously. The German delegates wanted international judges for all events who would have both original and final jurisdiction, but their proposal was rejected when the majority of the delegates agreed with Balck, who maintained that since the time would be barely sufficient to train an international qualified committee of judges, Swedish arbitrators would judge impartially and a second, international jury would be a guarantee to avoid dishonesty.

The German Olympic team was financially supported by the Reich (German Empire), some provinces, and a public collection, organized by the DRAFOS (German National Association for the Olympic Games). DRAFOS appealed to German patriotism by stating that ''our youth has to demonstrate an harmonious education and the strength and energy of our people and our nation. It's a patriotic duty that the German people, the people of Friedrich Ludwig Jahn, will be represented dignified [*sic*] at this international festival'' (Diem, *Die Olympische Spiele 1912,* p. 14). If a team of 200 Olympic competitors could be sent to Stockholm, there would be a good chance to give evidence of German power and excellence at the Games. But after achieving success in its public collection and building up an effective training system for the athletes, DRAFOS was shocked by the message that the Deutsche Turnerschaft, the German gymnastic federation, refused to participate in the Stockholm Olympics, although the central board of this organization had voted in favor of Stockholm the year before.

The argument was poor: the time for training was not sufficient. It was Ferdinand Goetz, chairman of the German Gymnastic Federation, who had decisively influenced this determination, reflecting the old controversy between sports and gymnastics. As a replacement for the gymnasts of the Deutsche Turnerschaft, a squad of students, prospective gymnastic teachers, was sent to Stockholm at the last minute, after the other athletes had already started their journey.

The stadium, erected on the grounds of the royal Djirgaden (zoological garden), was expressly built for sport but was suitable for festivals of all kinds. This fine edifice was inaugurated with grand ceremony on June 1, 1912. The great arena, with mighty arches, vaults, and towers, was designed by the Swedish architect Torben Grut and accommodated 22,000 spectators. In winter the arena could be converted into a skating rink for the people of Stockholm.

Gustav V and Crown Prince Adolf opened the Stockholm Olympics with appropriate speeches. Addressing himself to the king, the crown prince, representing the IOC, pointed out that physical culture, held in high esteem during antiquity, had once more obtained an honorable place in the life of the nations. Modern sport had become a counterbalance to specialized daily work and would maintain the health of the people. Athletic performances are instrumental in increasing interest in sport and in enlisting new men in the ranks of active athletes. These were new insights concerning the value of sport, and the king responded, ''May the noble thought be pursued by us . . . in such a manner that those connections will prove highly beneficial to the physical health and progress of the people'' (Hermelin and Peterson, *V. Olympiaden,* p. 159).

Diem admired the work the Swedish had done: they had not tried to imitate Greek art in their stadium design but had created a new style that reflected practicality and the Northern European tradition. Everything was well thought out and constituted a practical plan. For example, the large training ground near the stadium, the perfect organization and discipline at the opening ceremony, the procession of 4,000 sportsmen from twenty-five nations, the dipping of the flags in front of the king, the solemn prayer, and the hymn, ''A Mighty Fortress Is Our God,'' all contributed to the impressive beginning of the Games. Furthermore, there were several technical innovations: electric measurement of time and the photo finish, so that the judges could confirm their decisions with pictures. Most of the referees were military officers, supported by Swedish Boy Scouts.

The Games started with a lawn tennis tournament of men's singles and doubles, women's singles, and mixed doubles. The tournament attracted more entries than expected, although it was noted that the top players from England and Australia did not participate in Stockholm because the all-England championships were being played at Wimbledon at the same time.

The Olympic football tournament was the greatest soccer event ever staged. Many fine games were played during the five days of competition, especially the match between Great Britain and Hungary. The British team outclassed the Hungarians, 7–0, and won the final game against Denmark, 4–2, in front of the entire royal family. Diem was impressed: "What the English team demonstrated related to speed, playing together and technique was crowned by a fighting-spirit which could not be learned but only procreated by a race" (Diem, p. 122). This racial argumentation was also applied to the Danish, whose strong body structure and dynamic style of play outshone the seventh-place German team, with its lack of homogeneity, harmony, and team spirit.

The five days of gymnastic competitions were very successful, with no protests, no casualties, and no disturbances. Gymnastics comprised three different types of team competition in free exercises; exercises with poles, sticks, handlebars, and clubs; exercises on parallel and horizontal bars; vaulting horse with pommels; and exercises chosen by the leader. One of the events involved the free choice of exercises and apparatus. The Scandinavians based their system upon the Ling principles: firmness of form and exact execution of each movement, with the greatest attention paid to the bearing of the body. All the teams gave proof of skill and training, but the German team lacked in homogeneity. The Scandinavian countries finished first, second, and third in two of the events, while Italy, Hungary, and Great Britain won medals in the third. The German student team failed to win a medal, prompting Diem to note, "Altogether, the effectiveness of Swedish gymnastics is fascinating and the results indicate that strong, healthy and fit men were formed. . . . The gymnastical and sportive values of these Games have proved that for our sports world, preparatory training based on the Swedish system is very desirable" (Diem, p. 94).

The wrestling event demonstrated the recent changes in wrestling technique. The Swedes, Finns, and Hungarians were all excellent wrestlers, but the Finns were obviously the best in technical ability, strength, and endurance. Unfortunately in Stockholm there was a sharp conflict between the Swedish and Finnish judges, because the Swedish officials would not allow any dangerous or painful holds. So the Finns, threatened with disqualification, stopped using their brutal holds. It was evident that only standardized rules and the creation of an international federation for the sport would provide a way out of this dilemma.

Tug-of-war had been included in the Olympic Games since the Paris Games of 1900, but there were no specially trained tug-of-war teams. In the Games of London in 1908, two British teams, recruited from police forces, took the gold and silver prizes, but in Stockholm the strength of the London policemen was broken by the short, hard tugs of a well-trained Swedish team.

The American runners were heavy favorites and captured gold medals in the 100-meter and 200-meter dashes, as well as in the 400-meter and 800-meter races. In the final of the 1,500-meter run, an Oxford student, Arnold Jackson, won the race for Britain, while Hannes Kolehmainen of Finland captured the 5,000-meter and 10,000-meter runs. In the 5,000-meter race, Kolehmainen passed the favorite, Frenchman Jean Bouin, with a burst of speed in the final 25 meters and set a world record in the process. Another highlight of the Stockholm Olympics was the marathon. Here Kenneth McArthur of South Africa took the lead after the turning point and, in spite of terrible heat, entered the stadium 5 minutes in front of the next runner, his countryman Christian Gitsham. Americans won both the standing and running high jumps, as well as the running long jump. No fewer than eight Americans qualified for the final of the pole vault. The winner was Harry Babcock, a Yale student. Three Swedish athletes, encouraged by the Americans, swept the triple-jump medals. In the throwing competitions, the Americans and Finns were most prominent. The javelin and shot put events were divided into two contests: the best hand and the right and left hand. The latter contest was held only at the Stockholm Games.

In contrast to earlier Games, the program for Stockholm included both the pentathlon and the decathlon, all-around contests that showed what a high level of ability certain athletes had reached. The idea of multievent competition was based on the major principles of Swedish physical education and their significance for Swedish youth. The American Indian Jim Thorpe won the decathlon, followed by three Swedes. The modern pentathlon was included for the first time in the Olympics at the request of Pierre de Coubertin. This new competition comprised shooting, fencing, swimming, riding, and cross-country running. The first four places in the event went to Swedes, with George Patton, later a notable American World War II general, finishing fifth.

After the track and field events, Carl Diem noted the superior physical fitness of American athletes compared with his countrymen and urged a regimen of hard training in preparation for the Berlin Games of 1916. He emphasized that Germany "must bring up sportsmen of muscular strength, trained without any interruption, even without a pause during the winter, sinewy, coached in all branches of gymnastics" (Diem, p. 50).

The Swedish organizers had decided to route the cycling road race around Lake Mälar. Swedish athletes were well prepared after a winter of training on special machines, but "Okey" Lewis from South Africa led during the entire 320-kilometer (199-mile) contest, winning in a time of 10 hours, 42 minutes, 39 seconds. The Swedes did win the team competition in a close contest with Great Britain and the United States.

Swedish count Clarence von Rosen was responsible for including the equestrian competition in the Stockholm Olympic Games. Held for the first time in the Olympics, the riding events pitted cavalry officers from ten nations against one another in individual and team competition. Seven nations took part in the team event, with each team represented by four officers; the individual competition was a three-day affair of dressage, endurance riding, and show jumping. In the team event, a 50-kilometer distance ride and a cross-country ride with obstacles were the highlights. The Swedish team won both the individual and the team contests, beating out the Germans and the Americans and impressing Carl Diem, who wrote, "What Swedish officers showed was representative of military riding, an honorable work" (Diem, p. 148). But he questioned whether

equestrianism should be an Olympic sport, because only a person and his or her achievements and capabilities should be evaluated.

In addition to staging the athletic events, the Swedes showed that they understood how to celebrate festivals and entertain guests by an attractive cultural program and by receptions and celebrations that demonstrated Swedish hospitality. There were receptions organized by representatives of all sports. Among the most elegant were the festival honoring the IOC, the garden festival hosted by the king in the park of the royal palace, and two dinners given by the crown prince. According to Diem, "the most impressive celebrations were those festivals which united participants from all nations. . . . In the national park, Skansen, a magnificent natural museum, groups were introduced and guided in their mother-language by well-known scientists. The festival ended with music and songs" (Diem, p. 34).

The cultural highlight of the Games occurred Sunday, July 14, when the center of the stadium was transformed into an amusement park. A long table crossed the stadium for the crown prince and other dignitaries. A band played the national anthems of all participating nations. The crown prince, Balck, and Coubertin gave solemn speeches, and countless voices shouted "Hurrah" for the crown prince, who had been the principal promoter of the Games. A Swedish men's chorus of 3,000 voices sang impressively, fireworks lighted up the dark sky, and huge fires were lit on the towers of the stadium, illuminating wide parts of the country.

The Stockholm Olympics of 1912 were the first real world festival of sports with peaceful and fairly contested events, although by this time Europe was already split into two armed camps, the Entente and the Central Powers, and World War I was only two years ahead. Sweden, as a neutral country, could bridge the growing political gap and bring a hope of universal peace.

Nationalism had arisen at the eve of the 1912 Olympics when Bohemia and Finland demanded their "national" flag be raised in case of victory. Neither country was an independent nation but was part of Austria and Russia, respectively. Considering the athletic achievements of these two small countries, especially Finland, a compromise was found: in case of victory a Finnish or Bohemian streamer would be hoisted above the Austrian or Russian flag.

The Stockholm Olympics were not dominated by world's fairs like the 1900 or 1904 Games, nor were they burdened by discriminatory racial displays as in 1904. There was a minimum of the kind of political protests that had marked the 1908 Games, when women demanded the right to vote. There were no ideological conflicts as in the cold war period or any of the gigantism and commercialization that affect contemporary Games. Despite some instances of chauvinism the Stockholm Games were more private and far less technically sophisticated than the Olympic Games of the present. Drug problems did not exist. But we have to avoid a romantic backward glance. In some ways, the

Stockholm Games were great games, but the world has changed since that time, and new challenges and problems demand new solutions.

BIBLIOGRAPHICAL ESSAY

The Stockholm organizing committee's account of the Games is Erik Bergvall, ed., *The Official Report of the Olympic Games of Stockholm 1912* (Stockholm, 1913), translated by Evart Adams Ray. This book includes a complete list of competitors, photographs of winners, information on the facilities and the promotion of the Games, and reports on the art exhibition and music festival. The committee also published a number of other multilanguage programs, brochures, and regulation books for various events, as well as many others in Swedish only. There was no official report produced by the American Olympic Committee, but the British version is *The Official Report of the Olympic Games of 1912 in Stockholm* (London, 1912). The Swiss Olympic Committee published *Olympische Spiele Stockholm 1912* (Zurich, 1913), edited by Julius Wagner.

Carl Diem, *Die Olympischen Spiele 1912* (Berlin, 1912), and also available in a 1990 reprint, is the most valuable unofficial source. Diem was a close observer of the Stockholm Games, principally because the next scheduled Games were to be held in Berlin, and his commentary on the various ceremonies and each of the events reflects his expertise and his concern for the coming Berlin Games. Other sources in German are S. Hermelin and Erik Peterson, eds., *V Olympiaden* (Stockholm, 1912); Eugen Seybold, *Olympischen Spiele 1912* (Munich, 1912); and Julius Wagner and Guido Eichenberger, *Olympische Spiele 1912* (Zurich, 1912), a book probably quite similar to that Wagner edited for the Swiss Olympic Committee. A semiofficial U.S. report is James E. Sullivan, ed., *The Olympic Games, Stockholm, 1912* (New York, 1912). Sullivan was the secretary-treasurer of the Amateur Athletic Union and President William Howard Taft's official representative to the Games. This is primarily a straightforward account of U.S. participation at Stockholm, but it also includes an article by Princeton University professor and IOC member William Milligan Sloane, "The Olympic Idea—Its Origin, Foundation, and Progress." Another source in English is Ferenc Mezo, *The Stockholm Olympiad 1912* (Budapest, 1955).

Horst Ueberhorst

BERLIN 1916

THE GAMES OF THE VITH OLYMPIAD
(Never Held)

On their return trip from the first modern Olympics in Athens, German Olympic Committee officials discussed the prospect of holding the Olympic Games in Berlin. Germany felt an important link with the ancient Olympics. Long before the unification of Germany in 1871, the Germans viewed themselves and their vigorous culture as the reincarnation of the ancient Greeks. This attachment to the Hellenics was manifested in the excavation attempts of the ancient site of Olympia by German archaeologists. In the mid-eighteenth century, Johann Joachim Winckelman planned an expedition to Olympia to exhume the ancient stadium. The plan was suspended with Winckleman's death in 1767 but not forgotten.

A century later, Ernst Curtius, a professor at the University of Berlin, actively pursued Winckelman's objectives. In 1875, four years after the formation of the German Empire, Curtius led an expedition to Olympia, Greece. Within six years, he had unearthed the *altis,* where the ruins of the Temple of Zeus and Hera were uncovered. The German archaeologist's success could be attributed to the active support of Kaiser Wilhelm's son Frederick, who would succeed his father in 1888 and saw the methodical excavation as a great cultural undertaking. The German Reichstag generously financed Curtius's ambition from the state treasury. The German effort resulted in the unveiling of the ancient Olympic site where for a thousand years the Olympic Games had been held.

The German activity in Olympia and information about the discoveries themselves were published in scientific journals throughout Europe between 1890 and 1897 and helped to acquaint the Western world with the idea of reviving the Olympic Games. The Germans were able to bring to life the knowledge of Olympia, painting a clear and certain picture of the Olympic site and the procedures of the Games. Ernst Curtius suggested that a suitable undertaking for the intellectuals and educators of the late nineteenth century might be the revival of the Olympic Games.

This challenge was heard by many Germans, but actively pursued by Frenchman Pierre de Coubertin. In 1894, delegates from twelve countries met at the Sorbonne in Paris and agreed upon the revival of the Olympic Games. They determined that the Games would be held every four years, would embrace all modern sports, and the Olympics would be allotted to different countries instead of always being held at one location, as in ancient times. The first Olympic Games of the modern era was held in Athens in 1896. After the 1896 Games, the International Olympic Committee (IOC), which controlled the Olympic Games, awarded the second Games to Paris, the home of Coubertin and the site of an Exposition Universelle scheduled for the summer of 1900.

Preparations for a Berlin Olympic Games began in earnest at the turn of the century. In 1901, at the Olympic congress in Paris, German IOC member Willibald Gebhardt made a bid for the Olympic Games to be held in Berlin. The German Imperial Board for the Olympic Games was then established to organize national Olympic Games in the German Empire, to prepare participants for the international Olympic Games, and to achieve a more universal representation by uniting the various German organizations that promoted gymnastics. This board consisted of Berlin sport leaders and individual gymnasts, who did not permit themselves to be contaminated by their colleagues' hostility toward competitive sport.

The German Imperial Board for the Olympic Games established a committee to raise money and secure a location for the construction of a suitable arena for the future Games. An attempt to secure land from the German government failed, and a public collection fared only slightly better, raising only 1,000 marks. The committee members continued their search, and their attention eventually focused on a piece of land the Berlin Union Club was leasing from the Prussian Office of Forest Management. On this land, at the edge of the Grunewald forest, the Berlin Union Club had constructed a horse racing track. General Graf von der Asseburg, president of the German Imperial Board for the Olympic Games and member of the Berlin Union Club, convinced the imperial board that an athletic arena could be built on the natural depression within the oval track. Asseburg deduced that since the track and the arena would still be used for racing, the contract with the Prussian government would not be violated. While the imperial board was busy securing a location for the Berlin stadium, the IOC awarded the 1904 Olympic Games to St. Louis.

Shortly after the St. Louis Games, the IOC met in London. It rejected the German bid for the 1908 Olympic Games on the claim that it lacked evidence of governmental support at either the municipal or state level. Rome, which had the support of the Italian government and sports federations, was selected over Berlin. But in 1906, when Mt. Vesuvius erupted, killing 2,000 people and devastating the Italian economy, the Italian Olympic Organizing Committee withdrew Rome as the Olympic site. The IOC, meeting in Athens at the time of the announcement, invited Great Britain, rather than Germany, to take over the organization of the 1908 Games, and the British Olympic Association accepted. This rejection did not diminish the German desire to host the Olympic Games.

In 1909, the IOC met in Berlin to decide the site for the 1912 Games. Berlin and Stockholm both presented their credentials. Stockholm received the majority of delegates' ballots and was awarded the Games. According to Carl Diem, a member of the German Olympic Committee, the IOC members left Berlin impressed with German athletic attitudes and informed the German committee that it should begin serious planning for the 1916 Olympic celebration.

This announcement inspired German action. Shortly after the IOC meeting in Berlin, a first phase of stadium construction began with the building of a forecourt under the Grunewald horse track to house dressing rooms, a police station, and a first-aid station. That same year, Asseburg died and the presidency of the German Imperial Board for the Olympic Games passed to General Victor von Podbielski. Podbielski had been actively involved in German sport and had served with the Prussian government as postmaster general and later as minister of the interior. Podbielski's government connections helped to further the building of the stadium. He was able to arrange a loan of 2.75 million gold marks from the German government and to secure the notable architect Otto March to draw blueprints and direct construction.

The second phase of stadium construction called for the leveling of the floor of the natural depression in order to build a 400-meter foot race track. Around the perimeter of this track a 600-meter cycle track was constructed. Stands for 34,000 spectators were built into the sides of the depression, stopping slightly above the arena floor. At the northern edge of the arena a 100-meter pool was built surrounded by bleachers with seating for 4,000 spectators. To accommodate the predicted overflow crowds, a terrace was constructed around the top of the stands. All construction was below ground level so as not to impede spectators' views of the horse racing that took place at ground level. The German Imperial Olympic Committee was intent on creating a stadium that would exceed both London's and Stockholm's in accommodations for athletes and spectators and in architectural design.

As the building of the stadium continued, official word arrived in 1911 that the IOC had selected Berlin as the host for the VIth Olympics. The excitement and confidence of this news, however, turned to disappointment with the inferior athletic performances turned in by the German team at the 1912 Olympic Games. German athletes were lagging behind those of other European powers and the United States. Sport in Germany could not keep pace with the nation's commercial and military achievements. Through the first five Olympiads, the Germans had not won a single gold medal in any track or field event. The Germans believed that if the 1916 Berlin Olympics were going to be a success, athletic reform in Germany was necessary.

Every host nation had done extremely well in its Olympic Games, and Germany did not want to be an exception. The German Imperial Olympic Committee was intent on correcting the mistakes of the past and making the best possible showing at the Berlin Games. It concluded that German training techniques were lacking in effectiveness, and since American college athletes were the world's best in most track and field events, they viewed the American athletic system as an excellent model to follow. In 1913, the German committee sent a four-man contingent to the United States to learn American training methods, with the idea of adapting them to Germany.

The German commission, consisting of Carl Diem, secretary-general of the German Imperial Board for the Olympic Games; Lieutenant Walter von Reichenau, representing the Ministry of War; Joseph Wartzer, a prominent athletic coach in Germany; and Martin Berner, a young German sportsman and writer, spent almost two months in the United States. They visited U.S. military academies and universities in the Midwest, and hired Alvin C. Kraenzlein, a former Olympic gold medalist who knew German, as a coach for the German team.

Kraenzlein was expected to do for German athletics what Field Marshal von Moltke had done for the army in 1871: organize victory. To accomplish this task, the German Imperial Olympic Committee gave Kraenzlein complete control of German athletics. After his arrival in Germany, Kraenzlein told a *New York Times* correspondent that he witnessed a great athletic renaissance. He told the reporter that the Germans firmly believed their national life could only benefit from the healthy enthusiasm and rivalry found in athletic competition and in Olympic sports. This new athletic enthusiasm had been first manifested on June 8, 1913, when Kaiser Wilhelm dedicated the new Berlin Stadium, in celebration of his twenty-fifth anniversary as head of the German state. The dedication of the Grunewald Stadium was hailed as the ''greatest athletic exhibition Europe had ever witnessed,'' a combination of religious fervor and German military pomp. Some 30,000 athletes paraded around the stadium. The program consisted of games and the demonstration of athletic skills in honor of the kaiser. The closing speech, given by General von Podbielski, urged the 3 million members of German athletic societies to organize for victory in the upcoming Olympic Games. The encouragement of the Games by the kaiser, like that of Adolf Hitler twenty years later, conformed with German political policy and was looked upon by both leaders as an excellent instrument by which to carry out the German plan to impress the world with the achievements and accomplishments of the fatherland.

Many of the delegates to the IOC congress held at Lausanne in May 1913 had recognized this German enthusiasm and energy. The talk of the congress concerned the astounding thoroughness and organization for the Berlin Games conducted by the German organizing committee. An example of this thoroughness was the organizing committee's attempt to remedy a problem plaguing earlier Olympic organizing committees: how to house the hundreds of athletes participating in the Games.

The German Organizing Committee developed a novel plan of offering private training camps to all participating nations. The committee asked each nation to bear a proportion of the expense necessary for the construction of athletes' quarters near the stadium and then secured a large plot of land in the Grunewald pine forest for the purpose of building these dwellings. This location would afford each participant the opportunity to reside in seclusion within walking distance of the Olympic stadium. Each facility would include all the comforts of home, including private cooks specializing in that country's foods, and an adjacent athletic field. The Swedes were first to take advantage of the German offer, and they paid to erect a traditional Swedish country house for their athletes. The organizing committee, aware that many countries did not want to incur the cost of a building for a limited stay, also offered an alternate plan to house athletes in special portable barracks during their stay in Berlin.

Meanwhile, late in 1913, the German Imperial Parliament supplemented the private donations received by the German Imperial Board for the Olympic Games with an additional $75,000 in order to provide the German athletes and coaches with all ingredients necessary to guarantee victory in 1916. With a new stadium and a very supportive government, the 1916 Berlin Games looked as if they would be the best ever.

On June 4, 1914, the IOC met at the Sorbonne in Paris to celebrate the twentieth anniversary of the revival of the Olympic Games. At this meeting, the program for the 1916 Berlin Games was put into final form, and the five-ringed Olympic flag was unfurled for the first time. Robert Thompson, president of the American Olympic Committee, left the conference convinced "the Berlin Games would be the greatest ever held" because of the thoroughness of its preparation and organization and the lack of political controversy despite the nationalism and militarism building in Europe.

On June 28, 1914, while the Sorbonne Congress was still in session, a Serbian assassin shot and killed Archduke Franz Ferdinand, heir to the Austro-Hungarian throne, in the Bosnian capital of Sarajevo. A month later Austria-Hungary declared war on Serbia. Days later Germany sided with Austria-Hungary and declared war on Russia and France. By August 1914, Europe became engulfed in a war that touched all aspects of life, including the Berlin Olympic Games.

Coubertin, the IOC president, believed that the power of the Olympic movement was such that the Germans, who had wanted the Games since their revival, would reduce their belligerent conduct and complete their plans for the VIth Olympiad. He was wrong: Germany invaded neutral Belgium in August, and Britain joined the Allied Powers and entered the war against Germany.

The British also fought the Germans on the Olympic front. The British IOC contingent opposed Coubertin's insistence that Berlin be retained as the Olympic site for 1916. Theodore Cook, a British member, demanded the expulsion of the German members from the IOC. When his motion was defeated, Cook resigned from the committee in protest. According to Coubertin, the dream of Olympia had to be preserved, and Berlin would host the Games in 1916.

Others believed differently. Days before Germany declared war, Alvin Kraenzlein and his staff, fearing a devastating struggle in Europe, sailed back to the United States. Three months later, another American trainer, Jim McCoughlin, who had been hired by Denmark, returned to the United States because Danish Olympic officials were convinced that it would be impossible for the Germans to hold the Olympic Games in 1916.

The Germans disagreed. The German Imperial Board for the Olympic Games anticipated a short war and continued with their ambitious plans for the VIth Olympics. As the war progressed, the status of the Berlin Games remained in limbo. The German Olympic Committee firmly stated that Berlin was the only site for the 1916 Games, which would be held as planned. In November 1914, two months after the battle of the Marne, the IOC met in Lyons, France; Germany was not represented. Some Allied and neutral Olympic members called for moving the Games to a different site, but the Germans stood their ground.

In March 1915, the German Imperial Olympic Committee reported to IOC members that Germany was still making official preparations for the Berlin games and that only nations allied with Germany and neutral countries would be invited. Comte Justinien de Clary, president of the French Olympic Committee, promptly dismissed the German claim and said that he thought there could be no Olympics before 1920.

Many U.S. cities believed otherwise. Offers to host the 1916 Games arrived from Chicago, New York, Newark, Cleveland, San Francisco, and Philadelphia. Despite the protests of Comte de Clary and the growing movement to change the Olympic site, the Germans continued to claim that Berlin was the only possible site. Coubertin expressed his feelings concerning the 1916 Berlin Games in a March 1915 letter to the Associated Press:

The I.O.C. has not the right to withdraw the celebration of the Olympic Games from the country to which the celebration was given without consulting that country. The Sixth Olympic Games remain and will remain credited to Berlin, but it is possible that they will not be held. In olden times it happened that it was not possible to celebrate the games but they did not for this reason cease to exist. I consider all that is said and written on this subject now to be useless; the I.O.C. will not allow its hand to be forced. (*New York Times,* March 19, 1915)

Throughout 1915, battle followed battle as the war reached a stalemate. The German Imperial Olympic Committee continued to insist, however, that the Olympics would take place in Berlin at the end of the war. The summer of 1916 found European civilization at the brink of destruction and the Berlin stadium vacant. The Olympic flag of peace was not seen in Berlin. The flag of peace in Europe was not seen for another two years or the Olympic flag for another four years.

The fact that Berlin was selected to host the VIth Olympic Games was a recognition of the tremendous growth of interest in sport in Germany. The founding of German associations for bowling, cycling, swimming, skating, fencing, and lawn tennis during the late nineteenth century supported the new feeling in Germany of the importance of the spirit of competition and the pursuit of athletic records as opposed to the traditional views of the German Gymnastic Union. The Olympic Games provided imperial Germany an opportunity to demonstrate to the rest of the world that Germans were as successful in sport as they had become industrially and commercially. Through the first five Olympiads, however, the Germans did not achieve the athletic success they had anticipated. To remedy this situation, imperial Germany attempted to "Americanize" German sport by adapting American athletic ideas and methods for its sports associations. The year 1916 was to have been Germany's opportunity to demonstrate its athletic prowess and its ability to stage the best Olympic Games ever held. The German Imperial Olympic Committee had selected a team that it hoped was destined for Olympic victory, and the German organizing committee, with help from the imperial government, constructed Olympic facilities never seen before at Olympic Games. Imperial Germany's chance to shine athletically disappeared with World War I. Germany would have to wait until 1928 to participate in the Games and would once again be given the opportunity to be host eight years later. The preparations and the interest in sport spawned by the VIth Olympiad scheduled for Berlin in 1916 culminated in the success of the 1936 Berlin Olympic Games.

BIBLIOGRAPHICAL ESSAY

In the hundreds of books written about the Olympic Games since their revival by Baron Pierre de Coubertin in 1896, the 1916 Games are almost always neglected. Some books devote a page to them, but most address the contest with a simple statement, such as "The Great War of 1914–1918 precluded the conducting of the Games at Berlin in 1916." Nevertheless, there are materials available that provide information and insight into the VIth Olympiad.

Despite the fact that the Games never took place, the organizing committee did prepare an official report for the IOC, *Denkschrift zur Vorbereitung der VI. Olympiade, veranstaltet im Deutschen Stadion zu Berlin* (Berlin, n.d.), as well as *Olympische Spiele in Berlin 1916. Programme und allgemeine Beststimmungen* (Berlin, 1916), in German, French, and English editions.

Carl Diem, a leading advocate of sport in imperial, Weimar, and National Socialist Germany, in *Weltgeschichte des Sports und der Leibeserziehung* (Stuttgart, 1960), offers insight into the early German involvement in the Olympic movement, the formation of the German Olympic Committee, and the political and economic aspects of the VIth Olympiad. Diem's *Sport in Amerika* (Berlin, 1931) is an excellent source for information about his visit to the United States in 1913.

Karl Lennartz, a noted Olympic historian and director of the Carl-Diem-Institut in Cologne, has written a history of the 1916 Games, *Die VI. Olympische Spiele—Berlin 1916* (Cologne, 1978). See also Lennartz's "Die VI. Olympischen Spiele Berlin 1916," *Stadion* 6 (1980): 229–50. A book previewing the 1916 Games is Adolf Petienz, *Olympia 1916* (Berlin, 1914).

The *Olympic Games News Service,* published by the German organizing committee for the 1936 Games, was helpful because of its background material on the 1916 Games. Additional material for the 1916 Games can be found in the *Official Guide Book to the Celebration of the XI Olympiad* and *The XI Olympic Games, Berlin, 1936: Official Report* (Berlin, 1937), published in English by the German organizing committee. These sources reflected on the cancelled 1916 Berlin Games because of their impact on the 1936 Games.

The *New York Times* and *London Times* published statements made by IOC members during the war years of 1914–1915.

William Durick

ANTWERP 1920

THE GAMES OF THE VIIth OLYMPIAD

No other Olympic Games started their preparations with less time than did the VIIth Olympic Games, held in Antwerp, Belgium, in 1920. World War I had ended only twenty months before, and yet Baron Pierre de Coubertin was able to convince the cruelly damaged Belgian nation to host the first Olympic Games in eight years.

Situated on the Scheldt River, Antwerp is one of the most important seaports in the world. It lies in the Flemish part of Belgium. At the time of the VIIth Olympiad, the population of Antwerp, like many other Flemish cities, was still characterized by an outspoken sociocultural and economic division between a dominantly Francophone elite and a Flemish-speaking lower- and lower-middle-class majority.

The first Gymnastics Society of Belgium had been founded in 1839 in Antwerp. The city was the major gymnastics stronghold of the country, with Nicolaas J. Cupérus, the founding president of the Fédération européenne de gymnastique (FEG) in 1881, as one of its most influential exponents. Typical British sports such as rowing and association football had been adopted by some members of the Antwerp elite as early as 1851 and 1870, respectively. Sports like track and field, fencing, field hockey, equestrian events, and polo maintained an exclusive social status in the host country at that time. The popular physical activities among the lower and lower middle classes were professional cycling, in which several Belgians had excelled internationally, gymnastics, boxing and wrestling, and the traditional games of archery and *kaatsen* (balle pelote). Association football was quickly gaining in popularity as well. Although the war had seriously hampered regular competition, many of the best players had had a chance to play while serving in the military. The so-called Front Wanderers, a selection of Belgian soccer players, had competed behind the lines against British and French army teams, from which they had learned a lot.

In 1912 at the Thirteenth International Olympic Committee (IOC) meeting in Basel, the president of the Belgian Olympic Committee (BOC), Baron Edouard de Laveleye, made a bid for Belgium to host the 1920 Games. Originally it was intended that the Games would take place in the Belgian capital of Brussels, but Charles Cnoops, the vice-president of the Belgian Fencing Association, and others led a successful campaign on behalf of Antwerp. By 1914, when the site decision for the 1920 Games was to be decided, Antwerp had replaced Brussels as the preferred Belgian site.

Although the final decision was delayed because of the outbreak of war, French and Belgian representatives signed an agreement that Antwerp would host the Games if that city were liberated by 1920. Shortly after the armistice in November 1918, Coubertin approached the Belgian government to host either the 1920 or 1924 Games. Although the Belgians were skeptical at first, they agreed to host the 1920 Games after the Antwerp Provisory Committee pledged 1 million Belgian francs to help cover expenses. The final decision was made on April 5, 1919, at the Seventeenth IOC meeting in Lausanne, just sixteen months before the official opening of the Games. It was obvious that the choice of Antwerp was a political option, intended to give moral support to Belgium.

As a result of the late decision, the organization of the Games relied more on bravado and improvisation than on sound planning. On April 7, 1919, the BOC convened the Belgian sports federations in order to obtain their collaboration. Alfred Verdyck, the man who would become the major engineer of the Antwerp Games, was not glowing with enthusiasm when he was invited to this assembly. He and his colleague, R. W. Seeldrayers, had mixed feelings toward the whole operation. This was due to the fact that Count Henri de Baillet-Latour, influenced by some Antwerp sportsmen, had obtained the VIIth Olympic Games for Antwerp but in doing so had failed to consult the Belgian sports federations. After his return to Belgium, he organized an assembly of the sports federations. Verdyck and Seeldrayers, representing the Royal Belgian Football Association, were convinced that it would be impossible to set up in only one year an organization for which other countries, unaffected by war, had needed no fewer than four years. However, when they left the meeting, Verdyck had been appointed general secretary and Seeldrayers secretary-rapporteur of a committee under the presidency of Baillet-Latour.

The first stone of the transformed Beerschot Stadium was laid by Mayor Jan De Vos on July 4, 1919, and the Olympic stadium was officially inaugurated on Sunday, May 23, 1920, with demonstrations of the Antwerp Gymnastics Section and a choir of 1,200 singers. Since the official report mentions May 1 as opening date, there must have been two separate semiofficial openings, as confirmed later by the Antwerp newspaper *De Nieuwe Gazet.*

The entire Olympic enterprise is generally considered a magnificent piece of work on the part of the Belgians. Coubertin stated in his opening speech at the Eighteenth IOC Session on August 17 in Antwerp that ''in addition to the record of national honour, won in 1914, Belgium has now succeeded in setting a record of intelligent and rapid organization or—if I am allowed to speak in less academic but more expressive terms—a new record for its skill in improvisation'' (Coubertin, *L'idée olympique,* p. 81). Nevertheless, because of the lack of time, money, and materials, the standards of the 1912 Stockholm Games were not met. Although the stadium had been rebuilt and the running track had been newly constructed, there were many complaints. The silver medalist in the 1,500-meter race, Philip Noel-Baker, wrote that the track was slow and heavy. Rains left ruts and depressions in its surface, causing the runners constant worry. And it rained almost constantly during those August days of 1920.

Whereas the official report stressed the good accommodations provided for the visiting teams, this view was shared by only a minority of the participants. As spokesman for the British team, Noel-Baker described the accommodation in the Antwerp city schools, the catering, and the food as very good. But contradictory comments were heard from the mutinous American athletes, who had already rioted on board the *Princess Matoika* during their crossing. Whereas the athletes who had served in the navy were transported on board the cruiser *S.S. Frederick,* the majority of the army and civilian athletes were shipped on the *S.S. Princess Matoika.* There was nothing regal about the *Princess,* a rusty old troop carrier called in at the last minute to replace the broken-down *Great Northern.* It became a stirring crossing, known in American Olympic history as the "mutiny of the Matoika." The female athletes and a few officials had cabins on the top deck, but 108 male athletes bunked in troop quarters below decks. The sea was rough, the food was terrible, and the cream of the athletic world turned slightly sour. The American Olympic Committee was roundly denounced. Weight thrower Pat McDonald and swimmer Norman Ross acted as spokesmen for the riotous athletes. The only cheerful note was provided by Duke Kahanamoku, the Hawaiian swimmer who, with fellow Hawaiians, sang on deck while strumming a ukulele.

Things did not improve on arrival in Antwerp, where the male athletes were accommodated in a city school, while the women stayed at the YWCA Hostess House. The men complained about the lack of privacy and the absence of hot showers in their schoolrooms. Most outspoken was the Irish-American hammer thrower Pat Ryan, who spread the news that all athletes would get "cauliflower ears" sleeping on hard bunks with hay-filled pillows. Similar criticism was voiced by Swedish team members on their way home from Antwerp. When these allegations appeared in Dutch and German newspapers, the Antwerp sports magazine *Sport-revue* launched a counterattack, responding with reports about the behavior of Olympic participants outside the stadium. It accused some athletes, who had complained about Antwerp's high prices, of misbehavior in night bars and "mingling with venus kittens" (*Sport-revue,* September 21, 1920, p. 163).

Coubertin's opinion that the swimming pool was a "model of its kind" in the report of the American Olympic Committee was shared by the local population but certainly not by the American swimmers. Aileen Riggin recalled that she had never seen anything like it, it was a ditch that had been dug with an embankment on one side to be a protection in case of war. The water was entirely black and the coldest the American swimmers had ever encountered. The divers brought woolen stockings, socks, and mufflers to keep warm and gave each other rubdowns between dives.

Against the will of the Antwerpians, the soccer matches were played in several other Belgian cities, which wanted their share of the VIIth Olympic Games. The final match, however, was played in the Olympic Beerschot Stadium in Antwerp.

Boxing and wrestling, both popular in Antwerp, were staged in the auditorium of the Antwerp Zoological Society near the central train station and drew large crowds. The rowing contests were held on the canal of Willebroek near Brussels.

Even Coubertin qualified it an "anti-Olympic setting": walls of factories, reservoirs, and oil storage tanks so horrid that all attempt to hide its ugliness was abandoned. Yachting was moved to Ostend at the North Sea coast. Shooting events were held at the army camp of Beverloo, about 60 kilometers from Antwerp, except for running-deer shooting and trapshooting, which were staged near Antwerp. Next to track and field, there were more rifle and pistol shooting medals awarded than in any of other twenty-two events in Antwerp. A reporter from the *Echo de Paris* observed that "not even at Verdun were so many rifle shots heard."

During the Antwerp Games, the scars of the Great War were still omnipresent. For these first postwar Games, the Olympic ceremonies had been revised and highly ritualized. On the morning of the official opening day, August 14, 1920, a religious service was held in Antwerp Cathedral in remembrance of those who had lost their lives in the war.

For the first time in Olympic history, the Olympic flag was raised at the opening ceremony. According to Coubertin, this flag had been first displayed in Paris during the celebration of the twentieth anniversary of the reorganization of the Olympic Games in June 1914, but it had never appeared at an Olympic gathering. The five entwined multicolored circles on a white background symbolize the five parts of the world united by Olympism and reproduce the colors of every nation. This novelty became a favorite object for souvenir hunters. Wilfred Kent Hughes, who competed as a hurdler for the Australian team in Antwerp, remembered how the road leading to the stadium was bedecked with Olympic flags, "one of which, by some strange chance, was among my baggage on return to England" (Donald and Selth, *Olympic Saga,* p. 34). For the first time the Olympic oath was recited, spoken by the Belgian fencer Victor Boin, a former Olympic medalist and war pilot. A flight of doves, symbolizing the ideals of brotherhood and world peace, were ironically accompanied by the firing of a gun salute.

Germany and its former allies were not present. Although Coubertin had refused to exclude the former aggressors from the Olympic movement, he had worked out a diplomatic solution, leaving the task of the invitation to the organizing country. He believed that it would be unwise to let a German team appear in the Games before 1924. It was not long ago that the last German soldiers had left Belgian soil, and hostile feelings against the former invaders still ran high. On June 13, two months before the official opening of the Olympics, Antwerpians had watched a demonstration against the return of Germans. Soldiers and boy scouts were charged with the security tasks in the stadium, in which soldier-athletes of the victorious Allied nations wore their army uniforms during the opening ceremony. Although the weather at the opening day had been warm and sunny, attendance remained far below expectations. Photographs clearly show that the stadium was far from filled. King Albert, who had presided at the opening ceremony remarked, "All this is quite nice . . . , but it certainly lacks people" (*Les Sports,* August 19, 1920).

The 1919 Interallied Games in Paris had shown how the war had hampered the progress of sport. At these strictly military games, the Americans had won almost half of the competitions. One year later in Antwerp, however, American supremacy in track and field was seriously challenged by the remarkable achievements of the Finnish athletes. The legendary Paavo Nurmi, who made his first Olympic appearance in Antwerp, won the 10,000-meter and the 8-kilometer cross-country races. He was beaten in the 5,000-meter race by the eccentric Frenchman Joseph Guillemot, a victim of poison gas in the war, who took revenge for the defeat of his compatriot Jean Bouin at the 1912 Stockholm Games. The "gray eminence" of track and field, Hannes Kolehmainen of Finland, took the lead in the marathon at 30 kilometers and held it to the end, a victory that made him the most popular sport hero at Antwerp.

The brash American sprinter, Charles Paddock, won a gold medal in the 100-meter dash with a spectacular leap at the finish line. Only four years later, in Paris, the American hegemony in the sprint events would be broken by the British athlete Harold Abrahams. Contrary to the story told in Hugh Hudson's film, *Chariots of Fire,* Abrahams participated in Antwerp. He ran the 100-meter and 200-meter races but did not qualify for the finals. He also was a member of the British 4 × 100-meter relay team, which finished in fourth place.

America ruled the waves in the icy cold Antwerp swimming pool. Hawaiian Duke Kahanamoku repeated his Stockholm victory in the 100-meter freestyle, and his fellow Hawaiian, Warren Paoa Kealoha, won the 100-meter backstroke. Norman Ross, who had impersonated the role of Captain Bligh during the mutiny on board the *Princess Matoika,* won gold in the 400-meter and 1,500-meter freestyle events. American Ethelda Bleibtrey excelled among her swimming peers. She was the first female contestant to win three gold medals: 100-meter and 300-meter freestyle and 4 × 100-meter relay. Fourteen year-old Aileen Riggin won the springboard diving from both the 1-meter and 3-meter boards and thus became the youngest Olympic champion in history. Belgium lost in the water polo final against Great Britain 3–2. Belgian fans, quite unhappy with the decisions of the Swedish referee, started booing when the band played "God Save the King."

Belgian medals were rather scarce, except for archery, in which Hubert Van Innis won four gold and two silver medals. Archery then included popinjay shooting. Van Innis had also won this event, which involves shooting at a moving bird target at the top of a 33-meter mast, at the 1900 Paris Games. Along with the tug-of-war, popinjay shooting would not reappear on the Olympic program after 1920.

One of three American gold medal winners in boxing was Edward Eagan, a Yale student, who won the light-heavyweight event. Twelve years later, Eagan would make a unique Olympic comeback as a member of the winning American bobsled team at the Lake Placid Winter Games.

The Belgian public showed only scant interest in the whole Olympic happening. Some of the events, such as ice hockey and rugby, had never been seen before and appeared as exotic curiosities to the astonished spectators. Only swimming, boxing, and wrestling drew large crowds, although 40,000 invaded the stadium for the football final between Belgium and Czechoslovakia. A group of boys even dug a tunnel under a fence to gain entry. Belgium took an early lead through a penalty and scored a second goal in the twenty-eighth minute. The Czech players were very upset about the officiating by the British referee John Lewis, and the game got rougher. After a foul was called against one of their players, the Czech team left the field some minutes before the half. The Czechoslovakian team was disqualified, and the Belgians were declared Olympic champions. No other victory had been more enthusiastically acclaimed since the end of the war in Belgium. The spontaneous outburst of public joy that overtook the stadium acted as a catharsis for a battered population that regained some of its pride through football. From that point, football grew in popularity, to become the premier sport in Belgium.

In a formal address on August 17, 1920, in the Antwerp city hall, Coubertin had warned of the danger of mercantilism, which had already begun to menace sport. These words turned out to be prophetic, not only for the financial disaster of the Antwerp Games but also for the further evolution of the Olympic Games. In 1913, during the very first initiative to obtain the Games, the amount of 1 million Belgian francs had been promised by the Provisory Committee in order to make Antwerp the favorite among the possible candidates. These promises were never kept, and when the final accounts were made, a deficit of 626,022,500, Belgian francs was recorded. What had happened? Two rival factions had developed within the Provisory Committee. Opposing the Executive Committee was the so-called Festivities Committee, a consortium of Antwerp shipowners, exporters, and diamond traders formed to raise the promised million. This committee, consisting of "personalities absolutely alien to sport," according to the official report of the Games, managed to appropriate the prospective capital for its own aims. Moreover, the official report also noted that the committee had scheduled a series of pre-Olympic events, which had prematurely drained away the interest and money of the public from the actual Games. The official report also blamed the Belgian press, and especially the Brussels press, for its boycott of the Games. However, an analysis of fifteen Belgian and four foreign newspapers does not lend support to these contentions. On the contrary, it appeared that the four foreign newspapers covered the Games less fully than the Belgian papers did. In the face of these facts, the validity and objectivity of the official report of 1920 can seriously be doubted. On many occasions, the report appears as a plea written in defense of the brave but deceived men who had courageously taken up a task too heavy for their shoulders. It is not their integrity at fault here but rather their naive misreading of the economic situation in Belgium in 1920. At that time, the Olympics were still very much a symbol of conspicuous consumption. This lack of insight on the part of the organizers was clearly put into words by *Sport-revue* (August 15, 1920): "They have failed to understand that sport resides more in the soul of the people than in the higher circles.'' The whole Olympic enterprise was probably most accurately summarized in the weekly Flemish magazine *Ons Volk* (September 4, 1920): ''The Olympiads [*sic*] of Antwerp seem to have been successful with regard to the participation of the contestants. They failed with regard to the public interest.''

BIBLIOGRAPHICAL ESSAY

Primary sources for the first postwar Olympic Games are almost as scarce as genuine coffee and real butter must have been during the war years. The official report of the Belgian Olympic Committee is *Rapport officiel de Jeux des la 7ième Olympiade,* edited by Alfred Verdyck (Brussels, 1920), but it is inaccurate and incomplete. These shortcomings inspired Bill Mallon to write *The Unofficial Report of the 1920 Olympics* (Durham, N.C., 1992), which is the most comprehensive compilation of the results of the Games but does not touch their political or sociocultural aspects.

Some of the more interesting primary sources are the official reports of several national Olympic committees, such as the extensive *Report of the American Olympic Committee: Seventh Olympic Games Antwerp, Belgium 1920* (Greenwich, Conn., 1920). There are no official reports from the British or French Olympic committees, but one can find those reports from Sweden, Denmark, Finland, Italy, and Japan, all in the language of those countries. Another interesting source is the nicely edited brochure *Aurons nous la VIIe Olympiade à Anvers en 1920?* which was published in 1914 as part of Antwerp's bid for the 1920 Games. Another primary source was published as part of the Spalding Athletic Library, *VIIth Olympic Games: Antwerp 1920* (New York, 1920). Originals of the latter two works, together with original copies of the Belgian *Rapport officiel* and the Swedish and the Finnish reports, are held in the Sportmuseum Vlaanderen, Leuven, Belgium. For Coubertin's views, see his *L'Idee olympique* (Stuttgart, 1967).

Daily newspapers, magazines, and sport publications are valuable primary sources. Wilfried Mostinckx undertook a comparative quantitative analysis of fifteen Belgian newspapers and four foreign newspapers during the 1920 Games period. These results were published in 1983 in his licentiate thesis (under the supervision of Roland Renson) at the K.U. Leuven, Belgium, titled ''De Olympische Spelen van Antwerpen en hun receptie in de pers.''

The most important secondary work on the Antwerp Games is Roland Renson, *The Games Reborn: The VIIth Olympiad Antwerp 1920* (Brussels, 1995). Other secondary sources of interest are Keith Donald and Don Selth, *Olympic Saga: The Track and Field Story, Melbourne 1956* (Sydney, 1957); John Lucas, ''American Preparations for the First Post World War Olympic Games,'' *Journal of Sport History* 10, 2 (Summer 1983): 30–44, and Roland Renson, ''From the Trenches to the Track: The 1920 Antwerp Olympic Games'' in Norbert Müller and Joachim K. Rühl, eds., *Olympic Scientific Congress 1984 Official Report: Sport History* (Niedernhausen, Germany, 1985), pp. 234–244.

For the Interallied Games of 1919, see J. Mills Hanson, ed., *The Interallied Games: Paris, 22nd June to 6th July, 1919* (n.p., n.d.). A general account of the Olympics is Alexander Weyand, *The Olympic Pageant* (New York, 1952), notable because Weyand was a member of the U.S. Greco-Roman wrestling team in 1920 but failed to win a medal.

Roland Renson

PARIS 1924

THE GAMES OF THE VIIIth OLYMPIAD

In 1921, International Olympic Committee (IOC) president Baron Pierre de Coubertin appealed to the French Olympic Organizing Committee to endorse Amsterdam as the site of the 1928 Summer Games. French support for Amsterdam as host of the 1928 Games, predicted Coubertin, would be rewarded with the selection of a French city for the 1924 Games. Awareness that hosting the Olympic Games had become a prestigious honor was shown by the number of cities desiring to stage the 1924 Olympic Games. Interest in hosting had been expressed by the American cities of Los Angeles, Atlantic City, Chicago, and Pasadena. Rome, Barcelona, Amsterdam, Lyons, and Paris were among the European cities that had indicated an interest.

The economic conditions of the times rather than the concept of moving the Games around the world dictated the site selection of the 1924 Olympic Games. Many European countries were still coping with the lingering economic effects of World War I, and travel to the United States to compete would have posed financial hardships on many athletes and their national Olympic committees (NOC).

A *New York Times* sportswriter observed that interest in sport among French citizens had increased markedly since the Paris Olympics of 1900. Facilities such as Pershing Stadium and numerous halls for boxing, wrestling, and fencing constituted a basic infrastructure that could accommodate the international event. Less than a month before the IOC voted on a site for the VIIIth Olympic Games, Amsterdam officials withdrew their bid for the 1924 Games and requested the 1928 Olympic Games. Before the IOC voted for the 1924 site, French premier Aristide Briand offered enthusiastic moral and financial support from his government at a meeting of the French Olympic Organizing Committee. The French Olympic Games Committee showed political savvy by making the premier the honorary president of the committee. With influential support for Paris from Coubertin, the United States, and the Netherlands, the IOC announced on June 3, 1921, that Paris had been awarded the 1924 Olympic Games and Amsterdam the 1928 Games. This marked the first time two future sites had been selected together.

On the advice of Henri Pathe, commissioner of sports and physical education, the French Olympic Organizing Committee placed itself under the jurisdiction of the foreign minister, elevating the Games to a national level. The decision was based on the committee's view that the Olympic Games were a significant international entity. Not long after Paris had been awarded the Games, critics cast doubt on the ability of French officials to carry out their enormous task. Controversy over the suitability of Pershing Stadium and a lack of funds caused many Parisians to wonder if the IOC had made an error in its selection. Although the French government authorized the unprecedented appropriation of 20 million francs for the Games, delivery of those funds proceeded at a snail's pace. The president of the French Olympic Organizing Committee, Count Justinien de Clary, grew impatient with the slow government bureaucracy and borrowed money from banks to begin construction of venues.

The most important venue question concerned Pershing Stadium, an older facility named for the American general of World War I and used for the Interallied Games in 1919. The organizing committee, however, decided that the stadium was too small for the 1924 Games and that renovating it would be as costly as building a new stadium. Moreover, Pershing Stadium had been declared unsafe for spectators, and it was located in an inconvenient and undesirable part of the city. Because Paris municipal authorities had relinquished control of the Olympic Games to national authority, a portion of the government financial appropriation was used to construct a new stadium designed to accommodate the expected throng of visitors. In all, six government departments joined in the stadium project, thus further complicating matters. By June 1, 1922, organizational problems were worked out, and the committee announced that plans for the stadium would go forth. During these halcyon days of Olympic sport, financial considerations rather than environmental sensitivity dictated the stadium site selection. As a consequence, Colombes, a beautiful Paris suburb near the Seine River, became the center of Olympic construction.

By its thirtieth anniversary, the Summer Olympic Games had become a formidable international event despite World War I. Because of the military's use of sports for training and morale-building purposes during World War I, the pool of potential Olympic athletes was larger than ever. Since the first meeting of the IOC in 1894, additional men's events, as well as women's events, had become part of the Olympic program.

In addition, a special program of cultural events was planned to help commemorate the thirtieth anniversary. In an effort to extend the scope of the Olympic Games beyond athletic events, French officials invited all participating countries to submit entries for a truly international celebration of the arts. The French Olympic Organizing Committee coordinated the cultural activities through the French Ministries of Foreign Affairs and of Fine Arts; through its work, the arts were an important part of several subsequent Games.

The 1921 IOC Congress, meeting in Lausanne, voted to make sweeping changes in the program of the 1924 Games. Ninety delegates representing NOCs, international sport federations (IFs), and the IOC discussed the appropriateness of specific sporting events. The delegates adopted guidelines for the number of entries allowed in events and the organization of competitions, and it made substantial changes in the program. Some events, such as the women's 100-meter backstroke and 200-meter breaststroke, were added to expand opportunities for women; seven other sports were eliminated: the tug-of-war, the 3,000-meter walk, the 56-pound weight throw, rugby football, archery, and golf. Although the tug-of-war had made five consecutive appearances after 1900, the lack of participation caused its elimination with little regret. All morning contests, including preliminary heats, were dropped, thereby eliminating the lengthy day-long sessions that had caused so many objections at the 1920 Games. The delegates also made certain procedural changes so competition would be more uniform. Each IF appointed a five-member committee to control competition in its sport, removing that responsibility from the host country's organizing committee, which had often lacked the expertise necessary to conduct events in certain sports. While some of the eliminated sports were later readmitted to the Games, the IOC demonstrated its desire to exert more control over the staging of the Olympic Games.

Recognizing the economic impact of visitors and wishing to avert a reputation of unscrupulous hoteliers who might take advantage of tourists to the Olympic Games and to France, the organizing committee organized a bureau to arrange accommodations at reasonable prices in hotels and private residences for athletes, official delegates, and tourists. Hoteliers, tourist agencies, and the Olympic Accommodation Bureau worked out a plan to disseminate housing information to guests.

After the Paris Olympics, tennis was excluded from the Olympic Games as a result of conflicts between the International Lawn Tennis Federation (ILTF) and the IOC. Before the tennis competition began, Julian S. Myrick of the U.S. Lawn Tennis Association protested the inadequate facilities. Despite complaints from American players and officials about the playing conditions, the U.S. team clearly dominated the tennis competition, with victories in men's and women's singles, doubles, and mixed doubles. ILTF officials criticized the conduct of the tennis events and demanded that the organization be represented on the IOC. When the IOC refused to comply with the ILTF demand, the federation withdrew prior to the 1928 Games. The sport reentered the Olympic movement as a demonstration sport at the 1984 Los Angeles Olympics and was restored to medal status at the 1988 Seoul Olympics.

Amid controversies among athletes and officials, rugby football made a final appearance in the 1924 Olympic Games. A fight broke out during the France-U.S. rugby match and temporarily disrupted competition. Swift action by the International Amateur Athletic Federation (IAAF) and the IOC before the conclusion of the Games led to the termination of rugby because of limited spectator interest and few entries. By eliminating less popular sports, the IOC sought to ease the financial burden for host countries.

By January 1924, the town of Colombes, site of the Olympic stadium, was alive with Olympic spirit, and citizens were eagerly anticipating the Games when their streets would be teeming with visitors. The streetcar line had been improved, and plans for additional train service from Paris were well underway. New construction was evident, and lists of housing accommodations were already on display in front of cafés.

By May 1, the Olympic stadium was completed and presented to the various technical committees for inspection. The stadium provided covered seating for

20,000 spectators and standing room for an additional 40,000. There were dressing facilities for 1,200 athletes beneath the stadium, and electric bells summoned athletes from a waiting area 15 minutes before their events. The French Congress of Chronometry had designed new timing devices for accuracy and uniformity. The spacious and finely equipped swimming pool built on the outskirts of Paris at a cost of 8 million francs was the most modern in Europe.

The political climate created by World War I lingered, however. On April 12, 1923, the IOC announced that it would be inappropriate to invite the Soviet Union or Germany to participate in the Paris Olympic Games. The Bolshevik revolution in Russia was viewed suspiciously, and the German invasion of France during the war had not been forgiven. The IOC also voted not to replace deceased German IOC members before the Paris Olympics. Although Coubertin openly wished for the presence of German athletes, the IOC could not be swayed. Coubertin's ideal of universal peace through international sport would have to wait.

Coubertin never welcomed women as competitors. Following his dismissal as head of the 1900 Olympic organizing committee, women competed in tennis and golf. By 1924 golf was no longer on the Olympic program, but women could compete in tennis, swimming, diving, and a new event, fencing.

The fencing events were held at the Velodrome d'Hiver. Twenty-five contestants representing nine countries entered the inaugural women's Olympic fencing competition. Ellen Osiier of Denmark was the first woman Olympic fencing champion. She dominated her event with sixteen victories and no defeats and celebrated her accomplishment the next day by marching with her teammates in the opening ceremonies. The women's Olympic program consisted of sports that were available to those who had the means and the time to participate.

Forty-four nations were represented at the VIIIth Summer Olympic Games. Although the cultural competition had begun two months earlier, the elegant opening ceremonies were held in Colombes Stadium on the afternoon of July 6, 1924. The president of France, Gaston Doumergue, and other notables viewed the parade of nations from the Tribune of Honor. Adhering to the protocol that followed the language of the host nation, the South African delegation, Afrique de Sur, attired in green and white uniforms, led the athletes before the cheering spectators. The 1924 Games marked the appearance of more uniformity in the attire of each national team, and the freedom of national teams to select and design parade uniforms was recommended for future Games. When all of the delegations had assembled and faced the Tribune of Honor, Count Clary ascended the steps to the top of the rostrum and invited President Doumergue to declare open the Games of the VIIIth Olympiad. After an elaborate ceremony, including the release of hundreds of pigeons, French athlete Georges André recited the oath of the athletes, and the procession marched out of the stadium.

Scottish sprinter Eric Liddell rejected the opportunity to run the 100-meter race on Sunday because of his strong religious convictions. He made up for his lost chance in that event by winning a gold medal in the 400-meter race and a bronze medal in the 200 meters. Several other Olympians distinguished themselves by achieving impressive firsts or victories. In her second Olympic appearance, Aileen Riggin, a member of the famed Women's Swimming Association of New York, became the first competitor to win medals in both diving and swimming. After winning a silver medal in springboard diving, the 18 year old won a bronze medal in the first women's Olympic 100-meter backstroke. The Finnish trackmen Paavo Nurmi and Willie Ritola brought attention to their nation and distance running. Paavo Nurmi accomplished what no other Olympian had ever done when he won the 1,500- and 5,000-meter races within hours, setting Olympic records in each event. He increased his gold medal count by winning the individual cross-country event and contributing to Finnish victories in the cross-country and 3,000-meter team events. The American-trained Ritola set an Olympic record in the 10,000-meter race and a world record in the 3,000-meter steeplechase. In addition, he won a gold medal in the cross-country team race and silver medals in the 5,000-meter and individual cross-country races.

Newspaper correspondents and coaches debated the reasons for the outstanding performances of the Finnish athletes. Nurmi was the center of the numerous debates and theories. Some attributed his success to his diet of uncooked dried fish and black bread accompanied by baths in unheated water; others maintained that he was a beneficiary of the progressive Finnish educational system, which included compulsory physical training. Moreover, organized sport for all was promoted in every Finnish village.

In the presence of government officials and the diplomatic corps, the Olympic musical, literary, and artistic events began on May 2, 1924, in the Champs Elysées Theater. One hundred athletes presented the Olympic flag, and poetry reading and a dramatic production highlighted the occasion. The significance of the cultural events was realized during the closing ceremonies when the winners of the competition were awarded gold, silver, and bronze medals. The impressive finale featuring trumpets, flowing national flags, mounted dignitaries, and the national anthems of those winning the cultural prizes, was concluded with Coubertin's announcement that the VIIIth Olympic Games had concluded. These were the last Olympic Games Coubertin attended.

After the Olympics, the respected Louis de Brada Handley, coach of the American women's aquatic team, offered suggestions for future international competition. Transportation, the bane of athletes, had been woefully inadequate in Paris. Lengthy rides interfered with training schedules. Handley cited the 2-hour bus rides to the swimming pool at the Porte de Lilas, which shortened practice times and fatigued the athletes. The situation was alleviated somewhat when automobiles were made available; however, late drivers, insufficient numbers of cars, and breakdowns still posed problems. Despite objections from coaches, no changes were made in the content or scheduling of meals. Further complicating the athletes' schedule was the strict adherence to the rule that those who were late for meals were not to be served. The nearest restaurant was 2 miles from the living accommodations, and no transportation was provided. Handley suggested a more flexible schedule and a more appropriate menu for athletes.

The men lived in small frame structures accommodating two or three athletes at Rocquencourt, another suburb. Rocquencourt had been chosen because Olympic officials wanted to isolate the athletes from the temptations of Paris, but the athletes, especially those from cities, found the lack of recreation boring and the seclusion depressing. French officials no doubt were concerned about the cost of the Games and their responsibility for the safety of the athletes, but they overlooked specific needs of men and women in highly organized competition.

On July 28, 1924, the executive committee of the IOC met in Paris and issued a statement commending the French Olympic Organizing Committee for its preparation and organization. Complaints regarding officiating and spectator behavior had abounded during and after the Games. A special correspondent to the *Times* of London was so appalled that he wrote, "The death-knell of the Olympic Games . . . has been sounded." The *Times* correspondent was disillusioned with international sport after witnessing violent altercations between Hungarian and Italian foils competitors, riotous scenes at the France-U.S. football match, questionable calls by officials, and disagreements during the men's singles tennis finals. He deplored the loud boos, which drowned out national anthems during some awards ceremonies. The correspondent called for the elimination of events that involved fights, but the IOC chose to deal with problems in a more conservative manner. After an inquiry into boxing incidents involving Italian, French, and Argentine fighters, the IOC chose not to levy its own punishment but called on the NOCs to take appropriate action against the offenders.

The French organizing committee lost money because the Games had not been completed within the sixteen days of competition. The cultural events and the athletic competition had dragged on for nearly four months, contributing to the expense. Ticket sales were ineffective in reducing the debt, since, according to the newspapers, "nearly everybody in Paris seemed to have passes."

Following Coubertin's retirement as president of the IOC, the body conferred upon him the title of perpetual president of the Olympic Games. The honor was presented with the stipulation that it would never be conferred again. Coubertin felt secure in his announcement to retire because he believed the Olympic Games had overcome the obstacles of the past and achieved the status of a worldwide event.

Several controversies resulting from the 1924 Olympic Games were debated at the 1925 IOC Congress in Prague. Charles Sherrill of the United States sought the complete elimination of Sunday events, but the delegates trimmed only Sunday morning events. In other action, Sherrill successfully orchestrated an end to entry conflicts between national sport organizations and the IFs. His motion stated that an athlete could be entered only if the NOC was in accord with the national sport organization and the national organization was recognized by the appropriate ISF. In addition, the Congress declared that any professional athlete was ineligible for Olympic competition. The once-strict era of amateur sport was again revealed when those in attendance at the Congress voted to exclude athletes who received remuneration for the loss of wages while competing. Gustavus Kirby of the United States, a staunch believer in amateur sport and a stalwart member of the Amateur Athletic Union, suggested that those who wished to be paid for time devoted to sport should become professionals. Although the 1924 Games involved controversy resulting from growth, the event was recognized and praised by more people throughout the world than ever before.

BIBLIOGRAPHICAL ESSAY

Newspapers are among the leading sources of information for the VIIIth Summer Olympic Games. The *New York Times* provided insight into the bid cities, the site selection process, and the financial difficulties encountered by the French, and it covered the athletic events in detail each day of the competition. The *London Times* provided accounts of athletic events and the cultural competition, as well as spectator behavior and unruly play in some events. The London paper's special correspondent not only monitored the conduct of the Games but also detailed the protocol of the opening ceremonies. The *Chicago Tribune* also provided daily coverage of the Games.

The *Literary Digest* featured preparation for the Games, drawings of the venues, and controversy regarding spectators and athletes. Although the variety of sources for the 1924 Summer Games is limited, the *Literary Digest* published several articles during 1923 and 1924 that analyzed the performances of certain athletes.

The official report of the 1924 Games, published by the French Olympic Committee, is *Les Jeux de la VIIIème Olympiade Paris 1924, Rapport officiel du Comité Olympique français* (Paris, n.d.). Perhaps the best contemporary sources in English are Spalding Athletic Library, *Spalding's Official Athletic Almanac—1925* (New York, 1925), and Robert Thompson, ed., *Report on VIII Olympiad, Paris France, 1924* (New York, 1924), the American Olympic Committee's official report. The Canadian report is J. Howard Crocker, ed., *Report—Canadian Olympic Committee 1924 Games* (n.p., 1925), and the British version is F. G. L. Fairlie, ed., *The Official Report of the VIIIth Olympiad, Paris, 1924* (London, 1925). See also Willy Meisl, *Die Olympische Spiele: Paris 1924 in Wort, Bilde, Statistik* (Oldenberg, 1924).

There is relatively little secondary source material specifically on these Games. Apart from the usually brief mentions in the standard comprehensive Olympic histories, one is limited to Mark Jenkins, "An American Coup in Paris," *American Heritage* 40, 5 (July–August 1989): 66–71, which relates the story of the U.S. rugby team's gold medal at the Games and includes a number of photographs, and a biography, David P. Thompson, *Eric Liddell: Athlete and Missionary* (London? 1971), of the celebrated Scottish runner. Finally, the acclaimed 1981 film, *Chariots of Fire,* is set at the 1924 Games (see Appendix C: Olympic Films).

Paula D. Welch

AMSTERDAM 1928

THE GAMES OF THE IXTH OLYMPIAD

The Netherlands is a little country whose people do very big things. In the span of a few centuries, the citizens of this lowlands West European nation built an extensive canal and dike system to reclaim thousands of acres of land from the sea, including much of the land in the *polder* region of the country that includes the capital city of Amsterdam. Holland was also for much of the seventeenth century the most powerful seafaring nation in the world. The worldwide expansion of Dutch commerce that began during this period fueled the growth of Amsterdam as a center of trade, industry, and artistic creativity and paved the way for the International Olympic Committee (IOC) to select this beautiful city of canals, bridges, and tree-lined streets as the host of the IXth Olympic Games in 1928.

One other good reason Amsterdam followed Paris in the honor roll of Olympic hosts is that Dutch people relish physical activity. A visitor to the Netherlands today will observe people of all ages using bicycles as their primary mode of transportation. Another example of the Dutch people's strong sporting heritage is the 124-mile ice skating race, the Elfstedenstacht, which finds thousands of Dutch men and women gliding across canals that link the eleven cities of the northern province of Friesland.

In the summer of 1928, the Amsterdam Games (July 28–August 12) were centered around a new 40,000-seat track and field stadium built on reclaimed marshlands in the new Amsterdam south region. This area had been the focus of a large-scale building effort in the early 1900s to meet demand for industrial worker housing. Next to the main stadium was an outdoor swimming pool seating 1,500 and gymnasiums where the boxing, wrestling, and fencing competitions took place. While building the stadium on the soft, spongy lowlands soil highlighted Dutch ingenuity and industriousness in using every parcel of land in their small country, some participating athletes thought the track surface, which was composed of the same soil, was too soft for international competition. To remedy the problem, Dutch engineers worked feverishly in the days before the Games to provide a more solid footing to the running track. When the issue first came up, Major General Douglas MacArthur, the head of the American Olympic Committee (AOC), struck an upbeat note: "On the battlefield never believe reports of disaster. Leave it to Dutch engineering genius to produce a proper field for the games" (*New York Times,* July 21, 1928).

There were problems at the swimming stadium as well. At the pool, the water appeared to run uphill because of faulty construction. Because the swimming stadium was located in a swampy area and the necessary piling had not been used in the foundation, one end of the pool had sunk about 6 inches. Olympic venues that did work well included the fencing pavilion, whose "eight fine strips provided perfect lighting overhead and underfoot'' (*New York Times,* July 21, 1928), the equestrian facility at Hilversum, and the rowing venue in the Sloten Canal that found 10,000 cheering fans and assorted cows and sheep lining its banks for the dramatic eight-oared shell with coxswain race on the next-to-last day of the competition.

For these Games, there was no need to construct an Olympic Village because many of the teams, including the United States, stayed on ships moored in Amsterdam harbor. Other participating nations were housed in many of the city's splendid hotels.

The opening ceremonies for the Games took place on a Saturday afternoon under gray Dutch skies in front of a record-breaking 40,000 spectators at the track and field stadium. Adding a splash of welcome color to the events of the day were the nattily clad parading athletes from forty-six participating nations, an increase of two from the Paris Games four years earlier. Among the most sartorially splendid marchers were the South Africans, who were decked out in brilliant scarlet blazers and matching caps; the fez-wearing Turks; the pink-clad Belgians; and the American men with blue jackets with white trousers and straw hats and their female counterparts in white dresses. Drawing special notice from the crowd was the first German contingent to compete in the Olympics since World War I. The German squad, with their Eton jackets and stiff shirts, ''looked like ship stewards'' but were very impressive with their precise order of march (*New York Times*, July 29, 1928). Also displaying a military bearing was the Italian team, whose members wore army green and gave the Benito Mussolini regime's fascist salute as they passed the royal reviewing stand.

The American team was watched closely for their etiquette as they marched past the reviewing stand. Led by AOC head MacArthur, the Yankee squad continued the American custom of refusing to bow to or salute any foreign monarch and gave a correct eyes right as they passed in front of IOC president Count Henri Baillet-Latour and Holland's prince consort, Henry. The Netherland's reigning monarch, Queen Wilhelmina, did not attend the opening ceremonies, reportedly because of her religious-based objection to the fact that the competition would begin on the Sabbath.

Also absent from the opening ceremonies was the entire French contingent. The day before the Games began, a cantankerous gatekeeper refused to let French track and field athletes into the main stadium for a practice run. Following a few choice insults, the gatekeeper came to blows with Paul Mericamp, the general secretary of the French Athletic Federation. When the French team found out that the offending gatekeeper was still at his post the next day, they decided on the spot to boycott the opening ceremonies and threatened to withdraw from the Games. The former Dutch foreign minister was brought in to negotiate this burgeoning crisis with the French minister to The Hague; after an official apology was issued and a bottle of champagne presented to the French as a peace offering, the French decided that the gatekeeper's offense was not severe enough to force their absence from the Games. What the French did miss at the opening ceremonies was a spectacle of artillery salvos, bands, and hundreds of pigeons, as well as a colorful overflight of several airplanes. It was also at these ceremonies that the Olympic custom of torchlighting was introduced.

In the competition, the men's track and field events were dominated by the "Flying Finns." Paavo Nurmi, the 1924 Olympic star, duplicated his 10,000-meter-run victory, this time setting an Olympic record, and also finished second in the 3,000-meter steeplechase. Harry Larva, Willie Ritola, Toivo Loukola, and Paavo Yrjola added to the Finnish victory parade in the 1,500-meter, 5,000-meter, 3,000-meter steeplechase, and decathlon events. Canada's diminutive sprinter, Percy Williams, was the Games' individual star with victories in the 100- and 200-meter sprints. Japan's Mikio Oda became the first Olympic track victor from Asia, with a 49-foot, 11-inch leap in the hop, step, and jump event (now the triple jump).

In the marathon, Boughera El Ouafi, an Algerian who ran dispatches for the French Moroccan army behind the lines of the desert chieftain Abd El Krim in 1926, won a stirring race against more than 100 competitors in a time of 2 hours, 32 minutes, 37 seconds "across the typical Dutch landscape, between grim dikes and beside desolate marshes, punctured with tiny flower-decked windmills, under heavy watery skies through which the sun was unable to cast a single cheering ray" (*New York Times,* August 6, 1928). Ouafi's life would later have a tragic end; he was shot to death sitting in a Parisian café in 1959.

The American men's track and field squad was somewhat of a disappointment. Prior to the Games, MacArthur predicted team members would sew up "nine [individual] firsts" (*New York Times,* July 31, 1928) and stated, "This is the greatest team in our athletic history. Americans can rest serene and assured" (*New York Times,* July 29, 1928). In the end, the Americans fell three short of the predicted medal count, with six individual victories, along with two world records in the 4 × 100-meter and 4 × 400-meter sprint relays. The *London Evening Standard* speculated that the lackluster American performance could be blamed on "too much ice cream and lavish feeding" enjoyed by the U.S. athletes on board their ship, *President Roosevelt.* The *Standard* noted that the British athletes, including popular 400-meter hurdle victor Lord David Burghley, had consumed "hearty green salads" at their hotel. Hearing of this affront to the U.S. team's home base, T. V. O'Connor, chairman of the powerful U.S. Shipping Board, disclaimed any responsibility for diets on the *President Roosevelt.* "The principal complaint [of the English press] seems to be 'too lavish feeding.' This is a rather unique complaint about an ocean liner," noted O'Connor about shipboard fare of the time, which was certainly not up to the standards enjoyed on modern cruise ships (*New York* Times, August 1, 1928). MacArthur, who was already developing the keen sense of public relations that would serve him well during World War II, cabled O'Connor: "The American athletes have not only not failed, but have achieved a brilliant success compared to those of past Olympics. Guests who were entertained on board the *Roosevelt* were served the same fare always served to passengers. The standard of living on American ships is very high—much higher than on competing lines, perhaps. However, this is not a matter of reproach, but of gratification'' (*New York Times,* August 11, 1928). Then he released the contents of the cable to the press.

Food was not an issue in the women's events. Rather, the very fact that women were competing in track and field was a novelty. The IOC had long opposed the participation of women in track and field competition, with the aristocratic leaders holding to prejudices about ''amazon'' female athletes or to Victorian notions about the propriety of men watching scantily clad women compete. But the IOC was forced to change with the times, especially after the Federation sportive feminine international was formed and put on a highly successful track and field championship for women in Paris in 1922 and planned a ''Women's Olympics'' for 1926. On April 5, 1926, the IOC accepted the recommendation of the International Amateur Athletic Federation (IAAF) and voted to permit women to compete in gymnastics and track and field (women were already competing in Olympic swimming and diving events). The number of track and field events was limited to five (100-meter dash, 800-meter run, 4 × 100-meter relay, high jump and discus), which prompted a boycott by the British women.

In the first women's track event to be contested, Betty Robinson, a sixteen-year-old sprinter from Chicago, set a world record of 12.2 seconds in the 100-meter dash. In the high jump, Canada's Ethel Catherwood, the ''Saskatoon Lily,'' pleased the crowd with her winning performance of 5 feet, 2 inches.

The women's 800-meter run was the most consequential event of the Games. In the race won by Germany's Lina Radke, six of the nine contestants faltered at the end of a furious sprint to the finish line. Florence MacDonald of the United States was woozy for several minutes after the race, and even the second-place finisher, Kinue Hitomi of Japan, required medical attention before leaving the field.

Antifeminists in the press and in the IAAF seized on the race as evidence that women should be banned from running in events longer than 200 meters. For example, the *London Daily Mail* quoted doctors who said that female participants in 800-meter races and other such ''feats of endurance'' would become old too soon. IOC president Baillet-Latour joined the chorus and spoke out in favor of eliminating all women's sports from the Olympics and returning to the Greek custom of male-only competition. Representing women athletes before a special meeting of the IAAF in Amsterdam, Britain's Lady Heath rebutted Baillet-Latour's argument about women not having participated in the ancient Greek games. She retorted that neither were the hop, step, and jump, fencing, and pistol shooting part of the Greek Olympiads. Lady Heath then urged the IAAF members to ''let us help you raise your banners on the Olympic pole. We are now your comrades in industry, commerce, in the arts and sciences, why not in athletics? If you approve of athletics for women at all you must approve of participation in the Olympics. For women need the stimulus of matching their prowess against the world's best athletes quite as much as the men'' (*New York*

Times, August 8, 1928). Another proponent of female participation in the Games was a Dr. Bergmann, who as the examining physician of women athletes in Berlin, presented the IAAF leadership the astounding evidence based on ten years of experience that women athletes married and bore children just like nonathletes.

The protective males who governed the IAAF ended up deciding that the 800-meter event was too taxing for the "frail feminine gender," a decision that would last until the 1960 games. Also shunted aside for the time being were the women's long jump, shot put, and 200-meter race; the events that remained were the 100-meter dash and 4 × 100-meter relay, the 80-meter hurdles, the high jump, discus, and javelin throw.

Controversy was also part of the mix, as it is at many Olympiads, in the boxing hall. Decisions of referees led to raucous scenes following several of the bouts. After Belgium's Marcel Santos won a disputed decision over U.S. fly-weight (112 pounds) Hyman Miller, U.S. boxing coach Jacob Stumpf wanted to take the entire team out of the competition, but MacArthur curtly replied, "Americans never quit" (*New York Times,* August 9, 1928). And when Holland's Lambertus van Klaverens was awarded a decision over Argentina's Victor Peralta in the featherweight competition, the unhappy Argentine fans in the hall showered a few fisticuffs on the Dutch police.

A clear victor in the field hockey event was the team from India, which had begun international competition in the sports just two years prior to the Games. The Indian squad swept all its matches in Amsterdam and went on to an incredible thirty-game winning streak in the next six Olympics before losing to Pakistan in the final match of the 1960 Games.

Two American athletes who went from Amsterdam to further glory were swimmers Johnny Weissmuller and Clarence "Buster" Crabbe. Weissmuller lowered his Olympic record in the 100-meter freestyle, shared in a world record in the 4 × 200-meter freestyle relay, and was also on the U.S. water polo team. Weissmuller turned his Olympic victories into fame on the silver screen as he became the first of the movie Tarzans. Crabbe finished only third in the 1,500-meter freestyle but also headed to Hollywood, where he would take on the larger-than-life roles of Tarzan, Flash Gordon, and Buck Rogers.

On the water, the most exciting event in the Games may have been the men's eight-oared with coxswain final between the United States, represented by the University of California at Berkeley, and England, represented by the Thames Rowing Club. The U.S. squad beat the English eight by half a boat length in a race witnessed by 10,000 along the Sloten Banks. *New York Times* sportswriter Wythe Williams was most impressed by the performance of U.S. coxswain Don Blessing, who displayed "one of the greatest performances of demoniacal howling ever heard on a terrestrial planet. . . . He gave the impression of a terrier suddenly gone mad. But such language. And what a vocabulary! . . . One closed his eyes and waited for the crack of a cruel whip across the backs of the galley slaves" (*New York Times,* August 11, 1928). In contrast to Blessing's strong language, the British coxswain George Sulley futilely encouraged his rowers on with a more sedate call, "Up, up, up."

The Games came to an end with a ceremony at the track and field stadium. This time, the stadium was graced by the presence of Queen Wilhelmina, even though the ceremonies were held on a Sunday. The queen had warmed up to the competition after hosting a state dinner for the official Olympic party and had made one appearance at the stadium to witness an exhibition of the Dutch national sport of korfball. At the closing ceremonies, Wilhelmina shared the royal box with members of her family and various members of the Norwegian and Swedish royal families. The press was told that Wilhelmina was greatly interested in all things military and wanted to watch the conclusion of the Olympic equestrian competition, which resulted in a tie between the Dutch and Polish teams. The queen also presented medals to the winning athletes. And with the sound of bugles, cannons, and a band playing a final hymn filling the air of Amsterdam, the participants and the spectators headed home, knowing the athletes of the world would next assemble in a distant and relatively young city astride the Pacific Ocean, Los Angeles.

BIBLIOGRAPHICAL ESSAY

Records of the 1928 Summer Olympics may be found at the Municipal Archives of Amsterdam, Amsteldijk 67, 1074 HZ Amsterdam, The Netherlands, and at the Dutch Sportsfederation Library, Laan van de Poort 361, 2566 DA Den Haag, The Netherlands. Additional information is available at the IOC Archives in Lausanne, Switzerland, and in the Avery Brundage Collection at the University of Illinois Archives, Urbana, Illinois.

The official report of the Amsterdam organizing committee is George van Rossem, ed., *The Ninth Olympiad; Being the Official Report of the Olympic Games Celebrated at Amsterdam Issued by the Netherlands Olympic Committee* (Amsterdam, 1930). French and Dutch editions were published simultaneously. The committee also published *Rapport sur la preparation de l'organisation des Jeux de la IXe Olympiade à Amsterdam en 1928* (Amsterdam, 1927), *Catalogue de l'exposition au Musée municipal d'Amsterdam. 12 juin–12 aôut* (Amsterdam, 1928), a catalog of the art competition accompanying the Games, and a variety of daily programs and booklets detailing the rules and regulations of the competition.

The American Olympic Committee report is *Report of the American Olympic Committee; Ninth Olympic Games, Amsterdam, 1928. Second Olympic Winter Sports, St. Moritz, 1928* (New York, 1928); the Canadian report is M. M. Robinson, ed., *The Official Report of the IXth Olympiad 1928* (Hamilton, Ontario, 1929). The British version, edited by Harold M. Abrahams, is *The Official Report of the IXth Olympiad, Amsterdam, 1928* (London, 1928). The French Olympic Committee published *La Participation française aux jeux de la IXe Olympiade Amsterdam 1928* (Paris, 1928), and the Germans celebrated their return to Olympic competition in *Bericht uber die Beteiligung Deutschlands an den IX. Olympischen Spielen Amsterdam und St. Moritz 1928* (Berlin, 1928). Sport medicine scholars may wish to consult F.J.J. Buytendijk, *Ergebnisse der sportartlichen Untersuchungen bei den IX. Olympishe Spielen 1928 in Amsterdam* (Berlin, 1929), a collection of papers dealing with sport medicine published after the Games and based in part on data collected at the Games.

Excellent daily coverage of the Games can be found in the *New York Times,* whose correspondent, Wythe Williams, provided detailed, colorful reports of the events and pageantry of the Games from the American team's perspective. Williams was one of the few Americans correspondents on the scene, and his dispatches covered all of the major activities of the Games. As a passenger accompanying the team on the *President Roosevelt,* he had access to American Olympic Committee president Major General Douglas MacArthur and other U.S. officials and athletes. MacArthur's role in the AOC and the Amsterdam Games is detailed in John A. Lucas, ''USOC President Douglas MacArthur and His Olympic Moment,'' *Olympika* 3 (1994): 111–15.

Finally, the demonstration sport of korfball is described in Anthony Th. Bijkerk, ''Korfball at the Olympic Games,'' *Citius, Altius, Fortius* 2, 2 (May 1994): 20–23.

Edward S. Goldstein

LOS ANGELES 1932

THE GAMES OF THE XTH OLYMPIAD

When the International Olympic Committee (IOC) named Los Angeles the site for the 1932 Games at its meeting in Rome in 1923, no one could have foreseen economic disaster ahead. William May Garland, Los Angeles real estate baron, civic booster, and member of the IOC, made the case for Los Angeles in Rome. He returned home to his booming and optimistic city, where work soon began to renovate and expand the coliseum in Exposition Park into an Olympic stadium.

In 1925, California voters approved a $1 million bond issue to underwrite the Games. That same year the Los Angeles Organizing Committee for the Games of the Xth Olympiad (LAOC), chaired by Garland, rejected the possibility of replacing Amsterdam as host city in 1928. With sights still set on 1932, the city of Los Angeles voted a $1.5 million supporting bond issue.

By the end of the decade, however, boom had become bust, economic despair was settling over the world, and the organizing committee faced a gloomy prospect. War, its aftermath, and political boycotts have canceled or diminished Olympiads, but Garland's committee refused to give in to the devastation of the Great Depression. Olympic planners worked against constant, draining reminders of the depression, including record unemployment in California and the daily arrival in the state of refugees from the plains states, where severe drought had made farming impossible. Soup kitchens served the destitute of Los Angeles, some in the shadow of the coliseum. Sentiment ran against the "frivolity" of the Games. Pickets at the capitol in Sacramento called for them to be canceled, but the power and influence of the Los Angeles civic and business elite prevented that.

The Herbert Hoover administration offered no help. Hoover even declined to open the Games, breaking the tradition of heads of state presiding at the opening ceremony that dated back to King George of Greece in 1896.

Other nations hard-pressed economically hesitated to commit their teams to this longest Olympic journey to date. In mid-April 1932, with ticket sales and guarantees of participation near zero, Zack Farmer, general secretary of the LAOC, offered a plan for housing all athletes in an "Olympic village." When he had proposed this idea earlier, other nations rejected it, preferring secrecy and opposing fraternization among competitors. This time, however, by reducing the cost of feeding and housing an athlete to two dollars a day, the Olympic Village proved the salvation of the Games.

A scant three months before the scheduled opening, an athletes' village of 500 cottages rose west of the coliseum on 250 acres in the undeveloped Baldwin Hills section of Los Angeles. Organizers persuaded steamship and rail lines to cut fares on their nearly empty carriers; teams could then afford to travel from Europe, Asia, and South America.

The movie colony lent its prestige and charisma to the Olympic cause. In mid-July, Mary Pickford and Douglas Fairbanks, whose popularity knew no bounds, broadcast worldwide invitations to come for the Games, and the press began to report positively on preparations. Although it had hardly seemed possible ninety days earlier, 101,000 people paid two dollars each to crowd into the coliseum for the opening ceremony. Thousands more milled around outside.

One episode clouding the pre–World War II international political scene had some impact on the Olympic picture. Early in 1932, Japan had moved into the Chinese province of Manchuria and created the puppet state of Manchukuo; it then sought to send athletes from its pawn to the Games in Los Angeles. The IOC rejected the move, but the bid did spur China to send one lone athlete: Chung Cheng-liu, an unsuccessful competitor in the men's 200 meters.

Most political discord surrounding the 1932 Games was domestic, consisting of internal bickering in the American Olympic Association (AOA). Until then, the Olympic Games had been considered "eastern" or elitist by most Americans who had heard anything at all about them. Easterners, who predominated in AOA affairs, openly doubted the ability of Californians to oversee the planning and conduct of the Games.

After the associations's executive committee tentatively approved the formation of the LAOC in June 1929, Avery Brundage, president of the AOA, succeeded in muting further criticism and preventing true animosity from building. Final approval of the organizing committee, which the IOC required, came at the quadrennial meeting of the AOA in Washington on November 19, 1930. In a final echo of discord after the Games had ended, Californians contended that the easterners had let them down in fund raising.

The spotlight of Olympic politics focused on two issues: amateur purity and the participation of women. Half a century later, with women's events firmly established and Olympic athletes paid for medal-winning efforts, both elements seem quaintly dated.

Baron Pierre de Coubertin, in acclaiming the classical Greek athletic ideal of the young male athlete in the ultimate contest, saw no place for women in the modern Olympic movement. Nevertheless, women's swimming had entered the Olympic program in Stockholm in 1912 and fencing at Paris in 1924. Both sports enjoyed a measure of acceptance in the mid-1920s when expectations and ideas of what was proper for women still had a heavy Victorian cast. Track and field, however, bore marginal, even negative status. Intense championship competition for women in any sport drew condemnation in the United States, especially from physical education professionals and from the Women's Division of the National Amateur Athletic Federation (NAAF).

At Amsterdam in 1928, five women's track and field events made an Olympic debut on an experimental basis: 100- and 800-meter races, 4 × 100-meter relay, high jump, and discus. The collapse of exhausted runners at the end of the 800 meters amplified criticism. In an attempt to prevent women from competing in Los Angeles, the Women's Division of the NAAF petitioned the IOC in April 1930 to drop women's track and field. Their appeal followed a 1929 proposal by the new IOC president, Count Henri de Baillet-Latour, to eliminate all women's events as one way to trim the burgeoning program of the Games.

The IOC deferred final action until it met in Barcelona in 1931. By that time, Brundage, already a key American in Olympic affairs, had been enormously impressed by a women's track and field demonstration at the 1930 Olympic Congress in Berlin. Brundage was a representative to the IAAF and a member of its committee on women's sports, which recommended retaining women's events. Finally, in April 1931, the IOC called for the upcoming Xth Olympic Games to include women's swimming, fencing, and track and field, with the javelin throw replacing the 800 meters.

The issue of women's participation was settled in 1931, but the matter of amateurism was not resolved until the day before the 1932 opening ceremony. Acting on allegations that the brilliant and popular Finnish runner, Paavo Nurmi, had accepted financial rewards for races, the IAAF executive board ruled him a professional and barred him from competing in what would have been his fourth Olympiad. Judging this a blow to the Games' prospects and drawing power, one journalist wrote that the Games would now be "like Hamlet without the celebrated Dane in the cast." The outraged Finns threatened to withdraw the rest of their team from the Games.

On the media front, radio made its Olympic debut in the summer of 1932. Multimillion-dollar bidding wars for broadcast rights to the Games would have staggered the imagination of Games planners in 1932. Individual stations and networks were not permitted to broadcast directly from the coliseum or any other venue. Listeners settled for summaries of each day's events and occasional interviews with medalists.

The largest gathering of movie newsreel cameramen yet assembled for an international event covered every phase of the Olympic Games. Their films provided audiences worldwide with a taste of Olympic excitement in 1932, and they serve today as a priceless early record in celluloid.

By the time of the Nurmi decision, athletes from thirty-nine nations had arrived to warm California welcomes. Sizable parties of Japanese-Americans greeted the large contingent from Japan, including its powerful team of male swimmers. No other team had a more enthusiastic reception in Los Angeles than Germany's, met by an overflow crowd at the Santa Fe Station where two bands led hundreds in singing "Deutschland Uber Alles" at every opportunity.

Although the country remained locked in the depression, spectators flocked to Los Angeles. Cars with out-of-state license plates filled the city, and trains daily brought swarms of Olympic visitors. An occasional group even landed at Mines Field, the small municipal airport west of Inglewood that would become the Los Angeles International Airport. The organizing committee's fears that it might be throwing a party no one would attend proved groundless.

The Los Angeles facilities surpassed any previously provided by Olympic hosts. Four of the principal venues were clustered near Exposition Park: Olympic Stadium, Swimming Stadium, the State Armory, and the Los Angeles Museum of History, Science and Art, which housed entries in the arts competition.

Facilities at the Olympic Village included a small hospital, complete with x-ray and laboratory equipment. The bungalows of the Olympic Village drew magnanimous raves from the world's male athletes and team officials. In presenting the Olympic Village plan, Farmer had made clear that women would be excluded. They were housed separately in the Chapman Park Hotel just off Wilshire Boulevard near the Ambassador Hotel.

Usually critical American sports reporters employed such terms as "breathtaking" and "an architectural marvel" in assessing the refurbished Olympic Stadium. Renovations included new seating for 105,000, improvements to the dirt track surface, and the installation of a 20- by 30-foot scoreboard. Addition of a 107-foot-high torch to burn throughout the Games made possible the inauguration of that Olympic tradition.

The newly completed swimming stadium, with its state-of-the-art pool, stood in stark contrast to earlier sites that ranged from barely adequate to nearly unacceptable. The swimming stadium had permanent seating for 10,000 and temporary seats for 2,000 more.

The armory, which housed fencing competition, could accommodate 1,000. The 10,000-seat auditorium in the heart of the city was the venue for the boxing, wrestling, and weight lifting events. Pasadena's Rose Bowl hosted cycling. Rowing took place at Long Beach Marine Stadium which offered permanent and temporary seats as well as 2 miles of enclosed standing room along the course. The equestrian events were held at the Riviera Country Club near Beverly Hills, and yachting events took place off Los Angeles harbor.

No track team could use the coliseum track for training. Each morning during the week of July 25, buses arrived at the Chapman Park Hotel and the Olympic Village to transport athletes to various practice locations: high school fields, playgrounds, and athletic facilities at the University of Southern California and the University of California at Los Angeles (UCLA). Such planning was a welcome departure from previous years when nations often had to arrange for their own training sites.

During the week before the opening of the Games, teams trained in the swimming stadium pool at designated times; water polo and diving claimed morning hours. The Los Angeles Playground and Recreation Department reserved mornings for Olympic practice at such locations as Griffith Pool on Riverside Drive near Griffith Park and West Los Angeles Pool on Stoner Avenue. Teams also used the private pools of such landmarks as the Hollywood, Pasadena, and Los Angeles athletic clubs and the Ambassador Hotel.

In his presentation to the IOC in 1923, William May Garland had exploited the movie capital's worldwide celebrity by labeling Los Angeles a suburb of Hollywood. The crowded Olympic social calendar that greeted officials and athletes reflected the Hollywood connection along with the more formal bent of the civic elite.

Ballrooms and banquet halls at the Ambassador Hotel on Wilshire and the imposing Biltmore Hotel downtown provided sites for gala Olympic functions. Japan's Olympic committee, for example, hosted its American counterpart at an elegant banquet at the Ambassador. The formal Ball of All Nations honored athletes as special guests in the Coconut Grove nightclub at the Ambassador, and junior Olympic hostesses entertained athletes at another ball in the Biltmore's Sala de Oro. The Coconut Grove regularly attracted athletes, movie moguls and stars, Olympic dignitaries, and civic leaders.

Motion pictures captivated the world in the 1930s. Even had 1932 not seen the release of gold medal swimmer Johnny Weissmuller's first Tarzan film, Olympians would have reveled in social activities with a Hollywood link. The movie colony redeemed pledges of help made to Garland's committee and entertained the visitors royally.

Radio's immensely popular "The Breakfast Club" hosted Olympians at a broadcast, and athletes delighted in small gatherings at stars' homes. A star-studded luncheon and tour of the Fox Studios hosted by humorist Will Rogers was a social highlight for the women athletes.

Mary Pickford and Douglas Fairbanks had supported the Olympic Games since 1924 when they cheered their friend Charlie Paddock to a silver medal in Paris. Star-struck athletes coveted an invitation to Pickfair, their English Regency mansion, and the popular pair hosted a reception there for Olympians toward the end of the Games.

The Hollywood connection helped ensure positive and widespread publicity. Olympic stars became familiar names, and the Games themselves enjoyed greater popularity in the United States that year.

The Olympic Fine Arts Exhibition, mounted in the Los Angeles Museum of History, Science and Art, drew more than 348,000 visitors. It contained over 1,100 works—painting, sculpture, architecture, graphic arts, literature, and music—by artists of thirty-two nations.

Two giants in American letters, William Lyon Phelps and Thornton Wilder, judged the literary entries. It is worth noting that they awarded honorable mention to Avery Brundage's essay, "The Significance of Amateur Sport." Prize-winning paintings, watercolors, prints, and drawings bore such titles as *Struggle, Jackknife,* and *Stadium.* An honorable-mention award went to *Indian Ball Game,* by native American artist Blue Eagle. First prize for sculpture was awarded Mahonri Young of the United States for *The Knockdown.* Venerable Canadian sculptor R. Tait McKenzie's *Shield of the Athletes* placed third among medals and reliefs. Architectural design awards of lasting interest included second prize for Yale's Payne Whitney Gymnasium in New Haven, Connecticut, and honorable mention for the Stanford Stadium in Palo Alto, California. Awards in fine arts competition received ceremonial announcement in the stadium just as those for athletic events did. The victory stand, with medal ceremonies at the conclusion of each event, first appeared in 1932.

Nearly perfect weather graced the entire run of the Games in Los Angeles. This happy reality, together with improved facilities and conditions, virtually guaranteed that Olympic records would fall, and fall they did.

On Saturday, July 30, a capacity crowd settled into their seats in the coliseum under a blazing California sun. The opening ceremony established patterns and precedents for pageantry and showmanship. Hundreds of flags flew above the Coliseum. National banners and the five-ringed Olympic flag flanked the peristyle at the east end. The peristyle itself bore Coubertin's expression of the Olympic spirit: "The important thing in the Olympic Games is not winning, but taking part. The essential thing is not conquering, but fighting well."

A 250-piece band and a choir of 1,200 voices delivered impassioned music. With the delegation from Greece at its head, the parade of athletes marched crisply from the coliseum's main tunnel, drew up in columns across the field, and stood at attention.

Vice President Charles Curtis proclaimed the Games officially open. Artillery rounds saluted the lighting of the Olympic torch; the choir rendered the Olympic hymn; the Olympic standard rose to the top of the flagpole; and 2,000 pigeons flew to freedom. Following the Olympic oath, the athletes exited the stadium. The huge crowd remained seated. Although they stayed in response to a request to allow the athletes to clear the area, they had been deeply moved by this most impressive of Olympic opening ceremonies.

The 1932 Games proved salutary for the future of women in the Olympics and for women athletes in general. Women's events enjoyed significant popularity in Los Angeles. The women won the admiration of spectators and, through the press, the entire world. This was due in no small part to the publicity surrounding the performances of Mildred "Babe" Didrikson, the phenomenal all-around athlete from Texas. Generally conceded to have been the outstanding individual competitor of the Los Angeles Games, Didrikson went on to immortality as a pioneer and pacesetter in women's golf. In 1932, the versatile twenty-one year old electrified spectators in the first women's event of the Games with her world record–breaking first javelin throw. She won gold medals in two of the three events for which she qualified: the javelin and the 80-meter hurdles. The third event, the high jump, created one of the more enduring Olympic controversies. Women's rules in 1932 mandated crossing foot first over the bar. The judges ruled that Didrikson's rolling, horizontal jump was a head-first dive that disqualified her in a jump-off with teammate Jean Shiley, who won the gold medal.

For the Xth Olympic Games, officials went to great length to ensure confidence in the timing of events. They paid $6,000 for each of thirty-two Swiss government–certified watches used by timers.

In many respects, the Los Angeles Games represent a quantum leap forward, but electronic timing's day had not arrived. The United States used electrical timers at the men's Olympic trials that year, but the IAAF rules committee chose to stay with hand-held stopwatches for the Games themselves. The committee did approve the semiofficial use of the new Kirby photoelectric timer, a primitive device that simply prolonged timing controversies.

At its July meeting on timing devices, the rules committee dealt another technological setback to sprinters when they continued their ban on starting blocks. Use of blocks had been under discussion since Amsterdam, but in Los Angeles sprinters again carried trowels to the track to dig starting holes.

Olympic controversies, protests, and complaints about judging date back at least to the contentious London Games of 1908. Dispute marked many of the highlights of the 1932 Games but did nothing to mar their luster.

U.S. sprinters Eddie Tolan and Ralph Metcalfe finished so nearly even in the 100 meters that several judges and most spectators disputed the award of gold to Metcalfe. Tolan himself thought he had lost and congratulated Metcalfe before the final ruling was made. The popular Didrikson figured in another dispute when she took the 80-meter hurdles gold medal from Chicago's Evelyne Hall in what many considered a dead heat.

Dispute reached a highwater mark with the water polo match between Brazil and Germany. That 7–3 victory for the Germans ended in a minor riot at the swimming stadium. Brazilian players, incensed by their forty fouls in contrast to four called on Germany, charged at referee Bela Komjadi of Hungary, whose work had been roundly booed by spectators. Los Angeles police were summoned to protect Komjadi and to quell the melee that erupted.

Entrants in the 3,000-meter steeplechase were more sanguine in the face of a judging lapse. Finland's Volmari Iso-Hollo ran an extra lap to capture the gold medal because a substitute official neglected to flag the field on the final lap. During the officials' 2-hour delay in reaching a decision, no runner exercised his privilege of demanding a rerun of the tortuous grind.

Fortunately that contest for first place was not close. However, Iso-Hollo's teammate, world record holder Lauri Lehtinen, figured in a men's 5,000-meter controversy that had uglier overtones. Lehtinen twice swerved into a lane ahead of Ralph Hill, blocking the Oregonian's attempts to pass during the last 50 meters. The crowd roared its outrage when the judges awarded first place to the Finn. That judges' decision also required a 2-hour delay and carried the suspicion that, in the wake of the Paavo Nurmi affair, no judge dared risk further offense to Finland.

Rowing and the marathon provided memorable thrills without controversy. Some 80,000 people lining the course at Long Beach saw the University of California crew continue U.S. eight-oared domination with its thrilling come-from-behind victory over Italy. The runner in the lead when twenty-eight marathoners left the stadium still led when twenty returned, waving his white hat to the appreciative, roaring crowd. Juan Carlos Zabala, invariably labeled as a ''20-year-old newsboy from the Argentine,'' had cut a full minute from the record set at Antwerp in 1920.

The water polo imbroglio aside, swimming saw little discord. Excepting Clarence "Buster" Crabbe's gold medal for the United States in 400-meter free style, Japan virtually swept the men's events. Helene Madison, the premiere female freestyler of the day, took three gold medals home to Seattle. New York's backstroker, Eleanor Holm, and all the American divers won medals and notoriety, which would escalate for Holm enroute to Berlin four years later, when she was dismissed from the U.S. team for violating training rules on the transatlantic voyage to Europe.

The Games of the Xth Olympiad, begun in doubt, ended triumphantly. The August 14 closing ceremony paled but little beside the brilliant opening two weeks earlier. A crowd of 87,000 filled the coliseum that Sunday. A parade of nations' flags replaced the parade of athletes, many of whom had left Los Angeles immediately after their events in order to save money. Trumpet fanfare and artillery salutes marked the lowering of the five-ringed Olympic flag, which the mayor of Los Angeles accepted for safekeeping until it would rise in Berlin in 1936. The huge crowd joined massed bands and a thousand-voiced chorus in an emotion-filled moment, singing "Aloha" as the sun dropped below the horizon.

Approximately 1.25 million people had paid $1.5 million to attend events over the sixteen days. Optimism and tenacity had triumphed over a depressed economy to produce a financial profit for the Games and reward the Games planners with untold personal satisfaction. Los Angeles had staged a celebration that endowed the Olympics with much of the organization, color, and pageantry that have become traditions of the Games.

BIBLIOGRAPHICAL ESSAY

Essential to any work on the 1932 Games are Frederick Granger Browne, ed., *The Games of the Xth Olympiad, Los Angeles, 1932: Official Report* (Los Angeles, 1933), the report of the Los Angeles Organizing Committee (LAOC), and Frederick W. Rubien, ed., *American Olympic Committee Report: Games of the Xth Olympiad, Los Angeles, 30 July–14 August 1932. IIIrd Olympic Winter Games, Lake Placid, New York, 4–13 February, 1932* (New York, 1933). There is no collection extant of papers of the LAOC, but its 700-page report has superb photographs, a complete record of the competition, and details relating to housing, practice sites, and the like.

Five major libraries in the Los Angeles area have holdings relating to the 1932 Games. Varying in size and scope, collections can be found at the Los Angeles Public Library, in the Special Collections of the University of Southern California and Univeristy of California at Los Angeles, at the Paul Ziffren Sports Resource Center Library of the Amateur Athletic Foundation, and among papers housed in the Bill Henry Room of the Occidental College Library.

The Ziffren Center library holds transcripts of interviews with Olympians taped as part of the Athletic Foundation's oral history program. Videotapes from 1932 movie film of some events can be viewed. Other helpful items to be found there include a complete collection of the thirty-nine daily editions of the *Official Program, Games of the Xth*

Olympiad, Los Angeles, 1932, a complete set of the booklets that contain official regulations for the Games, and bound copies of 1932 editions of the *Los Angeles Times* and the *Los Angeles Herald-Examiner.* The *New York Times* is an excellent press source, but for the 1932 Games, the *Los Angeles Times* should be considered the newspaper of record.

Bill Henry and Patricia Henry Yeoman, *An Approved History of the Olympic Games* (New York, 1984), a general history first published in 1948, has special significance for the Xth Olympiad. Henry served as technical adviser and public address announcer for the Games in Los Angeles, and his daughter, Patricia Yeoman, continued efforts to keep the 1932 legacy alive.

The Los Angeles County Museum published *Olympic Competition and Exhibition of Art: Catalogue of the Exhibit* (Los Angeles, 1932) to accompany its contribution to the Xth Olympiad.

The Vance Bibliographies Series published Glenna Dunning, *The Olympic Games of 1932 and 1984: The Planning and Administration of the Los Angeles Games* (Monticello, Ill., 1985). It is intended for use by urban planners and historians, and, as the title implies, entries relate to planning and administration.

Al J. Stump, "The Olympics That Almost Wasn't," *American Heritage* 33, 5 (July–August 1982): 65–71, presents a short overview of the 1932 experience. The background of the Games is chronicled by John Lucas, "Prelude to the Games of the Tenth Olympiad in Los Angeles, 1932," *Southern California Quarterly* 64, 4 (Winter 1982): 313–17. A slender pamphlet by Franklin Kjorvestad, *The 1932 Los Angeles Xth Olympiad: Its Development and Impact on the Community* (n.d.), focuses on community impact.

Two books produced at the time of the 1984 Games contain material relating to 1932: Paul Zimmerman, *Los Angeles the Olympic City, 1932–1984* (Hollywood, 1984), and Delmar Watson and Miseki L. Simon, eds., *Xth Olympiad, Los Angeles, 1932* (South San Francisco, 1984), which contains an impressive collection of photographs.

A number of books contain interviews with or biographical material about individual 1932 Olympians. These include William O. Johnson, *All That Glitters Is Not Gold: The Olympic Games* (New York, 1972); Lewis H. Carlson and John J. Fogarty, *Tales of Gold* (Chicago, 1987); William O. Johnson and Nancy P. Williamson, *"Whatta Gal": The Babe Didrikson Story* (Boston, 1977); and Betty Lou Young, *Our First Century: The Los Angeles Athletic Club, 1880–1980* (Los Angeles, 1980). See also Arthur E. Grix, *Olympische Tage in Los Angeles* (Berlin, 1932), a diary of the Olympic Games by a German boxer then living in New York.

Finally, the archives of the Amateur Athletic Foundation of Los Angeles has a 31-minute videotape of Pathe newsreel coverage of the 1932 Games, made directly from 35-mm film footage.

Doris Pieroth

BERLIN 1936

THE GAMES OF THE XITH OLYMPIAD

The Berlin Olympic Games are infamous as a triumph of the theatrical self-portrayal of National Socialist Germany. The Games showed Hitler's state not only as a peace-loving host for the world's youth but also as a refuge for physical fitness and a home to a body cult, which led to grotesque results after the National Socialists seized power in January 1933. The Berlin Games came at the end of an era that had begun with the gymnastics movement of the early nineteenth century. Thus, the Berlin Olympics were a decidedly political affair. A description of the history of the Games therefore must first address the ideological background of the idea of sports in Germany.

At the close of the opening day of the XIth Olympic Games, a specially commissioned production, *Olympic Youth,* by Carl Diem, premiered in the newly constructed Olympic stadium in Berlin. This production, enriched with cultist elements, as was the entire ceremony, had a pseudo-religious component:

The magical circle of the historical-old and the godly-pious hovers over the modern incarnation of the Olympic games. The introductory festivities: the sound of bells, fanfare, oaths, flags, doves, symbols of light, signal consecration equal to that of a church festival without being the imitation of such, over everything rests a deep sense of emotion, comparable to a most religious hour. (Voigt, *Politik der Symbole—Symbole der Politik*, p. 168)

Due to its emphasis on heroic struggle and lamentation of the dead, this mass festival, with its 10,000 active participants, took on a political dimension. While at the outset of this *Weihespiel,* tumbling, eurythmic dances, and rhythmic, dance-like performances took place, the presentation continued in the style of an old Germanic, warlike duel. It culminated in a death march for the fallen hero, who was ceremoniously carried out of the arena, accompanied by the women's lamentations over the dead and the words of the choral leader:

Of all games
the holy purpose
prosperity of the fatherland
the fatherland's highest command
when in demand/self-sacrifice.

This type of *Thingspiel,* actually created as a form of entertainment, clarifies important aspects of the National Socialist ideology, youth cult, sacrifice for the fatherland, and the combination of mystic German and ancient Greek culture, which coincided with the concepts of the Olympic Games in an unfortunate way. In 1936, this contributed to the increased acceptance of the National Socialist Games among citizens and foreign observers.

The idea of holding Olympics in Germany has a long history. In 1916, the Olympic Games had been granted to Berlin. However, the outbreak of World War I prevented the Games from taking place there. As a result of the war and International Olympic Committee (IOC) arrangements concluded in the suburbs of Paris, Germany was not invited to the 1920 and 1924 Games. By granting Germany the 1936 Winter Games, Germany's former enemies signaled their readiness to reaccept Germany into the community of nations.

The 1936 Olympic Games were granted to Germany in 1928, during the time of the Weimar Republic. In that year, Germany had reached the height of its political reconciliation with France and its reintegration into the world of European nations. This was to change. After Hitler took power in 1933 and began a public campaign of discrimination against minorities and political opponents, critics abroad, particularly in the United States, loudly voiced their opposition to Germany's hosting the Games; some demanded a boycott. Foreign correspondents and diplomats denounced the totalitarian rule of the National Socialists: the press censorship, the brutal and organized discrimination against Jews, the public profession of Hitler's maxims, which he disseminated through his book, *Mein Kampf,* and the forced integration of the citizens into a community of peoples superior to all other peoples. Numerous German refugees reported abuse and killings in the German concentration camps. After a time, however, these horrific reports lost their impact. They were hardly noticed or were labeled as exaggerations. For this reason, Hitler's government was able to maintain a relatively good reputation abroad during its first few years in power. Hitler appeared able to reestablish the order lost during the Weimar Republic, and it appeared that Germany was on the way to becoming a reliable partner. Moreover, National Socialism was seen as the most effective bulwark against communism.

Only Jewish circles in the United States called for a boycott of the "Nazi Games." After some time, this initiative, supported by certain members of the press, did not fall on deaf ears in Europe. The emigrant organizations and the forbidden "proletarian athletes" joined in the U.S. demands for a boycott. Despite signs that Germany had become a totalitarian police state, the IOC, under the leadership of Count Henri de Baillet-Latour, insisted nonetheless on Germany as the host of the XIth Olympic Games. The IOC worked to prevent a boycott and to pressure the United States into participating. The absence of the United States, the world's greatest sports nation, would have reduced the idea of international unity inherent in the Games to absurdity. The acceptance of the National Socialists in Europe and the IOC's political agitation eventually led to fruitful results. A boycott did not take place: forty-nine nations with 3,980 athletes took part in the Berlin Games. With 427 athletes, the German hosts presented the largest team, larger than that of the United States, with 367 participants.

During the preparatory phase of the games, Germany appeared to make concessions to the rest of the world. Concurrently, however, National Socialism continued to show its brutality and contempt for human beings. The Nazis seized the opportunity to achieve a propaganda triumph through the Games, but in no way were the basic principles of National Socialist policy to change. Even if the world let itself be lulled into complacency by the National Socialist government's supposed concessions, the unparalleled and excellently equipped stadium, and the pompous organization, there were enough facts to contradict a peaceful European future: Hitler's occupation of the demilitarized Rhineland in violation of the Versailles Treaty in March 1936; the persecution of political opposition and the elimination of all pluralistic structures; and the disqualification of athletes due to their Jewish heritage. (A Jewish high jumper, Gretel Bergmann, spent the duration of the Games under house arrest to prevent her from speaking to foreign reporters, which likely cost Germany a gold medal in her event.) The "half-Jew" Helene Mayer was allowed to participate only because of her "Aryan appearance" and for publicity's sake.

The German government made no secret of the fact that in the end, an athletic contest between "Germans as Aryans" and "blacks as non-Aryans" was unacceptable to them.

One can unfortunately experience that often the free man must even fight with blacks, with Negroes, for the victory trophy. This is an unparalleled disgracing and a degrading of the Olympic idea. The old Greeks would turn in their graves if they knew what the modern man had made of their holy national games. (*Volkischer Beobachter,* 1932)

The next Olympic games take place in 1936 in Berlin. Hopefully the responsible men understand their duty. The blacks must be banned. We are expecting this! (*Volkischer Beobachter,* 1933)

The same went for the Jews, who at that time were banned from all sports organizations. This open discrimination was hardly noticed, and the Olympic idea, as represented by Pierre de Coubertin, had already been perverted.

Despite Germany's efforts, it was natural that foreigners still observed Germany with skepticism, and so Germany was forced to walk a fine line. A complete assertion of the principles of National Socialism in a time of difficult foreign policy would have been accompanied by too great a loss of prestige— and prestige was exactly what was needed. For external consumption, the propaganda machine portrayed National Socialist ideology as full of open-mindedness and tolerance. One such example of this is the handling of the American Jesse Owens. Despite his "lesser race," Jesse Owens, a favorite of the German public, easily dominated all "Aryan" athletes. He won four gold medals, in the 100-meter and 200-meter sprints, in the 4 × 100-meter relay, and in the long jump. Due to his popularity, it would not have been possible to subject him to the National Socialist discrimination machine. Nevertheless, Hitler found a way to avoid congratulating Owens and other black athletes for their victories by gladly and with great popular appeal congratulating German athletes at a ceremony after the Games.

Through supposed concessions, all of the IOC's latent doubts, prior to and during the Games, were easily dispelled. The IOC's members trusted in the assurances of the German representatives. Above all, they had faith in Theodor Lewald, who as a republican and coauthor of the Weimar constitution enjoyed an excellent reputation abroad. Those responsible were satisfied by the fact that the German national Olympic committee (NOC) was made up of individuals familiar to the IOC and the promise that all Olympic rules would be followed strictly. Additionally, Jewish athletes were to be permitted to participate on the German teams.

Theodor Lewald and Carl Diem, two men who had rendered great service to German sports and enjoyed positive international reputations, were entrusted with planning the Olympic Games. Lewald, born in 1860, was descended from the educated Jewish class. He pursued a civil service career and initially was active in diverse functions at the Reich Ministry for Domestic Affairs. Later he took on the responsibility as the Reich's cultural representative for the world's fairs in Chicago, Paris, and St. Louis and consequently was responsible for finances for the German Olympic teams in Paris and St. Louis. In this way he came in contact with the German sports movement. As representative of the Reich on the budget committee of the Reichstag, Lewald administered the finances of the 1916 Berlin Olympic Games. At the end of the war, he was undersecretary of state and carried out important political activities in the young republic.

Lewald used his growing political power to champion the return of German athletes to the international sports community. With his departure from politics in 1921, he dedicated himself to sports, which he later tried to keep from the grasp of the National Socialists, and to Olympic ideals. As the chairman of the first German umbrella organization for sports, the Reich Committee for Physical Exercise (Deutscher Reichsausschuss für Leibesubungen [DRA]), he was accepted into the IOC in 1926. Despite his international recognition, Lewald left his position as chairman of the DRA in 1933, after Joseph Goebbels, the Reich minister of propaganda, criticized his Jewish heritage in his newspaper, *Der Angriff*. Together with Diem, Lewald had directed the planning of the 1916 Games; the two men were a team, possessed by sports and the idea of the Olympics. As the DRA was disbanded and transformed into the National Socialist Reichsport Führerring, Diem and Lewald were removed from their offices. However, out of consideration for foreign opinion, both retained their responsibility for the Games.

For years, Carl Diem was one of the foremost German sports functionaries. He was born in 1882 into an upper-middle-class family. After finishing his primary education, he completed a sales apprenticeship, while also working at a number of sports newspapers. At the age of twenty, he was chosen to work for the sports league, the DSBfA, the German Sports Authority for Athletics (Deutsche Sportbehörde für Athletik) and was promoted in 1903 to its board of directors. In 1906, Diem accompanied the German team to the Games in Athens.

In 1908, he became the chairman of the DSBfA. Following the custom in the kaiser's Germany, Diem made contact with the military and the marines in order to encourage the institutionalization and the consolidation of individual sports organizations. A strong advocate of the Olympic idea and of sports, he became the general secretary for the German Imperial Committee for the Olympic Games (Deutscher Reichsausschuss für Olympische Spiele) in 1913 and thus Germany's first full-time sports executive. After World War I, Diem joined Lewald in advocating that the Games be conferred upon Germany.

Initially the NOC lacked government financial assistance to organize the 1936 Games. Funds were to be raised through the "Olympic-Penny," a supplement added on to the price of tickets for sports events, as well as a lottery and donations. More money could be saved through the use of existing facilities. In Grunewald near Berlin, an Olympic stadium that had been completed in 1916 was to be expanded to meet the needs of the 1936 Games.

Only gradually did the National Socialist government develop an interest in the project. As late as 1932, the Nazis opposed the choice of Berlin as the site, believing the Games to be a Jewish-run enterprise. After problems arose during the expansion of the Grunewald stadium, Hitler himself visited the construction site and immediately decided to rebuild all of the Olympic facilities in awe-inspiring dimensions. From that point on, financing was no longer a problem. With Nazi backing, there arose buildings of truly Olympian proportions. Planning and organization were no longer solely the concern of the sports organizations and the NOC but became a national preoccupation for which Hitler himself took on full responsibility. The stadium, constructed on the site of the old Grunewald stadium, offered room for over 100,000 spectators; according to Hitler's orders it was built not mostly of glass but of massive stone, in order to create additional employment. Through an opening in the stadium, an additional 100,000 visitors could follow the contests within the stadium from the neighboring grounds. Circling the stadium were many more equally monumental buildings, including an open-air theater, a 20,000-seat hockey rink, a 16,000-seat swimming pool, and a guest house with space for 400 female athletes. An Olympic Village provided accommodations for the male athletes, additional sites were constructed in other areas of Berlin, and facilities for the sailing events were built in Kiel.

The state increasingly controlled the substantive planning of the Games as well. The government resorted to the discriminatory measures that had been threatened in *Volkischer Beobachter,* although it tried to disguise them. Theodor Lewald, because of his Jewish heritage, was increasingly pressured to take a back seat during the planning stage. However, due to the trust that he enjoyed at the IOC, he could not be replaced by a National Socialist. Seven Jewish athletes who qualified for the Olympics were rejected due to their "insufficient achievements." To satisfy Lewald's promise to the IOC, some "half-Jews," Aryan-appearing Jewish athletes, were allowed to participate on the German team.

Additionally, the Games were used to integrate the population even further into an already functioning community cult. The entire population was to "share" in the preparations for the Olympic Games. A monthly newspaper, *Die Olympischen Spiele* (The Olympic Games), first appeared a year prior to the Games and in a short time reached a circulation of 60,000. Free information materials were sent to all European countries as well. The citizenry was urged by diverse and to some extent obligatory government initiatives to support athletic activities, and existing sports organizations were incorporated into a National Socialist umbrella organization.

While Olympic leaders and some governments demanded that politics must not be brought into sports in response to criticism concerning the choice of Germany as the host country, complying with this demand had not been possible for quite some time. The entire German society was already highly politicized. Despite press censorship and authoritarian actions against the opposition and ethnic minorities, Joseph Goebbels' propaganda efforts, through calculated information control and mass rallies, inspired strong feelings of shared purpose and the individual's allegiance to the state. The Olympic idea was incorporated into the National Socialist ideology, impressively documented in Leni Riefenstahl's film, *Olympia.*

The National Socialist Olympics was similar to other political mass events not only because of its social and political components but above all because it spoke directly to an ideological level. This suited the mass cult of National Socialism well because the bottled-up aggressions of the citizenry could be channeled in the same manner. Because the Olympics were attended primarily by Germans, while the competitions were international, the German audience developed a sense of national group consciousness. Anyone who defied the rules of the group in any way was attacked. The failure to salute Hitler at the times called for by the ceremony could have been dangerous for Germans. This controlled group consciousness is evident in the ceremonial course of all Nazi events. The Ministry of Propaganda understood how to emphasize these factors. The reports from the German broadcasters conveyed the impression within Germany that the Olympics were dominated by the Germans. The German team was the most successful and won the most (thirty-eight) gold medals, more even than the United States. The German reporters who covered the torch relay from Olympia to Berlin were highly motivated, despite extremely unfavorable circumstances. In Greece, the condition of the streets was catastrophical, and the extreme heat melted the plates used for the news recordings. The reporters sacrificed their drinking water in order to cool the recording plates. Nevertheless, the reporting was impressive and was an important factor in creating the Olympic fever that spread throughout Germany. There, as in other countries, the Olympics became something mystical. The widespread confusion of the antique Olympia with the Olymp Mountain created the impression that the Olympic flame was carried directly down from the home of the gods. Skillfully, propagandists stressed the supposed relation between the ancient Greek and ancient

German cultures. "Enter the stadium, become men, and learn how to fight" were the principles that coincided with National Socialist preferences for the military, sports, and a youth and body culture:

The Greeks had a general appreciation for the perfect human figure, for the sinewy, nude body. Art and athletics were unified in upholding this ideal of unadorned beauty in physical perfection. The peak of national civilisation was contemporaneous with the flourishing age in physical culture, and athletic achievements spurred the artists on to new heights. (*Die Olympischen Spiele* 4 [July 1935])

Following Carl Diem's idea, the Olympic flame was lit in Olympia for the first time and carried in a relay run to Berlin. The large-scale and precisely planned torch run, cheered and greeted from stadium to stadium by the respective populations, increasingly turned into a demonstration of support for the National Socialist ideology. In Vienna, where the political situation already was critical, the arrival of the torch carriers resulted in frenetic applause from the citizens. The applause was aimed not only at the Olympic ideals and myth but also at their organization and the supremacy they achieved through National Socialism, which now seemed to fuse with the Olympic ideals and myths. In Berlin, the Nazis used the gain in prestige through such an event to show the "new National Socialist Germany" in the best possible light. Superficial observers found what they sought: calm and order, cleanliness, and enthusiasm for a government that had managed to end the economic crisis and the political chaos of the Weimar Republic.

Thomas Wolfe described the atmosphere of that time in his novel, *You Can't Go Home Again* (1940):

It was the season of the great Olympic Games, and almost every day George and Else went to the stadium in Berlin. George observed that the organizing genius of the German people, which has been used so often to such noble purpose, was now more thrillingly displayed than he had ever seen it before. . . . The games were overshadowed, and they were no longer merely sporting competitions to which other nations had sent their chosen teams. They became, day after day, an orderly and overwhelming demonstration in which the whole of Germany had been schooled and disciplined. It was as if the games had been chosen as a symbol of the new collective might, a means of showing to the world in concrete terms what this new power had come to be.

But it was also clear that under the surface one could sense the regime's constant readiness to use force:

So the weeks, the month, the summer passed, and everywhere about him George saw the evidences of this dissolution, this shipwreck of a great spirit. The poisonous emanations of suppression, persecution, and fear permeated the air like miasmic and pestilential vapours, tainting, sickening, and blighting the lives of everyone he met. (Thomas Wolfe, *You Can't Go Home Again*)

From the very beginning, the Olympics were a National Socialist mass demonstration. As the runners handed over the torch on the German-Austrian border, the people in the streets began to celebrate. On many market squares, Hitler Youth played horns and trumpets, and church bells tolled.

The spirit of the Berlin Olympics is embodied best in Leni Riefenstahl's film, *Olympia.* Not only does the exacting reporting make this film an interesting documentation of the Games, but also the exceptional artistic achievement in the area of sports cinematography, particularly remarkable for the 1930s, remains admirable today. This combination of art and documentation created seismographic testimony of the National Socialist culture. The glorification of the human athletic physique is evident. The first part, "Festival of Nations," beginning at the Olympic stadium, establishes a link between the ancient Games and modern times. Accompanied by heavy Wagnerian music, the camera glides over a Greek set, then slowly zooms onto a statue of a discus thrower. The Greek past comes to life as the statue metamorphoses into a modern athlete. This setting turns into the 1936 Olympics. The second part of the 6-hour film, "Festival of Beauty," concentrates on the physical aesthetics of the athletes:

The film has often been described as a triumph of propaganda, but this is less than just. What it did was to record a triumph of propaganda, brilliantly capturing the militaristic nature of the organisation, particularly the opening ceremony; but its enduring merit is as a creative work of art. Even so, its director could not escape the consequences of her own close association with the Nazi leaders, which pursued her down the years with the tenacity of the Furies. (Hart-Davis, *Hitler's Games,* p. 242)

The Olympic Games had contradictory effects on foreign observers. On the one hand, they were impressed by the enormous achievement and the perfect organization, as was Thomas Wolfe. On the other hand, many commentaries evidenced fear and alienation. Sir Robert Vansittart, a high-ranking official in the British Foreign Office, recorded his impressions at the end of the Games; they are typical of many other observers:

These people are the most formidable proposition that has ever been formulated; they are in strict training now, not for the Olympic Games, but for breaking some other and emphatically unsporting world records, and perhaps the world as well. (Hart-Davis, *Hitler's Games,* p. 227)

To most observers, however, Germany, especially through its achievements and its production of the Games, proved its peaceful intentions and its wish to work with other nations. The National Socialists had ensured the participation of renowned artists, such as Carl Orff and Richard Strauss. The skillful combination of the Games with significant cultural events may have contributed more to the deception of the nation's public than did the perfect organization and the celebrated athletic fairness.

The Games ran smoothly, with no noteworthy problems. The athletic events and the awarding of the medals were interwoven with many cultural and social events. All athletes praised the organization, the hospitality, the facilities, and the sports venues. The 1936 Olympics in Berlin were responsible for introducing a number of activities and symbols still found at present-day Olympics; the Olympic hymn, the Olympic bell, the torch run, the youth and student camps, and the Olympic Congress testify to the efficacy of the Ministry of Propaganda.

The Games of 1936 were one of the greatest domestic and foreign policy successes of the Nazi regime. The triumphs of the German team and the praise the Games received abroad had a stabilizing effect on the system. On the one hand, Hitler had "proof" for the correctness of his theory of the master race; on the other hand, the German people began to believe in and support the government and its system. The German team, with its many wins, led the unofficial team standings. Two weeks after the conclusion of the Olympic "festival of peace," however, Hitler approved a memorandum on a "four year plan" that clearly indicated his determination to make political and military preparations for war. He had deceived the world.

BIBLIOGRAPHICAL ESSAY

A number of archives in Germany hold material on the Olympic Games of 1936. First are the Political Archives of the Office of Foreign Affairs (*Politisches Archiv des Auswärtigen Amtes*) in Bonn.

A very large collection is also held at the German Central Archives (*Deutschen Zentralarchiv*) in Potsdam, and the *Bundesarchiv* in the Koblenz Archives which contains a series of relevant documents. The film archives are particularly worth mentioning. Under the Akten zum Verhaltnis der Sportvereine zum Staat, Gerhard Granier, Josef Henke, and Klaus Oldenhage collected and edited the entire collection of Bundesarchives: *Das Bundesarchiv und seine Bestände,* Friedrich Facius, Hans Booms, Heinz Boberach, Harald Boldt Verlag, Boppard am Rhein O.J.

The Carl Diem Institute in Cologne, named for its founder, contains an archive holding all of the documents bequeathed by Carl Diem, cataloged as Korrespondenz Carl Diems, 1920–1936.

Additional sources of detailed information of the 1936 Olympics may be found in the Geheimen Staatsarchiv Preussischer Kulturbesitz, Archivstr. 12–14, 14195 Berlin, im Brandenburgisches Landeshauptarchiv, Sanssouci-Orangerie, 14469 Potsdam, or in Landesarchiv Berlin, Kalckreutherstr. 1–2, 10777.

In the United States, there is a substantial amount of primary source material on the Berlin Games in the Avery Brundage Collection, University of Illinois Archives, Urbana, Illinois. This collection includes clippings and other information on the Jewish problem and the threat of a U.S. boycott, bulletins from the Berlin organizing committee news service, copies of *Olympische Spiele,* a committee publication, and many programs, postcards, and photographs from the Games.

Published primary sources include the organizing committee's report to the IOC, *The XIth Olympic Games, Berlin, 1936: Official Report* (Berlin, 1936). German- and French-language editions are also available. The U.S. Olympic Committee report is Frederick

W. Rubien, ed., *Games of the XIth Olympiad, Berlin, Germany, and the IVth Winter Games, Garmisch-Partenkirchen* (New York, 1937), and the Canadian equivalent is W. A. Fry, ed., *Canada at the XIth Olympiad 1936* (Dunnville, Ontario, 1936). Former Olympian Harold M. Abrahams edited the British report, *The Official Report of the XIth Olympiad, Berlin, 1936* (London, 1937), and the French Olympic committee published *La Participation française aux jeux de la XIme Olympiade Garmisch-Partenkirchen-Berlin 1936* (Paris, 1937).

In keeping with its propaganda mission, the German organizing committee published a host of collateral documents in a variety of languages. Guidebooks, handbooks, rule books, regulations for the art competition, press manuals, and daily programs can all be found in German, French, English, Spanish, and Portuguese.

The Berlin Olympics have attracted more attention from historians, political scientists, and sociologists than any other modern Games. The two most comprehensive histories of the Games in English are Duff Hart-Davis, *Hitler's Games: The 1936 Olympics* (1986), a rather polemical study emphasizing the political background of the Games, and Richard Mandell, *The Nazi Olympics* (New York, 1971). Other works in English include Judith Holmes, *Olympiad 1936: Blaze of Glory for Hitler's Reich* (New York, 1971), which analyzes the Games as a successful propaganda effort and also includes many illustrations to emphasize the point, and Christopher Hill, *Olympic Politics* (1992), which examines the political connotation of sport, especially the Olympic Games. Articles touching on aspects of the politics of these Games include Bruce Kidd, "The Popular Front and the 1936 Olympics," *Canadian Journal of the History of Sport and Physical Education* 11 (1980): 1–18; and D. A. Kass, "The Issue of Racism at the 1936 Olympics," *Journal of Sport History* 3, 3 (Winter 1976): 223–35. For a viewpoint supportive of the proposed U.S. boycott, see Committee on Fair Play in Sports, *Preserve the Olympic Ideal* (New York, 1936?), and for analysis of the issue, see Carolyn Marvin, "Avery Brundage and American Participation in the 1936 Olympic Games, *American Studies* 16 (1982): 81–106, and Moshe Gottlieb, "The American Controversy over the Olympic Games," *American Jewish Historical Quarterly* 61 (March 1972): 181–213. See the *Los Angeles Times,* August 1, 1932, for evidence of early Nazi opposition to the Berlin Games.

Important works in German include Arnd Kruger, *Die Olympischen Spiele 1936 und die Weltmeinung Sportwiss* (Berlin, 1972), a study of the planning and staging of the Games within the political milieu of Hitler's Germany. Kruger also has a long chapter on the proposed U.S. boycott. Friedrich Bohlen, *Die XI. Olympischen Spiele, Berlin 1936* (Cologne, 1979), deals with the Games as a propaganda instrument and is extensively footnoted. Jurgen Bellers, *Die Olympiade Berlin 1936 im Spiegel der ausländischen Presse* (Munich, 1986), examines the coverage of the Berlin Games in newspapers of more than twenty-eight countries. The chapter on the United States cites the *New York Times* and the *New York Herald Tribune* almost exclusively. Thomas Schmidt, *Das Berliner Olympia Stadion* (Berlin, 1983), is a history of the stadium written on the occasion of its fiftieth anniversary. Two more general treatments of sports and politics that include much material on the Berlin Games are Willi B. Wange, *Der Sport im Griff der Politik. Von den olympischen Spielen der Antike bis heute* (1988), dealing with the ways in which sport is an instrument of political realism, and Rudiger Voigt (ed.), *Politik der Symbole—Symbole der Politik* (Opladen, Germany, 1989), in which sport is seen as an important symbol. Hans Joachim Teichler, "Zum Ausschluss der deutschen Juden von den Olympischen Spielen 1936," *Stadion* 15, 1 (1989): 45–64, discusses the exclusion of German Jewish athletes from the Games.

The Berlin Games are among the most pictorialized of the Olympics. Researchers interested in the visual impact of the Games should first view Leni Riefenstahl's *Olympia* (1938), the official film of the Games, and consult the many books and articles on her and her film (see Appendix C, documentary films). Other pictorial works include Hans V. Tischammer und Osten, *Zur Erinnerung an die XI. Olympiade: Berlin 1936* (n.p., n.d.), which, besides excellent illustrations, contains facsimile autographs of medal winners, and Walter Richter, ed., *Olympia 1936,* vol. 2 (Bielefeld, 1936), a pictorial book produced by a cigarette company with spaces for pictures of the Games that could be obtained by purchasing the company's product. Similar books exist for other Olympic Games, including the 1932 Los Angeles Games and the 1936 Winter Games at Garmisch-Partenkirchen.

Dietmar Herz and Angelika Altmann

TOKYO/HELSINKI 1940

THE GAMES OF THE XIIth OLYMPIAD
(Never Held)

Pierre de Coubertin revived the Olympic Games in 1896 with purist educational motives and with an eye on international harmony. The International Olympic Committee (IOC) council, initially representing nine Western countries, recognized Coubertin's determination and organizational genius and followed his lead in establishing criteria for the persistence of a pure competition between the world's best athletes. The magnitude and success of Olympiads during the subsequent century testify to the genius of these early efforts. However, although the international community endorsed these grandiose designs, ideals and dreams have not always overcome the complex realities of nationalism, opportunism, and delicate issues pregnant with secession and war. The agreement to hold the Olympics every four years in different cities did not anticipate what would take place from 1936 to 1940: the awarding of the same Olympics to Japan and then to Finland, with bombs rather than athletes leaving their marks at the unfinished Helsinki facilities.

The bidding campaign for the 1940 Olympic site, though less sophisticated than more recent efforts, portrayed a tranquil world in anticipation of a sequel to the XIth Olympiad. In 1936, victories for human rights had immortalized Olympic athletes, supplanted the Nazi medal count, and represented all that is good in athletic competition. The 1940 Games were to carry on this tradition, and the Olympic torch was cast as a symbol of international peace—a national prize more precious than the crown jewels. However, within the simple photo albums, blatant propaganda books, and ornate invitation bids, all intended to lure the XIIth Olympiad to their respective countries, were subtle prophetic hints of hidden national agendas and the realities of the frail political agreements haunting the 1930s.

The inside cover of Italy's booklet sported a picture of Benito Mussolini, the "First Sportsman," riding a horse. An army officer is the only visible audience, and the picture is captioned, "Stagnation weakens, Action strengthens—Mussolini." The ill-conceived bid booklet ended with the motto: "For the Honour of Our Country and the Glory of Sport."

Similar statements appeared in the opening paragraph of Japan's successful appeal for the selection of Tokyo, which the council granted at its Berlin meeting on August 31, 1936. The Japanese appealed to the dynamics of "human nature" and their leaders' understanding of the "natural impulse" of "competition." Ironically, these self-proclaimed proprietors of the human condition labeled World War I as "that catastrophic punctuation mark in the story of mankind's progress" and spoke of the ability to redirect human nature's competitive impulse "along sane, healthy, wholesome lines" (*Tokyo Sports Center of the Ori-*

ent, p. i). In 1938, Japan's military actions against China revealed that this impulse also flowed through the political veins of nationalism and imperialism.

The awarding of the Games to Japan in the light of its 1931 attack on Manchuria and the international political climate is one of the most telling statements of modern Olympic history. Japan's first proposal for the Games was delivered to the session of the IOC on July 29, 1932, in Los Angeles, just prior to the Xth Olympic Games. The year 1940 would be the 2,600th anniversary of the founding of the empire of Japan, and just months after the aggressive assault on Manchuria, the Japanese request still received favorable attention. The official IOC vote was 36–27, a controversial decision that sent conflicting messages to the world. Either the IOC members were oblivious to the possible problems with a Japanese site, or they were determined to keep politics and sports separate.

By 1936, political problems with any site selection in Asia or Europe were obvious. Hitler had renounced the Versailles Treaty, remilitarized the Rhineland, and was continuing to persecute Jews. Italy was acting with similarly aggressive tendencies in Ethiopia. The Chinese were in the throes of a political battle between the nationalists and communists, and both resented the Japanese for the Manchurian crisis and would soon battle them on Chinese soil.

The IOC's actions reveal the organization's awareness of the potentially explosive situation with Games at Tokyo. Nonetheless, after delegates to the (British) Empire Games Federation voted in 1938 to boycott the XIIth Olympiad if Japan were still at war, a frustrated Avery Brundage asked, "Why do the athletes meddle with politics—have they no foreign office?" He rejected a written request for postponement of the Games by A. C. Gilbert, an American Olympic Association member and former Olympian. And when Harvard's William J. Bingham resigned in protest from the American Olympic Association, Brundage responded, "The work of the committee will go on just the same." The IOC also ignored the protests of Chinese delegate C. T. Wang, and it had unanimously ousted American delegate Ernest L. Jahncke earlier for voicing dissent regarding the Berlin Games and German discrimination against Jews. At the time, Jahncke was the only American in the IOC who had spoken against any involvement with the Nazis. Brundage, who replaced Jahncke, later proclaimed that World War II was "the suicide of a culture," while persisting with the illusion of a XIIth Olympiad, that is, until the Soviet bombing of Helsinki shattered more than just his dreams.

This theory of the IOC's oblivious posture on international politics appears even more palatable when one considers its 1938 site selection decision for the 1940 Winter Games, which had been originally scheduled for Sapporo. The IOC considered Oslo but chose Garmisch-Partenkirchen at its London meeting in June 1939—less than three months before Germany's invasion of Poland on September 1, defending its choice on the grounds that Garmisch's facilities, used for the 1936 Games, were already in place.

Another factor in the decision for Tokyo was based on the financial advantages of competing in Japan. The mayor of Tokyo allegedly won some votes with his promise of $290,000 (1 million yen) in subsidies per foreign team if the Olympics were held in his city. No proof of that financial inducement exists, but it would have benefited struggling economies. In Japan, the news of the IOC decision was greeted with such a dramatic rise in the Tokyo stock exchange that city administrators called a three-day holiday. On March 29, 1938, Tokyo City's municipal assembly unanimously approved a 16 million yen Olympic budget.

After the beginning of war with China, Japan's imperial government withdrew its financial support (4.3 million yen), forcing the organizing committee into its last official duty: returning the Games to the IOC. Money had played a significant role from start to finish in the Japanese Olympic bid. The organizational and physical progress of Japan's preparations are summarized in the sixteen issues (197,500 copies) of the *Olympic News,* published from May 1937 to August 1938. In the last issue, "The XIIth Olympiad Tokyo 1940 Renounced," the national Olympic committee mentioned "the trouble with China" as the cause of forfeiture of the Games.

At the time of the return of the Games to the IOC, Japan was in the advanced planning stages for the event, with some construction in progress. Nearly all of the target dates for beginning construction of Olympic buildings were in October 1938 or later, and thus the cancellation of the games precluded most building activities. The original choice for the main stadium site was the Garden of the Meiji Shrine, a 125-acre complex in the center of Tokyo, famous for international sporting events. Although detailed plans were in hand and construction imminent, the Olympic organizing committee unanimously agreed to shift the center of the Olympics to Komazawa, a golf course and wooded area near the Meiji Shrine, since the latter could not be retrofitted with the proposed 100,000 seats. Construction of the Komazawa main stadium and the swimming stadium was abandoned. The promise of the Olympics did help Tokyo realize one of the Far East's largest hotels, the 628-room Daiit, which opened on April 27, 1938.

The forfeiture of the Olympics did not kill Japanese interest in sports. Over 15,000 Japanese youth had exhibited their commitment to sports with their voluntary service in Olympic construction projects. All-Japan Games were held instead of the Olympics, and the Japanese Amateur Athletic Association was reestablished in 1942.

The transfer of the XIIth Olympiad to Finland evoked a spirit of enthusiasm among the Finns, although tempered by the stark realities of time pressures and war possibilities. The Finnish Olympic committee took just twenty-four hours to respond to an offer that, in its own words, had "devolved upon Finland out of a clear sky on July 29th." Throughout its monthly publications are plans for makeshift arrangements and allusions to the international political scene. For example, the housing shortage would be alleviated by accommodation in private houses and apartments, with larger groups boarding in "schools, etc., or in tents." Ocean liners would serve as floating hotels, and a newly constructed nurses' training college and a cadet school would house some of the athletes.

Most of the sporting events were assigned to Helsinki's existing sports centers: an athletic stadium, an exhibition hall, a shooting range, two riding arenas, and a covered court club.

Although various buildings such as a swimming stadium and a velodrome were still needed, Finland was confident that the logistics of the Games could be met. The Finnish parliament voted a $5 million budget for the Games, and the Helsinki municipality granted an additional $2.5 million. In addition to the building needs, the earliest plans included a temporary stand alongside the rowing and canoe course at Taivallahti Bay. This facility was soon upgraded to include a permanent concrete stand seating 3,500 people, with provisions for 6,500 standing spectators. A two-story administration building and boat houses for 200 canoes were also planned for the bay site. A stadium had been built in 1934 with seating for 30,000 people, but an "Olympic gap" was left on the east side for additional seating in the event of a successful Olympic bid. By April 1939, the gap had been closed and the seating capacity doubled, with plans to add still more. The Finnish Olympic organizing committee (OOC) and civic authorities seemed undaunted by the challenges and worked indefatigably during the entire preparation process. The OOC came to be the voice not only of the amateur sports in Finland but also of most of its people. It was keenly aware of the international gratitude for Finland's efforts.

The OOC and the Helsinki city government were an administrative team. The tasks, "in view of the need for haste," were divided between OOC and a newly formed Olympic Games office, which administered construction related to public buildings along with many of the logistics of hosting an expected 100,000 visitors. By October 1939, the OOC and Games office had arranged housing for over 60,000 guests and could boast of having completed all competition buildings except the swimming stadium. The Games were scheduled for July 20 through August 4, 1940. In just two years, half the time normally allotted a host country, Finland was on track to complete all arrangements in good order and successfully host over sixty nations' teams. Perhaps the biggest obstacle to reaching this goal was finding enough qualified staff members from the relatively small population of Finland.

The summer and fall of 1939 were full of anticipatory sporting events. Taisto Mäki set a world record in the 5,000-meter race on June 16 in the renovated Olympic stadium. This occasion could not have come at a better time for Olympic publicity. The Finnish Open athletic championships were held during the last week of August, and on September 17, sixteen days after Hitler's invasion of Poland, Mäki established another record in the 10,000 meters.

Perhaps one cannot appreciate fully Finland's tenacious pursuit of the Olympics and desire to contribute positively to a troubled world without reading the Finns' contemporary accounts. The *Finlandia* papers are filled with anecdotal, humorous, and yet useful information for those preparing to visit Helsinki. The *Olympic-News Service* chronicled the official plans for public review. Through all of these accounts, a sense of Finnish exhaustion and exhilaration surfaces.

Appreciation, applause, and sympathy for their plight are certainly in order, and the granting of the Games to Helsinki at a later date was a well-deserved act of gratitude by the IOC.

The Finns went to great lengths to inform the world about their culture and to prepare for a peaceful and informative convergence of dozens of other cultures. However, this nation of goodwill ended its 1940 preparations with the acknowledgment that some ideologies are wrong and that the Olympic movement was not only one of the world's greatest institutions but also one of its greatest political hopes:

We [Finland] thought that even in time of war it was important to keep alive the Olympic idea, an idea that would unite all the nations of the world in a spirit of peace and brotherhood. We felt that it was our duty to arrange the Games at the very time when their significance, as a symbol of goodwill among the nations, was greater than ever. Shortly after having been entrusted with the Games we defined their aim: to be a feast which would awaken, in all individuals and nations, a desire for mutual understanding and hold before the eyes of a world, infected with discord and suspicion, the ideal of peace. . . . But when less than a year remained before the Games, bolshevik [*sic*] Russia attacked our peaceful people. . . . She disclosed her intentions by making air raids on the unfortified Olympic City killing women and children with bombs and machine guns. . . . We beseech you, our fellow athletes and sportsmen in all parts of the world, to think of Finland at this moment . . . which has been attacked without the slightest justification by a Great Power pursuing its bolshevist policy. (*Olympic-News Service,* January 1940)

The Finnish-Coubertin-Brundage perception of the Olympics still persists, and the Olympic movement has continued to gain respect as an institution for world peace and goodwill. Although the Games were not intended as a political force and although Brundage's typical response, "The Games must go on," is sometimes inappropriate, the Finnish perception of the Games is endorsed by most of the international community. Since World War II, countries have increasingly used the Games as a platform for carrying out certain political agendas. However, the Olympic movement remains one of the few institutions exuding the Finnish hope that all nations can be united in a spirit of peace and brotherhood.

BIBLIOGRAPHICAL ESSAY

Primary source materials for the XIIth Olympiad may be found at the Amateur Athletic Foundation of Los Angeles, 2141 West Adams Boulevard, Los Angeles, California, and at the Sports Museum of Finland, Olympic Stadium, 00250 Helsinki, Finland. The Avery Brundage Collection at the University of Illinois Archives, Urbana, Illinois, contains some correspondence, publications of the organizing committees, and newspaper clippings related to the 1940 Games.

The monthly publications of the Tokyo and Helsinki organizing committees describe the preparatory activities of the respective countries. For Tokyo, see *Tokyo Olympic News, XIIth Olympiad, 1940,* May 10, 1937–August 25, 1938; and for Helsinki, consult

Olympic News Service 1–10 (October 1938–October 1939) and *Finlandia News Service* 1–9 (1939). Other organizing committee publications include *Olympic Games XIIth, Tokyo, 1940. Report of the Organizing Committee on Its Work for the XIIth Olympic Games of 1940 in Tokyo until the Relinquishment* (Tokyo, 1938), the official report to the IOC, containing a historical overview of Japan's efforts to host the Olympics, copies of letters between Japanese officials and the IOC, and maps, photos, and blueprints of proposed venues. See also *Olympic Preparations for the Celebration of the XIIth Olympiad, Tokyo, 1940* (Tokyo, 1938), detailing the Japanese philosophy toward the Games and describing in considerable detail the planning for the Games and the influx of visitors to Tokyo; *Scenic Japan* (Tokyo, 1935), a touristic photo album; *Tokyo: Sports Center of the Orient* (Tokyo, 1933), a photo album that accompanied Japan's bid for the Games; the *Twelfth Olympiad Tokyo, 1940: General Rules and Programme* (Tokyo, 1938).

For Helsinki, the official report is *XIIth Olympiad Helsinki, 1940* (Helsinki, 1940); a German edition is titled *Olympische vorbereitungen fur die Feier der 12. Olympiade, Helsinki 1940 im 4. Jahr d. 11. Olympiad* (Helsinki, 1940). See also *XIIth Olympiad: Helsinki, 20th July–4th August 1940, Programme and Prices of Admission Tickets* (Helsinki, 1939); *Au Comité international olympique* (Helsinki, n.d.), a bidding letter from the civic authorities; and J. W. Rangell, Ernst Krogius, Urho Kekkonen, and Erik von Frenckell, "To the Athletes and Sportsmen of the World: Bolshevism and Humanity," *Olympic News Service* (December 1939). *Olympian Rome* (Rome, 1935), is a bidding propaganda book for that city's effort to host the 1940 Games.

The U.S. report is Frederick W. Rubien, ed., *Report of the American Olympic Committee 1940* (New York, 1940), which contains information on the preparation of a U.S. team for the never-held Games, Avery Brundage's report as chairman of the committee, and a listing of a "theoretical 1940 American Olympic team." A May 6, 1940, *New York Times* article describes tryouts for the "theoretical" team.

Three historical studies of the Games are Hajo Bernett, "Das Scheitern der Olympischen Spiele von 1940," *Stadion* 6 (1980): 251–90, which deals with the impact of the Japanese-Chinese and Russo-Finnish wars on the 1940 Games; Kumihiko Karaki, *Die aufgegebenen Olympische Spiele in Tokio 1940* (n.p., 1982), which presents the story of the 1940 Games from a Japanese perspective; and Harold James Olson, "Japan at the Olympic Games, 1909–1938: The Emergence of an Athletic Power" (master's thesis, California State Polytechnic University at Pomona, 1991).

Works that contribute to an understanding of the political climate surrounding the Games include John H. Herz, "The Territorial State Revisited: Reflections on the Future of the Nation-State," in *International Politics and Foreign Policy,* ed. James N. Rosenau (New York, 1969); John Lucas, " 'From Coubertin to Samaranch' ": The Unsettling Transformation of the Olympic Ideology of Athletic Amateurism, *Stadion* 14, 1 (1988): 65–84 and *The Future of the Olympic Games* (Champaign, Ill., 1992); and Robin Tait, "The Politicization of the Modern Olympic Games" (Ph.D. dissertation, University of Oregon, 1984). Finally, Gunnar Staalsett, "The Olympic Question?" *Christian Century* (March 16, 1994): 269–70, is a provocative sermon highlighting the Olympic charter in the face of war delivered by the general secretary of the Lutheran World Federation in Lillehammer, Norway, at the opening of the 1994 Winter Olympics.

Jerry A. Pattengale

LONDON 1944

THE GAMES OF THE XIIITH OLYMPIAD
(Never Held)

The XIIIth Olympic Summer Games did not take place because of World War II, "the suicide of a culture," as Avery Brundage observed. The Summer Games were scheduled for London, while the VIth Winter Games were awarded to Cortina d'Ampezzo, Italy. The International Olympic Committee (IOC) chose London over Athens, Budapest, Detroit, and Lausanne in the late 1930s.

On August 7, 1939, a gigantic Olympic preview was held at White City stadium, outside of London, where Americans won eight of the fourteen events. Less than a month later, on September 1, German troops invaded Poland, and athletic festivals became less important. Preparations for 1940 were dominated by the Tokyo-Helsinki competition for the Summer Games. Berlin viewed Tokyo's eventual success as evidence of an Anglo-Japanese alliance, especially after London withdrew its halfhearted bid for the Games. The fact that London withdrew in order to obtain the 1944 Games made less of an impression on Germany than the fact that Japan was the immediate beneficiary of the British decision.

Japan did not hold the award long. In 1937, the beginning of the Sino-Japanese War demonstrated that Japan was committed to a major military adventure in Asia. Under such circumstances, the Japanese returned the Games to the IOC, which conferred them on Helsinki, a replacement city suggested even before Japan gave up the Games. Japan held an all-Japan meet instead and planned later events that would include all the areas under the jurisdiction of the Greater East Asian Co-Prosperity Sphere.

The Winter Games, which ended up in Garmisch-Partenkirchen, were canceled because of Germany's belligerency, but there was still hope, at least in America, that the Summer Games would be held in Helsinki, though Finland had recently emerged from its 100 days of war with the Soviet Union. However, in April 1940, the Finnish Olympic Committee officially announced that it was necessary to cancel the Games. With the continuation of the war long past the date when any kind of preparations could be made for the 1944 Games, they too were canceled.

World-class athletes were deprived of their chance to compete in the 1944 Olympics, but some semblance of a hypothetical U.S. team can be seen from a list of expected winners for the All-American track and field team: 100-meter dash, Claude Young; 200-meter dash, Charles Parker; 400-meter run, Elmore Harris; 800-meter run, Robert Kelley; 1-mile run, Gilbert Dodds; 3-mile run, Oliver Hunter; 10,000-meter run, Norman Bright; marathon, Charles Robbins; 120-yard hurdles, Owen Cassidy; 440-yard hurdles, Arky Erwin; 3,000-meter steeplechase, Forest Efaw; 50,000-meter walk, Walter Fleming; high jump, Fred Sheffield; long jump, Barney Ewell; hop, step, and jump, Donald Barksdale;

pole vault, Cornelius Warmerdam; shot put, Earl Audet; hammer throw, Henry Dreyer; discus throw, Hugh Cannon; javelin throw, Martin Biles; and decathlon, Irving Mondschein.

In 1944, the fiftieth anniversary of the revival of the modern Olympic Games was celebrated at the IOC headquarters in Lausanne. London hosted the Games of the XIVth Olympiad in 1948, undertaking its second Olympic Games with more advance notice but more severe problems than was the case in 1908. The 1944 Games, it might be said, were merely postponed four years, giving London time to begin to recover from the war and allowing Helsinki until 1952 to prepare for an Olympic Games promised since 1938.

BIBLIOGRAPHICAL ESSAY

The IOC archives in Lausanne have some material on the XIIIth Olympiad, including the candidature reports, which describe events leading to the selection of London for the 1944 Games. There are no references to the 1944 London Games in the printed guide to the Avery Brundage Collection at the University of Illinois.

A few more general histories of the Olympics discuss the World War II years and the efforts of the IOC to keep the movement alive during difficult times. See Allen Guttmann, *The Olympics: A History of the Modern Games* (Urbana, Ill., 1992), and Alexander M. Weyand, *The Olympic Pageant* (New York, 1952), which has a chapter on the ''lost years.''

Martin J. Manning

LONDON 1948

THE GAMES OF THE XIVTH OLYMPIAD

Both the 1940 and 1944 Olympic Games were cancelled because of World War II. The 1940 Olympics had originally gone to Japan, with the Summer Games scheduled for Tokyo and Sapporo hosting the Winter Games. But the Japanese invasion of China caused the International Olympic Committee (IOC) to pull the Games out of Japan, with the summer Olympiad now going to Helsinki, Finland, and the Winter Games to Garmisch-Partenkirchen, Germany. When Germany attacked Poland less than five months before the opening of the Winter Games, and later when the Soviet Union invaded Finland, the IOC officially, finally, and mercifully canceled the Games of the XIIth Olympiad. The IOC had received applications for the 1944 Summer Games, the unlucky XIIIth, from Budapest, Lausanne, Helsinki, Athens, London, Detroit, and Rome. From a final list that included Detroit, London, Lausanne, and Rome, the IOC in June 1939 chose London to host the Summer Games, which of course would be cancelled, along with the Winter Games, which had been awarded to Cortina d'Ampezzo, Italy, because of the continuing hostilities. The Greeks at least had enough sense to halt warfare during the ancient Olympic Games.

After a twelve-year absence, the Olympic spectacle resumed in London with the Summer Games of the XIVth Olympiad. Immediately after the end of World War II the members of the IOC decided that it would be possible to stage the Games in 1948. The executive committee of the IOC convened in London, August 21–24, 1945, to select the venues for the 1948 Games. The cities of Baltimore, Los Angeles, Minneapolis, Philadelphia, Lausanne, and London all had expressed interest in hosting the Summer Games. The U.S. cities had strong support because of the enthusiasm shown by the Americans for the Olympics and their apparent willingness to back up that enthusiasm with finances. But the members of the committee decided that the American cities were too far away for affordable travel in the austere postwar years, so attention focused on London, the proposed site of the ill-fated 1944 Games. The fact that some of the facilities for the Games had been in place before the war helped London's cause. So in 1946 all the IOC members by a postal vote granted the Games of the XIVth Olympiad to London. As compensation for the Swiss not getting the Summer Games in Lausanne, the IOC awarded the Winter Games to St. Moritz in September 1946.

To London then fell the unenviable task of lighting the Olympic flame in a world vastly different from that of 1936. Although Germany and Japan had suffered terribly in the maelstrom of defeat and destruction of World War II, following the precedent of World War I these two losers received no invitations to participate in the Games. The United States with its ''atomic bombshells'' or ''giant firecrackers'' had now eclipsed Great Britain as the premier Western power. By 1946, the United States was beginning to take note of an expansionist Soviet Union, in a confrontation that by the time of the Games would be expressed in terms of "containment," and a "cold war," with "iron curtains" descending across Europe. Indeed it is ironic that London, the heart of the once-mighty British Empire, should be chosen as the site for the revival of the Summer Olympics, surely a time to revel in the joy of victory with the prospect of peace and prosperity that it held. But Great Britain emerged from the war a net loser, not a winner, with its power, prestige, and standard of living diminished and its empire ever more threatened. What allowed Britain to play any leading role at all in world affairs was the "special relationship" with the United States. With the economy in distress, many Britons were concerned about the high cost of the Games, particularly in light of the fact that Britain was still recovering from the war. Although the *London Evening Standard,* owned by Lord Beaverbrook, a staunch foe of the government, railed against the Games, polls showed that a majority of Britons supported them.

Financial hardship aside, some critics argued there should be no revival of the Games, because to encourage a display of nationalistic rivalry so soon after the war would be sheer folly. But the traditional supporters of the Games as a vehicle for the promotion of international understanding and brotherhood also had something to say. For example, Benjamin Welles, a *New York Times* reporter, wrote about the mystical Olympic moment when

for the British people, weary from two World Wars in thirty years and separated by only twenty-one miles from a Europe split and tense with international strife, the sight of young men and women from the Balkans, from Scandinavia, from Western Europe and from the Middle East, from the Moslem world, from the British Empire and from the Western Hemisphere . . . generally competing side by side, will have a tonic effect.

Like any other modern international sporting event, contemporary political issues had some impact on the London Olympics of 1948, particularly with regard to the participation of the Soviet Union in the Olympic movement. Although Russia had not participated in the Olympics since 1912, the Soviets had always been interested in sports, and by the time of World War II they wanted to participate actively in international sport. Some Olympic leaders, such as Avery Brundage, had always viewed the Soviets with a great deal of suspicion, stemming not just from a difference in political ideology but also from a belief that the Soviets might undermine the hallowed concept of amateurism. Brundage, then vice president of the IOC, became alarmed when he heard that the Soviets trained with the specific purpose of breaking world records. Brundage found the thought of someone getting paid for breaking a record particularly repulsive. He also believed that the true object of the Soviets in joining the Olympic movement was to humiliate the West, and therefore he adamantly opposed the admission of communists to the IOC. Although the London Olympics witnessed the first athletes from communist countries, and the first defections, the Soviet Union did not form a national Olympic committee and formally seek recognition and was therefore ineligible to receive an invitation to the Games. However, the Soviets did send observers to the Games, and they participated in the Helsinki Games of 1952. IOC officials also had to grapple with the question of the recognition of Israel, with the Arab countries threatening to boycott if the Israeli flag flew at the opening ceremonies. To avoid a potential flashpoint, the IOC, based on a technicality, excluded Israel from any participation in the Games.

A number of political incidents at the 1948 Games presaged the increasing politicalization of the post-1948 Olympic Games. A minor fracas developed when two swimmers from Northern Ireland were denied permission to compete for the team from Ireland. The Greek Olympic Committee protested to the IOC that communist Greek guerrillas had attempted to sabotage the Greek team during the opening ceremonies. An Italian reporter denied credentials to the Games accused the British government of harassing him because he was a communist. The British replied that they had enough evidence to consider him a threat. Romania pulled out of the Games because the Soviet Union and other Eastern bloc countries failed to get seats on the IOC. And a Soviet magazine questioned the motives of the U.S. Olympic Committee when it offered to feed all the athletes at the London Games. Such quarrels, some trivial and some not, would come to mark the postwar, media-dominated Olympics, for as historian Richard Espy has written in *The Politics of the Olympics*, ''The formative period for the postwar Olympics—1944–1948—was also the formative period of the post war world.''

Despite Beaverbrook's grumbling about costs, the Games seemed to go well, and as they went on, interest among Londoners increased. The number of competing nations reached fifty-nine, with over 4,000 competitors, of whom 385 were women. Track and field events for women were increased to nine with the addition of the 200-meter run, the long jump, and the shot put. Running events were conducted on a special temporary track laid at Wembley Stadium, built for the 1924–1925 Empire Exhibition, and other buildings from the exposition were pressed into service for radio, television, and the press. Athletes were housed in school buildings or at service camps in nearby Uxbridge and Richmond Park. Total expenditure came to about £750,000 and the whole affair made a modest profit of between £10,000 and £20,000. As with so much else in the postwar world, the United States was dominant in the 1948 Summer Games, capturing eighty-four medals, thirty-eight of which were gold, far ahead of Sweden, which finished with forty-four medals, including sixteen gold. Never again would the United States be so strong in a postwar Summer Olympics. The host country, Great Britain, did not fare that well, capturing twenty-three medals, with only three gold. Weather for the track and field competition was problematic, with rain falling nearly every day. Nonetheless, three competitors distinguished themselves despite the conditions. Fanny Blankers-Koen, a thirty-year-old Dutch housewife, known as the ''Marvelous Mama'' and the

"Flying Dutchwoman," captured the 200-meter dash to go along with her victories in the 100-meter dash and the 80-meter hurdles. She also anchored the
400-meter relay team. If Blankers-Koen had competed in the long jump, she
almost certainly would have won since the winning distance was nearly 2 feet
short of her world record. Among the Americans, the husky, handsome, sev-
enteen-year-old Robert Bruce Mathias from Tulare, California, won the Olympic
decathlon just eight weeks after competing in his first decathlon and seemed to
symbolize the new postwar American confidence. Whether pole vaulting on a
rain-soaked surface at night with the aid of a flashlight, or staggering, soaked,
weary, and hungry, to the end of the 1,500 meters and victory in the decathlon,
Mathias came to symbolize American grit and determination. His stunning performance in 1948 is considered one of the greatest Olympic exploits of all time,
and it made him an American hero and rocketed him into a political career. The
great Czech runner Emil Zatopek, called "The Machine," also made his debut
in London, winning the 10,000 meters in Olympic record time, thus setting
himself up for even greater accomplishments in Helsinki.

The track and field competition and the Games themselves ended on a note
that was both humorous and somewhat reminiscent of the controversies during
the previous London Games forty years earlier. On the last day of the competition, the 400-meter relay final took place before a crowd of 83,000 in Wembley
Stadium. The American team of Barney Ewell, Lorenzo Wright, Harrison Dil-
lard, and Mel Patton was expected to beat the British team easily—and indeed
it did, by a full 6 yards. But while the American team members celebrated their
victory, they heard the shocking news that they had been disqualified because
a judge had ruled that Ewell had handed the baton to Wright outside the legal
passing zone. The British team now mounted the pedestal to the strains of "God
Save the King." British honor had been preserved with this one and only victory
in track and field, something British fans had been yearning for during the entire
Games. But the story did not end there. The Americans appealed; the Olympic
jury of appeal made a careful study of the films of the race and reached the
conclusion that the pass had been perfectly legal. Two days after the event, it
was officially announced that the United States relay team had won, and the
British were forced to hand over their gold medals to the strains of "The Star-
Spangled Banner." Italy had to give up its silver medals to the British, and the
Hungarian team, now the fourth-place finisher, ended up with nothing. It was a
tragicomical end to the track and field competition.

A final assessment of the historical importance of the 1948 London Games
reveals a mixed bag. On the one hand, Richard Mandell lumps together all of
the games from 1948 to 1956 with the following comment: "However important
they were for their hosts and however tight the strain on the war-damaged
economies, they were not grandly expensive and did not have major political
consequences. . . . None of these festivals was significantly advanced in its techniques or festive trappings over the Winter and Summer Games in 1936" (Mandell, *Sport: A Cultural History,* p. 246). Perhaps Mandell is too harsh in his

assessment, because in many ways the 1948 Olympics—the revived, postwar version—did hint at the political tone and style that became more fully expressed in all subsequent Olympiads down to at least the Seoul Games of 1988. Also the 1948 London Games gave at least an inkling of the power of the Olympic image on film and television. The Rank Corporation produced the first color film of the Olympic Games in 1948. Television was in its infancy; there were some 80,000 television sets in Great Britain in 1948, and the number of people who saw the Games totaled only half a million, or about 1 percent of the British population. The London Summer Games of 1948 may appear modest in comparison to more recent Olympic extravaganzas, but they are hardly without consequence.

BIBLIOGRAPHICAL ESSAY

There appears to be no central repository for documents, records, ephemera, or other materials relating to the 1948 London Summer Olympics in London itself, so the place to look is at the archives of the IOC in Lausanne, Switzerland. The British Olympic Association should also be contacted directly for material. Other potential sources for the 1948 Games include the archives of the Greater London Boroughs, which can be accessed through the Greater London Archive Network (GLAN) and the BBC Written Archives Centre, Reading, Berkshire. Also, British government records in the Public Record Office in London may yield information on the government's involvement, and the British Library newspaper collection at Colindale, London, provides journalistic information.

The organizing committee's official report to the IOC is Lord Burghley, ed., *The Official Report of the Organizing Committee for the XIV Olympiad* (London, 1951). The committee also published a number of related works, including *Catalogue of the XIVth Olympiad Sport in Art Exhibition* (London, 1948), and *Olympic Games, London 1948. Official Souvenir* (London, 1948), as well as daily programs, a visitors' guide, and team handbooks. The British Olympic Association's report is Cecil Bear, ed., *The Official Report of the London Olympic Games* (London, 1948), while the U.S. counterpart is Asa S. Bushnell, ed., *Report of the United States Olympic Committee: XIV Olympiad, London, England; V Olympic Winter Games, St. Moritz, Switzerland* (New York, 1949), which provides a wealth of information about the participation of the United States in the Games, and is worth consulting.

Researchers may wish to consult Nelson C. Hart, Robert Kerr, and Alex Muir, eds., *Canada Competes at the Olympic Games 1948: Official Report of the Canadian Olympic Association, 1938–1948* (Montreal, 1948); Johann Bernhard, ed., *Iceland's Olympic Team at the Games in London 1948* (Reykjavik, 1949); and Kurt Gassman, ed., *Rapport sur la participation Suisse aux Jeux Olympiques de Londres 1948/Bericht über die Teilnahme der Schweiz an den XIV. Olympischen Spielen in London vom 29. Juli–14. August 1948* (Lausanne, 1948).

Among secondary works, Desmond Laing, *XIV Olympiad: An Illustrated Record* (London, 1948), provides an illustrated behind-the-scenes look at the people who made the Games possible. H. J. Osten, *Olympiade 1948* (London, 1948), and Arthur Heinzmann, *Die Spiele der XIV. Olympiade St. Moritz und London* (Zurich, 1948), are pictorial records. Richard Espy, *The Politics of the Olympics* (Berkeley, 1979) provides some insight into the political issues of these Games, while Richard Mandell, *Sport: A Cultural History* (New York, 1984) assesses the Games critically.

Readers may also wish to consult specific newspaper or magazine accounts of the 1948 London Olympics, such as ''American Athletes Sweep the Olympics,'' *Life,* August 23, 1948, pp. 28–32, or ''Golden Boys, the Californians,'' *Time,* August 23, 1948 p. 34.

Richard A. Voeltz

HELSINKI 1952

THE GAMES OF THE XVth OLYMPIAD

On July 20, 1952, 70,000 spectators filled the Olympic Stadium at Helsinki, Finland, to witness the opening ceremonies of the XVth Olympic Games. The formalities revolved around a celebration of Finland's sportive past. Finnish officials, in their bid to host the Summer Olympics in Helsinki, maintained that Finland deserved the honor because of its contributions to the Olympic movement. Finns, for example, had dominated Olympic distance running before World War II, and living legends from that era, Paavo Nurmi and Hannes Kolehmainen, who shared fifteen Olympic medals between them, participated in the festivities. Nurmi carried the Olympic torch into the stadium and ignited one of two Olympic flames, before passing the torch to several young relay runners, who carried it to the top of a 72.71-meter tower, erected to commemorate the Olympic record set by javelin thrower Matti Järvinen at Los Angeles in 1932. There, Kolehmainen, the grandfather of Finnish Olympic distance running, received the torch and ignited the other flame. Finally, Heikki Savolaimen, a champion gymnast of the 1930s and 1940s, recited the oath for the record 4,925 athletes who had gathered in Helsinki for what would be history's finest Olympic competition to date.

While the opening ceremonies of the 1952 Olympic Games provided Finland with a glance back at its Olympic past, the Games gave the world a glimpse of the economic and political dilemmas that would haunt future Games. Despite proposals to curtail the size of the Games, Helsinki staged what then would be the largest Olympic gathering up to that time, signaling a move toward larger and costlier spectacles. The participation of nations that had been geographically altered by cold war politics, such as Germany, posed a problem for the International Olympic Committee (IOC) on the eve of Helsinki, since the IOC could recognize only one team from specific geographic and cultural regions. China, represented by both the governments of the mainland communists and the exiled nationalists, posed a similar ordeal. The participation of the Soviet Union, the first by a Russian team in four decades, transformed the Olympics into a cold war battleground. Moreover, the Soviets introduced a controversial new performer to the Olympics, the state amateur, whose training and livelihood were subsidized entirely by government resources.

On June 21, 1947, the IOC, meeting in Stockholm, selected Helsinki from nine candidates to host the 1952 Summer Olympics. The IOC reached the decision on its second ballot, in which Helsinki received the fifteen votes necessary for approval, after missing affirmation on the first ballot by 1 vote. On the final ballot, Los Angeles and Minneapolis received 5 votes each and Amsterdam 3. Chicago and Philadelphia failed to receive any votes on either ballot. Europeans favored Helsinki over U.S. cities because many European nations, with their economies still recovering from war, could not afford to send a team to the United States. For many observers, however, the decision was considered a consolation for Finland, which had to withdraw from hosting the 1940 Summer Olympics because of its war with the Soviet Union. Moreover, the Finns, who had maintained that they should have hosted the 1948 Summer Olympics, were disheartened by the selection of London to host that event.

The IOC's decision to award Helsinki the 1952 Summer Olympics ignited passions of Finnish nationalism. On the day of the decision, radio stations in Helsinki interrupted programming to announce the good news, which sounded throughout the streets from loudspeakers mounted for the occasion. The Finnish national anthem followed the announcement, and Helsinkites stood at attention while flags were hoisted throughout the city. Eric von Frenckell, the deputy mayor of Helsinki and the president of the Helsinki Olympic Organizing Committee, thanked the IOC for the award and Finland's Scandinavian neighbor Sweden for withdrawing its nomination of Stockholm as a site for the 1952 Summer Olympics.

Helsinki embarked on major preparations for the Olympics after the Finnish parliament guaranteed the city 300 million Finnish marks ($1.25 million) for renovation of its sports facilities, construction of an Olympic Village, and other civic improvements. State and municipal funding for the Games appeared doubtful in late 1949, when a rift between the conservative Finnish Gymnastics and Athletic Union and the liberal Workers Athletic Union over representation in international sports federations angered the Social Democrats. While von Frenckell swore that he would finance the Games personally, even if he had to go begging in the streets, the issue was resolved when the two athletic unions agreed to share representation in the international sports federations and the Helsinki Olympic Organizing Committee. Olavi Sunanto, president of the Workers Athletic Union, and Aksli Kaskela, vice president of the Finnish Gymnastic and Athletic Union, both served as the vice presidents of the Helsinki Olympic Organizing Committee.

For the 1952 Summer Olympics, Helsinki refurbished the various stadiums built for the ill-fated 1940 Games. The main Olympic stadium, which had first been used for track and field competition in 1938, had its seating capacity increased from 60,000 to 70,000 and its track resurfaced and widened from seven to eight lanes. The seating capacity of the swimming and diving arena was increased fourfold to 8,000, and the pools were equipped with heaters, to maintain the water temperature above 24 degrees Celsius (75 degrees Fahrenheit). A new heated swimming pool was completed at Hämeenlinna, the site of the modern pentathlon. The Taivallahti rowing facility, first used in 1938, was replaced by one farther north, since the International Rowing Association considered the site too exposed to brisk ocean breezes.

Helsinki's paramount problem in preparing for the 1952 Olympic Games was providing housing for more than 5,000 athletes and team personnel. A new Olympic Village was required for the upcoming Olympics, since the one built for the 1940 Games had been converted into public housing. In the fall of 1950, construction began on a new village, near the original one at the Käpylä athletic grounds. Fourteen three- and four-story apartment buildings, similar to those built in 1939, were finished in late 1951. After the Games, these structures too became public housing units. Helsinki built a second Olympic Village at Otaniemi, site of the Finnish Institute of Technology, 6 miles from Helsinki. After the Games, this village became student dormitories. Finally, the Helsinki Nursing School at Töölö provided housing for female athletes.

In addition to housing the Olympic teams, Helsinki, with a population of only 400,000, also had to provide lodging for nearly 200,000 other Olympic visitors. Hotels, which could accommodate up to 4,000 guests, lodged the members of sixteen international sports federations and related organizations that held annual conventions in conjunction with the Olympics. Broadcasters, journalists, and media technicians also occupied the hotels. The Helsinki Olympic Organizing Committee made additional arrangements for other Olympic guests. By April 1951, the committee had arranged for over 100,000 visitors to stay in private homes, apartments, school dormitories, military barracks, and campsites throughout Helsinki.

Helsinki's preparations for housing illustrated the growing concern over the increasing size of the Olympic Games. In 1948, London's difficulty in providing room and board for a record 4,099 competitors encouraged the IOC to consider reducing the size of the 1952 Olympic program. In 1949 Avery Brundage, IOC vice president and the chief spokesman for streamlining the Olympic program, recommended reductions in men's gymnastics, rowing, and walking and women's track and field. Lauri Miettinen, president of the Finnish Athletic Federation and member of the Helsinki Olympic Organizing Committee, supported Brundage's proposals for reducing pedestrian events and women's athletics. However, the IOC's final decision was to retain the London program, increase the number of weight classifications in boxing, and expand women's gymnastics. To limit the number of contestants, the IOC decided to hold preliminary rounds in basketball, soccer, volleyball, field hockey, and water polo outside Helsinki before the official start of the Games. The IOC also voted to change the art competition to an exhibition, which the local organizing committee was responsible for administering.

The debate over the size and content of the program of the 1952 Summer Olympics paled in comparison to the IOC's dilemma in recognizing Olympic committees of nations geographically and politically altered after World War II. Of the former Axis powers, only Italy had competed in the 1948 Olympic Games; Germany and Japan, each still under military occupation, had not formed national Olympic committees. In 1951, the IOC recognized the Japanese Olympic Committee, organized under the supervision of General Douglas MacArthur, Supreme Commander of the Allied Powers governing postwar Japan. Recognition of a German Olympic Committee, however, posed a problem for the IOC, since two nations now existed where there was once one. In the fall of 1949, the western region, occupied by the Allied powers, formed the Federal Republic of Germany, and the eastern region, occupied by the Soviet Union, became the German Democratic Republic. Under IOC rules, only one Olympic committee and one team could represent a single geographic and cultural region.

In 1950, both Germanys formed national Olympic committees, but only the Federal Republic of Germany sought immediate recognition from the IOC. The West German Olympic Committee consisted principally of individuals who had belonged to the German Olympic Committee recognized by the IOC before the war. The IOC provisionally recognized the new organization, pending an apology for the atrocities committed by Germany during the war. Following the apology of the West Germans, the IOC executive committee recommended that the organization receive full recognition in 1951 and an invitation to participate in the 1952 Olympic Games. Meanwhile, the IOC learned of the formation of an Olympic committee by the German Democratic Republic and its application for membership to the various international sports federations. Faced with the dilemma of possibly having to recognize two separate German Olympic committees, the IOC urged the sports federations not to recognize the East Germans until it could deal with them at the 1951 IOC meeting.

In 1951, the IOC took up the German question. In their application to the IOC, the East Germans stipulated that only one organization should represent Germany. Western Europe and American IOC representatives maintained that the West German Committee fulfilled that purpose, providing a single Olympic committee to represent all of Germany. However, the Soviets and the Eastern Europeans supported the East Germans, contending that the German Democratic Republic, as a sovereign nation, should have its own national Olympic committee. Since the IOC failed to resolve the German question at Vienna, IOC president J. Sigfrid Edström postponed further deliberations until the executive committee met in Lausanne later that year. Before Lausanne, however, the Germans held a meeting in Hanover, in which the East demanded equal representation on a single German Olympic committee. At Lausanne, a more conciliatory East German contingent agreed to join in a single German Olympic team. The East German government, however, denounced the Lausanne agreement and demoted the members of the Olympic committee responsible for the agreement.

The rebuke of the Lausanne agreement was a setback to the IOC, which believed that persuading the Germans to form a single team would be a triumph for the Olympic movement. The IOC tried once more to bring about a compromise between the East and West Germans, by scheduling a special conference in Copenhagen. The Copenhagen conference was a disaster. The East Germans arrived in the Danish capital several hours late because of a circuitous train trip; exhausted, they wanted to rest before talking to the IOC Executive Board and the West Germans, but the latter groups demanded an immediate meeting. But the meeting never occurred, and all sides left Copenhagen without reaching any resolution. Edström then declared that only one team would represent East and West Germany at Helsinki. Despite continued efforts by the East Germans to negotiate with the IOC, the organization decided not to take up the German question again until after Helsinki. Since the East declined offers from the West to try out for the German Olympic team, no athletes from East Germany participated in the 1952 Summer Olympics.

The participation of China in the 1952 Summer Olympics presented the IOC with a similar dilemma. Following the communist triumph in China in 1949, the three-member Chinese Olympic Committee disbanded, with one member remaining in Beijing and the others taking up residence in Hong Kong and New York. In its place, the communists organized the All China Athletic Federation, which claimed authority over Chinese amateur sport. Throughout early 1952, the All China Athletic Federation approached the IOC for recognition and the Helsinki Olympic Organizing Committee for an invitation to the 1952 Summer Olympics. Meanwhile, the IOC heard nothing from the nationalists, exiled in Taiwan, about organizing an Olympic committee and participating in the Games. More important, the Finnish government recognized only the People's Republic as the legitimate government of China. Although the Helsinki Olympic Organizing Committee invited only the People's Republic to participate in the 1952 Summer Olympics, it received word that teams from the People's Republic and Taiwan, both representing China, would be coming to Helsinki.

As in the case of Germany, only one Chinese Olympic Committee could be recognized by the IOC, and only one team could represent China in the 1952 Summer Olympics. Since the communists and the nationalists were unwilling to form a single committee and team, Edström proposed that the IOC bar both the People's Republic and Taiwan from participating in the 1952 Summer Olympics and postpone a final decision on the two Chinas until 1953. However, the IOC agreed to permit both teams to compete at Helsinki, but only in those sports in which they belonged to international federations. The nationalist Chinese protested the ruling by withdrawing their one-man team from the Games. Globally, the decision was considered compensation for the People's Republic of China, which had been denied membership in the United Nations. In the United States, popular opinion condemned the decision because the People's Republic was an ally of North Korea in the ongoing Korean War. In the end, however, the People's Republic did not participate at all since its team did not arrive in Helsinki until July 29, just five days before the end of competition.

The entire weight of the cold war descended upon the 1952 Summer Olympics with the entry of the Soviet Union. Although invited to participate in the 1948 Summer Olympics, the Soviet Union had declined, maintaining that its athletes were not ready for international competition. Instead, Soviet observers attended the London Games and made careful observations. Between London and Helsinki, the Soviet Union had built an impressive athletic force, which made significant gains in nearly every Olympic sport, especially track and field. The Soviet Union won the European Track and Field Championships in 1950, and many of its female performers held world records in the weight throwing events by 1952. The sensational rise of the postwar Soviet athlete resulted from the development of a highly centralized and state-supported sports authority, which selected potential performers early in life, subsidized their training, and awarded them materially for championship and record-breaking performances.

Despite recognizing the Soviet Olympic Committee officially in 1951, the IOC still remained uncertain about the amateur status of Soviet athletes. As early as 1946, Brundage had warned Edström that the Soviets did not understand the meaning of amateurism, pointing out that Soviet athletes were trained at the expense of the state and paid for breaking world records. While Constantin Andrianov, head of the Soviet Olympic Committee, assured the IOC that his nation would uphold the amateur ideal, Brundage sternly questioned him about past allegations of state-supported training and cash awards. Andreanov answered that those practices might have occurred in the past but were no longer routine. He insisted that most athletes were either students supported by the state or government employees in civil service, education, or the military. Brundage, who doubted the sincerity of the Soviet's remarks, officially noted that different sportive ideals had polarized East and West and that state amateurism would be an ongoing dilemma for the Olympic movement.

Besides Brundage, officials of the U.S. government expressed concern over the entry of the Soviet Union into the Olympics. Before the Amateur Athletic Union (AAU) in December 1951, Richard B. Walsh, of the State Department, argued that the Soviets intended to use sport as an international propaganda tool, to demonstrate the advantages of socialism over capitalism through their athletic prowess. Ironically, Walsh called upon the AAU to counter the Soviet athletic threat through the promotion of democracy through American sportsmanship. In May 1952, Walsh and other American sports officials tried to persuade the IOC to permit a team of exiled Eastern European athletes, represented by the Union of Free Eastern European Sportsmen, to compete in the 1952 Summer Olympic Games. The IOC rejected the proposal, however, because the athletes came from several nations and thus did not represent a single geographic and cultural entity.

On June 3, 1952, the Soviet Union officially announced that it would participate in the Helsinki Games. Soviet officials demanded, however, that their team, as well as those from Eastern Europe and the People's Republic of China, be housed separately from those of the United States and Western Europe. The Finns, who wanted their Olympics to proceed without a major diplomatic rift, especially with the Soviet Union, assigned the Russians and their satellites to the Olympic Village at Otaniemi. Although the Soviets feared the influence of the West on socialist athletes, they nonetheless opened their camp to Western reporters and Olympians. However, the Soviets brought only their most trusted performers to Helsinki, leaving behind those considered politically unreliable, such as Heinno Lipp, the Estonian-born shot put and decathlon champion.

Despite the initial warmth of the Soviet Olympic team, a cold war chill settled over the competition, especially between the Soviet Union and the United States. Bob Mathias, the American Olympic decathlon champion, captured the tone of the Games when he remarked that defeating the Soviet Union was not the same as "beating some friendly country like Australia" (Richard Espy, *Politics of the Olympic Games,* p. 38). The rivalry between the Soviet Union and the United States was amplified by daily press accounts of the team scores. With outstanding performances in women's track and field and gymnastics, the Soviet Union assumed a lead over the United States that lasted until the last day of competition, when the United States, with powerful performances in swimming, basketball, and boxing, surpassed the Soviet Union for the team title. Prior to the start of the Games, the Soviets tried to persuade the IOC to recognize a team score at Helsinki, but the IOC rejected the idea because of its blatant identification with nationalism. Brundage, the IOC president-elect, remarked that nationalism would not tarnish the Olympics under his tenure.

If a single event dramatized the rivalry between the Soviet Union and the United States, it was the 3,000-meter steeplechase. Favored to win the race was Soviet Vladimir Kazantsev, who held the world record of 8 minutes, 48.4 seconds. His top American opponent, Horace Ashenfelter, a 27-year-old FBI agent, whose personal best time was 9 minutes, 6.4 seconds, seemed an unlikely threat. In the final, however, the American took the lead after the first kilometer, with the Russian running closely at his shoulder. Kazantsev pulled ahead the final 200 meters but stumbled after the final water jump. Ashenfelter, who successfully cleared the obstacle, won the race in a world record of 8 minutes, 45.4 seconds. American sportswriters quipped that never before had an FBI man allowed a Russian to follow him so closely.

The 1952 Summer Olympics witnessed more record-setting performances than any previous Games. Unquestionably, the outstanding achievement was the gold medal sweep of the long-distance running events by Czechoslovakia's Emil Zatopek. Zatopek, an army lieutenant, was the defending Olympic champion in the 10,000 meters. At Helsinki, he not only defended his 10,000-meter title, but he also captured the 5,000 meters as well, setting Olympic records in both events. No runner since Kolehmainen in 1912 had won both the 5,000 and 10,000 meters in a single Olympic Games. Zatopek also entered the marathon, a race in which he had no experience. After 20 miles, the Czech army officer moved ahead of his competition and won in an Olympic record of 2 hours, 23 minutes, 3.2 seconds. Although no other runner since has duplicated Zatopek's feat, Finland's Lasse Viren finished fifth in the marathon after winning the 5,000 and 10,000 meters at the 1976 Summer Olympics.

Whereas Zatopek, like other Eastern European athletes, returned to his homeland after the Games, Panait Calcai, a Romanian marksman, chose to remain in Helsinki and seek political asylum in the West. Calcai, who had been considered politically unreliable by Romanian authorities, initiated his escape by leaving a knapsack at Otaniemi. He was permitted to return to the Olympic Village to retrieve his belongings but with a Romanian secret police officer as escort. After they returned to Helsinki, Calcai told his escort that he was not returning to Romania, and a fight erupted between them. Arrested by Helsinki police for disturbing the peace, both were jailed but soon released from custody. As they were walking out of the police station, a bystander who had witnessed the fisticuffs motioned Calcai into his car, whisked him away to a private home, and introduced him to an underground organization that provided shelter and assistance to political refugees. A *New York Times* editorial lauded Calcai, who had finished sixth in the rapid-fire pistol contest, as a champion in the race for freedom.

Except for the Calcai affair, the 1952 Summer Olympic Games ended without any major incident. On August 3, 1952, the record sixty-nine nations marched into the Olympic stadium one last time, Edström made his final remarks as IOC president, the Olympic flame flickered out, and the mayor of London handed the Olympic flag over to his Helsinki counterpart for safekeeping until the 1956 Summer Olympics in Melbourne, Australia. For the people of Helsinki, who had sought the Olympics since 1935, the Games were a shining success, especially in the manner the city handled the record number of athletes, sports officials, media personnel, and spectators. For Finland, the Olympic year marked a major turning point, as the nation paid the final installment of war reparations to the Soviet Union. In that sense, the 1952 Summer Olympics were a celebration of Finnish autonomy as the country moved toward establishing cordial relations with its former enemy as well as the rest of the world.

For the Olympic movement itself, the 1952 Summer Olympics also marked a significant turning point. After Helsinki, the Summer Olympic Games became larger and much costlier affairs, leaving some hosts in great debt. The expense of the Olympics discouraged many potential hosts, even those that already had been awarded the Games, as when Denver, Colorado, residents voted against staging the 1976 Winter Olympics. The problem of recognizing Olympic committees and teams from nations by cold war politics was resolved in the settlement of the China question in 1959, as the IOC recognized the nationalist Chinese as Formosa, the name of the island held by the nationalists. The decision to use the name of the territory in which the Olympic committee operated provided a precedent for recognizing teams from East Germany, North and South Korea, and North and South Vietnam. For the next four decades, the Olympics served as a theater for the dramatization of the cold war tensions separating East and West. However, the introduction of the state amateur perhaps had the greatest impact on the Olympics, because in order to preserve the harmony between East and West, IOC officials tended to ignore the continued state support of athletes from the East, while vigorously enforcing the amateur code against athletes of the West. By establishing this double standard, the IOC itself ironically signaled the end of the late-nineteenth-century definition of amateurism.

BIBLIOGRAPHICAL ESSAY

The Avery Brundage Collection at the University of Illinois Archives, Urbana, Illinois, contains a substantial amount of primary source material for the Helsinki Games: organizing committee publications, newspaper clippings, data on film and television, and information on the political questions surrounding the Games. Other primary sources are housed at the Olympic Museum in the main Olympic stadium in Helsinki.

The chief primary source for this essay was the *XV Olympiad Official News-Service,* 16 vols. (November 1949–August 1952). This bulletin of the Organizing Committee for the Helsinki Games 1952 chronicles in great detail the local preparations for the 1952 Olympic Games. Much of this information is summarized in the committee's official report, Sulo Kolkka, ed., *The Official Report of the Organizing Committee for the Games of the XV Olympiad Helsinki 1952* (Porvoo, Finland, 1955). The Helsinki Organizing Committee also published a pamphlet, *Olympic Games, Helsinki, 1952* (1952). The British Olympic Association prepared two publications on the 1952 Olympic Games: Harold M. Abrahams and Jack Crump, eds., *Olympic Games; XVth Olympiad, Helsinki, 1952* (London, 1952), and Cecil Bear, ed., *Official Report of the XVth Olympic Games, Helsinki, July 19–August 3, 1952* (London, 1952). The U.S. Olympic Committee's official report is Asa S. Bushnell, ed., *United States 1952 Olympic Book: Quadrennial Report of the United States Olympic Committee* (New York, 1953). A Soviet publication that describes the rise of the Soviet athletes and their success at Helsinki is *Soviet Olympic Champions* (English trans.) (Moscow, 1954). The position of the U.S. State Department is best described in Richard B. Walsh, ''The Soviet Athlete in International Competition,'' *Department of State Bulletin,* December 24, 1951, pp. 1007–10. Popular magazines and newspapers, which provided thorough coverage of the Games, complement these sources.

For secondary literature on the 1952 Olympic Games, begin with Max L. and Reet Howell, ''The 1952 Helsinki Olympic Games: Another Turning Point?'' in Peter J. Graham and Horst Überhorst, eds., *The Modern Olympics* (West Point, N.Y., 1978), pp. 182–93. The Howells emphasize the entry of the Soviet Union, its rivalry with the United States, and the impact of the state amateur as making the 1952 Summer Olympics a turning point. The rise of Soviet sport and Soviet participation in the Olympics has attracted much scholarly attention. For that literature, begin with James Riordan, *Sport in Soviet Society: Development of Sport and Physical Education in Russia and the USSR* (Cambridge, 1977). Essays on the history, organization, structure, and function of sport in the Soviet Union, Eastern bloc, and China are in James Riordan, ed., *Sport under Communism* (Canberra, 1978). Other useful examinations of Soviet sport include Henry W. Morton, *Soviet Sport: Mirror of Soviet Society* (New York, 1963), and N. Norman Schneiderman, *The Soviet Road to Olympus: Theory and Practice of Soviet Physical Culture and Sport* (Toronto, 1978). For a more popular critique of Soviet sport, see Yuri Brokhin, *The Big Red Machine: The Rise and Fall of Soviet Olympic Champions,* trans. Glenn Ganelik and Yuri Brokhin (New York, 1977).

A thorough, scholarly treatment of the German and Chinese questions is Richard Espy, *Politics of the Olympic Games* (Berkeley, Calif., 1979). John M. Hoberman, *Sport and Political Ideology* (London, 1984), provides a Marxist critique of the rise of sport in the Soviet Union, East Germany, and China. For a broad consideration of postwar international sports, see David B. Kanin, ''Superpower Sport in Cold War and Détente,'' in Benjamin Lowe et al., eds., *Sport and International Relations* (Champaign, Ill., 1978), pp. 249–63. G. Carr, ''The Use of Sport in the German Democratic Republic for the Promotion of National Consciousness and International Prestige,'' *Journal of Sport History* 1 (Fall 1974): 123–36, examines the political and diplomatic context of sport in the German Democratic Republic. Useful, but too sympathetic to the East German sports system, is Doug Gilbert, *The Miracle Machine* (New York, 1980). Barclay F. Gordon,

Olympic Architecture: Building for the Summer Games (New York, 1983), provides a thorough examination of the design, construction, and renovation of the stadiums and Olympic Villages used during the 1952 Summer Olympic Games. For the story of Finland's contribution to Olympic distance running, see Matti Hannus, *Flying Finns* (Helsinki, 1990).

Adam R. Hornbuckle

MELBOURNE 1956

THE GAMES OF THE XVITH OLYMPIAD

Only one year after the end of the World War II, a group of Victorians banded together to bring the 1956 Olympic Games to Melbourne. The Victorian Olympic Council (VOC) had reserves of just 6 pounds, 7 shillings, 10 pence (less than 13 Australian dollars) when it reconvened in June 1946, its first meeting in seven years. It is not surprising that there was much laughter when Ronald Aitken moved a motion for the VOC to apply for Melbourne to host an Olympic Games. However, the motion was accepted unanimously.

Several Australian cities had previously put forward proposals to host the Olympics. Soon after the inaugural modern Olympic Games in 1896, Melbourne's *Argus* proposed that ''these new Games might offer themselves to the delighted gaze of Melbourne.'' In 1906, Richard Coombes, IOC member for Australasia, wrote in a letter to Baron Pierre de Coubertin that ''it is certainly hoped and expected that in due course the Olympic Games will be allotted to this part of the world.'' There were suggestions that Perth host the Olympics of 1916, then 1920. Sydney was proposed for 1930, the expected year of completion of the Sydney Harbour Bridge. Of course, the celebration of the Olympiad did not fall in that year; it is a pity that it could not have been foreseen that the completion of the bridge would be delayed until 1932.

Edgar Tanner, secretary-treasurer of the VOC, forwarded the VOC's proposal to the Australian Olympic Federation (AOF) in July 1946 and asked the IOC how to proceed with the bid. He gained support from the lord mayor of Melbourne, Sir James Connelly, and a former lord mayor (1940–1942), Sir Frank Beaurepaire. Beaurepaire's public profile in Australia and in the international Olympic movement was a key factor in the success of Melbourne's bid. He had won three silver and three bronze medals in three Olympic Games (1908, 1920, and 1924) and had been an official at the 1932 Olympics. Following his return from Los Angeles in 1932 he developed his automobile tires using the brand name ''Olympic.'' Beaurepaire assumed the presidency of the VOC in May 1947 and was instrumental in urging the Melbourne City Council to establish an invitation committee composed of influential media figures and businessmen. Friction arose because, apart from Beaurepaire, no member of the VOC or any sports organization was represented on this committee.

An extravagant invitation book, with additional copies bound in suede or merino lamb's wool, was sent to all IOC members and other international sports administrators and public figures. The book explained why Melbourne should become an Olympic Games host: Australia was only one of four nations to have been at every Summer Olympics and because of that it was more senior in the Olympic movement than any other competitor in the Southern Hemisphere; there was a concept of the Olympics as being a world games, and it was time for the event to be held in the Southern Hemisphere; and with the development of pressurized aircraft, it would take at most 30 hours to reach Melbourne, a time comparable to traveling to many other venues. The invitation book also claimed that Melbourne's bid had the "active interests of all athletic organizations, government and the people."

Although it was expected that the IOC would decide which city would host the 1956 Olympic Games at the London Olympics of 1948, the decision was postponed until the following year in Rome. Australians lobbied extensively during the 1948 Olympic Games; Beaurepaire and Connelly spent almost three months in London and Europe. In Rome in April 1949, Beaurepaire, respected among the IOC as an athlete-businessman, and the rest of the Melbourne delegation were the last to present their city's case to the IOC. Six U.S. cities were bidding, the main contenders being Detroit and Los Angeles. Other cities bidding were Buenos Aires, Mexico City, and London. Despite the competition, Melbourne won by a vote of 21–20 in the fourth round of balloting.

One would have thought that the magnificent Melbourne Cricket Ground (MCG) would have been the most appropriate choice for the main venue for the Olympic Games, but this was not an automatic selection. The Organizing Committee (OC), formed in October 1949, vacillated over six other sites. The OC and the trustees of the MCG negotiated from late 1949 to early 1952. A primary contention was whether this major cricket and football arena should be remodeled and resurfaced for an Olympic Games of a mere seventeen days' duration at the expense of one football and two cricket seasons. Over that period, three sites were successively designated as the main stadium. Originally it was Olympic Park. Then the Royal Agricultural Showgrounds (RAS), despite their location among sheep and cattle yards, abattoirs, and tanneries, had state and local government support. However, in 1951, alarmed at the cost of redevelopment of the RAS in a period of inflation and shortage of building materials, the state government indicated that it might have to withdraw its support for the Games unless the commonwealth government made a substantial financial contribution. In contrast to the earlier vision that the Games would boost development in Victoria, they were now seen as a burden on the economy. At the IOC meeting in Vienna in May 1951, Hugh Weir (IOC member from Australia) gave an ambiguous report of progress because the site of the main stadium venue had not been settled, and some felt that Melbourne should forgo the right to stage the Games.

At the next meeting of the IOC in Helsinki in July 1952, it was reported that Princes Park in Carlton was to be the main venue, but in 1953, Victorian premier John Cain, again alarmed at renovation costs of £2 million for a second stadium and in favor of utilizing the MCG, vetoed the proposal.

After a three-day meeting, which included Prime Minister Robert Menzies, it was finally resolved that the commonwealth government would pay half the costs of construction for the Games, which included modifications to the MCG, the swimming pool, and the velodrome, and for administration and promotion.

The balance would be financed by the Victorian government and the Melbourne city council. There was an agreement to share profits and losses, and the State Savings Bank of Victoria guaranteed £1 million to cover operating costs. Financing the athletes' village was resolved when Victoria received an advance of Commonwealth State Housing Agreement funds to erect a cheap public housing project in the suburb of Heidelberg.

Another issue of concern to the OC and the IOC related to Australia's strict quarantine laws, which prevented foreign horses from entering the country. As a consequence, the equestrian events were held in Stockholm June 10–17.

On the day IOC president Avery Brundage visited the MCG in April 1955, there were only six workers on the site because of a labor dispute. The irate Brundage administered a severe scolding to the MCG organizers (he later termed it "a mild atomic explosion") (Guttmann, *The Games Must Go On,* p. 159), accusing them of incompetence and intimating that, even at that late stage, several other cities (he seemed to favor Philadelphia) would be prepared to stage the 1956 Games. Although the Australians did not receive Brundage's anger well, the lambast seemed to work; there was much more cohesion among the individuals, committees, and agencies during those final eighteen months of preparation, as well as a positive mood of anticipation and diligence—only global war could jeopardize the success of these first Olympic Games to be held in the Southern Hemisphere.

On October 29, 1956, a mere twenty-four days prior to the opening ceremony on November 22, war broke out between Egypt and Israel. Britain and France joined in. On November 4, following attempts to liberalize the communist regime of Hungary, Soviet troops launched an attack on Budapest. Antagonism toward the Soviet Union and, especially, its Olympic athletes seemed inevitable.

The United States and the Soviet Union had emerged from World War II as dueling superpowers, and many thought the supremacy of their ideologies would be tested in the international sporting arenas. These world tensions affected the final preparation of the 1956 Olympic Games in several ways. The traditional torch relay bearing the Olympic flame from the altis at Olympia, Greece, was delayed a day because the conflict in the Suez Canal had affected flight schedules at the Athens airport. Fortunately, time was made up along the route. Cruise ships en route to Melbourne were forced to sail around the Cape of Good Hope. The Hungarian revolution caused the Hungarian Olympic team and officials to arrive in Australia one week later than scheduled.

The OC had anticipated a record number of teams and countries in Melbourne, but several countries threatened boycotts. Egypt, protesting the "cowardly aggression" of certain nations, was the first country to withdraw from the Games. Iraq and Lebanon also withdrew. Several nations boycotted to protest the actions of the U.S.S.R. in Hungary. The Netherlands Olympic Committee sent a gift of 100,000 guilders, the amount of money saved by not competing in Melbourne, to aid victims in war-torn Hungary. Dutch athletes, already in Melbourne, were recalled. Spain also withdrew. The Swiss Olympic Committee decided to send a team only if there was unanimity among the seven participating Swiss national sports federations; there was not. Otto Mayer, chancellor of the IOC and a Swiss citizen, appalled at the decision, was reported as stating, ''It is a disgrace that Switzerland, a neutral nation and the very country where the IOC has its head-quarters should set such a shameful example of political interference with the Olympic ideal.'' The Swiss Olympic Committee changed its mind and decided to send a team, but their indecisiveness meant that there was not enough time for the entire team to travel to Melbourne, so it withdrew. As late as November 13, five Scandinavian countries (Denmark, Finland, Iceland, Norway, and Sweden) had not made a firm decision to compete, despite collectively having more than 200 athletes in Australia. At a meeting of the Scandinavian Federation in Melbourne, it was decided that all countries would compete. Both the People's Republic of China and the island nation of Taiwan (Formosa) had been recognized by the IOC in 1954, but tension between these two Chinas was so great that mainland China withdrew from the Games.

Throughout the period of these conflicts and vacillations, the OC and other Australian officials worked hard to encourage nations to compete. In the weeks leading up to the Games, the chair of the OC, Kent Hughes, and the chief executive officer of the Games, Sir William Bridgeford, appealed to athletes and spectators to ensure that the true spirit of the Olympic Games would triumph. Internationally, Otto Mayer and Avery Brundage exhorted athletes and governments not to prevent the Olympic movement from fulfilling its humanitarian role in the interests of world peace and to keep politics out of the Olympic Games.

The withdrawals in October and early November caused some organizational problems. The number of athletes was reduced considerably. In the final analysis, ninety-one member nations of the IOC were sent invitations to participate; eighty accepted initially, and eleven subsequently withdrew (People's Republic of China, Egypt, Gold Coast, Guatemala, Holland, Iraq, Lebanon, Malta, Panama, Spain, and Switzerland). Ultimately, sixty-seven nations participated, bringing 2,813 male and 371 female competitors.

The IOC endorsed the holding of an arts festival instead of an arts competition at the IOC congress in Athens in May 1954; it was also decided that the festival be national rather than international in character. The festival was divided into sections: visual arts, literature, and music and drama. Visual arts included exhibitions of architecture and sculpture, painting and drawing, and graphic arts. The literature exhibition included early Australian examples of historical interest, books by Australian authors, and exceptional examples of book production in Australia. Music and drama was divided into three sections: theater and orchestral and chamber music. The OC contributed £4,000 to the civic committee toward the expenses of the arts festival. In addition, the World Congress on Physical Education, held during the week prior to the Games, attracted 350 delegates from more than thirty countries.

It was not until the mid-1950s that the IOC began to recognize the potential financial windfall to the Olympic movement that would flow from the sale of television rights. At this time, even IOC president Avery Brundage was wary of such an initiative, uncertain of its impact on the spirit of the Olympic Games. Four overseas companies made bids to the OC for exclusive newsreel and television rights in December 1955, with one London broadcaster offering £25,000. There was considerable opposition to this development. By April 1956, all television companies refused to pay for television rights to cover the Games because of a conflict over what was a news item and what was an entertainment package.

The chairman of the OC, Kent Hughes, met with people representing newsreel interests in New York in July 1956, and, aware that an average of 2 minutes of newsreel per day of the Helsinki Games of 1952 had been used, offered 3 minutes per day. However, American television newsreel interests requested 9 minutes daily: 3 minutes for each of three news broadcasts. It became clear, however, that no television entertainment departments and no film entrepreneurs would be interested in Olympic coverage if more than 3 minutes per day were granted to the newsreels. Eventually newsreel companies and international television networks boycotted the Melbourne Olympics. The OC decided on the production of a 16-mm color film plus a black and white film, thereby satisfying the requirements of the IOC, and a French film unit undertook to make a feature-length wide-screen color film.

Regular television transmission in Australia from stations in Melbourne and Sydney began in October 1956. The question of Australian television coverage of the Games was revived only a few days before the opening ceremony on November 22. Arrangements had been made with the local television stations to televise from any site where seating had been fully sold, and since this was the case with the main stadium (the MCG), as well as many other venues, the television companies were given the rights to televise daily. The charge for this live coverage, the first for a host nation, was a nominal payment to the OC because there were so few television sets—approximately 5,000—in operation.

In a unique arrangement, GTV9, a television station, and Ampol Petroleum joined forces to turn Ampol petrol stations into "television theatres" for people with no access to television sets in their homes. Community halls were also utilized, and many charity organizations contacted GTV9 and Ampol for permission to charge admission fees. For ten of the fifteen days of the Games, the three television stations (Channels 9, HSV7, and ABV2) provided more than 20 hours of coverage per day to Victorian viewers. A 16-mm film was flown to Sydney, allowing New South Wales to receive coverage each night.

A significant change in format from previous Olympic Games was the part of the closing ceremony that symbolized the Olympic philosophy of internationalism and goodwill. Throughout the Games, athletes, particularly medalists, were identified by nation, but the closing ceremony in Melbourne would be different. The idea was generated in a letter from John Ian Wing that Kent

Hughes received on the Wednesday of the final week of the Games. Wing, a 17-year-old Chinese-Australian, wrote:

The march I have in mind is different than the one during the Opening Ceremony and will make these games even greater, during the march there will only be 1 NATION. War, politics and nationality will be all forgotten, what more could anybody want, if the whole world could be made as one nation. Well, you can do it in a small way. . . . No team is to keep together and there should be no more than 2 team mates together, they must be spread out evenly, THEY MUST NOT MARCH but walk freely and wave to the public, let them walk around twice on the cinder, when they stop the public will give them three cheers. . . . It will show the whole world how friendly Australia is. (John Ian Wing to Keith Hughes, December 4, 1956, Australian Gallery of Sport and Olympic Museum)

It was not until lunchtime on the day before the closing ceremony that, with permission from the IOC president, arrangements were endorsed. It was a splendid closing ceremony. There was, as stated in the official report,

a prophetic image of a new future for mankind—the athletes of the world not now sharply divided, but . . . marching as one in a hotchpotch of sheer humanity, a fiesta of friendship. . . . A wave of emotion swept over the crowd, the Olympic Flame was engulfed in it and died; the Olympic flag went out in tears, not cheers, and a great silence. This, more than any remembered laurel of the Games, was something no-one had ever experienced before—not anywhere in the world, not anywhere in time.

Wing's vision of Olympism has become a tradition of the closing ceremony of every Olympics since 1956.

At the opening ceremony, athletes from Greece entered the stadium to the cheers of over 100,000 spectators. The Australian junior mile record holder, Ron Clarke, was the last of 3,500 torch bearers; the first relay runner on the host nation's soil was an Australian-born Greek, the second an Australian aborigine. When John Landy, the great sub–4 minute miler, pronounced the Olympic oath, spectators had difficulty following his version because he had been supplied with a different one from that printed in the program.

Australian athletes won a total of thirteen gold medals—their best ever performance. Overall, thirty-six Olympic and eleven world records were broken. The United States was dominant on the track, with Bobby Morrow a triple gold medalist by winning the 100- and 200-meter sprints and anchoring the 4 × 100-meter relay; Ira Murchison, Leamon King, Thane Baker, and Morrow broke the world record. In the 110-meter hurdles, both Lee Calhoun and Jack Davis recorded the same time of 13.5 seconds; Calhoun was awarded the gold and Joel Shankl came third, giving the United States a medal sweep. Americans won the gold and silver medals after a great struggle in the decathlon between the world record holder, Rafer Johnson, and Milton Campbell.

Like Morrow, Australia's golden girl, Betty Cuthbert, won three gold medals in the 100 and 200 meters and the record-breaking 4 × 100 relay. Ireland's Ron Delany shattered the hopes of many Australians by beating John Landy in the glamor track event, the 1,500 meters. Landy, who had become the second person to break the 4-minute mile two years earlier, won a bronze medal. A strategy of varying pace was successful for Soviet distance runner Vladimir Kuts in both the 5,000 and 10,000 meters. After finishing second to Emil Zatopek in the marathons of 1948 and 1952, Algerian Alain Mimoun, wearing number 13 on his French team singlet, won in 2 hours, 25 minutes.

Australians "scooped the pool" in swimming. Dawn Fraser made her Olympic debut and went on to win the 100-meter freestyle in Rome and Tokyo in 1960 and 1964, respectively. Murray Rose won three gold medals and Jon Henricks two. Their race against the United States in the 800-meter relay final, with John Devitt and Kevin O'Halloran as teammates, resulted in a world record time of 8 minutes, 23.6 seconds. Diving in the first enclosed diving pool used at an Olympic Games, America's Pat McCormick became the first ever to win consecutive gold medals in both the springboard and tower events.

Although there is much more known now about the cold war, those present at the Olympic Games in Melbourne seemed to embody the spirit of an Olympic truce, especially in relation to the athletes from the U.S.S.R. It was clear from their cheers and encouragement that the huge crowds in the main stadium appreciated the efforts of Kuts and the many successful Soviet women athletes in the field events. The magnificence of the male and female gymnasts from the Soviet Union, who won eight individual and two team gold medals, enthralled the many spectators at the West Melbourne Stadium.

There was, however, an infamous incident in the semifinal of the men's water polo match between Hungary and the Soviet Union. The Hungarians were leading 4–0 in the second half when two members of the Soviet team taunted the Hungarians by repeatedly calling them "fascists." At one stage the referee ordered five players out of the water for punching, kicking, and scratching. Although clearly exaggerating, a newspaper reported that the pool was like a "bloodbath" after Valentine Prokopov swam to Ervin Zador of Hungary and punched him in the eye while the ball was at the other end of the pool. As Zador clambered from the pool with blood streaming from his eye, the Swedish referee called off the match, declaring Hungary the winner. The crowd was incensed at the behavior of the Soviet team, and only the appearance of police, who had been waiting out of sight, prevented a riot.

On the other hand, not even the notorious 10-foot-high barbed-wire fence separating the men's and women's residences could prevent the blossoming romance of a Czechoslovakian and American; discus thrower Olga Fikotova and hammer thrower Harold Connolly, gold medalists in their respective events, later married in Prague.

For many Australians, as well as visitors to the first Olympic Games in the Southern Hemisphere, the 1956 Melbourne Games were an opportunity to comprehend the dictum, "It's not the winning but the taking part." These Games truly deserve to be known as the "Friendly Games."

BIBLIOGRAPHICAL ESSAY

The Australian Gallery of Sport and Olympic Museum (AGOS&OM), located at the Melbourne Cricket Ground, the site of the main stadium for the 1956 Olympic Games, has a permanent exhibition pertaining to the Melbourne Games. Many of the documents, the final *Official Report of the Organising Committee for the Games of the XVIth Olympiad Melbourne, 1956* (Melbourne, 1958), and other reports and press releases (many uncataloged) are located in the storage areas of AGOS&OM, along with an outstanding collection of memorabilia and artifacts (albums, letters, magazines, maps, charts, identity cards, certificates, diplomas, invitations, stamps and first day covers, postcards, posters, programs and other assorted publications). The most useful of the many donated collections are those of Doris Carter, Julius ("Judy") Patching, and George Moir. Many of the personal papers of Sir Frank Beaurepaire are also located in the AGOS&OM; the University of Melbourne Archives contains other papers of Beaurepaire and material relating to the Invitation Committee. The National Library of Australia holds the Kent Hughes Papers, which contain correspondence to and from the IOC. The library and the museum of the IOC in Lausanne, Switzerland, and the library of the International Olympic Academy in Olympia, Greece, house information about the Melbourne Olympics from countries other than the host nation.

The Victorian Olympic Council and the Australian Olympic Federation (both now known as committees) also hold extensive archival records and materials, including the official final report, and Bill Uren, *Olympic Games, Melbourne 1956: Australian Team Reports* (Melbourne, 1956).

Excellent sources in North America are contained in the Avery Brundage Collection, which is on microfilm and housed in several locations, including the University of Illinois at Urbana-Champaign; the Centre for Olympic Studies at the University of Western Ontario, London, Ontario; and the Fred Ziffren Resource Center at the Los Angeles Amateur Athletic Foundation. The Ziffren Center also holds a collection of the weekly syndicated newspaper columns from February to December 1956 by American journalist and Olympic athlete Ralph C. Craig.

In addition to the organizing committee's official report, the U.S. Olympic Committee's report is Asa S. Bushnell, ed., *United States 1956 Olympic Book. Quadrennial Report of the United States Olympic Committee* (New York, 1957); the British report is Cecil Bear, ed., *The Official Report of the XVIth Olympic Games Melbourne, 1956* (London, 1957); and the Canadian report is K. P. Farmer et al., eds., *Canada Competes at the Olympic Games 1956* (Montreal, 1956). See also G. F. James, ed., *The Art Festival of the Olympic Games, Melbourne* (Melbourne, 1956).

Several books have been published recently about Australia at the Olympic Games, especially Australian gold medalists; Gary Lester, *Australians at the Olympics—A Definitive History* (Melbourne, 1984), and Max and Reet Howell, *Aussie Gold: The Story of Australia at the Olympic Games* (Albion, Queensland, 1988), are most useful. The most recent and encompassing volume, which includes a substantial section on the Melbourne Olympics, is Harry Gordon, *Australia and the Olympic Games* (St. Lucia, Queensland, 1994). Other useful books are Keith Donald and Don Selth, *Olympic Saga: The*

Track and Field Story, Melbourne, 1956 (Sydney, 1957); Graham Lomas, *The Will to Win: The Story of Sir Frank Beaurepaire* (London, 1960); and Keith Dunstan, *The Paddock That Grew: The Story of the Melbourne Cricket Club,* 3d ed. (Surry, New South Wales, 1988), which includes a fascinating chapter (''Olympic Year'') about the effect of the 1956 Olympics on this very conservative cricket club.

The story of how Melbourne became the first city in the Southern Hemisphere to stage an Olympic Games is described by Ian Jobling in ''Proposals and Bids by Australian Cities to Host the Olympic Games,'' *Sporting Traditions* 11, 1 (November 1994): 37–56. Australian relations with IOC president Avery Brundage are detailed in Allen Guttmann, *The Games Must Go On* (New York, 1984). The first major use of television in an Olympic Games and the foreboding of what was to come has been told by Stephen Wenn in ''Lights! Camera! Little Action: Television, Avery Brundage, and the 1956 Melbourne Olympics,'' *Sporting Traditions* 10, 1 (November 1993): 38–53. Sasha Soldatow, *Politics of the Olympics* (North Ryde, New South Wales, 1980), and Hilary Kent and John Merritt, ''The Cold War and the Melbourne Olympic Games,'' in Ann Curthoys and John Merritt, *Better Dead Than Red* (Sydney, 1992), provide some background to the politics of the era. Shane Cahill's thesis, '' 'The Friendly Games'? The Melbourne Olympic Games in Australian Culture'' (master's thesis, University of Melbourne, 1989), is the outcome of thorough research of the preceding decade. See Dawn Fraser and Lesley H. Murdoch, *Our Dawn: A Pictorial Biography* (Birchgrove, New South Wales, 1991), and Harry Gordon, *Dawn Fraser* (Melbourne, 1979), for information on Australia's most celebrated gold medalist.

The three morning newspapers, the *Age,* the *Argus,* and the *Sun,* and the one evening newspaper, the *Herald,* provided excellent coverage of the preparations for the Olympics and proudly portrayed Melbourne as a progressive, international city that had successfully staged what was to become known as ''the Friendly Games.''

Ian Jobling

ROME 1960

THE GAMES OF THE XVIITH OLYMPIAD

The International Olympic Committee (IOC) met in Paris in 1955 to select the host cities for the XVIIth Olympiad. In a surprise move, it chose Squaw Valley in California, a remote and little-known resort, for the Winter Games. The popular choice for the Summer Games was Rome. By a vote of 35–24, the Roman proponents won easily over the second choice, Lausanne, Switzerland. The award of the Games was a continuation of the Olympic tradition of frequently holding the Games in the great cities of the world; they had previously been held in Athens, London, Paris, Los Angeles, and Berlin. The selection was also a method of repaying Rome for its long support of the Olympic movement and its longstanding desire to stage the games. Rome had been denied the opportunity to host the Games in 1904 and had been forced to relinquish them in 1908. When it had finally been chosen as the site of the 1944 Games, war had intervened, and the Games were canceled.

As an Olympic site, Rome was full of many classical associations and rich imagery. No doubt the images of athletes competing in the historical surroundings of the Eternal City cast a strong spell on the IOC selectors. From the gladiatorial combats once staged at the Colosseum to the chariots that raced around the Circus Maximus, the city was steeped in a sporting past that linked the ancient Games to the modern. The modern Games in Rome would be the biggest show in the world. New, unknown gladiators would fight to the end of their endurance in the same places where, centuries before, others had also striven to win.

Rome was the final site of the ancient Games, which had been moved there from Olympia when the Roman world superseded the Greek. The games were an integral part of the Roman sporting and religious scene until A.D. 3, when Theodosius I of Rome decreed the end of the ancient Olympics. This connection to the past, as well as the position of Rome as a modern and stylish city, was a powerful symbol of the Olympics: ancient yet modern, a place where nations came to compete, free from politics, among the vestiges of European classical civilization.

After hearing the news of Rome's selection, the Italian organizers mobilized to complete the construction that they had promised in their submission. The nation had been poorly equipped athletically but now spent at least $50 million to get ready. Most of the money went for new facilities, upgrading older ones built by Benito Mussolini in preparation for the 1944 Games, and planning venues that included ancient monuments as part of the structures.

In order not to overburden the population with additional taxes, the majority of the money was raised from the Italian soccer lottery, *Totocalcio,* a betting pool based on football results. In this way, the more the sporting public wagered, the more monies were raised for the Games. Italian fans, already passionate for soccer, quite painlessly supported the high cost of the spectacle that they would host and enjoy.

Italy's most prominent architect, Pier Luigi Nervi, was chosen to oversee the design of the new stadiums, coordinate the construction of new facilities, and integrate some of the venues into existing Roman sites. This task he accomplished brilliantly. Twelve magnificent venues were prepared in addition to the Olympic Village. The central location of the Games was the Foro Italico, which contains the Stadio Olimpico, a large stadium seating 100,000. Built by Mussolini for the 1944 Games, the stadium still contained the word *Duce* embedded in mosaics at many key points. This stadium was the site of track and field events, as well as the opening and closing ceremonies. Part of the same complex contained an arena that held the swimming and diving venues. Nearby, a modern velodrome seating 20,000 awaited the bicycle races.

Nervi was assisted by another famous Italian architect, Annibale Vitellozzi. Together they worked on the difficult problem of blending the ancient with the modern. For example, basketball, a modern game, was played in the large hall of the modern Palazetto dello Sport, seating 5,000. The grace and power of the gymnastics events were enhanced by the ancient monument of the Baths of Caracalla. Wrestling, one of the original sports of the ancient Games, was contested under the arches of the ruined ancient Basilica of Maxentius (Basilica di Massenzio). Only partially shaded by the arches, the competitors endured the heat and blazing sunlight of one of Rome's hottest months. Many events eventually had to be rescheduled to the cooler afternoon and evening. This time change frequently added even more drama to the contests, as it did in the marathon.

Up in the hills, a short distance from Rome, the rowing venue was created on Lake Albano at the foot of the pope's summer residence, Castle Gandolfo. The pontiff, who gave a personal audience to and blessing of all the athletes at the Vatican, took a keen interest in the Games and frequently watched the rowing competitions from his terrace. One hundred miles away, in the Bay of Naples, the sailing events were held.

The Olympic Village was an entirely new neighborhood built across the River Tiber from the main venues. New bridges over the river connected the village to the stadiums. The village was to become a new Roman suburb after the games. To offset the cost of construction, most of the homes had been purchased by Italian civil servants, who would move in as soon as the Games ended. Some three hundred Italian chefs were responsible for the feeding of the athletes and game officials. At night, the village and main venues were brilliantly lit, at a cost of $5.5 million.

New streets leading to the venues were built to cope with the hectic Roman traffic. To accommodate the thousands of athletes and visitors, many improvements to airports and train stations were completed, and numerous subways and overhead crosswalks were constructed.

The 1960 Rome Olympics were one of the least political Games of the modern era. Although there is always controversy within the Games over such matters as biased refereeing and dubious judging, there was little in the Rome Games to create a stir. Though it was the height of the cold war, the Americans and Russians were polite to each other and met as friendly sporting rivals. The nonpolitical nature of the Games was a triumph for Avery Brundage, the American president of the IOC. He had successfully negotiated two major issues into acceptable compromises and put off a third until after the Games were completed.

The first of these issues was the two Germanys question. Both the West and East German nations wanted to compete, and both had Olympic committees, but the East German committee had only provisional status within the IOC. Since both countries had competed at Melbourne in 1956 as a single team, it was preferred that they do so again. Although the political pressure from the Eastern bloc members was strong, the IOC was able to mediate with the two sporting organizations, which again agreed to compete as a single team, under a single flag and a single anthem. Seeing the united German team march into the stadium for the opening ceremonies, President Giovanni Gronchi of Italy, seated next to Brundage, remarked that IOC had worked a miracle. Brundage beamed and replied, ''In sport we do such things.'' It was perhaps his crowning moment.

The second major issue that arose before the XVIIth Olympiad was the two Chinas problem. Nationalist China, on the island of Taiwan (Formosa), called itself China and was recognized as such in the United Nations and by many nations, particularly the United States. Mainland China, known as the People's Republic of China (PRC), the communist state, insisted that only it could call itself ''China.'' It was a nation of over 600 million, one-fourth of the world's population. This issue was, of course, much bigger than the Olympics and was a hot topic of diplomatic discussion. The PRC was not a member of the IOC, but no one wanted to slight it over a bilateral dispute. The nations of the Eastern bloc and many of the nonaligned countries supported the PRC. After extensive discussion, the IOC executive board finally declared that the Olympic committee of any country could internally call itself whatever it wanted (in this case, Taiwan called itself the Olympic Committee of the Republic of China), but in international competition, the country name had to be consistent with the territory it actually ruled. Therefore, Taiwan could compete only under the name Taiwan (Formosa) and could not call itself China. The PRC, upset that Taiwan was not eliminated from international sport altogether, did not compete in Rome, but the compromise kept the Olympic movement together. The decision also set a precedent and allowed for other divided, previously unrecognized countries, such as East Germany and North Korea, to compete as separate teams. When the Taiwanese team entered the Stadio Olimpico for the opening ceremonies of the Rome Olympics, it marched in under a placard bearing the name ''Taiwan (Formosa).'' As the team approached the reviewing stand, the placard bearer whipped out a smaller sign saying, "Under Protest," and then quickly put it away. This brief gesture was the principal protest of the 1960 Summer Games.

The third issue was the question of South Africa and its policy of apartheid. With the decolonization of Africa in the early 1960s, the continent had become a hotbed of black nationalism, and these emerging nations were joining the IOC. Their criticism added to the concern of others in the IOC about allowing South Africa to compete because of their obvious violation of Olympic Rule 25, which proscribed discrimination of any kind. The African nations, strongly supported by the Soviet Union, accused South Africa of racial discrimination. The South Africans replied that blacks had only recently taken an interest in sports and that no "coloured" athletes had yet achieved international caliber. Brazil and other nations complained that their black soccer players had not been allowed to compete in South Africa. Some countries, such as New Zealand, sided with South Africa. Brundage finally intervened, stating that the IOC would accept the South African committee's explanation but that the whole issue would be investigated after the 1960 Games. After Rome, South Africa quit the IOC and began its long isolation from international sports.

It has always been the ideal of the Olympic movement to accompany the sporting events of the games with a series of festivals of the arts and sciences. Few cities have had notable success in this area. In Rome, however, one of the new buildings, the mammoth Palazzo delle Scienze (Palace of Science), was constructed specifically to house a magnificent display of exhibitions, entitled "Sport in History and Art." Professor Gulgielmo de Angelis d'Ossat and his assistants spent three years assembling the exhibits, which included contributions from over one hundred Italian museums and more than thirty libraries. The exhibits showed the role that sport had played in Italian life from ancient times to the end of the nineteenth century. Etruscan, Greek, Roman, and Italian works of art, rare manuscripts and books, photographs, and sculptures were displayed. The sporting images included frescoes from an Etruscan tomb, ancient Roman mosaics, and medieval paintings showing jousting, bullfights, and foot races. Apart from the high culture of the exhibits at the Palace of Science, many other events were scheduled around the Games, including reenactments of medieval soccer matches, horse races, and regattas. Finally, the first Paralympic Games for competitors with disabilities were held in Rome in 1960.

In keeping with the organizer's theme of a reunion of the ancient and modern Games in Rome, many old traditions were kept or reintroduced. The Olympic flame was kindled at Olympia, and runners carried it across Greece to an Italian ship, which brought it to Italy at Syracuse, in Sicily. From there, runners carried it to Messina, and again it traveled by boat to Calabria at the toe of Italy. Runners took it northward to Rome, passing through the ancient centers of Roman civilization until it finally arrived at the Stadio Olimpico for the opening ceremony. Gathered there were 5,902 athletes representing some eighty-four countries.

One of the format changes at the Rome Olympics, keeping with the desire to

make reference to the ancient Games, was the introduction of the modern pentathlon, a five-part military-derived competition that harkened back to the all-
around abilities of the ancient Olympic athletes. The events were cross-country
riding on horses supplied by the Italian cavalry, fencing, shooting, 300-meter
freestyle swimming, and a 4-kilometer cross-country run.

The Rome Olympics were significant because they heralded the start of a new
era of big business. The major change that affected the Olympics in 1960 was
money from the sale of television rights. In Melbourne in 1956, television stations had been asked to pay a fee to broadcast the Games. The stations had
absolutely refused to pay, arguing that the event was news, and access should
be free. By 1960, both broadcasters and organizers had become attuned to the
marketing possibilities of the Games and had recognized the public's desire to
be entertained by the sporting spectacle.

The Comite Olimpico Nazionale d'Italia (CONI), the organizers of the event,
had brilliantly used the Italian soccer lottery, *Totocalcio,* to fund the new construction. They then sold the television rights to make the games profitable. The
Columbia Broadcasting System (CBS) paid CONI $660,000 for the American
rights to film the events for later primetime telecast, while Eurovision broadcast
the games live for another $540,000. At the time, these were astounding sums
of money. Thereafter, the five Olympic rings became a marketing logo much in
demand. Avery Brundage and many of the older members of the IOC were
dedicated to the Olympic ideal of amateurism, fair play, and peace through sport.
Although frequently they had been involved in disputes over power and politics,
they had tried to keep commercialism out of the Games. This was an altruistic
stand, but it cost the IOC a great deal of money. Brundage, like many other
rich people, looked down on those who were interested in making money from
the Games and saw the ruination of the movement if it became too commercialized.

In 1959, the marquess of Exeter, one of the executive members of the IOC,
proposed a 5 percent tax on tickets to bring income into the organization. Of
this total, 3 percent would go to the local organizing committee and 2 percent
to the IOC. Brundage saw this as blatant profiteering and adamantly refused to
accept it. Brundage, however, had no control over the local organizing committee, and Guilio Onesti, head of CONI and Italy's leading IOC member, went
ahead with the sale of television rights over Brundage's objections. After the
games, CONI offered the IOC 5 percent of the proceeds, which the impoverished
IOC accepted. After the television money came in, the IOC increased its size,
expanded into much larger offices in Lausanne, and started to take on the luxurious image it currently holds.

Once the Games began, there was the usual excitement as athletes performed
exceptionally well. Notable in track and field was the achievement of Wilma
Rudolph, a young woman from Tennessee who won gold medals in the 100-
and 200-meter dashes and the 4 × 100-meter races. What was truly amazing
was that Rudolph, who ran so gracefully that the French called her *la gazelle,*

had been crippled as a child by illness. In the boxing ring at Rome, a shy young man from Louisville, Kentucky, came to international notice. Eighteen-year-old Cassius Clay, who was twice the Golden Gloves champion in America, competed in Rome as a light-heavyweight, where he used his stinging attacks and his great defensive skills to avoid the deadly left hand of the highly regarded Pole, Zbigniew Pietrzykowski, to become Olympic champion.

For many, the lasting memory of the Rome Olympics was the image of a slender, unknown Ethiopian running barefoot to victory along the Appian Way. Abebe Bikila, the marathon runner, was a soldier in the bodyguard of the Ethiopian emperor, Haile Selasse. He said he ran just for fun. The marathon course wound through both ancient and modern Rome. Starting in the evening because of the heat, the race finished in darkness. Beginning on the Via Fori Imperiali, the course ran past the Colosseum, past the Baths of Caracalla, and up the modern Via Cristoforo Columbo. At the start, no one knew who would go to the front; there were many runners, and most of them were unknown. After 20 kilometers, two runners were alone at the front, running together and pulling away from the pack: Rhadi Ben Abdesselem, the Moroccan, and Bikila. The last few kilometers were along the Via Appia Antica. Soldiers with flaming torches were stationed every 10 yards to mark the course in the darkness. Bikila and Rhadi raced past ancient walls, headless statues, and weathered inscriptions. As the course turned uphill, Bikila, running barefoot, increased his pace, and Rhadi gradually fell behind. When Bikila crossed the finish line at the Arch of Constantine, he was 26 seconds ahead of Rhadi. He was the first black African to win a gold medal in Olympic history, and it is noteworthy that his victory came in Italy, the invader and attempted colonizer of his homeland three decades earlier. The image of Abebe Bikila running through the ancient streets of Rome in 1960 symbolizes the emergence of a new world.

The organizers of the Summer Olympic Games in Rome in August 1960 achieved a remarkable success. The style and dramatic backgrounds of the sporting venues and the innate beauty of the city would not be rivaled until Barcelona, thirty years later. The lack of political controversy in the age of the cold war was a significant victory for Avery Brundage and the IOC executive board. The financing of the Games through the lottery was an original solution to the usual cost of hosting the event, and the sale of television rights brought an outright profit to the Games. The issue of broadcast rights was eventually bound to occur in an age of newer and better communications, but the money that poured into the IOC coffers altered the Olympic movement forever. After Rome, everything changed as commercialism took over the sporting world.

BIBLIOGRAPHICAL ESSAY

Primary sources of official Olympic materials are maintained at the International Olympic Committee (IOC) headquarters in Lausanne, Switzerland. Much of the material relating to the period of Avery Brundage's tenure, which includes the Rome 1960 Games, is available in the Avery Brundage Collection, 1908–1975, at the University of Illinois Archives. Specific materials relating to the Rome Games in the Brundage Papers include IOC correspondence and bulletins, Games programs, newspaper clippings, information on cultural programs, and some film footage.

The organizing committee's official report of the Games, edited by Romolo Giacomini and translated by Edwin Byatt, is *The Games of the XVII Olympiad, Rome, 1960: Official Report* (Rome, 1960). Other publications prepared by the organizing committee include *Games of the XVII Olympiad. Official Souvenir. Rome 1960* (Rome, 1960); *Olympic Rules and Sport Regulations/Regoli olimpiche e regloamenti sportivi* (Rome, 1960); and a catalog of an exhibition of sport photography, *Esposizione Olimpica di Fotografica Sportiva-Palazzo dello Sport* (Rome, 1960).

National Olympic committee reports on the Rome Games include Arthur G. Lentz and Asa S. Bushnell, eds., *United States 1960 Olympic Book: Quadrennial Report of the United States Olympic Committee* (New York, 1961); *Australia at the XVII Olympic Games, VII Olympic Winter Games* (Melbourne, 1960); Phil Pilley, ed., *The Official Report of the Olympic Games, XVIIth Olympiad, Rome, August 25–September 11, 1960* (London, 1960); *Die Olympischen Spiele 1960, Rom-Squaw Valley. Das Offizielle Standardwerke des Nationalen Olympischen Komitees* (Stuttgart, 1960); and *Canada Competes at the Olympic Games 1960* (Montreal, 1961).

Harald Lechenperg, ed., *Olympic Games 1960: Squaw Valley, Rome* (New York, 1960), is an excellent book that relates in great detail both the Summer and Winter Games of the XVIIth Olympiad. A short section is dedicated to each event, and the book is rich with photographs, color illustrations, and tables of results. Nonpolitical and noncontroversial, the book deals only with sports and the local atmosphere. Unfortunately, it contains no material on either the Italian organizers or the method by which the site was selected. Other secondary sources in English include Harold N. Abrahams, *XVII Olympiad, Rome 1960* (London, 1960), the account by the 1924 British sprinter who remained active in his country's sport administration; Neil Allen, *Olympic Diary: Rome 1960* (London, 1960); John A. Talbot-Ponsonby, *The Equestrian Olympic Games, Rome 1960* (n.p., 1960); and Naples Province, *Olympic Events: Events at Naples. XVIIth Olympiad Rome, 1960* (n.p., 1960).

Among articles related to the XVIIth Olympiad, see "Great Olympic Moments," *Ebony* 47 (December 1991), 47 (January 1992), and 47 (March 1992), which contains brief articles about Cassius Clay's battle for the gold medal as a light-heavyweight boxer, Wilma Rudolph's three gold medals in sprinting, and Rafer Johnson's gold medal in track.

Eric Leslie Davies

TOKYO 1964

THE GAMES OF THE XVIIIth OLYMPIAD

The history of Japan's abiding interest in staging the Olympic Games goes back to June 1930 when Hidejiro Nagata, the mayor of Tokyo, lobbied for his city as a possible site for the 1940 Summer Games. On October 28, 1931, the Tokyo Municipal Assembly approved a resolution inviting the Olympic Organizing Committee to visit Tokyo. In 1936, after the Thirty-fifth International Olympic Committee (IOC) General Session in Berlin, London withdrew from consideration for the 1940 Games, leaving Tokyo and Helsinki as the two remaining contenders. On July 31, 1936, when the voting took place, Tokyo won over Helsinki by a vote of 36–27 and was named the host city for the 1940 Games. Accordingly, an organizing committee, coordinated by Prince Tokugawa, was formed in Tokyo in December 1936 to begin the preparations. In July 1937, however, Japan and China went to war, forcing domestic wartime mobilization and the withdrawal of Tokyo as the host city for the 1940 Games.

Japan's second attempt to host the Olympic Games began in earnest in May 1952 during the Helsinki Games. On July 2, 1952, an official invitation to hold the 1964 Games in Tokyo was transmitted to the secretary of the IOC. On March 7, 1953, Japan's House of Representatives passed a resolution supporting Tokyo's bid; later the Tokyo Metropolitan Assembly approved a similar resolution. Japan also did a superb public relations job by showing prospective facilities to IOC president Avery Brundage during his visit in April 1955. On January 22, 1958, the Tokyo Olympic Preparatory Committee was established, consisting of representatives of financial institutions, the media, and the government. At the long-awaited Fifty-fourth IOC session in May 1958, with Emperor Hirohito present, Seichiro Yasui, Tokyo's governor, presented Tokyo's formal bid for the 1964 Summer Games. The following May, the IOC met in Munich and chose Tokyo over Brussels, Vienna, and Detroit.

Japan's efforts to make the Tokyo Olympics spectacular were tarnished by cold war political issues. The major controversy concerned the Games of the New Emergency Forces (GANEFO). Indonesia, which had been suspended by the IOC over the question of admitting teams from Israel and Taiwan to the Fourth Asian Games at Djakarta in 1962, had organized GANEFO and had persuaded the People's Republic of China (PRC) to take part in this event. The IOC had warned that countries participating in GANEFO would be ineligible to compete at Tokyo. As a result, Indonesia and North Korea were barred from the Tokyo Games.

Once Tokyo was selected, strategic planning for the Games began. Several renovation activities were undertaken in preparation for the Games. In particular, Meiji Olympic Park, Yoyogi Park, and Komazawa Sports Park were given priority, since a variety of events were to be staged at these venues. In addition, other facilities were constructed in Kanagawa, Saitama, Chiba, and Nagano. The land required for this purpose was leased by the Tokyo city government, which also contracted for the building of new access roads to the sites.

Road building was a major project, given the recent population increase of the Tokyo area. A comprehensive highway and road construction plan was prepared, with a completion date set for August 1964. The total cost of the project surpassed $200 million. In addition, two new lines totaling over 22 kilometers were added to the metropolitan Tokyo subway system, and improvements were made in the passenger ship–handling facilities at the port of Tokyo.

The three major coordinators of Games preparations were the Ministry of Education, the Japanese Amateur Sports Association, and the Tokyo Metropolitan Government. The Bureau of Olympic Preparations, created in October 1959, coordinated all the public works projects, and the Metropolitan Police Board was formed in March 1960 to handle matters of law and order at the Games. The Fire Defense Agency established a task force to ensure adequate emergency facilities.

Money for the Games came from the metropolitan and national governments, as well as from private donations. Between 1959 and 1964, the Olympic Organizing Committee raised $4.3 million from contributors.

As opening day approached, the renovation of the various sport complexes and the scheduling of the events were completed. Twenty-two different venues were employed in the Games, with the national stadium hosting the opening and closing ceremonies, as well as the track and field competition.

Excellent arrangements were made to house the athletes and officials during the Games. Some $555,000 from the metropolitan government and $1.1 million from the Shoko Chukin Bank was made available for loans to remodel Japanese inns, known as *ryokan,* to make them suitable for foreign visitors. Rooms in nearly 600 private homes were also rented to visitors. In addition, some 1,600 visitors were accommodated on five passenger ships berthed in Tokyo harbor. Finally, some visitors found lodging in schools, churches, and youth hostels.

Much attention was devoted to public transportation arrangements. On September 28, 1960, a special committee on transportation was created, consisting of representatives from government departments and sport organizations. This committee handled such matters as the entry formalities for arriving athletes and officials and their equipment and the complicated task of coordinating transportation to and from the different venues. The committee employed over 21,000 automobiles and 6,000 buses, in addition to trucks, jeeps, and helicopters. On the whole, the transportation system functioned smoothly during the Games.

Other aspects of the Games, such as entertainment for the participants, was also well handled. On the eve of the opening of the Games, some 40,000 attended a public reception at a local baseball field, including members of the royal family, IOC president Avery Brundage, members of the diplomatic corps, and foreign athletes and officials. The governor of Tokyo hosted a reception for IOC members and official Olympic committee representatives from participating nations. A Japanese dance performance, designated as one of the art exhibits of the Olympiad, was presented on October 1 as part of the Tokyo Arts Festival.

As happens in all Games, some athletes became Olympic heroes. Abebe Bikila, the Ethiopian marathon runner, won his second consecutive gold medal, despite having undergone stomach surgery just five weeks before the Games. His time of 2 hours, 12 minutes, 11.2 seconds was an Olympic record.

The performance of Al Oerter from the United States in the discus made him a folk hero. He too had triumphed over physical disabilities and won gold medals in three consecutive Olympics. His victory in Tokyo came in spite of a slipped disk and injured ribs.

Dawn Fraser, a 22-year-old sprint swimmer from Australia, won the 100-meter freestyle for the third consecutive time and set a third successive Olympic record. Don Schollander of the United States set three world and four Olympic records in winning gold medals in the 100-meter freestyle and 400-meter freestyle races, and as part of the U.S. team in the 4 × 100-meter and 4 × 200-meter freestyle relay races.

The Tokyo Games came to a spectacular conclusion with the staging of the closing ceremonies on October 24. The ceremonies were timed to coincide with sunset, and electronic bells played traditional music as Emperor Hirohito entered the royal box. In marched the athletes of the ninety-four competing nations. When the athletes finally had taken their places in the infield, Brundage formally declared the Tokyo Summer Games closed as the flame in the Olympic torch slowly disappeared. The scoreboard lit up with the word *Sayonara,* and then proclaimed, ''We meet again on Mexico City—1968.'' Thus ended the Tokyo Games, one of the most successful of modern times and a symbol of pride for all Japanese.

BIBLIOGRAPHICAL ESSAY

The Avery Brundage Collection at the University of Illinois Archives, Urbana-Champaign, Illinois, contains several boxes of material concerning the Tokyo Games, which took place near the midpoint of Brundage's tenure as IOC president. Among other items, these papers contain IOC correspondence, newspaper clippings, organizing committee publications, and information on the various cultural programs held in conjunction with the Games. The organizing committee's official report is *The Games of the XVIII Olympiad, Tokyo, 1964: The Official Report of the Organizing Committee* (Tokyo, 1964). The committee published numerous other works in English, including *Results of the Games of the XVIII Olympiad, Tokyo, 1964,* 4 vols. (Tokyo, 1964); *Tokyo Games Facilities/Les Installations des jeux de Tokyo* (Tokyo, 1964); and *Olympic Medical Archives* (Tokyo, 1964).

By 1964, the Olympic committees of most major participating nations were regularly publishing their own reports. See Arthur G. Lentz and Asa S. Bushnell, eds., *1964 United States Olympic Book* (New York, 1965); Doug Gardner, ed., *The British Olympic Association Official Report of the Olympic Games 1964* (London, 1965); Francis J. Shaughnessy et al., eds., *Canada Competes at the Olympic Games 1964* (Montreal, 1965); *Sport de France: Jeux olympiques Tokyo 1964* (Paris, 1964); *XVIII. Olympische Sommerspiele Tokio 1964* (Berlin, 1964); and *Die Spiele der XVIII. Olympiade, Tokio 1964. Das offizielle Standardwerke des Nationalen Olympischen Komitees* (Stuttgart, 1965).

Secondary works include diaries by observers and autobiographies of participants. See Neil Allen, *Olympic Diary: Tokyo 1964* (London, 1964); Christopher Brasher, *Tokyo 1964: A Diary of the XVIIIth Olympiad* (Tokyo, 1964); Dawn Fraser and Harry Gordon, *Below the Surface* (New York, 1965), the account of the three-time swimming champion; and Dorothy Hyman, *Sprint to Fame* (London, 1964), by the British runner who won a silver medal in the 100-meter race in 1960 but finished eighth at Tokyo. Finally, for the GANEFO controversy, consult the general books on politics in the Olympics as well as Ewa T. Parker, *GANEFO: Sports and Politics in Djakarta* (Santa Monica, Calif., 1964).

Mohammed B. Alam

MEXICO CITY 1968
THE GAMES OF THE XIXth OLYMPIAD

The 1960s was a decade of controversy and conflict, of ferment and protest: the Vietnam War escalated; international condemnation of South African apartheid intensified; the rapid move toward independence altered the political map of Africa; civil war in the former Belgian Congo led to the death of United Nations secretary-general Dag Hammarskjöld; the Cuban missile crisis carried the world to the brink of nuclear war; student unrest shook France, Germany, Japan, and the United States; rebellious popular behavior provoked often brutal responses in such places as Brazil and Uruguay; and the black civil rights movement in the United States brought change along with serious white resistance. In 1968 alone, assassins in the United States ended the lives of Martin Luther King, Jr., and Robert Kennedy, and violent confrontations marred the Democratic National Convention in Chicago, while in both France and the United States, university students raised their protests to new levels, and in China the Cultural Revolution raged on. Also that year the Soviet Union invaded Czechoslovakia to suppress a nationalistic and ideologically deviant movement.

Host Mexico and the Summer Olympics scheduled for October 12–27 could not avoid those forces. Perceived as most dangerous was a predominantly student protest and demand for change that began as a meaningless fistfight between two secondary school students but triggered an armed intervention by police and riot control troops. University students, particularly at the National University (UNAM), began to organize for action, eventually directing demonstrations, some quite impressive, and calling a general strike that only partially, yet noticeably, materialized. In turn, the army occupied the UNAM campus and continued to harass student leaders. The climax came on October 2 when troops surrounded a group of students and sympathizers in the Plaza of the Three Cultures or Tlatelolco, for the name of the surrounding neighborhood, as the area was known in the fifteenth-century Aztec capital of Tenochtitlán. Without cause or warning, the troops fired into the crowd, killing between 100 and 500 persons and wounding perhaps a thousand more. Following that "massacre," more protesters and suspected dissidents were arrested, tortured, or killed. Others were pursued for several years.

Well before that confrontation, at its Sixtieth General Session in Baden-Baden, Germany, on October 18, 1963, the International Olympic Committee (IOC) had accepted Mexico's City's bid, initially submitted on December 7, 1962, to host the 1968 Summer Olympics, rejecting similar invitations from Detroit, Lyons, and Buenos Aires. In anticipation of this victory, President Adolfo López Mateos had decreed in May 1963 the establishment of the organizing committee for the Games of the XIXth Olympiad, though it was not formally constituted until after the IOC decision. Following the Baden-Baden meeting, the government created an executive commission directed by a long-time sports promoter, General José A. Jesús Clark Flores; vice chairmanships were filled by Agustín Legorreta, for finance, and Pedro Ramírez Vázquez, for building, who were to be aided by eighteen specialized sections.

In June 1965 President Gustavo Díaz Ordáz chose López Mateos to fill the still-vacant chairmanship of the organizing committee, but due to declining health the former president stepped down after one year and was replaced by the architect Ramírez Vázquez. In October 1966 the committee created seven departments to carry out its functions: administration, sports technique, public relations, courtesies to visitors, control of installations, control of programs, and artistic and cultural activities. Now, with computer assistance and the aid of numerous government agencies and private companies, serious work began. The organizing committee also initiated a sophisticated campaign of publicity and public relations.

Many Mexicans viewed hosting the Games as a means to advance their country's long attempt to raise its global prestige and thereby earn greater acceptance as a place safe for tourists and foreign investors. The student movement of July–October 1968 seemed to threaten those dreams, which explains, though without excusing, the government's harsh reaction, especially at Tlatelolco. In addition to the 1968 Olympics, Mexican officials no doubt considered the impact of any social uprising on their obligation to host the 1970 soccer World Cup, another step in that long process of Mexican efforts to overcome five decades of foreign memory of its oft-cited revolution (1910–1920) and its status as a Third World country. Overlapping this concern was the perception that any prolonged instability would bring into question the hegemony of the ruling Partido Revolucionario Institucional (PRI) (Institutional Revolutionary party) and the authority of President Díaz Ordáz. Therefore, security for the Games was increased, whether necessary or not.

Meanwhile, within the IOC a potentially disruptive debate arose over the role of South Africa, which had been banned from Tokyo in 1964 because of racial policies offensive to the expanding body of black African states and to gradually more sensitive people in other world communities. Some eight months before the XIXth Olympiad, the IOC, based on a pledge from South African whites that they would modify their selection process to permit blacks to qualify, lifted the ban. In response, African nations announced plans to boycott the Games and soon had the support of countries in the West Indies, the Islamic world, and Eastern Europe, bringing to around forty the number of countries expressing their willingness to be absent from Mexico City. Finally the Soviet Union threatened to stay home. Attempts to negotiate a compromise failed, so a divided and reluctant IOC voted to withdraw the invitation sent to Pretoria. The Mexicans also chose to deny entry to all Rhodesian athletes, despite their country's promise to send an integrated team, because of perceptions that the governing regime was composed of white racists and that black Africans would again be offended.

Less directly political were several issues facing the IOC before and during the Games. Performance-enhancing drugs were not yet a source of intense pre-occupation, and irregular testing and observation brought only one expulsion: for alcohol abuse. Of greater importance to Olympic leaders was the suspicion that not all female athletes were truly female, either because of genetic irregularities or medical treatments. At least 640 females scheduled to compete were subjected to gender tests; none was disqualified.

As at the 1968 Winter Games in Grenoble, the IOC struggled to halt the spread of commercialism, at least among athletes, and thus the decline of amateurism as defined by the IOC. But the IOC was virtually powerless to stop the trend, and the Games, both Winter and Summer, generated a spate of stories about athletes who received gifts or kickbacks for their participation. A major source of income was the makers of sports equipment who paid athletes to wear their products and display their brand names conspicuously. Pressure to do this increased as television became more intrusive. Mexico City represented the first serious attempt at live broadcasting for a major market, the success of which would generate a television explosion at future Games. The IOC wanted the revenue, the manufacturers wanted the exposure, and the athletes wanted pay for their cooperation. This alliance would eventually bring openly professional athletes to virtually all Olympic sports, as fans and sponsors sought the best athletes, and the IOC could not disrupt the Games by banning so many obvious violators.

If Mexico's historic reputation and recent domestic unrest raised doubts about its ability to fulfill its Olympic responsibilities, even greater concern among some participant countries arose because of Mexico City's relatively high altitude of 7,400 feet. Critics predicted that this site, by far the highest in Summer Olympic history, would physically harm the athletes and distort the competition. To equalize the competitors, the British proposed that athletes be limited in the amount of time they could train above a certain altitude, an idea that received only mild support and was impossible to enforce. Mexican officials tried to reduce the nervousness by citing the number of local residents and foreign tourists who frequented the capital each year without obvious difficulty and by staging three pre-Olympic international sports competitions in which athletes experienced minimal problems. In the end, no nation withdrew from the Games because of the altitude issue. Of less concern were the growing congestion and pollution caused by the city's nearly 10 million inhabitants in an environment with too little air movement. A few alarmists did call attention to the intestinal discomfort often cited as a problem among foreigners visiting Mexico.

Ultimately 113 countries sent 5,531 athletes (4,750 males, 781 females) to participate in 182 competitive events involving eighteen official and two demonstration sports. In the end, by whatever means, athletes from forty-four countries carried home 174 gold, 170 silver, and 183 bronze medals. Track and field, with 780 males and 239 females representing ninety-two countries, was the leading category of athletic performance. All sporting events were held in and around Mexico City, except the sailing competitions, which were assigned to

Acapulco and its yacht club, 250 miles south on the Pacific coast. To house so many visiting athletes and conduct so many events, the Mexicans needed to prepare adequate physical facilities. The decision was made to take advantage of space all over the sprawling city, to maximize intercultural contacts, and to organize local services to meet the need: it was decentralized planning at its practical limits.

The Olympic Village for athletes was newly constructed south of the capital. The 5,000-unit complex combined large urban apartment blocks with varied open spaces and provided facilities to entertain the residents, aid in their training, and encourage them to mix across national lines. To the northeast of the village was the new 22,000-seat Sports Palace, with its masonry base capped by a copper-covered dome. Another new facility was the Olympic pool and gymnasium, a compound structure with both an aquatic center for swimming and diving and a small arena for volleyball. To the southeast, at the famous tourist site of Xochimilco, home of the floating gardens that date back to the fifteenth-century Aztecs, the Mexicans created a fine basin that served both rowing and canoeing. Other new structures included a prefabricated fencing arena, a velodrome next to the Sports Palace, and the partially roofed Aztec Stadium, privately financed, used in 1968 for Olympic soccer and then fully exploited during the 1970 World Cup.

Among the several renovated structures, the most used was the University City Stadium, renamed the Olympic Stadium, with a modernistic design and artwork based on indigenous motifs. This was the site of the opening and closing ceremonies and most of the track and field competitions. The refurbished National Auditorium in Chapultepec, with 12,800 seats, served successfully as the gymnastics venue. Weight lifting was held in the Insurgentes Theater, water polo in the UNAM pool, and target shooting on a military base.

Expanding on the Games' athletic content, Mexican officials, with encouragement from the IOC, sponsored cultural and academic activities equal to the number of Olympic sports and often integrated with them. Ninety-seven countries participated in the year-long Cultural Olympiad, offering such programs as international festivals of the arts, folk arts, sculptors, and poets; exhibitions of Olympic philately and of the history and art of the Olympic Games; exhibitions on space research and nuclear energy; ballet; an international youth film festival; an international meeting of young architects; an Olympic camp for world youth; and a presentation of the XIXth Olympiad in motion pictures and television. These events were held in museums and auditoriums, along busy thoroughfares, and in the city's green and spacious Chapultepec Park. Avery Brundage expressed hope that Mexico's expansive cultural program would mark a return to "the purity, beauty and simplicity" of the Olympic tradition.

Perhaps observers realized that this would be a special Olympic event when, at the opening ceremony, Norma Enriqueta Basilio, a 20-year-old hurdler, became the first woman in Olympic history to bring the Olympic torch into the stadium and carry it up ninety-two steps to light the Olympic flame, a feminist prize even Avery Brundage applauded.

Across the Games themselves, almost certainly the altitude did have an effect on performance, especially at the shorter racing distances and in field events, as well as among athletes who had trained extensively far enough above sea level; it often hampered those who had not. The sport that seemed to suffer most from the thin air was rowing; oxygen resuscitations were required on at least sixteen occasions. Still, uneven performances by athletes regardless of where they trained suggests a psychological dimension as well. For whatever combination of factors, these Games witnessed some remarkable feats; 252 competitors surpassed previous Olympic records in those sports that can meaningfully be measured precisely in time, weight, or points. In total, competitors matched or surpassed twenty-four world and fifty-six Olympic records.

It was in track and field that so many records fell; only twelve of thirty-eight track and field events failed to tie an old or produce some new record. Besides the altitude, track performances were surely improved by the new all-weather synthetic track, called Tartan by the 3M Company that developed and manufactured it. Its surface maintained uniform toughness and even resiliency, did not rut, and was impervious to weather. Competing mainly at the Olympic Stadium, men and women track and field participants combined to equal or exceed seventeen world and twenty-six Olympic records. In the five long-distance running events (1,500 meters and up) athletes from Ethiopia, Kenya, and Tunisia swept the gold medals, demonstrating both the benefit of their long-time mountain training and the increasing importance of their continent in the global sports arena. Highly acclaimed was Kipchoge "Kip" Keino of Kenya, whose time of 3 minutes, 34.9 seconds in the 1,500 meters easily beat the Olympic record of Herb Elliot of Australia and, in this race, his closest competitor, Jim Ryun of the United States, by almost 3 seconds and 20 yards.

Surely the most spectacular of the records was set in the long jump. First, Ralph Boston of the United States reached the world record in a qualifying leap on his way to a bronze medal. The next day he watched in amazement as the erratic but recently very successful Bob Beamon, who had won twenty of his last twenty-one meet competitions, reached the incredible distance of 29 feet, 2½ inches, almost 2 feet over the existing record of 27 feet, 4¾ inches, setting a mark that lasted some twenty-five years. It was a humid, overcast day, ideal for the long jump, yet only Beamon put together so impressive a performance.

Although aided some by the thinner air and lower gravitational force, U.S. high jumper Dick Fosbury and numerous pole vaulters, such as U.S. gold medal winner Bob Seagren, also benefited from new technologies and revised techniques. Gold medalist Fosbury forever changed high jumping with his head-first, stomach-up, flat-body leap, the "Fosbury flop," made less dangerous with the placement of a thick foam-filled landing pad instead of the traditional sand or sawdust pit; he won with a height of 7 feet, 4½ inches. The vaulters at last learned to take advantage of the fiberglass poles introduced a few years earlier to rise to new standards. Nine men cleared the historic Olympic barrier of 17 feet; Seagren won at 17 feet, 8½ inches. Less heralded but equally admirable was Al Oerter's fourth consecutive Olympic record and gold medal in the discus throw, a result of hard work and concentration.

In addition to the official Mexican desire to promote the host country and its willingness to spend for that purpose, the larger political atmosphere encroached on the Games in several ways, though local student activists who had generated such emotions over the previous two and one-half months were absent, due perhaps to a lack of organization, a fear of government brutality, or a sense of nationalistic interest in seeing the Games succeed; it will probably never be known for certain which determined the lack of further protest. What is certain is that spectators vigorously welcomed the Czechoslovakian delegation and adopted as one of their special heroines Vera Čáslavská, its highly talented gymnast, who became the symbol of suffering under communist aggression and, perhaps more generally, of small country resistance to great power domination. While Čáslavská could never drive the Soviets from her homeland, she, her fans, and her countrymen could take pride in her outstanding performance: four gold and two silver medals and the individual title, topping three Soviet stars and two East Germans. Even some other communist athletes cheered her on. After competing in three Olympics (1960, 1964, 1968), Čáslavská had earned seven gold and four silver medals.

Perhaps the most controversial and memorable political statement was that made by Tommie Smith and John Carlos of the United States. Teammates from San Jose State College, they had considered the suggestion of activist sociologist Harry Edwards to boycott the Games to protest mistreatment of blacks and denial of their human and civil rights and had helped him organize in 1967 the Olympic Project for Human Rights (OPHR). Eventually they chose to attend, though basketball great Lew Alcindor (later Kareem Abdul-Jabbar) did not, but they still sought a way to express their deep convictions. They got their chance when Smith won the gold and Carlos won the bronze medal in the 200-meter sprint. On the victory stand, during the national anthem, the two bowed their heads, closed their eyes, and raised their arms straight up, Smith's right and Carlos's left fists covered by black gloves, in the well-known black power salute; their shoeless feet showed only long black socks, a symbol of black poverty. For this act they were suspended from their national team and expelled from the Olympic Village. During the awards ceremony, silver medalist Peter Norman of Australia wore a badge supporting the OPHR that he received in advance from Smith and Carlos, in sympathy with their movement.

As the two militants were preparing to depart Mexico, three of their black teammates, medal winners in the 400-meter final, expressed their sympathy by donning black berets when entering the stadium to receive their medals. After winning the 4 × 400-meter relay, those three and a fourth runner mounted the victory stand, left hands under their jackets, saluted, and assumed the military at-ease position during the playing of the "Star Spangled Banner." Bob Beamon later demonstrated his solidarity by wearing black socks while trying another jump following his record leap.

Whether the appeal of 1936 Olympic hero Jesse Owens for black moderation mattered or not, not all U.S. blacks at the Games chose to protest. Wyomia Tyus impressively won the 100-meter sprint, becoming the first woman to win consecutive Olympic sprint titles, and she later helped the 400-meter relay team to a gold medal, yet she took no political action. Houston's George Foreman not only opposed the protest effort but marched around the ring waving a small U.S. flag after winning the gold medal in heavyweight boxing. Others may have remained silent out of fear of retaliation or because of money offers from sports agents or manufacturers.

After the Games had ended and the foreign athletes and media had departed, Mexicans assessed the impact of that unique spectacle. Official reports indicate that expenditures were higher than those of Rome in 1960 but well below those of Tokyo in 1964. The total outlay in U.S. dollars was $175,840,000 (93.9 percent spent within Mexico): $53.6 million for sports installations, $16.56 million for city works, $16.08 million for athlete housing in the Miguel Hidalgo Olympic Village, $12.72 million for accommodations for the cultural delegations in the Narciso Mendoza Village, and $76.88 million for organizing committee direct expenditures. All but the last item represented investments in permanent constructions to benefit the city and country in the future and were spent in conjunction with various government agencies such as the Ministry of Public Works and the Department of the Federal District.

To cover these costs, the organizing committee derived income from a range of sources: the Mexican government provided a subsidy equivalent to $56 million; committee activities, including ticket sales, brought in an additional $20 million. Of the latter, $6.41 million derived from international television rights; ABC alone paid $4.5 million for the U.S. market and sent a staff of 450 to handle production and transmission. Another $3.89 million more came from foreign services and royalty payments, while an additional $9.76 million was derived from local television rights, concessions, royalties, services, and contributions of in-kind goods and services by various private companies. To carry out its work, the organizing committee for a brief period in October 1968 employed as many as 14,000 people, though the number was generally much lower before September and dropped rapidly afterward. Independent of the committee, expenditures of the participating nations were estimated at over $2 million.

For this price Mexicans received not just the pleasure and profit of the Games themselves. In theory they indirectly benefited from the increased spending by visiting teams and tourists and an increase in tax collections. They also inherited a technologically superior television and communications system, a few pre-Hispanic archeological ruins exposed during construction, housing units in the two Olympic Villages, numerous works of art created especially for the occasion and left for public enjoyment, an improved athletic infrastructure, vast experience in organizing and conducting an elaborate global festival, and a sense of national achievement and pride. Simultaneously, Mexicans cheered their largest Olympic squad ever, 300 athletes in eighteen events, who gave their country its best results ever: three each of gold, silver, and bronze medals. It was hoped thereby that they did in fact improve their country's international image and stimulate long-term tourism and economic activity. Surely they paid a price, at Tlatelolco and in government spending, but for many, apparently it was a price worth paying.

Despite the alarming warnings, threatening outside forces, and obstacles within Mexico City, in the words of Bob Phillips, writing in the British report on the Games: "The ultimate winners of the Games were the Mexicans themselves, and their organisation at every venue was virtually beyond criticism." These Games were, in short, "the biggest and the best" since the Olympics were revived in the modern era. It is hard to disagree.

BIBLIOGRAPHICAL ESSAY

Considerable primary source material for the Mexico City Games is contained in the Avery Brundage Papers in the archives at the University of Illinois, Urbana, Illinois. Material related to the work of the organizing committee, the cultural events, the Rhodesian problem, and the Smith and Carlos dismissal may be found there, as well as a large collection of newspaper clippings, press releases, and five scrapbooks of material on the South African readmission question.

Among the published sources, the place to begin is Beatrice Trueblood, ed., *Mexico 1968*, 4 vols. (Mexico City, 1968). This is the official report of the organizing committee; the four volumes cover the country, the organization, the Games, and the cultural Olympiad. Before and during the Games, the committee published *Noticiero Olímpico* to communicate to the public its plans and scheduled events. Beginning in 1966, the committee also published *Mexico 68,* a series of forty newsletters in English, containing promotional material and background information on the Games.

Useful descriptions and analyses by foreign observers come from Bob Phillips, ed., *Official Report of the Olympic Games* (London, 1969), the official British Olympic Committee report; Francisco Echeverría and José María Múgica, eds., *Juegos Olímpicos-México 68* (Zallia, Spain, 1968), a Spanish summary, and Caetano Carlos Paioli, *Brasil Olimpico* (São Paulo, 1985), a Brazilian outlook. The official U.S. Olympic Committee report is Arthur G. Lentz and Frederick Fliegner, eds., *1968 United States Olympic Book* (Lausanne, 1968); the Canadian version is E. H. Radford and Francis J. Shaughnessy, eds., *Canada Competes at the Olympic Games 1968* (Montreal, 1969).

Additional insights into the construction projects completed for the Games are found in Barclay F. Gordon, *Olympic Architecture: Building for the Summer Games* (New York, 1983). Brazilian experts look at the construction and other technical and scientific aspects of sports performance in Mexico in Arthur Orlando da Costa Ferreira, et al., *Olimpiada-Mexico 68* (Brasilia, 1969). A critical British perspective of the altitude and facilities at these Games is found in Christopher Brasher, *Mexico 68: A Diary of the XIXth Olympiad* (London, 1968).

For discussions of the contemporary political atmosphere in Mexico, especially the student protests of 1968 and the government excesses at Tlatelolco, consult Barry Carr,

Marxism and Communism in Twentieth-Century Mexico (Lincoln, Neb., 1992), and Elena Poniatowska, *Massacre in Mexico* (New York, 1975). A consideration of how the 1968 Olympics fit into Mexico's long-term sports policy and its connection to larger domestic and foreign affairs is offered by Joseph L. Arbena, "Sport, Development, and Mexican Nationalism, 1920–1970," *Journal of Sport History* 18 (Winter 1991): 350–64. Armandow Satow traces the expanding role of Mexico in the Summer Olympics in a series of twelve articles published in July 1980 in the Mexican newspaper *Uno Más Uno.*

For an understanding of the meaning of the U.S. black protests in relation to the Games, consult Arthur R. Ashe, Jr., *A Hard Road to Glory: A History of the African-American Athlete since 1946* (New York, 1988); the series of introspective pieces contained in *Sports Illustrated,* August 5, 1991; and David K. Wiggins, " 'The Year of Awakening': Black Athletes, Racial Unrest and the Civil Rights Movement of 1968," *International Journal of the History of Sport* 9 (August 1992): 188–208.

An excellent illustrated history of the Games is Antonio Lavin, *México en los Juegos Olímpicos MCMLXVIII* (Tacubaya, Mexico, 1968), which also contains a survey of Mexican participation in the Olympics since 1928. A set of reminiscences of knowledgeable spectators is *Tafnot 68* (Los Altos, Calif., 1969), a *Track and Field News* publication based on a tour to the Games sponsored by the magazine.

Joseph L. Arbena

MUNICH 1972

THE GAMES OF THE XXth OLYMPIAD

With a long tradition of public interest in athletics and sports, German proponents of Olympism overcame the initial opposition of their national gymnastics societies to the international Olympic Games. By 1896, under the leadership of Willibald Gebhardt, Germany had joined the modern Olympic movement. The International Olympic Committee (IOC) awarded the 1916 Games to Berlin, but they were canceled due to World War I. The German team returned to Olympic competition in 1928 and finished second to the United States in total medals. In the summer of 1932, the IOC awarded the 1936 Olympic Games to Berlin. Adolf Hitler's Nazi party came to power in 1933. Under Hitler, the Olympics became a priority event to showcase the new regime's program to restore the shattered German economy. The racist ideology of the Nazis, however, created many problems and inspired groups in other countries to join a movement to boycott the Games. By the effective use of promises and some moderation of official policies, the German hosts avoided the boycott, staged the Games, and reaped a propaganda harvest in worldwide press coverage and Leni Riefenstahl's film *Olympia*. After 1936, the policies of the Nazi dictatorship were a major factor in polarizing the fascist-communist conflict in Europe, which led to World War II in 1939. The Holocaust and the destruction of the German economy during the war prevented German participation in the postwar Olympics until 1952. In 1960, IOC president Avery Brundage succeeded in persuading the Federal Republic of Germany (West Germany) and the German Democratic Republic (East Germany) to send a united team to the Rome Games. Though the German states were still occupied by North Atlantic Treaty Organization and Warsaw Pact troops, respectively, economic aid programs helped restore the West German economy, and the national devotion to sports brought both Germanys back into the Olympic movement. Meeting in Rome on April 22, 1966, the IOC awarded the 1972 Games to the German cities of Munich, Augsburg, and Kiel.

The Federal Republic hailed the 1972 Games as an opportunity to demonstrate the stability of the new government, the restoration of the economy, and German dedication to the ideal of peaceful competition in international athletics. In welcoming athletes of the world, German president Gustav Heinemann acknowledged that the Games alone would not ''be able to banish disputes and discord, violence and war from the world, even for a short time,'' but he welcomed them as ''a milestone on the road to a new way of life with the aim of realizing peaceful coexistence among peoples.''

Under the leadership of organizing committee chairman Willi Daume, the program was planned in meticulous detail. An astute German industrialist, Daume had been chosen for IOC membership in 1957. In April 1969, the organizing committee concluded a contract with the American Broadcasting Company (ABC) television network for $7.5 million for television rights and $6 million for the technical costs of producing the broadcasts. The Munich committee combined massive support from governmental agencies with television revenues and promotional fund raising to build a futuristic stadium, Olympic Village, sports arenas, and water sports sites. A new subway system connected these facilities with the center of the city. The principal Munich site was built on piles of rubble dumped after the postwar reconstruction of the bombed city. Under the direction of Otl Aichers, a graphic artist, coordinated colors and a series of sport pictographs were employed to negate the memory of the nationalistic propaganda themes of the Berlin Olympics.

At the IOC meeting before the Games, President Brundage recalled the controversies of the 1956, 1960, 1964, and 1968 Games and proclaimed that the Olympic movement was "strong, healthy and flourishing." He conceded that success brought greater "commercial and political intrusion" and urged that the rules relating to amateurism "should be made stronger and enforced more rigorously" (*Olympic Review,* 59 [Oct. 1972], pp. 346–47, 379). German president Gustav Heinemann acknowledged that the Olympic Games "have at no time been capable of bringing the peoples to refrain from violence." In deploring nationalism, he regretted that the 1936 Berlin Games "were abused by the then rulers in Germany for their purposes" (Wallburg-Zgoll, *Die Spiele der XX. Olympiade München,* 1972, p. 3).

By 1972, global television coverage had made the Olympics a venue for political protests as well as international athletic competition. Millions of viewers remembered the 1968 riots, boycotts, and Black Power protests in Mexico City. Before the Munich Games began, the IOC was faced with a widespread boycott by African nations and voted to bar the Rhodesian team. With an Olympic team from the German Democratic Republic competing for the first time, the stage was set for competition between the communist East and the capitalist West. Press officer Hans Klein provided luxurious quarters for 7,000 print, radio, and television journalists and technicians, while the athletes were housed in a new Olympic Village, consisting of series of high-rise apartments interspersed with lower, four-story buildings. Shops and transit facilities were nearby, and care was taken to ensure a parklike setting that would make the complex attractive as private housing after the Games.

The opening ceremonies occurred before 80,000 spectators on August 26 in the new Olympic stadium. Competition began the following day and lasted until September 11. The United States and the Soviet Union men's track and field teams each won six gold medals. Four additional gold medals were evenly divided between the West and East German teams. Finland's Lasse Viren won the 5,000-meter and 10,000-meter races, becoming only the fourth Olympian to do so in the same Games. The U.S. runner Frank Shorter won the marathon.

The East German women won six of fourteen women's track and field events, and the West German women won four events. In swimming, Mark Spitz of the United States won seven gold medals—four in individual events and three in team relays. Freestyle specialist Shane Gould of Australia won three gold medals as well as a silver and a bronze in the women's competition. U.S. swimmer Rick DeMont was disqualified after winning the 400-meter freestyle when traces of an illegal drug were found in his system during routine testing after the race. DeMont had taken asthma medicine the night before the race; team doctors were unaware that it contained a banned substance.

While the track and field and swimming events were well covered by the international television networks, the Munich Games marked the emergence of women's gymnastics with its coverage of Olga Korbut of the Soviet Union. The diminutive Soviet gymnast, who had made her team only as an alternate, captivated television audiences as she won two gold medals and a silver medal in individual competition. East Europeans dominated the weight lifting and wrestling events. American television viewers were dismayed when only one American won a gold medal in boxing.

In one of the greatest controversies of the Munich Games, the American basketball team lost to the Soviet Union in the finals, ending a sixty-two-game Olympic winning streak for the United States. The disputed 51–50 Soviet victory came after the game was twice resumed after the final horn had apparently sounded. The first resumption was on the order of the head of the International Basketball Federation; the second, amid great confusion, occurred because of a claim that the clock had not been properly adjusted after the first resumption of play. Impassioned appeals from the Americans, who had been leading 50–49 when the game ended for the first time, were unsuccessful, and members of the U.S. team refused to attend the victory ceremony to accept their silver medals.

In retrospect, the meticulous preparations of German hosts, the political boycott threats, and the thrilling performances by the athletes were overshadowed by an act of political terrorism. Early on the morning of September 5, eight Palestinians seized eleven members of the Israeli team in a raid on their apartments in the Olympic Village. Two Israelis were killed during the capture. After a day of siege and unsuccessful negotiations in which the terrorists demanded the release of more than 200 Palestinians jailed in Israel and two well-known German terrorists, the German police allowed the terrorists to move the hostages to the airport in anticipation of a flight to a Middle Eastern destination. As the terrorists and hostages made their way toward a waiting airplane, the police opened fire. In the ensuing gun battle, all of the remaining hostages and three of the Palestinians were killed.

After stormy meetings of the IOC's executive board and then the full executive committee during the afternoon and evening of September 5, the committee voted to continue the Games. At a memorial service on September 6, German president Heinemann spoke of his grief and sorrow. IOC president Brundage mourned the loss of ''our Israeli friends'' and observed that ''the greater and more important the Olympic Games become, the more they are open to commercial, political and now criminal pressure.'' He expressed confidence that the public would agree that the committee could not "allow a handful of terrorists to destroy this nucleus of international cooperation and good will we have in the Olympic Movement." He declared a day of mourning and announced that "the Games must go on" (Guttman, *The Games Must Go On,* pp. 253–54). Amid continuing criticism from Arab spokesmen and Western sports figures and columnists, the Munich Games ended on September 11.

The Munich Games had been a huge success for the television networks, and the resulting bonanza speeded the commercialization and professionalization of the modern Games. The Mexico City Games of 1968 had opened the American market. The efficient German arrangements at Munich facilitated worldwide coverage and produced over $12 million for the IOC and the international athletic federations. The tangible and intangible publicity benefits to Munich and Bavaria have continued. The terrorist murders of members of the Israeli team provided both journalists and academics with new opportunities to condemn Germany, the host committee, the IOC, and the Olympic movement. The superb facilities allowed the athletes to compete under favorable conditions and establish many new world's records.

BIBLIOGRAPHICAL ESSAY

For primary source material, the Avery Brundage Collection at the University of Illinois Archives, Urbana-Champaign, Illinois, contains about 5,000 documents on the plans, preparations, and events of the Games. Of particular interest are three folders of material on the Israeli tragedy and two folders on the Rhodesian problem.

English, French, and German accounts in a pre-Games bulletin, *Olympia in München* (Munich, 1970–1972), document the progress of Olympic plans and building construction. A. Louis Wallburg-Zgoll, *Die Spiele der XX. Olympiade München 1972: Hymne an den Sport* (Frankfurt, 1972), is an illustrated, multilingual tribute to the Olympic movement with photographs of facilities and an account of the "German Excavations at Olympia" exhibition in Munich. The organizing committee's official report is *Die Spiele: Der offizielle Bericht . . . der XX. Olympiade München 1972,* edited by Liselott Diem and Ernest Knoesel, 3 vols. (Munich, 1974). American participation is documented in the illustrated *1972 United States Olympic Book* (Lausanne, 1972), edited by C. Robert Paul, Jr. Two pictorial histories with German text, Harry Valérien, *Olympia 1972* (Munich, 1972), and Werner Schneider, *Die Olympischen Spiele 1972* (Stuttgart, 1974), cover the results of all major events. Werner Trockau, *München Olympia '72* (Alsdorf, Germany, 1972), is a paperback account of the Games. Plans for the yachting competition at Kiel are covered in Werner Istel, ed., *Olympic Yachting Kiel '72* (1972). The results are printed in *Kiel '72* (1972). Arnd Kruger, *Sport und Politik* (1975), discusses the Munich Games in the context of the German sports tradition.

For the architecture of the Olympic facilities, see W. D. Thiem, "XX Olympic Games, Munich," *Progressive Architecture* 53 (August 1972): 58–63, which discusses the stadium, sports and swimming arenas, velodrome, media center, and Olympic Village. Also of interest are R. Middleton, "Munich 1972," *Architectural Design* 42 (August 1972): 477–89; A. Best and D. Rowlands, "Munich Olympics," *Design* 285 (September 1972): 29–53; and V. Mahler, *Olympiastadion* 137 (October 1972): 26–33.

The first interpretive account in English after the Games was Hans Lenk's chapter, "The 1972 Munich Olympic Games: A Dilemma?" in Peter J. Graham and Horst Ueberhorst, eds., *The Modern Olympics* (West Point, N.Y., 1976), pp. 199–208. Allen Guttmann discusses the Munich Games at length in his biography of Brundage, *The Games Must Go On* (New York, 1984); the title of the book is taken from Brundage's remarks following the Israeli tragedy. Richard Mandell, *The Olympics of 1972, a Munich Diary* (Chapel Hill, N.C., 1991), provides an egocentric, aesthetic appreciation of the Olympics embedded in involuted prose and sociological hostility. Nevertheless, it is one of the best accounts of an Olympic spectacle. Mandell's view is that the Games were a financial success for Munich and Bavaria but an ideological and political failure for the IOC and the German government. For the Israeli tragedy, see Serge Groussard, *The Blood of Israel: The Massacre of the Israeli Athletes: The Olympics, 1972* (New York, 1975). Jim McKay, *My Wide World* (New York, 1973), recalls the Munich Games from his position as ABC's television host; it was McKay who kept millions of viewers informed as the tragedy unfolded.

Maynard Brichford

MONTREAL 1976
THE GAMES OF THE XXITH OLYMPIAD

The 1976 Olympics were experienced and have been remembered as a kaleidoscope of contradictory narratives and outcomes. Promised as "modest," "self-financing" Games, they ended up with such monumental facilities, constructed with such little regard for their cost, that the Montreal Games have become the byword for gargantuan extravaganzas. Yet the venues proved to be admirably suited for athletes and spectators, and the events were extremely well organized, enabling superb performances in virtually every sport. The heavy military security, the clumsy censoring of the Arts and Culture Program, and a last-minute walkout by African nations had little effect on the mood of participants; an internationalist, carnivalesque atmosphere reigned throughout. The Games provided a heady stimulus to the development of Canadian and Quebec sport and fitness and pioneered the development of new sources of Olympic revenues.

Montreal was a fitting site for Canada's first Games. Standing at the junction of the St. Lawrence and Ottawa rivers, it was founded in 1643 near a long-established Iroquois village as the jumping-off point for French exploration of the interior. It quickly became the center of the North American fur trade. By the nineteenth century, the Scottish and English merchants who emigrated after the 1763 French and Indian War had made it the leading economic, political, and cultural center of the new Dominion of Canada and the "cradle of Canadian sports." The male, middle-class Anglo-Montrealers who codified and publicized the first rules started an Olympic Club in 1842, and held "Montreal Olympics" in 1844. Pierre de Coubertin visited their successors during his North American field trip in 1889–1890, and they took an early interest in his Games. A Montreal police constable, Etienne DesMarteau, won Canada's first official Olympic gold medal in 1904, and Montrealers helped create the Canadian Olympic Committee (now Association) two years later. They bid for the 1932, 1956 (Winter and Summer), and 1972 Olympics, before beating Los Angeles and Moscow to win the right to stage them in 1976 at the IOC's Seventieth Session in Amsterdam in 1970.

But the politics of language, nationalism, and regionalism were to confound organizers' hopes for a smooth preparation of facilities and programs. During the 1960s, Quebec society was transformed by a broad state-led secularization and modernization often referred to as the "quiet revolution." Seeking to be *maîtres chez nous*, French-speaking Québeçois, the descendants of the original European settlers, aggressively challenged the Anglo-Canadian elite's economic and cultural hegemony, particularly the expectation that everyone speak English in the workplace and commerce. Though united in the desire for language rights, French-Canadians were divided about the best strategy to advance their interests within the Canadian federation. Quebec nationalists sought French unilingualism and ever greater powers for the provincial legislature—their "national government." Federalists like Pierre Trudeau, who became prime minister in 1968, championed a bilingual pan-Canadianism.

The largest and most visible English-Canadian presence in Quebec was found in Montreal, where they made up just 16 percent of the population. (French speakers comprised 64 percent and those from other backgrounds 20 percent.) The city was the site of the fiercest debates about the national question, the most volatile demonstrations for and against language laws, and a small but growing number of bombing attacks by Quebec revolutionaries against English corporations and federal institutions. Nationalism also fueled a growing militancy among the working class. These tensions evoked a deep resentment in the English-speaking majority in other parts of Canada. In the western provinces, many opposed federal bilingualism and felt Montreal and Quebec were unfairly favored while western economic problems were ignored. On this unpropitious terrain, the Trudeau government decided against financial assistance for Montreal's bid (though it promised full support for Vancouver's simultaneous bid for the 1976 Winter Games).

Charismatic Montreal mayor Jean Drapeau made oratorical virtue out of necessity in his presentation to the IOC, promising low-cost games. But his real ambition was to create a lasting symbol of *la survivance*, the will of French Canada to survive two centuries of English Canadian attempts at assimilation. (After Paris, Montreal is the largest French-speaking city in the world.) But he still needed federal funding for the necessary facilities. A succession of political crises hardened the federal government against Drapeau's increasingly urgent appeals. In October 1970, the revolutionary Front de libération de Québec (FLQ) kidnapped a British consul and a Quebec cabinet minister, provoking Trudeau to declare martial law. In 1972, a general strike led by nationalist trade unions rekindled the anxieties in and about Quebec. In the federal election of that year, western alienation reduced Trudeau's Liberal party to minority government status. It was only in 1973, when the province of Quebec reluctantly accepted responsibility for any deficit, that the Trudeau government agreed to create a lottery and a coin and stamp program to provide revenue for the Games. The organizers could finally budget with confidence. But the clash of nationalisms had cost them thirty-four months of precious time.

Preparations were complicated by the ambitious design Drapeau had encouraged French architect Roger Taillibert to devise for the main facilities in Olympic Park. Olympic Stadium was to include a fifty-story tower and a retractable roof. The engineering for the velodrome, a "giant arc of a roof sweeping over glass walls, rising higher and higher with no visible means of support, then sloping back to earth," was among the most complex in the world. Construction was frequently disrupted by Taillibert's penchant for last-minute changes, the incompetence of contractors hired for political connections, and strikes and stoppages, in the context of continuing federalist-separatist and English-French tensions, and rapid inflation. Most of the key decisions were made in secret by Mayor Drapeau. There was virtually no accountability to anyone else. It was only when the province assumed full responsibility for construction in November 1975 that significant progress began to be made. Uncertainty about whether enough would be completed in time kept the IOC and everyone else on tenterhooks until a few weeks before the opening ceremony. (As it was, Olympic Stadium was not completed until 1987.)

There was no end to the controversy. First came the China question. In 1970, as part of the bid, the Trudeau government undertook to honor the fundamental IOC requirement that it grant entry to all IOC-recognized participants, "pursuant to the normal regulations." Few at the time realized that this nebulous phrase bore any substance. But several months prior to the Games, the government indicated that the "usual regulations" would be used to bar athletes and coaches from the Republic of China (Taiwan), in accordance with the one-China policy it had adopted in 1970. A compromise was reached only 48 hours before the opening ceremony: the delegation would be allowed to enter Canada on condition that they be designated from "Taiwan" at the Games. At that point, the Taiwanese withdrew.

During the same week, while African runners were turning in record performances on the practice track at Olympic Park, African sports leaders sought some gesture of condemnation for the New Zealand rugby tour of South Africa then taking place in the aftermath of the apartheid regime's brutal suppression of the children's revolt in Soweto. The IOC chose to do nothing, arguing that rugby was not an Olympic sport. This seeming insensitivity, at a time when there were only five black IOC members in the forty-one national Olympic committees (NOCs) from Africa, so enraged the African political leadership that it ordered its athletes home. Twenty-two teams (including Iraq and Guyana) sadly but proudly departed, some after participating in the preliminary events. (Seven other African NOCs did not send teams to Montreal.) The walkout had a sobering effect on the international community. Within days, the two largest federations—International Amateur Athletic Federation and the Fédération internationale de football association—expelled white South Africa from membership. The IOC soon became a strong ally of the international campaign against apartheid sports.

The final embarrassment occurred four days before the opening ceremony. Shortly after midnight, work crews dismantled and destroyed an outdoor art and photographic exhibit along the marathon route that was mildly critical of the city's wholesale demolition of single-family housing, including a number of grand nineteenth-century mansions, to clear the way for high-rise apartments and commercial offices. (The artists were compensated five years later by a provincial court.) It underscored the mayor's dictatorial style and the antagonism between the Olympics, conservationists, environmentalists, and community advocates of alternative public investments, which had also plagued the Games from the beginning.

When the Olympics finally opened on July 17, 4,834 male and 1,251 female athletes from eighty-eight nations remained in the lists. The turmoil and conflict of the preparation period were quickly, if temporarily, forgotten.

In the first full day of competition, a tiny, seemingly fearless 14-year-old Romanian gymnast captured the public imagination. Nadia Comaneci scored an unprecedented perfect 10 on the uneven parallel bars, then immediately followed that feat with another perfect 10 on the balance beam. During the rest of the competition, she earned another five 10s and won the all-around title, the bars and the beam, and the hearts of the live and television audience. The Soviet women gymnasts were equally breathtaking. Nelli Kim also recorded two 10s and, with the graceful Ludmilla Tourischeva and ebullient Olga Korbut, extended their country's unbeaten record in Olympic team competition to seven straight championships. Though overlooked in the media frenzy around Comaneci and her rivals, the men's competition was just as exciting, with the team title decided on the final routine of the horizontal bar. Mituso Tsukahara scored a 9.9 to bring Japan its fifth straight crown. The individual champion was Soviet Nikolai Andrianov, who took home four gold, two silver, and one bronze medal.

Performances were also electrifying at the Olympic pool. World records were smashed or equaled in all but three of the twenty-six events. The United States dominated the men's competition, winning twelve of thirteen events, while women from the German Democratic Republic (GDR) won eleven of thirteen events, often in times once thought unattainable. Petra Thümer's new record of 4 minutes, 9.89 seconds in the 400-meter freestyle would have taken the silver medal in the men's event in Mexico just eight years earlier. The GDR's 17-year-old Kornelia Ender was the overall star, winning an unprecedented four gold medals (and a silver in the medley relay), including two in world record times within 27 minutes of each other.

In rowing, relative novice Pertti Karppinen of Finland took the men's single sculls in a masterfully paced race, overtaking the favorites in the last few meters. The GDR won five of the men's and four of the women's races, placing in every event.

Despite the absence of the Africans from the running events, track and field produced some stirring contests. West Indian runners Hasely Crawford of Trinidad in the 100 meters, Don Quarrie of Jamaica in the 200 meters, and Alberto Juantorena of Cuba in the 400 and 800 meters were popular winners of the men's sprints. Though favored in the 400, the tall, explosively striding Juantorena was not expected to have either the stamina or the tactical experience for the longer race. But in the final, he led from the break, fought off all challengers, and won convincingly in a new world record. Four days later he was equally impressive in the 400, winning in the fastest time ever recorded at sea level. Finland's imperturbable Lasse Viren achieved another remarkable double in the 5,000 and 10,000 meters (repeating his victories at Munich), outdistancing his rivals with brazenly gradual—but powerfully sustained—accelerations over the final laps. World records were achieved by American Edwin Moses (400-meter hurdles), Sweden's Anders Garderud (steeplechase), American Bruce Jenner (decathalon), and Hungary's Miklos Nemeth (javelin).

Among the women, the GDR was in a class by itself, winning nine events and nineteen medals overall. In the pentathlon, the three GDR competitors—Siegrun Siegl, Christine Laser, and Burglinde Pollak—finished just 5 points apart. The most popular victor was Poland's 30-year-old Irene Szewinska (Kirszenstein), already a six-time Olympic medalist, who pulled away from 18-year-old rival Christina Brehmer of the GDR in the last 100 meters of the 400 meters to win handily and set a new world record. The Soviet Tatanya Kazankina not only won her specialty, the 1,500 meters, but captured a hotly contested 800 meters, in which she had just been entered on the final day, in world record time.

Montreal was an excellent Games for spectators. The spacious Olympic Park, with four main venues and two practice tracks, handy eating establishments, souvenir kiosks, and picnic areas, immediately adjacent to the Olympic Village; the efficient Metro and bus system; and several open entertainment quarters facilitated a continuous, convivial festival. Olympic veterans say Montreal was the most spirited Games of the post–World War II period. But the Games did not give tourism the expected boost. Despite 3.25 million paid admissions, few hotels were completely full, and during the Games, taxi drivers staged a one-day tie-up of downtown traffic to protest the loss of business to the organizing committee's 1,035-car fleet. Many visitors were athletes and coaches themselves, who came to watch, trade pins, and talk—not to spend money. They camped, rode their bicycles, and ate packed sandwich lunches. Those who relied on television enjoyed greater and more sophisticated coverage than ever before. In Canada, the Canadian Broadcasting Corporation telecast 175 hours, five times what it had shown from Munich.

More than half the entered teams took medals home from Montreal, but few other Games have been so dominated by the athletic superpowers. Taken together, the U.S.S.R., the United States, the two Germanys, and Japan captured 60 percent of the medals. The Soviet model of sports development, cloned in its European satellites and Cuba, claimed half of all medal winners. The most noteworthy results were achieved by the GDR. With athletes drawn from a relatively closed population of just 17 million, it won forty gold medals, just seven fewer than the Soviet Union and six more than the United States (although the Americans won more medals overall). While it is now evident that many of those victories were enabled by performance-enhancing drugs, as was alleged at the time, they were also achieved by the dogged application of sports science to the material conditions of performance, the development of an extensive school sports system, and a regime of hard training. In the wake of the Games, a growing number of sports leaders beat a path to the German College of Physical Culture in Leipzig, where the GDR coaches were trained.

Competition for women in three sports—basketball, handball, and rowing—and four events was added to the program in Montreal. The example of so many strong, healthy, athletically talented women helped demolish the myths of female biological frailty, which frustrated the growing demands of Western women for sporting opportunities. But the messages were not unambiguously enabling. The celebrated success of Comaneci accelerated the "infantilization" of women's gymnastics and body image begun by Olga Korbut, the International Gymnastics Federation, and the American Broadcasting Company in Munich. The statuesque Ludmilla Tourischeva, the champion Comaneci dethroned, was the last physically mature female gymnastic star to win an Olympic gold medal.

The Games provided an important stimulus to both Quebec and Canadian sport and fitness. In Montreal, they left behind an impressive array of training halls, administrative offices, and skilled and confident francophone leaders. It was the beginning of a proud new age for Quebec sports. Although some of the new facilities proved too expensive to maintain for sports, the much-criticized Olympic Park has become a successful tourist attraction. At the same time, the stimulus of the Games persuaded federal decision makers to replace the inefficient, volunteer administration of the Olympic sports in Canada with a state-designed and -financed professional infrastructure. The resulting Canadian sport system has significantly improved opportunity for high-performance athletes. Federal spending on the Olympic sports increased five times between 1970 and 1976. The Games also contributed to the growing popularity of physical fitness. Although measurement is admittedly imprecise, national surveys indicate a 41 percent increase in participation between 1976 and 1981. The Olympic lottery generated $235 million for the Games, seven times the $32 million expected, thereby opening up a new source of revenue for cash-starved governments. The organizing committee's innovative approach to sponsorships, inviting competitive bidding for two-year agreements (compared to the three-month contracts in Munich) and granting exclusivity in product categories, paved the way for the heady commercialization of the 1980s.

Total revenue for the 1976 Olympics was $430 million, against operating expenses of $207 million. If staging the Games alone is considered, the 1976 Games generated a surplus of $223 million. It is only when the capital cost of building the facilities is entered that the shortfall became $1.2 billion. All three levels of government have contributed to the reduction of this debt. Montrealers finally paid off the city's share, raised through an annual property tax surcharge, in 1993. Consumers of tobacco in Quebec are still paying a special levy toward the province's Olympic obligations. The staggering burden of the Montreal facilities has led the IOC to revise the rules for Olympic financing, so that only facility rentals can be charged to a Games budget. The architect of this approach, Vice President Richard Pound of Montreal, contends that the host communities get the benefit of facility after use, so they should be expected to pay the lion's share of their cost. The nightmare of debt, during a period when the expectations for public services and the fiscal difficulties of governments are both increasing, has forced other Olympic boosters to be much more careful and accountable in their proposals for Games. In Calgary, the lessons of Montreal contributed to a much more open approach to planning the XVth Olympic Winter Games and a genuine attempt to involve citizens in staging them. In Toronto, they persuaded the city council to develop a ''social contract,'' including public and private sector obligations to share in any debt, to govern its 1996 bid. Ironically, as the cost and complexity of staging the Olympics continue to rise, the necessity for a democratic discussion and decision on whether and how to stage Games might well be Montreal's most important legacy.

BIBLIOGRAPHICAL ESSAY

The Canadian Olympic Association Archives in Olympic House, Montreal, contain the official final report, and all the published documents from the City of Montreal and the Comité d'organizateur des jeux olympiques (COJO). The collection has been well cataloged and organized. The remaining records are accessible but uncataloged in the Archives nationales du Québec in Montreal.

The National Archives of Canada (NAC) in Ottawa contain files on the federal government's responsibilities for Olympic security and the Olympic lottery, and the personal papers of COJO commissioner general and Loto Canada president Roger Rousseau. The NAC has a complete set of the videotapes of the television coverage and an extensive photo collection of the Games.

The three-volume *Report of the Commission of Inquiry into the Cost of the 21st Olympiad* (Albert A. Malouf, Commissioner, 1980) documents the mistakes, but Nick auf der Maur's muckraking *The Billion Dollar Game* (Toronto, 1976) is much more illuminating. There are also useful chapters on the Games and the Quebec political background in Brian McKenna and Susan Purcell, *Drapeau* (Markham, Ont., 1980). The annual reports of the Olympic Installation Board in Montreal detail the special Olympic taxes on the Games debt.

A useful window on the pan-Canadian politics of the Games is provided by the Parliamentary Debates on Bills C-196 (1973) and C-63 (1975), which provided federal financing for the Games, and Bill C-85 (1975), which gave the government temporary arbitrary powers to strengthen security for the Games. See also Rick Baka, ''Canadian Federal Government Policy and the 1976 Olympics,'' *Journal of the Canadian Association of Health, Physical Education and Recreation* 42, 4 (1976): 52–60; C. E. S. Franks et al., ''Sport and Canadian Diplomacy,'' *International Journal* 43, 4 (1988): 665–82; and Bruce Kidd, ''The Culture Wars of the Montreal Olympics,'' *International Review for the Sociology of Sport* 27 (1992): 151–64.

Doug Gilbert's almost daily reports and columns in the *Montreal Gazette* from 1970 to 1977 constitute a comprehensive source for the developments, controversies, events, and evaluations of the Games. In July 1991, the *Gazette* published David Stubbs' seventeen-part follow-up series on the stars of the Games.

Novelist Jack Ludwig's *Five Ring Circus* (Toronto, 1976) and John MacAloon's ''Festival, Ritual, and Television,'' in Roger Jackson and Tom McPhail, eds., and *The Olympic Movement and the Mass Media* (Calgary, 1989) provide the best accounts of the street life and festival.

Media analyses include Leon Chorbajian and Vince Mosco, ''1976 and 1980 Olympic Boycott Coverage,'' *Arena Review* 5, 3 (1981): 3–28; R. H. McCollum and D. F. McCollum, ''Analysis of ABC TV Coverage of the 21st Olympiad Games,'' in Jeffrey

Segrave and Donald Chu, eds., *Olympism* (Champaign, Ill., 1981); and Yakov Rabkin and David Franklin, "Soviet/Canadian Press Perspectives on the Montreal Olympics," in *The Olympic Movement and the Mass Media* (Calgary, 1989). The CBC's five-volume commentators' guide, *From Athens to Montreal* (Toronto, 1976), was prepared by Jack Sullivan.

                                                                              Bruce Kidd

MOSCOW 1980
THE GAMES OF THE XXIIND OLYMPIAD

The Moscow Summer Olympic Games of 1980 were remarkable in many ways. This was the first time in the history of the modern Olympics that a communist country had been selected to host the event. As subsequent events were to show, the choice proved controversial. The entry of Soviet troops into Afghanistan in December 1979, just over six months before the Games were to open, provided ''the peg on which to hand the boycott coat,'' as one anti-Moscow campaigner put it. The Moscow boycott campaign was launched by U.S. president Jimmy Carter and supported by the British, West German, Norwegian, Canadian, and Japanese governments.

Moscow also witnessed the change of the International Olympic Committee (IOC) presidency from Lord Killanin to Juan Antonio Samaranch, the entry of new nations into the Olympic arena—Angola, Mozambique, Vietnam, and Zimbabwe (whose all-white women's field hockey team won a gold medal)—and the first black woman to win a gold medal in a field event (Maria Colon, javelin). It was also the first Olympics in two decades that was not followed by a Paralympics—not through boycott but because the Soviet authorities refused to host Games for the disabled (since no disabled sport existed in the Soviet Union).

The IOC selected Moscow as the 1980 Olympic site at its Seventy-fifth Session on October 23, 1974, in Vienna; Moscow won the vote comfortably over its sole competitor, Los Angeles. At the time many felt the U.S.S.R. worthy of the honor: not only was it the most successful and versatile nation in Olympic history in sporting performance, but it was considered to have done much in Olympic forums to enhance the preeminent role of sport and the Olympic movement. It was a popular choice with both East European states (but not with all communist nations—China turned down its invitation) and many Third World countries whose political and sports causes had gained Soviet support in such matters as the banning of South Africa from the Olympic movement.

As for Western governments, despite their distaste for communism and the Soviet human rights record, it was generally thought that the appointment of Moscow as Olympic host might somehow make a contribution to the process of détente then underway. At the very least, it might encourage some liberalization within the country or even expose it to the world as a cynical violator of the Helsinki Accords.

Inasmuch as sport was, in effect, a political institution in the U.S.S.R., it was a relatively straightforward task to prioritize, within the centrally planned system, the building of Olympic amenities by July 1980. In the five-year breathing space between 1975 and 1980, Gosplan, the state planning agency, constructed or reconstructed the necessary facilities in the five Soviet cities scheduled for Olympic events: Moscow as central venue; Tallinn, Estonia's capital on the

Baltic, for yachting events; and the three cities in which preliminary soccer matches were to be played: St. Petersburg (then Leningrad), Kiev, capital of the Ukraine, and Minsk, capital of Belarus. The choice of five cities representing different Soviet republics (subsequently to become capitals of independent states after 1991) was a novel attempt to share Olympic kudos over a wide geographic area. By the summer of 1979, virtually all preparations were complete and a dress rehearsal was held at the Seventh U.S.S.R. Spartakiad Finals, involving 10,000 athletes, including over 2,000 invited from eighty-four foreign nations.

Moscow had adopted the motto of the Roman architect Vitruvius, "Utility, Durability, and Beauty," in developing its Olympic construction plan. It was claimed that all the new facilities had been envisaged in the Master Plan for the Development and Reconstruction of Moscow; the sports complexes were therefore distributed widely about the city so as to ensure their future use by all Muscovites.

Major events, including opening and closing ceremonies, were held in the Lenin Central Stadium, which had been built in 1956 (on the site of the pre-revolutionary Moscow River Yacht Club) but had been refurbished with new floodlights, electronic scoreboards, a Tartan track surface, and seating for 103,000 people. Swimming, diving, boxing, and basketball events were held in the new Olympic Palace of Sport, on Peace Avenue (Prospect mirla), covering nearly 16 acres. The swimming area, with its 50-meter pool, accommodated 7,500 and the diving area 4,500 spectators, while the partitioned boxing and basketball halls seated 18,000 and 16,000 fans, respectively.

The rowing, kayaking, and canoeing events took place on the Krylatskoe Rowing Canal built seven years previously for the 1973 European Rowing Championships; it had a basin 2,300 meters long and 125 meters wide, enabling eight sculls (or, as the official handout put it, "8 skulls") or eleven kayaks or canoes to race simultaneously. Cycling was held on a newly constructed wooden track (unhappily, of Siberian larch, which subsequently warped badly) in a velodrome at the same venue, with seating for 6,000.

Also new was the trade union–run Bitsa Park Equestrian Centre, covering more than 110 acres. Since equestrianism was a sport unknown to the great bulk of Muscovites (apart from thoroughbred racing at the Hippodrome Racetrack), it is hard to believe that the facility was one that actually fitted in with the master plan for Moscow.

Other sports planned for various parts of Moscow included wrestling and fencing at the Central Army Sports Club; handball at the Dinamo and Sokoloniki stadiums; gymnastics, volleyball, and judo at the Central Stadium's Palace of Sport; shooting at the Dinamo Club's Mytishchi base; field hockey at Dinamo's smaller arena; weight lifting at the Izmailova Palace of Sport; and soccer at various venues (the Lenin and Dinamo stadiums in Moscow, Dinamo stadiums in Kiev and Minsk, and the Kirov Stadium in St. Petersburg).

The Olympic Village in southwest Moscow, which subsequently became a housing estate, was a 15-minute ride from the Lenin Stadium and housed 12,000 athletes and officials in eighteen sixteen-story apartment blocks covering 263 acres. Two athletes were officially allocated to each room in the two- and three-room apartments, but owing to the boycott, many people did not have to share a room. Other amenities in the village included a 1,200-seat theater and a concert hall, two 250-seat cinemas, a dance hall, a disco, a library, and—novel to Moscow—amusement arcades. Sports facilities included tennis courts, swimming pools, saunas, and a training track. Another dent in Soviet mores was the Center for Religious Ceremonies, containing separate rooms for the various religions. Security measures were rigorously implemented on entry into the Village, which perhaps was just as well (in keeping Russians out), for the food supplied by the cafés and restaurants (catering 4,000 diners simultaneously) was far superior to what most Soviet people had ever seen.

The distaste in some Western circles for communism and the U.S.S.R. found expression in a spate of anti-Moscow articles in the press that appeared as soon as the 1980 venue became known. Reports said that the authorities were planning to remove all school children, prostitutes, and dissidents from the capital in time for the Games, a claim that was to be proved correct in the case of the last two categories. In Great Britain, British Olympic Association (BOA) officials struggled against what they perceived as a political campaign led by the right wing, supported by certain religious and human rights groups, and exploited by some MPs (members of Parliament) who took advantage of the publicity an anti-Olympic issue generated.

A new period in the anti–Moscow Games campaign began with the entry of Soviet troops into Afghanistan on December 27, 1979. It provided the campaigners with precisely the ammunition they needed. As Richard Palmer testified, ''It was the most intensive pressure that had ever been applied to sport.'' Following President Carter's lead, the British prime minister, Margaret Thatcher, called on the BOA on February 17, 1980, to ''approach the IOC urgently and propose that the Summer Games be moved from the Soviet Union.'' A few days later, she appealed to British athletes, over the heads of their national federations and the BOA, to boycott the Games, declaring that athletes had the same responsibility for the defense and preservation of freedom as other citizens. President Carter's special envoy on the boycott campaign, Lloyd Cutler, began his peregrinations around the world to urge other nations to join the U.S. boycott.

The pressure now became intense. In Britain, Robert Runcie, the new archbishop of Canterbury, published a strong statement against athletes' taking part in the Moscow Olympics, as did other church leaders, although the Methodists and Baptists left the decision up to the consciences of individuals. Big business began to withdraw offers of financial aid. The television networks, which had already spent millions of dollars on broadcast rights, announced that coverage of the Games would be drastically cut and not be shown during peak viewing hours.

Where Olympic associations did not join the boycott, governments put every obstacle in the way of athletes intending to participate in the Games. For example, the British government announced that special leave would not be granted to civil servants and army personnel hoping to compete in the Games. The Foreign Office withdrew the liaison services of the senior diplomat at the British embassy in Moscow who had been expected to act as British Olympic attaché, a post that traditionally went to a security forces person. The House of Commons approved of the boycott by a 315–117 vote, although a public opinion poll showed 70 percent of the public in favor of British athletes' going to Moscow. It was virtually impossible to have a dissenting voice heard in the media. Such was the hysteria that the British government prevented the review in the press of books with a contrary view, such as James Riordan's *Soviet Sport: Background to the Olympics.*

Despite all this pressure, the BOA decided by a 19–1 vote, with 4 abstentions, "for immediate acceptance of the invitation to Moscow." Subsequently, the yachting, field hockey, and equestrian federations voted against going to Moscow.

Like other Olympic associations that defied the U.S. boycott call, the BOA had to overcome enormous difficulties. Given the lack of funds, the troubled domestic atmosphere, and the government's refusal to allow the British state airline, British Airways, to fly anyone or anything involved in the Olympics to Moscow, British athletes and officials had to be ferried out to Moscow and back home only for the duration of their events, not for the whole Games. As a concession to the boycott campaign, it was decided that only the British chef de mission would take part in the opening ceremony and that the Union Jack would not be raised or the national anthem played in any ceremonies.

On May 27, 1980, the IOC announced that eighty-five countries had accepted invitations to compete in Moscow. Of the twenty-two nations that had won two or more gold medals in the 1972 and 1976 Olympics, only five had decided not to compete in Moscow: the United States, West Germany, Norway, Kenya, and Japan. The most conspicuous break in the boycott was paradoxically made by Western Europe, nations closely allied to the United States. In fact, the British team, consisting of 326 persons, was the fourth largest at the Games. Of course, in Britain there was no official government welcome home for the athletes and no recognition for gold medalists.

Like its quid pro quo, the communist boycott at the 1984 Los Angeles Games, the Moscow boycott was an abject failure. The Games went on, scarcely diminished, and Olympism gained in moral stature, while the boycott's protagonists soon disappeared from the historical stage.

All through the Games the Soviet organizers arranged cultural events featuring major orchestras, ballet and opera companies, folk troupes, and theater companies. Concerts were held in both traditional venues, such as the Bolshoi and the Tchaikovsky Concert Hall, as well as in the concert hall of the Olympic Village. Most athletes and team officials stayed away from many of the events, and the halls were more than half-empty, especially in the Olympic Village. This was not only due to pressures of sports preparation and athletic tastes but also to the fact that many delegations were forced to fly in and out owing to lack of funds because of the boycott. Nevertheless, the aim to inject a much-needed cultural ingredient into the Olympics was appreciated by those who took advantage of the cultural feast.

The cultural tone of the Olympics was set at the opening ceremony. At 4:00 P.M. on Saturday, July 19, the Games were opened by Soviet president Leonid Brezhnev, accompanied in the VIP delegation by Lord Killanin, IOC president, Juan Antonio Samaranch, the president-elect, and Ignaty Novikov, chairman of the organizing committee. Dmitri Shostakovich's *Festive Overture* had been chosen as the Olympic fanfare, heralding the entry into the Lenin Stadium of Greek chariots and young men and women wearing white Greek tunics and scattering rose petals along the track. They were followed by the parade of participants, most marching under their flag, but some marching beneath the Olympic flag and represented by a single token member or a Russian substitute. A special welcome was given to new members of the Olympic family: Mozambique, Angola, Vietnam, Laos, and Zimbabwe.

At the end of the parade, eight athletes carried out the unfurled Olympic flag, and it was hoisted up the flagpole, with twenty-two snow-white doves released into the air. The Olympic torch bearer now appeared: the three-time Olympic triple-jump champion, Victor Saneyev. He handed the torch over to the lofty basketball captain, Sergei Belov, who climbed up a pathway formed by white boards held on the heads of spectators sitting in the east stands. Once the flame was lit, the gymnast Nikolai Andrianov pronounced the Olympic oath on behalf of the athletes, and the former wrestling champion Alexander Medved spoke the oath on behalf of the judges and officials. A unique feature of this ceremony was the "Greetings from Space": a television picture of two Soviet cosmonauts that appeared on the electronic screen as they conveyed greetings from outer space to all athletes. Then began the colorful, beautiful, and multiethnic folklore display by over 16,000 artists from all over the country—so rich and moving that one hardly dared blink for fear of missing something. The closing ceremony was almost as exhilarating, culminating with the launching of a giant inflated Misha Bear, the Games' symbol, into the Moscow night air (he came down in the nearby grounds of Moscow University).

For Western nations, the Moscow Olympics and the boycott controversy brought to a head some of the tensions that had long been latent in the Olympic movement and in society generally. The first was the action of traditionalist, anticommunist groups who wished to see the abandonment of the Olympic Games as they were constituted. As long as the West was winning and could dictate sports policy, there was never a suggestion that the Olympics were too big, too political, too nationalistic, or unworthy of a particular country, even including Nazi Germany in 1936. The loss of this supremacy in sports forums caused such groups to conclude that the time had come to sever links with the Olympic movement and to form a West-oriented grouping of sports nations. Although these groups were defeated, the danger still exists of their seizing upon other international incidents to destroy the Olympic Games and fragment the structure of world sport.

The second tension that the boycott controversy made manifest in the West was that between the traditional amateur-elitist and the ascendant commercial-professional ethos. In those Western states attending the Moscow Games, it was the former that won the day. For traditional (and conservative) figures like the British Olympic president, Sir Dennis Follows, the marquis of Exeter, and Lord Killanin, the dominant credo in regard to sport had always been that it should be divorced from politics, government interference, and commercialism and should also represent a firm commitment to the Olympic ideal. British and French governments tended to espouse that philosophy too, particularly as it absolved them of any financial commitment to sport. The year 1980 changed all that. The Moscow Olympics marked the first time in which the democracies of the West became deeply involved in the government of sport. The notion that Avery Brundage had perpetuated for years, that international sport competition, like the Olympics, could flourish separately from governmental activity was finally laid to rest.

If the consequences of the Moscow Olympics were dramatic for Western states, they were resounding for the states of Eastern Europe, particularly the host country, the U.S.S.R. After its moment of sporting glory, the Soviet Union rapidly began to fall apart. Two years after the Games, Brezhnev died; five years after the Games, Mikhail Gorbachev came to power with his radically new policies of *perestroika* and *glasnost*. Nine years after the Games, the communist edifice crumbled throughout the eight nations of Eastern Europe; the Soviet Union followed suit and ceased to exist as a unitary state in late 1991.

It would be a bit extravagant to blame the Moscow Olympics for the demise of communism. And yet for many citizens of communist states in Eastern Europe and the Soviet Union, the 1980 Olympics brought tensions to a head, especially as the public was able to see the tensions in its own backyard. It is noteworthy that when the revolutions swept across Eastern Europe in late 1989, there was an intense debate about sport. Far from being at the periphery of politics, sport was right at the center. In Romania, athletes manned the barricades, with members of the Dinamo Club (the sports club sponsored and financed by the security forces), defending their patron, the Securitate, in opposition to army athletes of Steaua whose gold medalists in shooting were among those firing on the secret police. Romanian rugby captain Florica Marariu and teammate Radu Dadac were just two of the sports heroes who fell in battle. In East Germany, sports stars like Katarina Witt, Roland Matthes, and Kornelia Ender all complained of having their homes and cars vandalized by erstwhile ''fans'' angry at the privileges of the stars and their close identification with the communist regime.

The events of 1989 and subsequently in the one-time communist states demonstrated that to many people, sport, and particularly elite Olympic sport, was identified in the popular consciousness with privilege, paramilitary coercion (the two largest and best-endowed sports clubs in all communist states were the armed forces clubs and Dinamo), hypocrisy (having to pretend that communist athletes were amateur when everyone knew they were paid by the state and given either army officer sinecures or fictitious employment at industrial plants), and distorted priorities (the enormous sums of money that were lavished on sports stars and the Moscow Olympics, while sports facilities for the masses—not to mention hospitals, schools, housing, and consumer goods for the public generally—were poor and minimal). In the case of the non-Soviet nations, the Soviet sports structure was regarded as an alien, government-imposed institution.

The principal reason for the Soviet targeting of the Olympics to achieve world supremacy would seem to have been an attempt to gain recognition and prestige for the communist states and their brand of communism and thereby to advertise that brand, especially in the Third World, as being superior to the capitalist system. However, to many people in Eastern Europe and the U.S.S.R., the Olympic achievements and the Moscow Olympics diverted attention from the realities of living under communism. It is hardly surprising, then, that leaders in the post-*perestroika* period radically changed their scale of priorities. No longer seeing the need to demonstrate the advantages of socialism, they are trying to distance themselves from the state-directed economy and the totalitarian political system that failed so badly.

To the majority of the public in the communist states, especially the Soviet Union, the Moscow Olympics illuminated the vast gap between elite sport and the rest of society, the manipulation of sport for political ends, and the profligacy of pouring funds into a sporting spectacle for propaganda purposes when the economy was teetering on the brink of bankruptcy.

Notwithstanding the political shenanigans around the Games, the venues in the twenty-one sports were full, as always, of excitement, heroism, pathos, and memorable moments. In the absence of top rivals in some events, the Games presented opportunities for older athletes to grab the limelight unexpectedly one last time. The great Cuban heavyweight boxer Teofilo Stevenson won a record third gold, to add to the six Cuban boxing gold medals out of eleven gold medals. East German runner Waldemar Cierpinski took his second marathon gold. Another over-30s star was Ethiopia's Miruts Yifter, who won gold medals in both the 5,000-meter and 10,000-meter races. Other older winners were Britain's Alan Wells and Italy's Pietro Mennea, who took gold medals in the 100-meter and 200-meter sprints, respectively, and Britain's Daley Thompson, who won his second Olympic decathlon. In her last Olympic appearance, the great Romanian gymnast Nadia Comaneci won one more gold. However, as if to emphasize the thin line between success and tragedy, Russia's Yelena Mukhina broke her neck in gymnastics training just before the Olympics, paralyzing her from the neck down.

Whatever happened elsewhere in the world in July 1980 and whatever momentous events were to come in Russia, for those who attended the Moscow Olympic Games the overriding memory is of a magnificent sporting and cultural spectacle, an efficient if sometimes rigid organization, and an extremely joyful Games. And it did not rain once.

BIBLIOGRAPHICAL ESSAY

The Moscow organizing committee's official report on the Games is *Games of the XXIInd Olympiad,* 3 vols. (Moscow, 1981), published also in French and Russian editions. The British report, British Olympic Association, *The Official British Olympic Association Report of the 1980 Games* (London, 1981), includes a review of the boycott campaign in Great Britain. The U.S. version is *United States Olympic Book 1980* (Colorado Springs, 1980), although the U.S. boycott limits its coverage of the Moscow Games. The German Democratic Republic Olympic Committee, whose team participated, published *Spiele der XXII. Olympiade Moskau 1980* (Berlin, 1980); the Federal Republic of Germany, which joined the boycott, published *Moscow 80. Das Offizielle Standardwerk des Nationalen Olympischen Komitees fur Deutschland* (Munich, 1980).

A glossy Soviet publication on the Games, with many pictures as well as detailed information on preparations and events, is *Moscow '80* (Moscow, 1980), with text in English, Russian, French, and German. In addition to the official report, the organizing committee published a number of other books, including *Olympiada 80* (Moscow, 1980); *The Moscow Olympic Program of Cultural Events* (Moscow, 1980); and various others with compilations of participants, rules, event schedules, and results.

A number of congressional documents on the U.S. boycott have been published. The House of Representatives Committee on Foreign Affairs hearing on the question is *U.S. Participation in the 1980 Summer Olympic Games,* 96th Cong., 2d sess., on H. Cong. Res. 249 and H. Res. 547, January 23, February 4, 1980 (Washington, 1980); the Senate hearings are Committee on Foreign Relations, *1980 Olympics Boycott* 96th Cong., 2d sess. Another House of Representatives document of interest is *Alternatives to the Moscow Olympics,* a hearing before the Subcommittee on Transportation and Commerce of the Committee of Interstate and Foreign Commerce, 9th Cong., 2d sess., January 30, 1980.

A substantial number of secondary works exist on the boycott question. One of the first was James Riordan, *Soviet Sport: Background to the Olympics* (London, 1980), which argued against British participation in the boycott. Christopher Booker, *The Games War: A Moscow Journal* (London, 1981), attempts to place the Games in a political context dating back to 1974. James Riordan, "Great Britain and the 1980 Olympics: Victory for Olympism," in Maaret Ilmarinen, ed., *Sport and International Understanding* (Berlin, 1984), 138–44, emphasizes the failure of the boycott, while Hartford Cantelon, "The Canadian Absence from the XXIInd Olympiad—Some Plausible Explanations," in the same volume (pp. 145–51), discusses the Canadian position. See also Barukh Hazan, *Olympic Sports and Propaganda Games: Moscow 1980* (New Brunswick, N.J., 1982). A more recent analysis is Derick L. Hulme, *The Political Olympics: Moscow, Afghanistan, and the 1980 U.S. Boycott* (New York, 1990).

James Riordan

LOS ANGELES 1984

THE GAMES OF THE XXIIId OLYMPIAD

The decision of the International Olympic Committee (IOC) to award the 1984 Olympic Games to Los Angeles culminated decades of effort by the Southern California Committee for the Olympic Games (SCCOG) to bring the Games to Los Angeles a second time. Formed in 1939, seven years after Los Angeles hosted the Xth Olympic Games, SCCOG participated in every Olympic bid competition for the next thirty-nine years before achieving success.

The successful bid for the 1984 Games was a cooperative effort. SCCOG, headed by Los Angeles attorney John Argue, joined the City of Los Angeles, with strong backing from Mayor Tom Bradley. Despite the city's involvement, SCCOG and other private sources funded the entire bid.

Winning the bid was a two-step process. First, Los Angeles had to convince the United States Olympic Committee (USOC) to select Los Angeles as the American candidate city. Second, the city had to make a presentation to the IOC. Promising an economical, no-frills Games, Los Angeles successfully cleared the first hurdle in September 1977 when the USOC selected it over New York.

In the wake of the financially troubled Montreal Games, there were few cities eager to host the Olympic Games. In fact, the only other serious competitor was Tehran, whose bid was withdrawn voluntarily in 1977. Thus, Los Angeles was unopposed. On May 18, 1978, the IOC at its Eightieth Session in Athens provisionally awarded the Games to Los Angeles.

Final approval of Los Angeles' bid was subject to the city's signing a contract stating that Los Angeles would abide by all IOC rules, one of them requiring the host city to assume financial responsibility for staging the Games. Los Angeles officials, concerned about Montreal's experience and public opinion polls that indicated only 35 percent of Los Angeles voters favored public funding of the Games, balked at the IOC's terms.

Soon after the IOC awarded provisional host status to Los Angeles, Mayor Bradley, at the urging of private backers of the bid, created a committee of seven community leaders to continue negotiations with the IOC. The group named itself the Los Angeles Olympic Organizing Committee (LAOOC).

The impasse between the IOC and Los Angeles was resolved after weeks of negotiations in October 1978 when the IOC withdrew its demand that the city agree to assume financial liability. The IOC instead agreed to a plan whereby the privately financed LAOOC and the USOC would assume the financial risk. The USOC's willingness to become involved in the arrangement was motivated, in part, by the organizing committee's promise to share a portion of any surplus funds generated by the Games. The City of Los Angeles, LAOOC, IOC, and

USOC signed a series of agreements based on these principles, which concluded with a final contract executed on March 1, 1979.

The LAOOC incorporated formally on June 15, 1978. A twenty-two-person executive committee was formed in January 1979. Paul Ziffren became LAOOC chairman, and Peter Ueberroth was appointed president in late March. Ziffren was a prominent Los Angeles attorney who had been involved in state and national Democratic party politics for many years. The appointment of Ziffren, a pillar of the Los Angeles establishment, was not surprising. The selection of Ueberroth was another matter.

A graduate of San Jose State University, who had tried out unsuccessfully for the 1956 Olympic water polo team, the 41-year-old Ueberroth was virtually unknown to the general public. While still in his 20s, Ueberroth had founded a company called First Travel and developed it into one of the nation's largest travel agencies. His entrepreneurial spirit, business experience, and international negotiating ability gained in the travel industry impressed his early backers on the board of directors, such as Argue and David Wolper.

Throughout the planning and staging of the Games, Ueberroth was the central figure. The second in command on the LAOOC staff was the executive vice president and general manager, Harry Usher. Usher, who joined the organizing committee in early 1980, earned his B.A. at Brown University and a law degree at Stanford University, where he was an editor of the *Stanford Law Review*. Prior to his appointment, Usher had been an attorney in Los Angeles for many years, specializing in entertainment law.

The organizational structure of the LAOOC was fluid. The staff grew from a nucleus of 11 employees in 1979 to more than 1,700 by late May 1984. During the Games, the number of paid staff swelled to about 12,000. They were joined by 33,000 volunteers. Another 36,000 people worked for companies hired by the LAOOC to provide various services.

Because the LAOOC had no public funding, Ueberroth and the board had to devise ways to limit costs and maximize revenues. Central to their strategy was the use of existing sports facilities in southern California. Most major venues existed already. Although the committee spent millions of dollars refurbishing existing facilities, only three new venues—cycling, swimming, and shooting— had to be built anew. Corporate sponsors funded the swimming and cycling facilities.

Another way in which the organizing committee held down costs was to rely heavily on volunteers. Some worked for the LAOOC throughout the entire planning and staging of the Games; most, however, worked during the sixteen days of sports competition and the period immediately preceding and following the Games.

The LAOOC derived revenue from four major sources: sponsorships, television broadcast rights, ticket sales, and the sale of Olympic commemorative coins. Olympic sponsorship, giving companies the right to have their names associated with the Olympic Games in exchange for cash, goods, or services, was not a new concept. Ueberroth, however, refined the practice by reducing the number of available sponsorships while charging higher fees than ever before. The LAOOC offered three levels of corporate participation: official sponsor, official supplier, and official licensee. A total of 164 companies joined the program and contributed $126.7 million in cash, services, and products. This figure is somewhat misleading, though. The LAOOC structured the payment schedule so that it received much of the money up-front, thus enabling the committee to invest the payments. The committee earned more than $76 million from such investments.

The sale of television broadcast rights was an even bigger revenue source. ABC Sports and foreign broadcasters paid $286.8 million for the rights to broadcast the Games.

Ticket sales brought in $155.86 million, and the sale of Olympic coins accounted for an additional $35 million.

The LAOOC's strategy of controlling costs and generating revenue proved to be more effective than virtually anyone had anticipated. Several weeks after the Games, the LAOOC announced an estimated surplus of $150 million. That estimate grew to $195 million by year's end and to $225 million in a 1985 audit.

The announcement of the unexpectedly large surplus created considerable controversy. Many vendors who had done business with the LAOOC complained that they had provided products and services at reduced prices to support the cause of Olympism. A few volunteers argued that they should receive part of the surplus. And there were proposals to share the funds with Third World national Olympic committees (NOCs). In the end, though, the surplus was divided among the USOC, the national governing bodies (NGBs) of Olympic sports in the United States, and a newly formed youth sports foundation in southern California.

Organizers of the 1984 Games were responsible for staging competitions in twenty-one medal sports (the LAOOC counted diving, synchronized swimming, and water polo as part of swimming) and two demonstration sports, featuring a record 221 events.

The LAOOC in its earliest days concentrated on raising revenue. Once that was accomplished by the sale of television rights to ABC Sports in September 1979, identifying and securing sports venues became a top priority. The LAOOC acquired almost all of the necessary venues by early 1983.

During the summer and fall of 1983, the committee sponsored international competitions in archery, water polo, shooting, swimming, synchronized swimming, diving, cycling, rowing, canoeing, and gymnastics. These competitions, known collectively as LA83, were a dress rehearsal for the Olympic competitions in 1984. They provided an opportunity to test planning assumptions and served as the basis of final preparations for the following summer.

As the date of opening ceremonies drew nearer, the LAOOC underwent "venuization," a process designed to develop venue teams at each competition site comprising people from functional areas such as security, protocol, press operations, and food services. At each venue a commissioner was responsible for on-site management. All the sports commissioners were influential civic or business leaders. Their role was to serve as the liaison to the relevant international sports federation, while exercising some political clout at the local level. Many commissioners had little, if any, experience in the sport for which they were responsible. Technical expertise at each venue was supplied by a sports manager, who reported directly to the commissioner.

The geographic scope of the 1984 Games was enormous. In addition to widely dispersed sports venues, there were three Olympic Villages: at the University of California at Los Angeles, the University of Southern California, and the University of California, Santa Barbara. The Games encompassed approximately 4,500 square miles of southern California. Furthermore, early rounds of the soccer tournament took place in Maryland, Massachusetts, and northern California.

Olympic architecture in most Olympic cities has focused on the creation of new stadiums and arenas. Los Angeles, however, already had most of the necessary facilities. The task of architects and designers therefore was not to design sports facilities but rather to decorate them and the surrounding communities. In doing so, they hoped to create "a sense of place in a city without a center" and to persuade southern Californians to rally around the Games by creating a spirit of celebration and pageantry.

The LAOOC succeeded on both counts with a design scheme it dubbed "Festive Federalism," or "the Look." It featured pastel colors and unusual geometric shapes, presented through the use of banners, sonotubes, and fabrics mounted on bailing wire, chainlink fences, and scaffolding.

A year after the Games, an official LAOOC publication referred to the Look as the "single outstanding feature" of the Games. While that may have been true, the road to Festival Federalism was a convoluted one. Between 1979 and 1982 the organizing committee considered and rejected the work of several designers. There was tension throughout the process between a majority on the LAOOC who wanted a patriotic red, white, and blue theme and the executive vice president and general manager, Harry Usher, who wanted a less chauvinistic approach. Usher, despite pressure from other senior managers, held firm and selected the design concept of the Los Angeles design firm, Sussman/Prejza, which worked closely with architect Jon Jerde to make the Look a reality. The design plan was implemented at a cost of $12 million and 100,000 hours of labor devoted to installation.

The LAOOC, like any other organizing committee, was beset by a variety of obstacles and controversies. The committee's most serious problem, the Soviet-led boycott, reached a climax less than three months before opening ceremonies.

From the day that the IOC awarded the Games to Los Angeles, there existed the possibility of a Soviet-led boycott of the 1984 Games in retaliation against the American-led boycott of the 1980 Moscow Games. Sensitive to the problem, LAOOC representatives met several times with members of the Soviet Union's

NOC over a five-year period, beginning with Ueberroth's visit to Moscow in 1979 to attend the All-People's Spartakiade. In December 1983 a fourteen-person Soviet delegation made an eight-day visit to Los Angeles that concluded with the signing of a protocol agreement in which the Soviet NOC put forward several requests related to the entry of the Soviet Olympic delegation into the United States and housing arrangements for them in the Los Angeles area.

Contacts between the LAOOC and the Soviet Union's NOC took place against a backdrop of anti-Soviet political activity in California and the presidency of Ronald Reagan, who in 1983 called the Soviet Union the ''Evil Empire.'' Relations took a turn for the worse in September 1983 after a Soviet aircraft shot down a Korean Air Lines flight killing 269 passengers. The California legislature responded with a unanimous resolution of condemnation that included a clause demanding that athletes from the Soviet Union be banned from competing in the Los Angeles Games. Most legislators had not realized when they voted that the resolution contained the anti-Soviet clause. And although the legislature eventually rescinded the call for a ban, the U.S.S.R. reacted by pulling athletes out of the remaining LA83 events.

Meanwhile, a southern California citizens' group, the Ban the Soviets Coalition, demanded that the Soviet Union be barred from the Games. The group announced plans to gather a million signatures on petitions calling for the ban, but only about 10,000 people actually signed. Recognizing that the attempted ban would fail, the coalition also proposed protest demonstrations against the Soviet team in Los Angeles and the use of freeway billboards advising Soviet athletes how to defect.

The Reagan administration made no effort to deny entry to athletes from the Soviet Union. However, in March 1984 the administration did deny a visa to attaché Oleg Yermishkin, who had planned to accompany the Soviet team to Los Angeles. An anonymous administration source claimed that Yermishkin was a senior KGB operative.

In early April several stories appeared in the Soviet press criticizing preparations for the Games in stronger than usual terms. A particular concern, according to these articles, was the security of athletes from the U.S.S.R. The Soviet NOC issued a statement on April 9 charging that a campaign characterized by open threats of physical violence and harassment had been mounted in the United States against the Soviet Union's participation in the Olympic Games. The statement also complained about entry procedures for the Soviet Olympic delegation, which, according to the statement, violated the Olympic Charter. It demanded an emergency meeting of the IOC executive board to ensure U.S. compliance with the charter.

Responding to the escalating rhetoric, Ueberroth met with Soviet NOC representatives and top IOC officials in Lausanne, Switzerland. The Soviet representatives repeated their complaints. The meeting ended without resolution of the issues. The situation did not improve in the days that followed. On May 8,

1984, just hours after the start of the torch relay, the Soviet NOC announced officially that it would not participate in the 1984 Games.

Faced with the prospect of a Soviet boycott, the LAOOC responded by attempting to obtain commitments to attend the Games from more nations than had competed in Munich in 1972, thereby establishing a new record for participating nations. Toward this end the committee established a twenty-four-hour phone bank to call and cajole NOCs, sent envoys abroad, cabled and called embassies in Washington, D.C., and worked through American embassies in foreign countries in an attempt to contain the boycott.

The effort received a boost on May 12 when the People's Republic of China announced it would send a team. Several days later Romania also declared its intention to defy the boycott. On June 2, the deadline by which NOCs had to accept the invitation to send a team to the Games, the LAOOC was able to announce that 142 nations had accepted. A record number of 140 nations eventually did participate; 14 took part in the boycott led by the U.S.S.R.

The question of whether the boycott was inevitable or caused by events in the United States remains a matter of debate. Opinions among the principals within the United States government, LAOOC, and Soviet NOC were not unanimous in 1984 and remained divided in subsequent years. Although the prevailing opinion among Americans involved in the negotiations with Soviet representatives was that the boycott was unavoidable, some believed that Soviet officials were sincere in their expressed concerns about athlete entry and security and that the U.S. State Department undermined the LAOOC with its dogmatic cold war behavior.

Another major obstacle facing Ueberroth and the organizing committee was the Greek reaction to the LAOOC's plan for the torch relay. As a way of raising money for charities, the LAOOC decided to sell kilometers along the relay route. Companies or individuals could run in the relay only if they paid a $3,000 participation fee.

Many Greek sports officials and politicians, including the leftist mayor of Olympia, site of the eternal Olympic flame, objected to what they termed a defilement of a sacred Greek symbol. The Greek reaction was a reflection of both genuine opposition to the plan and political opportunism on the part of those who wished to capitalize on anti-American sentiment in Greek politics. The mayor of Olympia threatened to prevent the lighting ceremony from taking place in his city. Ueberroth countered by threatening to use a flame that already had been lit at Olympia and transported to IOC headquarters in Switzerland. The issue was resolved when the LAOOC agreed to halt remaining sales of kilometers and the Greek government permitted the lighting ceremony to take place at Olympia. Fearing demonstrations, however, the Greeks cancelled the traditional relay from Olympia to Athens. Before halting sales, the LAOOC raised nearly $11 million from the torch relay. The committee distributed the proceeds to several organizations, including the YMCA, Boys Clubs, Girls Clubs, and Special Olympics. The relay, which began on the same day that the

Soviet Union announced its boycott, covered 15,000 kilometers in thirty-three states and the District of Columbia and proved to be a major factor in galvanizing public enthusiasm for the Games.

The Olympic Arts Festival took place from June 1 to August 12 under the direction of Robert Fitzpatrick, president of the California Institute of the Arts. The festival featured nearly 900 presentations of dance, theater, music, film, and visual arts by American and international artists. The Times Mirror Company contributed $5 million to stage the festival; the LAOOC budgeted $3 million. Attendance at the festival totaled 1.3 million spectators.

Opening ceremonies took place on July 28 at the Los Angeles Memorial Coliseum before a live audience of 92,655 and 2.5 billion television viewers in the United States and abroad. Planned and staged by film producer and LAOOC board member David Wolper, the ceremonies were a great success by virtually all accounts. Highlights included a card trick in which the audience created the flags of the world, the flight of a man using a jet pack strapped to his back, and the flame lighting atop the stadium by the 1960 decathlon gold medalist, Rafer Johnson.

More than 7,000 athletes competed in Los Angeles. Yet the quality of competition clearly suffered from the boycott, especially in boxing, wrestling, gymnastics, weight lifting, and track and field. Still, athletes broke or tied thirteen world records and more than eighty Olympic records.

Among the memorable moments of the competitive program were the running of the first Olympic women's marathon, the on-track collision between runners Mary Decker and Zola Budd in the women's 3,000-meter final, Carl Lewis' four gold medals, Greg Louganis' superb diving performance, and the controversial disqualification of American boxer Evander Holyfield.

American athletes won 174 medals, far ahead of their closest rivals the West Germans, who won 59, and the Romanians, who took 53. The boycott of Soviet and Eastern European athletes gave Americans an opportunity to win medals in sports such as gymnastics and cycling in which traditionally they had not been top performers. That these victories were achieved in the absence of athletes from the boycotting nations did not seem to dampen the fervor of American spectators or the American media. In fact, before the Games ended, several athletes from other countries complained about the pro-American bias of ABC's television coverage, which was shown in the Olympic Villages.

Two potential problems that worried the LAOOC staff as they planned for the Games, smog and traffic jams, never developed during the sixteen days of competition. Air quality, at least by Los Angeles standards, remained good throughout the Games. Freeway traffic actually moved faster than normal because of the LAOOC's mobilization of public and private buses to carry spectators and the reduced number of vehicles on the roads during rush hours due to companies' voluntarily changing their regular business schedules.

The Games ended on August 12 with closing ceremonies at the coliseum again directed by Wolper.

The Games of the XXIIId Olympiad live on in the collective memory of Angelenos as a shining moment in the city's history when people cooperated with each other, institutions functioned well, and the traffic flowed. It remains to be seen what, if any, impact the inspirational memory of the Games will have as Los Angeles grapples with the litany of urban problems.

The 1984 Games firmly established the Olympic movement as a financially attractive endeavor with the potential to benefit host cities, corporate sponsors, and broadcasters. In the year following the Games, the IOC successfully launched its lucrative TOP program in which corporations agreed to pay tens of millions of dollars to become worldwide Olympic sponsors. The increased financial lure of the Olympic Games also was evident in the host city bid process that followed the 1984 Games. Whereas only Los Angeles had bid to host the 1984 Olympics, six cities presented bids in 1986 with the hope of hosting the 1992 Games.

In physical terms, the Games left behind a swim stadium, velodrome, shooting range, many refurbished sports facilities, and an administrative building on the UCLA campus. Most of the sports venues used in the Los Angeles Games, though, existed before 1984.

The local economic impact was substantial. Economics Research Associates, a Chicago research firm, estimated in a 1986 report that the Olympics brought $2.4 billion into the southern California economy.

The most tangible legacy of the Games was the Olympic surplus, calculated in 1985 at about $225 million. The USOC received 40 percent of the surplus, the NGBs of Olympic sports in the United States got 20 percent, and the rest, set aside for use in southern California, became the endowment of the Amateur Athletic Foundation of Los Angeles (AAF). The AAF began operations in 1985 with an endowment of $91 million. In the decade following 1984, the foundation invested $50 million in youth sport programs in southern California, while simultaneously increasing its assets to more than $100 million to ensure future funding in the community.

BIBLIOGRAPHICAL ESSAY

The Amateur Athletic Foundation of Los Angeles (AAF) sports library and the Special Collections Department of UCLA's University Research Library have excellent collections on the 1984 Games. The AAF materials are part of a larger Olympic collection that includes the official report, or what passes for the official report, of each modern Olympic Games. The 1984 materials include the official report; LAOOC brochures, guides, and programs; national team media guides; videos; photographs; musical works; posters; Harry Usher's office files; audiotapes and transcripts of interviews with more than 100 LAOOC staff, including Paul Ziffren, Peter Ueberroth, and Usher, conducted by *Los Angeles Times* reporter Kenneth Reich; the seven-volume ABC Sports 1984 Olympic research manual; United States Information Agency documents on the boycott; extensive newspaper clippings files; and numerous artifacts.

The UCLA collection is equally impressive, with nearly 1,700 archival boxes on the

1984 Games. Included are the official report, LAOOC publications, videos, and 130,000 photographs. More important for serious researchers, UCLA has thousands of pages of internal LAOOC documents and press releases. Special Collections has developed an index to the Olympic collection, and the staff is knowledgeable about the holdings.

The AAF and UCLA Special Collections maintain a good working relationship and will work together to assist researchers. Both collections are open to the public. An advance telephone call or letter will facilitate the use of either collection.

Official Report of the Games of the XXIIIrd Olympiad Los Angeles, 1984 (Los Angeles, 1984) is most the complete information source. *Olympic Retrospective: The Games of Los Angeles* (Los Angeles, 1985), published by the LAOOC, is a 596-page paperback that repeats, in condensed form, much information from the report and also a myriad of new statistics and details.

Peter Ueberroth, *Made in America: His Own Story* (New York, 1985), written with Peter Levin and Amy Quinn, presents the LAOOC point of view in a readable style enlivened by Ueberroth's observations of his contemporaries in sport and government. Kenneth Reich, *Making It Happen: Peter Ueberroth and the 1984 Olympic Games* (Santa Barbara, Calif., 1986), is a thoughtful, more critical examination of Ueberroth and the LAOOC corporate culture.

Economic Research Associates, *Executive Summary, Community Impact of the 1984 Olympic Games in Los Angeles and Southern California* (Chicago, 1986), analyzes the economic impact of the Games.

Several excellent articles on the Olympic design appear in *Design Quarterly* 127 (1985), which was devoted entirely to the 1984 spectacle.

Bud Greenspan's official film of the Games, *16 Days of Glory* (video, 1986), presents evocative portraits of individuals who competed in Los Angeles.

Doctoral dissertations on the Los Angeles Games include Harold Wilson, ''The Golden Opportunity: A Study of the Romanian Manipulation of the Olympic Movement during the Boycott of the 1984 Los Angeles Olympic Games'' (Ohio State University, 1993), and Susanna Levitt, ''1984 Olympic Arts Festival: Theatre'' (University of California, Davis, 1990).

In the popular press, *Sports Illustrated*'s articles were consistently reliable. The *Los Angeles Times* provided the most comprehensive journalistic coverage.

Wayne Wilson

SEOUL 1988

THE GAMES OF THE XXIVTH OLYMPIAD

Throughout the 1980s, the international Olympic movement underwent such a profound change that even the semiofficial biography of the International Olympic Committee (IOC) president Juan Antonio Samaranch was entitled *Olympic Revolution.* But rather than calling for a new order with the banging of drums and the clarion call of trumpets, the movement evolved, led by the Swiss-based IOC and driven by Samaranch, moving and swaying to the beat of world politics, and sometimes calling the tune itself, and plunged into global marketing, altering not just its own financial structure but the monetary basis of all international sport. The 1980s left behind forever the notion that sports, through such self-generating incomes as gate receipts, could be self-supporting.

Central to the evolution were the 1988 Games in Seoul, the twenty-fourth in the modern era, as the IOC likes to term them, an improbable venue when it was chosen by the IOC session in the Rhineland spa town of Baden-Baden in 1981. South Korea had scant tradition of Olympic involvement, was of little standing in international sport, was not high on the world's consciousness of Asia, and, most significant, was not recognized diplomatically by any of the communist states. In 1981, a year after Samaranch had taken over from affable Irish peer Lord Killanin as IOC president, the Olympic movement was in a period of high political uncertainty. It was a time of boycott. African, Asian, and West Indian states had either left or stayed away from the Montreal Games in 1976 because of their abhorrence of South Africa's apartheid system of separate racial development. In 1980, there had been the American-led Western boycott of the Moscow Games because of the Soviet presence in Afghanistan, and in 1984, there was the tit-for-tat boycott of the Los Angeles Games by communist states, with the notable exceptions of Romania and China (the latter dramatically thumbing its nose at Moscow by choosing the Games Moscow scorned to make its reappearance at an Olympics).

The selection of Seoul to host the 1988 Games immediately raised the prospect of a fourth consecutive boycott, a prospect that could have crippled the Olympic movement and grossly devalued the Games' insistence that it is a vehicle for international understanding, peace, and goodwill. Seoul's candidature was fortunate that because of the risks of boycotts, few cities then were lining up to host the Games and its only serious opposition was the Japanese city of Nagoya, the overwhelming favorite when the IOC members met in Baden-Baden. No one knows, then or now, what really influenced the ninety-odd IOC members who decided where the 1988 Games should be held; they are not delegates from their countries, and they need explain their decisions to no one. A noisy protest in Baden-Baden by environmentalists against Nagoya's candidature may have influenced some members to go for Seoul; a desire to spread the Games more widely (Japan had already hosted a Summer and a Winter Games) may have influenced others. The intense politicking within international sports and the role played by the chairman of Adidas, Horst Dassler, a man of great persuasion and monetary influence, may also have changed some minds. (An expert in the then little-known world of sports marketing, Dassler was something of a Father Christmas to financially strapped sports organizations, which then included the IOC.) Whatever the influences, Seoul prevailed over Nagoya, 52–27.

The outcome of the vote in Baden-Baden set Samaranch on a seven-year course of diplomatic shuttling rivaled in its air miles only by Henry Kissinger as he sought to avert yet another boycott or any other event that could disrupt or demean the first of *his* Games (Los Angeles had been chosen when Killanin was president, and Samaranch saw Seoul as the first of his era). Samaranch, unlike Lord Killanin or Avery Brundage, was not worried by the potential eventual size of Olympic Games and was open with his ambition for the Games to be a truly international sporting extravaganza for all sports and all countries.

The South Koreans were equally open about their motives for wanting to stage the Games. They were not the first country to see the Games as a window on their world as they sought, sometimes painfully and violently, to make the transition from military government to democratic rule and sought, like their neighbor, long-time antagonists and one-time occupiers Japan, to muscle their way into international trade. South Korea selected a decorative motif known as a ''Sam Taegeuk'' as the Games emblem and said it symbolized the harmony of man, heaven, and earth with the universe. It also symbolized the blending of traditional values and ideals with the much more pragmatic goal of making their way into the larger world.

Opposing that goal was their neighbor to the north, the communist state of North Korea, created by the Soviet Union in the area occupied by the Soviet army when Japan surrendered to end World War II. Under Kim Il-sung, the North Koreans coveted the South, which they had failed to gain by military means during the Korean War, and they looked to their communist allies for fraternal opposition to the Seoul Games. But as the South Koreans entered into a massive building and economic reconstruction program for the Games and as Samaranch flew around the world charming, persuading, and cajoling countries into committing themselves to the Games, the leaders in Moscow were both more liberal and more pragmatic than their predecessors. By the mid-1980s, Mikhail Gorbachev was in power, and the mood of boycott was fading as countries realized that there was more to be gained by being at the Games than there was by staying away from them. It was revealed that East Germany, then a powerful sporting nation, if through questionable means, had been desperate to go to Los Angeles in defiance of Moscow but was forced to fall into line. Those days were gone; Samaranch knew most of the communist states would be in Seoul.

The focus turned to North Korea, which had demanded that if the Games were going to go ahead in Seoul (and there was never any serious suggestion that they would not), Pyongyang should have its share of Olympic sports. In the interest of stability, Samaranch went along with the idea and organized a series of historic meetings between the two Koreas with the IOC as the broker, although there was no precedent for sharing the Games that are awarded to a city, not a country, and certainly not to a combination of countries. The North insisted on simultaneous opening ceremonies in Seoul and Pyongyang and a share of sports, notably the whole of the soccer tournament. There was a practical reason for this. Soccer's world governing body, Fédération Internationale de football association (FIFA), had suspended North Korea for refusing to play in an Olympic qualifying match, and Pyongyang saw the staging of the Olympic soccer tournament in North Korea as an ideal way of gaining reinstatement.

The negotiations between North and South were almost as protracted as the negotiations thirty years earlier that eventually led to the end of the Korean War. Underlying the proposition of shared Games was the knowledge that Olympic events are not played out in a vacuum. The quest for Olympic medals is accompanied by the electronic eye of television and thousands of journalists and commentators, and North Korea had to face the unpalatable fact that if some sports were on its hitherto closed territory, so would be the inquisitive hordes. This was something that could not be countenanced, and eventually the sharing plans foundered, but on the rocks of practicality, Samaranch telling them that planning required certain deadlines to be met. The North Koreans withdrew but left behind a suspicion rather than a threat that the Seoul Games might still somehow be disrupted, although it became evident as the Games approached that Pyongyang would risk losing much more than it could possibly gain if it attempted some form of disruption in a city that would be crowded with athletes and officials from communist states.

Just in case, security was stepped up along the border at the 38th Parallel and at the bizarre meeting points of Panmunjon, where North and South Korean soldiers—the latter backed by United Nations forces—daily stare each other down. And the United States found the need for military exercises in the region at the time of the Games, greatly increasing its naval presence in the Yellow Sea and the Sea of Japan.

South Korea's problems were not just with the communists. There was also television. The world's most pervasive information medium, it made its tentative Olympic beginnings at Berlin in 1936, and between 1960 and 1980 it underpinned the IOC's finances. Fees for the rights to exclusive coverage of the Olympics were dominated by the three American networks. For the 1960 Games in Rome, CBS paid $394,000 for its exclusivity, and by 1980, NBC paid $87 million—and lost heavily, because of the boycott. Rights fees took off in the early 1980s at two Games with "real time" coverage of the Games, Los Angeles in 1984 (ABC, $225 million) and the Winter Games in Calgary in 1988 (ABC, $309 million). Since the Games were in North America, finals in high-interest events were scheduled for prime time, and the scheduling of events was more or less what it would have been without television. The situation in Seoul, however, was different. Initially, the sports federations planned their Games programs without regard for television. In viewer interest terms, this primarily meant the International Amateur Athletic Federation (IAAF), controller of all track and field. On the advice of the International Management Group, one of the world's most successful sports marketing companies, Seoul sought a U.S. rights fee from television of something in the region of $750 million, an enormous sum in the best of times, but for the American networks, Seoul was not providing the best of times. Given the time difference, high-interest finals such as the 100-meter track clash—billed as a showdown between American Carl Lewis and Canadian Ben Johnson—would be late at night or early in the morning U.S. time. No American network would pay such an amount for dead-time viewing or, worse, delayed coverage.

NBC, which talked the Koreans down to $300 million for the rights, appealed to Samaranch, and he and other IOC officials gave the Koreans "guidance." At the same time, the Koreans and television executives leaned on the IAAF to alter competition times to suit peak viewing in the United States better. Eventually the times were changed (the 100-meter final was run late in the morning, Seoul time, exceptionally early for such a prestigious race), and NBC was happy. So too was the IAAF, which, according to journalists Vyv Simson and Andrew Jennings in *The Lord of the Rings* (1992), gained an extra $20 million from the Seoul organizers for changing the event times. Primo Nebiolo, IAAF president and one of the power players in international sports, denied that this payment was made.

When most people think of the Olympics, they may recall some of the athletic greats of past Games, such as Paavo Nurmi, Emil Zatopek, Vera Cáslavská, or Nadia Comaneci, or if they think of Seoul, they may think of Johnson and the doping scandal or the athletic feats of swimmers Matt Biondi or Kristin Otto. It is most unlikely they would think of, or even know of, the people who make the Games happen—those, often in appointed positions, who work behind the scenes to get the Games in the first place and then ensure their smooth running. People such as Samaranch and Nebiolo are world figures with as much political influence as any head of state, and sometimes more than many. Kim Un-Yong was not a name that was on many lips when Seoul won the Games or even when it staged them, yet he was almost a sixth Olympic ring. David Miller, the English journalist who wrote Samaranch's biography, described Kim as the second most influential man in the Olympic movement during Samaranch's tenure as president. He had been assistant to the prime minister; a diplomatic envoy in the United Nations, Washington, and London; and deputy director-general to the South Korean president; and he had moved in circles of tremendous power and influence. He led South Korea's bid for the Games, and thereafter no significant decision was made without his advice or input.

The world of politics in sport can be as byzantine and corrupt as the real political world, with a credo that the ends justify the means. For most of the world, the shadowy maneuverings behind the scenes, the power of the dollar, and the lust for real power are irrelevant when it comes to the Games themselves. The Games are judged on the quality of the sports events and the type of show the host city puts on. Seoul surpassed all its predecessors. It helped, of course, that the Olympic world was united for the first time since Munich in 1972, just six national Olympic committees choosing not to attend. North Korea (officially, the Democratic People's Republic of Korea) and Cuba would not compete unless the Games were held in both Koreas, Nicaragua stayed away because of difficulties at home, and Albania, Ethiopia, and the Seychelles did not respond to the invitations that the IOC sent. Normally it is the host city that issues the invitations, but the IOC took over to minimize the risk of offending those countries that did not recognize South Korea.

Reveling at being under the gaze of the world, the South Koreans described staging the Games as a "fantastic journey" on which they were guided by five themes they called the Quintessence of the Seoul Olympics and to which they gave the acronym, CLUE. "C" was for the Games of total *culture* (the biggest arts festivals staged in conjunction with a Games) and for the Olympics of *compassion* (events for the disabled and the funding of the Paralympics that followed the Games). "L" was for the Olympics of a future *legacy*. "U" was for the games of *unity*. And "E" was for the Olympics of a new *era*.

Much of the "Olympicspeak" centers on the themes of international understanding and peace and goodwill, phrases that can sound like empty rhetoric more in keeping with the United Nations than the real world of sporting endeavor that crosses all racial and socioeconomic boundaries. But events at an Olympics can give real meaning to the words, and this time, in the case of Seoul, truly the sporting world was united and the Olympics showed that no other force could so bring humanity together into harmony.

The Seoul Games were the largest in history—in size, technology, and publicity—and they were an exceptional success. Samaranch described them as the best Games there have been. Kim, the power behind the Seoul throne, afterward pointed to the success of the Olympics in areas where other international efforts have been dismal failures. He noted that the Olympics had led to South Korea's establishing diplomatic relations with many socialist countries and a trade office in the People's Republic of China. For South Korea, the 1988 Olympics brought about a significant change in the country's international standing.

The press chief at Seoul was Jae-won Lee, who in 1994 was invited to the Olympic Congress in Paris that marked the centenary of the Olympic movement. The Games, he said, provided a channel of communication for South Korea that previously had not existed, enabling it to have sporting relations as a prelude to diplomatic relations.

"This was the case at the Seoul Asian Games of 1986 and the Seoul Olympics in 1988," he said. "These two Games made it possible for Korea to open dialogues, compete together and to succeed in diplomatic relations with China and most Eastern European countries. In Korea, we are always mindful and grateful for the courage of sports leaders in China and Eastern Europe, and the inspiration we drew from the IOC. The Olympic movement changed our world forever and for the better'' (Lee, Jae-won, ''The Olympic Movement and International Understanding,'' paper presented at the Centenary Olympic Congress, Paris, August 1994).

The world was not entirely in peace and harmony at Seoul. One who was out of kilter was the Canadian sprinter Ben Johnson, who clearly had not heeded—or whose advisers had not heeded—a growing clamor within sport that the misuse of drugs had gone far enough. There have been reasons to suppose that some sports authorities have not pursued drug abusers as diligently as they should, or as thoroughly as they said they were, but there was no denying the growing international mood against drug abuse in sport. Johnson served to intensify that mood. Samaranch had warned as recently as Calgary, the Games before Seoul, that the IOC would do whatever it could in its power to rid the sports world of drugs.

There could have been no more public example of cheating than Johnson's. Before the Seoul Games, he and Carl Lewis were the most publicized athletes, and their meeting in the 100-meter final was the most anticipated event: the defending champion American against the world champion and world record holder. The final has been called the most-watched foot race in history, and perhaps it was, Johnson winning relatively easily with his right arm raised in a gesture of victory. But two days later it was revealed that he had tested positive for anabolic steroids, and his title was stripped from him. Subsequently his world record was removed from the record books, and Canada began a series of investigations into how it could have happened.

The sensational disqualification focused attention on drugs in sports like no other occurrence before it—and there had been plenty of them—but the only reputation to be sullied was Johnson's—not Seoul's and not the Olympics'. His exposure led to greater efforts around the world to stop the illicit use of drugs in sport and also to the realization that in modern sport the vast sums of money on offer are worth, to some, the price. Exposing those who use or misuse drugs is one step. The next problem confronting sports is exposing and eliminating those who supply and prescribe them. Johnson clearly did not act on his own.

The legacy of a united sporting world was not all that Seoul left the Olympic movement. It also gave it a new flag. The original Olympic flag, the five Olympic rings on a white background, was based on a design by Baron Pierre de Coubertin himself and made in the Au Bon Marché store near Coubertin's birthplace in Paris. It was first flown in 1914 on the occasion of the twentieth anniversary of the creation of the IOC but did not serve as a standard for the Games until 1920 in Antwerp. It had become worn with the years, and the IOC asked the Seoul organizers to come up with a new one. The Antwerp flag, as it had become known, was retired to the Olympic Museum in Lausanne, and its replacement was presented to Samaranch by Roh Tae Woo in 1985. Fittingly, it was wholly Korean made—from pure Korean raw silk and the needlework by the deft hands of women skilled in Korea's traditional methods. The impact of Seoul, both literally and figuratively, will hover over future Games cities.

BIBLIOGRAPHICAL ESSAY

Two widely contrasting books, David Miller, *Olympic Revolution, The Olympic Biography of Juan Antonio Samaranch* (London, 1992), and Vyv Simson and Andrew Jennings, *The Lord of the Rings: Power, Money, and Drugs in the Modern Olympics* (London, 1992), form the basis of contemporary research of the Seoul Games. Miller provides the orthodox, almost authorized version of Olympic history under Samaranch's presidency. Simson and Jennings provide almost the opposite: a study of the politicking and wheeling and dealing that are endemic to any multinational organization. The balance, as always, is somewhere in between.

The U.S. Olympic Committee's official report is *Seoul Calgary 1988* (Sandy, Utah, 1988); the Canadian version is David W. Ellis, *Canada at the Olympics, 1988* (St. Albert, Alberta, 1989). Various issues of the IOC's *Olympic Review* from the time of the awarding of the Games until their completion provided commentary and reportage on Seoul's organizational progress, as does *Seoul Flame,* the official newsletter of the Seoul organizing committee.

A useful view from within Seoul of the Olympics and their impact on Korean society came from Lee Jae-won, who was the press chief during the Games. He wrote *Seoul Olympics and the Global Community* (Seoul, 1992) and ''The Olympic Movement and International Understanding'' (paper presented at the Centenary Olympic Congress, Paris, August and September 1994). For other inside views, consult Park Seh-jik, *The Seoul Olympics: the Inside Story* (London, 1991); Kim Un-yong, *The Greatest Olympics: From Baden-Baden to Seoul* (Seoul, 1990); and Vincent J. Ricquant and C. S. Smith, *The Games within the Games: The Story behind the 1988 Seoul Olympics* (Seoul, 1988). Two other books that may prove useful are James T. Larson, *Global Television and the Politics of the Seoul Olympics* (Boulder, Colo., 1993), and Bill Toomey, *The Olympic Challenge, 1988* (Costa Mesa, Calif., 1988).

Simon Winchester, *Korea* (New York, 1988), and Bevin Alexander, *Korea, The Lost War* (London, 1989), provide insightful background on Korean politics and people. Daily coverage during the Games in the *Korean Herald* complemented my own personal observations.

Ron Palenski

BARCELONA 1992

THE GAMES OF THE XXVTH OLYMPIAD

Barcelona, considered one of the Olympic movement's perpetual bridesmaids, tried on four separate occasions to convince the International Olympic Committee (IOC) of its ability to host the Summer Olympics. In 1924, the Spanish city was considered a leading contender for the Games, but Paris received the award, with some help from native son and IOC president Baron Pierre de Coubertin. The city made a bid for the 1936 Olympics and built a stadium on the nearby mountain of Montjuic, only to have the IOC choose Berlin. Barcelona attempted to secure the 1940 Games canceled by World War II, and, finally, a poorly planned effort between Madrid and Barcelona for the 1972 Games ended in failure when Munich was selected as the host city.

Barcelona next pinned its hopes on a bid for the 1992 Games. The organizing committee focused the IOC's attention on the significance of 1992 to Spain: hosting the world during the five hundredth anniversary of Columbus' voyage to the Americas seemed appropriate, and Spain's entry into the European Community as a full partner deserved a celebration. In addition, the organizing committee prepared a conservative Olympic budget of $667 million, most of which would be secured by television rights and corporate sponsors.

Of the small field of candidates—including Amsterdam; Brisbane, Australia; Birmingham, England; and Belgrade, Yugoslavia—only Paris and Barcelona were considered likely choices. All of Spain supported Barcelona's bid; 65,000 young Spaniards offered to volunteer if Barcelona won the Games, and ninety-two members of the Catalan business community raised $10 million for the organizing committee's campaign. A promise was made to the IOC that 10 percent of excess revenue from a Barcelona Games would be shared with the IOC and with the Spanish Olympic Committee. The committee's final trump was Juan Antonio Samaranch, president of the IOC and a native of Barcelona. When asked what would happen if Barcelona lost a fifth time, one businessman replied, "Collective suicide." Such drastic steps proved unnecessary; this time the IOC overlooked Paris in favor of Barcelona.

The Olympics served several important functions for Barcelona. After four decades of economic and political oppression under the Franco regime, Barcelona wanted to show its principal rival, Madrid, the European Community, and, indeed, the entire world that the city could host a memorable international event. The Olympics also provided the city with the needed catalyst to overturn decades of neglect by hastening an infrastructure revitalization plan begun in 1980. The city's plan became a reality due to the efforts of one individual who ensured cooperation between the Barcelona Olympic Organizing Committee (COOB) and the city: Pascual Maragall i Mira, mayor of Barcelona and president of COOB. With just six years to work with prior to the Games, Maragall planned to turn Barcelona into a city that would serve the Olympic family and provide residents with a comfortable urban environment well into the twenty-first century.

In what art critic Robert Hughes described as "the most ambitious project of its kind that any government of a 20th-century city has tried," Barcelona began its preparations for the Olympic spotlight with a massive construction campaign for venues and urban improvements (*Art in America* [February 1991]: 110). The federal government spent more than $8 billion on the autonomous region of Catalonia and the city of Barcelona on approximately 300 Olympic-related infrastructure projects. One of the first steps in achieving the goal of a livable metropolis was the construction of a 26-mile ring road to divert traffic from downtown and submerged highways covered by walkways and gardens within the city. Additionally, the city replaced its 110-year-old sewer system.

To curb costs, COOB took great care in choosing existing buildings that could serve as venues and in commissioning innovative architects to enhance the city's design-conscious reputation. New facilities built on Montjuic truly made the mountain the crown jewel of the city. Arata Isozaki's Sant Jordi Sports Palace and plaza and Santiago Calatrava's futuristic telecommunications tower enriched the city's architectural heritage.

City planners concentrated on restoring the city's access to the Mediterranean waterfront, cut off since 1848 by rail lines and warehouses. The 175-acre site targeted for use as the Olympic Village proved critical to the redevelopment of central Barcelona. More than three dozen architectural firms participated in the design of the new neighborhood, composed of 2,000 apartments, with nearly half the site committed to parks. Additionally, residents of Barcelona regained access to the sea when a 3-mile stretch of beach was restored.

Living up to the ideal that all residents should benefit from the Games, infrastructure activity encompassed more than Olympic housing and venues. In addition to new facilities on Montjuic, Olympic planners methodically targeted venues for neighborhoods with little or no access to sports facilities. More than 700 apartments were demolished so that open plazas could be built in the city's older, more crowded neighborhoods. In total, Barcelona allocated more than $50 million to create or improve more than 200 parks, plazas, and streets. COOB paid twenty international artists approximately $250,000 each to create permanent works of art for the Olympic Village, and the city commissioned fifty works of sculpture for its new public spaces. Efforts to redesign the city earned for Barcelona Harvard University's 1991 Prince of Wales Award for Urban Design.

Despite accolades for Barcelona's modernization, the infrastructure improvements masked the difficulties COOB faced in hosting a world sporting event. The many factions in Barcelona had loud voices. In fact, the clash of disparate views threatened at times to derail the city's moment on the world stage. Most Olympic-related disputes pertained to the city's and the region's relationship with the government in Madrid. After decades of strife under Franco and living under the shadow of Madrid, Barcelona and Catalonia were determined to prepare for the Games with minimal assistance from the national government. Catalonia is an autonomous region with a distinct culture and language, and its officials wanted the Games to be Catalan, reflecting the region's character. It did not take much to persuade the IOC that Catalan should be the fourth official language of the Games, alongside English, French, and Spanish.

Yet the demands to capture the region's heritage continued. Catalonia formed its own Olympic committee, but the IOC denied its request to field a team separate from Spain's. To avoid an incident by Catalan extremists during the Games, Maragall permitted the Catalan flag to be raised beside those of Barcelona and Spain at all Olympic-related events and sites. Despite these concessions, the regional government sought undeserved credit for its role in the Games by spending $5.6 million on a global advertising campaign that geographically placed Barcelona in the "country" of Catalonia.

Unfortunately for COOB, all of its problems did not center on Catalonia's demands for a separate identity. Trouble started almost immediately when the Barcelona government was forced to work with the Generalitat of Catalonia, the autonomous regional government of which Barcelona is a part. The Generalitat and its president, Jordi Pujol, were conservative and did not share the socialist mayor's vision for remaking the city. Pujol, a political rival of Maragall, preferred to spend revenue on projects highlighting the city's attributes as a technologically superior business environment, a direct funding threat to Maragall's goals of a livable city. If it had not been for Spain's constitution, it might have been easy for Maragall to ignore the central government's demands. However, the federal constitution stipulated that government funds must be directed through the regional government to the city.

Catalonia's financial role in the Games led not only to a philosophical standoff but also to construction delays and increased costs. Pujol's government impeded construction on the ring road and blocked the development of a subway line to Olympic facilities on Montjuic. The din from the two governments' bickering led artist Javier Mariscal to comment that "the trouble with Barcelona is that there are too many Catalans in it," a statement that almost cost him the honor of designing the Olympic mascot, Cobi (*Financial Times,* March 17, 1988).

The effects of political posturing became evident in 1989 when the $80 million expansion of the Olympic stadium was completed, supposedly in time for the track and field World Cup. King Juan Carlos dedicated the new facility, but fiercely independent Catalans showed their disdain for the nation's figurehead by heckling him. Disaster plagued the stadium when two storms flooded the field and deluged interior rooms. Maragall, distressed by the treatment of the king and the disaster at the stadium, lamented, "I had hoped for evidence of progress, for momentum, for euphoria.... But it was not to be" (*New York Times,* September 26, 1989). Samaranch shared Maragall's embarrassment to such a degree that the IOC leader asked Spain's prime minister, Felipe Gonzalez, to intervene before the integrity of the Games was jeopardized.

Within six months of the stadium debacle, Maragall appointed a group of representatives from the local, state, and federal governments, COOB, and city agencies to oversee the remaining construction. Until the end of the Olympics, the decision makers set aside their differences and concentrated on completing essential projects.

No sooner had Spain's internal differences been resolved than the world political situation began to deteriorate. Little did anyone know the ramifications for the world and the Olympic movement when the Berlin Wall crumbled in November 1989. The accelerated pace of East Germany's demise hastened the decision to field a unified German team for the first time since the 1964 Summer Olympics in Tokyo. Questions surfaced immediately on how well the third- and fourth-ranked medal countries at the Seoul Olympics would fare as a single team.

Eastern Europe soon followed East Germany's lead as Estonia, Latvia, and Lithuania declared independence from the U.S.S.R. National Olympic committees were quickly formed for the Baltic states, and all were welcomed back into the Olympic family for the first time since the 1930s.

The continued existence of the Soviet sports machine was taken for granted even as plans were made to dismantle the Soviet Union and create the Commonwealth of Independent States. Arrangements were quickly made to field a Unified Team of athletes from the former Soviet Union, but this left many of the athletes feeling stripped of country and flag. The team members marched into the Olympic stadium under a newly designed Olympic flag and were announced as contestants for the Unified Team, not their homelands. Unlike the Albertville Olympics, however, medal winners stood to their country's flags and heard their national anthems at the Barcelona Games.

Despite the miracle of fielding a team under difficult political circumstances, the trip from the former Soviet Union to Barcelona was less than assured. In the waning days of the Soviet empire, the government halted its financial support of the central sports agency, Gossport. Deteriorating economic conditions and the development of independent states forced government leaders to cut Gossport's funding, but the timing could not have been worse for Winter and Summer Olympic athletes. The most stringent budget estimate required more than $5 million to send the team to Barcelona, but the Commonwealth countries could not or would not provide the needed economic support. Several Western corporations stepped in and provided the necessary support to send the Unified Team to the Games. Even then, the austere budget did not permit the athletes to stay and enjoy the Olympics after their performances.

The deteriorating situation in Yugoslavia also presented COOB with problems. That country's civil war and requests by breakaway countries caused the IOC and COOB to devise procedures to allow the new countries to be represented at the Games. The new states of Croatia and Slovenia were the first to receive IOC recognition, but the remainder of what once was Yugoslavia presented more difficult problems. Newly independent Bosnia and Herzegovina experienced daily bombardments by Serbs, and athletes from the former Olympic city of Sarajevo, including the 3,000-meter distance runner Mirsada Buric, continued to train despite sniper fire, bombings, and increasing hardship.

The IOC granted Bosnia and Herzegovina provisional membership just days before the opening ceremony, so the embattled country could march under its own flag. Conflicts with the United Nations military commander, who canceled the team's request for transport, almost prevented the country's participation in the Games, but the IOC made last-minute arrangements to transport the Bosnian team to the Olympics.

The remaining Olympians from Yugoslavia faced similar hardships reaching the Games. Team members from the new state of Macedonia could not compete under their nation's flag or name due to a dispute with Greece over the latter's historical rights to the name Macedonia. And members of the Yugoslavia Olympic Team were first denied entry to the Games because of United Nations sanctions. A last-minute appeal by the heads of state at the Group of Seven economic summit and a decision by the United Nations allowed athletes in individual sports to compete as individuals under the Olympic flag and anthem.

Not all the decisions facing the Olympic committee were so daunting. The IOC determined that South Africa had made sufficient headway in integrating its society to justify the country's return to the Olympic family. This decision to reinstate South Africa meant that no country would be banned at the 1992 Summer Games.

With a record number of countries and athletes participating, the city of Barcelona and COOB gave primary consideration to safety from terrorism. The terrorist group Basque Liberty and Homeland (ETA) had killed more than 700 people during the past two decades, and their ability to disrupt the Games was not taken lightly. City and COOB officials worked for months with terrorism experts from the United States, Israel, France, and other countries in developing a counterterrorism plan. Meanwhile, Spain and France cooperated in a manhunt for the leadership of ETA. Within months of opening ceremonies, French forces captured most of ETA's masterminds, but it was soon discovered that plans to disrupt the Olympics had already been disseminated throughout the organization. Two other terrorist organizations, El Grapo and Terra Lliure, presented similar threats when they detonated bombs in and around Barcelona in the months preceding the Games. To guard the city and the Olympic family against any unforeseen events, a squadron of 45,000 military and security forces was put in place. Nearly one-quarter of the Olympic security force underwent counterterrorism training.

Although two small bombs blew up a gas pipeline 40 miles outside Barcelona just before the Games opened, the Games themselves passed without incident. Barcelona even benefited from the increased police presence with a 20 percent reduction in common crime.

The only disruption left to harm the Games was a potential boycott. With the end of the cold war, it seemed unlikely that Barcelona would be afflicted by the political skirmishes that had tarnished the past three Summer Olympics, but two unlikely events brought the unwanted prospect of a boycott within the realm of possibility. The first issue concerned a stuffed African man called "El Negro," who had been on display in the small Spanish town of Banyoles since the late 1800s. African embassies in Spain began discussing an African boycott if the figure remained in place during the Games. But town officials in Banyoles, which served as the site of Olympic rowing competitions, would not budge. Even efforts by the IOC and Samaranch could not get El Negro removed. In the end, there was no boycott, and El Negro remained on display in Banyoles.

The second incident involved American Dream Team member Magic Johnson's admission that he was infected with HIV, the virus that causes AIDS. Brian Sando, Basketball Australia's senior director, publicly recommended that his players not compete against Johnson as he was a threat to their health. The Australian government quickly reprimanded Sando for his comments, and COOB stated that Johnson and other athletes infected with the virus were welcome to participate in Barcelona. Although the threatened boycott quickly faded, Sando's statement and Johnson's courage forced the Olympic movement to consider the threat of AIDS to athletes and the world at large. In fact, COOB was so concerned that it bought 2 million condoms for free distribution in the Olympic Village during the Games, and Samaranch promised Johnson IOC assistance in an AIDS education effort.

With the concerns of nations addressed, Barcelona was ready to welcome the world. Opening ceremonies dazzled millions of television viewers, as well as the Catalans in the stadium. To the delight of the crowd, King Juan Carlos spoke in Catalan, an act of conciliation that led to cheers rather than a repeat of the heckling he received in 1989. COOB ensured that other fragments of Catalan culture received center stage: the *sardana,* which had been outlawed under the Franco regime, was danced on the field, and the Catalan anthem brought tears to the eyes of the faithful.

Without doubt, the most memorable event of the evening occurred with the lighting of the Olympic flame. Disabled archer Antonio Rebollo shot a flaming arrow 230 feet from the floor of the stadium to the titanium dish above to light the Olympic flame, thus opening the largest Games in the history of the Olympic movement. The 1992 Summer Olympics fielded 9,959 athletes from 172 countries, all of whom received free accommodations during their competitions, another Olympic first. The Games expanded to twenty-six events with the addition of badminton and baseball as medal sports, while pelota, tae kwon do, and roller hockey became the last demonstration sports allowed in the Olympics. The Games also opened wider the doors to professionalism as professional sailors and basketball players competed for the first time. More countries provided their top athletes with cash bonuses. Spain offered its gold medal winners pensions worth $1 million. China provided gold medal winners $50,000 and a solid gold soda can, and Taiwan gave each member of its Olympic team $400,000. And for the first time, 257 competitors were awarded medals of solid gold valued at approximately $5,000 each.

During sixteen days, the Games created legends and produced spectacular stories. Jackie Joyner-Kersee of the United States captured her second Olympic heptathlon title. Swimmer Kiernan Perkins, the ''flying fish'' of Australia, broke his world record by 4.92 seconds in the grueling 1,500-meter freestyle. Chris Boardman of Great Britain broke the world record in the 4,000-meter pursuit with a revolutionary bicycle. The oldest world record in track and field was toppled when the U.S. relay team of Andrew Valmon, Quincy Watts, Michael Johnson, and Steve Lewis won the 4 × 400-meter relay. In all, thirty-two world records were set or broken, eight of those by athletes from the United States.

Even when world records remained intact, the Olympics generated memorable moments. Vitaly Scherbo of the Unified Team became the first gymnast in Olympic history to win six gold medals during one event. For the first time since 1932 in nonboycotted competition, a U.S. gymnast captured a gold medal in the horizontal bar. Xiaosahuang Li of China won a gold medal after performing the first triple somersault in Olympic gymnastics history. Of equal importance to the people of Spain was their national teams' best performance in history. Through the 1988 Games, Spain had won twenty-six medals; it won twenty-two medals in Barcelona.

The 32-year-old Linford Christie of Great Britain became the oldest runner in Olympic history to win the men's 100 meters, just one-tenth of a second off world record pace. Bruce Baumgartner of the United States became the first wrestler in Olympic history to stand on the medal platform at three Olympics. The women's marathon also produced the closest race in Olympic history, with Valentina Yegorova of the Unified Team finishing just 8 seconds ahead of Yuko Arimori of Japan. Gail Devers of the United States won the closest women's 100 meters since the Games adopted automatic timing in 1972. Devers's accomplishment was even more spectacular given that her legs had nearly been amputated eighteen months prior to the Games due to complications from Graves' disease.

Yet the Barcelona Games were not without controversy. Some critics remarked that professionals in the basketball tournament created a runaway show that eclipsed the twenty-five other events. The Olympic boxing tournament again led to disappointment, although a new scoring system had been introduced for Barcelona. The new system required judges to push buttons within 1 second of each other for a punch to count. The older judges' slow reflexes led to actual punches not being scored by the computer. A judge from Ghana failed to award points for any punches during two fights and was suspended. U.S. boxer Eric Griffin, considered a gold medal favorite, landed eighty-one punches during his last fight, but the judges scored only five of those. Judges awarded Rafael Lozano of Spain six scored punches, although his actual number of punches was fewer than Griffin's.

Drugs continued to plague the Olympics, with five athletes expelled for use of performance-enhancing substances. Another record of sorts was set during these Games: all three winners of the men's shot put had been suspended previously for drug use.

The level to which corporate sponsors have infiltrated the Olympic Games became more visible as well. As part of a $2.64 billion worldwide marketing campaign for the Games, corporate billboards on Olympic themes inundated the city, and venues remained partially full as sponsors, who collectively paid $250 million for sponsorship of the Games, refused to return unused tickets to COOB. Only complaints by broadcasters, who paid even greater sums for rights to cover the Olympics, led to a system in which individuals received temporary passes until a ticket holder claimed a seat.

Finally, Olympic history was made when the IOC stripped Unified Team weight lifter Ibragim Samadov of the bronze medal for his medals ceremony protest. Samadov, the world champion, tied for first place but was awarded the bronze due to his higher body weight. After throwing his medal to the floor and leaving the ceremony, Samadov became the first athlete ever to be punished by the IOC for a medal ceremony protest.

In spite of the more infamous moments of the 1992 Games, Barcelona produced one of the more memorable Olympics since World War II. There was no organized boycott, and athletes from sixty-four participating nations won medals, another record. Yet the cost for planning such an occasion was high. Taxes rose faster than inflation for the five years preceding the Games. Cost overruns ate the projected surplus. The original estimate of $30 million for the Sant Jordi Sports Palace soared to $89 million due to the structure's innovative design. Construction delays on the ring road contributed to a 50 percent increase in the original $1 billion budget estimate. When combined with the additional $600,000 needed to complete the Olympic Village and a $100 million loss due to a fall in the dollar's value, cost overruns left COOB with only a $3.8 million surplus instead of an anticipated $350 million. The original estimates for infrastructure improvements and related Olympic costs rose 300 percent from the original estimate of $2.37 billion (in 1992 dollars). The city felt the impact of these cost overruns within months of the closing ceremonies. Unemployment, which had fallen to 9 percent in the years preceding the Olympics, surpassed 12 percent four months after the Games. Prices soared, and business taxes increased 30 percent. City officials admitted prior to the Games that taxes would rise for five years after the Olympic Games to pay for all the city's improvements, but that open disclosure failed to stop angry calls for Maragall's job.

As Pascual Maragall attempted to remind the citizens of Barcelona, the Games provided the city with an excuse to overturn decades of neglect under the Franco regime. The city accomplished in six years what would otherwise have taken fifty to accomplish. The longstanding improvements to the city cannot be overlooked, nor can the organizers' success in hosting a successful Olympic Games.

ACKNOWLEDGMENT

I would like to thank the Honorable Pascual Maragall i Mira for reviewing this chapter.

BIBLIOGRAPHICAL ESSAY

The Barcelona Olympic Organizing Committee took steps to ensure that the efficiency of the 1992 Games could be replicated at any point in the future with the production of the *Official Report of the Games of the XXV Olympiad* (Barcelona, 1993). Although Olympic committees are bound by their contracts with the IOC to develop such a report, they are not required to offer it to the public, as Barcelona did. The four-volume set chronicles the depth of expertise developed by the organizing committee until its dismantling on July 25, 1993.

In addition to the final report, COOB began an archive well before the opening of the Games. The advance of modern technology enhanced the value and ease of use of this collection; all photographs and the extensive video library were copied on to laser discs, and the entire compilation of materials is cross-referenced on a database. The archive and the Olympic Gallery are located inside the Olympic stadium on Montjuic.

The official report of the United States Olympic Committee is *Barcelona Albertville 1992* (Salt Lake City, 1992); it contains abundant photographs, commentary, results, and pictures of Olympic team members. The media carried extensive coverage of the Barcelona Games from the development stage through the closing ceremonies. Of particular significance for a complete review of Barcelona's progress is *La Vanguardia,* a Barcelona newspaper. In the United States, the *New York Times* and the *Washington Post* carried significant articles on the development of the Games. After winning the 1996 Olympic Games, the *Atlanta Journal/Constitution* increased its coverage of every aspect of the Barcelona Olympics.

Important articles on the Olympic-related development of Barcelona appear in *Art in America* and *Architectural Record.* In addition, stories on financial matters can be found in the *Wall Street Journal, Financial World,* and the London-based *Financial Times.*

Two videos are important to note. Filmmaker Bud Greenspan continued his series of Olympic films with the production of *Barcelona '92: 16 Days of Glory.* The National Broadcasting Company, in conjunction with Blockbuster Video, produced a compilation of highlights from the 1992 Games.

Larry Maloney

ATLANTA 1996

THE GAMES OF THE XXVITH OLYMPIAD

Atlanta has striven to claim status as a competent world-class community ever since Union general William T. Sherman reduced the city to ashes during the American Civil War. Today Atlanta is a sprawling metropolis of 3 million people and arguably the most progressive city in the American South, yet few in the Olympic movement believed this first-time candidate was ready to host the Summer Games. To the surprise of its critics, though, Atlanta will see flames once again as the host of the 1996 Summer Olympic Games, the Centennial Games of the modern Olympic movement. Although the final chapter of the first Olympic century remains to be written, the notoriety of this largest world sporting event has left Atlanta with a task as daunting as postwar reconstruction. Heightened expectations for the centennial celebration have generated intense scrutiny and criticism that threaten to undermine the city's Olympic accomplishments.

The birthplace of the ancient and modern Olympics, Athens, was initially considered the natural choice to host the Centennial Games; regardless, its chronic pollution and Greece's political instability precluded a fait accompli in the host city selection process. Of the five remaining competitors—Atlanta; Belgrade, Yugoslavia; Manchester, England; Melbourne, Australia; and Toronto, Canada—three produced bids strong enough to challenge Athens' claim. Melbourne last hosted the Olympic Games in 1956 and used a compelling "Time for Another Continent" slogan. The Melbourne committee thoughtfully recognized the financial burden of an Australian Games on national Olympic committees by budgeting $40 million to subsidize athlete travel and accommodation costs. Toronto's media and communications facilities had few rivals in North America, and the city carried the United Nations distinction of being the most multicultural city on earth. Atlanta's strengths, however, overcame those of the competition. The International Olympic Committee (IOC) Evaluation Commission ranked Atlanta highest for its infrastructure and facilities. More IOC representatives visited Atlanta than any other bid city, and Billy Payne, a local lawyer and president of the organizing committee, circled the globe for two years meeting with IOC members. Atlanta surpassed the competition's international credibility through the participation of Andrew Young, former mayor of Atlanta and former U.S. ambassador to the United Nations.

Two components of Atlanta's bid swayed IOC members. First, Young assured African IOC delegates that Atlanta's civil rights history and reputation for racial harmony proved the city could host a successful multicultural Olympics. Second, Atlanta's organizing committee proposed a substantial revenue-sharing package. Like Barcelona's financial package for the 1992 Olympics, the Atlanta committee planned to distribute 10 percent of excess revenue to the IOC, with an additional 10 percent targeted for the national organization, the U.S. Olympic Committee (USOC). Atlanta surpassed Barcelona's generosity by offering to disburse half of the remaining surplus to national Olympic committees (NOCs) around the globe.

The fierce competition for the 1996 Games culminated at the IOC session in Tokyo in September 1990. The campaign to host these Olympics had cost the bidding cities more than $100 million, of which Atlanta spent an estimated $7.3 million. Candidate financial expenditures reached such exorbitant heights that the IOC later enacted new regulations to curb excessive and unnecessary bidding costs, including a $200 limit on gifts to voting members.

The decision on the 1996 Olympic city required five rounds of voting. Athens won the first two rounds of voting but began to lose ground, finally succumbing to Atlanta on the fifth ballot, 51–35. Efforts to discredit Atlanta began shortly after IOC president Juan Antonio Samaranch announced the results. Athens led the unsuccessful competitors in suggesting that Atlanta had won because of a conspiracy organized by Atlanta-based Coca-Cola, the oldest corporate supporter of the Olympic movement. The Greek newspaper *Eleftherostypos* declared, "The Olympic flame will now not be lit with oil, but with Coca-Cola." Spyros Metaxas, the outspoken president of the Athens committee, went further, emphatically stating that Athens would never again bid to host the Olympic Games. Evidence of Athens' and Melbourne's bitterness toward Atlanta resurfaced a year later when they informed the German periodical *Der Spiegel* that some bid cities had bribed IOC members. In its article, *Der Spiegel* alleged that Atlanta bought the votes of eighteen IOC members with promises of free heart surgery in the United States, gold credit cards, up to $120,000 in cash, and college scholarships for their children. Isolated incidents occurred during the selection process that coincided with the allegations of bribery. For example, one IOC official suffered a heart attack while visiting Atlanta, and the bid committee and the hospital covered the medical expenses as a professional courtesy. However, no evidence exists to confirm that Atlanta willfully attempted to undermine the bidding process.

Atlanta's troubles extended beyond international headlines and the bruised egos of competitors. U.S. newspapers criticized Atlanta as a second-tier city with a plethora of fast food restaurants and a dearth of culture. Charges of nepotism were leveled against the Atlanta Committee for the Olympic Games (ACOG) as relatives of city officials and ACOG board members received paid staff positions. City leaders questioned the committee's ethics when former staff members, as well as city officials, received contracts for Olympic goods and services. Critics likened the computer-generated mascot, "Izzy," to a large blue sperm. Even the state flag's confederate battle insignia fueled editorial criticism. Georgia governor Zell Miller felt the flag's historical links to slavery and segregation conveyed the wrong message about the new American South, but his attempt to have the flag redesigned derailed when political extremists mobilized on both sides of the issue and polls indicated that 59 percent of the state's citizens opposed its redesign.

ACOG unwittingly fueled national criticism by selecting controversial communities to host Olympic events. The committee chose Atlanta's neighbor to the north, Cobb County, to host preliminary volleyball competitions. Soon thereafter, the county's conservative government passed a resolution stating that homosexual lifestyles were not compatible with the community's values. The resolution created a firestorm extending beyond Cobb County's borders. Gay rights groups challenged ACOG, stating that the committee's pledge "to reunite the family of man in the profound bond of the Olympic spirit" was a farce if gay athletes and visitors felt unwelcome at venues. Gay activists demanded that Cobb County be dropped as a site, or they would "shut Atlanta down" during the Games. Four-time gold medalist Greg Louganis, an openly gay athlete, appealed to ACOG to drop the site. After the Cobb County Commission refused to alter its stance on the resolution, ACOG moved the preliminary volleyball competition to downtown Atlanta.

ACOG's efforts to include golf on the 1996 program proved controversial as well. Although IOC members informed ACOG there was insufficient time to approve golf for 1996 and openly questioned the sport's elitist image, the committee continued to lobby for the sport and made the fatal mistake of choosing the Augusta National Golf Club as the proposed venue. Augusta National's reputation for excluding women and minorities caused residents of Atlanta to question ACOG's judgment. The Atlanta city council shared the community's misgivings and wrote to Samaranch asking that he oppose the Augusta golf course. ACOG finally dropped its campaign after Samaranch publicly stated that the proposal had only a "slim possibility" of being approved.

Previous Olympic cities endured similar bouts of unfavorable publicity and persevered to host successful Games, but claims of discrimination raised against ACOG had explosive potential. Atlantans expected ACOG to cure the city's social ills by building new roads, providing housing for the homeless, and creating good jobs for the unemployed. Little did they understand that the committee's sole purpose was to host the Olympic Games, not to improve the city's infrastructure or the plight of the poor. Citizen groups attacked ACOG for failing to address the city's most pressing problems; city council members suggested that Games officials were unwilling to work with a predominantly black council. The location of Olympic venues fueled calls of racism when ACOG moved the planned tennis facility from an unsupportive white suburb, while black neighborhoods near the proposed Olympic Stadium felt helpless in their fight to change that venue's location. Community wrath toward ACOG culminated with a speech by Martin Luther King III, a county commissioner and the son of the slain civil rights leader, who declared, "Greed, exclusivity and elitism have become the symbols of Atlanta's Olympic movement, all things that my father fought against—and they are all reflected in the [stadium] deal before us, the rich and affluent on one side, the poor and hopeless on the other side" (*Atlanta*

Journal/Constitution, March 6, 1993). It began to appear that international sporting events were exempt from the city's tradition of racial harmony.

ACOG's contract with the IOC did not require the committee to undertake community improvement programs, and as a private entity, the committee had no legal obligation to the city's disadvantaged residents. However, the organization's leadership felt that all the city's residents should benefit from the Games and therefore made substantial commitments to assist Atlanta's poor and minorities. First, ACOG adopted strict equal opportunity standards. Minority- and female-owned companies received more than 40 percent of all Olympic contracts, a milestone that surpassed the performance of both the city and county governments. The committee also established a policy that favored bids including minority subcontracting. ACOG set similar standards in its hiring practices; 32 percent of the committee's management consisted of minorities, and 35 percent represented women.

ACOG's minority enrichment strategy encompassed the entire state with the development of a program to assist the state's underprivileged. The committee stated repeatedly that the 40,000 Olympic volunteers would be chosen based on their history of volunteer service. The warning proved successful, and the largest training program for volunteers in the history of the Olympic movement was born. More than 540,000 volunteers joined the Olympic Force, a multiyear training program designed to improve impoverished communities and assist the state's youth before the Olympic Games.

In addition to the Olympic Force, ACOG supported a program at predominantly black Clark Atlanta University to provide up to 1,200 students with the technical training needed for 700 available jobs with the Olympic broadcast network. Donations were made to establish training programs for residents around the Olympic stadium interested in Olympic construction jobs, and the committee awarded contracts to organizations employing the homeless.

Certain neighborhood groups surrounding the Olympic stadium were adamant in their opposition to its construction. Already living in the shadow of Fulton County Stadium, residents felt a second sports structure nearby would lead to further deterioration of the neighborhood and lower property values. With support from the Urban Land Institute in Washington, D.C., stadium residents persuaded the city to demolish the older facility after the Games. As part of the package in which ACOG agreed to demolish the existing stadium, the committee appeased residents with a package of minority employment and training programs.

No less important was the committee's and the city's efforts to improve dilapidated Olympic neighborhoods. More than 50 percent of Atlanta's impoverished families reside in the downtown area, where the majority of Olympic activities are scheduled. The proliferation of inner-city neighborhoods scarred by urban decay led one city planner to state, "It doesn't take a genius to figure out what the story's going to be in 1996. The splendor of the Olympics amid the squalor of Southern poverty. Boy, that's written all over every tabloid in the world'' (*Atlanta Journal/Constitution,* April 5, 1992). When the city faced an avalanche of necessary projects to complete by 1996, ACOG and the business community stepped in to assist Atlanta's poorer neighborhoods. Atlanta-based foundations funded redevelopment projects, and a consortium of banks loaned $120 million to build or refurbish homes and apartments in Olympic neighborhoods. ACOG worked with nonprofit groups to build homes near the Olympic stadium. The committee funded construction of two of the stadium homes, and more than 200 ACOG employee volunteers assisted with construction.

Atlanta's laudable steps to ensure a role for the city's minority community received less recognition than deserved. However, circumstances beyond ACOG's control threaten to undermine the memory of the Centennial Games, for which ACOG will shoulder the blame. For instance, funding for the Olympics spectacle continues to soar as each host city attempts to improve on the success of its predecessors. Atlanta likely will follow the pattern and surpass Barcelona's extravaganza, but revenues have not kept pace with burgeoning expectations. Lackluster economic performance in the United States increased the burden of convincing corporations of the 1996 Games' worth, and IOC financing requirements dampened ACOG's ability to finance the Olympics. The IOC sought to avoid a situation in which both the USOC and ACOG competed for funds from the core group of U.S. Olympic supporters and asked that both organizations join forces to finance their programs. Consequently, individual corporate sponsorships for the 1996 Olympics raised an unprecedented $40 million, of which ACOG received only $28 million.

Companies initially balked at paying the sponsorship fee, principally due to the downturn in the U.S. economy. Television rights are a case in point. Payne predicted in 1990 that U.S. television rights would sell for an extraordinary $600 million, a $199 million increase over the rights for Barcelona. With the advent of the recession, ACOG quickly lowered its projection to $500 million, and the IOC delayed negotiations, hoping the economy would improve. In a move that might indicate a decline in the commercial value of the Olympics, U.S. television rights finally sold to the National Broadcasting Company (NBC) for $456 million, only $6 million above the figure ACOG needed to meet its budget projections.

Meanwhile, costs continue to soar. The original estimate to host the Games for $1.01 billion climbed to $1.6 billion. Projections for surplus revenue of $132 million dwindled to zero due to higher costs and promises to the city's minority community. For example, estimates for the Olympic stadium jumped from $145 million to $209 million after ACOG agreed to cover post-Olympic demolition costs for Fulton County Stadium. Escalating costs caused a certain degree of anxiety among IOC members. ACOG's organizational structure and charter ensured that Atlanta and state residents would be shielded from any Olympic deficit. If the committee failed to raise sufficient funds, plans for an extravagant Centennial Games would have to be curtailed. The prospect of trimming Olympic luxury to meet a restricted budget prompted IOC member Dick Pound to announce, "We will never award the Games in the future to a city in the United States or elsewhere, which has no significant public sector commitment, either in the form of a financial contribution or at the very least, in the form of a guarantee to meet the necessary costs of organizing the Games" (*Atlanta Journal/Constitution,* May 18, 1994).

Although ACOG vowed to host the Games without taxpayer assistance, the city of Atlanta made no similar claim. It is estimated that Atlanta needs up to $500 million to complete necessary infrastructure improvements by the time of the opening ceremonies. To date, $250 million in federal funds for city improvements have failed to materialize. Additionally, the Georgia state legislature offered no state funding and blocked attempts by the city to raise revenue through a 1 percent increase in the city's sales tax and a surcharge on tickets to sporting and cultural events. The financial logjam left a sour taste in the mouths of Atlanta's taxpayers; polls indicated that half the city's residents were resigned to paying higher taxes to support Olympic-related development. Ultimately voters accepted the grim reality and approved $149 million for critical infrastructure improvements, far short of the $500 million needed.

The continuing evolution in world politics could have a greater impact on the outcome of the 1996 Games than anything anticipated at the local level. Samaranch closed the 1992 Olympics with statements that more than 200 countries could be represented in Atlanta and that a ceiling for athletes would be set at 10,500. The limit on participants could require some nations to drop younger athletes with promising futures due to restrictive team quotas. Part of the anticipated explosion in new countries rests within the boundaries of the former Soviet Union, as members of the Commonwealth of Independent States (CIS) plan to field individual teams in Atlanta. Yet funding for many of these teams has been difficult to secure given more pressing needs. Russia is the only CIS member to implement an Olympic finance program, predominantly funded with proceeds from a national lottery. Without similar efforts by other CIS countries, it is likely that the quality of competition from the former Soviet states will decline.

A more pressing problem for ACOG is its ability to protect the world's athletes. The increase in terrorist activity on American soil during the 1990s could make the Centennial Games a coveted target for terrorists in search of media attention. Consequently, Atlanta may be forced to adopt more oppressive security measures than those used for the Barcelona Games. Equally important to ACOG is any initiative that could restrict participation at the 1996 Games. Two issues are important to highlight. First, when Atlanta bid for the Games, President George Bush promised entry to all the world's athletes. Under the Clinton administration, it is unclear whether that promise will hold. In 1993, the U.S. State Department prohibited Libyan athletes from attending the World University Games in Buffalo due to that country's support of terrorism. If the U.S. political process interferes with the admittance of athletes on these grounds, as many as seven nations could be barred from participating in Atlanta.

Second, it remains to be seen whether China will participate in the 1996 Games. When Beijing bid for the 2000 Summer Olympics, the U.S. House of Representatives passed a resolution condemning the city's candidacy on grounds of China's human rights abuses. More than half the U.S. Senate signed a letter requesting that the IOC choose another city. Since Sydney, Australia, defeated Beijing, the Chinese government may use the U.S. government's interference in the selection process as an excuse for its failure, thus leading to a boycott of the Atlanta Games. The absence of China at the 1996 Games could drastically affect the quality of competition. China won fifty-four medals in Barcelona, sixteen of them gold.

The effect of international political events on the 1996 Summer Olympics remains to be seen, but if the collective experience of past Olympic cities holds true, early problems and setbacks with ACOG's Olympic plans will have little if any impact on the committee's ability to host a spectacular Centennial Games. The hostility expressed by the 1996 bid cities and Atlanta's critics will give way to the excitement of athletic competitions. Even the city of Atlanta, which experienced considerable anxiety upon witnessing the metamorphosis of Barcelona, will obtain the remaining funds from the state or federal government or local taxpayers to prepare for the onslaught of Olympic visitors. Yet to be determined are the lasting impact Atlanta will derive from hosting the world and the legacy the organizing committee will leave behind to guide future host cities through the Olympic movement's second century.

BIBLIOGRAPHICAL ESSAY

The production schedule for this book dictated that the chapter on Atlanta be written two years prior to the opening of the Olympic Games. Consequently, significant events during the final two years of the development process are not reported in this chapter. Similarly, few publications were covering the 1996 Games at this early stage. The principal sources used for this chapter were the *Atlanta Journal/Constitution* and materials provided by the Atlanta Committee for the Olympic Games. Other articles appeared in the *New York Times,* the *Washington Post,* the *Wall Street Journal,* and *Business Week.*

Larry Maloney

SYDNEY 2000

THE GAMES OF THE XVIITH OLYMPIAD

Australia is one of only two countries to have been represented at each Olympic Games (the other is Greece), and the 1956 Olympic Games were held at Melbourne. It is interesting to note that Melbourne gained the right to hold the 1956 Games by 1 vote (21–20); otherwise, they would have gone to Buenos Aires.

The next attempt to secure the Games for Australia was when Brisbane entered the race for the 1992 Games. Brisbane was eliminated in the third round of voting, Barcelona gaining 47 votes in that round to Brisbane's 10. Melbourne then bid for the 1996 games but was also eliminated in the third round, Athens and Atlanta being tied with 26 votes each at that point.

Sydney's successful bid for the 2000 Games in 1993 gained immeasurably from the failed bids of Brisbane and Melbourne, not only in the preparation of documentation but also in the international contacts and goodwill that resulted from their highly professional efforts. The buildup for Sydney's bid was arduous yet additive, with three premiers of New South Wales, Neville Wran, Nick Greiner, and John Fahey, each making contributions to the process and keeping long-term objectives in mind. Although Melbourne was bidding for the 1996 Games, Sydney's plans for the development of Homebush Bay, the 2000 Games site, went on unabated. When Melbourne was defeated, Sydney went into action a month later, Premier Greiner announcing the formation of a Sydney Olympic Games Review Committee under Chairman the Hon. B. G. (Bruce) Baird. The so-called Baird Report was to be crucial in the planning of the bid.

Three Australian cities attempted to secure bidding rights from the Australian Olympic Committee (AOC): Brisbane, Melbourne, and Sydney. At the executive board meeting of the AOC on November 16, 1990, Sydney was provisionally endorsed. This became a final endorsement by the end of 1990, following further negotiations with the New South Wales government and the city of Sydney. At that November meeting, John Coates was elected as the new president of the AOC; his leadership and knowledge were vital to the Sydney bid.

Some funding problems had to be resolved with the federal government, but when it was agreed that the New South Wales government could extend its global borrowing limits by $300 million over three years, Greiner announced on the same day—November 26, 1991—that construction would begin as soon as possible on stage 1 of the Olympic site at Homebush Bay.

In May 1991, Rod McGeoch, a prominent solicitor, became the chief executive officer of Sydney Olympic 2000 Bid Limited (SOBOL), a public company limited by guarantee and incorporated within New South Wales in full compliance with corporate law. This organization took on the responsibility of conducting Sydney's candidature for the 2000 Games. It was governed by sixteen directors, who constituted the executive board of the company. The directors, along with thirty members of the company, made up the bid committee, which represented a cross-section of community, government, business, and sporting interests. Various commissions were established, the key ones being Strategy, Sports, Cultural, Finance, Building, and Communications.

The steady and guiding hand of John Coates was soon in evidence. He produced a paper, "The Process of Bidding for an Olympic Games," in March 1991, which was a brilliant summary of the steps to be taken to ensure a successful bid. It was the beacon that led the way.

In August 1991 a distinctive symbol was selected. The logo represented the dawn of a new century and the flame of the Olympic torch and profiled the shell-like roof of Sydney's great landmark, the Opera House.

The team was now gathered, the staff was off and running, and the symbol was in place. There were just over two years to convince the International Olympic Committee (IOC) that Sydney was the logical choice for the 2000 Games. At this time, there were eight contenders attempting to achieve sport's highest prize: Tashkent, Brasilia, Sydney, Beijing, Manchester, Milan, Istanbul and Berlin. In June 1992, Nick Greiner, the father of the Olympic bid, left the premier's office and was succeeded by John Fahey.

A considerable coup for Sydney was its selection as the site of the 1991 General Association of International Sports Federations (GAISF) conference. Many of the leading figures in the world of sport, including up to thirty IOC members, attended, among a total of 400 visitors from thirty-nine countries. Other events staged in 1991 were the World Youth Soccer championships, the Women's Pentathlon championships, and the World Amateur Boxing championships. The Sydney bid organizers were clearly demonstrating to the world that they could stage sporting events of international significance. Lobbying also began in earnest in 1991 and accelerated in 1992 and 1993.

One of the most important events was the November 1992 General Assembly of the Association of National Olympic Committees (ANOC) in Acapulco, Mexico. At this meeting, Australia, through John Coates, threw down one of its trump cards: free travel to Australia for athletes, coaches, and officials if Sydney got the Olympic Games. The projected cost was $24.5 million.

On February 2, 1993, Sydney went one step further, offering $8.32 million to transport sporting equipment to Sydney. This was considered of greatest assistance to the equestrian sports, yachting, and canoeing. Aid for African athletes was another late development. A Homestay Program was yet another innovation, with free accommodation for more than 20,000 relatives and friends of overseas athletes promised if the Sydney bid were successful.

On September 23, 1993, the IOC's ninety members assembled in the Salle des Etoiles of the Sporting d'Ete, Monaco's open-air cinema and concert plaza. Each of the five remaining cities in contention had 45 minutes to make its final presentation, including 15 minutes for questions. The order was Berlin, Sydney, Manchester, Beijing, and Istanbul. At 5:00 P.M., the IOC Inquiry Commission, chaired by Gunnar Ericsson of Sweden, presented its report on the five bid cities and answered any questions from IOC delegates.

At 6:00 P.M., voting commenced. It was a secret vote, with the city receiving the least number of votes in each round eliminated until one city had at least 46 votes. IOC president Juan Antonio Samaranch (who did not vote) announced the name of the city that dropped out of the race at the end of each round of voting. He did not reveal the votes received by the other cities in the elimination rounds. When one city obtained an absolute majority, the session concluded. None of the IOC members, including Samaranch, knew in advance the final result. During the voting, Swaziland delegate David Sibandze pulled out of the voting after two rounds, explaining that he had to return home urgently to take part in an election. Only eighty-eight delegates voted in the final round; Bulgarian IOC member Ivan Slavkov had been detained in his own country for political reasons. At 8:30 P.M., Samaranch came to the podium at Louis II Stadium, where the scene had shifted for the much-awaited announcement. There was an Australian delegation of 200 in the audience. The Olympic anthem was played. Samaranch took the envelope from his inside pocket, fumbled with it, and said: "The International Olympic Committee wishes to thank the five bidding cities—Beijing, Berlin, Istanbul, Manchester and Sydney—for their efforts in presenting their bids and promoting the Olympic Movement."

He opened the envelope and stared at it, and then said: "The winner is . . . Sydney."

The final vote was:

First round: Beijing, 32; Sydney, 30; Manchester, 11; Berlin, 9; Istanbul, 7 (eliminated)

Second round: Beijing, 37; Sydney, 30; Manchester, 13; Berlin, 9 (eliminated)

Third round: Beijing, 40; Sydney, 37; Manchester, 11 (eliminated)

Fourth round: Sydney, 45; Beijing, 43

The only time Sydney was in front was in the final vote. When Manchester was eliminated, 8 votes committed to it went to Sydney and 3 to Beijing. It might be argued that the European and United Kingdom–aligned votes basically won the day for Sydney, but one can never be certain, as earlier votes could have shifted.

Why was Sydney successful? Numerous reasons have been advanced, and some combination of them worked together to persuade a majority of voting IOC delegates to favor Sydney in the final round. Sydney had been the recommended choice of the IOC Inquiry Commission, while Beijing had been rated below Manchester and Berlin. Part of the reason for this was the excellence of Sydney's technical bid that was presented to the IOC. The early start on the facilities at Homebush Bay and the assent of each international sport federation to the plans were important components of the bid.

Politically, Sydney offered the safest site. All levels of government and all political parties supported Sydney's bid, as did the AOC and the national press, which rarely printed a critical story on the bid process. No one campaigned against Sydney, as many did against Beijing (including members of the U.S. Congress) and Berlin. Moreover, Sydney promised a safe Games, with minimal security problems with respect to international terrorist organizations or domestic minority groups.

Sydney's bid offered distinctive cultural features. The 2000 Games were portrayed as a festival for athletes, with excellent weather, comfortable accommodations, and financial inducements. Sydney also offered a host of multicultural advantages; a city of 140 different ethnic groups and radio programs in sixty-five languages had appeal to virtually every IOC delegate. Finally, Sydney proposed an extensive cultural program, highlighting the diverse cultures of the Pacific, to accompany the Games. This cultural extravaganza would be spread over four years and include festivals celebrating the aboriginal experience, the age of exploration, Australian visual and performing arts, and, to go along with the Games themselves, a series of programs expressing humanity's quest for peace.

It may just have been that Sydney marketed its bid better than its rivals did. The company handling Sydney's candidacy produced award-winning videos, hired a firm to boost the city's image in Europe, and emphasized the community spirit behind the bid. The presentation at Monte Carlo was highly professional and very effective, and the multifaceted lobbying that went on behind the scenes for years was also very well handled.

BIBLIOGRAPHICAL ESSAY

Most of the records related to Sydney's successful bid for the 2000 Games are at the Sydney Organising Committee for the Olympic Games (SOCOG) library in Sydney. This library was established in June 1991 at the beginning of the bidding process and accumulates materials concerning the forthcoming Games, although the principal concern is the management of the Games rather than sport. Because the primary function of the library is to provide information to the SOCOG staff and to corporate and government departments that have contacts with SOCOG, public access is quite limited and will remain so until after the Games. Public information centers have been established in several locations, and the library expects to have a database available via Internet by 1996. For further information, contact Melissa Petherbridge, Director, Information Systems, SOCOG Library, GPO Box 2000, Sydney, NSW, Australia 2001.

Published reports and a clipping file on the 2000 Games are held at the Australian Sport Commission's National Sport Information Centre in Belconnen, ACT, Australia. This center also has information relating to the failed bids of Brisbane and Melbourne to host the 1992 and 1996 Games. Write to Greg Blood, Services Librarian, National Sport Information Centre, P.O. Box 176, Belconnen, ACT, Australia 2616.

Major sport libraries in the countries of the other contending cities may have the bidding books from those cities. For example, Axel Nawrocki, *Berlin 2000* (Berlin, 1993), is an elaborate four-volume boxed set extolling the virtues of Berlin as host for the 2000 Games and may be found in libraries in Germany.

Finally, the *Chicago Tribune* published a series of articles, September 12–26, 1993, analyzing the bid of each of the five finalists for the 2000 Games and the impact of the victory on Sydney. Australian newspapers no doubt covered the process in even greater detail.

Max L. Howell

One of the first women's Olympic events was golf. Here the U.S. team competes in the Paris Games of 1900. © IOC. Courtesy of the International Olympic Committee.

The British curling team on parade at the opening ceremonies of the first Olympic Winter Games, Chamonix, France, 1924. © IOC. Courtesy of the International Olympic Committee.

Bob Mathias, U.S. decathlon winner, accepting his medal at awards ceremony, Helsinki Games, 1952. Courtesy of University of Illinois Archives, Avery Brundage Collection.

1912 Olympic star Jim Thorpe (left) and Avery Brundage (right) at 1952 U.S. Olympic Committee fund-raising telethon. Courtesy of University of Illinois Archives, Avery Brundage Collection.

Cultural competitions or exhibitions have always been a part of each Olympic celebration. This photograph shows the architectural design exhibit held in conjunction with the 1956 Summer Games in Melbourne. Courtesy of University of Illinois Archives, Avery Brundage Collection.

The IOC conducts its business at periodic sessions in elegant locations such as this palace in Rome. Courtesy of University of Illinois Archives, Avery Brundage Collection.

New IOC member Juan Antonio Samaranch (far left) serving as guide to Avery Brundage (second from right) and other IOC officials in Barcelona, 1967. Courtesy of University of Illinois Archives, Avery Brundage Collection.

The Olympic torch relay has been a standard part of the Games since 1936. Here a runner carries the torch through the streets of Mexico City prior to the start of the 1968 Summer Games. Courtesy of University of Illinois Archives, Avery Brundage Collection.

The Villa Mons-Repos in Lausanne, Switzerland: Coubertin's home and headquarters of the International Olympic Committee from 1921 to 1968. Courtesy of University of Illinois Archives, Avery Brundage Collection.

Avery Brundage at the grave of modern Olympic movement founder Pierre de Coubertin in Lausanne, Switzerland. Courtesy of University of Illinois Archives, Avery Brundage Collection.

Before Olympic Villages were built specifically for the Games, athletes were housed in existing facilities. For the Stockholm Games of 1912, athletes stayed in the Military College, shown here. © IOC. Courtesy of the International Olympic Committee.

A summer view of the ski jump at Garmisch-Partenkirchen, Germany, site of the 1936 Winter Games. Courtesy of University of Illinois Archives, Avery Brundage Collection.

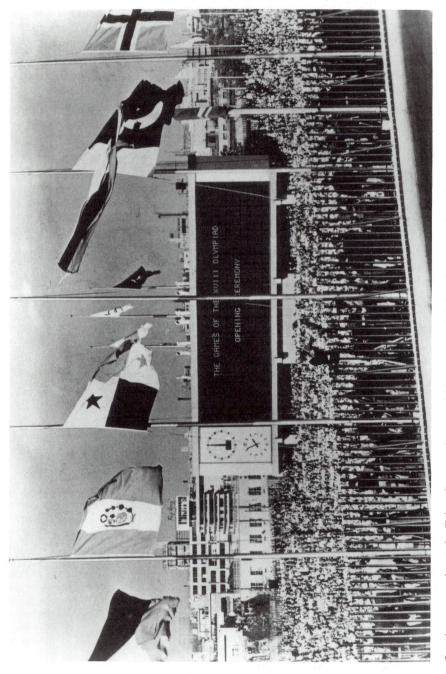

Opening ceremonies at the Tokyo Summer Games, 1964. Courtesy of University of Illinois Archives, Avery Brundage Collection.

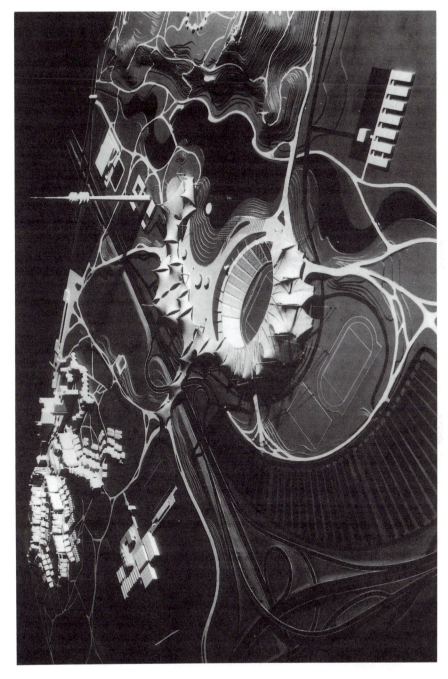

Architectural model of facilities for Munich Summer Games, 1972. Courtesy of University of Illinois Archives, Avery Brundage Collection.

The main entrance to the Olympic Park, Quai d'Ouchy, Lausanne, Switzerland, where the new Olympic Museum is located. Photograph by John E. Findling.

PART II

THE WINTER GAMES

CHAMONIX 1924

1st OLYMPIC WINTER GAMES

When plans for reviving the modern Olympic Games were underway in 1894, figure skating was among the sports proposed for the competitive program. However, nearly three decades passed until winter sports were officially sanctioned. Opposition from the Scandinavian countries prevented the introduction of winter sports until 1908, when skating was included in the London Olympics. Resistance to winter sports centered on the inability to conduct competition at the same time and in the same venues as the Summer Games. Another obvious problem for some countries was the lack of mountainous regions suitable for skiing. The 1912 Stockholm Olympic Organizing Committee refused to conduct winter competition because of a lack of facilities. Eventually Olympic organizing committees were persuaded to divide the program into separate entities because of the growing interest in winter sports.

Baron Pierre de Coubertin, founder of the modern Olympics, viewed winter sports as truly amateur endeavors and especially valuable because they were "so pure in their sporting dignity." The popularity of winter sports, particularly in Europe, and the organization of winter sports federations established the foundation for international competition. While the appearance of figure skating in the 1908 London Olympic Games was overshadowed by more established Summer Olympic sports, the event did acknowledge winter sports as legitimate competitive events at an Olympic level. Men from five nations and women from three nations skated at the London Olympic Games.

In 1920, additional impetus to winter sports competition occurred prior to most of the events of the Antwerp Games. A modest program of winter sports, including ice hockey and figure skating, attracted athletes from nine countries. Although the International Olympic Committee (IOC) did not sanction the competition, the success of the experiment could be measured by the level of competition and the enthusiastic competitors. Like most other athletic events that have reached worldwide prominence, the winter sports in Antwerp and their unofficial association with the Olympic movement began inconspicuously. The success of this competition provided winter sports enthusiasts with sufficient evidence to convince the IOC that a quadrennial program of winter sports could develop into an international event.

At its meeting in Paris on March 22, 1922, the IOC announced that skating events would initiate the 1924 Olympic competition, as part of a separate program of winter sports. In 1925 at the IOC Congress in Prague, the IOC officially sanctioned the Olympic Winter Games and retroactively declared the competition at Chamonix the 1st Olympic Winter Games. The 1925 congress also determined that summer and winter competition would take place in the same year and, if desired by a national Olympic committee, in the same country. The 1924

Games coincided with the thirtieth anniversary of the revival of the Games and were an important milestone for Coubertin, who wished to conclude his term of office after the Games were held in his native France. He successfully negotiated his wishes, and the town of Chamonix was chosen to begin the events of the anniversary year.

France had largely recovered from the devastating effects of World War I. Hosting the Winter and Summer Olympic Games was an additional indication that the country had overcome the destruction left by the invading German army. Most of the railroad lines destroyed during the war had been rebuilt by 1921. Although the national debt had reached nearly 40 million francs in 1924, there were numerous signs of economic recovery. Unemployment was nearly nonexistent, with the reconstruction of 22,000 factories boasting modern equipment.

At Chamonix, French officials had to overcome hotel shortages. The population of the winter resort was 3,000; fewer than 2,000 visitors could be accommodated. French Olympic Games officials worked with local citizens to find space for another 1,000 visitors by placing beds in the corridors, ballrooms, and billiard parlors of hotels and inviting private citizens to open their homes. But this was still woefully inadequate, since between 20,000 and 30,000 visitors were anticipated. By November 1923, about 65 percent of the hotel rooms in Chamonix had been reserved for Olympic committee members, athletes, trainers, officials, and newspaper correspondents. In order to accommodate the majority of spectators, the French Olympic Committee referred guests to hotels in Aix-les-Bains and Annecy and provided twice-daily excursion trains to and from Chamonix. In addition, special bus service was made available to Olympic visitors. French officials boasted of a new aerial railway line built to carry passengers from Chamonix to the Alguille de Midl. While not built specifically for the Chamonix Games, the railway was scheduled to be completed before the competition began. The special mountain rail line consisted of two eighteen-passenger cars, designed so that one car ascended while the other descended.

Athletes from sixteen nations entered the first Olympic Winter Games. The program included ice hockey, bobsledding, figure skating, skiing, and speed skating, but women could compete only in figure skating. It was not until 1948 that women were admitted to skiing and 1960 that speed skating was sanctioned for women. The staid members of the IOC were reluctant to approve endurance events for woman or traditionally masculine sports for women, since medical opinion questioned the effects of such events on a woman's childbearing ability.

The first Olympic Winter Games athletes assembled at the city hall in Chamonix on January 25, 1924. After four days of slushy thaw, the precedent-setting opening ceremonies were enhanced by cold weather and blue skies, and thousands of spectators gathered in the small Alpine town to view the festivities. A total of 408 men and women, nearly all of the athletes and officials, took part in the festivities. The procession, led by the French Blue Devil band and the Austrian team, paraded through the streets of the city to the Olympic skating rink, where they were reviewed by Count Clary, president of the French Olympic Games Committee, and marquis de Polignac. Gaston Vidal, undersecretary of state for physical education, presided over the opening ceremonies.

The 500-meter speed skating race was the inaugural event of the first Olympic Winter Games, and Charles Jewtraw of the United States became the first gold medalist of the Olympic competition, beating his personal best by 2 seconds and winning over twenty-six other skaters from ten countries. The first gold medal in women's Olympic Winter competition went to an Austrian figure skater, Herma Planck-Szabo. In that same event, 11-year-old Sonja Henie, who would become one of the most famous and successful Olympic champions, finished last among the eight skaters from six nations who competed. In an era before indoor rinks, skaters formulated their strategy by considering not only their opponents but also the weather conditions. The women's school figures were skated in nearly ideal outdoor conditions, but during the free skating phase of competition, the ice was hard and brittle and the weather unusually windy and cold. The outstanding Olympian in these Games was Thorlief Haug of Norway, who won gold medals in the 18-kilometer and 50-kilometer cross-country skiing races and in the Nordic combined event.

The twelve days of competition culminated at the medal presentation during the closing ceremonies on February 5, 1924. Coubertin presided over the festivities in the same outdoor rink where the eager athletes had awaited the start of the Games. Although media coverage of the 1st Olympic Winter Games was not as extensive as it was for the Summer Games, leading American and European newspapers sent correspondents to chronicle the event.

The Games were successful in many respects, but financial losses detracted somewhat from the overall celebration. Costs ran to 3 million francs, but gate receipts totaled only 250,000 francs. Attendance was estimated at no fewer than 3,000 each day, but many entered on free passes. Perhaps to ensure larger crowds than the poorly attended Antwerp Games, officials had offered free passes not only to the Olympic family but also to others in an attempt to fill the stands. Financial backing came from the city of Chamonix, the department of Haute Savoie, and the French government. There were reports that French officials had anticipated a financial shortfall. Apparently the French Olympic Committee members were guided more by their enthusiastic support for the Olympic Games and the prestige of hosting the event than by their desire to make the Olympics a financial success.

Success was measured by the enthusiastic crowds and the apparent high level of athletic performances in the individual events and the exciting ice hockey competition. Canada and the United States had each scored four victories when they met in the gold medal game. The main topic of conversation among sports enthusiasts on the eve of the championship match centered on which style of play would dominate: the smooth Canadian teamwork or the stellar individual effort by the Americans. The largest crowd of the Games filled the stands, purchased standing room space on roofs of nearby houses, and even perched atop chimneys to watch the Canadians dominate the game, 6–1, to claim the Olympic championship.

For the first time, the death of a former head of state cast a shadow over Olympic competition. Just as the hockey match ended, the announcement of former U.S. president Woodrow Wilson's death transformed the upbeat Olympic mood to a somber homage. After a moment of silence, the Olympic and U.S. flags were lowered to half staff while the band played the "Star Spangled Banner." Athletes and spectators paid tribute to the wartime leader; some linked Chamonix's gathering of the peoples of the world to Wilson's League of Nations.

Perhaps feeling secure in knowing that the Winter and Summer Olympic Games could stand alone as truly distinct international events, Coubertin announced his retirement as president of the IOC on November 16, 1924, revealing his intentions to relinquish his official position while continuing his ardent support of the Olympic movement.

BIBLIOGRAPHICAL ESSAY

Because the Chamonix Olympic Winter Games were the first official Olympic program of winter sports, there are only limited sources and brief references to the event. Although there was no official report prepared, the French Olympic Committee published *Resultats des concours des jeux d'hiver organisés par le comité Olympique français* (Paris, 1925), which is a listing of the official results.

Newspapers provide the most detailed descriptions of the Games. Don Skene of the *Chicago Tribune* wrote a series of articles chronicling the Games from start to finish. His description of the opening ceremonies on January 26, 1924, provides some insight into the protocol of the early Olympic Winter Games. The *New York Times* covered other aspects of the Games, including problems encountered by small resort towns unaccustomed to dealing with large numbers of visitors. Additionally, articles in the *Times* of London describe the daily events and athletes of the leading nations. Although the IOC does not support the concept of awarding points and declaring national winners, the newspapers devised point systems and identified the dominant nations.

Secondary literature on the Chamonix Games is also limited. John Lucas, *Saga of the Modern Olympic Games* (New Brunswick, N.J., 1980), includes some interesting facts about the Olympic Winter Games. *The World Almanac and Book of Facts,* edited by Robert Hunt Lyman (New York, 1925), includes background information about postwar France, including rail and building reconstruction, industrial power, government, and general economic status.

There has been some scholarly work on the origins of the Winter Games. A good starting point is Ron Edgeworth, "The Nordic Games and the Origins of the Olympic Winter Games," *Citius, Altius, Fortius* 2, 2 (May 1994): 29–37. See also Erich Kamper, *Encyclopedia of the Winter Games* (Stuttgart, 1964), which includes a short history of the Games' origins, as well as a brief account of the Chamonix Games; Kristen Mo, "Norwegian Resistance against the Winter Olympics of the 1920s," in *The Olympic Games Through the Ages: Greek Antiquity and its Impact on Modern Sport,* edited by Roland Renson et al. (Athens, 1991); Johannes Palliere, *Les Premiers jeux d'hiver de*

1924: La Grande bataille de Chamonix (Chamberg, France, 1991); Pierre Arnaud and Thierry Terret, *Le Rêve blanc: Olympisme et sports d'hiver en France: Chamonix 1924, Grenoble 1968* (Talence, France, 1993); and Michel Clare, ''Chamonix 1924,'' *Olympic Magazine* 1 (February 1994): 30–32.

Paula D. Welch

ST. MORITZ 1928

IID OLYMPIC WINTER GAMES

The Winter Olympic Games were officially christened at the 1925 International Olympic Congress (IOC) in Prague. Following the successful competition at Chamonix, the congress voted to declare the 1924 Games the first Winter Olympic Games. The congress also decided to allow the host of the Summer Games the option of holding the Winter Games. This decision, a turning point for the IOC, placed the leadership of the organization in an uncomfortable situation.

In 1921, long before the decision was made to hold Winter Games on a regular basis, the IOC had selected Amsterdam as the host for the 1928 Summer Games. Amsterdam had competed for the right to host both the 1912 and 1924 Olympics but had failed because of a lack of marketing skills and political clout. Los Angeles was the main competition for the 1928 Games, but the IOC was reluctant to give the home field advantage again to a traditional Olympic power. The Netherlands, neutral in the recent war, was a politically expedient place to host the returning German Olympic team.

The IOC's immediate concern, once the decision was made to continue the Winter Games, was to select a site. By 1925, considerable doubt had arisen as to the ability of the Dutch to provide proper facilities for the Summer Games; the Dutch certainly could not be expected to provide the site for the second Winter Games. Negotiations between the Dutch and French Olympic committees, apparently unsanctioned by the IOC, concluded that the 1928 Winter Games would be again held at Chamonix. Premier Edouard Herriot and the French Ministry of Foreign Affairs authorized the French Olympic Committee to undertake the organization of the 1928 Winter Games at Chamonix and promised to provide whatever support necessary.

The arrangement was criticized, however, by IOC president Pierre de Coubertin, who noted that "the celebration of the Olympic Games is awarded to a city, not to a country, and can not be split under any pretext" (*New York Times*, January 17, 1925). Coubertin's decision brought with it a flurry of criticism from nations lacking the physical environment to hold both summer and winter events. The French, understandably critical of Coubertin's position, responded negatively. In 1926, the French Senate politicized the issue by refusing to grant the French Olympic Committee's request of 2 million francs to prepare a team in 1928. The French Chamber of Deputies had passed the measure by a wide margin, and the surprising Senate refusal brought about Herriot's involvement in the matter, and it was quickly resolved. Chamonix, as a conciliatory measure, was declared a site for preliminary events. The controversy over splitting Winter and Summer Games between countries was not resolved permanently until some years later.

The final decision was made to hold the Games in neutral Switzerland, where the political environment would be more receptive and site development would not be a primary concern. The area around St. Moritz was already a popular and well-established haven for winter enthusiasts. The IOC's decision to hold the Winter Games at St. Moritz was further influenced by Coubertin's awareness of the political concerns surrounding the Games. German athletes would be participating for the first time since 1912. The political climate of 1920 and 1924 had not warranted an invitation, and the likelihood of German participation in 1928 was received with considerable hostility. The Belgian National Olympic Committee, for example, voted to protest the admission of Germany to the 1928 Games. Despite Belgian efforts, however, the Germans did compete at St. Moritz and although considered a dark horse to win a number of events placed no better than third in any event.

The Swiss Olympic Committee (SOC) and the St. Moritz Organizing Committee, led by M. C. Nater, directed physical preparations for the 1928 Winter Games, which progressed rapidly. Workers built a special pavilion for dignitaries, seating 400, and a 5,000-seat grandstand for spectators. The Swiss also constructed the world's highest ski jump. Designed especially for the 1928 Games, the vertical height was an impressive 310 feet, and ski jumpers at St. Moritz far exceeded the distances attained at Chamonix.

Swiss leaders, including the president, hosted banquets on the eve of the St. Moritz Games for members of the various national committees and the IOC in order to show Swiss appreciation for the privilege of hosting the Games. The hospitality, facilities, and success of the Games were impressive enough to bring the Games back to St. Moritz twenty years later.

The St. Moritz Games ran from February 11 to February 19 and attracted a total of 495 competitors, of whom only 27 were female. The program was still very limited, with only thirteen events for men and two for women, and one event, 10,000-meter speed skating, was cancelled due to poor ice conditions. Curling, contested at Chamonix, was dropped from the program at St. Moritz. As expected, Norway dominated the second Winter Olympic Games, with seven first-place medals, including the first of three consecutive figure skating medals for Sonja Henie. In addition, the Norwegians garnered three ski titles and a first and a tie for first in speed skating. Sweden finished second, with three first-place finishes, the United States and Finland tied for third with two, and Canada along with France rounded out the field of gold medal winners with one each. Canada's gold medal came in ice hockey, which its team, made up of University of Toronto students who had won the Canadian championships, dominated as no other team has before or since. The Canadians won their final three games by scores of 11–0, 14–0, and 13–0.

The U.S. team, not surprisingly, gave a weak showing while winning one gold medal in bobsledding and one in skeleton, a kind of one-man sledding event contested only at St. Moritz. The winning four-man bobsled team was recruited from Americans living abroad. The U.S. speed skaters and women figure skaters, favored to win their events, made a disappointing showing. Under the leadership of the American Olympic Committee president, General Douglas MacArthur, the U.S. team had been plagued from the beginning by disputes over the selection process. The controversy was particularly disturbing to those who had hoped to maintain a united front to foreign rivals. Psychologically, the incident was particularly devastating to the U.S. speed skating team.

The dispute concerning the speed skating team was a particularly trying one for MacArthur and the American Olympic Committee. The Amateur Skating Union of the United States and the International Skating Union both claimed the right to send the U.S. team to St. Moritz. The decision was delayed by Jeremiah T. Mahoney, chairman of the legislation committee of the Amateur Athletic Union, and Frederick Rubien, secretary of the American Olympic Committee, until the day after team members had sailed aboard the Scandinavian liner *Oscar II* for Europe. The turmoil created by the dispute regarding the legitimate skating team was indicative of a much larger problem facing the maladministered American Olympic team. Many American coaches were concerned that holding trials for places on the various teams within a few months of the Games was too exhausting for the athletes. One solution, apparent to many, was to hold Olympic trials one year before the Games.

Disagreement over the selection process was not limited to the American Olympic Committee. Several other questions remained unresolved on the eve of the 1928 Winter Games. The troublesome difficulty of the IOC in defining amateur status loomed as a dark cloud. Another potential problem was a proposal to sell newsreel rights to the Olympic Games. The IOC managed to avoid this problem at St. Moritz, but it became a serious controversy just prior to the Summer Games at Amsterdam.

At their conclusion, recently elected IOC president Henri Baillet-Latour declared the second Winter Olympics a success. Some observers had expressed concern that Coubertin's resignation in 1925 would have a negative effect on the Games, but Baillet-Latour presided over Games at which attendance exceeded expectations and controversy was minimal.

BIBLIOGRAPHICAL ESSAY

Information related to the 1928 Winter Games held at St. Moritz, Switzerland, is extremely limited and difficult to find. Few of the available sources are in English. The *Rapport général du comité executif des IImes jeux olympiques d'hiver et documents officiels divers* (Lausanne, 1928), along with the *Resultats des Concours des IImes jeux olympiques d'hiver organises à St. Moritz* (Lausanne, 1928), and the *General Rules and Program of the 2nd Olympic Winter Games* (Lausanne, 1928), are all available at the IOC Archives in Lausanne, Switzerland. The Swiss Olympic Committee also published a newsletter, *Bulletin officiel du Comité Olympique Suisse,* for several months in 1927 and early 1928. The official French report is Comité Olympique Français, *La Participation française aux jeux de la IXe olympiade: Saint-Moritz, Amsterdam 1928* (Paris, 1929).

Some information, as well as the American Olympic Committee's official report, *Sec-*

ond Olympic Winter Sports [sic], St. Moritz, 1928 (New York, 1928), is available at the U.S. Olympic Committee Library, Colorado Springs, Colorado. Carl J. Luther, *Olympische Wintersport* (Zurich, 1929), contains good photographs of the Games. The best review of the emergence of winter sport in St. Moritz is Stuart Stevens, ''The Chuting Party,'' *Ultra Sport* 3, 11 (December 1986): 42–49.

The most pertinent English-language dissertation related to the events of the 1928 Winter Games is Donald E. Fuoss, ''An Analysis of the Incidents in the Olympic Games from 1924 to 1948, with Reference to the Contribution of the Games to International Good Will and Understanding'' (Ph.D. dissertation, Columbia University, 1951). Fuoss emphasizes the international political environment of the 1920s as it related to athletic competition.

Donald C. Simmons, Jr.

LAKE PLACID 1932
IIId OLYMPIC WINTER GAMES

Prior to 1932, the village of Lake Placid, New York, located in the heart of the famed Adirondack forest preserve, was little more than a regional summer and winter vacation haven. Much of the activity in the tiny community centered around Melvil Dewey's Lake Placid Club, a summer resort catering to New York vacationers. In 1905 Dewey made the decision to keep the club open for the winter, thus setting the stage for the development of winter sports in Lake Placid. Such development proceeded rapidly. By 1921, Lake Placid had its own ski jump, speed skating facility, and ski association and was emerging as one of America's premier winter sports facilities. From February 4 to 13, 1932, this small community would play host to a relatively new venture in the Olympic movement, the Winter Games.

Bringing the Olympics to Lake Placid was not easy. Probably the biggest obstacle organizers had to face in securing the winter Games was the job of proving to the International Olympic Committee (IOC) that Lake Placid was an Olympic-caliber winter sports center and thus a legitimate potential host. Lake Placid did have somewhat adequate facilities, but it was not as well known in the winter sports world as European resorts like St. Moritz, the host of the 1928 Games. One advantage for Lake Placid was that in 1929, the 1932 Summer Olympic Games had been awarded to Los Angeles, and it had been an unofficial practice of the IOC to keep the Winter and Summer Games in the same country. While this custom made Lake Placid's chances more promising, other American locales, such as Lake Tahoe, Yosemite Valley, and Denver, sites closer to southern California, also were interested in hosting the Games. Furthermore, Montreal and Oslo, Norway, were being considered in case the Americans were unable to provide necessary funding and facilities.

The responsibility of securing the Games for Lake Placid rested with one man, the secretary and eventual president of the Lake Placid Club, Godfrey Dewey, the son of the club's founder, Melvil Dewey. Dewey had convinced both local and state officials of the possibility of hosting the Winter Games. In March 1928, the town of Lake Placid had formed a committee to prepare a bid for the Games. Franklin D. Roosevelt, governor of New York, had convinced the state legislature to back the Lake Placid bid and to authorize part of the needed funds. Early in 1929 Dewey and his Lake Placid delegation sailed to Lausanne to present the advantages of their venue. By the time of this trip, the prime competition Lake Placid faced came from a group of Californians intent upon keeping the Winter and Summer Games together in the Los Angeles area.

While none of the American sites completely satisfied the IOC as far as the development of their facilities was concerned, Dewey was able to convince the committee that Lake Placid was the best equipped. On April 10, 1929, despite an angry protest from the California group under the impression that the Winter and Summer Games should be staged in the same locale, the 1932 Winter Olympic Games were awarded to Lake Placid.

The village of Lake Placid and New York State quickly rallied to provide leadership for the development and preparation of their Olympic venue. Franklin Roosevelt provided funding to establish a temporary state commission, which included representatives from the Lake Placid Olympic Committee (LPOC), the New York State Assembly, and the state conservation department. Dewey became president of the LPOC and was the most influential person in the organization of the Games. Avery Brundage, who had just succeeded Graeme Hammond as president of the American Olympic Committee (AOC), was involved in publicizing the Games and providing equipment and training facilities for the American athletes.

Yet it was the LPOC, led by Dewey, that had the biggest task on their hands: preparing the community to play host to the nations of the world. The committee estimated that preparations and provisions would be needed for 600 contestants from twenty-five nations (sixty-five nations were invited, but not all were expected to accept the invitations) with 8,000 spectators expected daily. The bulk of the site development centered around the construction of a bobsled run and a stadium, which could be used for the opening and closing ceremonies, speed skating, and ice hockey. Shortly after the IOC chose Lake Placid to host the games, the New York legislature approved a bill providing $125,000 for the construction of the bobsled run. The committee hired Berlin bobsled designer Stanislaus Zentzytsky to build the structure, which turned out to please both the competitors and the IOC.

The only major problem the Lake Placid developers faced in their preparation for the Games was a New York law that forbade the removal of trees from the forests of the Adirondacks. The construction of the bobsled run directly violated this ''forever wild'' ordinance, since it required that approximately 2,500 trees be cut down. Protests from local environmentalists caused Dewey and his committee to appeal to Governor Roosevelt for a constitutional amendment. After heated debate in the state assembly, the environmental faction was appeased and construction permitted on the bobsled run.

Mother nature also provided a scare for Lake Placid organizers. The village received virtually no snowfall during the two months prior to the Games. Worse, New York was hit with an unusual heat wave in mid-January. Temperatures jumped to 50 degrees, ice rinks thawed, and the U.S. bobsled team was forced to cancel practice because the bobsled run was unusable. Fortunately for the organizers, the temperature dropped a few days later, and a winter storm dumped 6 inches of snow on the village.

Besides the local debates over the environment and issues regarding individual sporting events, there were no serious political controversies surrounding the Games. President Herbert Hoover was invited to open the Games but was unable to attend, paving the way for his prospective election opponent, Roosevelt, to handle the task. Using the opening ceremonies as another political campaign stop, Roosevelt's message, broadcast nationwide over the National Broadcasting Company (NBC) and Columbia radio networks (the two networks that provided coverage of all the athletic events), called for world peace. During the festivities Eleanor Roosevelt took a ride down the newly constructed bobsled run, delighting the crowds gathered for the opening ceremonies. Roosevelt's role in convincing the New York legislature of the viability of the games in Lake Placid cannot be overestimated in importance.

The Lake Placid Games brought some new ventures in Olympic winter sports. A controversy centered around the style of the speed skating competition. Traditionally, competitors skated against the clock in these events, with those skating the three fastest times receiving medals. Dewey proposed an American "pack-style" of skating, especially for the distance events, which saw athletes skating against each other rather than against the stopwatch. Dewey believed that pack skating was not only more entertaining but allowed all the competitors to participate at once, providing the same ice conditions for all the skaters. Dewey's suggestion was approved by the IOC, but after American victories in some of the early events, European skaters protested to the International Skating Union (ISU). The ISU upheld the protest, forcing the races to be rerun, but unfortunately for the Europeans, the Americans won those races too. Lake Placid also saw the emergence of women's speed skating as an Olympic sport and dogsled racing and curling as demonstration sports.

The biggest issue facing the Lake Placid organizers was an economic one: worldwide economic depression. During the two months before the Games, nation after nation withdrew teams from competition due to their inability to finance their athletes, and other nations greatly reduced the size of their teams. The number of withdrawals due to the depression caused Sweden and other nations to propose a postponement of the Games until better economic conditions prevailed. The problem was greater for European nations because of the costs of getting to Lake Placid. In addition, Canada, France, and Sweden complained that the Americans were not providing a high enough exchange rate on their respective currencies.

The AOC under Avery Brundage worked with state and federal government agencies to do everything possible to enable European teams to attend the Games. The North Atlantic Passenger Agreement reduced ship fares up to 20 percent for athletes traveling to the Games, and President Hoover exempted foreign participants from usual passport and visa fees. Hoover's gesture was particularly welcome in the light of the strict immigration requirements imposed on those coming to America. The United States even offered to finance the German hockey team's trip to America, an offer eventually accepted by the Germans. Even with these measures, a smaller than expected number of athletes competed. When the closing date (December 24, 1931) for applications arrived, seventeen nations, accounting for 364 athletes, had accepted invitations. Participating nations were Austria, Belgium, Canada, Czechoslovakia, Finland,

France, Germany, Great Britain, Italy, Japan, Hungary, Norway, Poland, Romania, Sweden, Switzerland, and the United States.

The host country provided most of the excitement in the competition. Twenty-one-year-old Jack Shea, a Lake Placid native, won the first gold medal of the Games in the 500-meter speed skating event and later went on to win the 1,500-meter event. Irving Jaffee of the United States captured both distance speed skating races, winning the 5,000- and 10,000-meter events. Sonja Henie of Norway, who had won the gold medal in women's figure skating at St. Moritz, charmed spectators by winning her second gold medal at Lake Placid. Edward Eagan, a member of the victorious U.S. four-man bobsled team, became the first man to win gold medals in both the Winter and Summer Games. He won the light-heavyweight boxing title in the 1920 Summer Games at Antwerp.

The total cost of the Lake Placid Olympics was $1.05 million, most of which was spent on the construction of the bobsled run and the Olympic stadium. Funding came from a variety of sources. The town of North Elba (in which Lake Placid village is located) passed a $200,000 bond issue in 1929 with the hope that the money would cover all the expenses of the games. The community was promised that their costs would eventually be reimbursed through ticket sales. Unfortunately for the citizens of North Elba, the $200,000 fell well short of the expenses required to stage the Games, and proceeds from ticket sales did not exceed the amount of the bond. The bulk of financial assistance came from the New York State legislature. The state appropriated $500,000 for the construction of facilities: $125,000 for the bobsled run and $375,000 for the completion of the Olympic stadium. Perhaps Dewey's greatest accomplishment was in convincing the state to allocate such funds in the light of the depression.

Overall, the 1932 Lake Placid Olympics were rather small and simple. The small size of the Games created an atmosphere that was not conducive to any major controversies or political issues. In 1932 the Winter Olympic Games had yet to achieve the prestige and popularity that the Summer Games enjoyed; the quiet simplicity of Lake Placid did not further enhance the worldwide image of the Winter Games. Yet for those Lake Placid organizers seeking to establish their community as one of the world's leading centers for winter sports and provide an event centered around the athletes rather than the venues, the Games proved to be a success.

BIBLIOGRAPHICAL ESSAY

Historical material, especially secondary sources, is limited on the history of the Winter Olympic games and especially scarce for the 1932 Games because the Great Depression caused such limited participation.

For historians willing to take the challenge of providing the historical community with new interpretations of the Lake Placid Games, the official records of the games are held by the Olympic Regional Development Authority (ORDA) located on Main Street in Lake Placid, New York. The bulk of the material is accessible to researchers. The records include minutes of all meetings of the organizing committee and records of the committee's lobbying of state and federal officials, including the International Olympic Committee.

There does exist an official report of the Lake Placid Games edited by George M. Lattimer, the director of the Olympic Publicity Committee. The work, *Official Report: III Olympic Winter Games: Lake Placid 1932* (Lake Placid, N.Y., 1932), provides statistics chronicling the finances, events, and development of the Olympic movement in Lake Placid. The organizing committee also published *Setting the Stage for the III Olympic Winter Games* (New York, 1932) and *Official Souvenir Book of the III Olympic Winter Games* (New York, 1932), and a *News Bulletin,* issued between October 1930 and early 1932. The official Canadian report is W. A. Fry, ed., *Canada at the Xth Olympiad 1932* (Dunnville, Ontario, 1932).

Without a doubt the most complete journalistic coverage of the local, developmental, and political issues surrounding the Lake Placid Games is the *New York Times.* The *Times*'s in-depth reporting makes it the most useful source of information on the Games. The national scope of the *Times,* coupled with the local interest of the Games in New York, provide for quite thorough coverage. The *Lake Placid News* also provides insight to local issues affecting the games.

The most thorough historical monograph on the Lake Placid Games is a local history written by Lake Placid residents George Christian Ortloff and Stephen C. Ortloff, *Lake Placid, The Olympic Years, 1932–1980: A Portrait of America's Premier Winter Resort* (Lake Placid, 1976). The work is quite popular in nature, but it does provide information on the history, politics, and preparations surrounding the Games. It is also helpful in placing the Games into their local context. Another useful piece that places the Games in a historical context with other Winter Games is Marc Onigman, ''Discontent in the Olympic Winter Games, 1908–1980,'' in *The Modern Olympics,* edited by Peter J. Graham and Horst Ueberhorst (West Point, N.Y., 1976). Onigman provides one of the few scholarly treatments of the 1932 Lake Placid Games, with much of his research stemming from *New York Times* accounts.

Historians and other researchers interested in the Games should contact Mrs. Seymour McKenzie, the Lake Placid town historian, or the archivist of the Olympic Regional Development Authority for further information.

John Fea

GARMISCH-PARTENKIRCHEN 1936
IVth OLYMPIC WINTER GAMES

When German Olympic officials, eager to erase the disappointment of the canceled 1916 Berlin Games, won the right to organize the XIth Olympic Games of 1936, they also became hosts to the IVth Winter Olympic Games. While these Winter Games may have been treated initially as a mere sideshow to the summer event, they assumed greater importance after the seizure of power by Adolf Hitler and the National Socialist party in January 1933. As an opposition party, the Nazis had been predisposed against the modern Olympic movement for political and ideological reasons, but they revised their position once the minister for popular enlightenment, Joseph Goebbels, and others recognized the international propaganda potential inherent in the Olympics, particularly the Summer Games in Berlin. Senior Nazi officials would work alongside leading non-Nazi Olympic functionaries to ensure that the Garmisch-Partenkirchen Games would be the grandest in history, not only to glorify the Olympic movement and to show German athletic prowess but also to convince the world that Berlin, despite Germany's oppressive political culture, was a suitable venue for the Summer Games later that year. This desire to collect international prestige for Germany would often overshadow mere sporting ambitions to cast doubt upon the true intentions of the organizers of the Garmisch-Partenkirchen Games.

Three vacation areas submitted bids in 1933 to host the 1936 Winter Games: Schreiberhau, Braunlage-Schierke, and Garmisch-Partenkirchen. A combination of factors favored the candidacy of the neighboring Upper Bavarian resorts of Garmisch and Partenkirchen. The two towns had the necessary infrastructure and experienced personnel to host such a large competition. There was a tested ski jumping facility in Partenkirchen, good cross-country trails, excellent ice surfaces, and a challenging bobsled run already in operation. The nearby presence of the Zugspitze, Germany's tallest mountain, provided insurance against a lack of snow that had plagued previous Winter Olympics. Local sports officials from the Garmisch and Partenkirchen ski clubs and the Riessersee sport club had organized multisport competitions, including the annual Winter Sport Week, for years. And the proximity of Garmisch and Partenkirchen to the large cities of Munich and Innsbruck, combined with plenty of accommodations for German and international spectators, created the possibility of attracting large crowds to the contests that would bolster both short- and long-term economic prospects. These advantages of the Bavarian site were enough to convince IOC officials to select Garmisch and Partenkirchen in May 1933.

The Nazi leadership also favored the Garmisch-Partenkirchen bid. Bavaria was home to the National Socialist party, with Munich serving as party headquarters and Nuremberg playing host to the annual party conventions. The natural alpine beauty of the Werdenfelserland region, with its impressive landscapes, mountain peaks, and blue Bavarian sky, provided the perfect backdrop for the awe-inspiring ceremonies favored by the Nazis. The national government would spare no expense in preparing the area for the Games; such a grand spectacle required magnificent facilities to match the beautiful scenery and international fanfare of an Olympic Games.

Karl Ritter von Halt, a German IOC member since 1929, presided over the organizing committee (OC). He served as a member on the Berlin OC as well as president of the International Handball Federation. Ritter von Halt appointed Peter von Le Fort, an officer of the Partenkirchen ski club, as executive secretary, and other notables, including the mayors of Munich, Garmisch, and Partenkirchen, a military officer, a duke, and several government officials, took places as OC members. Also present were Reich sport leader Hans von Tschammer und Osten, who would become president of the German Olympic Commission, and Munich banker Friedrich Döhlemann, who served as the OC's vice president/treasurer. The committee began its work on June 1, 1933, and received its charter in August. Le Fort's appointment exacerbated tensions between Garmisch and Partenkirchen officials, and Nazi town councilors in Garmisch fought for the dismissal of Le Fort from the OC. The Reich Sport Office deemed this action to be a "violation of leadership principle" (*Führerprinzip*), and Garmisch officials later paid for their indiscretion when the two towns were merged in 1935, with Partenkirchen benefiting from the administrative consolidation.

Despite this local friction, the planning of the Games proceeded relatively smoothly, with organizers conducting their business on a small-scale, personal level. A general secretariat coordinated the financial advisory committee, legal counsel, the venue construction office, and the various event committees (in addition to those offices responsible for media relations, ticket sales and advertising, and traffic coordination). Separate subcommittees for ice, bobsled, and skiing events operated in both construction and event areas. A total of 2.6 million Reichmarks (RM), including a RM 1.1 million grant from the Berlin government, covered the costs of facilities construction and other organizing expenses. Despite the existence of functioning venues in the area, organizers planned the construction of a new ski stadium, an ice arena with an artificial ice surface, new cross-country trails, and a state-of-the-art bob run. All facilities, with the exception of the ice arena, were finished by the winter of 1934–1935, thus allowing them to be tested in competition before the Olympic Games in 1936.

Organizers incorporated the existing ski jump on the Gudiberg into a new ski stadium. Workers renovated the old jump in the style of the famed Holmenkollen facility in Norway for use in the Nordic combined event and built a new, bigger jumping facility adjacent to the old jump for the special jumping event. The Partenkirchen municipal construction officer, supported with technical assistance by the International Ski Federation (FIS), oversaw this construction. The stadium, designed to accommodate 40,000 spectators in the stands and 60,000 in total, would serve as the site of the opening and closing ceremonies, and eventually 80,000 fans would squeeze into the facility to watch Birger Ruud win the special jumping competition. (Officials turned away 50,000 more spectators and set up loudspeakers outside the stadium to allow them to follow the activities inside.)

The frozen Riessersee, one of Germany's oldest winter sport venues, was the site for ice hockey, speed skating, and the German national winter sport of *Eisschiessen,* an indigenous form of curling. Two hockey rinks were located in the infield of the speed skating oval, and the *Eisschiessen* rinks stood adjacent to the south side of the oval. To the east of the lake was the new bob course, designed by Stanislaus Zentzytsky, the Polish engineer who had designed the 1932 Olympic bobsled run at Lake Placid. Organizers also built a new ice arena, with seating for over 2,000 and room for 10,000 spectators in all, to host the artistic skating events. The open air arena, featuring an artificial ice surface of 10,000 square feet, was completed in 1934, but adjustments to the facilities were made through the end of 1935.

New events in addition to the national folk sport of *Eisschiessen* made their way onto the Olympic program in Garmisch-Partenkirchen. Alpine countries finally succeeded in overcoming the resistance of the Scandinavian bloc to have Alpine skiing competition included in the Winter Olympic Games. A combined event, consisting of a downhill race and two slalom runs, was scheduled for both men and women. After 1936, Alpine skiing would find a permanent place in the Winter Olympics. Another program addition as a demonstration sport was military ski patrol, a forerunner of the present-day biathlon. While many countries in Europe and the United States participated in military ski patrol competitions, the inclusion of the sport may also be interpreted as a gesture to appease Nazi officials, who looked favorably on any sporting activity that could be combined with military training. These additional contests boosted the number of competing athletes over the 1,000 mark for the first time in the history of the Winter Games.

As important as making a positive sporting impression was to the organizers, enhancing Germany's international prestige also ranked high on the OC's list of priorities. Olympic officials, whether out of a sense of ideological conviction or based on a simple strategy of survival, had resigned themselves to working together with the Nazis to make the Winter and Summer Games powerful political statements of the reborn German nation. Leading functionaries, including Carl Diem, organizer of the XIth Summer Games, knew that just one incident might be enough to endanger the Berlin event, especially in the light of a boycott movement in the United States. Diem expressed his concerns to Ritter von Halt and urged that any evidence of institutionalized anti-Semitism be removed from the roads between Munich and Garmisch-Partenkirchen, as well as from the host towns. Efforts were made to prevent any public demonstrations of anti-Semitic behavior in order to preserve a hospitable climate that would win favorable world opinion regarding Berlin's summer festival. While Diem has been honored by the Olympic movement for his painstaking efforts to promote international sport, he has also been vilified for his collaboration with the Nazi leaders in preparing the 1936 Berlin Games. Historians claim that the exchange with Ritter von Halt shows that Diem opposed anti-Semitism not from an ethical standpoint but from a practical one: bad international press would fuel the fires of the boycott movement and prevent Germany from gaining international prestige from the Olympics. While the debate over Diem's motives may continue in the future, what cannot be argued is the test-run nature of the Garmisch-Partenkirchen event in relation to the XIth Summer Games. The experience acquired in Garmisch-Partenkirchen would help German Olympic leaders with their planning for Berlin.

Over 6,000 SS and SA troops performed bodyguard functions for Adolf Hitler when he opened the Games on February 6. Ritter von Halt stated in his opening address, ''We Germans want [also] to show the world that, faithful to the order of our Führer and federal Chancellor [Hitler], we can put on an Olympic Games [that will be] a true festival of peace and sincere understanding among peoples.'' Organizers took great care to control the image of the Games in the international press; foreign photographers did not receive credentials to work in Garmisch-Partenkirchen, thus forcing the international press corps to rely on German photos that had received official approval for distribution. The OC wrote newsletters and arranged briefings for foreign journalists to control the message. Organizers achieved some measure of success in this enterprise; most American newspapers sent their Berlin political correspondents (who had no expertise in sports) to cover the Games, and these journalists reported mostly favorable stories about the organization of the Games and the events themselves. Sonja Henie's third gold medal in figure skating, the ski jumping of Birger Ruud, and the American victory in the two-man bobsled competition provided enough positive material to relegate the only major sporting controversy of the Games, the gold medal–winning British ice hockey team and the questionable citizenship of some of its Anglo-Canadian members, to a supporting role in press coverage. The media did nothing to fuel movements to boycott the Berlin Games that summer.

For all their efforts to awe an audience of foreign spectators, German organizers need not have made such a fuss. There were only 2,000 foreign athletes and spectators in the area for the Games. Still, the 1936 Garmisch-Partenkirchen Games proved to be impressive enough to merit the award of the Vth Olympic Games to be held in 1940. In the postwar era, Garmisch-Partenkirchen has served as a popular ski resort and winter sport competition site. The 1978 World Alpine Skiing Championships took place in Garmisch-Partenkirchen, and town officials continue to bid for major competitions as a means of boosting the local economy.

BIBLIOGRAPHICAL ESSAY

The official repository of the records of the 1936 Winter Games Organization Committee is the German Federal Archives, Potsdam Branch (former German Central Archives,

Division I, of the German Democratic Republic), Berliner Str. 98-101, Potsdam, Germany. Once thought to be lost, these records are once again available, thanks to German unification. Twenty boxes of material are listed in the archive's catalog, but a significant portion of the documents, including some that may shed light on the relationship between the Nazis and the OC, are not available. The records are cataloged under "70 Or 1"; the archive will promptly photocopy its catalog upon request for a small fee. Although Garmisch-Partenkirchen officials will happily refer researchers to Potsdam, the town archive retains some documentation pertaining to the Games as well as other memorabilia.

The official report on the Games, prepared by the Garmisch-Partenkirchen organizing committee, is *Amtlicher Bericht hrsg. vom Organisationskomitee die IV. Olympischen Winterspiele 1936, Garmisch-Partenkirchen e.V.* (Berlin, 1936). The committee also published a number of other works, some in German, French, and English. See *Offizielle Ergebnisse der IV. Olympischen Winterspiele 1936 in Garmisch-Partenkirchen* (Berlin, 1936) and *Bericht des Präsidenten des Organisations-Komitees der IV. Olympischen Winterspiele 1936 Dr. Ritter von Halt* (Garmisch-Partenkirchen, 1935). The report published by the American Olympic Committee is Frederick W. Rubien, ed., *Games of the XIth Olympiad, Berlin, Germany and the IVth Winter Games, Garmisch-Partenkirchen* (New York, 1937). The French Olympic Committee's report is *La Participation française aux jeux de la XIme Olympiade Garmisch-Partenkirchen—Berlin 1936* (Paris, 1937).

There has been little written about the Garmisch-Partenkirchen Games in English; most works have focused on the Berlin Summer Games. William Shirer devotes several entries of his *Berlin Diary* (New York, 1941) to the Games, paying attention to news coverage of the event by foreign newspapers and criticizing the naiveté of several of the American correspondents. A short article about the skiing events is Nicholas Howe, "1936: Garmisch-Partenkirchen," *Skiing* 40 (September 1987): 56.

The availability of secondary material in German is not much better. Arnd Krüger's *Die Olympischen Spiele 1936 und die Weltmeinung* (Berlin, 1972) is the most complete analysis of the organization of the 1936 Winter Games from a scholarly standpoint, yet this analysis is a sidelight to Krüger's excellent investigation into world public opinion and the Summer Games. The community of Garmisch-Partenkirchen published a fiftieth anniversary retrospective of the Games, *50 Jahre Olympiasport—Garmisch-Partenkirchen 1936–1986* (Garmisch-Partenkirchen, 1986), which contains reprinted material from contemporary accounts written by organizers, in addition to results, pictures, and details about facility construction. Garmisch-Partenkirchen's continued prominence as a winter sports competition site has kept the town in the media spotlight. Students should survey German newspapers and periodicals (particularly the Munich-based *Suddeutsche Zeitung*) for coverage of the town and its history.

Jon W. Stauff

SAPPORO/ST. MORITZ/GARMISCH-PARTENKIRCHEN 1940

OLYMPIC WINTER GAMES
(Never Held)

During the Thirty-sixth Session of the International Olympic Committee (IOC) in Warsaw in 1937, Japan received the honor of hosting the Vth Olympic Winter Games in Sapporo, one year after Tokyo had been awarded the 1940 Summer Games. According to an IOC decision in 1926, the country hosting the Summer Games had priority for the site of the Winter Games.

Werner Klingeberg, a sports consultant paid by the German government, worked as a technical adviser to the IOC. At the Thirty-seventh Session of the IOC, held in Cairo in 1938, Klingeberg reported that the financial and organizational requirements for Sapporo were assured, with Hokkaido's government providing a budget of 1.25 million yen ($356,426). During the Cairo session, the IOC member from China, Chen-ting Wang, pleaded via telegram for a change of the Games site because of the Japanese invasion of China the preceding year. Despite concerns over the increasing politicization of sport and evidence of Japan's militarism and expansionism, the IOC remained committed to the Japanese site.

The IOC encountered problems with the International Ski Federation (FIS) almost immediately after the Cairo session, resulting in drastic changes to the Olympic program. According to FIS regulations, ski instructors were allowed to compete in the Olympics; according to the IOC amateur code, they were not. The FIS rejected the IOC's demands to exclude "professional" skiers and insisted on its own right to determine the amateur status of its members. Because a compromise between the FIS and the IOC could not be reached, the IOC canceled the Alpine ski competition for the 1940 Winter Games. Meanwhile, the external and internal political pressures upon Fuminaro Konoe's government in 1938 caused a reduction of the financial commitment to the Games. Initially, the Japanese Olympic Committee (JOC) tried to cope with the setbacks, but on July 15, 1938, one year after the beginning of the war with China, the committee informed the Japanese public that both the 1940 Summer and Winter Games were canceled.

The choice of Helsinki on July 18, 1938, as the new location for the Summer Games gave hope to Oslo's bid for the Winter Games. On September 3, however, the executive committee of the IOC, meeting in Brussels, decided to award the Games to St. Moritz, the host of the 1928 Winter Olympics. St. Moritz had the necessary sporting facilities and in 1928 had demonstrated its ability to organize an impressive Olympic Games. By October 1938, the program for the Games, scheduled to begin in February 1940, had been completed, with competition in figure skating, speed skating, ice hockey, bobsled, and military patrol, and with ski jumping and slalom as demonstration sports. The Swiss organizing committee (SOC) intended to circumvent the dispute with the FIS by making ski jumping a demonstration sport, but after further consideration of the position of the FIS, the committee canceled the event. The IOC was notified of this decision during its Thirty-eighth Session in London in June 1939; it gave the Swiss a week to reconsider, but the Swiss refused to reinstate ski jumping. In a secret vote, the IOC, seeing no alternative, took the Games away from St. Moritz and awarded them to Garmisch-Partenkirchen in the German Alps. Never before had the IOC removed a city as a Games host.

Garmisch-Partenkirchen's selection as a substitute site for the 1940 Winter Games had been facilitated by the appointment of Karl Ritter von Halt to the IOC executive board in 1937; at the same time, Theodor Lewald had been forced to resign his IOC membership because of his Jewish ancestry and was replaced by the politically reliable General Walter von Reichenau. These changes increased German influence within the Olympic movement, and in May 1939, a month before St. Moritz was replaced, IOC president Henri Baillet-Latour confidentially asked Ritter von Halt whether Garmisch-Partenkirchen could host the Winter Olympics again. Sports officials around the world had been impressed by the Berlin Games of 1936 and were not particularly concerned by the politics of the National Socialist regime, although many others regarded it as inhumane and monstrous. By 1938, the Jewish pogroms had begun, and in March 1939, German troops occupied all of Czechoslovakia in violation of the Munich Agreement. By this time, sport had become officially a part of the state apparatus with the foundation of the Nationalsozialistische Reichsbund für Leibesübungen on December 21, 1938. Among other things, this party-affiliated organization was responsible for international sport exchange.

The German government agreed to host the Winter Olympics in Garmisch-Partenkirchen but refused to recognize an independent Czech national Olympic committee. To keep the IOC happy, however, the Germans did not require Czech athletes to compete under the German flag, although they did not acknowledge Czech sovereignty. Official IOC statements have always emphasized the political neutrality of sport, but many saw the decision to award the 1940 Winter Games to Garmisch-Partenkirchen (and therefore to Nazi Germany) as acceptance of and even support of the German political situation and thus a political victory for National Socialism. Sport as an effective international symbol of peace became a propaganda tool and reflected one aspect of Nazi Germany's foreign policy.

A day of skiing with more than 12,000 participants, an impressive display of mass sport, had been planned for the Games. The event would feature Hitler, who at the end of his speech would donate skiing huts to Germany and other nations. Following a military demonstration, the 3-hour event would end, as it had in Berlin in 1936, with Richard Strauss's "Olympic Hymn." Invitations coupled with the generous promise to pay for all internal travel costs and to reduce the accommodation fee to only three reichsmarks (RM) per person per day was meant to sidetrack any international boycott movement before it could start.

Eighteen nations quickly accepted the invitation to Garmisch-Partenkirchen: Argentina, Belgium, Bohemia, Bulgaria, Estonia, Finland, France, Greece, Great Britain, Hungary, Italy, Latvia, Liechtenstein, the Netherlands, Norway, Slovakia, the United States, and Yugoslavia. On July 1, 1939, the initial meeting of the German Organizing Committee (GOC) was held. In addition to agreeing to finance extensions to the skating rink and ski stadium, Hitler provided 6 million RM for the construction of a 50-meter indoor swimming pool. A torch relay from the site of the first Winter Games in Chamonix, France, via St. Moritz, to Garmisch-Partenkirchen, an innovation designed to appeal to the public, was planned.

The GOC intended to have an extraordinary meeting to clarify the amateur status dispute with the FIS, but this meeting never took place. Instead, the question of the justification of the Winter Olympics arose as a result of the public conflict with the FIS over amateurism. Opponents of the Winter Olympics regarded the Games as competition to the FIS-sponsored world championships. In the summer of 1939, the Scandinavian countries, Poland, France, the Netherlands, and Switzerland spoke in favor of a rejection of the Winter Olympics. After reports of this controversy reached foreign newspapers, the GOC, to save the Games, invited 1,235 foreign athletes and promised to assume full travel and accommodation costs. Travel to Olso after the Games would be facilitated so that athletes could still take part in the FIS world championships.

World War II began with the German invasion of Poland on September 1, 1939, only twelve weeks after the IOC's decision to award the Games to Garmisch-Partenkirchen. On September 9, a progress report on site construction for the Games was published; it was impossible to halt construction without returning the Games to the IOC. Hitler demanded the continuation of site work for another three weeks. On September 26, one day before the surrender of Warsaw, Hitler again insisted on an accelerated completion of the Olympic facilities. Shortly after, all work on the site was halted because the workers were needed elsewhere. It was only in November, however, that the Reichsportführer informed the IOC that the Ministry of the Interior, which was responsible for sport, had decided to return the Games to the IOC. According to an IOC resolution of 1938, the Olympic Games could not be held in a war zone. Officially, this decision was based on the refusal of the British and French governments to restore world peace.

Despite the cancellation of the Games, Hitler tried to safeguard the chances of organizing his massive winter spectacle. On December 27, 1939, Hitler ordered the finance minister to continue the construction of facilities at Garmisch-Partenkirchen, using local workers. The Fourth Winter Sport Week, intended to be a substitute for the Winter Olympics, inaugurated the newly built sport complex at Garmisch-Partenkirchen. This international event, important for Nazi foreign policy, was to be honored with the presence of fifteen IOC members as well as representatives of the various sport federations from those European nations not yet participating in the war. The significance of the event was dimmed when the important neutral skiing nations—Switzerland, Sweden, Norway, Finland, and the Netherlands—declined to participate. All 182 athletes who did participate came from nations linked to or dependent on Germany: Italy, Yugoslavia, Hungary, Romania, and Bulgaria.

BIBLIOGRAPHICAL ESSAY

The German Organizing Committee published an official report about its preparations for the Games, *Vorbereitung zu den V. Olympischen Winterspiele 1940 Garmisch-Partenkirchen* (Munich, 1939), edited by Carl Diem. No similar reports appear to have been prepared by committees representing Sapporo or St. Moritz, although each did publish other works. The Sapporo committee published a program and book of regulations in German and French editions in 1938, and the St. Moritz committee published *Projet de programme* (Geneva, 1939).

The sport historian Hajo Bernett has written several works bearing on the 1940 Games. His article, ''Das Scheitern der Olympischen Spiele von 1940,'' *Stadion* 6 (1980): 251–90, examines the impact of the Sino-Japanese and Russo-Finnish wars on the 1940 Games. Two books, *Nationalsozialistische Leibeserziehung. Eine Dokumentation ihrer Theorie und Organisation* (Schorndorf, 1966) and *Sportpolitik im Dritten Reich* (Schorndorf, 1971), take a broader look at sport in Hitler's Germany, as does Carl Diem, *Der deutsche Sport in der Zeit der Nationalsozialismus* (Cologne, 1980), a publication of the Carl-Diem-Institut. See also Dieter Steinhofer, *Hans von Tschammer und Osten: Reichssportführer im Dritten Reich* (Berlin, 1973), and Hans-Joachim Teicher, *Internationale Sportpolitik im Dritten Reich* (Schorndorf, 1991), for other perspectives. Arnd Krüger comments on the 1940 Games in ''Deutschland und die Olympische Bewegung (1918–1945),'' in Horst Ueberhorst, ed., *Geschichte der Leibesubungen* (Berlin, 1982), pt. 2, vol. 3, pp. 1026–47.

For information on the Sapporo effort, consult Kunihiko Karaki, ''Die Aufgegebenen Olympischen Spiele in Tokio 1940,'' *Hitotsubashi Journal of Arts and Sciences* 23 (December 1982): 60–70.

                                                        Swantje Scharenberg

CORTINA D'AMPEZZO 1944

OLYMPIC WINTER GAMES
(Never Held)

After the members of the International Olympic Committee (IOC), in the Thirty-fourth Session at Warsaw in 1937, had, with the exception of Sigfrid Edström, unanimously supported the continuance of the Winter Games and had reached an agreement to stage the Vth Winter Games in Sapporo, the representatives from Oslo, Cortina d'Ampezzo, Montreal, and St. Moritz advanced their cases for hosting the VIth Winter Games in 1944. St. Moritz, citing its successful experience with the 1928 Games, had submitted its application as early as March 1935; Montreal, which did not submit its formal application until July 1938, emphasized its existing infrastructure. The application from the national Olympic committee of Italy, promoting Cortina, did not arrive until shortly before the Thirty-sixth Session in London in September 1939. At that session, after the representatives had reported on the progress of their plans to host the 1944 Games, a majority of the thirty-five members present voted for the Italian winter resort of Cortina d'Ampezzo. St. Moritz finished second in the voting, its chances ruined by a conflict between the International Ski Federation (FIS) and the Swiss Olympic Committee over the program of competition and the eligibility of ski instructors.

Shortly after the London session, World War II began with Hitler's invasion of Poland. The Soviet invasion of Finland on November 30, 1939, forced the Finnish organizational committee to abandon its plans to host the XIIth Summer Games in Helsinki in 1940. Meanwhile, on November 25, 1939, the president of the IOC, Henri Baillet-Latour, informed the national organizing committees that the 1940 Winter Games, originally scheduled for Sapporo and then moved to Garmisch-Partenkirchen, were cancelled and that the fate of the 1944 Winter Games was uncertain. By 1943, the fate of the Cortina Games was clear: "Even if the war should end this year, as some optimistic people believe, it would still be too late to hold the 1944 games," wrote James F. Simms, an official of the United States of America Sports Federation, to Avery Brundage, the head of the U.S. Olympic Committee.

By order of Baillet-Latour, neither IOC executive committee meetings nor sessions were held during the war, nor was the admission of new IOC members or national Olympic committees decided upon. Once again, war had put the future of the Olympic Games in doubt. For Brundage, the virtual suspension of IOC activity was frustrating; many long-time members of the IOC were dead, and others had not been heard from since the beginning of the war. "We will have our hands full in getting the Olympic machine operating after the war," he wrote Edström. In the Western Hemisphere, an alternative appeared to be the Pan-American Games, planned for 1942, but the entry of the United States into the war in 1941 delayed the inauguration of those games until 1951.

In general, there was a stagnation of Olympic activity during the war, although at the beginning of 1944, more frequent correspondence among IOC members indicated a gradual reactivation of the organization. In 1944, the fiftieth anniversary of the founding of the IOC was solemnly celebrated on a modest scale in Lausanne. With the slogan "Revival of the Olympic Games," the continuation of the Olympic ideal was recaptured. By the first postwar session of the executive committee in August 1945 in London, IOC leaders, including Edström and Brundage, had already agreed that the 1948 Olympic Games would take place in any case.

BIBLIOGRAPHICAL ESSAY

There is a good deal of correspondence dealing with the question of the 1944 Winter Games in the Avery Brundage Collection at the University of Illinois Archives, Urbana, Illinois. As president of the U.S. Olympic Committee, Brundage carried on a steady correspondence with Baillet-Latour, Edström, and other significant figures in the IOC. Information on the various IOC sessions at which the wartime Games were considered may be found in the session minutes and reports; these can be found at a number of repositories, including the IOC archives in Lausanne, the Center for Olympic Studies at the University of Western Ontario, London, Ontario, and the Brundage Collection.

Astrid Engelbrecht
Translated by Jamey J. Findling

ST. MORITZ 1948

VTH OLYMPIC WINTER GAMES

The Swiss welcomed the decision to hold the 1948 Winter Olympic Games in St. Moritz, Switzerland. Unlike the situation in England where there had been much criticism of the decision to host the 1948 Summer Games due to food, housing, and transportation shortages, St. Moritz welcomed the economic opportunities afforded by hosting such an international event. Despite its isolation from the events of World War II and the emerging cold war, St. Moritz had not emerged from the conflagration unscathed. It was not the same thriving tourist haven that had hosted the Winter Games some twenty years earlier. The rise and fall of Nazi Germany had dealt a severe blow to its neighbor so dependent on tourism for its livelihood. A number of hotels and restaurants had been forced to close as the war progressed, and the influx of tourists had virtually ceased. The war in Europe had forced the closure of 20 percent of the hotels and restaurants in and around St. Moritz.

The total cost of hosting the Games was 350,000 Swiss francs (about $82,325). St. Moritz guaranteed 120,000 francs, nearly one-third of which was raised from a hotel tax. The Swiss national government promised to provide more than one-half of the required revenue. Some of the funding provided by the Swiss government was generated through the sale of special Winter Olympic stamps. The set of four stamps was quite popular and contributed significantly to the ability of the Swiss to provide adequate facilities for the events. Additional revenue came from the sale of tickets, which ranged in price from 40 Swiss francs to 200 Swiss francs. One distinct advantage that St. Moritz had over London was that its former Olympic facilities were virtually intact. The increased popularity of the Winter Games required more accommodations for the larger crowds and the greater number of teams participating, but this was viewed as an opportunity for economic revival. The Swiss Organizing Committee estimated that 1,200 athletes, 400 Olympic officials, 400 media personnel, and 20,000 spectators would come to St. Moritz, a number that, it was hoped, would rejuvenate the region's sluggish economy. Other than an expansion of seating capacity and improvement of facilities, including the renovation of the ski jump built for the 1928 Games, major improvements were not necessary.

The tumultuous international environment was also a factor in the IOC decision to select St. Moritz as host. St. Moritz, in a neutral country, was the ideal postwar site for the Winter Games. Not only was there ill will between the former belligerents, but also the emerging cold war was rapidly becoming a consideration. The Soviet Union did not participate in the Winter Games at St. Moritz, but it did send official observers; the Soviets were beginning to display an interest in competing in the Games. The Soviet magazine *Ogonysk* on December 23, 1947, predicted the defeat of the United States and charged that

American propaganda was a "psychological attack intended to frighten the weak-nerved." The cold war was well a fact of life by 1948, as governments that owed allegiance to Moscow were already established in Poland, Hungary, Romania, Bulgaria, and Czechoslovakia. Of these, only Poland and Czechoslovakia were well represented at St. Moritz.

Despite the neutrality of the Swiss, the Winter Olympics were riddled by controversy even before they began. Lebanon, the only Arab state entered at St. Moritz, threatened to withdraw less than a month before opening day if the all-Jewish team representing Palestine displayed a Zionist flag. The Lebanese minister to Switzerland, Jamiel Miekaui, argued that since Palestine was not a nation, it should not be allowed to compete. Fortunately for the host committee, the entire controversy was avoided when Hans Roth, director of the Palestinian team, withdrew its entry on the grounds that the team would not have adequate time to prepare for the Games. Roth denied reports that the decision was influenced by the Lebanese complaint. Less than four months later, the Jewish provisional government proclaimed the establishment of the independent state of Israel, and future Olympic hosts would be forced to deal with the controversy.

As had occurred following World War I, several nations that had been defeated in World War II were not invited to participate. The IOC officially explained that neither Germany nor Japan possessed a legitimate government to which an invitation could be sent. Italy, Austria, Bulgaria, Hungary, and Romania, all of which had allied with the Nazis, did send teams, although their presence was not well received by all parties. Several of the teams were rumored to include former Nazis. On at least one occasion, the Swiss government refused to grant a visa to an Austrian ski jumper despite the claim he had been "de-Nazified."

The issue so concerned the Norwegians and the Yugoslavs that they formally protested to the IOC. They claimed that despite efforts by the Swiss government to screen potential Nazis, the Austrian team still included three soldiers who had fought with the German army. The entire incident might have led to an uncomfortable international incident had it not been for the efforts of Jean Carle, acting president of the International Ski Federation. Carle came to the defense of the Austrian athletes by stating that all three accused had been conscripts in the army and had not voluntarily enlisted. Carle's argument that "they could not help it" seemed to satisfy all parties, and the official protests were withdrawn. The unstable political climate proved to be a justifiably grave concern of the organizing committee.

The United Press story of the opening day's events properly described it as the "wildest day in international sports history." With the possible exception of the president of the Swiss Federation, Enrico Celio, who proclaimed the Winter Games a "symbol of the new world of peace and goodwill," there was no peace or goodwill to be noted. To begin with, it was discovered that two of the three American bobsleds had been tampered with the evening before the start of the festivities. Nuts on the sleds were allegedly loosened, and one was almost completely unscrewed on the main bolt holding the steering mechanism of one sled. The perpetrators were never discovered, but this greatly contributed to an atmosphere of ill will in the event. The U.S. team placed guards at strategic points following the incident to protect the team's equipment. This surely added to the frustration already felt by a U.S. team lacking a flag or a recording of "The Star Spangled Banner" needed for the opening ceremony and, hopefully, several awards ceremonies. At the last minute, bobsledder Jack Heaton obtained an American flag from a local hotel and carried it during the opening ceremonies. A copy of the national anthem was provided by John Carter Vincent, a former American diplomat living in Switzerland.

The most controversial incident of the 1948 Winter Games, which threatened to cancel the entire celebration, was a dispute over which of two rival teams was the legitimate U.S. Olympic hockey team. Ironically, the dispute was almost identical to the one regarding the legitimacy of the American speed skating team during the 1928 Winter Olympics at St. Moritz. Two teams arrived from the United States, each claiming to be the legitimate U.S. team. In response, the IOC executive committee ruled that inasmuch as there were irregularities on both sides, neither the team of the Amateur Hockey Association (AHA) nor the team of the Amateur Athletic Union (AAU) would be allowed to compete. The Swiss Olympic Committee, however, defied the IOC ruling and declared in a formal statement that the AHA team was qualified to participate. The chairman of the United States Olympic Committee (USOC), Avery Brundage, responded by declaring that if the AHA team competed, the USOC would withdraw all of its team from participation in the Games.

The incident came close to derailing the Winter Games when Mayor Carl Nater of St. Moritz threatened to withdraw his city's offer to host the Games if the USOC carried out its threatened boycott. The Swiss Olympic Committee stood its ground, and the Games continued as planned with USOC participation. In one final defiant protest, the AAU hockey team marched with the USOC and Brundage in the opening parade while the AHA team stood with the crowd. During the hockey competition, several reporters noted that some members of the AAU hockey team cheered each time the AHA team's opposition scored. The confusing and frustrating event surely distracted the AHA team, which despite the controversy still managed to finish fourth in the competition.

Combine the U.S. hockey dispute with a Canadian-Swedish fistfight, speed skating rules protests, allegations of hotel price gouging, and the accidental shooting of a Swiss policeman by a competitor in the winter pentathlon, and it is clear that the Games were neither peaceful nor filled with much goodwill. The act that was truly symbolic of the frustration that the IOC and Swiss committee must have felt was the theft of the historic Olympic flag, which had originally been presented to the IOC in 1920 at Antwerp. To make matters even worse, the flag that replaced it above the stadium was also stolen.

IOC president Sigfrid Edström declared the Games a success but called for reforms in the often contradictory rules. He showed his frustration with the controversies when he announced his intent to resign his position after the 1948 Summer Olympics in London. Edström later changed his mind and remained in office until 1952.

Despite all of the difficulties faced by the organizers, the Winter Games of 1948 proved to be one of the most competitive in Olympic history. Unlike previous Winter Games, dominated by one or two national teams, the gold medals at the 1948 Games were distributed among ten of the twenty-eight competing nations. Sweden, Norway, Switzerland, and the United States won the most gold medals. Several new events were added to the program. The skeleton sledding event returned to the program for the first time since 1928, and men's and women's downhill and slalom Alpine skiing races were added. A winter pentathlon was included in the program as a demonstration event.

BIBLIOGRAPHICAL ESSAY

Much of the research for these Games must be done with the help of the various official reports that were published following the event. The official report is Swiss Olympic Committee, *Rapport général sur les Ves jeux olympiques d'hiver St-Moritz* (Lausanne, 1951). The Swiss Olympic Committee published a descriptive account in German and French, *XIV. Olympiade. V. Olympische Winterspiele St. Moritz 1948* (Lausanne, 1948). The organizing committee for the Games published *Reglement général et programme des Ve jeux olympiques d'hiver* (Zurich, n.d.). See also Austrian Olympic Committee, *V. Olympische Winterspiele in St. Moritz 1948* (Vienna, 1948); and, for the United States, Asa Bushnell, ed., *Report of the United States Olympic Committee: XIV Olympiad, London, England; V Olympic Winter Games, St. Moritz, Switzerland* (New York, 1949). The Avery Brundage Collection at the University of Illinois Archives, Urbana, Illinois, has a limited number of clippings and daily programs from these Games.

Secondary sources in English are scarce. Researchers interested in the political climate of the Games should consult Donald E. Fuoss, "An Analysis of the Incidents in the Olympic Games from 1924 to 1948, with Reference to Contribution of the Games to International Good Will and Understanding" (Ph.D. dissertation, Columbia University, 1951). Avery Brundage's position on the ice hockey controversy is explained in Allen Guttmann, *The Games Must Go On* (New York, 1984). Dick Button, the American figure skater and gold medalist at St. Moritz, recounts his experience in *Dick Button on Skates* (Englewood Cliffs, N.J., 1955).

German-language sources include Max H. Willy, *V Olympischen Winterspiele* (Freiburg, 1948), a summary of the Games with some background information; *Olympia: Fest der Volker St. Moritz-London 1948* (Vienna, 1948); and Gerhard Bahr, *Olympische Tage im Engadin: V. Olympische Winterspiele in St. Moritz von 30.1.1948-8.2.1948: ein Bilderbuch* (Nurnberg, 1948), a book of photographs.

Donald C. Simmons, Jr.

OSLO 1952

VITH OLYMPIC WINTER GAMES

At its annual session in 1947, held in Stockholm, the International Olympic Committee (IOC) voted to award the Olympic Winter Games of 1952 to the city of Oslo, Norway. The Oslo bid successfully defeated those of Cortina D'Ampezzo, Italy, and Lake Placid, United States, on the first ballot. Oslo thus became both the first capital city and the first Scandinavian city to host the Winter Games.

The IOC's choice of Oslo seems to have been based on several factors. First, Oslo had expressed its desire to host the Winter Games as early as 1936, when it offered to stage the 1940 Games. However, the tradition of allowing the city awarded the Summer Games the privilege of also organizing Winter Games dictated that the 1940 Winter Olympics would be organized by Japan. They were scheduled to be held in Sapporo. Of course, neither the Summer nor the Winter Games of 1940 were held due to World War II.

Second, after the war, when London agreed to host the 1948 Olympic Games, it declined to exercise its option of organizing the Winter Games and suggested that Oslo stage them instead. However, Oslo refused because of the Norwegians' wish to focus their attentions and resources on rebuilding their war-torn country. Norwegian officials decided to wait and bid for the 1952 Winter Games. Thus, on August 22, 1946, the Oslo city council voted to submit its bid. At this early stage the municipality of Oslo agreed to finance the construction and maintenance of the various venues, a pledge of support that boosted the strength of the bid. When the time came for the IOC to make its decision, the city commanded a positive profile due to previous national and international interest in staging the Games in Norway. In addition, Oslo's strong technical bid influenced the choice.

Oslo's chances were heightened by the drawbacks of its principal competitors. Lake Placid had already hosted the 1932 Olympic Winter Games, and travel to the United States was a financial hardship for many of the European teams that made up the majority of competitors. Cortina D'Ampezzo's bid, coming as it did from a German ally in World War II, might not have been seen by IOC members in 1947 as a prudent choice.

Once granted the Winter Games, the Norwegians promptly created an organizing committee composed of four municipal and four sport organization representatives. In 1948, a second Norwegian, Olav Ditlev-Simonsen, Jr., became a member of the IOC. Ditlev-Simonsen was made chair of Oslo's organizing committee and took over the responsibilities of guiding its work as well as delivering progress reports to the IOC.

The most important municipal representative on the committee was Brynjulf Bull, Oslo's mayor. Because of the municipality's heavy financial investment in the Games, the mayor clearly had a vested interest in staging them successfully and economically. The city of Oslo granted 10.7 million Norwegian kroner (about $1.5 million) over a five-year period to pay for the costs of the Games.

Though Oslo had many good winter sports facilities at the time of its bid, an enterprise of this magnitude required the renovation of existing facilities and the construction of new ones. Oslo's most famous facility was (and still is) the world-renowned Holmenkollen ski jump. This facility was renovated to accommodate a restaurant and shops underneath the jump's takeoff ramp. Although spectator seating was quite limited, there was standing room for more than 130,000 in the immediate area of the jump, and reports from the 1952 Winter Games indicate that this number of people did in fact attend the jumping competitions.

Other facilities for skiing were constructed at Norefjell, 75 miles from Oslo, and Rodkleiva. It was at these venues that the Alpine skiing events were held. Because of Norefjell's distance from Oslo, accommodations were built at the site for the competitors. The access to Norefjell was also enhanced by improving roads and bridges. Unfortunately, there was an unusual lack of snow in February 1952, and it was only through the efforts of a large number of volunteers and the military in moving snow from nearby areas that the downhill courses were made raceworthy. The scarcity of snow forced the organizers to reschedule some events and limit training time for the competitors. Despite these inconveniences, all the scheduled races were held.

For the opening and closing ceremonies and the skating events, Bislett Stadium in Oslo was chosen. When renovations were completed, it accommodated 27,000 spectators, but there were only 3,000 seats. This was no problem for the Norwegians, who were accustomed to standing at sport competitions.

Construction of the ice hockey facilities aroused controversy. Although the IOC had removed ice hockey from the Winter Games program after the fiasco in 1948 at St. Moritz, the Norwegian organizing committee hoped that hockey would be returned to the program. Despite the uncertainty, the Norwegians decided to propose several arenas for ice hockey matches in the hope that the dispute between the IOC and the International Ice Hockey Federation would be resolved before the Games.

The International Ice Hockey Federation demanded that the main arena for the competition, Jordal Amfi, have an artificial ice surface to ensure the best possible conditions for the matches. The Norwegians were extremely reluctant to proceed with such an expensive project, especially when it was not clear whether the competitions would take place. But they finally capitulated and began work on renovating the stadium to provide an artificial ice surface; in 1950, the dispute between the IOC and the International Ice Hockey Federation was resolved, and hockey was placed on the program for the Olympic Winter Games.

The venue for the bobsled competition was also the cause of some discussion. The cost of constructing a permanent course was deemed to be prohibitive, especially since the sport had little popularity in Norway. Hence, the organizing committee decided to go ahead with the construction of a temporary bobsled run built entirely of snow and ice. Under the direction of Swiss experts, the course was constructed in 1951. It worked well enough for the process to be repeated in 1952.

Besides the competition venues, accommodations for competitors, coaches, and foreign spectators, as well as communications facilities for the influx of journalists, had to be constructed cr renovated. Three Olympic villages were constructed for competitors and coaches in the Oslo area. International sports federation personnel and IOC members occupied most of the hotels in Oslo. To accommodate tourists, the organizing committee created a system of billeting Olympic visitors in private homes in Oslo. This strategy provided space for 6,000 people.

Although the VIth Olympic Winter Games were not beset with the politically motivated difficulties of other Olympic competitions, several contentious issues arose, most notably the question of inviting German athletes to participate in the Games. Anti-German feelings, underscored by memories of the Nazi occupation forces, were still prevalent in Norway during preparations for the Games. As the official report of the Games noted, public discussions on this particular topic ''were rather lively.''

The case of a Norwegian speed skater, Finn Hodt, provides a good example of the feelings of some Norwegians at that time. The Norwegian Skating Union had proposed Hodt as a member of the speed skating team, but the Norwegian Olympic Committee rejected him because he had been a Nazi collaborator during the war.

A similar situation developed within the IOC during this period. Some IOC members were opposed to retaining German members who had joined the IOC before the war. The greatest controversy revolved around Karl Ritter von Halt, a former Nazi and organizer of the 1936 Winter Games. Despite the protests of some of the IOC members, President J. Sigfrid Edström did not allow a vote to be taken on the issue, and the Germans remained members of the IOC. However, it is significant to note that Ditlev-Simonsen claimed in a 1951 letter to Avery Brundage that Ritter von Halt had promised that he would not attend the 1952 Winter Games.

Interestingly, the IOC executive committee also recommended in 1950 that the Germans not participate in Norway. However, this recommendation was never acted upon by the general session of the IOC, and the West Germans, whose national Olympic committee had been recognized by the IOC, eventually took part in the Games at the invitation of the Norwegians. In sum, the Germans were well received by the Norwegian people as representatives of a new and democratic West Germany. Although the East Germans also had a national committee by 1952, its status had not been resolved by the IOC, and, as a consequence, they were not invited to Oslo.

In 1951, the Soviet Union, also on the fringe of international sport, indicated that it wished to become involved in the Olympics. Its national Olympic com- mittee had been recognized by the IOC, and there was considerable speculation as to whether the Russians would send a hockey team to the Winter Games. However, because the Soviet application to join the International Ice Hockey Federation was not made in time, they were denied participation. (In order to participate in the Olympic Games, a country must have its national federations controlling the various sports recognized by the corresponding international fed- erations.)

As with earlier summer Games, a torch run was incorporated into the cere- monies arranged for the Winter Games; however, instead of starting in Olympia, Greece, the 1952 torch run commenced in Morgedal, Norway, and was carried out entirely on skis. The reasons for this unusual format were twofold. First, Morgedal was the birthplace of one of Norway's most famous skiers and, sec- ond, skiing had long been an integral part of Norway's history and culture. Like previous torch runs, the flame entered the stadium shortly after the parade of athletes from the thirty nations represented at the Games.

Although Olympic competitions are normally declared open by the head of state of the country in which they are being held, the Oslo Games were officially opened on February 15, 1952, by Princess Ragnhild, granddaughter of the head of state. She was given this honor because her grandfather, Haakon VII, and her father, Crown Prince Olav, were in London attending the funeral of George VI of England.

The program of the VIth Winter Games was similar to that of the 1948 Games in St. Moritz, with the addition of the giant slalom event for both women and men and the 10-kilometer Nordic (cross-country) event for women, and the dropping of the Alpine combined event for men and women. The women's giant slalom was won on February 14 (it was held one day before the official opening because of scheduling requirements) by Andrea Mead Lawrence of the United States, who also won a gold medal in the slalom event. To the delight of the local fans, a Norwegian, Stein Erikson, won the men's giant slalom. Finnish skiers swept all the medals in the 10-kilometer cross-country race.

In keeping with most previous Winter Games, a demonstration sport was placed on the program. Although there had been suggestions within the IOC for displays of curling and military patrol on skis, the Norwegians opted for bandy, a sport that may be likened to soccer on ice. It is primarily a Scandinavian sport; only Norway, Sweden, and Finland fielded teams.

The Winter Games, as usual, saw certain athletes achieve star status. As ex- pected, the Scandinavian countries dominated the Nordic ski events. The Nor- wegians were delighted by the fact that one of their speed skaters, Hjalmar Andersen, won three gold medals. Of note also was Germany's successful return to the Games. West German teams won both the two- and four-man bobsled events. Making good use of the laws of momentum in their victories, the com- bined weight of their four-man team was an astounding 1,041.5 pounds (472 kg). (Because of the spiraling weights of the teams, the international federation for bobsled and toboganning decided just prior to the Games to limit the weight of future teams to 880 pounds.)

Ice hockey was reinstated in the program of the Games, and eight teams competed. As in 1948 there was some controversy, although this time it concerned the conduct of several teams and players. The rough play of the U.S. team offended many Norwegian spectators. In fact, after the Games had concluded, an editorial in an Oslo paper suggested that the behavior of the U.S. players lowered the Norwegian opinion of the United States so much that Norway's opinion of the Soviet Union might improve.

A more blatant example of cold war attitudes may be seen in the Soviet press reaction to the silver medal won by the U.S. hockey team. By tying the Canadian team 3–3 in its final game, the U.S. team vaulted into second place in the standings, forcing Sweden and Czechoslovakia to play for third. The Soviet press immediately accused the Canadians and Americans of conspiring to produce the tie, terming it a typical example of bourgeois capitalist cheating. Naturally both accused teams denied the charge.

The political and economic consequences of the VIth Olympic Winter Games for Oslo were perhaps not as pronounced as for other host cities; however, the Norwegians did benefit from the construction of new facilities and the renovation of old ones. For a country in which a large segment of the population was physically active, these improvements were welcomed. With regard to the Olympic Villages, one was turned into a hospital's staff residence, while another provided homes for senior citizens and old-age pensioners.

Economically the Games were a major expense for Oslo's citizens, particularly since the municipality provided the bulk of the funding, which came from local residents. Of course, the Games drew a large number of foreign visitors to Oslo, helping to offset the costs. Furthermore, the publicity created by the Games boosted tourism in ensuing years. Finally, it may be argued that the Games helped provide a psychological boost to most Norwegians recovering from the effects of the war.

In summary, the VIth Olympic Winter Games were relatively uneventful compared to many other Olympic festivals. The organizing committee was congratulated on its effectiveness, particularly in the light of the sometimes difficult weather conditions. The IOC members, at least, were impressed with the Games. They awarded the Olympic Cup of 1952 to Oslo for its excellent job of organizing the Winter Games. The VIth Olympic Winter Games saw the issue of Nazi Germany put to rest and provided a preview of the cold war attitudes between East and West that became much more evident several months later during the Summer Olympics of 1952.

BIBLIOGRAPHICAL ESSAY

The most comprehensive source of information on the VIth Olympic Winter Games is the official report of the organizing committee. The English version, *Olympic Winter*

Games Oslo 1952, edited by Rolf Petersen and translated by Margaret Wold and Ragnar Wold (Oslo, 1952), contains a wealth of information on the preparations for the Games as well as a report on the athletic competitions. This report is not easily obtainable due to the small number printed. Besides the one held by the IOC, there is another located at the International Olympic Academy, Olympia, Greece.

A similar report, P. Chr. Andersen, *The Olympic Winter Games Oslo 1952* (Oslo, 1952), contains much of the same information as the official report but in abbreviated form and with greater focus on the competitions. The Centre for Olympic Studies at the University of Western Ontario, London, Ontario, Canada, has a copy of this work. The U.S. official report is Asa S. Bushnell, ed., *United States 1952 Olympic Book: Quadrennial Report of the United States Olympic Committee* (New York, 1953), and the Canadian report is James Worrall et al., eds., *Canada Competes at the Olympic Games 1952: Official Report of the Canadian Olympic Association, 1948–1952* (Montreal, 1953). The West German version is *Die Olympische Spiele 1952, Oslo und Helsinki, das Offizielle Standardwerk des Nationalen Olympischen Komitees* (Frankfurt/Main, 1952).

The papers of Avery Brundage, IOC president from 1952 to 1972, provide a comprehensive source of information on the IOC's involvement with the Oslo Winter Games. This includes several letters to Brundage from the chair of the organizing committee, Olav Ditlev-Simonsen, Jr., as well as newspaper clippings, press releases, and programs. The Brundage Papers are held by the University of Illinois Archives; a printed catalog of the collection is available.

Several IOC publications mention the Oslo Games. The *Bulletin du comité international olympique* 27 (1951): 35–36 has a report on the preparations for the Games. *Bulletin du comité internationale olympique* 1 (1952): 4 also contains information on the Oslo Winter Games.

The National Olympic Committee of Norway published several news bulletins prior to the Games. These were entitled the *Olympic Winter Games News Bulletin,* nos. 1–4 (1951–1952). Copies may be found in the Brundage Papers.

Gordon MacDonald and Douglas Brown

CORTINA D'AMPEZZO 1956

VIITH OLYMPIC WINTER GAMES

The 1956 Winter Olympic Games were held at Cortina d'Ampezzo, Italy, situated in a huge natural amphitheater in the northern part of Italy and with a population of nearly 7,000 people.

In the fourteenth century, Cortina was governed by the Venetian Republic and in 1515 was annexed to Tyrol. It passed to Austrian hands during the Napoleonic wars at the Treaty of Campo Formio in 1797, which was reaffirmed at the Congress of Vienna in 1815. Cortina remained under Austrian rule until World War I. When Italy entered the war, its army occupied Cortina in May 1915, and the town remains a part of Italy today.

Winter sports had not appeared in northern Italy until early in the twentieth century when skiing and ice skating were introduced; in 1905, bobsledding was seen in a rudimentary form. Ice hockey made its first appearance in 1911, and although Italian athletes competed in winter athletic contests throughout the world, they were not recognized as other Italian athletes were.

Italian winter sport enthusiasts were interested in promoting their athletic interests, as well as opening the northern area of Italy to tourist trade. The Winter Olympics, first contested at Chamonix, France, in 1924, seemed an appropriate vehicle to open this area of Italy to tourism and promote interest in winter athletic endeavors.

Count Alberto Bonacossa spearheaded the drive to have Italy host an Olympic event. The count, an excellent Alpine skier and figure skater, held the Italian skating title from 1914 until 1928. His wife, Marisa, also an Italian figure skating champion, from 1920 to 1928, aided the count in the campaign to have the Winter Games at Cortina. Bonacossa became a member of the International Olympic Committee (IOC) in 1925, affording him a favorable position to promote Cortina. He encouraged the town council of Cortina d'Ampezzo to prepare a bid for the 1944 Winter Games and solicited the cooperation of the Comitato Olimpico Italiano (CONI).

The IOC met in London, June 6–9, 1939, and awarded Cortina the 1944 Winter Olympic Games. The Dolomite community had won over Montreal and Oslo on the second round of voting. World War II, however, ended Cortina's hopes and preparations for the 1944 Games.

Immediately following the war, Count Bonacossa began working again to bring the Winter Games to Cortina. At a meeting in Milan in the fall of 1946, the council of the Italian Winter Sports Federation asked Cortina to prepare a bid for the 1952 Winter Games. Under Bonacossa's leadership, an Italian delegation attended the IOC meeting held in Stockholm in June 1947, where it presented Cortina's bid for the 1952 Winter Olympics. Competition came from

Oslo and Lake Placid, and the final vote saw eighteen favoring Oslo, nine for Cortina, and one for Lake Placid.

Determined to try again for the 1956 Games, the Italian delegation got a break since the IOC was to meet in Rome, April 24–29, 1949, for the selection process. Montreal, Colorado Springs/Aspen, and Lake Placid were Cortina's rivals this time, but the IOC voted overwhelmingly for Cortina.

With the selection of Cortina for the 1956 Winter Games, excitement ran high. Count Bonacossa, so instrumental in ensuring Cortina received the bid, died on January 30, 1953. CONI now set a time line that would aim at producing an outstanding Olympic event. On July 26, 1950, a budget was established, and on December 20 the task of developing a master plan for the Olympics was put into the hands of a committee. On October 24, 1951, CONI decided to send observers to the Oslo Winter Olympics in February 1952, and on November 29, 1951, it set the dates of the Cortina Games as January 26–February 5, 1956. On March 27, 1952, CONI, in concert with the Italian government, established the Interministerial Committee with representatives of the local authorities in Cortina and various governmental agencies to ensure a well-organized Olympic spectacle. On March 25, 1953, CONI turned over authority for the 1956 Games to the committees organizing them, coordinated by an organizing committee composed of the two Italian members of the Olympic Committee, Count Paolo Thaon di Revel and Giorgio de Stefani, respectively the chair and the secretary-general of CONI, the two chair of the national winter sports federations, the prefect of the province of Belluno, and the mayor of Cortina. On July 15, 1954, Count Revel was appointed chair of the organizing committee.

The final agreement on the program for Cortina was reached at the IOC meeting in Athens in May 1954. The program was the same as that of the Oslo Games, except that a 30-kilometer cross-country skiing race and a women's 3×5-kilometer relay were added. However, the Soviet Union's request for the inclusion of women's speed skating was rejected.

CONI took advantage of the good look they had at the facilities at the 1952 Oslo Games. Twelve observers were sent to Oslo with instructions to bring back as much information as they could. Even after the Oslo Games had ended, CONI kept in close touch with the Norwegian committee. Compared with the spectacular building program developed at Oslo, Cortina's facilities were lacking. The Italian town had no suitable ice stadium; the old ski jump needed a tremendous amount of work; the ski runs did not meet international standards; the bobsled run, in spite of recent work, was far from being acceptable; and, worst, there was no speed skating rink.

The ice stadium was of special concern since skating was to be the focal point of the Games. The committee, which had to build not only the stadium but also a network of access roads, succeeded remarkably well in its task. The stadium, dedicated in October 1955, had seats that rose almost vertically from the rink level and featured an open view of the nearby Dolomite mountains. There was permanent seating for about 7,500 spectators, and the addition of temporary seats allowed more than 14,000 to see the featured Olympic events. The locker rooms and other ancillary facilities were also first rate.

The organizing committee decided to replace the old ski jump with a new, technologically advanced facility. A new "snow stadium," seating 6,000, was built for the cross-country events. The south-facing grandstand was planned to provide the best light conditions for television and motion picture cameras. The bobsled run had been in place since 1928, when it had been used during the International University Winter Games. In 1936 it had been modernized similar to the runs at St. Moritz and Garmisch-Partenkirchen. The World Bobsled Championships were held on the new run in 1939, with outstanding success. In 1948 the run was again rebuilt and the turns reconfigured according to the latest standards. After the 1956 Winter Games were awarded to Cortina, CONI took steps to have an outstanding bobsled event. World bobsled championships were held in Cortina in 1950 and 1954, with the latter event serving as a dress rehearsal for the 1956 Olympics. Moreover, Italy's victory in the 1954 races heightened public interest in the sport as the Olympics approached.

Among the logistical problems involving the Games were the construction of new roads in the area to take care of the increased traffic, the upgrading of the local railway, and the number of new telephone and electric lines strung to facilitate the print and electronic media that covered the competition. Except for speed skating, all of the events were held near Cortina and were easily accessible to athletes and spectators alike. Hayes and Carol Heiss Jenkins, members of the U.S. team, recalled, "We felt as a real team because we could see our fellow Americans compete and our friends in other events could watch us perform in the skating. The events were held within easy walking distance" (interview, Hayes and Carol Heiss Jenkins, February 1993).

Speed skating presented a difficult problem. The organizing committee had planned for these races to be held at Lake Miswina, a little over 11 miles from Cortina. Although many officials were skeptical of these races' being held at this site, the selection proved to be an outstanding choice. The absence of wind due to the location of lake and the excellent condition of the ice contributed to the setting of one world record, the equaling of another, and the shattering of all current Olympic marks. While the skating on Lake Miswina was highly successful, the skiing events suffered from a lack of snow. Alpine units of the Italian army, which had done a great deal of work in the preparations for the Games, were now called upon to move tons of snow to cover bare spots.

Politically the East and West Germans competed as a single unit, as the IOC had decreed. The Cortina Games were held early enough in the year to escape the problems that the Summer Games, held in Melbourne in November and December, faced.

The Cortina Games marked the first appearance of Soviet athletes at a Winter Olympics, although the U.S.S.R. had competed in the 1952 Summer Games held in Helsinki and had sent observers to the Winter Games held in Oslo in

1952. In Cortina, Soviet speed skaters stunned the world by capturing the 500-, 1,500-, and 500-meter events, and the U.S.S.R. hockey team skated off with Olympic gold, ending the Canadian domination in that event. The U.S.S.R. also won the women's 10-kilometer cross-country skiing event and captured the 4 × 10-kilometer cross-country relay. The impact of the Soviet athletes was felt immediately and took the Winter Games to a higher level of competition.

The individual star of the VIIth Winter Olympics was skier Anton "Toni" Sailer of Austria. Sailer won the slalom and the giant slalom and was the clear favorite to win the downhill event, since he held the course record. Just before his run, however, Sailer broke one of his straps and could not find a replacement. Faced with withdrawal from the event, Sailer used straps from the skis of Hansl Senger, the Italian team trainer, and went on to win his third gold medal, making him the first ever to win all three Alpine events at the same Games. His Olympic victories put him in the elite company of trackman Jesse Owens who won four gold medals at the Berlin Olympics in 1936; Thorlief Haug, a Norwegian skier who won three skiing events in cross country and jumping at the 1924 Winter Games; Hjalmar Andersen, a Norwegian speed skater who won the three speed skating events at Oslo in 1952; and the Czech distance runner Emil Zatopek, who won the 5,000-meters, 10,000-meters, and marathon at the 1952 Helsinki Games.

In figure skating the Americans dominated both the men's and women's events. In the men's events, Hayes Alan Jenkins took top honors, followed by Ronald Robertson and Hayes' brother, David Jenkins. Jenkins' triumph followed Dick Button's Olympic wins in 1948 and 1952; David Jenkins took the gold medal at the 1960 Winter Olympics at Squaw Valley. Tenley Albright of the United States won the gold medal in the women's figure skating event, with Carol Heiss of the United States second. Heiss won the gold medal in 1960 and later married Hayes Jenkins.

The Cortina Games were notable for the tremendous amount of work the Italians did to prepare the site and for the entrance of the Soviet Union into competition. The Soviets led the medal count with a total of sixteen, including seven gold; no other national team captured more than four. The Games were remarkably free of the cold war political turmoil that marked other Summer and Winter Games of this era, leaving spectators and journalists free to be dazzled by the individual achievements of Toni Sailer, Hayes Jenkins, and Tenley Albright.

BIBLIOGRAPHICAL ESSAY

The organizing committee's official report to the IOC is *VII Giochi Olimpici Invernali/ VII Olympic Winter Games* (Cortina d'Ampezzo, 1956), in Italian and English; there is also a French edition: *VII. Jeux olympiques d'hiver Cortina d'Ampezzo* (Cortina d'Ampezzo, 1956). The committee published the usual daily programs, rules booklets, and site descriptions. The U.S. Olympic Committee report is Asa S. Bushnell and Arthur G.

Lentz, eds., *United States 1956 Olympic Book: Quadrennial Report of the United States Olympic Committee* (New York, 1957). The Canadian report is K. P. Farmer et al., eds., *Canada Competes at the Olympic Games 1956* (Montreal, 1956), and the German version is *Die VII. Olympischen Winterspiele 1956 Cortina d'Ampezzo, das Offizielle Standardwerk des Nationalen Olympischen Komitees* (Stuttgart, 1956). The Italian Olympic Committee (CONI) prepared a report, *VII Giochi Olimpici Invernali/VII Olympia Games—Cortina d'Ampezzo* (Rome, 1956), in Italian and English, as well as a pre-Games publication, apparently designed to attract people to the Games, *Olimpiade nelle Dolomiti, dalle Tofane all tre cime di Lavaredo. Edita in occasione dei VII Giochi olimpici invernali, Cortina d'Ampezzo 26 Gennaio–5 Febbraio 1956* (Milan, 1955).

Since Avery Brundage was president of the IOC during the Cortina Games, his papers at the University of Illinois Archives contain considerable material related to the Games. In addition to clippings and daily programs, researchers can find pre-Games reports and other publications of the organizing committee and a competitors' questionnaire used in Cortina.

For background on the tangled history of Cortina and the surrounding region, consult Charles A. Gulick, *Austria from Habsburg to Hitler,* vol. 1 (Berkeley, 1948); Karl R. Standler, *Austria* (New York, 1971); and Z. A. B. Zeman, *The Break-Up of the Hapsburg Empire, 1914–1918* (London, 1961).

Most secondary works on the 1956 Winter Games are in German, and many of those are noncritical works featuring lovely photographs of winter in Cortina. But researchers may want to consult Carl Diem, *Die Olympischen Spiele 1956. Cortina d'Ampezzo, Stockholm, Melbourne* (Stuttgart, 1957), for the views of the most notable German Olympic leader. See also Werner Eberhardt, *VII. Olympische Winterspiele, Cortina d'Ampezzo 1956* (Berlin, 1956); Harald Lechtenperg, *Olympische Spiele, 1956: Cortina, Stockholm, Melbourne* (Munich, 1957); and Martin Maier, *So war es in Cortina* (Vienna, 1956).

Allan W. Hall

SQUAW VALLEY 1960
VIIITH OLYMPIC WINTER GAMES

Squaw Valley was the Brigadoon of Winter Games, a community that magically appeared out of the wind-blown snow of California's Sierra Nevada range and then disappeared. The ice arena that witnessed the U.S. hockey team's miraculous gold medal performance is gone; the ski jump is in disrepair; a ski training center for Olympic hopefuls failed for lack of funds. Attempts to turn the Olympic site into a world-class resort were stalled for years by rivalries among property owners. Although the area remains a popular destination for West Coast skiers, tourists three decades after the Games regularly bemoan Squaw Valley's lack of amenities.

What remains, however, is the land itself: a natural bowl ½ mile wide and 2 miles long carved into the eastern face of the Sierras at 6,200 feet above sea level. Towering above are three alpine peaks; the tallest, Squaw Peak at the western end, rises steeply to 8,885 feet. The valley is located nearly astride the California–Nevada state line, overlooking Lake Tahoe, 40 miles southwest of Reno and 200 miles northeast of San Francisco. Add to the terrain the copious snows that blanket the Tahoe Basin each year, and Squaw Valley becomes the ideal location for the world's finest athletes to celebrate their skills.

That, at least, was the dream of Alexander C. Cushing, a socially prominent New York attorney and avid skier who first visited the valley in 1947. Cushing was so taken by the land that he purchased 574 acres, raised $400,000 from friends back east, among them Laurance Rockefeller, and moved his family west to start a ski resort. When Cushing learned in December 1954 that the United States Olympic Committee (USOC) would entertain bids from communities hoping to host the 1960 Winter Games, he saw an opportunity to promote California tourism in general and his own properties in particular. He quickly won expressions of support from California's publicity-conscious governor, Goodwin Knight, and the state's two U.S. senators. State senator Harold Johnson, whose district included Squaw Valley, agreed to file legislation in Sacramento guaranteeing $1 million in site development funds if Cushing managed to win the USOC's endorsement. "None of them thought I had a chance," Cushing recalled, "but they naturally couldn't go on record saying they were against the Winter Olympics coming to California." (Melvin Dursing, "The Great Winter–Olympics Fight," *Saturday Evening Post,* February 22, 1960, pp. 35, 73).

The chances of that actually happening, all agreed, were slim. When Cushing arrived at the USOC meeting in New York in January 1955, Squaw Valley's facilities included one chair lift, two rope tows, and a modest lodge. His rivals included such well-established winter sports centers as Aspen, Colorado; Sun Valley, Idaho; and Lake Placid, New York, host of the 1932 Winter Games. Extolling Squaw Valley's natural beauty and California hospitality, as well as his pledges of support from the state's establishment, Cushing persuaded the USOC to back his bid for the 1960 Games.

Rushing back to California, Cushing hurriedly raised a $50,000 campaign fund to sell Squaw Valley to the International Olympic Committee (IOC), scheduled to meet in Paris in June. Most of the money came from investors in the Squaw Valley Development Company, who saw an opportunity to garner badly needed publicity for their struggling resort, although the possibility that Squaw Valley would be chosen still appeared remote. Squaw's rivals for the bid included St. Moritz, which had successfully hosted the Games in 1928 and 1948, Garmisch-Partenkirchen, the 1936 site, and Innsbruck, the acknowledged favorite.

Clearly unable to compete with the European candidates in terms of facilities, Cushing chose to make the valley's unspoiled environment his selling point. He would offer the IOC an ideal Olympic venue built from the ground up. "Psychologically," he recalled, "this was our knockout punch. Ours would be a healthy, unadorned games, in a clean, simple atmosphere, free from commercial pressure and public interference" ("The Great Winter-Olympics Fight," p. 73).

Squaw Valley's presentation was dedicated to the theme, "Restoring the Olympic Ideal to the Winter Games." An Olympic Village with a common dining room would be constructed to feed and house the world's athletes, a first for the Winter Games. Venues would be clustered within walking distance of the village, not scattered across the countryside. Costs, Cushing promised, would be reasonable; transportation and living accommodations would not exceed $500 per athlete. Finally, Cushing argued, it was time for the IOC to acknowledge geopolitical realities of the postwar world. The time had come for a member of what he described as the Pacific family of nations to host the event.

On June 15, 1955, on the second ballot, IOC members cast 32 votes for Squaw Valley and 30 for Innsbruck. By the narrowest of margins, the 1960 Winter Games had been awarded to the obscure California ski area. Squaw Valley's obscurity was underscored at the closing ceremonies of the 1956 Games at Cortina d'Ampezzo. The mayor of the host city of the next Games traditionally takes part in the festivities, but Squaw Valley was an unincorporated village with no local government. IOC member John J. Garland of Los Angeles was drafted to fill in on behalf of his home state.

That Squaw Valley was awarded the Winter Games is a testimony to the promotional skills of a politically clever resort owner from a state synonymous with self-promotion. Cushing had arrived in Paris with a plaster scale model of the valley and glossy brochures depicting unbuilt facilities. Delivering on the promises made to the IOC would prove a formidable task.

Financing the Games was an immediate problem. The original $1 million appropriation was inadequate. The centerpiece of the games, the 8,500-seat Blyth Memorial Arena, which would be the scene of the opening and closing ceremonies as well as figure skating and hockey, was budgeted at $4 million. Infrastructure for the Olympic Village, including a sewage treatment plant, had to be constructed. The state's share of the cost quickly escalated to $2.4 million, then $4 million, and eventually $8 million. Reluctant legislators balked. Although much of the site would revert to state park land after the Olympics, Cushing and other private developers would reap the profits.

Governor Knight and his successor, Edmund "Pat" Brown, however, stood firmly behind the project. California was the fastest growing state in the Union but still suffered from a nagging inferiority complex. The Olympics represented an unparalleled opportunity to promote the state on the world stage. The possibility that California might not take advantage of this opportunity and forfeit the Games was unthinkable. A new state agency, the California Olympic Commission, was created to coordinate development at Squaw Valley and administer the games. H. D. Thoreau, great-grandnephew of the famous writer, was appointed managing director of the Games.

Cushing had expected to chair the organizing committee but was eased out of the process in 1956 as the budget soared. San Francisco businessman Prentis Cobb Hale, Jr., headed the Olympic Organizing Committee and rallied private support for the Games. The committee provided Cushing two free tickets to the Games, but he had no official connection with the project he had made possible.

At some point between the IOC's vote in 1955 and the opening ceremonies, the idea of a rustic, intimate Games was forgotten. This was, after all, California. Walt Disney was enlisted as pageant director and promised a spectacle no one would soon forget. The Olympic Village would be decorated with giant snow sculptures made of plaster, which, Disney insisted, looked like actual snow. The athletes would be treated to nightly entertainments hosted by television personality Art Linkletter, including a "western night" featuring a frontier saloon motif and highlighted by a mock gunfight with movie cowboys. Such Hollywood touches, as well as the proximity of Nevada's glittering gambling casinos, caused several European delegates to worry that the combination of western informality and show business would taint the Games, one expressing the fear that Squaw Valley would be "a second Disneyland" ("All Set for the Games," *Sports Illustrated,* February 18, 1960). Addressing the IOC in San Francisco five days before the Games began, IOC president Avery Brundage also seemed to have Disney in mind. "Sport," he warned, "must be amateur or it is not sport at all, but a branch of the entertainment business" (*New York Times,* February 14, 1960).

The Olympic facilities themselves were, if not exactly rustic, tightly bunched in the valley, and athletes could walk from their rooms to most of the events. The only venue outside Squaw Valley was the Nordic skiing course, located 12 miles away at McKinney Creek. Several Scandinavian nations noted the course was more than 6,000 feet above sea level and worried that the thin air would ruin the races. While the cross-country racers worried about the altitude, they at least knew they would have races to run. Citing a lack of potential entrants and the high cost, the organizing committee announced it would not build a bobsled course. The sport had been a fixture since the 1924 Games, but the bobsledders' protests were ignored. They held their own world championships in Cortina d'Ampezzo two weeks before the Squaw Valley Games.

New technologies were introduced. For the first time, both the indoor and outdoor skating rinks were artificially refrigerated, and electronic timing and scoring devices were installed to determine medalists and flash results to the press. Organizers hoped to reduce traffic congestion by directing spectators to outlying parking lots paved with packed snow and sand and delivering them to the venues by bus.

As costs mounted, Congress and the state of Nevada pitched in to fund construction. By 1960, the cost of turning Squaw Valley into an Olympic site totaled $15 million. The final bill, including indirect expenses such as the accelerated completion of the interstate highway linking San Francisco and Reno and the expansion of Reno's municipal airport, eventually reached an estimated $20 million.

As the organizers rushed to complete construction, cold war rivalries threatened to disrupt the Games. The China question posed the most serious danger. The United States refused to recognize the People's Republic of China, insisting that Taiwan's nationalist regime represented China. The People's Republic had withdrawn from the IOC in 1958, but the nationalists remained a problem. The IOC voted that the Taiwan government could not represent China either, triggering threats of reprisals from Congress and pro-nationalist groups in the United States. As a compromise, the IOC allowed Taiwanese officials, who had no Winter Games athletes in any case, to attend because they had been invited prior to the decertification vote. India, fearful of offending the People's Republic, withdrew. East and West Germany were willing to field a joint team, but the State Department refused to issue visas to the full complement of East German officials and journalists, claiming the delegation included spies and propagandists. Again a compromise was reached.

Despite a blizzard that tangled traffic and forced a brief delay in the opening ceremonies, Squaw Valley welcomed the world on February 18, 1960. Nearly 800 athletes from thirty nations were on hand, along with 12,500 paying spectators. For the first time, a television audience watched the ceremonies live across the United States. Disney came through in lavish style: a chorus of 2,500 accompanied by a 1,200-piece band performed as 1952 gold medalist Andrea Mead Lawrence skied down Papoose Peak bearing the Olympic torch. She passed the flame to speed skater Ken Henry, who circled the outdoor rink before lighting the ceremonial torch atop the Tower of Nations. As he did, 2,000 pigeons, feathered stand-ins for doves of peace, were released from inside the arena and swirled overhead. A few stragglers stayed behind and roosted in the eaves, making encore appearances from time to time throughout the Games.

The blizzard that nearly disrupted the ceremonies forced a one-day delay in the downhill skiing events and reminded organizers that too much snow could prove as problematic as too little. French ski official Robert Faure noted Squaw's proximity to Donner Pass. ''The history of America's march westward,'' he observed, "is full of tragic adventures of pioneers perishing in the snow" ("Squawk Valley," *Time,* February 8, 1960, p. 50). Once the remains of the blizzard were cleared away, however, neither the weather nor the altitude played a significant role. Attendance picked up, and the athletes provided several memorable performances, with a surprising number coming from members of the host team.

Figure skaters Carol Heiss and David Jenkins captured gold medals, while Americans also claimed silver medals in the women's and pairs events. Penny Pitou, the leading U.S. hope for a skiing medal, captured two silvers, trailing Germany's Heidi Biebl in the downhill and Switzerland's Yvonne Ruegg in the giant slalom. Teammate Betsey Snite finished second to Canada's Anne Heggtveit in the slalom.

The most astounding U.S. victory, and one of the most unlikely triumphs during the Games, came in ice hockey. The underdog Americans upset Canada, 2–1, and the Soviet Union, 3–2, thanks to the acrobatic play of goalie Jack McCartan and the scoring of brothers Bill and Roger Christian. The United States clinched the gold medal with a come-from-behind 9–4 victory over Czechoslovakia. Reporters eager to detect signs of a thaw in the cold war made much of the fact that Soviet hockey captain Nikolai Sologubov visited the U.S. locker room before the final period of the gold medal game and urged the weary Americans to rejuvenate themselves with oxygen. "The big joke," McCartan later admitted, "was that the guys who didn't take the oxygen were the ones who scored the goals" ("The Way It Used to Be." *Time,* February 11, 1980, p. 8).

Sweden's Kars Lestander captured the biathlon, a skiing and shooting event contested for the first time at Squaw Valley. Lestander logged the fifteenth fastest time over the 20-kilometer course but was perfect on each of his twenty rifle shots. Veikko Hakulinen of Finland, the 1952 gold medalist in the 50-kilometer cross-country race, narrowly missed recapturing his title as he finished behind teammate Kalevi Kamalainen, but he helped his nation capture the 40-kilometer relay by overtaking the leader in the final 50 meters.

Women's speed skating was also contested for the first time at Squaw Valley, and the Soviet Union's Lidia Skoblikova won gold medals in both the 1,500- and 3,000-meter races. The Soviet men dominated their events as the U.S.S.R. claimed six gold medals in speed skating. Overall, the Soviet Union claimed twenty-one medals, including seven golds, more than any other nation. The combined German team took four gold medals home. The United States, Norway, and Sweden each won three.

The Games closed with another Disney-produced ceremony on February 28. Total paid attendance for the eleven days was 240,904, fewer than the 300,000 whom organizers had hoped for, but still a record. Visitors to the valley, however, were only a fraction of the total audience.

The Columbia Broadcasting System (CBS) purchased exclusive rights to the Games for $50,000 and found it difficult to sell enough advertising before the

Games to cover its investment. As the Games went on, however, and American athletes encountered unexpected success, audiences for the network's nightly coverage increased steadily. The medium was still testing its wings in 1960, but as *Sports Illustrated* marveled after the Games, "It soared triumphantly over Squaw and bore a whole nation of sports fans into new heights of excitement."

The Olympic site was turned over to California's State Division of Beaches and Parks two days after the closing ceremonies. As critics feared, it became a white elephant, requiring continuing subsidies as commercial developers found they could not generate enough revenue to maintain the facility. The Squaw Valley Games, which Alexander Cushing had promised would be "unadorned, clean and simple" and a throwback to simpler days, were in fact symbolic of modern times.

Frankly conceived to yield private profit, the Squaw Valley Games became a public project. Government funding was rationalized on the grounds that the Olympic site would become a recreation area for the people, albeit one operated by private corporations. The intermingling of state and corporate interests fueled the U.S. postwar economic boom, a boom that was most explosive in California, where the defense and aerospace industries, utterly reliant on government support, led the economy.

The organizers also consciously turned their back on the elitism of posh European resorts and embraced American popular culture. Squaw Valley was, in fact, another Disneyland, an artfully created artificial environment. After Squaw Valley, network television cameras and the viewers at home, not spectators at the site, would become the primary Olympic audience. The unexpected success of the 1960 Winter Games as television entertainment presaged the vast audiences and multimillion dollar television contracts that would radically alter future Games.

BIBLIOGRAPHICAL ESSAY

The California State Archives in Sacramento hold the records of both the California Olympic Commission and the State Division of Beaches and Parks, as well as legislative documents concerning state appropriations both before and after the Games. Among the holdings are design blueprints for Squaw Valley's buildings. No specific user's guide is available, but the archives are indexed in a topical card catalog. Since the valley lies within the boundaries of the Tahoe National Forest, more information on the development of Squaw Valley may be found in the files of the U.S. Forest Service, Department of Agriculture, held by the National Archives and Records Administration, Washington, D.C.

Los Angeles Times columnist and Olympic Games historian Bill Henry served as official public address announcer for the Squaw Valley games. His papers, including Olympic memorabilia, are in the Occidental College Library, Los Angeles. The Avery Brundage Papers at the University of Illinois contain material from the organizing committee, newspaper clippings, photographs, programs, and press releases, as well as information on the Disney pageants and some newsreel footage of the Games.

Official reports include Robert Rubin, ed., *VIII Olympic Winter Games, Squaw Valley, California, 1960: Final Report* (Sacramento, 1960); the organizing committee's report to the IOC, Arthur G. Lentz and Asa S. Bushnell, eds., *United States 1960 Olympic Book: Quadrennial Report of the United States Olympic Committee* (New York, 1961); and K. P. Farmer and E. H. Radford, eds., *Canada Competes at the Olympic Games 1960* (Montreal, 1961). See also the German report, *Die Olympische Spiele 1960, Rom-Squaw Valley. Das Offizielle Standardwerk des Nationalen Olympischen Komittees* (Stuttgart, 1960).

Secondary literature on the Squaw Valley Games is limited. Aside from the standard general histories of the Olympic Games, see Harald Lechenperg, ed., *Olympic Games 1960: Squaw Valley, Rome,* translated by Benjamin B. Lacy, Jr. (New York, 1960), for a detailed if plodding chronicle of the event. The Disney contribution is described in John Ormond, ed., *The Pageantry Story* (Burbank, Calif., 1960).

The most thorough contemporary newspaper coverage of the Games may be found in San Francisco's dailies, the *Chronicle* and the *Examiner.* The *Los Angeles Times,* under sports editor Paul Zimmerman, offered fewer column inches but better writing. The tone of the California dailies can best be described as euphoric, testimony to the state's psychological as well as material investment in the Games' success. *Sports Illustrated*'s coverage of the Games, spearheaded by Roy Terrell, was exemplary. Among general interest magazines in the period leading up to the Games, the *Saturday Evening Post* and *Life* provided some coverage, and *Time* and the *Nation* occasionally examined the mushrooming cost of the Games with a jaundiced eye.

The best evidence of the Squaw Valley Games would be kinescopes of CBS-TV's eleven days of coverage, anchored by Walter Cronkite. Some footage survives in scattered form at the network and in the hands of private collectors, but neither the Museum of Television and Radio in New York nor the UCLA Film and Television Archives in Los Angeles, the most accessible sources, holds a copy.

Newsreels were still alive in 1960 and present an alternate source of visual evidence that should not be ignored. The Brundage Collection and the UCLA Archives, for instance, both include the Hearst Metrotone footage of the Games, and excerpts are available at audiovisual centers across the country.

Tim Ashwell

INNSBRUCK 1964

IXTH OLYMPIC WINTER GAMES

Innsbruck first entered the bidding to host the Winter Olympics in the mid-1950s with an effort to secure the 1960 Games. The Austrian provincial capital was matched against St. Moritz, Switzerland; Garmisch-Partenkirchen, West Germany; and Squaw Valley, United States. The International Olympic Committee (IOC) struggled with the decision, delaying voting for several hours as the committee debated and called back the Innsbruck and Squaw Valley delegations for further descriptions of their facilities and plans.

The result came as a major surprise, and for the first time in twenty-eight years the Winter Games were awarded to a non-European city. Unofficially, Squaw Valley edged the Tyrolean city by a count of 32–30, leading local newspapers to decry the defection of two European delegates who voted against Innsbruck: "European envy, Europe's inherited disease, caused the defeat." The *Tiroler Nachrichten* echoed the bitterness, saying of Squaw Valley that "with the help of the Olympic Games, they want to polish up a bankrupt or nonexisting winter resort." But Austrian organizers persevered, and in May 1959 they were awarded the 1964 Winter Games. Innsbruck, receiving 49 votes, was selected on the first ballot, outpolling Calgary, Canada, and Lahti, Finland.

Austrians viewed the selection of Innsbruck as host city as ratification of the progress their nation had made since World War II. After emerging from the Third Reich in 1945 and Allied occupation in 1955, Austria embarked on a period of sustained economic growth coupled with a burgeoning spirit of national consciousness. Austria enjoyed full employment and lack of labor strife and gave credit to the "social partnership," the system adopted to allow corporatism, state intervention, and compromise to create consensual settlement of controversial issues. This "Austrian model" helped place the nation on a par technologically and economically with other leading Western European countries.

Innsbruck, capital of Tyrol province and home to 100,000 people, shared fully in this economic optimism. Austrian officials had dedicated about twenty million of Marshall Plan funds toward the development of ski resorts in the western provinces, and with Toni Sailer's 1956 sweep of Alpine gold medals, they stood poised to capitalize on their investment. By 1964 Austria was the world's leading exporter of ski equipment and the second largest producer behind West Germany. The Inn River valley enjoyed a full measure of the dynamic economic development, becoming a major continental summer tourist destination. The western provinces of Tyrol, Salzburg, and Carthinia led the way in attracting foreign visitors: tourism accounted for 9 percent of Austria's per capita national income, and revenue from foreign tourists grew to $362.4 million by the end of 1963. Otto Spitz, Austrian trade delegate to the United States, spoke for many when he said "We are hoping that the Olympics will establish Innsbruck and the Tyrol as one of Europe's top sports and tourist attractions."

Toward that end, organizers spent nearly forty million preparing for the Games. A new ski area was carved out of the mountains at Axamer Lizum 12 miles from Innsbruck to accommodate the Alpine events, a new ice stadium was constructed in the city, the Nordic venue at Seefeld was renovated, a new bobsled and luge course and two ski jumping hills overlooked the city, and eight eleven-story apartment buildings were erected to house the athletes. A fifty-foot screen was erected to hide from view the only remaining building damaged by World War II bombs. Private businesses also built several new hotels and restaurants, ski lifts, and parking lots, and area roads and bridges were fortified to handle the expected onslaught of some 150,000 daily visitors. Organizers planned to move the spectators through a bus system connecting the widely scattered athletic venues and banned private automobiles from outlying sites.

The physical arrangement of the Innsbruck Games drew criticism as the Olympics progressed. The dispersed events and inaccessibility of the Olympic Village—athletes were housed 10 miles from the city behind chain-link fences patrolled by armed guards and were rarely seen on the streets of Innsbruck—detracted from the usual festival-like atmosphere. Only the hockey and skating events took place within the city.

But all of these carefully crafted plans were endangered by a factor the organizers could not control: the weather. Temperatures persistently climbed above freezing, and rain denuded the slopes of snow. The warm weather and paucity of snow continued a recent Winter Olympics tradition. Piute Indians had been called in to perform ritual snow dances on the eve of the 1960 Games at Squaw Valley, and Cortina's 1956 Games were salvaged only when thousands of cubic meters of snow were trucked in from distant areas. Innsbruck pundits remarked that snow was as scarce as American gold medal winners, and a standing joke held that the lord mayor, Alois Lugger, had damaged his knees by constantly praying for snow.

The snow famine was no laughing matter to Olympic organizers. With no significant snowfall for seven weeks and facing the mildest winter in fifty-eight years, officials called on 3,000 Austrian soldiers to deliver 40,000 cubic meters of snow to the ski courses. Snow was trucked in from distant sites and then hauled up the slopes on wooden sleds where soldiers hand-packed the courses. An additional 20,000 cubic meters was held in reserve, and six artificial snow-making machines were imported from the United States, and workers labored around the clock to preserve the thawing bobsled and luge runs.

The cause of this unseasonable weather was the *foehn,* the dry, downslope wind blowing from the south that caused both temperature and anxiety to soar. Local lore said the *foehn* induced melancholy, befuddled people's thinking, and encouraged suicides. Some schools cancelled examinations when the *foehn* blew, and many considered it an inauspicious omen to begin new ventures under its influence.

The warm weather threatened to cancel the Austrian national bobsled championships the week prior to the opening of the Olympics. Hubert Spies, head of the Alpine organizing committee, adamantly declared that there be no training delays for skiers. But lugers and bobsledders were plagued by haphazard practice schedules due to the uncertain conditions, and Alpine skiers noted the menacing quality of their icy courses.

On January 23, the same day as organizers held a full-scale dress rehearsal of the opening ceremony complete with the lighting of the Olympic flame, tragedy struck. British bobsledder Kazimirez Kay-Skrzypeski was killed in an accident during a training run. Two German lugers and an American bobsledder also suffered injuries in separate mishaps. When another British luger was seriously hurt practicing the next day, International Federation officials agreed to install wooden lips at the top of the steepest curves in order to lessen the danger.

The run of bad luck continued. On January 26, 19-year-old Australian skier Ross Milne died after striking a tree on the Patscherkofel ski course. Two other serious accidents and a near miss by Prince Karim, the aga khan of Iran (who would place fifty-third of eighty-eight in the giant slalom and fifty-ninth of seventy-seven in the downhill), persuaded officials to cancel the following day's practice session and inspect the trail for hazards. This disastrous beginning to what should have been a sporting frolic raised troublesome questions. Some argued that the Alpine events be split into two separate divisions, one for nations with a skiing tradition and one for non-Alpine countries.

Such a radical plan could not be implemented for the 1964 Games, but officials did react to the carnage by ordering additional safety precautions. Two extra compulsory gates were added to the men's downhill run at Patscherkofel, a trail now known to the European press as the ''Course of Fear,'' and hundreds of tree trunks lining the run were padded with straw. The women's downhill course at Lizum was shortened due to a lack of snow at the top, and three compulsory gates were added to control skiers' speed. Three doctors stood at each finish line, trails were patrolled by rescue squads, and helicopters were held ready to evacuate seriously injured athletes and reach inaccessible areas. Further adjustments to the ski trails would be made throughout the competition in an attempt to control speeds and limit injuries, but the icy courses continued to frustrate officials and threaten athletes. Ironically, a female British spectator suffered a fractured skull when a toboggan careened off the course during the women's event. In tribute to the deaths, throughout the Games all flags were flown at half-staff and a black mourning ribbon was attached to the Olympic banner.

Under this cloud of injury and death, the opening ceremonies were held January 29 at the base of the Bergisel ski jump, the first time the Winter Games were not begun at an ice arena. Adolf Schaerf, the Austrian president, and Heinrich Drimmel, chair of the Austrian Organizing Committee and the nation's minister of education, welcomed a record 1,332 athletes from thirty-six nations who would compete for thirty-four gold medals. The simple ceremony was attended by more than 50,000 spectators. They witnessed Austrian Paul Aste take the Olympic oath on behalf of all the athletes. Aste injected a significant change to the oath, which traditionally had ended with the words "for the glory of the sports and the honor of our countries." In an effort to rid the Games of a measure of the nationalism that inherently attached itself to the competition, Aste dropped *countries* from the ending and substituted the word *teams.* His admirable intentions were lost on some, however. Yuri D. Mashin, chair of the Soviet Union's Central Council of Soviet Sport Societies, believed "feelings of patriotism may play a decisive role" in deciding who earned medals. He proudly observed that fifty-five of the seventy-four Soviet competitors were members of either the Communist party or the Young Communist League.

In addition to the modification of the athletes' oath, the Innsbruck Games were notable for several important innovations and format changes. The sport of luge was entered on the Olympic roster for the first time, and the ski jumping competition was divided into 70-meter and 90-meter events. Bobsledding returned after a four-year hiatus. Perhaps the most significant advance came in figure skating, where computers were used for the first time as judging aids. The International Business Machines (IBM) company provided $2.5 million worth of equipment that proved a major improvement over the laborious and time-consuming hand calculation of complex scores. Results were posted within seconds of the performance rather than the usual wait of up to several hours. Along with figure skating, eleven other data feeding points at competition sites relayed information to a processing center at Innsbruck University. IBM found it necessary to bring along a backup power generator for the computers. Local facilities were strained by the extra demands of the new Olympic installations, let alone the requirements of the arcane tabulating machinery.

The most notable athletic performance belonged to Soviet speed skater Lidia Skoblikova, who became the first competitor to win four individual gold medals in a single Olympics. The 24-year-old Chelyabinsk physiology teacher triumphed in the 500-, 1,000-, 1,500-, and 3,000-meter events. She rejected the stereotype of stocky peasant Siberian women as muscular and masculine, claiming that "skating makes us more feminine." Innsbruck also marked the first time that sisters won gold medals. French skiers Christine and Marielle Goitschel finished first and second, respectively, in the women's slalom, then traded places in the giant slalom. Marielle caused a stir in the Village after her victory by announcing her engagement to French skier Jean-Claude Killy. Killy was unaware of the arrangements, and later Marielle admitted that it was all a hoax.

The Innsbruck Games were the occasion at which Avery Brundage announced that South Africa would be barred from the upcoming Tokyo Summer Games due to its policy of racial segregation in sports. The IOC also granted full recognition to the national Olympic committees from Algeria, Nigeria, Congo Brazzaville, and Sierra Leone, bringing to 114 the number of nations fully vested in the Olympic movement. Grenoble, France, was chosen narrowly over Banff, Canada, to host the 1968 Winter Games.

Predictably, Innsbruck did not escape without a share of controversy. Both men's and women's figure skating finals were marked by protests concerning biased judging. The U.S. hockey coach complained that his squad was unfairly matched against European professionals, and the Canadian hockey team boycotted the medals ceremony. They were one of three teams to finish with identical 5–2 records behind the unbeaten Soviets but were denied a medal when the tie-breaking system was based on goals allowed in all seven games. The Canadians demanded a four-game basis, but Sweden and Czechoslovakia were awarded medals instead. Two German athletes were stripped of their silver medals when it was determined that they were professionals. After France dominated the Alpine skiing events, a sore point for the proud Austrians, Rupert Zimmerebner, chief of mission for the Austrian ski team, criticized his squad's dedication and training habits. Still, the home team performed well, capturing four gold, five silver, and three bronze medals, to finish second in the unofficial medal standings behind the Soviet Union, which collected twenty-five medals, including twelve gold.

Off the field, American officials decried the rough treatment three of their athletes received at the hands of Innsbruck police after they were charged with stealing a car and resisting arrest. The charges were later reduced, but Judge Franz Obholzer refused any court discussion of the alleged brutality. In other incidents troopers were accused of roughing up female spectators, and several newsmen claimed that they were harassed by police. Five Iranian students were arrested for parading with anti-shah banners, and another twenty-five were detained after demonstrating for the release of their countrymen. One week after the closing ceremony, three Missoula, Montana, students were given suspended sentences for stealing flags hoisted at the Games. The recalcitrant souvenir hunters were warned to avoid Austria in their future travels.

In a grim reminder of the pall that hung over the opening of the Games, soon after the Olympic flame was extinguished, two competitors were killed in a freak accident. German Barbi Henneberger and American Wallace "Bud" Werner were buried under a Swiss avalanche while filming a skiing movie.

The Winterspiele at Innsbruck ended on February 9, 1964. The Games surmounted tragedy, contention, and uncooperative weather. Trade delegate Spitz placed the spectacle in an economic perspective, maintaining that "revenues from the Games will be small compared to the total investment. We'll get back our investment in the Olympics, all right. But it will take some time. At least two or three seasons."

BIBLIOGRAPHICAL ESSAY

A significant amount of primary source material for the 1964 Innsbruck Games may be found in the Avery Brundage Collection at the University of Illinois Archives. Brundage was president of the IOC at this time, and his papers include information on Innsbruck's bid to host the Games, on films and television broadcasts of the Games, as well as a range of organizing committee publications, clippings, and press releases.

The official report of the organizing committee is Friedl Wolfgang and Bertl Neumann, *Official Report of the IXth Olympic Winter Games Innsbruck 1964* (Vienna, 1967). The report was also published in German and French editions. The committee published souvenir books, daily programs, and reports of the results, often in multilingual editions, as well as *IX. Olympische Winterspiele Bulletin,* a multilingual newsletter published intermittently between September 1961 and May 1964.

The U.S. Olympic Committee report is Arthur G. Lentz and Asa S. Bushnell, eds., *1964 United States Olympic Book* (New York, 1965), which covers both Summer and Winter Games. The British counterpart is Doug Gardner, ed., *The British Olympic Association Official Report of the Olympic Games 1964: 18th Olympiad, Tokyo, October 10–October 24; 9th Winter Olympic Games, Innsbruck, January 29–February 9* (London, 1965). Francis J. Shaughnessy, J. H. Bowden, and E. H. Radford, eds., *Canada Competes at the Olympic Games 1964* (Montreal, 1965), is the official report of the Canadian Olympic Association, while *Die VIII. Olympischen Winterspiele Innsbruck 1964, das Offizielle Standardwerk des Nationalen Olympischen Komitees fur Deutschland* (Stuttgart, 1964) tells the official German story, even while misnumbering the Games.

Secondary literature about the Games is sparse, especially in English. Harald Lechenperg, *Olympic Games 1964: Innsbruck-Tokyo* (New York, 1965), is a pictorial survey. Christopher Ondaatge and Gordon Currie, *Olympic Victory* (Toronto, 1967), recounts the victory of the Canadian bobsled team. Kurt Bernegger et al., *Olympia Innsbruck 1964* (Innsbruck, 1964), chronicles all aspects of the Games.

The *New York Times* and *Sports Illustrated* provided good coverage of the competition during the Games.

For those seeking to understand the host country, a good starting point is William M. Johnson, *The Austrian Mind: An Intellectual and Social History, 1848–1938* (Berkeley, 1983), which provides an interesting overview of the thinking that has shaped Austria. Kurt Steiner, ed., *Modern Austria* (Palo Alto, Calif., 1981), gives an excellent summary of the political, cultural, and social forces at work in the nations, while John Fitzmaurice, *Austrian Politics and Society Today: In Defence of Austria* (Basingstroke, England, 1990), examines the less fortunate characteristics of Austrian public life. Fitzmaurice deals with the provincialism, pragmatism, and absence of open debate on key issues that have marked postwar Austria, arguing that they have produced a weak ethical climate in politics.

John J. Kennedy, Jr.

GRENOBLE 1968

XTH OLYMPIC WINTER GAMES

When French president Charles de Gaulle officially declared open the Xth Olympic Winter Games in Grenoble, France, on February 8, 1968, the future of the Olympic Winter Games had rarely looked bleaker from the perspective of the International Olympic Committee (IOC). With President Avery Brundage at the lead, the IOC and the Olympic movement seemed to be completely at odds with the Winter Games. Almost every aspect of the Games in Grenoble came under criticism for one reason or another. Excessive political intervention, commercialism, organizational headaches, and even the attitudes of the athletes were regarded as contradictory to the true spirit of the Olympic Games. Despite the shadow of criticism and controversy, the Olympic Winter Games of Grenoble saw the emergence of several Olympic heroes and the beginning of some enduring Olympic traditions. In all, 1,065 male and 228 female athletes from thirty-seven countries participated in these first broadly televised Olympic Winter Games. There were also 1,545 accredited members of the press in Grenoble. The competitions ran for an unprecedented thirteen days, February 6 to 18, 1968.

The Dauphine city of Grenoble began its effort to host the Xth Olympic Winter Games in 1960. The bid became official on December 30, 1960, when the mayor of Grenoble, Albert Michallon, officially informed Brundage of the city's application to host the games. The prefect of the Isère, François Raoul, and president of the Dauphine Ski Committee, Raoul Arduin, are recognized in official reports as the initiators of the bid. Even at this early date, Brundage was notorious for his antagonistic attitude toward the Winter Games movement. At the IOC executive committee meeting in Rome in 1960, he asked the IOC to reconsider its support of the Winter Games beyond its commitment to Innsbruck in 1964. For Brundage, the Winter Games did not reflect the high standard of amateurism befitting Olympic endorsement. He pointed his finger at the international sport federations and the national Olympic committees for not strictly applying the amateur rules to the athletes under their jurisdiction.

Grenoble began the preparations required of any bidding city immediately. By the end of 1962, the organizing committee had received several important local government and commercial subsidies amounting to 170,000 francs. These efforts helped Grenoble to be chosen as the host city for the Xth Olympic Winter Games during the IOC General Session in Innsbruck, Austria, on January 28, 1964. After three ballots, Grenoble finally won the bid over Calgary, Canada, 27–24. There was some suggestion that the IOC selected Grenoble as a consolation prize to France, since Lyon had been unsuccessful in its bid to host the 1968 Summer Olympic Games. Just two days before Grenoble was selected, the life of the Winter Games had been given a temporary reprieve at an IOC executive committee meeting in Innsbruck. The IOC decided it would commit itself to the Winter Games until the close of the 1972 Games. Once again, the IOC stressed that the national Olympic committees (NOCs) had to enforce the amateur code more stringently.

Grenoble marked the beginning of a new era in Olympic Winter Games. The Games had become a huge media event, and hosting them meant extensive capital investments. It is difficult to determine the actual cost of any Olympic Games because of the immense capital involved and the many indirect expenses that the hosting region incurs. The official report from Grenoble indicates a total expenditure of $240 million, or just over 1 billion French francs. *Giganticism* was the descriptive word Brundage and other critics used when referring to the phenomenon that appeared to be enveloping these Games.

Not long after Grenoble won the bid, issues that would become synonymous with the Games began to surface. In 1965, the IOC began questioning the host committee's decision to hold events at six distant venues throughout the Dauphine region. Only the skating (speed and figure) and ice hockey events would be held in Grenoble itself. The other events were scheduled for Autran (cross-country skiing), St. Nizer (90-meter ski jumping), Villard de Lans (luge), Chamrousse (Alpine skiing), and Alpe D'Huex (bobsled). The long distances between venues forced the organizers to plan for three separate Olympic Villages—the main one in Grenoble and the other two in Chamrousse and Autran. Early on, the IOC was concerned that this arrangement would be detrimental to the spirit of the Games. At the end of the Games, most observers maintained that a single athletes' village is most desirable and most in keeping with the intended experience of the Olympic Games. The Grenoble organizing committee justified the three separate Olympic Villages by explaining that it was necessary to accommodate the technological advances that were becoming part of the Games. Critics claimed that the strategy was really intended to accommodate the technology of television. The organizing committee recouped $2 million from the sale of television rights, a significant contrast to the $936,667 that the Innsbruck organizers received in 1964. According to the director of technical services for the organizing committee, Jean-Paul Courant, the number of athletes did not increase from the previous Games in Innsbruck, but the number of press representatives increased at a "rate which can almost be described as disturbing." (Courant, "Tenth Winter Olympic Games," *IOC Academy Proceedings,* 1969). Compromising the athletes' experience at the Olympic Games in favor of creating larger and more spectacular media events has, of course, become an ongoing theme for Olympic Games organizers.

Not only were there concerns about the athletes' village, but the selection of the competition venues was also severely criticized. The bobsled and luge tracks were the most controversial. The installations were extremely expensive and received too much direct sunlight, which continually melted the ice and made them unsuitable for racing except in the very early morning. The schedules for bobsled and luge competitions were continually altered, and in one instance the number of runs used to determine the championship had to be reduced because of deteriorating track conditions.

The logistical and economic feasibility of hosting bobsled and luge events at the Olympic Winter Games has become a persistent theme for the IOC and host organizing committees. Costs, environmental damage, and the esoteric nature of the sport are issues that contribute to this ongoing debate. The exclusivity of participation in these sports is often used to criticize the Olympic Winter Games within the context of a truly universal sport movement. There may be some truth to the argument that the Winter Games are simply an event for the wealthy nations of the Northern Hemisphere.

The Grenoble Games held a political significance for France that brought national government personalities into the picture. With the competition sites at distant corners of the Dauphine region, safe and efficient travel between venues was an important consideration. Schemes for road development became the primary responsibility of the national government. Eventually, a national government committee headed by Prime Minister Georges Pompidou was established. Consequently, President Charles de Gaulle and Prime Minister Pompidou projected prominent images of French nationalism during the Games. With de Gaulle, the symbol of French nationalism, and Brundage, the staunch symbol of Olympism, both vying for a platform in Grenoble, it is surprising that the athletes received any media attention.

There is evidence from a 1965 IOC executive committee meeting that French government interference with the French NOC and the Grenoble organizing committee was exceeding the IOC's level of tolerance. While Brundage was openly critical, the French became defensive. In the official report of the Games, Count Jean de Beaumont, an IOC member in France and president of France's NOC, offered a lengthy defense of the French government's role in the Games. The grateful recognition he offered stands in defiant contrast to Brundage's report. This dispute evidently stemmed from an earlier disagreement, with cold war overtones, between Brundage and the Soviet representative on the IOC, Constantin Andrianov, over government involvement in the staging of Olympic Games.

A cold war issue of much greater significance involved the recognition of an independent team from East Germany. The IOC had already recognized the NOC of East Germany (GDR). At this time, the North Atlantic Treaty Organization (NATO) had blocked East German delegations from traveling to NATO countries by forcing NATO members to deny them entrance visas. The NATO initiative was a protest against the international travel restrictions that the GDR imposed on its private citizens, seen as a basic human rights violation. As a NATO member, France was obligated to uphold the organization's policy. While the IOC was prepared to recognize a separate team from East Germany, the French government was in a position to bar the East German Olympic delegation from entering the country. The question of their participation was answered, however, in 1967 when the president of the Grenoble Organizing Committee,

Albert Michallon, received confirmation from Prime Minister Pompidou that the French government would take no action to block the entrance into France of the East German Olympic team. Consequently, the Olympic Winter Games in Grenoble saw the beginning of a new era in international sport. Although the East German performances in Grenoble were unremarkable, their presence made an impact. Ironically, the East Germans' debut was marred by a scandal in the women's luge event. After the East German women had recorded three of the four fastest times in the women's single event, they were disqualified after it was revealed that they had heated the runners of their sleds.

Although South African participation in the Olympic Winter Games in Grenoble was not an issue, the debate over their reinstatement into the Olympic movement was raised at the IOC General Session held on February 1–5, 1968, just before the Games. Beginning in 1961, the South African issue had become a permanent agenda item at IOC meetings. Once the IOC members had voted (by mail ballot for those who could not attend the Grenoble session), the announcement came that South Africa had been accepted back into the Olympic family. The results of the vote were 37 in favor of reinstatement, 28 opposed, and 7 abstention. The possibility of a South African team's participating in the Summer Olympic Games in Mexico City was the obvious consequence, but the accompanying significance of this message was repugnant to many members of the international sport community. Without hesitation, some threatened to boycott the Summer Games. In the *New York Times,* stories of athletes' boycotting indoor track and field meets in New York City nearly eclipsed the final coverage of competition from Grenoble. With the African nations encouraging a broad Soviet-led boycott of the Mexico City Games, the IOC eventually reconsidered its decision and backed down from its proposal to readmit South Africa.

Of all the peripheral events and issues surrounding the Olympic Winter Games in Grenoble, Avery Brundage's crusade against commercialism was the most memorable and one of the most embarrassing for the Olympic movement. Although he was critical of the commercialism that pervaded every winter sport, his primary target was Alpine skiing. Brundage's attack on the ski industry and individual athletes was truly exceptional, even by his standards. By allowing their images to be used in advertising and receiving under-the-table payments, the Alpine skiers, in Brundage's opinion, had gone too far. He refused to participate in any of the medal ceremonies for the Alpine events, and a year after the Games, he spearheaded an unsuccessful campaign to have the medals won by these skiers returned to the IOC.

The most notable effort to rid the Games of rampant advertising was a proposal to have the trademarks removed from the athletes' skis. The IOC negotiated with the Federation internationale de ski (FIS) prior to the games to ensure Brundage that this would in fact occur. At the last minute, the FIS informed the IOC that this was not a feasible solution. The skiers, coaches, and manufacturers protested that tampering with their cosmetics would alter the balance of the skis and create technical difficulties for the skiers. As an alternative solution, the FIS proposed that skis be confiscated from the athlete immediately after their descent. This would prevent them from displaying trademarks while posing for photographs. The IOC seemed reasonably content with this solution until a newspaper photograph showed Jean-Claude Killy, an outstanding French skier, accepting congratulations from a friend and prominently, but probably inadvertently, exposing his Rossingnol ski gloves to the photographer. A significant personality at the center of the FIS/IOC negotiations was the Austrian, Marc Hodler, who was the IOC treasurer and the president of FIS. In its history, the IOC has never lacked for examples of conflicting interests within its membership.

When the effort to rid the Olympics of commercialism was juxtaposed with the IOC decision to welcome South Africa back into the Olympic movement, the media recognized the opportunity to scrutinize the values of the movement and, in particular, those of Avery Brundage. When the IOC made its official statement about South Africa's reinstatement on February 17, the press had already covered Brundage's outspoken criticism over the Games' commercialism. The media characterizations were most unflattering, particularly in France. Following the IOC vote to reinstate South Africa into the Olympic movement, for example, a French journalist working for *Le Monde* described the IOC and Brundage as racist. Indeed, when the Olympic flame was extinguished on February 18, it would have been difficult to find many supporters for Brundage outside the IOC membership. The media played a key role in questioning the social and cultural priorities established by the IOC.

Placing the political and administrative controversies aside, two true sport stories emerged from the 1968 Olympic Winter Games in Grenoble. Rightly so, these are the stories of athletes who, despite being targeted in the IOC's crusade against commercialization, established themselves as icons in Olympic history by virtue of their athletic talents. The dashing Alpine star from France, Jean-Claude Killy, and the elegant figure skating ingenue from the United States, Peggy Fleming, are still synonymous with the athletic excellence that is often overlooked in analytical Olympic history. Killy carried France's expectations for Olympic greatness long before the Games were officially opened. He had been the leading international skier the year preceding the Olympic Games. A lengthy profile of Killy in the *New York Times Magazine* speculated that he could win everything. By the end of the Games, the forecasts were proved correct, and Killy duplicated the 1956 feat of Austria's Toni Sailer by winning gold medals in all three Alpine events. While it is important to note that Killy's medals did not all come without controversy themselves, the combination of circumstances, good and bad, that surrounded his victory at these Games has made an indelible mark in the Olympic history books. To list and discuss the many events that have contributed to the Killy legend would take an entire book. Regardless, it is worthwhile mentioning one matter that is illustrative of the discussion on commercialization. Brundage's threats to purge the Olympic Games of Alpine skiing and its growing commercialism was likely a factor that ultimately contributed positively to Killy's image at the Games. Brundage naturally implicated Killy in the issue of commercialism. The direct and public criticism for accepting endorsements from ski manufacturers (whether true or false) became trivialized or regarded as just another adversity for Killy, the athlete, to conquer in his quest for Olympic triple gold. Clearly the Olympic audience was far less critical of the athletes' forays into the marketplace of sport than was the IOC.

How ironic that Killy, the demon of commercialism in Brundage's eyes, has sustained his prominent role in the international Olympic movement even after a period of some twenty-five years. Jean-Claude Killy retired from amateur skiing shortly after the Grenoble Olympics but remained a prominent sport figure in France. As an important footnote to the Xth Olympic Winter Games, Killy became the copresident of the Olympic Winter Games Organizing Committee in Albertville, France, for the 1992 Games. In two of the three Winter Games hosted by France, Killy has been the most prominent and popular French personality involved. In the greater scope of Olympic history, Killy is not remembered as an athletic hero embroiled in controversy but rather for his athletic accomplishments at the 1968 Olympic Winter Games in Grenoble and his long involvement with the Olympic movement.

Peggy Fleming's fame as an elegant sport heroine has also lasted to the present day. She demonstrated that her presence in the Olympic movement was more than just a sparkle. As the world figure skating champion of 1967, she was clearly favored to win the gold medal at Grenoble, and she did with relative ease. Despite the lack of suspense in the competition itself, Fleming's personality captured the media's affection. The Fleming image fit into the stereotype of the Olympic Games ice princess that probably began in earnest with Barbara Ann Scott in 1948 and persists even today, in large part because of the attractiveness of the sport on television. Although the Grenoble Games took place in the era of racial and gender equal rights awareness, it is clear that women's issues had not infiltrated the thinking of the sports press. While the coverage on Fleming rarely described her athletic attributes, her personality and the nature of figure skating reinforced the media's ideal of a female Olympian. According to the American press, the future of women's events in the Olympic Games looked promising because there were also some "good lookers" among the female cross-country skiers. The *New York Times* described how female Nordic skiers in Grenoble were slimmer and prettier than the "burly and buxom" athletes from the Innsbruck Games (*New York Times,* February 6, 1968). The stereotyping of Killy and Fleming, the dashing Alpine playboy and the demure skating princess, are parallel media images that seem to be repeated at each Olympic Winter Games.

The Austrian equivalent of Jean-Claude Killy, Karl Schranz, deserves brief mention. For Schranz, the 1968 Games may be considered the beginning of an Olympic nightmare for Austria. Many enthusiastic fans of Alpine skiing during this era felt that Schranz was unjustly disqualified after marking the fastest time in a rerun during the slalom event, a dispute that gave Killy his third gold medal of the Games. This was only the beginning of Schranz's frustration with the Olympic movement. The clear favorite for gold medals in 1972 Games in Sapporo, Schranz was singled out by the IOC for alleged violations of amateurism and banned from amateur competition. This was the climax of Brundage's crusade against commercialism.

Controversy dominated the Olympic Winter Games of Grenoble. As host, the Grenoble Organizing Committee was in a difficult position because of the inevitable problems associated with hosting an event of an unprecedented scale. At the same time, the IOC was attempting to resolve problems that confronted the future of the Olympic movement and looked to the Games in Grenoble for ways in which its position could be supported. It is difficult to say if these Games represent a turning point in the history of the Winter Olympics, but certainly specific issues came to the forefront in Grenoble. This is evident by the establishment of an IOC commission to examine and report on the future of the Olympic Winter Games. As the Games in Grenoble closed, the IOC, and specifically Brundage, were predicting a showdown between the Olympic movement and the forces of nationalism and commercialism at the Sapporo Games in 1972. The Karl Schranz episode is evidence that this showdown did, in fact, materialize.

BIBLIOGRAPHICAL ESSAY

Regrettably, few scholarly books examine the Olympic winter Games from a true social or cultural perspective. Although some excellent academic books study the modern Olympic Games and the associated Olympic movement, the Winter Games phenomenon is usually eclipsed in the overall analysis.

This essay relied most extensively on the two-volume official report, *Xes jeux olympiques d'hiver: Grenoble 1968* (Grenoble, 1968) published by the organizing committee in Grenoble. It lists the results, describes the investments and venues in the Dauphine region, lists expenses, explains the administrative structures needed to host the Games, and includes reports from key individuals. Prior to the Games, the organizing committee also published a series of sophisticated bulletins under different titles. See, for example, *Xes jeux olympiques d'hiver: Rapporte préliminaire* (Grenoble, 1967) and *Grenoble—Dauphine—Ville Olympique—France* (Grenoble, 1965). These hard-cover volumes resemble promotional books for the Dauphine region, although occasionally there is some interesting information on the committees and the construction details of the venues. Neither the official report nor the bulletins are easily obtainable. Jean-Paul Courant, the technical services director for the Games, discussed his experience in "Tenth Winter Olympic Games," *IOC Academy Proceedings* (Athens, 1969).

National Olympic committee reports may be useful. The U.S. report is Arthur G. Lentz and Frederick Fliegner, eds., *1968 United States Olympic Book* (Lausanne, 1968). For Great Britain, consult Bob Phillips, ed., *The Official Report of the Olympic Games, 1968: XIXth Olympiad, Mexico City, October 12–27: Xth Winter Olympics, Grenoble, February 6–18* (London, 1969). E. H. Radford and Francis J. Shaughnessy edited Canada's report, *Canada Competes at the Olympic Games 1968* (Montreal, 1969), and the West German version is Walter Umminger, ed., *Die X. Olympischen Winterspiele, Grenoble 1968. Das Offizielle Standardwerke des Nationalen Olympischen Komitees* (Dortmund, 1968). Competing in their first Winter Games, the East Germans published *X. Olympische Winterspiele Grenoble 1968* (Berlin, 1968), and *Olympiamannschaft der DDR, Olympische Winterspiele 1968* (Dresden, 1968) to chronicle their effort. It appears that during this era, the team leaders who wrote the final Olympic Games reports for the NOCs were given some liberty to interpret and describe the team's experience. One is not likely to find recent NOC reports displaying the same candor as those from the 1968 Games. Contemporary NOC reports are generally much more formal and written in a guarded, diplomatic tone.

The Avery Brundage Collection, at the University of Illinois Archives, is a valuable source for researchers in virtually any area of Olympic studies, including the 1968 Winter Olympics. These archives hold personal correspondence between Brundage, IOC members, leaders of the international sport federations (IFs), national Olympic committees (NOCs), and Olympic Games organization committees. Information pertaining to the Grenoble Olympics Games is located in several sections of the collection, and there is a useful printed guide. Microfilm copies of the Brundage Papers are held by other libraries and archives around the world.

Newspapers are excellent primary sources for analyzing the media's interpretation of the Olympic Winter Games in Grenoble. A cursory survey of the *New York Times, The Times* (London), and *Le Monde* (Paris) provides a valuable glimpse at the media's response to the athletes, the competitions, and the persistent issues of commercialism and nationalism.

Wolf Lyberg's translation and annotations of minutes from the IOC's general sessions and executive committee meetings are an important source for tracing the history of IOC debates regarding South Africa, commercialism, and East Germany's entrance into the Olympic movement. These translations also describe the IOC's monitoring of the preparations and progress of Olympic Games organizing committees. Copies of these minutes are available at the IOC Archives in Lausanne and at the Centre for Olympic Studies at the University of Western Ontario, London, Ontario, Canada.

Finally, a journalistic account, *Olympic Report—1968* by James Cootes (Bristol, England, 1968), provides an interesting and thorough account of the competitions in Grenoble and Mexico City. Although there is a British bias, this book is an objective and concise description of the Xth Olympic Winter Games. Another firsthand account is L. R. Hesler, *The Winter Olympics: Scrapbook of the 1968 Winter Olympic Games* (Knoxville, Tenn., 1968)

Douglas Brown and Gordon MacDonald

SAPPORO 1972

XITH OLYMPIC WINTER GAMES

As in earlier Olympiads, the authority of the International Olympic Committee (IOC) came under a severe test when shortly before the selection of the sites for the Summer and Winter Games of 1972, the international federations of the twenty-one Olympic sports voted on locations they preferred for the Games. According to news accounts, this action was a clear challenge; previously, the international federations had simply expressed to the IOC their preferences for selection. While only the IOC had the right to select sites for the Games, the international federations proclaimed their right under the Olympic charter to boycott an unpopular choice.

Among the acceptable choices for the 1972 Winter Olympics were Banff (Canada), Salt Lake City (United States), and Sapporo (Japan). Newspapers at the time indicated that the United States was unlikely to host the Winter Games so soon after the 1960 Games at Squaw Valley and that Sapporo was considered too far away. The chances for Sapporo dimmed considerably following the tragic crash of a Boeing 727, which killed 133 passengers on a flight from Sapporo to Tokyo in February 1966, not long before the April balloting. The path seemed clear for the Canadian favorite.

On April 26, 1966, the 1972 Summer Olympics were awarded to Munich as expected, but the choice of Sapporo for the Winter Games came as a shock to all, especially to the promoters of Banff. Banff had lost the bidding for the 1968 Games by 1 vote and had been expected to win the 1972 vote. The actual vote of the IOC was not revealed, but it is interesting to note that Sapporo won the balloting on the first round.

Banff had appeared to have the unanimous support of the international sports federations; however, the site was strongly and actively opposed by the Canadian Wildlife Association (CWA), which feared that the invasion of the Lake Louise area near Banff would be a disruptive influence on the wildlife. Evidently the IOC felt that it had enough problems without compounding the situation by angering activist bird watchers. Rumors circulated that the head of the IOC, Avery Brundage, raised the issue just prior to the vote. Other members of the committee lent credibility to the rumors by indicating that Banff lost the vote on this issue alone.

This selection was not the first for Japan, which had hosted the 1964 Summer Games. By the mid-1960s, Sapporo, located on the northernmost island of Hokkaido, was the ninth largest city in Japan, with a population of more than 500,000 and was a thriving industrial center. Tsuneyoshi Takeda, president of the Japanese Olympic Committee, announced that the games would be held during the last two weeks of February to coincide with the traditional snow festival, although later, the dates of February 3 to 13 were set to match more closely the dates of other Winter Olympics.

Naohiro Dogakinai, a Japanese bobsledder, civil engineer, and retired civil servant, acted as a major booster of Sapporo during the selection process. As organizer and head of the Hokkaido Comprehensive Development Institute, he often emphasized the potential for development on this land-rich island of Japan as opposed to the crowded, overdeveloped area around Tokyo and Osaka. Naohiro stated that the inhabitants of Hokkaido would be able to attract new industry while protecting the environment.

The 1964 Olympics had provided a needed boost for the economy of Tokyo, and Hokkaido officials hoped that the 1972 Olympics would provide a catalyst for economic development and increased tourism. Rich in natural resources and fish, Hokkaido lagged behind the other islands of Japan in economic development because of its severe climate. While Hokkaido had one-fifth of the land area in Japan, only 5 percent of the population lived on this frigid island. Naohiro and others praised the new technology, which would allow them to overcome the snow and cold conditions. These Olympic Games were seen as the turning point for Hokkaido, the basis for a changing image, and the invitation to join the twentieth century. Visionaries dreamed of the construction of a 36-mile tunnel to join Hokkaido with the rest of Japan. Other plans involved the construction of a major pipeline to carry natural gas between the islands. Such improvements would surely make Hokkaido in general, and Sapporo in particular, the hub of a northern economic sphere that would include the Soviet Far East, Alaska, and Canada.

In February 1971, Sapporo held an international sports week to try out the $25 million worth of facilities constructed for the Games. In addition, the city was able to test its civic mettle and hospitality. International visitors declared the sports week a complete success and complimented the Japanese on their preparation so far in advance of the Games.

The Japanese Olympic Committee budgeted $27 million for operating expenses; the national and local governments and area businesses spent $500 million for new roads, a new state house, and a subway. This level of spending was much less than half of that spent for the Tokyo Games, but it was a tremendous investment for the Sapporo area. Economists predicted that the investment would generate an additional $500 million in related business activities.

In early 1972, Sapporo prepared for the onslaught of international competitors and spectators. Respectable businesses warned their female employees to smile but keep their distance from the foreigners, and nightclub operators offered high pay to women who would move to Hokkaido. Press reports during the Games indicated that these entertainers earned as much as a junior executive. When nightclubs closed at midnight, some hostesses accompanied their male guests to one of Sapporo's 450 *Tsurekomi Yado,* motels where room rates were quoted by the hour. Journalists were also amazed at the number of Turkish baths available to Olympic participants and visitors, where women were available to lather up clients and serve as human washcloths.

Prior to the opening of the Games, the weather threatened to be uncooperative. Mild temperatures created slushy ski slopes and thin ice. By the end of January, however, the *Doka Yuki,* or Siberian storms, began to dump enormous amounts of snow on the area. While experts argued over the quality of the now-powdery slopes, local officials, including Naohiro, visited Shinto shrines and prayed for good weather.

This Winter Olympics was also preceded by freak accidents, including that of a West German coach who was injured when he skated into an approaching snowplow while testing the ice rink and two American bobsledders who were injured when their sled crashed during a practice run. In spite of everything, foreigners were impressed by the apparent calm and control of the Japanese. Robert Petersen, director of the American Cultural Center in Sapporo, said, "If you see someone slap a last-minute coat of paint on, you can bet it was planned that way three years ago" (*New York Times,* January 27, 1972).

Not surprisingly, political overtones crept into the 1972 event. The East Germans became upset when the Japanese customs officials impounded their salami for sanitary reasons. The North Koreans were outraged and refused to enter the Olympic Village after the hosts, who used both Japanese and English names for participating countries, used only the English "North Korea" because there was no acceptable Japanese translation for this nation, which is not recognized diplomatically by Japan. In frustration, Japanese officials imposed an English-only rule for all official country designations. Internally, the nation endured a political scandal when two former Japanese ski team officials were convicted of having diverted training funds to their own use in the form of new cars and entertainment.

More important, the continuing dispute over the professionalism of amateur athletes was raised again in May 1971 when the International Ski Federation (FIS) met in Yugoslavia for its Twenty-eighth Congress. A controversy had erupted when IOC president Brundage had demanded the exclusion of ten prominent skiers who had participated in a ski camp at Mammoth Mountain, California. Since they had been compensated for their participation, Brundage deemed them professionals. France, Austria, Italy, West Germany, Yugoslavia, and Switzerland all threatened to boycott the Winter Games if Brundage followed through on his demand; the FIS indicated that the Scandinavian nations would follow suit and that it would organize a separate world skiing championship in place of the Olympics.

Backing off from his threat to expel the ten skiers, Brundage announced in December that Olympic athletes, and skiers in particular, would not be allowed to display advertising logos, in accord with an IOC regulation that stated, "No advertising of any kind whatever is allowed in the Olympic area, either on things or on people." Moreover, he admonished the athletes to observe strict discipline during the opening and closing ceremonies. This warning received superficial support from the FIS, whose president, Marc Holder, stated that medalists would be required to remove trademarks from skis before having their pictures taken. Moreover, photographers at jumping events would be allowed to take pictures between jumps only if the brand names of skis were turned away from the camera.

Holder arrived in Sapporo on January 27, 1972, to express his support for the upcoming Games and assure the Japanese Olympic Committee that his organization had no intention to boycott. Rather, he stated that it would organize a separate world championship in Europe the following spring if the IOC banned the skiers accused of professionalism. A few days later, the IOC barred Karl Schranz, Austria's Alpine star, from participation for having had his picture taken while holding a popular brand of skis, whose logo was clearly visible. Without hesitation, the FIS announced that it would hold a world championship the following spring to allow Schranz to participate.

Following this confrontation, Brundage became known derisively as the Abominable Snowman. Although he believed that many skiers were guilty of professionalism, Schranz was the only participant barred from competition. He returned to Austria but requested that the other Austrians remain in the competition. Upon his return to Austria, Schranz was given the Austrian Order of Merit and promptly retired. Brundage was burned in effigy. In August 1972, a frustrated Brundage urged the IOC to eliminate the Winter Olympics after the 1976 games in Denver, Colorado.

The Sapporo Games opened February 3, 1972, with 1,232 competitors from thirty-five nations on hand. In contrast to the controversy over amateurism just before the Games, the events themselves passed without major incident. Ard Schenk of the Netherlands won the 1,000-meter, 5,000-meter, and 10,000-meter cross-country (or Nordic) ski races, and Marie-Theres Nadig of Switzerland defeated the favored Annamarie Proell of Austria in two of the three women's Alpine skiing events. U.S. women speed skaters won two gold medals, one silver medal, and one bronze medal, and Francisco Fernandez Ochoa of Spain won his country's first ever Winter Olympic medal on the 70-meter ski jump; it was the first Olympic gold medal of any kind won by a Spaniard since 1928.

BIBLIOGRAPHICAL ESSAY

Sources relative to the Sapporo 1972 Winter Olympics are limited in scope and difficult to access. The Avery Brundage Collection at the University of Illinois Archives contains a variety of organizing committee documents, clippings, and a cassette recording related to the Games. Very few of the available references are published in English; most sources are written in French. Available in multiple languages at the International Olympic Committee Archives, Lausanne, Switzerland, as well as at other major repositories, are Japanese Olympic Organizing Committee, *The 11th Olympic Winter Games: Sapporo 1972. Official Report* (Sapporo, 1972), available in French and English; *Program for the Clos-*

ing Ceremony (Sapporo, 1972), available in French, English, and Japanese; and *Preparations for XI Olympic Winter Games, Sapporo 1972* (Sapporo, 1971), available in French and English. The committee also published, in a variety of languages, a guidebook, a press guide, and an edition of sports regulations. Various participating nations published their own official reports. See Austrian Olympic Committee, *München 72— Sapporo 72. Das offizielle Werk des Österreichischen Olympischen Comites* (n.p., 1972); British Olympic Committee, *The Official Report of the Olympic Games, 1972: XXth Olympiad, Munich, August 26–September 11: XIth Winter Olympics, Sapporo, February 3–13* (London, 1973); Federal Republic of Germany Olympic Committee, *Die Spiele der XX Olympiade Winterspiele Sapporo 1972, das Offizielle Standardwerk des Nationalen Olympischen Komitees für Deutschland* (Freiburg, 1972) and *Die Olympiamannschaft der Bundesrepublik Deutschland. Sapporo 1972* (Dusseldorf, 1972); German Democratic Republic, *XI. Olympische Winterspiele Sapporo 1972* (Berlin, 1972); Swiss Olympic Committee, *Sapporo/München 1972. Rapports sur la participation suisse aux jeux de la 20e olympiade* (Lausanne, 1972); and C. Robert Paul and Frederick Fliegner, eds., *1972 United States Olympic Book* (Lausanne, 1972).

The most insightful English-language dissertation is Udodiri Paul Okafor, "The Interaction of Sports and Politics as a Dilemma of the Modern Olympic Games" (Ph.D. dissertation, Ohio State University, 1979). This should not be overlooked by anyone interested in the study of the international political environment of the modern Games and athletic competition.

Two *Sports Illustrated* articles are worthy of note: William Johnson, "The Big Man Lowers His Olympic Boom," January 17, 1972, pp. 18–19, and William Johnson, "As Smooth as Silk in Sapporo," February 22, 1971, pp. 17–19.

The success of German, Austrian, and Swiss athletes at Sapporo produced several celebratory books in German. See Karl Erb, *Die goldenen Tage von Sapporo. Olympische Winterspiele 1972. Die Schweizer Erfolge* (Derendinger/Solothurn, West Germany, 1972); Erwin Flieger, *Sapporo 1972. Das Olympiawerk der Stiftung Deutsche Sporthilfe* (Zurich, 1972); Ferdi Huber and Armin Och, *Schweizer siegten in Sapporo. Dank an unsere Madaillen-Gewinner* (Zurich, 1972); and Kurt Lavall, *Die Sieger von Sapporo* (Dusseldorf, 1972).

Donna Addkison-Simmons

INNSBRUCK 1976

XIITH OLYMPIC WINTER GAMES

In his 1972 farewell address to the International Olympic Committee (IOC), President Avery Brundage expressed his wish that "the Winter Olympics receive a decent burial in Denver." Brundage had long despised the "Frostbite Follies" for their overtones of professionalism and commercialism and their lack of universal appeal. "This poisonous cancer must be eliminated without further delay," he declared (*New York Times,* February 6, 1973). His wish was almost realized, but last-minute transplant surgery revived the patient.

Denver, Colorado, was awarded the 1976 Winter Olympics in May 1970. Denver had mounted a $750,000 campaign beginning in 1963 to win designation, promising to stage the Games at a cost of $14 million. Its closest rival, Vancouver, Canada, estimated the festival would cost $65 million, and its chances were further damaged when Montreal was selected to host the 1976 Summer Games. The IOC appeared unwilling to grant both Games to the same country, and Denver emerged victorious in the third round of voting. Sion, Switzerland, and Tampere, Finland, had also campaigned for the Games.

Part of Denver's attraction for the IOC was the allure of simple, low-cost Games modeled after Squaw Valley, rather than the increasingly commercialized spectacle that many saw evolving out of Grenoble. Colorado organizers claimed that 80 percent of the required facilities were already in place, and they promoted the state's ability to host a compact, easily accessible sporting festival financed with public and private funds. But Denver organizers, so adept at wooing the IOC decision makers, were abject failures at courting the voters of Colorado. A series of public relations gaffes, unreliable cost estimates, and slipshod planning by the organizing committee conspired to take the luster off the award of the Games. Citizen concerns about environmental degradation to fragile mountain areas, obsolete athletic facilities, and the propriety of committing state funds to a ten-day sporting event when the state faced pressing social problems coalesced to endanger Denver's host status. On November 7, 1972, Colorado voters soundly rejected a referendum to allocate $5 million to fund the 1976 Games, effectively ending the state's efforts.

The new IOC president, Lord Killanin, noted that Denver's abdication posed a serious threat to the continuation of the Winter Games: "I am sure that there will be some people in the IOC who will favor winding up the Winter Olympics altogether" (*New York Times,* November 9, 1972). Killanin later wrote that Avery Brundage "was delighted when things began to go wrong in Denver," and surmised that Brundage gladly would have used the withdrawal as a convenient means to terminate the Winter Games had he still been in office (Killanin, *My Olympic Years,* p. 57).

But Killanin, usurping Brundage's policy, determined that the Games must go on. An IOC spokesman admitted immediately after the Denver debacle that it was "impossible at this time to speculate what will happen, but there is no shortage of towns which appear willing to take over" (*New York Times,* November 9, 1972). Indeed, even as Colorado voters went to the polls, anxious organizers from numerous cities lined up to lobby for the Games. The list of interested cities comprise a veritable Who's Who of prospective winter sports capitals: Lake Placid, New York; Squaw Valley, California; Salt Lake City, Utah; Sion and St. Moritz, Switzerland; Trentin and Cortina d'Ampezzo, Italy; Vancouver, Canada; Grenoble and Chamonix, France; Tampere, Finland; Oslo, Norway; and Innsbruck, Austria.

Several of these cities had hosted past Winter Olympics and were counting on their existing sports infrastructure to defray the costs of holding the festival. Sion was an early dropout, citing the short time left for construction of facilities; Innsbruck, Lake Placid, and Chamonix were viewed as the favorites.

Some of the contending cities were hampered by intrinsic defects. Both Salt Lake City and Lake Placid were dependent on state and federal funding, surely a sore point after Denver's demise, and Tampere lacked facilities for Alpine skiing. Organizers there proposed to hold skiing events in Sweden. Chamonix's bid did not include the staging of luge or bobsled events due to the exorbitant cost of constructing the run.

Meeting in Lausanne, Switzerland, the IOC selected Innsbruck on February 4, 1973, to hold the Games in just three years. No announcement of the vote was made, but it did not appear to be unanimous. Killanin declined to discuss the merits on which Innsbruck was selected or why the others were rejected. He did observe that "the IOC is rethinking the whole question of allocation of the Games," particularly for the Winter Olympics, since relatively few cities could conduct a winter sports festival. Barely one-fourth of the countries with national Olympic committees participated in winter sports, leading critics to allege elitism in the Winter Games.

One important innovation that grew out of Denver's withdrawal was what became known as the "Undertaking." The IOC had an agreement with Denver, but it was not a legally binding contract. Subsequent host cities would be required to post a surety bond and sign a contract that guaranteed they would uphold their obligations as host city.

Speculation concerning the selection of Innsbruck centered on the widespread respect felt within the IOC for Mayor Alois Lugger, the efficient manner in which the 1964 Games had been conducted, the availability of nearly unlimited funds from Austrian skiing and tourism concerns, and the IOC's need to restore its tarnished image in Austria. National hero Karl Schranz had been disqualified from the 1972 Sapporo Games when it was determined that he was a professional, and Brundage had been hanged in effigy and pilloried in the Austrian press. Awarding the Games to Innsbruck was seen as recompense for the affront.

Austrian chancellor Bruno Kreisky was pleased with the decision, saying, "The only thing we cannot guarantee is a sufficient quantity of snow" (*New*

York Times, February 6, 1973). Once again, the Tyrol was plagued by a mild winter, and on January 6, 1976, with the Games less than a month away, organizers opted to enact "Operation Snowlift." One thousand truckloads of snow were hauled in from Brenner Pass, and ski runs were painstakingly hand-packed by soldiers, as in 1964. But organizers were given a reprieve when a storm dropped 3 feet of fresh powder on the city the week before the opening of the Olympics.

Creeping giganticism was a major concern for IOC members as they met at their Seventy-seventh Session just prior to the Games. Innsbruck, with many facilities in place from 1964, had spent $148 million to stage the Games, along with an undetermined amount for security. The price tag for Grenoble's Olympics had reached $250 million, and costs were at more than $1 billion for Sapporo. Meanwhile, the Summer Games slated for Montreal were threatened by soaring costs, unrealistic planning, and unanticipated labor problems.

Killanin took this opportunity to warn ambitious cities to think carefully and budget well before applying for future Olympics. He spoke of the need to cut costs and for cities to carry out their responsibilities when hosting the Games. Many observers thought that the problem of bigness could be alleviated by eliminating particular sports from the Olympic program, but Killanin declined to pursue that course.

A more immediate concern for the 1976 Games was security. Innsbruck marked not only Killanin's debut as IOC president but also the first Olympics since the tragic terrorist massacre at Munich. Heightening the tension was the assault on the headquarters of the Organization of Petroleum Exporting Countries (OPEC) in Vienna six weeks before the Games. Three had been killed and eighty taken hostage. Fear of terrorist attacks was so great that the shah of Iran cancelled his plans to attend the Olympics, despite having rented an entire luxury hotel at Iglis.

To meet the threat, Innsbruck organizers assigned 5,000 specially trained police and soldiers to the Games. The specter of armed troops at athletic venues offended some, but a police official declared that "the highest possible measure of security demands a visible presence. The picture of peaceful Games will suffer a little. Police with steel helmets and machine guns will be a part of the normal street scene during the Games" (*New York Times,* January 25, 1976). Olympic officials were hesitant to disclose the amount allocated for security, but Herwig Herbert of the Austrian Organizing Committee said the costs would certainly run into the millions of schillings. The Austrian magazine *Profil* estimated security measures would cost 30 million schillings ($1.7 million), not including the soldiers, whose expenses were borne by the federal government.

Karl Heinz Klee, secretary-general of the Austrian Organizing Committee, said that security at the Olympic Village would be exceptional. Special photo identification cards were required for entry, and the recently completed eleven-story buildings were clustered behind 2-meter cyclone fencing equipped with electronic sensors. Armed police with guard dogs patrolled the perimeter of the village, and floodlights illuminated the complex at night. The village housed 1,650 athletes and officials, with men and women in separate buildings. Klee, an Innsbruck attorney, said that 2,000 elite policemen would be supervised by Austria's top federal security officials. The two-to-one security-to-athlete ratio might have diminished the charm of the spectacle, but Austrian organizers were determined to thwart any terrorist disruptions.

When the Olympic Village opened on January 27, word quickly spread that security measures were not as airtight as the hosts had initially indicated. "Men can't come to our part of the Village, but we can go to their quarters," confided a female Austrian luger (*New York Times,* January 28, 1976). The eighty-nine members of the Austrian team gave President Rudolf Kirchschlaeger pledges of good sportsmanship at the Baroque, a former royal palace. He urged them to think not only of medals but to compete fairly and be prepared to give their best.

As the opening of the Games approached, organizers had a paradox to contend with. Starved for snow until recently, they now prayed for clear skies. The ski courses were deemed perfect, as evidenced by a parade of record-breaking practice runs. Recent snowfall had freed soldiers from the onerous task of preparing trails, and now they could concentrate on guard duty. Press photographers complained that the soldiers were patrolling so diligently that they were unable to get good angles for their pictures. Newsmen covering the Games received requests from police to report any suspicious or threatening telephone calls, and a special form was distributed to reporters to help them determine if callers spoke in a "firm, hoarse, or affected voice."

The opening ceremony was held on February 4 before 60,000 spectators at Bergisol Stadium, site of the ski jumping events. Two torches, in honor of the two Olympics held at Innsbruck, were carried by 1964 Austrian medalists Josef Feistmantl and Christl Hass and used to ignite the Olympic flame. Franz Klammer took the athletes' oath for the 1,054 participants from thirty-seven nations, while gray-coated policemen conducted random searches of bags and packs throughout the crowds. The aura of monumental ceremony surrounding recent Olympics was muted here. Innsbruck strove to achieve a more human-scale, lower-key approach throughout the Games. Indeed, after having been through the spectacle before, a mild air of ennui pervaded the city, and seats were readily available for most events. Traffic jams were rare.

Competition started well for the home team. Franz Klammer, balancing the fate of the entire Austrian winter tourism industry on his skis, raced to victory in the downhill. Soon there was talk of renaming the Patscherkofel course the Klammerkofel in his honor. But the Austrians would go without another gold medal until the final event of the Games, when Karl Schnabl won the 90-meter ski jump. The medal drought caused local rooters to upbraid national sports officials. Ski coach Toni Sailer only half-jokingly suggested that the massive police presence was there to guarantee his personal safety.

The undisputed queen of the slopes was a 25-year-old West German waitress,

Rosi Mittermaier. She won the slalom and the downhill, on the same course on which she suffered a serious injury the previous year, and placed second in the giant slalom, missing an Alpine sweep by twelve one-hundredths of a second. Mittermaier's efforts proved to be the best overall Alpine performance by a female in Olympic history. Soviet skier Galina Kulakova became the first woman to capture four Nordic golds, but the bronze she received in the 5-kilometer individual race was taken away after she tested positive for a banned substance, ephedrine, a nonprescription decongestant, to clear up a case of the sniffles.

The medical commission deemed other acts less innocent, however. Czech team physician Otto Trefny was banned for life after giving hockey captain Frantisek Popisil codeine to combat the flu. The team was forced to forfeit a victory but battled on to a silver medal.

Another major controversy emerged when the IOC, acting on complaints from communist states, withdrew accreditation from the staffs of Radio Free Europe (RFE) and Radio Liberty. RFE, founded by the U.S. Central Intelligence Agency and financed by the agency until 1971, had been accredited to cover Olympic Games since 1952, but Eastern European nations objected that its application had not been formally channeled through a national Olympic committee. U.S. secretary of state Henry Kissinger called the IOC's actions "a craven capitulation," but the decision stood.

The Games were not without a humorous side. Hoping to show off the refrigerated bobsled run with retractable awning they hoped would become a long-term tourist attraction, organizers prodded Mayor Lugger to take a ceremonial ride down the track. The mayor unbuttoned his trousers to ease his ample girth into the narrow sled and sped away. At ride's end he emerged from the sled, waved triumphantly to the press and spectators, and his pants fell to the floor.

As the Games progressed, the fine weather continued, and even the presence of troops and police grew less obtrusive. Soldiers and guards relaxed as the week wore on, and conditions helped athletes mount a concerted assault on Olympic records. The top five finishers in the women's 500-meter speed skating race broke the previous mark, and the first ten did so in the 1,500-meter event. East German sledders won all five bobsled and luge events, and the Soviet hockey squad skated to its fourth consecutive gold medal. Once again, the Soviet Union topped the unofficial medal table, winning a total of twenty-seven medals and thirteen of the thirty-seven gold medals awarded.

The closing ceremony was held amid tight security on February 15. Killanin, visibly relieved that the Games had proceeded without major disturbances, paid tribute to the Austrian organizers and addressed the issue of encroaching professionalism, maintaining that open competition was a possibility for the future but that it was too soon to welcome professional athletes to the Olympics.

The nation that Pope John Paul I called "an island of the blessed" must have appeared heaven sent to Lord Killanin. Facing the possible demise of the Winter Olympics, Austria had hosted a peaceful, efficient, and successful Games when they were most needed. Innsbruck, the ancient city of medieval walls, narrow alleys, and Baroque churches, had stepped forward at a time of crisis and glittered like a jewel among Olympic cities.

BIBLIOGRAPHICAL ESSAY

The official report on the 1976 Innsbruck Games is *Endbericht/Rapport Final/Final Report/Zakdyuchitedbnuii Otchet. XII. Olympische Winterspiele Innsbruck 1976* (Innsbruck, 1976), with text in various languages. The committee also published the usual assortment of daily programs, souvenir pictorial books, and guidebooks. The U.S. Olympic Committee report is *1976 United States Olympic Book* (Munich, 1976); the committee also published *United States Olympic Winter Sports Teams . . . Media Guide* (n.p., 1976). For the British version, see British Olympic Association, *Olympics '76: British Olympic Association Official Report* (London, 1976), and *Official Handbook of Great Britain's Team: XIIth Olympic Winter Games. Innsbruck 1976* (Kettering, 1976). For West Germany, the report is *Innsbruck 76. Das Offizielle Standardwerk des Nationalen Olympischen Komitees fur Deutschland* (Munich, 1976); for East Germany, it is *XII. Olympische Winterspiele Innsbruck 1976* (Berlin, 1976). The Austrian official report is Thaddaus Podgorski, ed., *Olympische Winterspiele Innsbruck '76* (Vienna, 1976).

Denver's withdrawal as host city is admirably explained in Mark S. Foster, ''Colorado's Defeat of the 1976 Winter Olympics,'' *Colorado Magazine* 8 (Summer 1976). Foster shows how the convergence of numerous political and social trends brought about the referendum's defeat.

An interesting inside perspective of the machinations surrounding the Denver abdication and Innsbruck selection is found in Lord Killanin (Michael Morris), *My Olympic Years* (New York, 1983). Killanin's book illustrates the clublike atmosphere in which IOC dealings took place, although his pronouncements should be taken with a good deal of skepticism. A more balanced look at the broader political context is available in Richard Espy, *The Politics of the Olympic Games* (Berkeley, Calif., 1979), and Allan Guttmann, *The Olympics: A History of the Modern Games* (Champaign, Ill., 1992).

Pictorial works on the Innsbruck Games include *Innsbruck-Montreal 1976: The Pictorial Record of the 1976 Games* (Montreal, 1976); Graham Fulton-Smith, *Olympics 1976: Montreal, Innsbruck* (New York, 1976); Kurt Bernegger, *Innsbruck '76—Tirol, Austria—4.2.—15.2 Olympische Winterspiele 1976* (Vienna, 1976); Hubert Burda, *Innsbruck 76—All Die Siege* (Offenberg, West Germany, 1976); Teddy Podgorski and Helga Zoglmann, *Olympische Winterspiele Innsbruck 1976: Daten, Fakten, Berichte* (Vienna, 1976); and Karl Schranz, *Olympische Winterspiele '76 Innsbruck* (Salzburg, 1976). The last-named book is nominally authored by the Austrian skiing champion.

For an excellent account of the political, cultural, and social forces that have molded Austria, consult Kurt Steiner, ed., *Modern Austria* (Palo Alto, Calif., 1981), and John Fitzmaurice, *Austrian Politics and Society Today: In Defence of Austria* (Basingstoke, England, 1990).

                                                                        John J. Kennedy, Jr.

LAKE PLACID 1980
XIIIth OLYMPIC WINTER GAMES

"Welcome World, We're Ready" read the blue and white banner flapping from the wall of the newly built Olympic Center in the tiny village of Lake Placid, New York (population 2,731). This small Adirondack vacation resort, quite an unlikely candidate for America's premier winter sports facility, would serve for the second time as host to the Olympic Winter Games.

Since hosting the IIId Winter Olympics in 1932, the citizens of this community were eager to recapture the world's most prestigious winter sporting event. Lake Placid had bid unsuccessfully for every Winter Olympiad since 1956. Their appeal to the International Olympic Committee (IOC) for the 1980 Games was the same used in all previous attempts including the 1932 Games: "Bring the Games back to the athletes by providing a simple venue without spectacular production."

If the IOC were to choose an American site for the 1980 Games, Lake Placid was the logical choice. The community had already hosted an Olympic Games, it possessed America's only championship-caliber bobsled run, and it had hosted various international winter sporting events, including the World University Games in 1972. The relationship between the United States Olympic Committee (USOC) and the IOC was a rocky one, however. The city of Denver, Colorado, had won the right to host the 1976 Winter Games but was forced to withdraw its bid after the state of Colorado refused to appropriate the necessary funds to stage the event. Frustrated with what it perceived to be American red tape, the IOC turned to a city it could trust: Innsbruck, Austria, which had hosted the Winter Games in 1964.

There was no clear-cut favorite to win the bid to host the 1980 Games. Despite the Denver incident, Lake Placid had as good a chance as the other competitors, which included Vancouver, Canada; Lahti, Finland; and Chamonix, France. Members of the Lake Placid Olympic Committee had hoped that the Olympics would provide much-needed growth in the local economy, where the unemployment rate was twice that of the rest of the state. The only obstacle to a competitive bid was the acquisition of necessary federal, state, and local funding to improve aging facilities, construct new facilities, and provide initial operating expenses.

When Lahti, Chamonix, and Vancouver all dropped out of the running due to lack of financial support, Lake Placid pleasantly found itself as the only contender. Lord Killanin, president of the IOC, however, threatened to reopen bids or cancel the Games entirely if Lake Placid could not obtain the financial support needed. Reverend Bernard Fell, director of the Lake Placid Olympic Bid Committee, estimated that $22 million in state and federal funds were needed to stage the Games. This initial funding came in the form of $12 million in federal funds to build a new arena, a 90-kilometer ski jump, and an Olympic Village and $10 million in New York State funds to be used to improve the ski center at White Face Mountain, the bobsled run, and various cross-country ski trails. On October 23, 1974, in Vienna, Austria, the Lake Placid Olympic Bid Committee became the Lake Placid Olympic Organizing Committee (LPOOC) as it was awarded the right to host the XIIIth Winter Olympic Games.

Leadership in the LPOOC during the five years of preparation before the games was constantly in flux. Scandal, death, and financial struggles led to a constant shuffling of officers. Only Bernard Fell remained a constant in the LPOOC leadership, and even he changed offices during the period. The first president of the LPOOC, Ron MacKenzie, who worked closely with USOC president Robert Kane and executive director Donald Miller to secure the games for Lake Placid, suffered a fatal heart attack in December 1978. The office was passed to Fell, a Methodist minister who had served as the chairman of the bid committee. In February 1979, behind schedule in the construction of new facilities and over budget, the LPOOC called Petr Spurney to serve in the role of general manager. Spurney, a financial troubleshooter who commanded a $100,000 salary, was well known for his performance in pulling the 1974 Spokane Expo and the 1976 Bicentennial Freedom Train out of threatened bankruptcy.

The LPOOC also had to deal with major site development problems. In January 1977, an Austrian ski official expressed doubt as to whether Lake Placid could host the Games because the site was so far from being ready. Innsbruck and Grenoble, France, were mentioned as possible substitute sites in case Lake Placid failed to complete construction on time. The old Lake Placid arena, which played host to winter athletes such as Sonja Henie in 1932, needed to be refurbished, as did the bobsled run on Mt. Hoevenburg. The Olympic Village would be built 7 miles west of Lake Placid in the town of Raybrook, and Intervale would host the ski jumping competition. The Alpine skiing event would be held at Whiteface Mountain, and Lake Placid High School would double as the Olympic press center. By February 1978, construction had begun and was on schedule. What appeared to be a straightforward job on paper, however, resulted in a series of problems that brought severe criticism of the LPOOC's ability to stage the Games.

The first hurdle the LPOOC faced was an environmental one. The entire Adirondack region had the status of a state park. The state had declared that the region was to be "forever wild" and not to be disturbed by commercial developers. Environmental organizations claimed that the construction of the 260-foot-high 90-kilometer ski jump tower would mar hikers' view of nearby mountain peaks. Furthermore, the jump was being built too close to the farm where nineteenth-century abolitionist John Brown was buried, thus destroying the character of the historic site. Other environmentalists protested the widening of ski trails on Whiteface Mountain and the general commercialization of the small, quiet, Adirondack resort town. Most of these protests were quelled through legislation, but they did hinder the speed of site development.

An even more intense debate raged over the construction of the Olympic Village. Upon completion, the village would serve as the social center for Olympic athletes. It would contain souvenir shops, medical and dining facilities, a movie theatre, a barber shop, a post office, and a discotheque. While athletes during the Games looked with favor on these amenities, the primary issue of controversy surrounded the village living quarters and the role that the village would play after the Games.

In order to secure the necessary funds for construction of the village, the LPOOC turned to the Federal Bureau of Prisons. This government agency would provide the $47 million needed to complete the project, in exchange for its utilization as a federal minimum security prison after the Games. Controversy swirled over the idea of housing Olympic athletes in a "prison." Athletes complained that the quarters, or "cells," were too small. The housing plan called for four Olympians to dwell in rooms designed to accommodate two prisoners. Athletes from several nations refused to live in the village due to the close quarters as well as the distance of the village (7 miles) from the athletic venues. Local protests over the building of the prison in Lake Placid came from blacks and church groups who complained that the prison was built too far away from any major city, creating difficulty for family members who would have to travel long distances to see imprisoned loved ones.

Other problems in site development abounded. The building of the ski jumps and the hockey rink was delayed due to the bankruptcy of the steel supplier. Numerous questions over the safety of the newly built facilities embarrassed LPOOC officials. As late as January 1, 1980, there were still questions about the safety of the ski jumps and the luge run. Construction was delayed on the Olympic fieldhouse when part of the newly remodeled roof collapsed.

In January 1978 federal authorities conducted an investigation of the LPOOC for possible "financial irregularities" in its preparation for the Games. The investigation by the Department of Economic Development Administration came in the light of the multimillion dollar deficits in construction and administrative costs accrued by the LPOOC. Chief fund raiser John Wilkins was removed from his position after being charged with nepotism in awarding construction contracts and failing to submit his Ramada Inn hotel to Olympic board rate controls. While Wilkins was caught in his impropriety, other Lake Placid landlords and small business owners also became motivated by greed. Due to the limited housing available in the village, property owners rented their homes for the duration of the Olympics for prices as high as $60,000. Often tenants were evicted from apartment buildings to make room for incoming guests willing to pay premium prices for accommodations in the village.

Probably the greatest problem the LPOOC faced, aside from financial difficulty, was that of transportation. With little housing available in the village, spectators were forced to find lodging as far as 2½ hours from Lake Placid.

The large quantity of daily traffic that would enter Lake Placid, coupled with the fact that the only access to the village was through three two-lane roads, caused the LPOOC to prepare for a transportation nightmare. The Adirondack airport was upgraded to handle larger aircraft and the Utica–to–Lake Placid train line, which had carried the bulk of traffic for the 1932 Lake Placid Games, was remodeled and reopened. Just 51,000 spectators were permitted into Lake Placid daily, with only athletes, residents, and dignitaries permitted to drive cars into the village. The rest of the spectators were transported on shuttle buses from parking lots located 10 miles away from the village.

Once the Games began, the intricately developed system of transportation failed miserably. Due to a shortage of buses and scheduling mix-ups, spectators were stranded at events in the freezing cold. Some 14,000 luge spectators waited for over 2 hours on the first night of competition at Mt. Hoevenburg. Spectators often lined up ten deep for two city blocks waiting to attend events for which they were already late. New York governor Hugh Carey declared a transit emergency on the second day of the Games for the purpose of obtaining more state snowplows and buses. In describing the first few days of the Games in the light of the world political situation, *New York Times* columnist Dave Anderson quipped, "The good news is that the Soviet Union is ready to withdraw its troops from Afghanistan. The bad news is that the Lake Placid Olympic Organizing Committee has the contract to bus them out." While conditions improved as the Games went on, the transportation nightmare was never totally resolved.

The original $22 million budget for the development of the site and operating expenses did not last long. The LPOOC was in constant need of funds to keep the project afloat. After numerous pleas to federal, state, and local government agencies, the final budget was set at $150 million with $73 million coming from the federal government, $30 million from the New York state legislature, $15.5 million from television revenues, and a projected $13 million from ticket sales. In July 1977 the New York State Assembly established a special Olympic lottery with the hope of raising $100 million to build and maintain Olympic facilities.

On the international scene in 1980, the cold war was clearly reaching a boiling point. In December 1979, the Soviet Union had invaded Afghanistan, causing President Jimmy Carter to consider a boycott of the 1980 Summer Olympic Games in Moscow. Throughout the early part of 1980, a political battle was waged between Carter, who wanted the Olympics moved to another site due to Soviet aggression, and IOC president Lord Killanin, who was intent on keeping the Games in Moscow.

At the outset, the effect of the proposed Moscow boycott on the Lake Placid Games was unclear. Carter rejected the idea that the Soviets should be barred from Lake Placid, but a larger fear was that the Soviets would boycott Lake Placid and trigger a larger boycott of all Eastern bloc countries (possibly one-quarter of the thirty-seven participating countries). In order to save the Lake Placid Games, Carter and Secretary of State Cyrus Vance faced a delicate decision over the timing of the official announcement to boycott the Moscow Games. However, fear of an Eastern bloc boycott of Lake Placid was quelled when the Soviets publicly announced their decision not to boycott. They vowed not to "work counter to the spirit of the Olympic games" by participating in a boycott. The statement served both as a tonic to the LPOOC and as an indirect criticism of Carter's proposed policy toward the Moscow Games.

The other major international controversy surrounding the Lake Placid Games centered around the IOC's decision late in 1979 to reinstate mainland China. The People's Republic of China would be permitted to send athletes to the Olympic Games for the first time since 1952. The IOC made provisions for them to compete under the name "People's Republic of China," utilizing China's national anthem and flag. This decision by the IOC had major implications for the island of Taiwan. Prior to mainland China's reinstatement, Taiwan had been competing in the Olympics as the Republic of China and had been utilizing the Chinese flag and anthem. The IOC agreed to let Taiwan continue to send athletes to the Olympic Games provided they changed their flag and anthem and competed under the name Chinese Taipei.

The Taiwan Olympic Committee refused to accept the new conditions. Courts in both Switzerland and New York State heard appeals from Taiwanese athletes seeking to compete at Lake Placid under the "Republic of China" banner, but all attempts to override the IOC decision failed. The Taiwanese team, upon arrival in Lake Placid, was not permitted entrance into the Olympic Village when they displayed Republic of China identification cards. In a show of nationalistic pride, the eighteen-member Taiwanese team left the Olympic Games just prior to the opening ceremonies.

Despite its isolated location in the Adirondacks, Lake Placid was prepared, with future tourism obviously in mind, to "sell" the region to the world through a well-planned cultural program. The federal government appropriated $1.5 million for the development of a cultural program that director Carol Hopkins called "the most in-depth arts festival that's ever been done in the United States." The festival included exhibitions in sculpture, photographs, films, and music. Performances in the Lake Placid area were held by the Los Angeles Chamber Orchestra and the Cantelina Chamber Players. A large children's art program demonstrating children's artwork from 135 countries was initiated by the United Nations Children's Fund. However, the decision to stage most of the cultural exhibits in Plattsburg, New York, 47 miles from Lake Placid, led to sparse attendance and inadequate conditions for performers.

The Olympic competition itself was fueled by cold war and nationalistic expressions, especially in the light of recent Soviet activity in Afghanistan and the proposed Moscow Olympic boycott. A renewed patriotism surrounded the games, especially among Americans. The spectacular victory of the U.S. ice hockey team sparked a national celebration that touched the entire country. The excitement was not merely in response to the medal round victory of the United States over a clearly superior Soviet hockey team, but in the light of current events, the triumph symbolized to many an ideological victory over an evil, aggressive empire. Even Jimmy Carter used the victory to his political advantage by calling the hockey team ''modern day heroes,'' perhaps hoping such a feeling of national self-esteem would help voters overlook American hostages in Iran, the Moscow Olympic boycott, and a drab economy.

Any discussion of athletic achievement at Lake Placid cannot overlook the feats of American speed skater Eric Heiden. Heiden captured American interest by skating to five gold medals, one in every speed skating event. Other multiple medal winners were Sweden's Ingemar Stenmark and Liechtenstein's Hanni Wenzel, who won gold medals in the men's and women's slalom and giant slalom ski events respectively.

For the LPOOC, the publicity surrounding the U.S. ice hockey team and Eric Heiden took some of the pressure off the organizational problems it had throughout the Games. Aside from the transportation problems, the LPOOC had to deal with an unusually warm winter that failed to produce adequate amounts of snow on the area until two weeks before the Games began. Local businesses were not turning the profits they had hoped for, due mainly to the few number of cars permitted into the Olympic village.

Six months after the Games were completed, the LPOOC found itself with an operational and construction deficit of over $8 million. When the Carter administration refused to provide additional funds requested by the LPOOC, the committee was forced to turn to the state legislature. In a final attempt to avoid bankruptcy, the LPOOC sold all the Olympic facilities to the state of New York for $6 million.

After financial, organizational, and political difficulties, the village of Lake Placid did not take long to return to its quiet simplicity. But its opportunity to serve as host to the world's greatest winter athletes would surely leave an indelible mark on the community for generations to come.

BIBLIOGRAPHICAL ESSAY

The Winter Olympic Games have always taken a back seat to the size and splendor of the Summer Games. The plight of the Winter Games in sport historiography is not much better, if not worse. Very little has been written on the Winter Olympic Games in general, thus making secondary literature on specific Games such as Lake Placid even more difficult to find.

For historians interested in providing the historical community with new interpretations of the Lake Placid Games, the official records of the 1980 Games are located at the Lake Placid Olympic Museum, Lake Placid, New York. All material is cataloged and indexed, and records are accessible to researchers. For further information, contact director Marie Goff at the museum.

The organizing committee's official report on the Games is *Final Report/Rapport final* (Lake Placid, 1981); a separate publication, *Official Results of the XIII Olympic Winter Games—Lake Placid 1980* (Lake Placid, 1980), chronicled the results. The committee also published the usual variety of programs, media guides, and handbooks for the

Games. The Canadian official report is Pierre Labelle, ed., *L'Equipe olympique cana-dienne/The Canadian Olympic Team: XIII. Winter Olympic Games/XIIIe jeux olympique d'hiver* (Montreal, 1980), and the British Olympic Association's report is *Sport: Official British Olympic Association Report of the 1980 Games* (London, 1981). See also the West German report, *Lake Placid 80. Das Offizielle Standardwerk des Nationalen Olym-pischen Komittees fur Deutschland* (Munich, 1980), and the East German report, *XIII. Olympische Winterspiele Lake Placid 1980* (Berlin, 1980)

The most complete journalistic coverage of the local, developmental, and political issues surrounding the Lake Placid Games is the *New York Times.* The *Times*'s in-depth reporting makes it the most useful source of information on the Games. The national scope of the *Times,* coupled with the local interest of the Games in New York, ensures thorough coverage.

The most thorough historical monograph on the Lake Placid Games is a local history written by Lake Placid residents George Christian Ortloff and Stephen C. Ortloff, *Lake Placid, The Olympic Years, 1932–1980: A Portrait of America's Premier Winter Resort,* (Lake Placid, 1976). The work is quite popular in nature, but it does provide information on the politics and preparations surrounding the Games and is helpful in placing the Games in their local context. Unfortunately, the book covers only site development to 1976. For another valuable monograph, see the Associated Press's *In Pursuit of Excel-lence* (New York, 1980). Still another useful piece that places the Games in their his-torical context with other Winter Games is Marc Onigman's "Discontent in the Olympic Winter Games, 1908–1980," in *The Modern Olympics,* edited by Peter J. Graham and Horst Ueberhorst (West Point, N.Y., 1976). The work was published prior to the Lake Placid Games but is valuable for understanding the role Lake Placid has played in the bidding for previous winter Olympics.

Most other secondary literature on Lake Placid consists of books and articles focusing on the politics surrounding the Moscow Games boycott of 1980 and Lake Placid's in-direct role in the politics of the boycott. Most references to Lake Placid in such works, however, are usually in passing. Two such monographs are Derick L. Hulme, Jr., *The Political Olympics: Moscow, Afghanistan, and the 1980 U.S. Boycott* (New York, 1990), and Baruch Hazen, *Olympic Sports and Propaganda Games: Moscow, 1980* (New Bruns-wick, N.J., 1982). While not directly discussing Lake Placid, Allen Guttmann, "The Cold War and the Olympics," *International Journal* 43 (1988): 554–68, is helpful for the political background to the Olympics and the cold war.

The best analysis of the environmental debates surrounding the Adirondacks and the Games is Jane Eblen Keller's "Olympics Illuminate the Long War over the Future of the Adirondacks," *Smithsonian* 10 (February 1980): 42–51. Books and articles abound on individual Olympic athletes and competitions, especially on the U.S. Olympic hockey team. A concise analysis of the hockey victory is E. M. Swift, "A Reminder of What We Can Be," *Sports Illustrated,* December 22–29, 1980, pp. 30–46. Numerous popular books and documentaries can also be found on the team, including *Miracle on Ice* (New York, 1980), which later aired as a television movie.

John Fea

SARAJEVO 1984
XIVth OLYMPIC WINTER GAMES

The 1984 Winter Olympics was the crowning achievement for both the city of Sarajevo and the country of Yugoslavia. It was a statement made by an entire nation that had advanced to the point where it was able to organize and host an Olympic Games. The 1984 Olympics demonstrated the promise of Yugoslavia and Sarajevo, seventy years after the one event that left the city's name indelibly etched on the pages of history, the June 1914 assassination of the Archduke Franz Ferdinand that contributed to the onset of the World War I. What could be considered an even greater tragedy is how the promise the Olympics showed for Yugoslavia was lost and how only nine years after the completion of the Games many of the competition sites lay in ruin, just some of the many victims of a terrible civil war. But for two weeks in February 1984, the world looked to Sarajevo as the center of athletic competition, where all nations could meet and set aside their animosities. The XIVth Winter Olympics gave Sarajevo a chance to shine as never before.

Sarajevo was first mentioned in the late 1960s as a potential site for the Winter Olympics. An international study completed in 1968 stated that Yugoslavia, and the Sarajevo area in particular, would be a suitable location for a Winter Olympics if the proper facilities could be developed. The Organization for Economic Cooperation and Development (OECD), based in Paris, prepared a report concluding that the creation of a winter sports industry in Yugoslavia would help the nation's economy. Officials in Sarajevo decided to combine these ideas and use the Olympics to turn the area into a center for winter tourism that would continue to draw people long after the Games had ended. That Sarajevo should compete for the Winter Olympics was first proposed in the early 1970s, and contact with the International Olympic Committee (IOC) was established in 1971. In 1977 the city set up committees to prepare a bid for the 1984 Games, which were awarded at the Eightieth Session of the IOC on May 18, 1978, in Athens, Greece. In January of that year a group of French cities withdrew from the competition, leaving Sapporo, Japan, and Göteborg, Sweden, along with Sarajevo, as the three candidates for the Olympics. In the second round of voting, by a count of 39–36 over Sapporo, Sarajevo was awarded the XIVth Winter Olympic Games.

Although the entry of Sarajevo into the competition for the Winter Olympics was initially a surprise, the city had several advantages over the other contenders. The scheduled events were to be located in a compact area, with no site more than 15 miles from the city. It also had long been an area for winter sports, and Yugoslavia had hosted the world and European figure skating championships, ice hockey tournaments, and World Cup Alpine ski races. The two other sites had major disadvantages that made them less attractive as host city for the

Games. Göteborg's plan was to have the events at widely scattered locations that would require the use of air transport, which was not a practical method for the movement of thousands of spectators. The original budget for the Swedish Olympics was very expensive, and the proposed cost continued to escalate. Sapporo also was not looked on as favorably as Sarajevo as a potential Olympic site. The Winter Games had been there just six years before, and areas of the world that had never hosted an Olympics were considered more desirable. The Sapporo area in northern Japan had the same problem as Göteborg, with long distances between sites that would require the construction of miles of access roads and a four-lane highway.

One of the two major reasons the IOC awarded Sarajevo the XIVth Winter Olympics was that the Games would help an area that needed the boost an Olympic connection would provide, especially in terms of tourism. A second reason was that the Olympic spirit and influence would move into a new territory, that of Eastern Europe and the communist bloc, and help bring that area closer to the rest of the world. This was the first time a Winter Olympics was held in a developing country, and it was a chance for a communist nation to prove that it was up to the challenge.

Sarajevo city officials were extremely proud of the award and intended to use the Olympics as a means of stimulating the city's growth as a winter sports resort and tourist attraction. The original budget for the Games was $160 million, and the level of popular support for them was shown when a referendum for higher taxes to pay for construction was approved by 96 percent of the voters. This occurred despite difficult economic times in Yugoslavia, with an inflation rate of 50 percent, a large trade deficit, a $20 billion foreign debt, and high unemployment. It did not seem that the weak economy could handle the cost, but after the death of Marshal Josip Broz (Tito), the leaders of Yugoslavia were determined to host the Games as a matter of national pride and to prove that they were worthy successors of his legacy. It was also an opportunity for Yugoslavian athletes to perform in front of their fellow citizens.

The most important Yugoslav officials for the XIVth Winter Olympic Games were Branko Mikulić, president of the organizing committee; Ahmed Karabegović, the secretary-general; and Anto Sučić, then mayor of Sarajevo, who became president of the executive committee. They kept a tight rein on all aspects of planning and funding for the Games, which contributed to their success. The full organizing committee, appointed in April 1980, made the decisions on the program of activities and construction of facilities necessary for the competition. The sports facilities were constructed in consultation with the appropriate international sports federations to ensure they conformed to all regulations. The majority of the sports venues were completed by the end of 1981 and were ready for competition in December 1982, more than a year before the start of the Olympics.

The finances needed to support construction in the first few years after the Games were awarded came from the Yugoslavian government and funds borrowed from banks and the IOC. Money came later from foreign market revenues, which was the largest single source of income. The marketing of the Winter Olympics was a great success for Yugoslavia and the main reason the Games ultimately showed a profit. The money from the sale of television rights, sponsorships, licensing agreements, donations, advertising, tickets, and other sources totaled over $100 million. The largest part of this funding came from ABC Television, which bid $91.5 million for the U.S. broadcast rights. Two-thirds of the total, or $61 million, went to the organizing committee, and the other third, $30.5 million, went to the IOC. Yugoslav Television also produced extensive coverage of the Games, which amounted to more than 200 hours for worldwide transmission to an audience of more than 2 billion people. Although a socialist country was the host of these Olympics, there was no hesitation on its part to associate with capitalist institutions and corporations in order to raise money. Sports were supposed to be above political influences, so it was not hypocritical to accept capitalist money to support the Olympics. The organizers of the Olympic Games were realists as well as socialists and knew they had to have the cooperation of corporate sponsors in order to acquire the necessary funding. There was no other way to host the Winter Olympics successfully.

That the Games were well organized financially was shown by the fact that the original budget of $160 million was reduced to $135 million by finishing construction projects ahead of schedule and canceling the construction of some roads, ski lifts, and parking lots. This contrasted sharply with the 1980 Winter Olympics held in Lake Placid, New York, which was originally budgeted at less than $100 million but ended up costing $185 million and leaving a large deficit. Olympic money transformed Sarajevo into a respectable winter resort that became a source of pride for Yugoslavia.

All the existing sports facilities in the Sarajevo area were built after World War II. In 1978, these consisted of one sports arena with artificial ice, cross-country and biathlon tracks on Mt. Igman and downhill and slalom courses on Mt. Jahornia. Sports facilities that needed to be constructed were Alpine skiing runs, 70- and 90-meter ski jumps, two indoor and one outdoor ice rinks for speed skating, and a combined bobsled/luge run. In addition to this work, construction and remodeling had to be carried out for facilities to accommodate athletes, officials, other members of the Olympic delegations, and the press. The Olympic Village built for the athletes housed over 2,200, and the village for the press had room for 8,500 people. Both were begun in 1982 and completed the next year. Construction work on the competition venues began during the summer of 1979 when skiing trails were laid out on the three mountains around Sarajevo used for the Games. Mt. Bjelašnica was the site of the men's downhill race course, which in order to match international ski racing rules had to have an 800-meter vertical drop but was discovered to be 9 meters short. The problem was solved when a four-story lodge was built on top of the mountain with a restaurant on the third floor where the starting gate was located. This raised the course to the required height. It was also necessary to remodel the 55,000-seat

Koševo stadium, which would be used for the opening ceremonies, as well as the Zetra Arena for ice hockey and figure skating, which seated over 8,500 people and was the site of the closing ceremonies.

Extensive work had to be done with the infrastructure in the Sarajevo area, including the construction of a new road network nearly 100 miles (160 kilometers) in length. The railway station and airport were remodeled and expanded, water and sewage networks and power lines were improved, and fifteen hotels were built or remodeled. The Olympics raised the standard of living in Sarajevo with improvements that would not have been carried out otherwise. This construction greatly increased the tourism capabilities of the area; local leaders hoped these facilities would establish Sarajevo as a thriving ski center and lead to greater numbers of tourists bearing hard currency from the West.

Numerous publications and five films informed people of the progress of work on the XIVth Winter Olympic Games and highlighted the tourist and recreational potential of the Sarajevo region and all of Yugoslavia. The promotion of the Olympics in Yugoslavia included an exhibition entitled "Sarajevo—Olympic City," which discussed the economic possibilities of the Games and the development of tourism. Two of the Olympic films, *Welcome to Sarajevo* and *Sarajevo Is Building,* were involved in the promotion along with the mascot for the Games, Vučko the Wolf. Eighty thousand visitors saw the exhibition in Sarajevo. An international exhibit, "One Thousand Olympic Exhibitions in the World," was a thematic poster exhibition presented in over 1,000 cities on six continents. It was shown in Yugoslavian diplomatic and business sites and cultural and information centers.

The IOC continued its defense of amateurism in the Sarajevo Olympics by upholding the International Ski Federation's ban on champion skiers Ingemar Stenmark of Sweden and Hanni Wenzel of Liechtenstein from the Games for having accepted appearance money. More controversy surfaced just before competition began when the United States alleged that the Canadian hockey team had players who had signed professional contracts and were therefore ineligible. A compromise was eventually worked out with the IOC whereby five men from three Olympic teams who had competed in the professional National Hockey League (NHL) were withdrawn by their countries before the start of hockey competition, while any players who signed professional contracts but had not played were still eligible. The only other eligibility issue occurred when a member of the Mongolian cross-country ski team was found to have used banned drugs and was subsequently disqualified from the 50-kilometer race. With the exception of these relatively minor problems the Games proceeded with a minimum of controversies and disagreements.

The XIVth Winter Olympic Games were the largest staged, with forty-nine nations represented, an increase of twelve over 1980, and the most athletes ever in competition—over 1,500. Thirty-nine medal events were held in a format that included one new event from previous Winter Olympics, the women's 20-kilometer cross-country ski race. Spectators filled all of the hotels in a 100-mile radius around Sarajevo, forcing 25,000 tourists to stay in private homes in the city. One thousand buses were used to transport athletes, officials, and the press between competition sites, hotels, and the Olympic village. This was one area of concern for the organizing committee, since they did not want a repeat of the nightmare at the 1980 Winter Olympics in Lake Placid, where transportation was undependable at best.

The Winter Olympic Games officially began on February 8, 1984, with a 90-minute opening ceremony that cost nearly $250,000 and featured 7,000 young ballet dancers. The Yugoslav figure skater Sanda Dubravčić lit the Olympic flame. Although the ceremony was a success, problems with the weather began almost immediately. The pre-Olympic competitions held in Sarajevo the year before had been affected by a lack of snow on the mountain ski runs. There was some concern this might happen again, and as a precaution snowmaking machines were made available. The problem during the Olympics, however, was too much snow and blizzard-like conditions. The men's downhill race, originally scheduled for the first full day of competition, was postponed three times before it was finally run one week late. The delays ensued when a storm hit the afternoon of February 9 and lasted four days. The violent snowstorms on Mt. Bjelašnica featured steady winds of 90 miles per hour with gusts up to 130, and deposited almost 3 feet of new snow on the mountain, producing conditions with visibility of less than 100 feet. All Alpine events were called off for the first four days but were rescheduled and eventually made up with little trouble. Air transport for visitors was also hurt by the storms, with the Sarajevo airport shut down for two days. But excellent work by the Yugoslav snow removal crews, including hundreds of students, kept the roads passable and ski runs in good condition. The delays caused by the weather were the only real interruptions in an otherwise trouble-free Olympic Games.

The 1984 Winter Olympics featured several fine performances. Katarina Witt of East Germany won the first of her two gold medals in women's figure skating, and her teammate Karin Enke set a world's record in the women's 1,500-meter speed skating race. Women speed skaters recorded the finest efforts of the competition, with the only Olympic records of the Games being set in all four events. The highlight of the Olympics for Yugoslavia was when Jurij Franko won the host country's first-ever Winter Olympic medal by earning a silver in the men's giant slalom. Although this might have been the high point for the people of Sarajevo and Yugoslavia, the Games themselves represented the culmination of years of hard effort and showed what the country was able to accomplish. The XIVth Winter Olympic Games closed with an impressive ceremony attended by 8,500 people in the Zetra Arena on February 19. The promise of national cooperation turned out to be short-lived; Yugoslavia was torn apart only seven years later in a bloody and destructive civil war.

The Winter Olympics was a great success for the organizing committee, which realized a profit of 2 billion Yugoslav dinars, or $10 million, based on the exchange rate in September 1984. The rapid rate of inflation in the country during this time caused the value of the Yugoslav currency to fall dramatically, making it very difficult to determine at any one time the accuracy of the finances for the Games. The surplus was used to develop sports and tourism in the Sarajevo area. The Olympic Games provided the city with a debt-free winter resort to attract foreign tourists who previously had been familiar only with the summer beaches along the Adriatic coast. The success Sarajevo enjoyed with the Winter Olympics, however, was not shared by all. ABC Television had much lower ratings than expected for the Games, which affected the amount networks bid for television rights in the future. This was a serious concern because it limited the amount of money Olympic committees could expect to receive from this most important of revenue sources. A major cause of the low ratings was a lack of live coverage in the United States due to the 6-hour time difference between Sarajevo and New York City and the fact that all of the winners were known by the time the broadcasts began each evening.

The Winter Olympics had a positive effect on the culture and economy of Sarajevo, exactly what the organizers had intended. It promoted the development of winter sports in Yugoslavia with the establishment of new sports clubs and an increased interest among young athletes. Many of the facilities built for the Games were adapted for use after the Games as business establishments—shops, warehouses, catering facilities, department stores, and parking garages. The computer center for the Olympics was utilized as a commercial and banking center, and the Olympic Village became a housing development. The new airport, hotels, post offices, restaurants, and remodeled railroad station improved the quality of life in Sarajevo. It also created 9,000 jobs, supplied training for personnel who worked during the Games, and gave them new skills for future employment.

The glow of Olympic success did last for a time, with a continuation of cultural programs including ballet, drama, and music, and a brief upsurge in economic conditions. But at the end of 1985 Yugoslavia was still beset with severe economic problems, with yearly inflation of 80 percent and a national unemployment rate of 13 percent. The real disaster began with the breakup of the country in 1991, followed the next year by the civil war that engulfed Sarajevo and Bosnia. The sites that had previously hosted thousands of cheering spectators on the mountains around the city now held artillery that rained down destruction. Hotels and ski resorts where athletes had once competed for an Olympic gold medal were destroyed. Although the Yugoslav civil war represented the worst in a people, the 1984 Olympics proved they could put aside their age-old animosities and accomplish what was not thought possible: to host a successful and memorable XIVth Winter Olympic Games.

BIBLIOGRAPHICAL ESSAY

Official records of the Organizing Committee of the XIVth Winter Olympic Games 1984 at Sarajevo should be held by the Archives of Bosnia and Herzegovina on Save Kovačevića 6 in Sarajevo. As of 1996, access to these records is not known, but they are not readily available because of the civil war.

An archival collection that contains important material on the 1984 Olympics is the Olympic Collection, 1976–92 (Record Series 26/20/137) in the University Archives at the University of Illinois at Urbana-Champaign. It is a collection of publications on the Summer and Winter Olympics with items on the Sarajevo Olympics including promotional brochures, the Organizing Committee's final report, and the Yugoslav Olympic newsletter, *Sarajevo '84* (1984–1987).

Several published works on the 1984 Winter Olympics provide excellent accounts. Two previews of the Olympics are Slobodan Stajić et al., *Sarajevo '84: All on the Games* (Sarajevo, 1984), which describes in detail Sarajevo's architecture, its cultural and historical heritage, and the athletic facilities and courses built for the competition, and Phyllis and Zander Hollander, eds., *The Complete Handbook of the Olympic Winter Games: 1984, Sarajevo, Yugoslavia* (New York, 1983), a U.S. television viewers' guide to the Olympics that contains articles on Sarajevo, ABC Sports television coverage, and a section on each of the events with a history of its origin and a preview of the leading medal candidates.

A comprehensive summary is Organizing Committee of the XIVth Winter Olympic Games 1984 at Sarajevo, *Sarajevo '84: Final Report* (Sarajevo, 1984), the authoritative source on the planning that organized the Games and includes information on finances, the Olympic officials and organizational structure, and the construction of athletic and accommodation facilities. Dick Schaap, *The 1984 Olympic Games: Sarajevo/Los Angeles* (New York, 1984), is a fine documentation of the 1984 Olympics published by ABC Sports. It is a day-by-day review of the competition with a human interest look at the athletes.

Several journal articles provide a view of the 1984 Winter Olympics at various stages in its history. An article that examines the cities in competition for the Games is "Candidate Cities for 1984," *Olympic Review* 127 (May 1978): 276–84. Helmut Koenig, "Sarajevo: A Miracle in the Balkans," *Physician and Sportsmedicine* 11 (September 1983): 146–48, 153, describes the preparations Yugoslavia made for the Olympics, and an excellent summary of the Winter Olympics is Milomir Niketić, "XIV Olympic Winter Games, Sarajevo 1984," *Yugoslav Survey* 25 (November 1984): 3–22. Finally, the *Yugoslavian Tourist Review,* a publication of the Yugoslavian Tourist Board, contains considerable information on the Games in its 1984 (vol. 1, no. 1) and February 1985 (vol. 1, no. 3) issues.

Three newspapers that gave in-depth coverage of the Sarajevo Olympics are the *Times* (London), the *New York Times,* and *USA Today.* The *Times* (London) provided a view of the Olympics from a perspective different from that of newspapers in the United States, with interesting commentary on the use of professionals in Olympic competition and the manner in which Yugoslavia conducted the Games. The *New York Times* coverage of the Olympics was thorough, with a number of articles on the disappointing performance of U.S. athletes, especially the hockey team's attempt to defend its 1980 gold medal. Probably the most expanded look at the 1984 Winter Olympics was provided by *USA Today.* This was the first Olympics the newspaper covered after its inception in 1982, and each issue dealt extensively with the U.S. team and events surrounding the Games. The journalistic style is more popular than that of the other newspapers, but it does provide some information on the Winter Olympics not found elsewhere.

There are two videos available on the Sarajevo Olympics: *1984 Winter Olympics*

Highlights by ABC Video Enterprises, which is 60 minutes in length and covers the highlights of each event, and *A Turning Point: The Official Film of the XIV Winter Olympics* (1984), an IOC production.

Robert Dunkelberger

CALGARY 1988
XVTH OLYMPIC WINTER GAMES

Calgary's fourth bid to host the Winter Olympic Games was granted on September 30, 1981, at the Eleventh Olympic Congress in Baden-Baden. Under the auspices of the Canadian Olympic Development Organization (CODA), formed in 1957 and reorganized in 1978, a select group of local economic and political elites lobbied at home and abroad, spending $2.5 million to persuade International Olympic Committee (IOC) delegates to select Canada as host of the 1988 Winter Games. What followed was a massive and elaborate campaign by a newly formed organizing committee, Olympiques Calgary Olympics (OCO), to guarantee the support and enthusiasm of Calgarians in hosting the highly valued Olympic caravan. Olympic ideologies, constantly reshaped and articulated by the IOC according to the cross-currents of particular global relations, had long ago permeated Canadian society, so much so that any resistance to hosting the festival was rapidly submerged, and the integrity of Olympic discourse, with a history of contradictions in practice, was never questioned.

OCO successfully translated the Olympic aura with its attendant ideologies into a cultural happening of volunteering, spectatorship, and celebration, whose residual substance is still visible in the city of Calgary. Facilities, venues, and the idea of hospitality were defined as symbols of identity for Calgarians. Citizens were mobilized on a massive scale to donate time and money as the responsibility for the image of the city, the province of Alberta, and all of Canada was linked inextricably to the success of the Games. Funding for what became known as the billion-dollar Games was provided by the most lucrative television contract ever signed for an Olympic Games, support from all levels of government, sponsorships from international, national, and local corporations, and other monies raised by OCO. An important part of global image construction during the festival was a weakly contrived government- and OCO-sponsored program of native involvement in some of the ritual aspects of the Games and a large exhibition solicited from collections around the world of native artifacts removed from Canada during the European invasions of past centuries.

The building of elaborate Olympic facilities, frequently cited as a legacy to be left behind for the benefit of Calgarians, and the idea of showcasing the city to the whole world were well-established practices and articulated to delineate measures of success prior to the Games. OCO was able to achieve its prescribed goals while attracting little damaging public criticism in the process. IOC president Juan Antonio Samaranch called the festival "the best organized Olympic Winter Games ever" (*Olympic Review* 243 [1988]:4.)

The city of Calgary, once an outpost for the Northwest Mounted Police, a Canadian Pacific Railway town, home since 1912 to different forms of the internationally renowned Calgary Stampede, a rodeo-based civic festival, and oil capital of Canada since its discovery in nearby Turner Valley in 1914 has been faced with varying, sometimes contradictory images.

The capitalist work ethic dominates the oil-driven economy and ways of thinking in Calgary, with an emphasis on a trickle-down distribution of wealth and resistance to any form of federal control in economic matters. The tourism programs of the local and provincial governments emphasize the mountain playgrounds, surrounding wilderness, and the western character of the Stampede; yet the contradictory images of Calgary as a modern, dynamic, business-minded city are promoted just as fervently. The bid committee for the 1988 Winter Olympic Games emphasized these cultural and geographic elements as assets in their extensive lobbying program for hosting privileges. But when the status of host city was granted over Falun and Cortina d'Ampezzo, the organizing committee adopted a vigorous, resilient, and impersonal corporate business strategy in operating all aspects of the Olympic building and staging process.

The board of directors of the organizing committee was male dominated, eventually consisting of twenty-nine members, including lawyers, justices, businessmen, and politicians; former premier Peter Lougheed was appointed the twenty-ninth member. From the successful bid to the closing ceremonies, the individuals exerting the most influence on all aspects of the Games, including media and political relations, signature facilities, and official ceremonies, were: Frank King, chemical engineer, oilman, and chief executive officer of OCO; Bill Pratt, former manager of the Calgary Stampede and president of OCO; Ralph Klein, mayor of Calgary; and Roger Jackson, former Olympic gold medalist, president of the Canadian Olympic Association (COA), dean of the Faculty of Physical Education at the University of Calgary, and member of the OCO board of directors. As part of the bid to the IOC and throughout the establishment of venues and construction of facilities, it was clearly emphasized that Calgary would not experience the same financial problems as Montreal had in 1976. In the final few years leading up to the Games, it was evident that a profit was forthcoming and that endowment funds, secured in financial contracts with funding sources for post-Games maintenance of facilities, would be considerable. The domineering approach adopted by the OCO was borrowed in part from Peter Ueberroth's management of the 1984 Games in Los Angeles. In the midst of many firings and resignations within OCO, Ueberroth gave an inspirational speech suggesting that such things were part of the process. King maintained that OCO would not be remembered for its methods in the accomplishment of tasks, and Pratt was known for his intolerance of ''bullshit and wimps'' (*Maclean's* [February 1988]). Men and women who were at odds with upper-level management were fired or forced to resign; abuse of volunteers, philosophical differences, or a restructuring of responsibilities were most commonly cited as reasons for leaving or dismissal.

David Leighton was hired as president of OCO in 1982 at a salary of $100,000 but resigned under pressure five months later, citing differences in management philosophy. It was suggested that he was not a team player, wanted to use paid employees, and had lost the confidence of the board of directors. Bill Pratt was chosen to replace Leighton, and immediately a volunteer labor strategy similar to that used during the Stampede became fundamental to the Olympic project. The "let's get it done" philosophy of Pratt, at the expense of cordial interpersonal relations, was often cited as a manifestation of administrative efficiency. Conflicts were defined as miscommunications in public and media relations; challenges and criticism were thus structured so as not to interfere with administrative methods and the completion of physical or ideological projects. A three-man committee of OCO members was selected to review the management of the organization following Mayor Klein's threat of a public inquiry. As a result of the report, Frank King was promoted from his volunteer leadership position within OCO to the $150,000 chief executive officer's post in 1986.

Under a reorganized OCO, more full-time staff were hired and 75 volunteer committees were formed, along with over 200 subcommittees. By the end of the Games over 9,000 volunteers, working countless hours, were mobilized by OCO. The unveiling of cultural programs, an arts festival, a nationwide torch relay, and increased national and international media attention as the Games drew closer served to create local enthusiasm. Record levels of unemployment, empty office and warehouse space, and housing vacancies in the years prior to the Games helped to legitimize the massive amounts of construction taking place, under the auspices of job creation, global attention for business investment and tourism, and the legacy of facilities to be left for Calgarians.

ABC television bid an unprecedented $389 million for the broadcast rights to the Olympics. International official sponsors, licensees, distributors, and corporate donations, principally in goods and services, provided funds as well. OCO distributed television income toward facilities and services, while the federal, provincial, and local governments contributed $506 million toward construction and the upgrading of existing sites. OCO guarded the official symbols vehemently, investigating some 300 businesses and individuals and launching fifty-two lawsuits related to the protection of over 200 Olympic-related symbols and words. The "Miss Nude Olympics" at a local bar, for example, was changed to the "Miss Nude O-Word."

After Calgary was chosen as host city for the XVth Winter Games, resistance to staging the Games related to financial concerns, administrative conflicts, and site controversies. All sites for events, with the exception of the speed skating oval, which had not been chosen, were changed after the presentation of the original bid in Baden-Baden. The most controversial site change was to develop Mount Allan for downhill skiing events rather than following the original plan of utilizing Mount Sparrowhawk and Mount Shark. Many groups argued that Allan was a poor selection because of possible environmental damage and its capacity to sustain an adequate ski slope during and after the Olympics. Fifteen years of research on Allan, conducted by the Canadian Forestry Service, suggested that average snowfall was far below the standard required for a ski resort.

John Read resigned from OCO over the decision, charging that Alberta premier Peter Lougheed had personally ordered the organization to select Allan for development, providing a winter complement to the provincially funded $140 million golf facility at Kananaskis. The $27 million development, funded for the most part by the provincial government, was called Nakiska, the Cree word for "meeting place." A $5 million computerized snowmaking apparatus was installed at Nakiska to offset possible problems due to lack in snowfall or chinook winds.

The Olympic Saddledome, a civic symbol and home to the National Hockey League's Calgary Flames, was under construction before the bid was secured. Bill Pratt served as project manager for the $98 million facility, funded eventually by the three levels of government and OCO. Unlike other venues, the Saddledome cost exceeded budget by $16.5 million.

Ski jumping, luge, and bobsled venues were originally planned for the nearby town of Bragg Creek. After some local resistance and sentiment that the facility should be located closer to Calgary, the OCO decided to purchase land on the Paskapoo slopes just outside the city limits. The federal government handled the design and construction of the $72 million Olympic Park. Practice and competition ski jumps were constructed, facing northward, along with an artificially cooled, combined bobsled and luge track despite warnings that westerly chinook winds could prove dangerous to ski jumpers. A first-class training center and athletes' accommodations were also constructed on the site. A private donation matched by the federal government funded the building of an Olympic Hall of Fame.

The town of Canmore hosted the biathlon, cross-country skiing, Nordic combined, and disabled Nordic skiing events at the $17 million Nordic Centre. Construction was justified as a tourism venture to support the town's economy that had long depended on mining. Some thought, however, that such a facility was too distant from Calgary to be maintained as a training center and was both too challenging and not scenic enough for recreational skiers. Some competitors resided at an athletes' village in Canmore, but the main athletes' village consisted of seven residence halls at the University of Calgary. The federal government, provincial government, OCO, and the university combined interests in conjunction with a previously planned expansion to the Faculty of Physical Education. As a result, $103 million worth of new facilities were constructed, including a $40 million speed skating oval. For the first time at the Winter Games, speed skating events were held in a fully enclosed structure. University students were forced to relocate to accommodate athletes, and classes were cancelled during the Games.

Canadians were initiated into the Olympic experience through a cross-country, 18,000-kilometer (11,160-mile) torch relay sponsored by Petro Canada, involving some celebrities and 6,520 public participants selected from 6.5 million applications. The $50 million excursion lasted eighty-eight days, with the torch leaving Signal Hill in Newfoundland and traveling by runner, boat, snowmobile, airplane, and helicopter to the opening ceremonies at McMahon Stadium in Calgary. The base of the torch resembled the Calgary Tower, a city structure transformed during the Olympics into a giant torch visible for 15 kilometers. Affiliation with the Olympic Games proved to be profitable for Petro Canada; it was reported that during the torch relay, gasoline sales increased by $23 million per month.

Another component of OCO's elaborate program of mobilizing support for the Games was the distribution of Olympic Education Resource Kits to 13,500 elementary schools across the country. Children were educated on the value of the Olympic movement and were encouraged to be excited about the festival. Almost a half-million students in Alberta were involved in Olympic-related curriculum projects leading up to the Games, a significant element in generating contrived excitement in a structured cultural context.

OCO's operations were slighted somewhat by a ticket scandal engineered by the ticketing manager, James McGregor. Known as "Jiminy Tickets," McGregor had required U.S. customers to pay face value in their currency to his company, World Tickets. He was later charged with fraud, theft, and mischief. Further controversies unfolded when ticketing supervisor Kenneth Melnyk revealed that Olympic insiders such as the IOC, international sport federations, and national Olympic committee members, along with Games sponsors and suppliers, would receive 50 percent of the allotted tickets for Olympic events. Complimentary ticket distribution to the so-called Olympic family and its guests was an IOC policy. OCO was forced to redistribute some tickets when it was charged with providing preferential treatment to staff members. To satisfy the public anger over ticket distribution, additional seating was added to some venues.

The IOC demanded the usual luxury treatment for its members, families, and guests. For each member of the Olympic retinue, a luxury sedan and driver was provided. Over 700,000 kilometers was logged by the 216 automobiles. These dignitaries joined 60,000 spectators for the colorful, elaborate opening ceremonies at the newly expanded McMahon Stadium. Over 8,000 performers participated, with costumes made by 1,600 volunteers. For the first time, seating was provided for the athletes to watch the spectacle after their entrance.

The Olympic program was expanded to sixteen days to allow for an extra weekend of prime time television viewing. Warm chinook winds gusting to almost 60 miles per hour forced the rescheduling of thirty events. With the performances of Matti Nykanen of Finland, Yvonne Van Gennip of Holland, skaters Katarina Witt and Debi Thomas, Brian Boitano and Brian Orsor whose competitions were translated into epic proportions, and the accomplishments of Raisa Smetanina of the Soviet Union, winning her ninth medal in her fourth Olympics, the Games unfolded as had been promised in pre-Olympic publicity. For the Calgarians and visitors, individual characters, rather than elite Olympic athletes, received the most public attention. Ski jumper Michael Edwards of Great Britain, nicknamed "Eddie the Eagle," and the Jamaican bobsled team became the focus of controversy for officials, satirical heroes for the spectators, and salable commodities for small-scale profiteers. The celebrating and competitive anomalies were a break from contrived experiences but were absorbed readily by the powerful Olympic culture.

OCO billed the Olympic Arts Festival as the most comprehensive and longest-running event ever held in association with the Winter Games. Over 600 exhibitions and performances in the visual, literary, film, and performing arts were presented over five weeks, at a cost of almost $13 million. The most intense resistance to the Games was conducted against ''The Spirit Sings'' exhibition, sponsored by Shell Canada and the federal government and hosted by the Glenbow Museum. In organizing the exhibition, six curators spent five years examining over 6,000 displaced native and nonnative artifacts from collections around the world. The Lubicon Cree called on museums to boycott the exhibition in protest of the many years of abusive treatment of Cree by the federal government. A land settlement had been promised in 1940, and, in the meantime, many natives had been arbitrarily removed from lists officially recognizing their status; trapping lands within a 10-mile radius of the community were destroyed by oil development. Alberta's native affairs minister suggested in 1984 that the Lubicon Cree did not even exist. The United Council of Churches and United Nations Human Rights Committee reported, however, that oil companies and the government had taken actions with serious consequences to the tribe. As a result of Chief Bernard Ominyak's lobbying, twenty-nine museums refused to participate in the exhibition, and 700 Mohawks in Quebec voiced their support of the Lubicons along the route of the torch relay. In general, the federal government promoted native involvement in official ceremonies, medal insignias, and cultural activities to avoid criticism during the Games; OCO was accommodating in order to secure its financial partnership with the government and to suit the usual Olympic requirements of spectacle.

OCO successfully delivered its legacy of facilities, carrying the signature of prominent Games organizers; further, profits of over $30 million were registered, and endowments for the operation of facilities and staging of sporting events were established. While the University of Calgary houses some of the best facilities in North America, with some accessibility to the public, most of the Olympic legacy remains for elite athletes. Hence, venues tend to promote sport spectatorship rather than participation. Since the dismantling of OCO, assets and endowments under the administration of CODA have given that organization considerable power in controlling facilities and distributing funds to sport-related endeavors. Partnerships established with government and corporate sponsors were crucial sources of revenue and aided in the absorption of cultural resistance, while bringing the business of corporations closer to the daily lives and cultural experiences of Canadians. Thousands of Canadians were mobilized and animated through this event, particular images were portrayed to the world, and Calgary continues to bear the physical and ideological residue of a Winter Olympic city.

BIBLIOGRAPHICAL ESSAY

For an overview of sources pertaining to the Calgary Olympics, see Gretchen Ghent, "Bibliographical Notes and Sources of Information," in John Tewnion, *The University of Calgary and the XV Olympic Winter Games* (Calgary, 1993). A comprehensive and accessible collection of materials exists in the University of Calgary Libraries including: OCO '88, *Rapport officiel des XVes jeux olympiques d'hiver—XV Olympic Winter Games: Official Report* (Calgary, 1988), progress reports, newsletters, press releases, curriculum resource kits (*Come Together: The Olympics and You*), media guides, regulations, terms related to the XVth Olympic Winter Games, facts, and information. Gretchen Ghent and her research assistant, Hillary Munroe, abstracted all records and publications from the Games. Lists of holdings may be obtained through Internet, and over 1,200 citations to periodicals can be located through the CD-ROM, SPORT Discus. The University Library Special Collections contains a copy of all public and semipublic documents. The official repository for records of the Games is the city of Calgary Archives. The records consist of documents, contracts, agreements, correspondence, photographs, posters, artifacts, audiotapes, and broadcast videotapes from OCO '88, the city, individuals, and private agencies. Public accessibility is excellent.

For other collections, see the Amateur Athletic Foundation of Los Angeles library; Canadian Olympic Association, Montreal; and the Olympic Hall of Fame at Canada Olympic Park, J. Thomas West, director. The communications media department at the University of Calgary holds the *Official 1988 Calgary Winter Olympics* video by ABC Sports, a highlight production. Also in the film library are 500 hours of video highlights from the Games. An extensive collection of photographs is housed at the Glenbow Museum in Calgary. An attractive pictorial version of the Games is found in Lloyd Robertson and Brian D. James, *XV Olympic Winter Games: The Official Commemorative Book* (n.p., 1988).

For an anecdotal autobiographical diary of the Games, see Frank W. King, *It's How You Play the Game* (Calgary, 1991). A critical assessment of the Games and their implications for the city is provided in Chuck Reasons, ed., *Stampede City* (Calgary, 1984), particularly "It's Just a Game? The 1988 Winter Olympics." Dominique Nguyen, ed., *Les Jeux olympiques: Calgary 1988* (Bordeaux, 1988), contains a series of articles on the Games dealing principally with their urban impact in such areas as tourism and the city's image. J. R. Brent Ritchie analyzes marketing in "Promoting Calgary through the Olympics" in Seymour H. Fine, ed., *Social Marketing* (Boston, 1990). For good analysis of particular issues, see Harry H. Hiller, "The Urban Transformation of a Landmark Event: The 1988 Calgary Winter Olympics," *Urban Affairs Quarterly* 26 (September 1990): 118–37, and "Impact and Image: The Convergence of Urban Factors in Preparing for the 1988 Calgary Winter Olympics," in Geoffrey J. Syme, *The Planning and Evaluation of Hallmark Events* (Aldershot, England, 1989), pp. 119–31; Valerius Geist, "Bighorn Sheep and the Calgary Winter Olympics," *Probe Post* 9 (February 1987): 20–24; Herbert and Patricia Kariel, "Tourism Developments in the Kananaskis Valley Area, Alberta, Canada and the Impact of the 1988 Winter Olympic Games," *Mountain Research and Development* 8 (1988): 1–10; C. F. Feest, "Glenbow Incident: The Spirit Sinks," *European Review of Native American Studies* 1 (1987): 61–63; and M. Myers, "Glenbow Affair," *Inuit Art Quarterly* 3 (Winter 1988): 12–16. The following periodicals provide extensive additional information on various aspects of the Games: *Alberta Report, Maclean's, Windspeaker,* and to a lesser extent, *Olympic Review, Time,* and *Saturday Night.*

K. B. Wamsley

ALBERTVILLE AND SAVOIE 1992
XVITH OLYMPIC WINTER GAMES

Michel Barnier was a 17-year-old spectator at the 1968 Grenoble Winter Olympics when fellow Frenchman Jean-Claude Killy won his gold medals. Barnier became a young political star as a deputy in the National Assembly representing the Savoie department, while Killy became an entrepreneur in that part of Savoie where he lived and skied, known as "L'Espace Killy." Killy and Barnier became friends and met at one of the many Savoie resorts, Val d'Isère, on December 5, 1981. Both were interested in expanding the Savoie department's tourist economy, which was hampered by the area's outdated transportation system. They agreed that the way to showcase the Savoie as a winter resort area and therefore get the much-needed improvements quickly was to host a Winter Olympics.

A state or region, however, could not sponsor a Games; a city was needed. If one of the ski resorts were chosen as the lead city, the others might refuse to participate. In addition, the Savoie resorts were all small and hard to reach. Hence, the obvious choice became the slightly larger, easily accessible town of Albertville, although Barnier knew that even most French people had no idea just where Albertville was located.

On June 11, 1982, Barnier and Killy presented their idea to Albertville's mayor, Henri Dujol, and the town council. Barnier, now head of the department's regional council, Killy, and Dujol announced the bid on December 11, 1982. The race to the Olympics was on.

Thirteen cities were bidding for the Games of 1992, spending more than $100 million in the process. For the Winter Games, Albertville was joined by Cortina d'Ampezzo, Italy; Falun, Sweden; Sofia, Bulgaria; Berchtesgaden, West Germany; Lillehammer, Norway; and Anchorage, the United States. It was the first bid for Albertville, Anchorage, and Berchtesgaden, which had been the winter playground of the Nazi elite. Cortina had hosted the Games in 1956 but had lost in its bid in 1988. Falun and Sofia represented countries that had never hosted Winter games, although Falun had bid four times before, withdrawing twice, and failing in 1984 and 1988. Berchtesgaden had more facilities in place than any of the other cities, all within a 25-mile radius. By contrast, Albertville offered snow venues spread over a 650-square-mile area and nothing but promises to build ice venues.

The Ninety-first IOC Session was held in Lausanne, Switzerland, in October 1986. Albertville's winning hinged on Paris's bid for the Summer Games failing, which was almost certain. IOC president Juan Antonio Samaranch had engineered Paris's entry to compete with his home town of Barcelona, and IOC members knew their president wanted Barcelona to win. If Albertville won, the strong Paris bid would necessarily fail, since the last time the same country had hosted both the Summer and Winter Olympics was 1936.

Albertville's bid was presented October 15, beginning with a film by Robert Enrico. Then Barnier, Killy, and French prime minister Jacques Chirac spoke. Chirac spoke for both Paris and Albertville and was so persuasive that it looked as if Paris would win. Instead, to preserve Barcelona's bid, the groundswell for the French bid was switched to Albertville. Voting for the Winter Games was conducted first on October 17, before that for the Summer Games, and in the longest election in Olympic history, Albertville won on the sixth ballot, with 51 votes to Sofia's 25.

Once the bid was won, the real work began. Killy became committee president on January 13, 1987. A skeleton staff had been in place since 1983, and venues had been selected in October of that year. However, the IOC wanted a streamlined Games, which meant eliminating several resorts as venues. The former hero, Killy, now had to be the villain, angering the owners of the resorts left off the revised list. There were calls for him to resign, including one from a fellow 1968 gold medalist, Marielle Goitschel, who managed one of the excluded resorts. Disenchanted with the lack of unity, Killy resigned on January 29, 1987.

The organizing committee, officially titled the Comité d'organization de jeux olympiques d'Albertville et de la Savoie, known as COJO, was formally created on February 24, 1987, with Barnier as president. Samaranch, however, wanted Killy back. Killy relented and became co-president of COJO in April 1988.

Even scaled down, the Albertville Games were still the most decentralized in history, with ten venues spread over 650 square miles of the French Alps. There were several athletes' villages instead of the central Olympic Village of past Games, and this feature was unpopular with the athletes. The host city of Albertville staged the opening and closing ceremonies, as well as the speed and figure skating events. In "L'Espace Killy," the Val d'Isère resort hosted all the men's Alpine events except slalom; Tignes hosted the freestyle skiing events. Les Trois Vallées staged the ski jump and Nordic combined events at Courchevel, hockey and the women's Alpine events at Méribel, and men's slalom at Les Menuires. Speed skiing took place at Les Arcs, bobsled and luge at La Plagne, cross-country skiing and biathlon at Les Saisies, and curling at Pralognan-la-Vanoise. Tignes and Albertville also hosted the Paralympic Games for the disabled.

The organizing committee took pride in the fact that for the first time, the question of environmental protection was considered in the planning for the Games. Nevertheless, protestors outside the stadium prior to the opening ceremonies recited a litany of environmental horrors the Games had brought. For a gondola lift between Méribel's ski run and the Brides-les-Bains' main athletes' village, the French government removed protection on a forest preserve, allowing 100 acres of trees to be cut down. Thirty-five million cubic feet of earth were removed from various mountainsides to build ski runs and parking lots. The ski jumps were anchored in place because they were built on unstable ground caused by a high water table.

Perhaps the largest environmental (and economic) disaster was the bobsled and luge run, the white elephant of every Winter Games. Located at La Plagne, it had to be propped up several times because it was built over an old mine and kept sinking into the ground. It was also in direct sunlight and would not naturally freeze. The budget skyrocketed from $12 million to $37 million as 40 tons of ammonia were brought in to freeze the track. In December 1990, the run was closed due to an ammonia leak. Sirens were put in place and gas masks were given to the residents of nearby La Roche because of the leak and the fact the track was built in an avalanche zone.

Despite those environmental problems, Albertville was in the forefront of the green Europe in its use of facilities; most structures built for the Games were reused, dismantled, or sold. The 33,000-seat stadium at Albertville was built on temporary scaffolding and sold to Barcelona for the Summer Games. The speed skating track was converted into a running track with a rubberized surface. The figure skating rink's 9,000 seats were reduced to 1,200, and most of the space became offices. The COJO offices were in a technical college, which converted them to their original use upon COJO's dissolution. The Méribel hockey rink had only 1,750 permanent seats out of 6,000, with the rest of the building converted into shops, restaurants, offices, and housing. The press center at La Léchère became a conference center. The "finish" stadiums for spectators at the ski events were sold, along with 450 other prefabricated buildings.

To provide for the ice events, five skating rinks were built in the area. Pralognan-la-Vanoise, with a population of just 650, contributed to building an ice rink (reportedly $3,400 per inhabitant), hoping to host a glamour event. Instead, Pralognan received the decidedly unglamorous demonstration sport of curling, with a $400 per day maintenance cost, and the residents voted the village administration out of office. Four villages were on the verge of bankruptcy by the eve of the Games; Brides-les-Bains had a $10 million deficit, incurred in building a casino, town hall, and the main athletes' village.

While the resorts were going into debt, COJO created several sponsorship categories to lure corporations into joining the worldwide Olympic program. In honor of Pierre Coubertin, there was the "Club Coubertin," a sponsors' organization consisting of some of the largest companies in France: Crédit Lyonnais (banking), Renault, Bis (temporary personnel), AGF (insurance), Evian, Candia-Yoplait, Alcatel (telecommunications equipment), France-Télécom (television), Thomson SNCF (French railway), La Poste (post office), and IBM. In addition to Club Coubertin, there was the Club des Quinze, composed of fifteen sponsoring companies including Club Med, whose Val d'Isère resort was the skiers' village, and Arthur Andersen Consulting, which had helped prepare the Albertville bid. There were also twenty-four official suppliers and twelve authorized dealers.

Another major source of funding for the Games was $289 million from the sale of television coverage to the European Broadcasting Union, Australia's Nine Network, Japan's NHK, Canada's CBC, and America's CBS (which accounted for $243 million). CBS won the Games on May 25, 1988, with a bid that was $68 million more than that of NBC, $43 million above the IOC minimum, and part of an astounding $3.6 billion CBS spent on sports, in an ultimately successful attempt to boost ratings. CBS had not carried an Olympics since it had pioneered U.S. Olympic coverage in 1960 at Squaw Valley and Rome and finished selling advertising time only two days before the Games began. However, despite the mostly taped, commercial-heavy coverage, the network attracted a large audience and won fifteen of sixteen nights of prime-time coverage, the most ever for a Winter Olympics.

The American telecast was revolutionary in many respects. In addition to 116 hours on CBS, 45 hours were carried by cable network TNT (Turner Network Television), which paid $50 million to CBS for the rights to cover Albertville and Lillehammer. CBS's on-air talent was a mix of sports and news personalities, as it had been in Squaw Valley and Rome, with no single prime-time anchor, as ABC and NBC had used in their Olympic broadcasts. Paula Zahn of the news department and Tim McCarver of the sports department shared the duties.

For the first time, coverage was edited at the remote site and transmitted via fiber-optic cable, microwave, and Eutelsat (European domestic satellite) to the International Broadcast Center at Moutiers for either further editing or broadcast. CBS did not trust on-site recording and carrying the tape back to Moutiers to do the broadcast, due to unpredictable weather and road conditions. Instead of building a master control room at Moutiers, CBS shipped two remote trucks to the Games. Even the anchors' studio sets were preassembled and tested in the United States before being sent to France. In keeping with the recyclable nature of the Games, all the broadcasting materials were packed up and shipped to Lillehammer for the next Games.

Albertville was billed as the "First Games of the New World Order"—the first Olympics since the collapse of communism. Calgary had been dominated by the Soviet Union and East Germany, countries that did not exist any more. The remains of the Soviet Union became the Unified Team on January 24, 1992, consisting of athletes from Russia, Ukraine, Belarus, Kazakhstan, and Uzbekistan. The team wore matching CCCP uniforms ordered from Yugoslav manufacturers prior to the dissolution; the left sleeve bore the athlete's home republic name, the right, its flag. They marched under the Olympic flag and used the Olympic anthem. While the Unified team did get an Adidas sponsorship, the athletes were busy selling U.S.S.R. souvenirs in the athletes' villages to obtain hard currency.

The former Soviet republics of Latvia, Estonia, and Lithuania fielded teams for the first time in fifty-six years. In fact, Latvian bobsledders Janis Kipurs and Zintis Ekmanis, former medal winners for the Soviet Union, had manned barricades in the May 1990 independence movement. The Latvians bartered use of the only luge run in the former Soviet Union for airline tickets and hotel rooms at foreign competitions.

Germany fielded a joint team for the first time since 1964, and the former East Germans had to adjust to the loss of state subsidies. Bobsled driver Harald Czudaj admitted he had informed on teammates to the East German secret police, the Stasi, but those same teammates supported him. Yugoslavia split into Yugoslavia, Croatia, and Slovenia. Almost all the Yugoslavian winter athletes and all medal winners in prior Games had been Slovenians. Slovenia team officials gave their previous year's uniforms and advice to the Yugoslavian team, but the Slovenian skiers refused to share lockers with the Yugoslavs.

In an interview with *Europe* magazine (January–February, 1992), Killy stated his goal for Albertville on the eve of the Games: "I would like them to go home with the feeling that they spent time on another planet, the planet of the French Olympics." The spectacle surrounding the Games was designed to accomplish this. The torch run began on December 14, 1991, when a special Concorde flight brought the flame from Athens to Paris. The flame was carried by 5,598 runners, all young people born between 1971 and 1976, on a fifty-seven-day course across the twenty-two regions and sixty departments of France, including the island of Corsica. Every night when the flame stopped, there was a special Olympics light and sound show by Jean-Michel Jarre in the most historic part of the city or town in which the procession found itself.

The world was welcomed to the "Planet of the French Olympics" on February 8. To the sounds of otherworldly percussion, the 1,808 athletes marched in behind women costumed as snow globes, labeled with the French names of the sixty-three countries fielding teams. The elaborate opening ceremony continued as 300 professional dancers and 1,500 local performers acted out a bizarre futuristic tribute to winter sports. The "Marseillaise" was sung a capella by a 12-year-old girl; on hearing the bloody lyrics from such an innocent voice, many French citizens added their voices to the call for the song's alteration. French figure skater Surya Bonaly, who is black and at the time claimed to be from Reunion Island off Africa (she was actually from Nice), gave the athlete's oath, which led to racist telephone protests to COJO.

Then the Games began. Over 900,000 tickets were sold, 20 percent over estimates. The weather, which had dumped too much snow in previous weeks, precipitating an avalanche at Christmas, cooperated, postponing only one event (women's giant slalom) for only one day. Otherwise, the fifty-seven events produced 330 medals in twelve sports: Alpine skiing, bobsled/luge, biathlon (with women competitors and electronic targets for the first time), cross-country skiing, figure skating (without compulsory figures for the first time), hockey, Nordic combined, ski jump, speed skating, short track speed skating (becoming a full medal sport), freestyle skiing (moguls, a first-time full medal event); demonstration events of aerial, ballet and speed skiing; and the demonstration sport of curling. Participating in these twelve sports were 1,318 men representing all competing countries and 490 women representing forty-nine countries. Most of the women had to take a new femininity test, the *sry* gene test, which replaced the Barr body count test. The French medical ethics committee protested because the test is often inaccurate, but the French government refused to carry the protest to the IOC.

Germany led the medal count with twenty-six, followed by the Unified Team (twenty-three), and Austria (twenty-one). The United States finished sixth, leading once again to criticism over its poor showing. Actually Albertville marked the best performance by a U.S. team overseas since 1952, with nine of the eleven medals (and all the golds) won by women, but four of the medals were won in events not even contested at Calgary.

The medals were the traditional gold, silver, and bronze with a distinctive engraved center of Lalique crystal, which did cause problems. Austrian bronze medalist Stefan Kreiner dropped his medal while packing, and it shattered. Killy himself replaced it, admonishing Kreiner to be careful; there would not be another one.

Italian Alberto Tomba became the first Alpine skier to defend his gold (in the giant slalom) and American Bonnie Blair the first woman speed skater to defend her gold (in the 500-meter race). The Unified Team's cross-country skier Lyubov Egorova was the most decorated athlete of the Games, with three golds and two silvers. Fellow cross-country skier Raisa Smetanina became the oldest medal winner (at age 40) and most decorated athlete in Winter Olympics history: first to win in five consecutive Games and winner of the most medals (four golds, five silvers, one bronze) in a career. Slalom skier Annelise Coberger of New Zealand won Oceania's first Winter medal; speed skater Qiaobo Ye won the People's Republic of China's first medals (in the 500- and 1,000-meter races). Finland's ski jump sensation Toni Nieminen became the youngest gold medalist ever by one day, at 16 years and 259 days.

For all the superlatives, some simply competed for their country's honor, and, with their hopeless performances, once again there came calls to limit the Games to the best, especially after a Moroccan skier was so slow in giant slalom that the next skier passed him and after the Puerto Rican bobsled team flipped over for a mile of its run. The British team limited its membership to those ranked in the top fifty of a particular sport, leaving home the hero of Calgary, ski jumper Eddie "The Eagle" Edwards. But in rebuttal to those calls, there was surprise silver medalist Paul Wylie, an American figure skater who had never finished in the top five at a world championship, and had made the American team by one-tenth of a point. He gave the performance of his career and won the Olympic Spirit Award.

The closing ceremonies on February 23 were yet another bizarre musical spectacle accompanied by drums, including a tribute to Lillehammer featuring a Viking ship and a giant polar bear float. The ceremonies were shadowed by the absence of the Swiss team, mourning the Games' only fatality, speed skier Nicholas Bochatay, who died in a training accident.

The Games did accomplish some of Savoie's objectives. The high-speed TGV trains began running to Albertville. A four-lane highway was built linking Albertville to Lyons, France, and Geneva, Switzerland. Albertville built a new hospital, cultural center, and five new hotels. Tourism rose during the summer of 1992, and by the winter, area hotels reported record occupancy, with ski lift receipts up 60 percent in Les Trois Vallées; a quarter of the visitors had never been to the area before but had seen the Games on television. But Brides-les-Bains' famous waters were mortgaged for the next thirty years, taxes were up 15 percent in Méribel, La Plagne's bobsled track must remain open for at least three years to pay its debt, and regional unemployment rose from 7.5 percent to 10 percent. The Games ended with a deficit because of a greater number of athletes (400 more than Calgary) and journalists (7,000 from 120 countries) than anticipated and the costs of the ski jump and luge run. The final cost estimates varied from $692 million to $800 million. In the end, the French government and the Savoie department paid the $52 million deficit, split 75 percent to 25 percent.

Killy and Barnier received the Olympic Order in Gold at the conclusion of the Games. Barnier won reelection in March 1993, and Killy was named the president of Amaury Sports. Overall, Albertville had been a rousing success, with no disasters, no delays, and no scandals.

BIBLIOGRAPHICAL ESSAY

The archives of the Albertville Games probably reside with the Comité national olympique et sportif français in Paris. The published record is *The Official Report of the XVI Olympic Winter Games of Albertville and Savoie* (Paris, 1992); a copy is at the Amateur Athletic Foundation in Los Angeles. The foundation also possesses research materials and other information from CBS related to the television coverage of the Games.

Books previewing the Games include Daniel and Susan Cohen, *Going for the Gold* (New York, 1992), on the Winter Games, aimed at younger readers, and the more in-depth Martin Connors, Diane L. Dupis, and Brad Morgan, *The Olympic Factbook* (Detroit, 1992), which covers both Albertville and the Summer Games in Barcelona. The U.S. Olympic Committee's *Barcelona/Albertville 1992* (Salt Lake City, 1992) provides an overview of each event, with U.S. finishes, and lists all U.S. team members.

Journalistic sources provide the most information on Albertville. The April and May 1992 issues of *Olympic Review* provide an overview of the Games. Sally Jenkins, "New Allegiances," *Sports Illustrated*, February 24, 1992, pp. 38–41, discusses the Eastern European competitors' problems, as does Mark McDonald, "Tough Sledding," *Dallas Morning News,* February 7, 1992, and Jere Longman, "New World Order," *Sporting News,* January 13, 1992, p. 47. The *Anchorage Daily News*'s series on that city's bid, "Reaching for the Rings," beginning October 9, 1986, is worth pursuing as is William Oscar Johnson and Anita Verschoth, "Olympic Circus Maximus," *Sports Illustrated,* October 27, 1986, pp. 39–43, also on the bidding process. Ken Stephens, "Disposable Olympics," *Dallas Morning News,* November 24, 1991, provides an excellent account of the building of the Games' facilities. For information on Jean-Claude Killy, see Randy

Harvey, "Can the French Re-Enlist Killy?" *Los Angeles Times,* March 1, 1988, and Olivier Margot, "Killy rêve encore du 'Petit Prince,' " *L'Equipe,* February 8, 1992, and "Je n'ai peut-être pas d'avenir," *L'Equipe,* February 29, 1992.

The environmental impact of the Games is thoroughly discussed in Margaret Schilling, "Will the Olympics Kill the Alps?" *World Press Review* 39 (February 1992): 47. The impact of the Olympics one year later is detailed in Christopher Clarey, "Albertville Learning to Turn Gold, Silver and Bronze into Green," *New York Times,* February 13, 1993. For a preview of the Games and an English-language interview with Killy, see Ester Laushway, "Spreading the Olympic Spirit," *Europe* (January–February 1992). For CBS ratings, see Steve McClellan, "Olympic-Size Ratings for CBS," *Broadcasting,* February 17, 1992, pp. 6–7. The Olympics from a U.S. perspective is analyzed in John Powers, "US Fails to Scale Olympic Heights," *Boston Globe,* February 23, 1992.

CBS produced two videos: *1992 Winter Olympics Highlights* and *1992 Winter Olympics Figure Skating* (CBS/Fox Video, 1992). One feature film, *The Cutting Edge* (1992), recreates inaccurately the Calgary and Albertville figure skating competitions; the skating was choreographed by 1980 men's gold medalist Robin Cousins.

Michele Lellouche

LILLEHAMMER 1994
XVIITH OLYMPIC WINTER GAMES

When Norway's Crown Prince Harald first heard of Lillehammer's intentions to bid for the Winter Olympics, he declared, "You must be kidding" (Matti Mathisen, "The Road to the Olympic Games," *Destination Lillehammer* [1989], 5). Herein lies the beginning of a tale as rich as Norwegian folklore, in which an implausibly small community set its sights on hosting a premier sporting event and succeeded not only in preparing one of the greatest Winter Olympic Games in history but also in presenting the Olympic movement with a variety of innovative programs that will affect future host cities for years to come.

By the early 1980s, the tiny community of 23,000 and the surrounding region had fallen under the shadow of the west coast's booming oil trade; the prospect of better livelihoods lured Lillehammer's young residents, particularly its women, away from Norway's listless interior. City leaders considered a bid for the 1992 Winter Games as a panacea for the region's declining fortunes. Skepticism from across the country did not deter the bid committee from pursuing the Games with vigor, stating that "Lillehammer was born for the winter Olympic Games." (Matti Mathisen, "The Road to the Olympic Games," *Destination Lillehammer* [1989], 8). The International Olympic Committee (IOC) considered such a claim premature, especially since some IOC members consistently misidentified the city as Hammerville. The Games eventually went to Albertville as France's consolation prize for Paris' impending loss of the 1992 Summer Games to Barcelona. However, the IOC decision to alternate the Winter and Summer Games every two years, starting in 1994, prevented Lillehammer's organizing committee from brooding long over its loss.

The committee quickly formulated plans to bid for the XVIIth Winter Olympic Games. Lillehammer orchestrated a campaign that presented the city as the winter sports capital of the world, due to the fact that Norway's athletes owned more Winter Olympic medals than any nation other than the Soviet Union. Organizers proudly boasted that Lillehammer was the only city in the world with a skier on its coat of arms. Additionally, the bid committee promised to hold compact Games that would not alter Lillehammer's character, all on a frugal budget of 1.8 billion Norwegian kroner (NOK) ($280 million). Nevertheless, a Lillehammer Olympics appeared remote. Numerous presentations to the Olympic family on the city's virtues could not convince the IOC of Lillehammer's readiness for the world stage. Østersund/Åre, Sweden, and Sofia, Bulgaria, led the field of four candidates. Only Anchorage appeared to have less backing, in part due to its proximity to the 1988 Winter Olympics in Calgary.

Lillehammer's bid committee had all but conceded defeat by the time of the IOC decision at Seoul's Games in 1988. Several organizing committee leaders left Seoul prior to the vote, and the executive director told other bid cities they did not stand a chance. Surprisingly, a majority of the IOC's members failed to agree. Although IOC votes are confidential, rumors circulated that the IOC decision was influenced by an incident that tipped the scales in Lillehammer's favor. Østersund/Åre supposedly lost because of a controversy between Sweden and the Soviet Union. Prior to the vote, Sweden accused a Soviet submarine of violating its territorial waters, resulting in a retaliatory Soviet vote for Lillehammer. Sofia lost favor as other IOC members swung toward hosting the Games in smaller cities with predictable winter weather, a reaction to Calgary's size and erratic snowfall.

Before the celebration over Lillehammer's victory faded, the immense undertaking of the city's commitment began to weigh heavily on its citizens and the entire nation, and with good reason. The realistic cost of staging the Games surpassed every worst-case scenario; instead of a $280 million Olympic commitment, Lillehammer's residents faced a $1 billion expenditure. Local and national leaders realized the city could not absorb such a financial burden. To avoid international embarrassment, the Norwegian parliament agreed to assume financial responsibility for all cost overruns, but parliament's support came with the price of greater authority in the decision-making process. The government created the Lillehammer Olympic Organizing Committee (LOOC) to oversee preparation of the Games, with the central government retaining a majority voice in economic development issues. Two nonnegotiable government demands worked to Lillehammer's favor: site placement and personnel appointments. The central government, refusing to fund an event that would forever change Lillehammer while generating few residual benefits to the region, demanded that more venues be dispersed throughout the region, a violation of Lillehammer's original promise of a compact Games. However, the government's demand increased the likelihood that the venues would continue to be used long after the Olympic flame was extinguished. The ensuing battle for new sports facilities among the region's municipalities caused rifts in the organizing committee and finally brought about the departure of Ole Sjetne, LOOC's president. The timing of Sjetne's resignation provided the government with the opportunity to select a new president, industrialist Gerhard Heiberg. The subsequent addition of Henrik Andenaes as managing director secured the government's control of Lillehammer '94.

Parliament's request for broader site dispersal enlarged the scope of the Games as they became a showcase event for the entire country. LOOC capitalized on the world spotlight by creating a seamless image for the Games that promoted Norway's unique cultural heritage through architecture and design. Design teams from throughout the country worked to create some of the Olympic movement's most celebrated structures. The "Viking Ship" in Hamar, so called for its roof design resembling an overturned ship, proved to be an engineering marvel with wooden roof beams spanning more than 100 yards. Project engineers accomplished this task by developing a new laminated glue technique for wood that surpassed the structural strength and fire safety of steel. Architects used the same technology to build the "Northern Lights" skating hall, the largest building in the world to use wood for structural support. Norwegian engineering prowess also made possible the world's largest in-mountain arena, the ice hockey hall at Gjøvik. Workers blasted a cave in the mountain over a period of more than nine months and removed more than 29,000 truckloads of debris. The completed space had perfect acoustics, increasing its usefulness after the Games, and remained at a constant temperature, thus saving money. Asian businessmen flocked to the mountain hall to study the feasibility of similar structures in their overpopulated nations.

The design and marketing program for LOOC matched the boldness of the venues. The organizing committee developed a theme for the 1994 Winter Games that was distinctly Nordic and reflective of the country's heritage, yet at times they received inspiration from unlikely sources. Prior to Lillehammer's selection by the IOC, Mexican artist Javier Ramirez Campuzano, the son of IOC member Ramirez Vasquez, sent the bid committee an unsolicited drawing of a mascot he felt embodied Norway. LOOC quickly adopted Håkon, based on a thirteenth-century member of the royal family, as the Olympic mascot. The later addition of Kristin, another ancient royal personage, made the pair the first child mascots in the history of the Olympic Games. The most successful design concept, however, threatened to eclipse not only the mascots but also the striking Northern Lights Olympic logo. A 4,000-year-old Norwegian cave drawing of a man on skis inspired the design of twelve primitive sport pictograms that took the country by storm. Unlike design themes from previous Games, the pictograms and the logo embodied Norway's love of the season and its sports. The committee guaranteed that this love would not be cheapened through the sale of plastic trinkets. LOOC choose thirty-six companies to make higher-priced, high-quality items that served a function in daily life, and Olympic fans voiced their approval through the sounds of clanging cash registers. LOOC budgeted $3.5 million for royalties from the sale of Olympic-related merchandise and was surprised to find it set a Winter Olympics record, with more than $20 million.

The extraordinary Olympic sales figures were indicative of the frenzy building among Norwegians for the Games. Early versions of Lillehammer Olympic pins sold on the black market for up to $200. Norwegians mailed 1.8 million applications for the 900,000 tickets available in that country. In the middle of the night, Olympic-crazed Norwegians surreptitiously removed special manhole covers bearing the Olympic logo. The most amazing indicator of Olympic hysteria, however, was the daily countdown t-shirt auction. Each day for 1,000 days, a t-shirt bearing the number of days remaining until the Games was auctioned off on Lillehammer's main street. The auctions raised more than $300,000 for LOOC, with the final t-shirt selling for a remarkable $7,500.

Lillehammer's Olympic Games encompassed more than the tangible results of t-shirts, pictograms, and mortar: a deep respect for the environment guided the development and design of the entire Olympic program to such an extent that the IOC revised its procedures for selecting host cities. During the bidding process, Prime Minister Grø Harlem Brundtland pledged to protect Norway's environment during the Games. Her promise carried weight: she chaired the United Nations Commission on Environment and Development. Moreover, the government required Lillehammer to meet environmental guidelines before pledging to underwrite the Games. Despite this national commitment, a cosmetic environmental initiative might have resulted if not for a standoff between LOOC and environmental activists over the Akersvika bird sanctuary in Håmår. Environmental groups claimed placement of the Viking Ship building on the shore of the sanctuary would disrupt migratory bird patterns and they demanded another site for the speed skating venue. LOOC ignored those demands, claiming that building plans were completed and construction ready to begin. Tempers had reached a flash point when IOC president Juan Antonio Samaranch arrived in Norway to review Olympic development, at which time the environmental groups accosted him in Hamar. The unrelenting stubbornness of LOOC and the environmentalists prompted Samaranch to suggest mediation on the Viking Ship site. The resulting modifications were slight: planners moved the venue away from the shoreline and rotated the structure slightly so that visitors would not disturb the sanctuary's residents.

The most important change brought about by mediation, however, was the new perception that business and environmentalists could work toward common goals. The negotiations laid the foundation for a constructive dialogue and the development of the first green Games. Environmental groups received $100,000 per year from the government to create Project Environment-Friendly Olympics as an umbrella organization to work with LOOC. Representatives from LOOC, the project, the affected local governments, and the Ministry of the Environment met once each week to review and discuss development issues. LOOC hired an environmental coordinator to review all aspects of Olympic planning, a decision that attested to the ability to undertake large-scale building projects while protecting natural habitats. To avoid radical alterations of the landscape, LOOC reversed the curves at the Hunderfossen bobsled-luge track to hug the mountainside, and designers outlined a Lysgårdsbakkene ski jump that complemented the contours of the mountain. Schoolchildren helped plant "Olympic forests" and transplanted rare wildflowers from construction sites, while developers faced fines of up to $7,500 for felling trees marked for protection by LOOC and the environmentalists. All venues incorporated the latest energy-saving techniques, such as recirculation of waste heat and computer-monitored thermostats. In all, environmental design lowered energy consumption at Olympic sites by 30 percent.

The green campaign expanded beyond the actual management of Olympic venues. LOOC instituted a green office protocol, including recycling and the purchase of products meeting strict environmental standards. Corporate sponsors signed contracts that included environmental clauses, in which they pledged to provide services and products that minimized environmental impact. In most cases, packaging for equipment was stored and reused after the Games. Lillehammer city leaders instituted a strict ban against billboards and other visual pollution that would alter the city's character. Sponsor recognition was limited to discreet banners affixed to light poles or small signs carved from Norwegian woods. Strong efforts were made to cushion the impact of the projected 100,000 daily visitors to the Olympic region. Edible plates made of potato starch and cutlery produced from cornstarch were composted, and Coca-Cola recycled all its paper cups used during the Games. Even the Olympic torch, constructed of a specially designed recycled glass concrete, burned propane gas. The most notable signs of the green campaign to limit waste, however, were the medals draped around athletic necks. Granite excavated from the ski jump became the core element in the unique design of the Olympic medals, the first to combine stone and precious metals.

LOOC's environmental profile made a lasting impression on the country and the Olympic movement. More than 25 percent of Norway's municipalities adopted LOOC's green office protocol, and the IOC implemented environmental requirements for future organizers.

LOOC's efforts to preserve the natural habitat while undertaking a development campaign of grand proportions highlighted the committee's concern that the 1994 Winter Olympic Games be more than just another athletic competition. In addition to protecting the environment, the organizing committee believed the Olympic movement had veered from the goals of the Olympic charter, which call for efforts to "contribute to building a peaceful and better world." LOOC felt it was time not only to entertain the world but also improve humankind, particularly its children.

LOOC worked with the city of Lillehammer and Norwegian relief agencies to establish the first-ever Olympic humanitarian program. Olympic Aid became their effort to raise awareness of the plight facing children in war-torn Sarajevo, the host of the 1984 Winter Olympics. The first phase of the two-year initiative began during the closing days of Barcelona's Games. Olympic Aid distributed posters to all athletes that showed a small photograph of the Games of Sarajevo with a larger, overwhelming photograph of a Sarajevo child wrapped in bandages. The awareness and fund-raising campaign continued when Olympic Aid organized a day of Olympic Solidarity involving every Olympic city through Atlanta, the host of the 1996 Games. The two events raised NOK 27 million ($4 million) for the children of Sarajevo. LOOC recognized soon after that other children around the globe needed the Olympic community's support too, so additional programs were established to build schools in Eritrea, to fund a rehabilitation center for the youth of Beirut, and to educate children in Guatemala and Afghanistan.

The grand ideals of world peace and solidarity represented during the Olympic Games moved spectators and athletes alike to support Olympic Aid. Johann Olav Koss, the Norwegian speed skating champion and Olympic Aid ambassador to Eritrea, challenged his countrymen to contribute NOK 10 for each Norwegian gold medal won during the Games. The people of Norway responded to his appeal individually and through community fund-raising drives. The IOC offered to match Koss' and other athletes' contributions with equal donations to the Sarajevo campaign. In all, the generosity of visitors and the citizens of Norway helped Olympic Aid raise NOK 65 million ($9 million) for the five relief efforts.

Despite Lillehammer's noble intentions to expand the boundaries of the Olympic movement, more sensational events held the public's attention, the most famous of which involved Albertville bronze medalist Nancy Kerrigan. An attacker clubbed Kerrigan on the knee during the U.S. Olympic figure skating trials in January. A police investigation later tied the assailant to figure skater Tonya Harding, who had won the Olympic trials due to Kerrigan's injury. Other Harding confidants, including her bodyguard and her husband, were arrested in a plot to improve Harding's chances of winning a medal by preventing Kerrigan from competing in Lillehammer. Their efforts failed, as the U.S. Olympic Committee (USOC) selected Kerrigan for the Olympic team, and her injuries healed rapidly. The bungled conspiracy also cast suspicion on Harding's role in the plot. Despite Harding's pleas of innocence, the USOC attempted to remove her from the Olympic team. Harding's lawyers responded with a $25 million lawsuit against the USOC, resulting in a delay of any disciplinary action against Harding until after the Games.

The Kerrigan-Harding incident added a touch of sensationalism that increased the Games' visibility, but the event Norwegians called "Wounded Knee II" caused less concern for IOC members than the prospect of an icy reception from the host country. The IOC's penchant for fine living conflicted with the Norwegian preference for simple lifestyles. Many Norwegians believed that Samaranch was blatantly lobbying for the country's valued Nobel Peace Prize, specifically because of his public statements and efforts to stop the fighting in Sarajevo and end apartheid in South Africa. Prior to the Games, a Norwegian poll found that 58 percent of those polled held negative views toward the IOC. Two teenagers sharing those sentiments were caught painting a message, "Samaranch Go Home," and a swastika on a downtown wall the week prior to opening ceremonies. Several IOC members indeed made plans for an early departure in case actions turned more hostile.

When the Games opened, though, the populace's suspicions gave way to a rousing show of support for the Olympic movement, and unfortunate pre-Olympic events were soon eclipsed by the extraordinary moments of the Games, starting with the lighting of the Olympic flame. Organizers improved upon Barcelona's archer and flaming arrow by routing the Olympic flame down the ski jump. Stein Gruben, a last-minute replacement, made a successful jump with the torch that thrilled an anxious audience still shaken by 1988 Olympic bronze medalist Ole Gunnar Fidjestøl's skull-rattling crash during his final practice run. Gruben's spectacular jump acted as the precursor to equally magnificent competitions. Johann Olav Koss set the standard of excellence during the Games and cemented his destiny as a Norwegian sports icon by winning an unprecedented three gold medals in world record time in the 1,500-, 5,000-, and 10,000-meter speed skating events. Bonnie Blair became the most decorated U.S. Winter Olympic athlete with her gold medals in the 500- and 1,000-meter speed skating races, for a career total of five gold medals and one bronze. Blair also became the only American athlete to repeat gold medal performances in the same event (the 500-meter race) in three consecutive Winter Games. Her success, however, was overshadowed by the long-awaited triumph of her teammate, Dan Jansen. In his fourth Olympic Games, Jansen overcame the personal tragedy of his sister's death during the 1988 Games to win the 1,000-meter speed skating race in world record time and capture his first Olympic gold medal in his final event.

Lillehammer also produced a hockey final to rival the excitement of the United States' legendary win over the Soviet Union in 1980. Sweden and Canada battled one another to a 2-point tie after regulation play and a 10-minute overtime. The game was decided using the 1992 rules change of a shoot-out, requiring one player to attempt a goal against the opponent's goalie. The score remained tied after the first round of shoot-out play, but Sweden won the heart-throbbing game in the second round.

Skiing records also dominated these Games. Italian skier Alberto Tomba, notorious for his social life, became the first to win medals in three Olympics with his silver medal in the slalom; he also tied the record for total Alpine Olympic medals with five. Swiss Alpine skier Vrenie Schneider became the first woman to win three gold medals in that sport. Andreas Schönbächler of Switzerland and Lina Cherjazova of Uzbekistan became the first competitors to win gold medals in the new medal sport of freestyle skiing aerials. Russia's Lyubov Egorova and Norway's Bjorn Daehlie tied the career gold medal record for women (six) and men (five) with their performances in the women's 20-kilometer cross-country relay, the 10-kilometer pursuit, the 5-kilometer classical style race, the men's 15-kilometer cross-country pursuit, and the 10-kilometer classical-style cross-country race, respectively.

The expectation of high drama at women's figure skating came true as well. Nancy Kerrigan was ready to compete by the opening of the Games, but Harding crumbled under the pressure of the investigation and the media's intense scrutiny. Other skaters, such as the 16-year-old orphan from Ukraine, Oksana Baiul, maintained the pressure on Kerrigan to skate the best performance of her career. Baiul's status as the favorite to win the ice skating competition was threatened the day prior to the finals when, during practice, she collided on the ice with another competitor. Despite three stitches on her shin and a back injury, Baiul skated in the finals with the assistance of an IOC-approved painkiller. Critics and spectators alike felt Baiul's performance failed to match Kerrigan's technical excellence. Artistic merit, however, indisputably belonged to Baiul. Baiul and Kerrigan tied for total points, but Baiul won with the closest margin possible due to a tenth of a point lead in the tie-breaking artistic category. The best performance Harding could manage was a broken shoelace and an opportunity to reskate her program, leaving her in eighth place overall.

In all, Lillehammer produced a spectacular Olympic Games. Even record cold temperatures and more than 50 inches of snow failed to dampen the spirits of spectators and athletes alike, with the possible exception of the 112 individuals who suffered fractures or broken bones while maneuvering on snow-compacted surfaces. Norway's love of sport became evident by the way predominantly Norwegian crowds cheered for all athletes, not just their own. Yet as fate would have it, Norwegians cheered more for their countrymen than any other national team, as Norway won twenty-six medals, the most the country ever won at the Winter Games. Crowds surpassed all expectations and broke records with 88 percent of all seats sold, an accomplishment that aided the committee in surpassing its financial projections. The success of ticket sales and the marketing campaign helped LOOC earn an estimated NOK 400 million ($57 million) surplus, the majority of which will be used to maintain venues. The only sector of Lillehammer's Games to lose money was the cultural festival ($1.3 million), which organizers blamed on low attendance due to the record cold temperatures.

It is certain that the IOC and a majority of the sports-loving public will never again mistake Lillehammer for fictitious Hammerville. Certainly LOOC's adroit handling of the Olympic Games enhanced Norway's reputation for management, design, and quality. The Norwegian construction industry hoped its creativity and adeptness would lead to building contracts in other countries, and LOOC offered the world two important gifts: greater stewardship of the environment and a system for the Olympics to assist those in need. It is too early to determine the long-term benefits the region will reap from hosting the Games, however. As Barcelona discovered, hosting a successful Olympics does not protect a community from the whims of the global economy. Lillehammer has no guarantee that the new facilities and international recognition will improve the economy sufficiently to keep its young people, particularly women, in the region. Lillehammer's city leaders have ideas, however, on the best approach to keep the world's eye on Norway. In case the region cannot sustain the magic created during sixteen days in February 1994, Lillehammer plans to bid for the 2010 Winter Olympics.

ACKNOWLEDGMENTS

I would like to thank Mr. Torstein Rudi of LOOC's public relations department and Nita Kapoor of Olympic Aid for their assistance in locating up-to-the-minute financial figures.

BIBLIOGRAPHICAL ESSAY

Several official publications by the Lillehammer Olympic Organizing Committee documented the Games from infancy to closing ceremonies. The Norwegian publisher, J. M. Stenersens Forlag A.S., published a series of official books, beginning with Knut Ramberg, ed., *Destination Lillehammer* (Oslo, 1989). Stenersens also released *This Is Norway,* ed. Arne Bonde, in 1992. See also *The Official Book of the XVII Lillehammer Olympic*

Games (Oslo, 1994), another organizing committee publication. The *Final Report* of the organizing committee was published in hard copy and CD-Rom versions in 1995.

In addition to larger works, several publications were used to develop this chapter, including "Building an Environmental Policy and Action Plan for the International Olympic Committee," by the Project Environment-Friendly Olympics and the Norwegian Society for the Conservation of Nature (1992); "The Olympic Environmental Message," published by LOOC (1993); *The Greening of Sports: The Third Dimension of the Olympics,* published by the Ministry of Environment (Oslo, 1994); and "An Environmentally Friendly Olympics: The Norwegian Example," also published by the Ministry of Environment (Oslo, 1993), all of which provide in-depth information into the development of LOOC's environmental program. Small pamphlets published by LOOC were used to develop this chapter as well, and direct communiqués with Olympic Aid provided supplemental information on its efforts.

Of particular significance for a complete review of Lillehammer's Olympic Games are the *New York Times* and the *Washington Post,* both of which carried extensive coverage of the Olympics. The *Atlanta Journal/Constitution* covered the Games in depth in preparation for the 1996 Summer Olympics in Atlanta. National magazines such as *Time* and *Sports Illustrated* covered Lillehammer extensively during the Games.

Two videos are important to note. Filmmaker Bud Greenspan continued his series of Olympic films with the production of *16 Days of Glory: Lillehammer '94,* and CBS produced a compilation of sports highlights from the 1994 Games.

Larry Maloney

NAGANO 1998

XVIIITH OLYMPIC WINTER GAMES

On June 15, 1991, the International Olympic Committee (IOC) selected Nagano, Japan, as the host city of the 1998 Winter Olympics. In the final round of voting, Nagano beat out Salt Lake City, 46–42; other contenders—Aosta, Italy; Jaca, Spain; and Oestersund, Sweden—had been eliminated in earlier rounds. Salt Lake City officials had mounted a serious bid but failed because of the several Olympics held in North America in recent years and the fact that Atlanta is hosting the 1996 Summer Games. Nagano also put together an impressive bid package that included a pledge to pay the transportation and housing costs of those participating in the Games.

Nagano, a popular winter resort city of 350,000 located 110 miles northwest of Tokyo, had lost out to Sapporo, Japan, for the right to host both the 1940 and 1972 Winter Games. Although the 1940 Games were never held, Sapporo did host the 1972 Games, so 1998, in a sense, was Nagano's turn. The city's organizing committee announced plans to spend $563 million to stage the Games, while taking full advantage of Japan's technical expertise. The total cost of the Games, including collateral facilities, may approach $6 billion. These expenditures, most of which will be borne by Japanese taxpayers, will cover the costs of constructing a high-speed railway between Tokyo and Nagano and widening several highways through the mountainous terrain between the two cities.

The early stages of Games preparation have not been free of problems. Environmentalists are concerned that the impact of Games-related construction will damage relatively undeveloped mountain forest areas, as well as the agricultural resources of the mountain valleys. Others are concerned about problems that might arise from the relatively mild winter weather of Nagano (the southernmost Winter Olympic site), where rain, instead of snow, frequently falls.

Japan's recent political turmoil has also had an impact on the 1998 Games. In a general sense, the political difficulties, including revelations of corrupt behavior, have, according to some observers, dampened the national enthusiasm for the Games that had been an important factor in the success of the 1964 and 1972 Games in Japan. Instead, there is an attitude of cynicism and indifference. The political problems involve, among others, Yutaka Nishizawa, the mayor of Hakuba and a member of the organizing committee, who in 1994 admitted accepting a $200,000 bribe from a construction company in return for a contract to build a sewage treatment plant. Though the plant was not directly linked to the Nagano Games, Nishizawa was, and the incident fueled the feeling that similar bribes were being offered in Games-related matters. In addition, there have been allegations that IOC members were bribed in order to secure their votes and ensure Nagano's victory. When asked to account for the $28 million it spent to make its proposal to the IOC, the Nagano bid committee announced that it had lost its ledger books and therefore could not document its expenditures.

The Columbia Broadcasting System (CBS) won the rights to broadcast the Games on television and radio for $375 million, a Winter Games record. Since CBS's rivals, ABC, NBC, and the Fox network, chose not to bid for the broadcast rights, the $375 million figure was worked out in negotiations between the network and IOC officials. Although the cost of the broadcast rights seemed very high to many observers, CBS asserted that the amount was simply a realistic figure based on inflation projections, the anticipated growth in the advertising market, and the increased interest in the Winter Games, and figure skating in particular. However, the large time difference between Japan and the United States will force CBS to show some events on tape rather than live, and this will weaken the appeal of the broadcast for some viewers. Nonetheless, the network, which broke even in its telecast of the 1992 Albertville Games, remains confident that it will do as well in Nagano.

As of 1996, there are still two years before the opening ceremonies at Nagano, and much will happen that will affect the staging of the Games. Nagano, now shouldering a $1.3 billion municipal debt, may be forced to renege on its promise to pay transportation and housing costs for perhaps as many as 2,000 athletes, and the city may require the assistance of the IOC, so successful in its marketing efforts in recent years, to ensure a successful Games.

BIBLIOGRAPHICAL ESSAY

The archives of the Amateur Athletic Foundation in Los Angeles is the best place to research materials on the Nagano Games. For the most part, these materials relate to the bidding process for the Games. The collection includes *1998 Nagano Japan* (n.p., 1991), a six-volume presentation prepared by the Nagano Winter Olympics Bidding Committee, and a variety of materials related to Salt Lake City's efforts to win the right to host the Games. Among these materials are the IOC questionnaire that Salt Lake City's bid committee completed; a two-volume presentation, *Salt Lake City 1998* (Salt Lake City, 1990); a formal bidding document, *Salt Lake City: A Bid to Host the XVIII Olympic Winter Games* (Salt Lake City, 1989?); a technical questionnaire completed for the U.S. Olympic Committee; a special issue of *Utah Business* dealing with the proposed Games; and Alex Kelner, comp., *Utah's Olympics Circus* (Salt Lake City, 1989), a collection of articles, illustrations, and songs opposing the idea of the Games' coming to Utah.

Bid materials from Jaca, Spain, and Aosta, Italy, may be found at the archives as well. These include *Jaca '98* (n.p., 1991), a five-volume boxed bid presentation with additional information on computer disks, and *Aosta: An Olympic Vocation* (n.p., 1990), a four-volume bid presentation from Aosta, with a 10-minute video presentation.

The *New York Times* provided some coverage of the Nagano Games. See the *Times* for June 16, 1991, on the selection of Nagano, and for August 30, 1991, November 29, 1992, January 19, 1994, and August 19, 1994, for articles on preparations for the Games.

John E. Findling

APPENDIX A: THE INTERNATIONAL OLYMPIC COMMITTEE

The International Olympic Committee (IOC), described in the *Olympic Charter* as the "supreme authority of the Olympic Movement," is responsible for the spread of modern Olympism, the philosophy that is basic to this global organization. This philosophy is expressed in the charter as

a philosophy of life, exalting and combining in a balanced whole the qualities of body, will and mind. Blending sport with culture and education, Olympism seeks to create a way of life based on the joy found in effort, the educational value of good example and respect for universal fundamental ethical principles. The goal of Olympism is to place everywhere sport at the service of the harmonious development of man [*sic*], with a view to encouraging the establishment of a peaceful society concerned with the preservation of human dignity.

The Olympic movement, which the IOC governs, ensures that Olympism is spread throughout the world by means of Olympic sport festivals and the various educational, artistic, and sport development programs it supports.

The primary way that the IOC ensures that this occurs is through the celebration of the Olympic Games based on the fundamental philosophical principles of modern Olympism, but other publications and educational programs exist to enhance the development of Olympism. The charter is "the codification of the Fundamental Principles, Rules and By-laws adopted by the IOC. It governs the organization and operation of the Olympic Movement and stipulates the conditions for the celebration of the Olympic Games."

At the second meeting of the IOC in Athens (1896), delegates voted that each nation should form its own national Olympic committee (NOC) and that each NOC would be eligible to have a representative on the IOC. In addition, the powers of the IOC and its president were defined and the relationship between the IOC and the various NOCs spelled out. Many of the policies approved in 1896 remain in the current version of the charter. With this authority, the IOC is able to control the individuals (especially athletes), organizations (clubs and regional/national sport bodies), the Olympic Games, and other games (e.g., Universiade, Pan American) that seek recognition under its charter. This policy dates back to the founding meeting in Paris in 1894.

Although the presidency and headquarters of the IOC were to change with each Olympiad, this did not occur. During the 1901 meeting in Paris, Pierre de Coubertin, first elected in 1896, was reelected president for a ten-year term. Six years later, this term was extended for another ten years. Therefore, the head-quarters in the early years of the movement were located in the private office of Coubertin's home in Paris. Since 1915, the headquarters have been located in Lausanne, a beautiful city on Lac Leman and a favorite location of Coubertin. The city had been a site for IOC sessions and congresses beginning in 1908. As Coubertin felt a need to ensure the administrative continuity of the movement and protect its archives, he relocated the headquarters in Lausanne, a safe haven during World War I. Switzerland's neutrality has resulted in a number of other international organizations' locating their offices in this country.

In Lausanne, the IOC was first housed in the Casino de Montenon (1915–1921). As the size of the IOC, its archives, and museum grew, the Villa Mons-Repos (1921–1968) became the headquarters and served also as Coubertin's home. Several other buildings have housed different elements of the IOC and its secretariat since 1915. Currently the Château de Vidy (1968–present) and its new administrative annex, Olympic House (1986–present), make up the main headquarters. They contain facilities for the secretariat, meetings, publications, translation, and public and legal relations, as well as the president's office. The three principal buildings, land for new buildings, and rent for temporary locations have been provided free by the city of Lausanne.

On June 23, 1993, a new museum, research center, archives, and library opened in Ouchy, the port town adjacent to Lausanne. This new building replaces an older facility in downtown Lausanne and areas within Olympic House in Vidy. The IOC also has a residence (Villa Gruaz) near the headquarters and two offices in downtown Lausanne that house other IOC activities.

In June 1894 a congress was held at the Sorbonne in Paris, at the initiative of Coubertin, ostensibly to discuss sportive matters but, according to Coubertin's memoirs, to establish a modern version of the ancient Greek Olympic Games. Some seventy-eight delegates from ten countries attended these meetings. Discussions centered on two main topics: amateur sport and the revival of the Olympic Games.

On June 23, 1894, several decisions were accepted in a plenary session, including the establishment of a modern cycle of Olympic Games. Several rules for these Games were set, as were the first two host cities: Athens (1896) and Paris (1900). Thirteen individuals (including some not in attendance) were se-

lected as members of the newly named Comité international des jeux olympiques. Demetrios Vikelas of Greece was appointed president since the first
games were to be held in Athens. Father Didion's motto of "Citius, Altius,
Fortius" (faster, higher, stronger) was accepted as the official motto of the new
movement. The congress closed as it had opened, with ceremonies and other
festivities to celebrate both ancient and modern sport. This pomp, ceremony,
and absolute adherence to protocol became a hallmark the IOC in all of its
activities.

In July 1894 the first *Bulletin* of the IOC was published. This publication was
the main source of information about the Olympic movement. It appeared spo-
radically after 1896 and has been revived under other titles, including the current
one, *Olympic Review*. Generally *Olympic Review* contains the minutes of meetings, decisions of congresses and sessions (and executive board meetings after
1921), the status of both individual and organizational members, and Olympic
stories. Today, a wide variety of publications (two journals—*Olympic Review*
and *Olympic Message*—the speeches of the president, the charter, manuals on
holding Games, histories, as well as postcards, posters, comics, and other related
items) emanate from the IOC.

The IOC remained a small body well into the twentieth century. It had fifteen
members in 1896, twenty-five in 1901, forty-eight in 1914, sixty-five in 1930,
and seventy-three in 1939. Currently, the IOC has ninety-five members, including seven women. The first female members, Pirjo Haggman and Flor Isava-
Fonseca, were selected in 1981. In 1990 Isava-Fonseca became the first female
to be elected to the executive board.

New members were selected at the whim of Coubertin until 1902, when a
postal vote was initiated for the whole IOC to approve new members. This
procedure was apparently discontinued in 1939, although many other decisions
continued to be made this way well into the 1970s. When the executive board
(EB) was established in 1921, one of its tasks was to put forward individuals
for membership. Currently, members are suggested by their NOCs and are then
approved by the EB for ratification at the next regular IOC session. There have
been exceptions to this rule, the most recent being in 1992 when the president
was given permission to appoint two members and to circumvent the rules on
language, domicile, and the maximum number of members per country.

In the early years of the IOC, any country belonging to the movement could
have at least one IOC member, and some had up to three. Currently the maximum number of members any country can have is two, if it has hosted a Summer
or Winter Games. The size of the IOC has been a continuing problem for the
movement. With 183 member NOCs and with several countries having two
members, it is possible that the IOC could easily replicate the United Nations
in size and organizational difficulty. Now certain countries are deemed to be
represented by members who are on both the IOC and one of the regional
associations of NOCs. The regional associations are the Association of NOCs
of Africa (ANOCA), the Olympic Council of Asia (OCA), the Pan American

Sports Organization (PASO), the Association of European NOCs (AENOC), and the Oceania NOCs (ONOC). These regional associations belong to the Association of NOCs (ANOC), which holds a general assembly every two years, with its executive council meeting twice yearly. The regional associations meet every year, and their executives meet on a regular basis. These NOC organizations are part of the Olympic family.

In 1908 at its Tenth Session in London, the IOC defined the criteria for membership, length of term, and total number of members. Each member represents the IOC in his or her country, lives in that country, ensures that its NOC follows the charter, and is conversant in either English or French, the official languages. An oath of admission to the IOC pledges that each member will support the charter. Members must attend the annual session, participate on one of the many permanent or ad hoc commissions of the IOC, or hold office on one of the other world sport bodies the IOC recognizes.

As of 1992 there have been 389 members on the IOC. Originally IOC members were elected for life, but currently, individuals selected as members after 1966 must retire from active participation at age 75. If a member has ten years of service (and retires or resigns for good reason), he or she becomes an honorary member at retirement. This allows them to attend the sessions as nonvoting delegates and go to the Games. Members may also be labeled *décommissionaire,* that is, expelled from membership on the IOC for not attending sessions or "knowingly jeopardizing the interests of the IOC or act[ing] in a way which is unworthy of the IOC."

Until it was abolished at the end of 1975, members had to pay an annual membership fee that varied from 50 to 250 Swiss francs. Many members failed to pay this amount and were declared *décommissionaire.* Other members, of course, died (many on the long journeys they had to make to attend the meetings, which were mainly in Europe), resigned, changed their country of residence, or lost interest. It is interesting to note that the EB and the general membership have also refused to accept retirements and resignations.

The session is the annual general meeting of the Olympic movement. At the beginning of the movement, the meetings of the IOC were identified as congresses, but that term is now used for separate, less regular meetings, which are concerned with particular topics or issues. Three of these congresses were held when a change of presidents occurred. The first took place in 1925 when Coubertin was replaced by Comte Henri de Baillet-Latour. The second was in 1972 when Lord Killanin replaced Avery Brundage. The 1981 congress was held the year after Juan Antonio Samaranch replaced Lord Killanin. The most recent congress took place in June 1994 in Paris to mark the centennial of the IOC's founding. The charter now stipulates that congresses will be held every eight years.

The congresses are important in the history of the Olympic movement for two key reasons. First, they deal with fundamental issues of global sport. The IOC holds a distinctive position in that it was established during a period when few national sport bodies (now NOCs) and few international sport governing bodies (IFs) existed. Therefore, the congresses dealt with many basic issues that still take considerable organizational effort: standardization of the rules, equipment, and officiating and judging; financing and organizing the Games and their facilities; eligibility (especially the issue of amateurism); the establishing, promoting, and expansion of NOCs and IFs; sport pedagogy; sport hygiene; and, most important and regularly, developing the program of the Summer and Winter Games. The reports of the congresses of 1921, 1925, 1930, and especially 1973 and 1981 are voluminous, attesting to this complex and difficult task.

Congresses also hear the reports of commissions. From the very first meeting, commissions have controlled the operation of the Olympic movement. Many of the commissions have continued to operate since the early days of the movement, and there are now eighteen commissions, some permanent and some ad hoc. The currently operating commissions deal with the International Olympic Academy, eligibility, apartheid and Olympism, athletes, culture, finance, medical issues (which has several subcommittees), the Olympic movement, new sources of financing, the Olympic program (with subcommittees for Summer and Winter), press, radio and television, Olympic Solidarity, sport for all, and the Coordination Commission for the Olympic Games (for and with upcoming Summer and Winter Games organizing committees). The president now decides when a commission is needed and when its work has finished and serves ex officio on all commissions.

Other advisory groups and individual consultants also carry out duties under the IOC's guidance. Councillors exist for the council of the Olympic Order, the council of the Olympic movement, and the court of arbitration for sport. Advisers are also used for juridical matters, marketing, the Olympic coin and stamp programs, technical matters regarding television, preparation for the Olympic Games, and relations with Switzerland and with developing countries. Clearly, this committee structure has served an important role in carrying out the IOC's work under the charter.

Sessions have been held every year except during the world wars. Although the Winter Games began in 1924, it was not until 1936 that sessions were held in conjunction with each of the Games. The IOC returned to the single annual meeting format after the cycle of Games was separated in 1994. It is possible to see from the minutes of these sessions and from the evolution of the charter that considerable work has been put forth to elaborate the charter, to manage the Olympic movement's influence, and to control the expansion of international sport. This work is ongoing as circumstances change.

Cities around the world compete in an intense bidding process to host sessions, which are elaborate ceremonies with formal speeches, cultural activities, dinners, balls, receptions, and other social activities in addition to the business meetings. A strict protocol is followed at these meetings, based on one's position and length of service on the IOC. This protocol also applies to attendance at the Games and other IOC-related activities.

The workload of the IOC increased dramatically once the Games gained stability and recognition after 1912. In 1921 an executive board was established to meet more frequently for carrying out routine business and proposing an agenda to the annual session. The EB structure has varied over time. Other than the president, it has had from one to four vice presidents and from three to six members at large. Currently, there are four vice presidents and five (of a possible six) members at large. According to the charter, the vice presidents and members at large must rotate off the EB every four years and are not eligible for immediate reelection. The terms are staggered to provide continuity on the EB.

The EB began its work on October 1, 1921; its first recorded meeting minutes are dated November 7, 1921, in Paris. Before 1962, the EB generally met annually, although it convened more frequently in those years when Games took place. From 1962 to the present there have been more frequent meetings, with four the standard since the 1970s. A perusal of the EB minutes shows the immense increase of work this board carries out.

Although the session is theoretically central to the operation of the IOC, the EB has come to hold a very important power position since 1980. The IOC has a much more corporate orientation today than in its earlier history. The current president, Juan Antonio Samaranch, has worked full time for the IOC. Not since Coubertin has a president had such a presence in the daily operation of the movement. This centralization of power has stirred controversy in the light of the egalitarian philosophy of Olympism that guides the IOC. Much of the business of the IOC is now shrouded in secrecy, which supports those who criticize the organization and its operation.

The secretariat is the bureaucracy that handles the IOC's daily operation. The size and elaboration of the secretariat have changed with the growth of the IOC. In the early days of the movement, Coubertin was very much the key figure in ensuring that business was done. He was the secretary-general for the first meetings and wrote prodigiously about the movement in the *Bulletin/Olympic Review* and in his memoirs. The executive "board" of the pre-1921 period was very much like that of a sport club in that the members filled various roles to carry on the operation of the group. Translators and transcribers were selected on an ad hoc basis, especially for the recording of the minutes and results of the congresses.

Around 1923, non-IOC members first joined the secretariat. The EB could name a chancellor and secretary to assist the president with IOC business. The chancellor helped organize meetings and assisted the secretary with other services and duties, such as copying the minutes. Lydia Zanchi, a part-time employee from 1926 to 1946, handled many of the administrative tasks in these early years. Her work in maintaining the integrity of the IOC was particularly vital during World War II when EB members were unable to meet regularly. In 1946, Zanchi became the IOC's full-time secretary, a position she held until her retirement in 1966.

Much of the recent growth of the secretariat came after the appointment of

Monique Berlioux as secretary-general in 1969. Berlioux was actually the director of press and public relations in charge of the *Olympic Review*; however, she filled the role of secretary-general in addition to her press directorship until 1973, when she became the full-time secretary-general. A technical director, Arthur Takac, was also appointed on a full-time basis at this time. Through her strength of character and capacity to work, Berlioux took control of the secretariat and moved it through an expansion and rationalization process, which has led to the current structure. Her reports, including suggestions for changes in the structure of the secretariat, were extensive and detailed. From her reports to the sessions and the EB meetings, it is possible to see how formalized the organization became under her guidance.

The secretariat grew from a staff of twelve in 1969 to thirty-five in 1978 and then eighty-three by 1986. Although there was a growing need for employees, difficulties were encountered with attracting and retaining them. A good deal of this problem had to do with obtaining Swiss work permits, but some apparently stemmed from Berlioux's leadership style. Berlioux's power in organizing and operating the IOC eventually resulted in a conflict with Samaranch, which led to her removal in 1985. She was replaced by Raymond Gafner, who acted as administrative delegate until 1989, when the current director, François Carrard, was appointed.

The entire secretariat has undergone considerable change since 1980, and change will likely continue as programs expand and new facilities open. A detailed description of the organization's structure continues to be an agenda item at EB meetings as the IOC struggles to keep pace with its expansion.

Today the secretariat has over one hundred full- and part-time employees with others working in contract positions outside the main buildings. Turnover continues to be fairly high, mainly due to the ongoing problem of Swiss work regulations. The complexity of the movement can be seen in the twelve directorships under a director-general, who has an administrative delegate to assist with daily administrative tasks. The secretary-general is also responsible for the departments of archives, publications, the *Olympic Review,* and personnel. Each of these directorates and departments is further divided into specialized tasks.

This expansion will also continue as the requirements of the Olympic family continue to grow. From the beginning, IOC controversies with NOCs and especially the IFs have increased. Because the IOC was formed when few of these organizations existed, many of the early congresses and executive board meetings and sessions wrestled with the problem of establishing globally acceptable rules, regulations, and eligibility requirements, as well as the constant controversies over which sports to include in the Games and which sport organizations to recognize.

NOCs and IFs meet regularly with the IOC; some meetings bring together all three groups, but most are bilateral. The IOC continues to grant recognition to new NOCs as the world map changes and to new IFs. Currently thirty IFs have status as International Olympic Federations, and eighteen have status as recognized international federations. As the NOCs have formed larger umbrella groups, so have the IFs. These include the Association of Summer Olympic International Federations (ASOIF), Association of the International Winter Sports Federations (AIWF), Association of the IOC Recognized International Sports Federations (ARISF), and the IF umbrella organization, the General Association of International Sports Federations (GAISF). Each of these associations is recognized by the IOC. Also the IOC gives its patronage to a number of regional games and IF championships.

As revenues have risen since the 1960s, ways of sharing in the television, sponsorship, and licensing monies have led to refined programs. In the 1990s, The Olympic Programme (TOP) and Olympic Solidarity are the principal ways in which the NOCs share in the wealth. Other cost-sharing agreements exist with the IFs and the Olympic Games organizing committees (OGOs). The OGOs are established to organize each Games and are the fourth member of the Olympic family. During each Olympiad, billions of dollars are generated through these programs. This situation contrasts sharply with the days when member fees were practically the only source of operating funds for the movement. Today the IOC, several NOCs, and many of the IFs have considerable incomes, investments, and healthy contingency funds.

Over the years, the IOC has changed from a volunteer organization to a professionally managed corporation. The IOC had long sought legal status to provide tax relief and security to its operation. Furthermore, it has sought exclusive rights to the use of its symbol, flag, motto, emblems, and anthem. When the IOC gained legal status as an international nongovernmental, nonprofit organization from the Swiss Federation in September 1981, it could bring the movement into a new phase of existence. It marked a considerable evolution of this organization, one that continues to become more complex and corporately intertwined.

BIBLIOGRAPHICAL ESSAY

There is no significant body of literature on the IOC. As the IOC encompasses the Olympic movement, this is understandable. Most of the works focus on the whole movement so that one must extract and piece together elements on the IOC. The *IOC Charter* (Lausanne, 1992) is the central source of the rules, guidelines, and policies of the movement. The IOC has also published promotional monographs on the movement that describe the nature of the IOC. See, for example, *The Olympic Movement* (Lausanne, 1987). A book edited by former director Monique Berlioux, *Olympism* (Lausanne, 1972), is another in-house publication that describes the workings of the IOC. Berlioux also has contributed an entry in the Killanin and Rodda collection, *The Olympic Games: 80 Years of People, Events and Records* (New York, 1976).

The IOC has a vast archives that contain the minutes of meetings for the sessions and executive board meetings and documentation on the commission meetings and activities. Swedish NOC member Wolf Lyberg has made extremely useful summaries of the sessions and EB minutes. Although they have been vetted and lack, in certain cases, the detail now contained in annexes to the minutes, they allow scholars the opportunity to follow the development of the IOC. The IOC and its secretariat are often leery of people attempting entry to the IOC's collection. It is difficult to gain access without assistance from the staff.

The IOC has published the memoirs of Coubertin, first in a small monograph and later in a large boxed volume, as well as the speeches of Brundage, Killanin, and Samaranch, and the results of the Varna and Baden-Baden congresses, among other items. In 1994, the IOC published two significant works: a three-volume centennial history, *1894–1994: The International Olympic Committee, One Hundred Years,* edited by Raymond Gafner et al., and Norbert Muller, *One Hundred Years of Olympic Congresses, 1894–1994: History, Objectives, Achievements.*

Nikolai Gueorguiev, a former Bulgarian NOC member who now works for the IOC, has studied the Olympic program over the years, and his unpublished manuscripts, available at the IOC archives, reveal much about the evolution of Summer and Winter Games events. In "Analyse du programme olympique" (1987), Gueorguiev notes that the IOC in 1912 divided Olympic sports into three categories—indispensable, desirable, and admissible—each bearing certain criteria, and has proceeded from that point. A second study, "Analyse du programme des jeux olympiques d'hiver" (1988), traces the development of the Winter Games program, and a third, "La Participation nationale aux jeux olympiques d'hiver" (1989), surveys the nations that have participated in the Winter Games between 1924 and 1988. Gueorguiev's works indicate the steady growth of events and participants in the Summer and Winter Games that by the 1990s became a matter of considerable concern to the IOC and host cities due to logistical and cost problems. See Jere Longman, "Less Is More, More or Less," *New York Times,* January 22, 1995, for a brief discussion of the dilemma.

For information on the International Olympic Academy (IOA) in Greece, consult the IOA's descriptive pamphlet, *International Olympic Academy* (Athens, 1983); Nina Pappas, "History and Development of the International Olympic Academy, 1927–1977," a typescript history available at the University of Illinois Archives; and Carl Diem, ed., *Olympic Academy* (Frankfurt, 1961), a series of papers on the IOA presented at the Fifty-eighth IOC session in Athens. This publication also includes a fairly extensive bibliography compiled by Hubert Jachowski. For a study of the IOC's periodic congresses, consult Norbert Muller, "Idee und Geschichte der Olympischen Kongresse," *Stadion* 6 (1980): 129–56.

Books on or including the IOC that have an analytical focus include Jean Leiper, "The International Olympic Committee: The Pursuit of Olympism 1894–1970" (Ph.D. dissertation, University of Edmonton, 1976), and chapters in Dwight Zakus, "A Preliminary Examination of the Dialectical Change in 'Modern' Sport and of the Intervention of the Canadian State in Sport between 1968 and 1988" (Ph.D. dissertation, University of Edmonton, 1988). Other secondary works with information on the history of the IOC include John MacAloon, *This Great Symbol: Pierre de Coubertin and the Origins of the Modern Olympic Games* (Chicago, 1981); Allan Guttmann, *The Games Must Go On: Avery Brundage and the Olympic Movement* (Urbana, Ill., 1984); and Lord Killanin, *My Olympic Years* (London, 1983).

Dwight H. Zakus

Demetrios Vikelas

Little known and not as celebrated as Coubertin, Brundage, or other International Olympic Committee (IOC) presidents, Demetrios Vikelas (also spelled Bikelas), is no less important; he was the first president of the IOC. The creation of the IOC and his election as president in 1894 constitute the beginning of the modern Olympic movement.

According to David C. Young (1988), Vikelas was the most educated and the most worldly of all IOC presidents. He was born in 1835 on the island of Syros in Greece. Shortly after, his family became refugees during the Greek war of independence. As a youth, Vikelas spent time in Odessa, Constantinople, and Syros. In 1851, he left Syros and moved to England, where he joined two of his uncles who were merchants and eventually became quite wealthy. Here he was able to perfect his knowledge of English. In addition to working with his uncles, Vikelas continued his education at the University of London, where he studied architecture, German, Italian, and French. At the age of thirty, he married a wealthy Greek heiress, Calliopi Jeralopolou, and shortly after became a full partner in his uncles' business. By the time Vikelas reached age thirty-five, he was extremely wealthy, having made his fortune in the London, Athens, and Paris mercantile and banking industries.

Vikelas had not been married long when his wife developed a serious illness which would render her an invalid. Vikelas retired, and the couple moved to Paris. Here, Vikelas dedicated his time and efforts to his wife's comfort and rediscovered his first love: literature. He translated many of Shakespeare's works into Greek and found time to write a great deal about Greek affairs and educational topics.

In 1893, he created the Institut Melas for the creation of kindergartens throughout Greece, outside of Athens. A loyal Greek, he sent money to nationalist insurgents on Crete and collaborated in the founding of a Greek school in London. His knowledge of and devotion to Greece and Greek culture were influential and important in regard to his handling of the negotiations and organizing the details of the 1896 Athens Games.

Vikelas, who was by no means a sports enthusiast, considered his election as IOC president to be somewhat coincidental and destined. In February 1894, Vikelas received a letter from a friend, Alexander Fokinos, asking him to take his place as a delegate representing the Panhellenic Gymnasium Club of Athens at the International Athletic Congress which was to be held in mid–June at the Sorbonne in Paris. Vikelas' first inclination was to decline, but upon learning that the organizer of this endeavor was Baron Pierre de Coubertin, an acquaintance with whom he shared many of the same qualities: panhellenism, patriotism, and a devotion to the cause of education, he accepted the invitation. The

Demetrios Vikelas, IOC president, 1894–1896. © IOC. Courtesy of the International Olympic Committee.

outcome of this Congress was Vikelas' election as president of the committee to reestablish the Olympic Games. Although Vikelas was surprised at his election, he accepted the responsibility with pleasure and took his official duties seriously as he began the tedious task of setting the wheels in motion for the 1896 Games.

Accounts vary as to the extent of Vikelas' involvement in the organization of the first modern Olympic Games. According to Young in "Demetrios Vikelas: First President of the IOC," Vikelas did almost all the work. Young states that it was Vikelas who met with officials in Athens, Vikelas who got them to agree to host the first "modern" games, and Vikelas who tended to the public relations, sent out invitations and made arrangements to use various facilities in the city. Young also concludes that it is Vikelas who is responsible for the Olympic tradition and the Olympic spirit of good will that still exists today.

Although most other historians believe Coubertin deserves the credit for the "Olympic Idea" and for the reestablishment of the modern Games, Young is quick to note that Coubertin was too busy with planning his upcoming wedding to participate in the organization of those first games. Young further notes that Coubertin, who was serving the IOC as the secretary-general, failed in his attempt to recruit French and British teams, and was remiss in his management of IOC officials. Most interestingly, Young notes that perhaps Coubertin would not have been the important IOC figure as he is known today if it were not for Vikelas. In early 1895, Coubertin's interest in the Olympic movement waned and he submitted his resignation to the IOC; Vikelas refused to accept it.

Other accounts of Vikelas' Olympic involvement and tenure as IOC president, depict Vikelas as a mere marionette in Coubertin's grand scheme. According to John MacAloon, Vikelas' success in implementating and organizing the early preparations for the Games was merely an illusion that Coubertin later had to rectify.

Nevertheless, historians do portray the organization of the 1896 Games as tedious due to internal political and financial problems. Vikelas deserves recognition for his role in organizing these Games. Except for a brief absence, in which he returned to Paris to bury his wife, Vikelas was the instrumental figure throughout the development of the first modern Olympic Games. Vikelas worked well with IOC officials and fullfilled his IOC presidental duties with determination and enthusiasm. The only controversy encountered during Vikelas' tenure as IOC president was a disagreement with Coubertin in regard to future Olympic Games. Since the 1896 Games were so successful, the Greeks decided to claim the Olympic Games as their own; they wanted all future Games to be held in Athens. This is ironic when one considers that it took great effort on Vikelas' part to convince the Greeks to host the 1896 games. Coubertin was adamant that the Games would be international in scope, and as such should move around the world. Although Vikelas agreed with Coubertin that indeed the Olympic Games should be international, his Greek pride and fierce loyalty to his country led him to sympathize with his compatriots, and he lobbied in their favor. Coubertin rejected all proposals on this matter. Vikelas tried to compromise, proposing instead "in-between" games in Athens. Again Coubertin declined, determined to internationalize future Olympic Games. The two had heated debates and their relationship became strained. In late 1896, Vikelas resigned as president of the IOC, although he remained very active in the organization until 1899, and his friendship with Coubertin survived the disagreement. Interestingly, a successful "in-between" Games did take place in Athens in 1906. Coubertin gave the event the IOC's blessing, but he did not attend and labeled the games as "unofficial."

Vikelas died in July 1908. At the end of his life, Vikelas returned to the cause of Greece, locked in seemingly endless conflict with Turkey. He remained active in the literary field, writing and editing several books, and he continued to be involved with activities which promoted education. In 1904 he organized a large conference on education in Athens, out of which came an education museum. In 1905, he served as the Greek delegate to the Olympic Congress in Brussels and accepted the 1906 intermediate Games as "Jeux Olympiques Internationaux d'Athens."

Young gives a heartwarming account of Vikelas as a lover of all people and a philanthropist. Despite Vikelas' modest reputation, he was a serious man who gave all his interests his utmost consideration, especially his role as the first IOC president. His obscurity is not at all deserved.

BIBLIOGRAPHICAL ESSAY

Primary sources regarding Demetrios Vikelas are somewhat limited. Information is available at the IOC Archives in Lausanne, Switzerland, which includes correspondence between Vikelas and Coubertin, as well as Vikelas' writings. Among Vikelas' writings, two articles relate to the Olympics: "Les Jeux Olympiques Internationaux," *Estia* [Athens] (1895): 146, and "Les Jeux Olympiques dans le passé et l'avernir. Memoire présenti au Congrès de 1894 au nom de la Société Panhelleneque d'Athens," *Bulletin Officiel du CIO*, 1, 2 (October 1894): 3–4.

Secondary sources of use to researchers include two in-depth and insightful articles. David C. Young gives an enlightening account in "Demetrios Vikelas: First President of the IOC," *Stadion* 14, 1 (1988): 85–102. Researchers who are able to read French may wish to consult Yves Pierre Boulongue's, "Les presidencies de Demetrios Vikelas et de Pierre de Coubertin," in Raymond Gafner, ed., *Un Siècle du Comité Internationaal Olympique: L'Idée—Les Présidents—L'Oeuvre* (Lausanne, 1994).

See also Pierre de Coubertin, "Demetrios Vikelas," *Revue Olympique* 8 (September 1908): 131–32, and brief passages concerning Vikelas' role in the 1896 Games in Allen Guttmann, *The Olympics* (Urbana, Ill., 1992) and John J. MacAloon, *This Great Symbol: Pierre de Coubertin and the Origins of the Modern Olympic Games* (Chicago, 1981).

Kimberly D. Pelle

Pierre de Coubertin

Baron Pierre de Coubertin was born on January 1, 1863, the son of an old Italian family that had lived for nearly five hundred years in France. An ancestor, Pierre Fredy, was ennobled by Louis XI, whom he served as chamberlain, in March 1477. In 1822, Coubertin's grandfather, Julien-Bonaventure Fredy de Coubertin, was made hereditary baron by *lettres patents,* in the general reorganization of privileges under Louis XVIII.

At the age of 12, Pierre de Coubertin was one of the first forty students to inaugurate the new Jesuit college, Externat Saint-Ignace, in Paris. He attended this school for seven years. To his parents, it was very important that he received a Christian education. Through that education, they hoped to smother their son's freethinking and rebellious nature. Although at home Pierre was a rebel, in the hierarchical and peer group environment of the college, he was, at least in his behavior, a conformist.

As one of the three top students at Externat Saint-Ignace, Pierre earned an appointment to the French military academy. Within a few months of his matriculation in 1880, however, he resigned. By this time, he had already become interested, mostly through republican professor-reformers, in the rebuilding and modernization of the educational system and the army.

Although he entered law school in 1884, studying law was the last time Pierre de Coubertin bowed to his father's wishes and made a last, half-hearted attempt at a conventional higher education. In his father's opinion, law was the only option left for a man of this class who had refused entrance into the army. In 1885 Coubertin quit law school; his father never acknowledged his son's subsequent projects and achievements. Coubertin then enrolled in the Ecole libre de sciences politiques. During that time the young humanist became deeply involved in the idea of the reform of the educational system based on what he had observed during visits to England.

In 1883, Coubertin made his first trip to England. Although this visit was in part a result of his inability to settle down, it was also a step toward his new purpose: to make inquiries into the English educational system. He planned to visit several colleges and universities, but whether his name became associated with that of a great pedagogical reformer occasioned the trip to England or was its outcome is hard to say. It was the ideas of Hippolyte Taine, a moderate intellectual and provincial lawyer's son, that brought Coubertin to England. It is almost certain that he read Taine's book about English education before his departure. Taine investigated as many neighborhoods, schools, parks, associations, and social groups as he could for his ethnographic studies. In England, Coubertin learned Thomas Arnold's theory about the principal element in male education: sports. Arnold had become headmaster of Rugby school in 1828 and

Pierre de Coubertin, IOC president, 1896–1916, 1919–1925. Courtesy of University of Illinois Archives, Avery Brundage Collection.

raised the institution to the rank of a great public school. He was not an innovator in teaching methods, but his aim was to reform Rugby school by making it a school for gentlemen. His system of school sports, student self-government, and postgraduate athletic associations could, Pierre de Coubertin felt assured, *rebronzer la France,* after the disastrous Franco-Prussian War of 1870–1871 and would help to build up a lasting democratic society, as the English had. Sports would be the key element to fulfill this goal and to reform the French school system. During the 1880s school sport competitions started in Paris. For the first time, high school students played soccer; then the Racing Club de France was founded. In 1888 Coubertin published the results of his studies on the British educational system, which were more or less a reflection of Arnold's theories.

Coubertin's next goal was the formation of a committee designed to be responsible for physical education in schools. He was very interested in finding a proper name for his committee but at the same time had to be careful not to alarm parents, many of whom were skeptical about the value of physical education. The committee, introduced for the first time on May 29, 1888, consisted of five members; however, in reality the committee *was* Pierre de Coubertin. The other members, such as president Jules Simon, a republican professor-reformer, thought it was enough to lend the committee their names, experiences, and good reputation. Coubertin did not find too many supporters for his committee but did publish some helpful articles in journals and newspapers. These helped increase the power of the 26-year-old Coubertin, who then arranged a room at the Sorbonne as an assembly hall for the committee. As a meeting place, the Sorbonne could help convince people of the seriousness of the movement. Besides, if Coubertin could be successful in getting into the Sorbonne, people like Jules Simon would believe in him more.

For the world's fair of 1889 in Paris, Coubertin sent out a questionnaire to all large high schools and universities in Great Britain, the British empire, and the United States to determine whether Arnold's theory was understood and accepted. Additionally, he wanted to know how far the theory had been implemented and how other nations handled new educational systems, especially sports. In case he got positive answers, he hoped to persuade educators in France to adopt Arnold's theory. Sports and school reform became increasingly his vocation. Most of the responses he received showed that universities and colleges utilized sport, despite the fact that they did not acknowledge Arnold. At Coubertin's instigation, the committee, in pioneering work, published a small guidebook promoting sports in school. However, opponents feared that the influence of other nations could disturb their own nationality and raise the influence of Great Britain.

In July 1889 Coubertin traveled to the United States and Canada to visit several universities, colleges, and high schools and to examine the organization of the sports clubs in these countries. He knew that he would come back to France with much more evidence to prove the educational value of sport activities. In December Coubertin returned to Paris, convinced that promoting sports was the right path. His program was the realization of "sport and freedom" in that he wanted to achieve freedom through sport activities. For the next two years, he edited the *Revue athlétique*. During this time he traveled to Scotland, visiting an old friend who had established a sports center. This friend had also sent a trophy to Athens for the winner in an athletic competition. Engraved on the trophy was the word *Olympics*. That word was an inspiration for Coubertin; now he knew what he was looking for to popularize the idea of sports: Olympic Games. These Olympics had been essentially religious affairs, and the Greeks had always proclaimed a sacred truce for them and for the people traveling to and from Olympia. For Coubertin, this would be the key: with the help of sport, it should again be possible to bring nations together. At the same time, Olympic Games would make sport so popular again that it would be easy to introduce it into French schools.

Coubertin recognized that for the French, celebrations were something very attractive. Therefore, he hoped that in the form of an international celebration, the Olympic Games could become reality and that he could rally support from his country. Despite the fact that the way to Olympic Games was exhausting, Coubertin was convinced by the end of 1890 that he would reestablish the Games. His conviction had been enforced through the archaeological discoveries in Olympia between 1875 and 1881, which had not been completely analyzed until 1890. The name *Olympia* could be found in most newspapers and magazines, which helped make it more popular. Many articles were published about the excavations by the expedition of Heinrich Schliemann as well as about the ancient Olympic Games. Consequently, *Olympic* became a well-known word.

Coubertin never doubted that Olympic Games could be successful only in an international context. This seemed even more possible after American athletes journeyed to Paris in July 1891 for a series of competitions. However, the moment to start an Olympic campaign in Paris was, as Coubertin wrote in his 1908 book, *Une Campagne de 21 ans,* not quite right. Hence he started the campaign in the countryside, although financial support was difficult to obtain while maintaining independence from the government. The year 1892 was a hard one for the movement, but Coubertin thought that direct contact between French athletes and sports-minded nations would bring so much recognition that nobody would call the relationship into question. Athletes should work together, independent of their nations, for the same idea: sport. And this idea was again very close to the Olympic ideal. The Olympic Games should bring nations together, overcome national disputes, and serve as a symbol for peace. Coubertin thought that at least one reason for the flowering of Greece during the so-called Golden Age had been sport and the ideal of the Olympic Games.

As he wrote in *Une Campagne de 21 ans,* if Germany excavated the rest of Olympia, why should France not give back Olympia its grand style? The idea of reestablishing the Olympic Games became paramount for Coubertin. He lectured at the Sorbonne in November 1892 about sports in the past, the renewal of the Olympic Games, and the export of athletes as a basis for peace within all of Europe and the rest of the world. From the reaction, he learned that the Olympic Games were something that happened in history but nothing one can renew.

Therefore, instead of promoting the Olympic Games as the subject of the next conference, planned for June 1894, he mentioned the renewal of the Olympic Games only in a paragraph. With help of such conferences he hoped to gain more support and popularize his idea of a new Olympic Games. This idea became more concrete in a letter to foreign sports clubs in January 1894. His notion of creating international cooperation was much more difficult than he had thought, since most athletes thought that international competition in a variety of sports would reduce the importance of their own sport, and most did not believe in sports other than their own. Although there was great resistance to his idea, Coubertin never gave up. Finally the conference took place in June 1894 at the Sorbonne. On the last day, the delegates decided to revive the Olympic Games and elect an International Olympic Committee (IOC). The first Games were scheduled for Paris in conjunction with the international exposition in 1900. During the conference, it was decided that six years would be too long a period to wait for the Games. Since Paris would be hosting the exposition and the Olympic Games in 1900, the delegates decided to give the honor of hosting the first modern Olympic Games in 1896 to Athens.

In addition, the conference decided to form commissions on hygiene and education. The first one published a short guide on hygiene for athletes, and the second one, under the presidency of a Sorbonne professor, contained essays about international education. Although both commissions were of utmost importance for Coubertin, his main interest was the formation of the IOC.

After his success, Coubertin's next step was to convince Greece to host the first Games. Initially, it refused, for financial reasons. Coubertin was afraid that Greece would resist, and so he went to Athens. Within the government, a majority opposed the idea because of the political and economic situation in Greece. The Greek government was too weak to survive a financial loss on a project that the majority of the population found useless. Coubertin thus faced a major challenge. It was a very arduous path for him; he supplied plans, constructions, cost estimates, and a brochure at his own expense. Finally, the Greek Olympic Committee decided to host the Games. Believing in its success, they were no longer interested in Coubertin and did not want to give him credit for the initiative and the idea of the first Olympic Games. Now, convinced of the idea, they wanted to take the credit for themselves. As he wrote in *Une Campagne de 21 ans*, Greece refused to mention his name and the influence of France for reviving the Games. The Games were such a success that the Greek government wanted to institutionalize them in Athens, but Coubertin intended to make the Games as international as possible, and the next Games were already planned for Paris. Again, his diplomatic talent was much needed. He went to his former ally for the Olympic Games in Athens, the crown prince of Greece, and persuaded him of the idea of moving the Games from place to place. The crown prince finally convinced the king, who acknowledged the virtue of the idea. After such an acknowledgment, Coubertin received many unfriendly letters from Greeks who wanted "their" Olympic Games back.

Immediately after the first Olympic Games, Pierre de Coubertin knew that four years would be a long time to wait for the next festival and that something related to the Games must happen during this period. Under difficult circumstances, he succeeded in organizing a conference in Le Havre, France, to give consideration to pedagogical problems. After this conference, the idea of a Greek Olympic Games was finally dead; no one considered again that anything or anybody else other than the IOC could be responsible for the implementation of Olympic Games. In addition, the Greeks lost their interest in the Olympic Games in 1897 when Turkey declared war on them.

The next Olympic Games took place in Paris, and again it was difficult for Coubertin to organize them. This time, he was not as successful as he had been in Athens. The Games in Paris were the result of power struggles and a very bad organization. Therefore the next conference was even more important: the IOC had to prove its stability and capacity to implement the Olympic Games in the future and to choose locations for future Games. Coubertin again devoted all his energy to develop the Games, and though the Games of 1904 in St. Louis were again a disaster, there was significant success in that the IOC was building strength. His future work could be directed more toward the movement itself. The next Games, in London in 1908, were much more successful and well organized, despite numerous controversies. Now, though, political problems were arising: the Russians tried to prevent the Finns from displaying their flag, and the English did the same to the Irish. In the competition, the British won a disproportionate share of the medals, which led to protests over the rules and the judging by France, Canada, Italy, Sweden, and especially the United States. The dispute between Great Britain and its former colony was so acute that it almost put an end to the Olympics. Once again the diplomatic skills of Pierre de Coubertin quelled the dispute.

The Games of 1912 in Stockholm were a well-organized success, with a total of 4,742 athletes from twenty-seven different nations participating. During this time, the next Games were planned for Berlin. In ancient times, all wars were suspended during the period of the Olympics. In modern times, the reverse has been true. Although Coubertin suggested a truce during the Games, World War I forced the cancellation of the 1916 Olympics. Coubertin himself took a leave from his duties as IOC president while he fought for the French in the war, and Godefroy de Blonay of Switzerland served as interim president until 1919. An Egyptologist and linguist, Blonay taught at the University of Neuchâtel and became a member of the IOC in 1899 and a founding member and first president of the Comité Olympique Suisse in 1912. Blonay became a member of the IOC's executive board in 1921 and served until his death in 1937.

After his return to the IOC presidency in 1919, Coubertin faced postwar

Olympic Games that were frequently characterized by political struggles and a global depression. The last Olympic Games during Coubertin's lifetime were in Berlin in 1936. Only eleven months before his death, Coubertin's voice echoed around the Berlin Olympic stadium, through a gramophone recording and loud-speaker. Some 110,000 people in the stadium, listeners to an overseas radio network, were the first commercial television audience to hear his famous words: ''The important thing in the Olympic Games is not winning but taking part. Just as in life, the aim is not to conquer but to struggle well.''

The man who renovated the Olympic Games, who held the presidency of the IOC from 1896 to 1916 and from 1919 to 1925 and was elected as honorary president for life, died a lonely man. In 1895 he had married Marie Rothan, the daughter of family friends, and they had a couple of happy and successful years. But then everything changed. Exhausted by his projects, war, and depression, the Coubertins could not maintain their living standard. But the fates of their children were the real source for their deep depressions. The first-born, Jacques, became retarded after his parents left him in the sun too long when he was a little child. He died when he was 56. Their daughter, an intelligent girl, was overwhelmed by her guilt-ridden mother and left alone by her father, who was perpetually away on his missions. She suffered emotional disturbances, never married, and never found peace in her life. Marie and Pierre de Coubertin blamed each other and tried to console themselves with two nephews who be-came substitutes for their own children. The nephews were killed at the front in World War I, ending the ancient Coubertin line with the death of Pierre de Coubertin. He died on September 2, 1937, in Geneva and was buried in the Bois de Vaux in Lausanne, almost within sight of the present IOC headquarters. According to his last will, his heart was buried in Greece at the Archaia Olym-pia.

BIBLIOGRAPHICAL ESSAY

A remarkable book by Pierre de Coubertin is *Une Campagne de 21 ans (1887–1908)* (Paris, 1909), which describes his efforts to reestablish the Olympic Games. His other works deal mainly with his studies of education and French history: *L'Education en Angleterre: collèges et universités* (Paris, 1888); *Essais de psychologie sportive* (Lausanne, 1913); *La Chronique de France* (Auxerre, 1900–1904); *L'Evolution française sous la Troisième République* (Paris, 1896); *France since 1814* (London, 1900); and *Pierre de Coubertin: Textes choisis* (Zurich, 1986).

Noteworthy books on Coubertin's life and work are John J. MacAloon, *This Great Symbol* (Chicago, 1981), the best biographical study in English; Yves-Pierre Boulongne, *La Vie et l'oeuvre pédagogique de Pierre de Coubertin* (Montreal, 1975); Charles vi-comte de Bouthillier-Chavigny, *Justice aux Canadiens-français! A m. le baron Pierre de Coubertin* (Montreal, 1890); Louis Callebat, *Pierre de Coubertin* (Paris, 1988); and Kurt Zentner, *Pierre de Coubertin! Ein Beitrag zur Entwicklung des modernen Sports* (Borna-Leipzig, 1935). Available on microfiche is Thomas Alkemeyer, *Vom Wettstreit der Nationen zum Kampf der Voelker: Aneignung und Umdeutung der olympischen Idee im deutschen Faschismus: der Olympismus Pierre de Coubertins und die Olympischen Spiele von 1936 in Berlin* (1994).

Ute Schwabe

Henri de Baillet-Latour

Belgium became a modern nation in 1830, some sixty years prior to Baron Pierre de Coubertin's creation of the modern Olympic movement. While Coubertin dreamed the Olympics would promote world peace and harmony, the leaders of Belgium—a country long renowned for its culture and commerce but not for its military prowess—had the less grand objective of staying out of harm's way in a Europe set apart by hostile nations and alliances. One young Belgian whose life was intertwined with Coubertin's vision and Belgium's fate was Count Henri de Baillet-Latour. Born March 1, 1876, in Brussels, Baillet-Latour joined Coubertin's fledgling International Olympic Committee (IOC) in 1903 and gave the next four decades of his life to the organization, the last sixteen of them spent as Coubertin's successor. Baillet-Latour's custodianship of Coubertin's dream would end upon his death in 1942 with the world at war and his country occupied by the same Nazi regime that hosted Berlin's controversial 1936 Olympic Games.

Baillet-Latour, while thirteen years younger than Coubertin, fit in nicely with the aristocratic gentleman's club atmosphere that long characterized the governance of the IOC. The cigar-smoking Belgian was owner of several racehorses and the president of the elite Jockey-Club de Bruxelles. His conception of the Olympic movement scarcely differed from Coubertin's. Baillet-Latour helped organize the Third IOC Congress, held in Brussels in 1905, an occasion "at which the idealistic spokesmen for internationalism gave voice to their dreams for a more pacific world unified by a common commitment to amateur sport" (Guttmann, *The Olympics,* p. 28). The congress also featured debate over the concept of amateurism, with the Olympic barons attempting to exclude members of the lower classes from competition, despite the universal aims of the Olympic movement. Shortly after, Baillet-Latour organized Belgian participation in the 1908 London and 1912 Stockholm Games.

Two years after the Stockholm Games, Europe's peace was shattered; the guns of August fired in Belgium, as German armies used the small nation's countryside as an invasion route to France. The 1916 Games, scheduled for Berlin, were never held. When the war ended with Germany's defeat, the IOC voted in 1919 to place symbolically the first postwar games in Belgium's port city of Antwerp. Baillet-Latour distinguished himself by helping the Antwerp committee organize the massive undertaking despite having only a year's lead time and a scant budget. The following year he was rewarded with a nomination

Henri de Baillet-Latour, IOC president, 1925–1942. Courtesy of University of Illinois Archives, Avery Brundage Collection.

to the IOC's newly formed five-member executive board. And at the IOC's 1925 congress in Prague, following two rounds of balloting, Baillet-Latour was elected to an eight-year term as president, to succeed the retiring Coubertin.

During Baillet-Latour's first term, a major issue on the IOC's agenda was the question of women's sports. In 1929, Baillet-Latour argued before the executive board for limiting women athletes to the "suitably feminine" sports of gymnastics, swimming, tennis, and figure skating, but a decision was postponed until after the Berlin congress of 1930. Holding to the common prejudice that participation in track and field would turn women into "masculine Amazons," Baillet-Latour proposed to track and field's governing body, the International Amateur Athletic Federation (IAAF), meeting in conjunction with the congress, that the five women's track and field events introduced at the 1928 Games be eliminated from the 1932 Los Angeles Games program. American delegate Gustavus Kirby angrily counterproposed that if women were banned, a special congress be summoned to consider the elimination of men's track and field. The IAAF then voted to continue supporting female inclusion, and the full Olympic congress also followed suit.

The Berlin congress was also fateful as its organizers successfully pressed the IOC in 1931 to award the 1936 Summer Games to their city. On January 24, 1933, six days prior to Adolf Hitler's accession to power, the Organisationskomitte for the Berlin Games was formed. The Nazi party's bitter ideological views about race and religion extended to sport, with Nazi spokesman Bruno Malitz condemning modern sports for being "infested" with "Frenchmen, Belgians, Pollacks and Jew-Niggers," who had been allowed "to start on tracks, to play on the soccer fields and to swim in the pools" (Guttmann, *The Olympics,* p. 54). Propaganda minister Joseph Goebbels convinced Hitler, however, that the Games would be an opportunity to showcase Germany's vitality and organizational expertise and to promote their particular brand of National Socialism. Baillet-Latour was concerned from the start about Hitler's intentions and intervened in 1933 to force the Nazis to retain the two principal organizers of the Berlin Games—Theodor Lewald and Karl Ritter von Halt—after it was disclosed that Lewald's father was a Jewish convert to Christianity and von Halt had Jewish ancestors.

The right of Jewish athletes to participate on the German national team became the focus of worldwide attention as the IOC met for its 1933 congress in Vienna. At the congress, which reelected Baillet-Latour to a second eight-year term by a 48–1 vote, the president pressed Germany's three IOC members for written assurance from their government that German Jews would have the right to participate in the Games. He did receive such an assurance and declared it to be "satisfactory."

Despite this promise, the Nazis moved quickly and brazenly to exclude German Jews from private German sports clubs and to deny them use of public sports facilities. Jewish athletes who had a chance to make the team, including world-class high jumper Gretel Bergmann, were eventually denied fair tryouts.

As a result of negative publicity about the Nazi regime, a significant movement to boycott the Berlin Games arose in Great Britain, Canada, and the United States. American IOC member Ernest Lee Jahncke, who had served in the Herbert Hoover administration as assistant secretary of the navy, published an appeal in the November 27, 1935, *New York Times* calling for Baillet-Latour to meet his ''duty to hold the Nazi sports authorities accountable for the violation of their pledges. . . . Let me beseech you to seize the opportunity to take your rightful place in the history of the Olympics alongside of de Coubertin instead of Hitler.'' Baillet-Latour was furious at this public airing of the IOC's business and promised Avery Brundage that he was ready to come to the United States to combat the ''Jewish'' boycott campaign. He had recently visited Hitler, who had assured him that the charges against Germany were false. Baillet-Latour told Jahncke that the president's duty was to execute the will of the IOC, which was steadfastly committed to the Games. He subsequently supported Jahncke's replacement by Brundage on the IOC. Four months later, when Hitler violated the Versailles Treaty by sending armed soldiers into the demilitarized Rhineland, Baillet-Latour told a press conference that only an armed conflict would prevent holding the Games in Berlin.

Baillet-Latour's motivation is still the subject of some historic controversy. One interpretation of his actions holds him to the mistaken belief that allowing the Germans to host the Olympics would somehow reduce Hitler's aggressive instincts. The less generous explanation is that he was so determined to have the Olympics go forward as scheduled that he willingly overlooked German violations of the Olympic code. Despite Baillet-Latour's statement that the IOC would not interfere with the internal policies of other countries, when questions were raised about the Nazi regime's discriminatory practices, he did assert IOC prerogatives in his dealings with the Nazis over the actual conduct of the Games. Shortly before the 1936 Winter Olympics in Garmisch-Partenkirchen, he demanded that Hitler have anti-Semitic signs around the city removed, stating that during the Olympics, the host city becomes ''sacred Olympic territory'' of which he was the master. Astonishingly, Hitler complied. During the Berlin Games, Hitler left the Olympic stadium in order to avoid being placed in the position of having to shake the hands of the black American gold– and silver medal–winning long jumpers Cornelius Johnson and David Albritten. Baillet-Latour subsequently told the führer that he must invite all the victors to his box or none of them. Hitler decided to save his greetings to German athletes for a post-Games celebration. Thus, Hitler did not actually refuse to shake the hand of America's four gold medal winner Jesse Owens, as popular myth holds.

As the Berlin Games wound down, Baillet-Latour attended a grand dinner given by Hitler for Olympic notables and sat next to the wife of the Nazi Youth leader, Baldur von Schirach. She remarked on how well ''the great festival of youth, peace and reconciliation'' was going. Baillet-Latour replied, ''May God preserve you from your illusions, madame! If you ask me, we shall have war in three years'' (quoted in *New York Times,* June 15, 1986). He was absolutely right. Germany invaded Poland on September 1, 1939, and by the following spring had occupied Belgium. With the world engulfed in war, the 1940 Winter Games, originally scheduled for Sapporo, Japan, and then moved to Garmisch-Partenkirchen, were cancelled. The same fate struck the 1940 Summer Games, which were set first for Tokyo and then shifted to Helsinki. During the winter of 1940–1941, the German sports officials Carl Diem, Karl Ritter von Halt, and Reichssportsführer Hans von Tschammer und Osten visited Baillet-Latour and told him that Hitler had a grandiose plan for a new order in postwar sports. Coubertin's dream was to be transformed literally into the Nazi Olympics that would be held "for all time" in a 450,000-seat *deutsches stadium* built by Hitler's favorite architect, Albert Speer. Baillet-Latour never lived long enough to see the crumbling of this nightmare vision; he died of a stroke on January 6, 1942, shortly after hearing his son had died in a free Belgium army exercise in the United States and exactly two years and five months prior to the day when the Allied invasion of Normandy hastened the end of the Nazi empire.

While the events of World War I and II provide dramatic bookends to Baillet-Latour's life in the Olympic movement, he should also be remembered for his steady leadership of the IOC after Coubertin and for keeping the basic amateur and male-oriented structure of the games intact during the interwar period.

BIBLIOGRAPHICAL ESSAY

Count Henri de Baillet-Latour may be among the least chronicled of the IOC presidents. He never wrote about his own life and experiences in the Olympic movement, and his papers have not been collected and made public. Scattered letters to or from Baillet-Latour may be found in the IOC Archives in Lausanne and in the Avery Brundage Papers, University of Illinois Archives.

The best secondary source for a study of Baillet-Latour's regency over the IOC is Allen Guttmann, *The Olympics: A History of the Modern Games* (Urbana, Ill., 1992). Guttmann's history details Baillet-Latour's involvement in early Olympic congresses and his role in organizing the 1920 Antwerp Games, which brought him into prominence within IOC circles. Guttmann writes with knowing authority about Baillet-Latour's relationship with Pierre de Coubertin and about his role in the events leading up to the 1936 Berlin Games.

For more detailed insight into Baillet-Latour's involvement in the controversial Berlin Games, consult the various sources dealing specifically with those Games, and especially Duff Hart-Davis, *Hitler's Games* (London, 1986), which provides a dramatic overview of the events leading up to the Berlin Olympics and is very critical of the role of Baillet-Latour in allowing the Games to go forward, despite clear warning signs that the Nazis would use the Games as a propaganda vehicle and would violate the nondiscrimination clause of the Olympic charter.

Edward S. Goldstein

Sigfrid Edström

On a per capita basis, no other set of countries has had greater success in the modern Olympics than those of Scandinavia. Born into cultures that cherish the outdoor life, Scandinavia's sons and daughters have dominated competition in the Winter Games and more than held their own in such disparate Summer Games events as boxing, sailing, wrestling, and track and field. In the first modern Olympics in Athens in 1896, Sigfrid Edström ran the 100-meter sprint for his native Sweden. His best time in the event was an impressive 11 seconds flat. In Olympic affairs, however, Edström was more of a marathon man; he served the International Olympic Committee (IOC) for thirty-one years, and guided it as acting president from 1942 to 1946 and as president from 1946 to 1952.

Like Baron Pierre de Coubertin, Edström was of aristocratic stock. He was born November 21, 1870, in Gothenburg and was educated there and in Zurich as a civil engineer. In 1899 he married Ruth Miriam Randall, an American. Edström became president of the Swedish General Electric Company in 1903. Although he remained an industrialist all his life, Edström's avocational focus turned toward athletics when the Olympics came to Stockholm in 1912. For those Games, Edström was director and vice president of the organizing committee and a member of the stadium building committee. During the Stockholm Olympics he began a lifelong friendship with American decathlete Avery Brundage. Enthused by the success of the Stockholm Games, Edström became a founder and first president of the International Amateur Athletic Federation (IAAF), track and field's governing body.

In 1921, Edström joined future IOC president Count Henri de Baillet-Latour as a member of the first five-member executive board of the IOC. One of Edström's first significant actions was to counter traditional Scandinavian opposition to a separate Winter Olympic Games by voting to allow the IOC to give its patronage to the Week of Winter Sports, which was held in Chamonix, France, in 1924. Until then the Scandinavian countries feared a Winter Games would diminish the appeal of their traditional skiing competitions. At the IOC's 1925 congress in Prague, the body voted to adopt the Winter Games as an official part of the Olympic program.

The IOC also debated the issue of amateurism at the Prague Congress. Edström argued that compensating athletes for the time they spend away from work would "open up the floodgates" to professionals from the lower classes. The IOC agreed but did allow for athletes to be reimbursed for their expenses for periods up to fifteen days. Seven years later, just prior to the 1932 Olympic Games in Los Angeles, Edström, acting as president of the IAAF, disqualified

Sigfrid Edström, acting IOC president, 1942–1946, IOC president, 1946–1952. Courtesy of University of Illinois Archives, Avery Brundage Collection.

from competition the great Finnish runner Paavo Nurmi after allegations that Nurmi was being paid to run.

Edström also shared the prejudice of his time against the participation of women in strenuous athletic events. In 1924, his IAAF voted to sanction women's track and field events in general but not to advocate their inclusion in the Olympic Games. But Edström did not count on the popularity of "Women's Olympics" put on by the fledgling Fédération sportive feminine internationale and its leader, Alice Milliat. In 1926 he met with Milliat and agreed to recommend to the IOC that women be allowed to compete in five athletic events, beginning with the 1928 Games in Amsterdam.

In the events leading up to the controversial 1936 Berlin Olympics, Edström supported the IOC's official position that the Olympics should go on as scheduled, no matter how outrageous the actions of the Nazi government towards its people. By 1934, when it became clear that German persecution of its Jewish citizens was increasing and might lead to an international backlash against the Games, Edström wrote Brundage a letter that in part excused Germany's anti-Semitism and called for keeping Jews "within certain limits" even in the United States.

Less than four years after the Berlin Games, war engulfed Europe, and IOC president Baillet-Latour found himself unable to focus on his Olympic duties from his occupied Belgian home. Edström, IOC vice president since 1938 and a neutral-country citizen, was the logical choice to supervise IOC business. And when Baillet-Latour died of a stroke in 1942, Edström became the acting IOC president. One of Edström's first actions was to recommend to the other IOC members that Avery Brundage become second vice president.

In August 1945, Edström, Brundage, and Britain's Lord Aberdare met in London to discuss the revival of the Games. While Aberdare had lost his optimism and wondered if the Games should be resumed as if the horrors of World War II had never occurred, Edström and Brundage persuaded him that the Games were more necessary than ever. Later, by a mail ballot of IOC members, London (Summer) and St. Moritz, Switzerland (Winter) were selected as the Olympic sites for 1948.

In 1946, at the IOC's first postwar session in Lausanne, Switzerland, Edström was elected president by acclamation. The IOC members then attempted to deal with a pent-up demand for new Olympic events. They considered but rejected petitions for the inclusion of archery, baseball, gliding, team handball, polo, roller skating, table tennis, and volleyball. (Of these sports, volleyball was accepted in 1964, archery and team handball in 1972.)

During the next important IOC session, held in 1951 in Vienna, delegates passionately debated whether IOC members who had been associated with the deposed regimes of Germany, Italy, and Japan should be allowed to remain in the organization. Edström called some of the accused members—including his longtime acquaintance from Germany, Karl Ritter von Halt—"old friends" and refused to put the matter to a vote, despite the protests of a number of members whose homelands had been occupied by German forces during the war.

Edström's reign as IOC president wound down as the cold war continued and as the athletes of the communist world were welcomed into the Olympic movement. As early as 1947 Edström indicated to Brundage that he was willing to allow communist nations to compete in the Olympics, but the aging capitalist drew the line at endorsing the election of communists to the IOC board. The Soviet Union was given permission to compete in the Games at the IOC's May 1951 Congress in Vienna. (Although czarist Russia had participated in the Olympics, the Soviet Union under Lenin and Stalin had withdrawn from the Games and sponsored its own workers' games.)

The question of Chinese Olympic participation following the bloody civil war between communists and nationalists was a more difficult one for the IOC leadership. On the eve of the 1952 Games in Helsinki, the mainland communists and the Chinese nationalists on the island of Formosa (now known as Taiwan) each claimed to be the sole legitimate representative of Chinese athletes, and both angered Edström with their political harangues. A compromise proposal to allow the individual sport federations to recognize either the communists' or the nationalists' athletes failed; the nationalists boycotted the Games because the communists were expected to be present, and the communists arrived too late to compete.

Edström's IOC also wrestled with the classic cold war issue of divided Germany. At the IOC's Vienna session in 1951, the national Olympic committee from democratic West Germany was officially recognized and requested to include representatives from communist East Germany. Years of fruitless negotiations aimed at achieving this objective followed. At a 1952 meeting in Copenhagen, a furious Edström was left waiting for 9½ hours for a meeting to begin because the East German negotiators refused to walk 300 yards to his hotel. Eventually the East Germans did form a common team with the West Germans from 1956 through 1964. From 1968 through 1988, the two Germanys competed as separate teams. After the Berlin Wall fell in 1989, a reunified German team appeared in the 1992 Games.

In his final official act, opening the 1952 Summer Games at Helsinki, Edström said, ''We hope the Olympic Games will allow a respite from political tensions and that international understanding will increase among the youth of the world as a direct result of their intermingling and participation during the Games.'' Sigfrid Edström died in Stockholm on March 18, 1964, shortly after the Winter Olympics were held in Innsbruck, Austria, still under the shadow of the cold war.

In his Olympic career, Edström was both participant and administrator, competitor and rulemaker. While his faith in the Olympic movement contributed to the expanding role of sport in world society, his inner-circle clannishness led to decisions that stressed exclusion over inclusion. In these ways, Edström reflected the fascinating times in which he was one of many memorable lords of the rings.

BIBLIOGRAPHICAL ESSAY

Neither the IOC nor the Brundage Papers at the University of Illinois has extensive material relating to Edström's life and career. The IOC Archives has a number of circular letters Edström wrote to IOC members during World War II as an "Olympic Bulletin." These letters are also available in the Brundage Papers, as is correspondence between Brundage and Edström and an assortment of newspaper clippings from the years of Edström's presidency.

Among secondary works, the most useful is Allen Guttmann, *The Olympics: A History of the Modern Games* (Urbana, 1992), which focuses on the organization and ideology of the Olympic movement rather than on the Games themselves. Guttmann recognizes that from the start, the Games have been influenced by politics and represent an important twentieth-century social movement. His description of Edström's role in IOC wrangling over such issues as amateurism, women's participation, and the recognition of communist countries is quite riveting. Much of this is elaborated in Guttmann's biography of Brundage, *The Games Must Go On: Avery Brundage and the Olympic Movement* (New York, 1984).

Edward S. Goldstein

Avery Brundage

In 1997, one year following what will certainly be a festive celebration in Atlanta of the hundredth anniversary of the Olympic Games, the International Olympic Committee (IOC) will choose the organization's eighth president. Among that successful candidate's predecessors, none occupied the position during more difficult times of upheaval than did Avery Brundage. Brundage, for twenty years (1952–1972) the czar of Olympic affairs the world over, at one time or another was embroiled in almost every conceivable issue that hounded the IOC: eligibility, commercialism, nationalism, race, politics, giganticism, and a good many more. On each issue, Brundage's public stance and problem-solving approach was consistent and unyielding: there was no room for compromise. It was either Avery's way, or the highway, so to speak.

There is nothing in Avery Brundage's lineage that suggests an aristocratic strain. He was born in Detroit of working-class parents on September 28, 1887. Such an egalitarian background is distinctively at odds with that quality consistently identified with the organization he would come to preside over longer than any other president, with the exception of the Olympic *renovateur* himself, Baron Pierre de Coubertin. Brundage's parents were easterners from upstate New York. His father was a stonecutter by trade. The Brundages moved to

Avery Brundage, IOC president, 1952–1972. Courtesy of University of Illinois Archives, Avery Brundage Collection.

Chicago when Avery was 5 years old. Shortly afterward, Avery's father abandoned the family, prompting his mother to turn the family domicile into a boarding house. Though never as destitute as Horatio Alger's enterprising youthful urban heroes, Avery "hustled a buck" just as industriously. He became a *Chicago Tribune* paperboy at 12. When he was 13, Brundage won a city-wide newspaper essay contest; his prize was an expense-paid trip to Washington to witness William McKinley's second inauguration. He enrolled at the R. T. Crane Manual Training School (popularly known as Crane Tech) where he was a solid student, mixing after-school athletics with a daily schedule of 9:00 to 5:00 classes, a 7-mile trolley ride to and from school, and a 2 hour predawn stint of newspaper deliveries. Clearly young Brundage knew hard work, discipline, tenaciousness, sacrifice, and, at the same time, the need for setting priorities. While admired characteristics, his constant practice of them to an ascetic degree later made him a wearisome figure to his IOC colleagues and world sport leaders, most of whom believed that the context of a changing world had isolated Avery.

Brundage entered the University of Illinois in 1905 and four years later graduated with a degree in civil engineering. By any standard of measurement, he left behind an enviable student-athlete record. His academic standing merited membership in two honor societies; his athletic pursuits in track and field earned him an Intercollegiate Athletic Conference (Big 10) discus championship in his senior year; his extracurricular student energies gained him a position on the *Daily Illini* newspaper staff, chairmanship of the Senior Stag (the university's gala annual prom), and affiliation with two literary organizations. Brundage's college life had been busy. He was driven to succeed, to prove that a poor boy could make it in the types of forums where all too often only the wealthy or politically connected made it. Another Brundage characteristic also had been demonstrated. Overly serious, genuinely zealous in the pursuit of mission, abrupt, even acerbic to those who did not subscribe to his way of doing things, Brundage did not exemplify the nature of the individual usually so actively engaged in campus life. There is evidence that Brundage was something of a loner, neither particularly well liked nor sought after by his classmates. Indeed, Brundage never did enjoy a wide circle of friends during his lifetime—business and athletic associates, yes, but close friends, no.

Almost immediately after graduation, Brundage went to work as a construction superintendent for the well-known Chicago architectural firm of Holabird and Roche. With borrowed money he established his own construction company in 1915. But once an athlete, always an athlete. Brundage joined the Chicago Athletic Association's "Cherry Circle" track and field team in 1910, training himself to compete in what was then called the "all-around" competitions (100-yard dash, high jump, broad jump, hammer throw, pole vault, 120-yard high hurdles, mile run, 880-yard walk, and 56-pound weight throw). He placed third in the 1910 national championships for the event, fourth in 1911, and first in 1914, 1916, and 1918. Brundage's skill as an "all-arounder" made him a serious candidate for two new Olympic events planned for Stockholm in 1912, the decathlon and pentathlon. In western regional trials, he placed high enough in both events to be selected for the U.S. Olympic team. His Olympic performance, though an improvement over that achieved previously in America, by no means matched that of the legendary Jim Thorpe, who won both events with stunning performances. Brundage placed sixth in the pentathlon and failed to complete the decathlon, dropping out of the event's final test, the 1,500-meter run. For Brundage, a man of unusual discipline and willpower, failure to complete the event was not only a contradiction but probably a severe embarrassment too.

Upon his return to Chicago, Brundage immersed himself in business affairs and continued his association with the Chicago Athletic Association. Leaving track and field competition, Brundage turned to handball, an activity for "older" sportsmen. Eventually he won the city championship and was at one time ranked among the top ten players in the nation. It was the sport of handball that launched Brundage's long and fruitful affiliation with the Amateur Athletic Union (AAU) of the United States. Following dedicated service with the Central Association of the AAU, he served as chairman of the national handball committee from 1925 to 1927. By 1926 Avery Brundage had become a recognized figure in the power venues of AAU administration. In 1928 he was elected president of both the AAU (serving until the fall of 1935, except for 1933) and its Olympic arm, the American Olympic Association (AOA). By the early 1930s, when Brundage had reached his mid-40s, he had become an American sports czar faintly reminiscent of the storied James E. Sullivan of a bygone era.

America's confrontation with Germany and the Nazi regime's trusteeship for staging the Games of the XIth Olympiad in Berlin propelled Avery Brundage into the international Olympic spotlight. A festering confrontation arose between those national sports federations and AAU officials who favored American Olympic participation in 1936 and those who did not. Brundage, a staunch believer that sport should be held apart from politics, championed the participation argument. New York judge Jeremiah Mahoney, president of the AAU in 1935, led the adversarial position of nonparticipation. In an extremely close vote of delegates at the AAU convention held at the Commodore Hotel in New York City in December 1935, Brundage's point of view prevailed. An American Olympic team went to the Berlin Games, an occasion that showcased the track and field exploits of African Americans, particularly Jesse Owens. With the death of American IOC member Charles Sherrill in June 1936 and the ouster from the IOC in the same year of American boycott supporter Ernest Jahncke, Brundage, the leader of the fight to keep America in the 1936 Games, became an obvious candidate to join William G. Garland as IOC members from America. Brundage's selection (or "co-option," as the IOC terms it) was confirmed at the IOC's Thirty-fifth Session in Berlin in July 1936. Though a fresh face on the IOC, Brundage lost little time in climbing its internal structure to power and authority. In 1937 he replaced the recently deceased Baron Godefroy de Blonay of Switzerland on the powerful executive board.

Olympic matters aside, Avery Brundage was making a name for himself in other fields of endeavor. His construction business in Chicago flourished. Capital and influence accrued. In the years ahead he would need money. He estimated that in his position as IOC president, he spent $75,000 annually on travel and administrative costs associated with Olympic duties. Brundage was also interested in politics. Reflecting his business and administrative style, his political position was almost always on the far right. He was a confirmed Republican and an isolationist in foreign policy matters. Outspoken, sometimes volatile, generally resolute, Brundage was often at odds with individuals and groups of opposing thought and action. At times he spoke publicly on boiling world issues, including his perception of Germany and Japan in the late 1930s—Germany defended Western civilization from the onslaught of communism; Japan, basically friendly, wanted only peace with America. Postures like those, together with a streak of anti-Semitism, often kept Brundage in hot water during the turbulent 1930s and 1940s.

Brundage's Olympic life was not dormant during the years of World War II when the Summer Games of the XIIth and XIIIth Olympiads were cancelled, as were the Winter Olympics in 1940 and 1944. Partially motivated toward keeping America involved in international sport during the war years, Brundage was among those who revived interest in the concept of Pan-American Games, the first edition of which was planned for Buenos Aires in 1942. The Argentinian dream of organizing the first Pan-American Games in 1942, however, was delayed until 1951.

Meanwhile, Count Henri Baillet-Latour had succeeded Coubertin as president of the IOC in 1925. When the Belgian aristocrat died in Brussels in 1942, Olympic leadership passed to the IOC's first vice-president, Sigfrid Edström of Sweden. During the wartime years of the 1940s, Brundage helped Edström maintain contacts with IOC members, irrespective of the geography that dictated the residence of each with respect to the Allied-Axis conflict. Brundage's IOC executive committee membership and his zeal to aid in Olympic matters prompted Edström to suggest his name for the second vice-president position, a distinction the Chicagoan assumed at the IOC's first postwar executive committee meeting held in London in 1945. More and more as the 1940s passed, Brundage publicly pontificated on Olympic problems, often being viewed in America as the real leader of the IOC. In Lausanne in 1946, at the IOC's first postwar general session, Brundage was acclaimed first vice-president. His sponsor was Edström, whose wife was American and who, in fact, was a former Chicago school teacher. With the 82-year-old Edström voicing no desire to continue as IOC president after the Helsinki Games in 1952, Brundage became an obvious heir apparent. In a rousing election that progressed through twenty-five rounds of balloting, he prevailed over England's Lord David Burghley, an Olympic gold medalist at the Amsterdam Games and an individual who would joust continually with Brundage on all sorts of Olympic issues during the 1950s and 1960s. In the end Brundage's election to the IOC presidency boiled down to his proven administrative expertise in American and international Olympic matters.

Brundage served as president of the IOC for a period of twenty years, passing the gavel of leadership to Michael Morris, Lord Killanin, following the tragic conclusion of the Munich Games in the summer of 1972. During that period, Brundage faced almost all of the major issues that to greater or lesser extent continue to be viewed as Olympic problem areas. The earliest issues were those surrounding the amateur-professional dichotomy, followed by problems caused by the aftermath of World War II and the collapse of colonial empires and fracture of former Olympic countries into two or more national-political entities.

Brundage's confrontation with forces in contradiction with Rule 26 (eligibility) of the IOC statutes was perhaps the most vexing of all issues confronted in his long Olympic career. Born and bred in the turn-of-the-century atmosphere of a sporting amateur myth inherited from England, the hard-working Brundage, who claimed that his "athletic journey" had always been undertaken simply for the joy and satisfaction of it all, held no sympathy for those whose involvement in sport might be motivated by a quest for records and the payoffs that might accrue in the form of cash, goods, jobs, or the type of recognition that eventually converts into financial gain. Again and again throughout the years of his presidency, Brundage stood astride the bridge of the Olympic ship ready to do battle with those in violation of his perception of the amateur athlete. He warmed up to the task in 1947 when he noted that an adoring Ottawa had given its Canadian figure skating darling, Barbara Ann Scott, a canary-colored convertible for winning the gold medal at the world championships. He was quick to warn that Scott's amateur status for the Olympic Winter Games scheduled for St. Moritz the following year might be jeopardized. An alarmed Ottawa citizenry "temporarily reclaimed" the automobile, and the Canadian press vilified Brundage. Scott eventually won the Olympic women's figure skating title in 1948, and shortly after, as Brundage fumed, the convertible was returned to her custodianship.

For twenty years Avery Brundage warred with all challengers, including many of his IOC colleagues, on the issue of eligibility. For the most part his campaign to preserve the exclusive atmosphere of Olympic amateurism can be viewed as a grudging retreat against the forces of change. Though Brundage admonished that "broken time" payments to Olympic athletes would spell "the end of the Olympic Movement as it now exists" (and he was right), IOC members pushed for a more lenient eligibility code. Arguing that the paradox between striving to achieve the Olympic motto, "Citius, Altius, Fortius," and the commensurate training time and support infrastructure necessary to pursue the quest made liars, cheaters, and hypocrites out of Olympic aspirants, the IOC took the first in a series of steps that has led today to the participation of full-fledged professionals in the Games, of which the so-called U.S. Dream Team basketball contingent in Barcelona is the most celebrated example. Despite Brundage's condemnations against such action, the IOC's Rule 26 was modified in 1962 to allow national

Olympic committees to administer "broken time" compensation to athletes for the support of "dependents suffering hardship." In hardly the blink of an eye, "suffering dependents" became "suffering athletes." Brundage, who continually railed against putting interpretations of important Olympic statutes in the hands of NOCs, whose very existence was rooted in nationalism, had every reason in the years ahead to say, "I told you so!"

As Brundage reached the end of his tenure as IOC president, he gathered himself for one last kick at the eligibility can. Like a petulant schoolboy, he made sure that it was one of vigorous dimensions. The sport was Alpine skiing; the issue, constant association by most international-caliber athletes in that sport with the skiing industry's manufacturers and resort sites for remuneration in hard cash, "kind," or both. Brundage was never a vigorous enthusiast of the Winter Games. To him, the Summer Games by themselves were too big, and getting even more so with each passing Olympiad. The toll on IOC resources and energies in any one Olympic year was mindboggling, especially in those years of limited financial resources, of which the Brundage presidential years certainly were characteristic. It is a pity that Brundage never thought of alternating the Summer Games with the Winter Games in even-numbered years, a formula that was implemented in the 1990s.

Of all those Olympic athletes, in both an individual sense and a generic sport sense, whom Brundage monitored relative to encroachments on the Olympic eligibility code, none elicited his anger as much as did Alpine skiers. Sojourning around the globe on the world ski circuit, brandishing ski equipment emblazoned with manufacturing logos to millions of admiring television viewers, and flaunting an athletic jet-set lifestyle was more than Brundage could tolerate. After numerous confrontations with the International Ski Federation on the issue, Brundage's frustration boiled over. He moved to strike Alpine skiing entirely from the program of the 1972 Winter Games in Sapporo. Brundage's IOC colleagues prevented such a drastic procedure from occurring, but they were persuaded to support the disqualification from the Games of Austria's Karl Schranz, the most illustrious Alpine ski performer in the world and, at the same time, the individual Brundage considered to be the most blatant violator of amateur standards. The entire Austrian ski team reacted by threatening to boycott the Sapporo Games. Schranz, now a martyr, convinced them to participate. He subsequently flew home to Vienna, where he was greeted as a hero by thousands of fellow Austrians and presented with a gold medal for "service to the state." Schranz's disqualification was hardly full satisfaction for Brundage. His alienation from Alpine skiing continued for the rest of his life.

The geopolitical results of World War II presented severe problems for the modern Olympic movement, and Avery Brundage was left to wrestle with virtually all of them. A charter member of the modern Olympic movement, Germany was fractured into two states, East and West. Indeed, the whole of Europe was separated into East and West political-economic spheres, Korea into North and South, and China into the People's Republic of China on the mainland and the Republic of China on the island of Formosa. Following the war, too, many of the colonial empires of Germany, Italy, Portugal, Belgium, England, France, and the Netherlands in Africa, Southeast Asia, and Oceania were dissolved, replaced by scores of newly independent countries. There are several ways in which new countries can be recognized internationally. One is to join the United Nations. Another is to establish a national Olympic committee and join the world sports community. For new countries this was an easy matter. For those old regimes now split in two, the task was not so easy. Although solutions to the problems concerning North and South Korea and the two Chinas issue were delayed until well after his death, Brundage could not escape the German question.

Germany, as had been the case following World War I, was excluded from participating in the first postwar Olympic Games, in London in 1948. Brundage, a close friend of Germany's NOC leaders Karl Ritter von Halt and Carl Diem, labored mightily to have Germany readmitted to the modern Olympic movement. But following World War II, Germany was split into the pro-Soviet East and the Allied-sponsored West. The German Democratic Republic (East Germany or GDR) argued for its own Olympic autonomy. The Federal Republic of Germany (West Germany or FRG) argued that it represented all Germans. Prolonged negotiations in late 1951 and early 1952 between IOC authorities and representatives of both East and West Germany aimed at having one combined German team for the Helsinki Games resulted in stalemate and acrimony. West German athletes participated at Helsinki; East Germans did not. Under the urbane leadership of Hans Schöbel, a noted Brundage ingratiator, East Germany was finally successful in establishing an NOC in 1955 and gaining IOC recognition, but with the proviso that they would compete in combined German status with the West Germans. When the combined German Olympic team appeared for the 1956 Winter Games in Cortina d'Ampezzo, Italy, and for the Summer Games in Melbourne, its composition heavily favored West German athletes by a ratio of about three to one. Roughly the same scenario prevailed in 1960 at Rome. Shortly afterward, in August 1961, East Germany sealed itself off from its western brethren by erecting the Berlin Wall and implementing a menacing frontier along its entire western border. Despite a West German boycott of all sporting relations with the East in retaliation, the IOC continued to insist on a single team to represent all Germany at Tokyo in 1964. Both sides were furious over this dictum. To Brundage's credit, he patiently moved each side toward compromise, but it took fourteen meetings of the national Olympic committees of East and West and nearly a hundred sessions of dialogue among Germany's national sports federations before a combined German team appeared in Tokyo.

By the mid-1960s more and more international sports federations were recognizing the GDR as a separate and distinct entity at world and regional championships. This fact had some influence on the IOC's allowing a separate East German team to compete at Mexico City in 1968, though the official flag of both East and West was the Olympic banner with the familiar five-ring symbol.

No German, East or West, could quibble with the anthem played at medal ceremonies for German winners of gold—the "Ode to Joy" from the final movement of Ludwig von Beethoven's Ninth Symphony. With Brundage's friend Schöbel co-opted to the IOC in 1964 replacing West Germany's deceased Karl Ritter von Halt, the GDR finally owned the type of franchisement that could pay dividends. Partly because of Schöbel's IOC activities, partly because of Brundage's personal sponsorship, and partly because of pressure from the Soviet Union, the IOC voted 44–4 at its Sixty-seventh General Session (Mexico City, 1968) for acceptance of the East Germans, an acceptance that guaranteed them their own flag, their own anthem, and, of course, their own team. It was ironic that the GDR's first appearance in a Summer Olympic Games was at Munich in 1972. The appearance at the opening ceremonies of the GDR team, basking in the condition of complete autonomy, provided Brundage with his most satisfying moment at his last Olympic Games.

The China question, somewhat akin to the German situation, provided Brundage with continual headaches. First, and completely unlike the German case, Brundage had no cronies among Chinese Olympic folks to whom he could relate in convivial fashion. Second, the atmosphere for dialogue with Olympic officials from the People's Republic of China was consistently compromised by Brundage's frequently haughty and intransigent manner, a demeanor that grated against the international naiveté of Chairman Mao Tse-tung and his Olympic coterie. But when all was said and done, the entire issue boiled down to the argument presented by both the People's Republic of China on the mainland and the Republic of China on Formosa that each exclusively represented all Chinese on Olympic matters. Following a two decade–long civil war, the triumph of Mao's communist forces over Chiang Kai-shek's nationalists in 1949 resulted in the defeated nationalists' escape to Formosa, where "business as usual," including Olympic business, was carried out under the name of the Republic of China. On the mainland resided almost 1 billion Chinese, citizens of a new regime, the People's Republic of China.

The cleavage between the two Chinas rallied sharp political-economic lines in the context of global politics. All too familiar with class struggle, emerging countries in the communist world were sympathetic to the plight of the People's Republic of China, despite its stance of self-imposed isolation. On the other hand, the United States had been a supporter of nationalist China since early in the century. It continued political recognition of, and aggressive commercial relationships with, Taiwan (the nationalists' name for the more archaic Formosa). Conversely, in its postwar strategy of containment, the United States shunned the People's Republic of China. Brundage, a personification of American capitalism, was most often viewed by communist Chinese leaders as simply a "faithful menial of the U.S. imperialists." Every move that he made to work toward a solution of the two Chinas problem was immediately interpreted by sports officials from the People's Republic as simply another reflection of a U.S. foreign policy aimed at aggrandizement of Taiwan. Brundage, in turn, accused the Chinese communists of continually mixing politics with sport in their dialogue with him on the issue of Olympic Games participation. Though communist China made a cameo appearance at the Helsinki Games in 1952 (one swimmer actually competed), the Brundage–People's Republic of China confrontation became an enduring stalemate, one that in the end forced a bitter Chinese resignation from the modern Olympic movement in 1958.

With the crusty Brundage retired in 1972 and the more conciliatory Lord Killanin in the presidency, with the People's Republic of China's expanded representation in various international sports federations, with United Nations membership and increasing diplomatic recognition, with the death of Mao in 1976 and the advent of Deng Xiao Ping and a China bent on entering the modern world, indeed, with the IOC's growing realization that the international Olympic movement could not truly be called international if it continued to exclude almost one-third of the world's population, the People's Republic of China was admitted to the Olympic family in 1980. Taiwan was told that it might remain in Olympic good standing if it no longer insisted on being called the Republic of China and accepted the designation of Chinese Taipei. Though initially defiant at this rebuff, in the end it acquiesced. In Los Angeles in July 1984, an Olympic power of the future took its place among the competing nations. It might have been far sooner had Brundage worked as diligently on the Chinese issue as he had on the German problem.

Avery Brundage hated confrontations that mixed national or global politics with sport. Most of the time they sorely tested his patience and occupied time he would have liked to spend on other items of Olympic business. In the South African apartheid issue, he met one of the few outright defeats that he experienced in his twenty-year presidency. Seeking international recognition as a first order of business after ridding themselves of European colonial domination, emerging African nations joined the modern Olympic movement in the 1950s. The nation on the African continent with the longest Olympic affiliation was South Africa, its athletes having competed since 1908. Since the days of early Dutch settlement and subsequent British stewardship, however, the country functioned under a strict racial policy of apartheid: whites ruled; colored and black lived with scant social, political, and economic franchise. Only white athletes represented South Africa at the Olympic Games. Such blatant racial discrimination and resulting political hegemony angered millions of black Africans. In an effort to apply world pressure on South Africa for destruction of apartheid, African nations protested to Olympic officials that the IOC was in violation of its own fundamental principle that no athlete be excluded from Olympic competition because of race, religion, or politics. Opportunities for membership on the South African Olympic team, it was argued, were prevented by virtue of race. Remaining united in their quest, African countries gathered support from the Soviet Union and other countries in the communist bloc, as well as many Third World countries, in an effort to exclude South Africa from the modern Olympic movement unless its policy of apartheid was obliterated.

Brundage, a long-time friend of Reginald Honey, South Africa's IOC member, continually rebuffed the African bloc's argument, asserting over and over again that "the Olympic Games cannot be shaped by politics." As other world-wide sanctions of a social, economic, and political nature were meted on South Africa and as it refused to budge on the issue, black Africa played its trump card, threatening a wholesale boycott of Olympic Games to which the South Africans were invited. Tokyo in 1964 and Mexico City in 1968 withdrew their invitations to South Africa in the face of possible boycott. Brundage called this action outright blackmail. Still, he procrastinated on getting tough with an Olympic country obviously in violation of family rules. With gathering world opinion and sanctions exerted against South Africa, together with rising African influence in the halls of IOC decision making, Brundage's recalcitrance to take action was finally brushed aside. In 1970 the IOC voted to banish South Africa from the Olympic family. Though African nations won the battle against Avery Brundage and South Africa, they failed to win the war. A resolute South Africa continued to cling tenaciously to white hegemony. Startling domestic events in the early 1990s, in which the IOC had no role, finally brought an end to the evil doctrine. It is difficult to imagine, if Avery Brundage had still been alive, how he would have greeted the tides of change in South Africa, change from which he dismissed himself from playing a role of possible great influence.

Avery Brundage, an exponent of sustaining Olympic participation only for amateurs, of trying to keep the Games from gaining unmanageable size, and of separating them from harm at the hands of both domestic and international politics, was also intent on protecting the Olympic image from contamination by commercial forces. Though an alert watchdog over liaisons between Olympic athletes and commercial firms, an action that usually elicited prompt censure from him, Brundage nevertheless was at last drawn to compromise his consistent hard-line stance on the subject. It was the beckoning hand of television that intruded into Brundage's austere world of divorce between amateur sport and commercialism.

Though a primitive form of television had been present in Berlin in 1936 and again in London in 1948, the happy marriage between sport and television did not really commence until television sets became commonplace in American homes by the mid-1950s. Networks soon realized that sporting extravaganzas were especially attractive program fare. The World Series, bowl games, and college basketball were early targets for the three big American television networks. Attraction to the Olympic Games followed. When Australian Olympic officials charged with organizing the Melbourne Games in 1956 argued with local and international television networks on the distinction between Olympic news coverage and Olympic entertainment programming, the result was that the Games went untelevised except for scant coverage by two local stations, and then only at venues where the seats had been sold out.

A principle for future IOC revenue acquisition had, however, been established. If the Games were desired as entertainment viewing, that is, for television programming beyond a brief news report, then television would have to pay for the privilege. By the time of the 1960 Winter Games in Squaw Valley and the Summer Games in Rome, the IOC had enlarged its Media Statutes (Rule 49) to include television rights. The chief architect in all this was Avery Brundage. Though a commercial relationship of this nature was decidedly repugnant to him, the thought of throwing thousands of dollars into the hands of others for absolutely no return consideration was even more repugnant. Brundage and the IOC joined with the organizing committees of the Squaw Valley Winter Games and the Rome Summer Games to negotiate the sale of television rights to CBS for $50,000 and $394,000, respectively.

How did Brundage rationalize this marriage of convenience? Besides the obvious folly of allowing American business enterprise to capitalize on the Games for little or no investment, the pragmatic Brundage knew that if a major source of revenue were not found, the future of the modern Olympic movement was in dire jeopardy. The fact of the matter was that when Brundage assumed the presidency in 1952, the IOC operated at an annual deficit of more than $3,000. Television rights fees could solve the financial problem, and besides, television might be used in such a way as to help promote a worldwide understanding of the concept and philosophy of Olympism, rather like a form of electronic religion.

Despite all this, Brundage was not particularly progressive when it came to television matters. The shrewd business mind that had earned him millions in the construction industry in Chicago was consistently outmaneuvered by the negotiating strategies of television moguls. Olympic television rights fees sold to American networks for each Olympic Games during the Brundage presidency increased at a minuscule rate when compared to the percentage increases achieved by his successor twice removed, Juan Antonio Samaranch.

Avery Brundage died in Garmisch-Partenkirchen, Germany, on May 8, 1975. He was 87 years old and had been involved with the Olympic movement for over sixty years. As his legacy unfolded, detractors and defenders pronounced their judgments. "Obdurate, outwardly unfriendly, dictatorial, crusty bureaucrat, cultural conservative, personification of frigidity and false cleanliness, intransigent, unswerving, obstinate," and a good many more similar terms, have been used to describe Avery Brundage as he led the modern Olympic movement through the problem-laden years between 1952 and 1972. Other terms were also used to describe him: "thoroughly honest, honorable, principled, a man who dedicated himself and much of his life to serving the modern Olympic movement." For many who knew him and dealt with him on various Olympic issues, a positive memory of Avery Brundage will be difficult to manage. His detractors outweighed his defenders several times over. For them, unkind images of Brundage's railing against enlargement of the Olympic Games due to expanded opportunities for women athletes; pernicious penalties meted out for even the most minor violations of Olympic regulations; and a consistent stance on issues in terms of black and white, never anything in between, will always override anything remotely favorable one might remember. Lastly, his detractors will always point at his crass handling of the Black September massacre and its aftermath at the final Games under his IOC custodianship, those of the XXth Olympiad in Munich in 1972. Nevertheless, for those who decry the Olympic movement's contemporary subservience to commercial forces, deplore the nonsense of such a happenstance as America's basketball Dream Team, castigate the myriad instances of the Olympic Games being manipulated by politics and politicians, and carp at the ever-growing immensity of the great festival and its conversion to what we have always understood to be the connotation of showtime, Avery Brundage will most certainly be recalled for having been the last serious barrier of resistance in preventing such questionable character from enveloping the late twentieth-century version of a noble one-hundred-year-old ideal originally visualized by a dedicated Frenchman named Pierre de Coubertin.

BIBLIOGRAPHICAL ESSAY

Avery Brundage has probably elicited more serious scholarly writing than any other figure in Olympic history, including the baron de Coubertin. One reason for this is that he saved almost every document pertaining to his life in sports. In his will he made provisions for his papers to be donated to the archives of his alma mater, the University of Illinois. Thus, for research on Avery Brundage, the fundamental primary sources are to be found in the Avery Brundage Collection (ABC), the original version of which is at the University of Illinois. A microfilm copy of the ABC can be found at the Centre for Olympic Studies at the University of Western Ontario in Canada. The microfilm version of the ABC numbers some 150 reels of material, including letters, reports, IOC and USOC minutes, observations, reactions, reminiscences, and newspaper clippings of Avery Brundage's athletic and Olympic career. An absolutely indispensable index of the ABC is Maynard Brichford, comp., *Avery Brundage Collection: 1908–1975* (Cologne, 1977). Another important repository is the IOC archives in Lausanne, Switzerland. Far less in volume and more haphazard in organization are the records of the U.S. Olympic Committee in Colorado Springs.

Some biographical treatments of Brundage exist. The best, without question, is Allen Guttmann, *The Games Must Go On: Avery Brundage and the Olympic Movement* (New York, 1984). Of far lesser note is Heinz Schöbel, *The Four Dimensions of Avery Brundage* (Leipzig, 1968), available in both German and English. Many works explore the relationship between Brundage and various problem issues. Of those, the following bear the most credibility based on the primary source record examined. For Brundage and Olympic television matters, see Stephen R. Wenn, "A History of the IOC and Television: 1936–1980" (Ph.D. dissertation, Pennsylvania State University, 1993); and Stephen R. Wenn, "An Olympian Squabble: The Distribution of Olympic Television Revenue, 1960–1966," in *Olympika: International Journal of Olympic Studies* 3 (1994): 27–48. For the best review of Brundage and his confrontation with the two Chinas issue from the point of view of both English and Chinese sources, see Dongguang Pei, " 'A Question of Names': The Two Chinas Issue and the People's Republic of China in the Modern Olympic Movement" (master's thesis, University of Western Ontario, 1995).

For particularly enlightening observations on Avery Brundage and his entanglement with the South African, Chinese, and amateur-professional questions, written from the perspective of Brundage's successor, see Lord Killanin, *My Olympic Years* (London, 1983). For discussions of Brundage and the German question, see Christopher R. Hill, *Olympic Politics* (Manchester, 1992), Richard Espy, *The Politics of the Olympic Games* (Berkeley, 1979), and John Hoberman, *Olympic Crisis* (New York, 1986).

Robert K. Barney

Michael Morris, Lord Killanin

Michael Morris, Lord Killanin, joined the Olympic movement in 1951, inspired by the idealism of the founder of the modern Olympics, Baron Pierre de Coubertin. Killanin wanted to help build a system of games that would reflect the values of the Olympic charter—those of fair competition without interference by politicians. He would eventually preside over the International Olympic Committee (IOC) for eight of the most turbulent years in the history of the organization. But, in his own words, "long before that I was to become acquainted with two of the forces that have come more and more to darken the idealism inspired by Coubertin and put the whole Olympic movement at risk: politics and violence" (Killanin, *My Olympic Years,* 32).

Michael Morris, born on July 30, 1914, is, in the words of John Hennessy, a "strange mixture of patrician and commoner." The Dublin, Ireland, native inherited the title of third baron of Killanin in 1915 upon the death in World War I of his father, Lieutenant-Colonel George Henry Morris of the Irish Guards. In 1918 Killanin's mother, Dora Maryan, remarried; her second husband, Lieutenant Colonel Gerard Tharp, possessed the financial means to ensure an excellent education for his stepson.

Killanin was educated at Eton, the Sorbonne in Paris, and Magdalene College, Cambridge. Although young Killanin was an avid amateur boxer, rower, and equestrian, he received little recognition as an athlete. After receiving a B.A. from the Sorbonne, he embarked on a career in journalism and served in the House of Lords.

Killanin was on the editorial staff of Dublin's *Daily Express–Daily Mail* from 1935 to 1939, where he served as special war correspondent during the Sino-Japanese War of 1937. Before World War II interrupted his newspaper career, Killanin was a political columnist for the *Daily Dispatch,* where he and other journalists edited a chronicle of the Munich talks entitled *Four Days.*

Killanin served in the 30th Armed Battalion during World War II, rising in rank to brigade major in 1943. In 1945, he married Mary Sheila Cathcart, the daughter of an Anglican minister, with whom he had one daughter and three sons. Killanin continued to write, eventually publishing a total of six books and several screenplays. In addition, he directed several films, including *The Quiet*

Michael Morris, Lord Killanin, IOC president, 1972–1980. © IOC. Courtesy of the International Olympic Committee.

Man, with John Ford. Killanin's interest in the film industry led to his appointment to the Government Committee on the Film Industry in 1957 and as chairman of the Dublin Theater Festival in 1958. The activity for which he is best known, however, is his involvement in the Olympic movement, beginning in 1951 when he joined the Olympic Council of Ireland.

Killanin once said his "Olympic life began not through any prowess at sport, but by trying to resolve disputes and squabbles," a skill he would need later as president of the IOC (Killanin, *My Olympic Years,* 23). Although Killanin was committed to the idea of a united Ireland, not just politically but also in sports and business, he was seen as a conciliatory figure, acceptable to all sides. He supported the cause of the Irish Republican Army but denounced their methods, while his peerage and service during World War II gave him credibility to the Northern Ireland Protestants. The political division of the country was reflected in its national sporting associations; some represented a united Ireland, while others, despite claims that they represented the entire country at an international level, did not field united teams. In 1951, because Killanin's political views were acceptable to all sides, Major General W. R. E. Murphy of the International Amateur Boxing Association and Patrick Carroll, president of the Irish Amateur Boxing Association, asked Killanin to become president of the Olympic Council of Ireland, an "all-Ireland" body.

As president, Killanin managed to arrange partial government financing for Ireland's teams. His desire to unite all sporting events on a national basis was only partially successful, however; he never achieved the desired unity in Irish track and field or cycling. After his election, Killanin was asked to replace J. J. Keane, the first president of the Olympic Council of Ireland, on the IOC. In 1952, Killanin attended his first meeting of the IOC in Oslo, Norway, as a nonvoting participant. He attended the 1952 Helsinki Games as a member of both the IOC and president of the Irish Olympic Council.

International politics, an issue that plagued Killanin throughout his tenure in the IOC, became a problem during the planning of the Helsinki Games. The Eastern bloc countries, competing in the Games for the first time since the war, requested separate quarters for their athletes. According to Killanin, the IOC granted this request because of a desire to bring these countries back into the Games. Even during his first session in the IOC, Killanin objected to the use of the Olympic Games as a political tool.

The question of professionalism on the part of Olympic athletes also arose at Helsinki. The participation of Finnish runner Paavo Nurmi during the opening ceremonies raised the ire of many IOC members. The International Amateur Athletic Federation (IAAF) had stripped Nurmi of his amateur status in 1932, and several members considered him unfit to participate in any way in the Olympics. This was the first of many dealings Killanin had over the question of professionalism in the Olympic movement.

An ironic event occurred during the Helsinki Games when sportswriter Arthur MacWeeney suggested to Killanin that he might someday become president of the IOC. MacWeeney believed future presidents of the IOC should come from small countries that would not leave the IOC "fettered with its politics." Killanin took the statement in jest, because he had no desire at that time to hold the office and because he did not believe he could afford to serve in the position. In later years, however, MacWeeney's statement became prophecy; Killanin advanced through the ranks until he was elected president of the IOC in 1972.

Coubertin had formed the IOC in 1894 to popularize his ideas of universal sportsmanship and goodwill without political encumbrance, to appeal to governments for support of their athletes on a nonpolitical basis, and to provide an international governing body for the Olympic Games. Despite Coubertin's ideal of an organization without political biases, the IOC has always mirrored the world political situation. At the beginning, IOC membership consisted primarily of individuals from countries that represented the great powers. Although countries are supposed to have only one representative, powerful countries often have more than one on the IOC. As more and more countries create sanctioned national Olympic committees (NOC), the IOC has slowly gained members from Third World countries, but the voting members are still predominantly white and European. Until recently, the rules of the IOC required all participants to speak either French or English, helping to reinforce the hegemony of Eurocentric people over the organization.

The membership of the IOC elects a president for eight years. The president is then eligible for reelection for four-year terms. The nature of the IOC, which meets annually during non-Olympic years and biannually during the years of Olympic Games, gives considerable day-to-day power to the president. The president chairs a nine-member executive board that meets two or three times a year, includes three vice presidents, and makes most of the IOC's decisions.

The president and executive board of the IOC elect new members to what Killanin referred to as "the most exclusive club in the world." With a membership that includes heads of state, peers, princes, counts, knights, pashas, and rajahs, the IOC is based on an almost hereditary system. Although Killanin has defended this aspect of the IOC, self-perpetuation has caused the IOC to be extremely resistant to change and slow to solve internal problems. Although IOC rules state that members are to vote on matters independently and not by instruction of their government, it is unrealistic to expect people so intimately tied to the political structure of their own countries to be able to act on behalf of the IOC when an issue is contrary to their countries' own national interests. Despite its appointment policies, the IOC, once elected, is a nominally democratic organization, which depends on the votes and participation of all members.

The IOC also depends on nonmembers to help organize and run the Games efficiently. Although the IOC has gradually assumed charge of all the logistical planning of the Olympics, it sets up commissions to deal with the technical aspects of running the Games. Generally IOC members head these commissions, but experts are brought in to consult with each commission. A strength of the

IOC is that it has recognized the necessity of utilizing consultants in such fields as television coverage, medicine, security, and the press. Delegation of certain responsibilities to experts has not only improved the presentation of the Games but has, particularly in regard to television rights, substantially improved the financial health of the IOC. If not for the increase in revenue generated by television rights to the Olympic Games, Killanin might never have been elected president of the IOC. Before the IOC added money generated by television rights to its holdings, the IOC president was obliged to use a substantial amount of his own money to perform the duties of his office.

Although Killanin lacked the wealth of many of his predecessors, his ability to mediate disputes and smooth rough situations was an asset for the IOC even before his presidency. These talents were especially important when, in 1966, Killanin was appointed *chef de protocol* of the organization. As the name of the office implies, the person holding this office is responsible for instructing the other members and their spouses about the rules and procedures of the IOC. In addition, he or she is responsible for making certain all members are informed about how to behave during social functions. Given the social and political positions of many IOC members, this can be a very sensitive task, especially when instructing delegates about what information can or cannot be repeated during breaks in IOC congresses. As *chef de protocol,* Killanin had to meet every member of the IOC, an aspect he considered vital to his future appointment as president. Killanin's first job of major importance and his first dealings with international politics as an IOC representative came the next year, however.

South Africa's system of apartheid had, for several years, received criticism from many countries involved in the Olympic Games. In 1963 the IOC had demanded that the South African NOC end all racial discrimination in sports. When the South Africans refused to integrate sports, they were asked to resign from Olympic competition. Political pressure from South African groups led the IOC to send a commission to determine whether the South Africans were in compliance with IOC standards of equal treatment and facilities for all athletes regardless of race, religion, or nationality. Killanin was appointed chair of the commission. Killanin's commission discovered that although the South African NOC had tried to comply with the IOC standards, the government would not allow them to integrate national sports teams. Appalled at the level of discrimination toward black athletes, the commission reported that South Africa was still in violation of IOC guidelines. Despite the commission's report, members of the IOC voted to invite South Africa to participate in the Mexico City Olympics. The vote was followed by a strong reaction against the compromise, including a threat by several nations to boycott the Mexico City Games. Eventually the IOC withdrew the invitation, but only after severe criticism from several countries. Killanin resented the fact that the report from his commission had not received the attention it deserved, and he believed that the political turmoil generated over the issue severely damaged the reputation of the IOC.

In addition to his other tasks, Killanin was unanimously elected to fill a position on the executive board of the IOC in 1967. His experience in journalism was an asset when, in 1969, he was appointed chairman of the press committee. He formed an easy rapport with journalists at press conferences and said he "understood what journalists required, and as I made their lives a little easier and brought some clarity out of the mystery of the way the Olympic Movement worked, I gained respect." Killanin considered the posts of *chef de protocol* and chairman of the press committee to be the two most important positions he held on his way to the presidency of the IOC. His tenure as vice president, however, was also instrumental in his eventual election to the presidency.

At the 1968 IOC session before the Mexico City Olympics, Killanin was elected vice president of the IOC, after turning down an invitation to run for the presidency. Killanin declined and accepted the vice presidency, but he began to realize he might vie for the top position upon the resignation of Avery Brundage. Immediately after Killanin's election to the vice presidency, he was exposed to one of the first situations where political controversies surrounding the Olympic Games ended in violence and threatened to disrupt the Games.

Student demonstrations had plagued Mexico City for several months before the 1968 Summer Games. Although IOC members were aware of the protests, most members were under the impression that they were merely an extension of student protest that had occurred in the United States and Europe throughout the decade. The students in Mexico City, however, were not demonstrating to draw attention to political ideals but were objecting to the extremely uneven distribution of wealth in Mexico. Many students were furious that the government would spend enormous sums of money to host the Olympic Games while the majority of Mexican citizens lived in poverty. On the day Killanin arrived in Mexico City, an armed battle between students and the police resulted in the deaths of 267 students and injuries to 1,200 others. Brundage called an emergency session of the IOC, and members discussed the possibility of canceling the Games but voted to continue as planned. The violence that occurred at Mexico City left a deep impression on Killanin:

This was my first experience of violence at the Olympic Games and its sequel was exceptionally tight and oppressively visible security arrangements. The carrying of the Olympic torch to the top of the huge pyramid at Teotihuacan prior to the opening ceremony was, in itself, immensely dramatic. Yet for me it was marred by the armed guards who were stationed everywhere in full battle gear and with loaded rifles. (Killanin, *My Olympic Years,* 49)

In addition to the student riots, Mexico City was the site of nonviolent political protest. Some black athletes from the United States boycotted the Games, and two track athletes on the victory stand greeted the national anthem by wearing black and raising their fists in support of the U.S. black power movement. The Czechoslovakian team received a standing ovation from the crowd in response to the invasion of that country by Warsaw Pact armies. After Mexico

City, political agendas were no longer covert, and the Olympics became an open forum for political issues. Unfortunately, Killanin's first experience of violence would not be his last. While Killanin was president-elect of the IOC in 1972, violence once again disrupted the festivities of the Games; this time Olympic athletes were the victims.

Killanin was elected president of the IOC in 1972 at the IOC Congress that was held before the Munich Games and took office after the Games were over. The president-elect was attending the sailing events in Kiel when he was informed that eight armed Palestinian terrorists had invaded the Israeli quarters in the Olympic Village. One Israeli athlete was dead. Nine other athletes and two of their bodyguards had been taken hostage and would be executed before the next morning. Killanin described the event as a "time of nightmare and confusion." Killanin was very critical of the way IOC president Avery Brundage handled the incident, mainly because of Brundage's insistence on handling every aspect of the affair himself. Brundage refused to keep IOC members apprised of the way the event was developing; at one point IOC members were erroneously informed that the hostages were free. He made crucial decisions without consulting IOC members and, most reprehensibly to Killanin, used the memorial service to chastise African countries that were threatening to boycott the Games for political reasons.

Brundage's ill-timed remarks led a number of countries to threaten to boycott the Games. The executive board, infuriated at Brundage's remarks, demanded that Brundage apologize for his remarks. The board also demanded to be included in any further action taken in the name of the IOC and, at the request of the West German government, continued the Games but canceled all receptions, music, and the closing ceremonies. The Palestinian attack was the most heinous incident in modern Olympic history and a horrifying example of political manipulation in the Olympic Games.

Although the terrorist attack was the most extreme incident during Killanin's IOC career, political issues connected with the Games continued to plague the Irishman. Killanin was determined to use his presidency to build a better organization that would follow the goals of Coubertin more closely. To that end, he was instrumental in trying to resolve a dispute that had occurred when the Chinese mainland became communist. In 1952, when Killanin first joined the IOC, Olympic organizations in Taipei, Nanking, and Peking each claimed to be the NOC recognized by the IOC before World War II. During Brundage's tenure, the IOC recognized only Taipei, eliminating athletes from the People's Republic of China (PRC) from Olympic competition. Killanin resolved to bring the PRC back into Olympic competition. By 1981 both Chinas were participating in the IOC, despite continuing political disputes that threatened to keep both nations out of the organization.

The China issue provided the 1976 Montreal Olympics with one of several political problems that threatened the Games. Canada had recently resumed diplomatic relations with mainland China, which demanded that Canada not recognize Taiwan. Killanin worked out a compromise that would allow Taiwan to compete but not to use "Republic of China" in its name. However, Taiwan rejected Killanin's compromise, refused to participate, and ended the problem for 1976. Killanin, disappointed that the Taiwanese would not compete, was quickly embroiled in another political situation that jeopardized the Games.

In July, days before the beginning of the Montreal Games, a number of black African nations threatened to withdraw from competition if New Zealand were allowed to participate. The prime minister of New Zealand, Robert Muldoon, had decided to allow rugby players to compete in South Africa, angering the other African nations. After several days of negotiation, twenty-eight African nations pulled out of Olympic competition just 24 hours before the beginning of the Games. The 1976 Games also hosted a few minor demonstrations by Ukrainians against the Soviet Union, but they were nonviolent and the protestors were arrested quickly. Killanin was now primed for the Moscow Games in 1980, which would serve as a battleground for even more political controversy than Montreal.

The IOC had voted almost unanimously to allow Moscow to host the 1980 Olympics. The Soviets agreed to allow competitors from all nations, except those with ties to South Africa, to enter. Israel, in an attempt to show that it believed the Games were very important, suspended diplomatic relations with Pretoria. Until late 1979, it appeared that Killanin's last Olympics would go smoothly.

In December 1979, the Soviet Union invaded Afghanistan. By the second week of January 1980, Killanin was receiving suggestions from the United States that the Games be moved. By February these suggestions turned to demands. Killanin explained to Lloyd Cutler, one of President Jimmy Carter's counselors, that the IOC had no right to dictate the foreign policy of a country and that the Games should be apolitical and not used for political manipulation. Killanin was very angry that Carter would make demands on the IOC and, for one of the few times in his IOC career, assumed a nonconciliatory attitude toward the U.S. president. After meeting with Cutler, Killanin asked for a meeting with the executive director of the U.S. Olympic Committee (USOC), Donald Miller, and its president, Robert Kane. Killanin then traveled to Lake Placid for the Winter Games, where he met with the two, who assured him that the USOC was autonomous and could resist political pressure. Unfortunately, Killanin and the USOC representatives learned later that the USOC was subject to U.S. laws under the Amateur Athletic Act of 1978.

Killanin continued to negotiate the IOC's position before the Games at Lake Placid began. Secretary of State Cyrus Vance gave the opening speech at the Games, infuriating Killanin because of its demand that the IOC cancel the Moscow Games. Killanin considered the speech outrageously political and offensive to the Soviet Union. He was convinced that the hard line taken by Carter toward the Moscow Games was not only because of his moral outrage at the invasion of Afghanistan but also was an attempt to bolster his sagging political popularity. Regardless of his motive, Carter ordered a boycott of the Moscow Games.

When Carter's stand was bolstered by firm support from British prime minister Margaret Thatcher, Killanin became concerned that if other countries joined the U.S. boycott, the Games would be jeopardized. Killanin presented a firm statement to the IOC reiterating the purpose of the Olympic Games and the apolitical nature of the IOC and NOCs. He emphasized that many NOCs were in a difficult position if their governments ordered a boycott, but they had a duty to the amateur athletes who had trained for competition in the events. Finally, Killanin emphasized his personal responsibility to see that the Olympic Games went on as scheduled.

Despite Killanin's protests, the United States persisted in the boycott and was supported by Saudi Arabia and Israel. After the U.S.S.R. exiled dissident Andrei Sakharov on January 22, 1980, a number of Western European nations joined the boycott. Ironically, the British did not officially boycott the Games but allowed their athletes to participate on an individual basis. The boycott of the Moscow Games left Killanin extremely bitter toward the United States and Jimmy Carter in particular. He believed the boycott was proof of the severe damage that could occur when political issues were allowed to interfere in the Olympic Games.

When Killanin was elected to the presidency in 1972, he agreed to serve one eight-year term. Although several members of the IOC urged him to run for reelection, he refused, and in 1980 he turned the reins of the IOC over to Juan Antonio Samaranch. Killanin retired to Dublin where he lives with his wife, Pauline.

The events of the 1980 Games provided an ironic end to the IOC presidency of Killanin. The Irishman had worked throughout his IOC career to end political manipulation of the Games, but his presidency was dominated by issues tied to politics and nationalism. The violence and political manipulation that occurred during the 1972, 1976, and 1980 Olympic Games threatened to tear apart the very foundation of the Olympic movement. Through the leadership of Killanin, however, the IOC survived and emerged a stronger, more vital organization.

BIBLIOGRAPHICAL ESSAY

Although there are some Killanin papers at the IOC archives in Lausanne, Switzerland, most still are in family hands. The Avery Brundage Collection at the University of Illinois Archives, Urbana, Illinois, contains some papers relevant to Killanin's work on the public relations and press commission between 1966 and 1971.

Killanin's autobiography, *My Olympic Years* (London, 1983), reveals his opinions on key issues, but its factual recounting should be corroborated with other sources. One of these is Christopher Hill, *Olympic Politics* (Manchester, 1992), which has detailed accounts of the China controversy and the Moscow boycott. The relationship between Killanin and his predecessor, Avery Brundage, is described in Allen Guttmann, *The Games Must Go On* (New York, 1984).

The political controversies of the Killanin years are analyzed in Richard Espy, *The Politics of the Olympic Games* (Berkeley, 1979), and David B. Kanin, *Political History of the Olympic Games* (Boulder, Colo., 1981). See also the bibliographical essays following the chapters in this book on the 1972, 1976, and 1980 Games for titles of books and articles specific to those Games.

Kathy Nichols

Juan Antonio Samaranch

Juan Antonio Samaranch, the seventh president of the International Olympic Committee (IOC), was born in Barcelona, Spain, on July 17, 1920, the son of Francisco Samaranch Castro, a textile manufacturer, and Juana Torello Malhevy. He received a good education at business schools and the German College before the outbreak of the Spanish Civil War. In that conflict, he was drafted into the Popular Front army of the existing government and served as a medic but apparently deserted and spent the rest of the war hiding in Barcelona, although sources differ on his activities at this time.

In 1940, Samaranch passed a state examination qualifying him to be a *perito mercantil,* or business appraiser, and he went to work in his family's business, Samaranch, S.A. During the early 1940s, he developed interests in sport, first as a boxer fighting under the name of ''Kid Samaranch'' in the Catalonia championships and then as a player and promoter of *hockey sobre patinas* (roller hockey), a variation of the game played on roller skates. In 1943, he became coach of the Royal Spanish Athletic Club and wrote articles for *La Prensa* under the pen name ''Stick.'' Two years later, he led the effort of the Spanish Roller Hockey Federation to be admitted to the International Federation of Roller Hockey, and in 1946 he attended the international congress of the sport in Montreux, at which Spain was admitted to the international federation. In 1950, he joined the executive council of the international federation, a prelude to Barcelona's hosting the world roller hockey championships the following year, at which Spain won its first world title.

In 1951, Samaranch, perhaps emboldened by the Spanish roller hockey victory, ran for the Barcelona city council but lost. He continued his association with the roller hockey federation, however, and by 1954, he had become vice president of the international federation, president of the Spanish federation, and a Barcelona city councilman, representing the Movimiento party of the authoritarian national government of Francisco Franco. In 1955, he became a provincial deputy and also vice president of the organizing committee for the second Mediterranean Games, held in Barcelona, and in 1956, he was appointed to the Spanish Olympic Committee and headed the Spanish team to the Winter Games held that year in Cortina d'Ampezzo, Italy.

Juan Antonio Samaranch, IOC president, 1980–present. © IOC. Courtesy of the International Olympic Committee.

Between 1960 and 1975, Samaranch's influence increased in both the Olympic movement and Spanish politics. He led the Spanish team to the Rome Games in 1960 and the Tokyo Games in 1964. As early as 1955, he began cultivating a close relationship with Avery Brundage through flattering letters and telegrams; he might have been named to the IOC earlier than 1966 had Spain ever hosted an Olympic Games. Brundage engineered his appointment to the IOC in 1966; the next year, Samaranch rose to the presidency of the Spanish Olympic Committee. He sought a position on the IOC executive board in 1968 but had to settle for the post of chief of protocol. In 1970, he succeeded in joining the IOC's executive board, and in 1974 he was named vice president, making him the most likely successor to Lord Killanin, the current president.

Meanwhile, Samaranch continued to be active in Barcelona and Catalonia business and political affairs. He left the city council in 1961 but remained visible in the city by serving on the boards of several real estate firms and banks and continuing to represent Barcelona as a provincial deputy. But sports were clearly commanding more of his time; he left the provincial council in 1967 and sold the family business, which he had taken over in 1957 after his father's death, in 1968. Five years later, however, political fortune came his way again when he was elected president of the deputation of Barcelona, one of the most important political posts in Catalonia and one closely tied to the Franco regime.

Franco died in 1975, and Spain returned to a democratic form of government nominally headed by King Juan Carlos. Samaranch's ties with the Franco regime brought political difficulties for him in Barcelona, and he was no doubt grateful to resign his presidency of the deputation in order to become Spain's first ambassador to the Soviet Union in 1977. His work in helping the Moscow organizing committee plan the 1980 Summer Games and his efforts to minimize effects of the U.S.-led boycott of those Games convinced the Soviets to swing their support to him in the IOC presidential election in 1980, which he won rather handily over Willi Daume of West Germany, James Worrall of Canada, Lance Cross of New Zealand, and Marc Hodler of Switzerland.

Under Samaranch's presidency, the IOC has undergone vast changes. Its annual budget swelled from 5.8 million Swiss francs in 1981 to 24.4 million Swiss francs in 1990; its assets soared from $2 million in 1980 to more than $105 million in 1990. Samaranch is the first IOC president since Coubertin to work full time at the job; his primary residence is Lausanne. In many ways, Samaranch has pushed the IOC into the realities of late twentieth-century political and economic life, earning in the process heated criticism from those who believe that his policies have trampled the original ideals and meaning of the Olympic movement as Coubertin conceived it a century ago. Much of the new direction for the IOC began with the important and productive IOC Congress at Baden-Baden in 1981, the organization of which was Samaranch's first major task as president.

Politically, Samaranch has done much to raise the visibility of the IOC in world affairs. He worked futilely to get the Soviet Union and other boycotting nations to come to the Los Angeles Games in 1984, but he was more successful in dealing with the political controversies that swarmed around the Seoul Games in 1988. There he was able to soothe the feelings of the North Koreans after their demand to co-host the Games was rejected and to prevent a threatened boycott by other communist nations that had no diplomatic relations with South Korea and asserted that coming to Seoul would present unacceptable security risks. There was no boycott, and the Games were concluded without significant political disturbances.

Samaranch and the IOC were also closely involved in the South African question. When South Africa, which had been suspended from the Olympic movement in 1964, began to move away from its strict apartheid policies, Samaranch sent a delegation to the country to help create a mixed-race sports commission there and provided $2 million for training facilities for black athletes. The IOC rerecognized South Africa in 1992, and Nelson Mandela was Samaranch's guest at the Barcelona Games that year.

As the Soviet Union and Yugoslavia both collapsed in the late 1980s and early 1990s, the IOC moved quickly to recognize the newly independent countries that resulted from the political upheaval. The IOC recognized the Baltic states of Estonia, Latvia, and Lithuania in 1991 soon after they joined the United Nations and, after they had created national Olympic committees, invited them to send teams to the Albertville Games. Other former Soviet republics, not yet part of the UN, were invited to join what was called the Unified Team, and five did so. Croatia and Slovenia, formerly parts of Yugoslavia, came to the Albertville Games, and Samaranch convinced UN authorities to lift their boycott on Serbia and Montenegro with regard to the Olympics so that athletes from those states could participate as individuals in the Games. Samaranch carries out much the IOC's diplomacy personally by frequent travel; as of the summer of 1994, he had visited 182 countries, including the 15 Soviet republics.

An even more visible and controversial aspect of the Samaranch regime has been its embrace of professionalism for the athletes and commercialism for the Games. Samaranch has lobbied the international sport federations, which control eligibility rules for Olympic participants, to open the Games to professional athletes, a move he has defended as only fair, since most countries without significant professional athletes give large state subsidies to their Olympic athletes, making them de facto professionals. His success in this regard was seen most dramatically by the presence of the "Dream Team" of U.S. professional basketball players at the Barcelona Games. But most other sports, including tennis and hockey, now allow professionals to compete in the Olympics.

The commercial success of the 1984 Los Angeles Games elevated the Olympic movement into the world of big business and modern commercialism. Television rights had already demonstrated that large amounts of money could be generated for the Olympic movement, and in 1985, Samaranch tried to take control of commercialism through the creation of TOP (The Olympic Programme), an extensive marketing effort that quickly became an important revenue producer for the IOC and lessened the dependence on the sale of television rights for income. TOP was the creation of International Sports, Culture and Leisure Marketing of Lausanne (ISL), an agency whose majority owner was Horst Dassler, the chairman of the Adidas Company, a giant sports equipment manufacturer, who was believed to have been influential in ensuring Samaranch's election to the IOC presidency. By the end of the 1980s, ISL had paid some $15 million for its exclusive contract with the IOC and had developed TOP-1 for the Seoul Games and the more successful TOP-2 for the Barcelona Games. Although television rights still constitute nearly 50 percent of IOC income, the sale of sponsorships accounts for more than 30 percent, with other income coming from licensing programs and ticket and souvenir sales.

Much of the additional money generated has gone to support Samaranch's efforts to increase the humanitarian work of the IOC. He has increased IOC cooperation with the UN and its humanitarian agencies, as well as with other nongovernmental organizations, sensing that the IOC can be helpful in certain areas like drug education and AIDS prevention. He created a department of international cooperation focusing on such areas as the environment, education, and economic development, and he worked hard to persuade the UN to declare 1994 the International Year of Sport and the Olympic Movement. In 1981, Samaranch brought about the creation of Olympic Solidarity, an aid program to NOCs, especially those in developing countries. Originally created in 1961 as an IOC aid committee to the newly independent countries of Africa and Asia, Olympic Solidarity became a semiautonomous agency within the IOC, although the IOC president serves as its chairman. Between 1983 and 1992, the agency distributed $95.7 million to NOCs around the world. One of the largest recipients was the U.S. Olympic Committee, which received $1.5 million, but each NOC is guaranteed enough to send six athletes and two officials to an Olympic Games.

The substantial changes Samaranch has brought to the IOC have not come without criticism and controversy, much of which concerns the power and authority Samaranch has assumed during his years in the presidency. One telling example of this is the conflict with Monique Berlioux. Berlioux had worked for the IOC since the 1960s and had risen to the influential position of executive director. There she wielded great authority during the terms of Brundage and Killanin, who spent most of their time away from Lausanne. When Samaranch became president in 1980 and made the post his full-time occupation, conflict developed between him and Berlioux, who was used to running the organization with a good deal of independence. They clashed over the growing commercialism of the IOC and the contract with ISL, and they each supported their home city as host for the 1992 Games—Samaranch favoring Barcelona, Berlioux championing Paris. By 1985, the differences between the president and the director had become irreparable, and the IOC executive board demanded Berlioux's resignation.

Later in the 1980s, the executive board granted Samaranch the right to name two additional IOC members on his own authority, without screening or approval by the IOC, as was customary. Samaranch used this privilege to appoint Primo Nebiolo, the head of the International Amateur Athletic Federation (IAAF), to the IOC. Although there was logic in Nebiolo's appointment—the IAAF is the largest and most influential of the international sport federations— Nebiolo's selection raised much controversy, since he had been linked with cheating scandals in world championship track and field meets in the late 1980s. Samaranch brushed off the criticism by stating that the IOC had granted him the authority to make independent appointments and that nothing had ever been proved against Nebiolo.

Samaranch, who is expected to retire at the end of his current term in 1996, has been a highly influential president. His pragmatic policies with respect to the inclusion of professional athletes into the Games and the acceptance of corporate largesse into the organization have significantly changed the character of the Olympic Games. While his critics (and there are many) say he has ruined the ideals of amateurism and brought the Games into the brutal and corrupt world of contemporary politics while making himself into a kind of imperial being, his supporters maintain that he has only done what has been necessary in order to keep the Olympic flame alive in the modern world, a world vastly different from that in which Pierre de Coubertin kindled the modern Olympic movement a century earlier.

BIBLIOGRAPHICAL ESSAY

The main body of Samaranch's papers is at the Biblioteca de l'Esport, Generalitat de Catalunya, Valencia 3, 08015 Barcelona, Spain. The IOC Archives in Lausanne also possess considerable material relating to the Samaranch presidency, although some material of recent origin is likely to be closed to researchers.

There have been two recent biographies of Samaranch in English, representing wildly differing points of view. David Miller, *The Olympic Revolution: The Olympic Biography of Juan Antonio Samaranch* (London, 1992), is a favorable treatment of the life and career of the IOC president by the chief sportswriter for the *London Times.* Vyv Simson and Andrew Jennings, *The Lords of the Rings* (London, 1992), is so critical of Samaranch, his political past in Spain, and his management of the IOC that he has filed suit against the authors for defaming the organization. A more balanced biography, though one written in a traditional Spanish style often baffling to English-speaking readers, is Jaume Boix and Arcadio Espada, *El Deporte del Poder: Vida y Milagro de Juan Antonio Samaranch* (Madrid, 1991). A short sketch of Samaranch's life can be found in *Current Biography Yearbook 1994,* pp. 508–12.

Christopher R. Hill, *Olympic Politics* (Manchester, 1992), John A. Lucas, *The Future of the Olympic Games* (Champaign, Ill., 1992), and Allen Guttman, *The Olympics: A History of the Modern Games* (Urbana, Ill., 1992) all contain considerable material on the progress of the Olympic movement and the IOC under Samaranch's leadership. Articles on Samaranch and his policies include William O. Johnson, ''Goodbye, Olive Wreaths; Hello, Riches and Reality,'' *Sports Illustrated,* February 9, 1987, pp. 168–74;

Mark Mulvoy et al., "A Presidential Pardon," *Sports Illustrated,* August 3, 1992, pp. 82–83; Andrew Jennings, "Eyes on the Prize," *New Statesman and Society,* September 17, 1993, pp. 18–19; and Karel Wendl, "The International Olympic Committee in the Years 1980–1994," *Proceedings,* 2d International Symposium for Olympic Research, London, Ontario, October 1994.

Finally, during Samaranch's tenure as president, the IOC has significantly increased the range of its publications, which offer insight on what the organization believes its primary accomplishments to have been. Apart from the public relations nature of the narrative, these publications often provide statistics and illustrations not found elsewhere. The *Olympic Review* chronicles the ongoing activities of the IOC and occasionally publishes historical articles. *Message olympique/Olympic Message* is an occasional publication of the IOC; number 37 (September 1993) is devoted to the new Olympic museum that opened in June 1993. The museum has its own publication, *Olympic Magazine,* highlighting its exhibits and also publishing some historical articles. See also *Olympic Solidarity: The Last Ten Years* (Lausanne, 1993), for a review of the first decade of the assistance program begun during Samaranch's presidency.

John E. Findling

APPENDIX B: THE U.S. OLYMPIC COMMITTEE

Although American athletes participated in the inaugural Games of the modern Olympics, there was no permanent, formal organization representing the U.S. contingent competing at Athens in 1896. The early, pre-Olympic committee era was, nevertheless, not without some semblance of leadership. That the U.S. team was able to participate in the 1896 Athens Games, for instance, was largely the result of the energy and charisma of James E. Sullivan, founder of the Amateur Athletic Union (AAU). Later, in 1900, A. G. Spalding, a prominent publisher and sporting goods manufacturer, took the reins from Sullivan and became the first president of America's Olympic movement.

Despite the efforts of Sullivan, Spalding, and others, the Olympic movement in America suffered from a lack of coordinated and unified administrative support. Prior to the establishment of a formal organization, and even after the creation of the U.S. Olympic Committee (USOC), the early years of the U.S. Olympic movement were defined by chaos, competition, and cooperation, with the last rarely being the definitive characteristic. A collage of forces including the AAU, the National Collegiate Athletic Association (NCAA), large colleges, national sports federations, and prominent individuals vied for control of the Olympic movement. Under the prevailing arrangement, several sports had little or no representation in matters of administration and often found themselves overlooked or underrepresented in the selection of positions on the U.S. Olympic team. Power struggles between factions claiming to represent different sports and between the AAU and NCAA often occurred, resulting in protests, resignations, and ultimately the disruption of the larger objective of fielding quality American athletes for the Olympic Games. So too was this informal system unable to deal effectively with issues such as the provision of adequate training facilities, the financial needs of athletes, or institutional fund raising.

A case in point was the Olympic effort after World War I. Because national priorities were directed toward the war effort, America's Olympic movement was woefully unprepared for the 1920 Antwerp Games. As a result, U.S. athletes found themselves traveling aboard crowded troop ships whose cramped and uncomfortable facilities were not conducive to training. The embarrassment resulting from public criticism of the spartan conditions available to the U.S. Olympic team led to changes in the way the Olympic movement was organized.

A 1921 meeting at the New York Athletic Club produced a proposal to organize the U.S. Olympic effort under a single, formal administrative structure: the American Olympic Association (AOA), the predecessor of the USOC. In 1940 the AOA was renamed the United States of America Sports Federation; the name was again changed in 1945 to the United States Olympic Association (USOA); the current designation of the USOC came in 1961. The establishment and growth of the USOC has been, at times, a laborious and politicized process, with many events serving to shape the organization that exists today.

In 1950, for example, action by the federal government (PL 805) gave the USOA a federal charter as a private, nonprofit corporation, and with this the ability to receive tax-deductible contributions. This would prove invaluable in addressing the financial demands of the U.S. Olympic movement.

In part due to the rather poor showing of U.S. athletes against Soviet and East German competitors at the 1976 Games, attention was again focused on improving the U.S. Olympic movement, resulting in the formation of the President's Commission on Olympic Sports. The commission recommended significant changes in the Olympic organization. On July 1, 1978, USOC headquarters moved from New York City to its present location in Colorado Springs, Colorado. Possibly the most important public action in strengthening the USOC was the enactment of PL 95-606 in 1978. The passage of the Amateur Sports Act named the USOC as the official coordinating organization for athletes and sports on the Olympic and Pan-American Games programs. The USOC was also charged with promoting participation and opportunities in sports and physical fitness for the general public.

The Amateur Sports Act, like the 1950 charter, aided fund-raising efforts and the financial health of the USOC by granting the organization exclusive rights to symbols associated with the U.S. Olympic movement, such as the USOC emblem and five Olympic rings, and protected words like *Olympic* and *Olympiad.* In addition, the U.S. Treasury boosted USOC finances by introducing its Olympic commemorative coins series.

Today the USOC is the primary force in America for sports in both the Olympic and Pan-American Games and, more generally, is the body leading the country's sports and physical fitness efforts. The USOC is also recognized by the International Olympic Committee (IOC) as the primary organization in America representing the Olympic movement. In the 1990s, the USOC stands as an internationally recognized institution managing a multimillion dollar budget that provides state-of-the-art training facilities and educational, financial, and competitive support and opportunities for American athletes.

The common perception of the USOC is of a committee that spearheads the U.S. Olympic movement in the four years between the Olympics and organizes the U.S. Olympic team during the actual Games. While this is true, such a view fails to capture the diverse tasks the USOC fulfills for both the Olympic movement and, in a broader capacity, America's athletic and physical fitness communities. As the stated mission of the USOC declares, "The USOC is the guardian of the U.S. Olympic Movement and is dedicated to providing opportunities for American athletes of all ages."

As the principal organization leading America's Olympic effort, the USOC provides financial, educational, training, and medical support systems for Olympic athletes and hopefuls that better enables them to meet the rigorous training demands associated with Olympic-caliber competition.

The USOC also resolves conflicts involving athletes or sports organizations participating in the Olympic and Pan-American Games and coordinates athletic activity in the United States pertaining to international competition. It oversees sports-related organizations within the Olympic movement and maintains exclusive administrative jurisdiction over American participants in the Olympic and Pan-American Games. The USOC maintains relationships with the corporate community and government in America and with international organizations, including the International Olympic Committee (IOC).

Although the USOC is a private, apolitical body, it performs tasks typically associated with a public sector institution, serving as an advocate for U.S. cities bidding to host Summer or Winter Games and reviewing, voting on, and endorsing potential host cities. Cities and sites for the U.S. Olympic Festival and Olympic trials are also set by the USOC.

In a more general role, the USOC provides basic fitness, athletic, and competitive opportunities for American athletes of all ages and skill levels. Moreover, it advocates and provides programs to foster the development of quality coaches, trainers, and sports officials. More recently, the committee has pursued a commitment to encourage and assist with athletic activity and opportunity for elements within American society such as the physically disabled, women, and ethnic minorities, who have been underserved in sports endeavors.

Changing times have mandated that the USOC address numerous emerging issues such as drug and steroid use, testing, and counseling; the status of amateurism in Olympic sports; and administrative restructuring of its own organizational apparatus. All the while it must continue to upgrade its fund raising, athlete development, training facilities, and public relations activities.

Fund raising is a priority undertaking for the USOC, as the USOC receives no permanent funding from the government and the success of its mission is, to a degree, tied to having adequate financial resources. A principal source for USOC revenue is the business community. Corporations provided just over 40 percent of the USOC total budget for the 1992 Games, and it is anticipated that nearly half of the USOC budget for the 1996 Games will come from corporate sponsorship. Roughly forty-five companies sponsored the 1992 Games, donating tens of millions of dollars in return for exclusivity in their product area as an official Olympic sponsor and for rights to use official Olympic-related logos and items in product packaging and advertising. In addition to corporate sponsors, the USOC generates some 28 percent of its funds from Olympic television revenues, 11 percent from direct mail solicitation, 8 percent from miscellaneous fund-raising efforts, 7 percent from the U.S. Treasury's Olympic commemorative coins, and 4 percent from sales of souvenirs at Olympic Spirit stores.

The USOC is often described as ''an organization of organizations.'' This description is quite accurate, as the USOC comprises numerous member organizations (see Table 1) within its umbrella of responsibility and representation. Member organizations consist of each of the sports in the Olympic and Pan-American Games programs, Olympic-affiliated sports organizations, community-based multisport affiliates, education-based multisport organizations, and representative bodies from the U.S. armed forces and the world of disabled athletics.

Although it is clearly an organization comprising organizations, the administrative structure of the USOC is a two-tiered system composed of a board of directors and an executive committee. The most visible leader of the U.S. Olympic movement, however, is the USOC president, who is assisted by six senior USOC officers: three vice presidents, a secretary, a treasurer, and a representative to the IOC. As such, there is more than one governance council operating the USOC.

The board of directors, with 119 members (102 voting members), functions much like a legislative body. In this capacity it sets forth the objectives of the USOC, votes on or confirms administrative officers, and has power to amend the USOC constitution and bylaws, admit new members, and terminate undesirable members. Meeting three times a year or as necessary, the board includes USOC officers, past USOC presidents, IOC members, Olympic/Pan-American sports organization members, a contingent of athletes, and representatives from each of the many other affiliated bodies.

The executive committee, the administrative unit of the USOC, has responsibility for the implementation of the business and operational affairs of the USOC, according to the guidelines set forth by the board of directors. The chief administrative official of the USOC is the executive director. Elected by a majority vote of the board, the executive director is awarded a salary and benefits package and, to assist in the management of USOC business, the services of a staff. Furthermore, the executive committee is served by an executive council. Headed by the executive director, the council meets as often as is necessary to fulfill its function of administrative oversight. Membership on this council numbers twenty-one, with eighteen having voting rights, and includes USOC officers, IOC members, athletes, representatives from Olympic/Pan-American sports organizations, and from affiliated organizations.

Table 1
USOC Member Organizations

Olympic/Pan Am Games Sports Organizations

National Archery Association
U.S. Badminton Association
U.S.A. Basketball
U.S. Bobsled and Skeleton Federation
U.S. Tenpin Bowling Federation
U.S. Cycling Federation
American Horse Shows Association
Field Hockey Association of America
U.S. Figure Skating Association
United States Judo, Inc.
U.S. Modern Pentathlon Association
American Amateur Racquetball
  Association
U.S. Sailing Association
U.S. Ski Association
Amateur Softball Association
U.S. Synchronized Swimming, Inc.
U.S. Taekwondo Union
U.S. Tennis Association
United States Water Polo
U.S. International Speedskating
  Association
U.S. Amateur Confederation of Roller
Skating
Athletes Congress
U.S. Baseball Federation
U.S. Biathlon Association
U.S.A. Boxing, Inc.
American Canoe Association
U.S. Diving, Inc.
U.S. Fencing Association
U.S. Field Hockey Association
U.S. Gymnastics Federation
U.S.A. Hockey
U.S. Luge Association
U.S. Rowing Association
National Rifle Association
U.S. Soccer Federation
U.S. Swimming, Inc.
U.S. Table Tennis Association
U.S. Team Handball Federation
U.S. Volleyball Association
U.S. Weightlifting Federation
U.S.A. Wrestling

USOC-Affiliated Sports Organizations

U.S. Orienteering Federation
U.S. Squash Racquets Association
Triathlon Federation
Underwater Society of America
United States Sports Acrobatics
  Federation
American Trampoline and Tumbling
  Association
U.S. Curling Association
U.S.A. Karate Federation
American Waterski Association

Community-Based Multisport Organizations

Catholic Youth Organization
Jewish Community Centers Association
U.S. National Senior Sport Organization
National Exploring Division, Boy Scouts
  of America
National Association of Police Athletic
  Leagues
American Alliance for Health, Physical
  Education, Recreation and Dance
Boys and Girls Clubs of America
Amateur Athletic Union
National Congress of State Games
YMCA of the USA
YWCA of the USA

Table 1 (continued)

Education-Based Multisport Organizations

National Association of Intercollegiate Athletics

National Federation of State High School Associations

National Collegiate Athletic Association

National Junior College Athletic Association

Armed Forces Organization

U.S. Armed Forces Sports

Disabled in Sports Organizations

American Athletic Association of the Deaf

Dwarf Athletic Association of America

United States Cerebral Palsy Athletic Association

National Handicapped Sports

National Wheelchair Athletic Association

Special Olympics International

U.S. Association for Blind Athletes

The USOC, despite having jurisdiction over the U.S. Olympic movement, does not act alone in leading America's Olympic efforts. For instance, at the international level, each sport has an International Federation (IF) responsible for governance of that sport. The IF establishes the rules for the sport and sets eligibility standards for athletes. These federations conduct the events and competitions involving their respective sports at the Games.

The IOC is the governing body of the Olympics, with control over Olympic sites, invitations, rules and protocol, and what sports are on the Olympic program. Furthermore, the USOC must work with the national governing bodies (NGB) that represent each individual sport in the United States. Of course, the USOC is dependent financially on corporate sponsors, private donors, and public fund raising as well as contributions from cities and states hosting Olympic festivals, trials, and Games. Clearly, the USOC is not alone in carrying the torch of the U.S. Olympic team, although it is the principal organization leading the U.S. Olympic movement.

To be sure, old challenges continue to confront the USOC, yet each passing year seems to bring higher public expectations for the U.S. Olympic team at home, increased competition internationally, and sensitive and complex issues that require considerable attention and resources. Underlying all of these issues, however, has been an image problem resulting from much criticism. Deservingly or undeservingly, despite the patriotism and purpose that define the mission of the USOC, the committee has frequently been criticized in the press and is widely perceived as being too bureaucratic, wasteful, and politicized. While the United States has enjoyed considerable success in the Olympics, critics contend that the USOC has detracted from its athletes' performance and is in need of substantial reform.

In examining the image problem, part of the explanation may be inherent in the task facing the USOC, but it is also necessary to consider the charges of scandal and ineffectiveness leveled against the organization. In 1991, for example, the resignation of USOC president Robert Helmick was surrounded by controversy. Part of the controversy included criticism of the USOC itself for not being forthcoming about the reasons behind Helmick's resignation. The USOC special counsel's office eventually released a report criticizing Helmick for conflicts of interest in his personal business relationships. In the wake of the Helmick incident, William Hybl, Helmick's replacement, resigned only a year into his tenure as president over rumors of ethical problems.

The year before Helmick's resignation, the USOC was in the news for its highly publicized buyout of two USOC officials in order to purchase the services of a new USOC executive director, Harvey Schiller. News of this kind did nothing but add to existing public skepticism of the organization. Additionally, critics maintain that the USOC has spent money lavishly on executive items such as travel, lodging, and meals while underfunding athletes.

Perhaps the most politicized and sensitive event the USOC has faced was the boycott of the 1980 summer Games in Moscow. Following the Soviet invasion of Afghanistan in December 1979, the U.S. government moved to boycott U.S. participation in the upcoming Games. At the behest of the Carter administration, both houses of Congress voted overwhelmingly in January 1980 not to send a team to Moscow. In April 1980 the USOC voted by a two-to-one margin not to accept an invitation to the Moscow Games.

Although the United States was joined by a number of other countries in the boycott, the U.S. government was leading the movement, and public opinion in America seemed to support the decision, the USOC did not come away from the boycott decision without criticism. The larger question concerning keeping the Olympic Games above the fray of politics was raised, and twenty-five athletes brought suit against the USOC because of the boycott. In *DeFrantz* v. *USOC*, the plaintiffs claimed that in preventing athletes from competing in the Games, the USOC had exceeded its statutory powers and abridged the constitutional rights of U.S. Olympic athletes.

The questioning the USOC endured concerning mixing politics with the purity of the noble ideals of the Olympics is not without precedent. Olympic tradition was breached at the 1968 Mexico City Games by the American medalists in the 200-meter dash, Tommie Smith and John Carlos, who raised gloved, fisted hands and looked downward while on the victory stand during the playing of the U.S. national anthem. This display at the 1968 Mexico City Games was a political gesture pertaining to discrimination toward African Americans in the United States and led to the protestors' being quickly sent home. Race has been a persistent political issue the USOC has faced in recent years. Not only have athletes in general not enjoyed success in gaining positions of influence on USOC committees or in the USOC administration, but certain groups have been underserved in broader athletic opportunities. The USOC, for instance, has been criticized for failing to fill enough administrative positions with African Americans. The appointment, however, of the first African American, LeRoy T. Walker, to the presidency of the USOC in 1992 underscores the changing times and

Table 2
USOC Leadership

USOC Presidents		*USOC Executive Directors*	
1900–1904	A. G. Spalding	1950–1965	J. Lyman Bingham
1904–1906	David Francis	1965–1973	Arthur G. Lentz
1906–1910	Caspar Whitney	1968*	Everett D. Barnes
1910–1912	F. B. Pratt	1973–1985	F. Don Miller
1912–1920	Robert M. Thompson	1985–1987	George D. Miller
1920–1924	Gustavus T. Kirby	1987–1989	Baaron B. Pittenger
1924–1926	Col. Robert M. Thompson	1990–1995	Harvey W. Schiller
1926**	William C. Prout	1995–	Dick Schultz
1926*	Henry G. Lapham		
1926–1927	Graeme H. Hammond		
1927–1928	Douglas MacArthur		
1928–1953	Avery Brundage		
1953–1965	Kenneth L. Wilson		
1965–1969	Douglas F. Ruby		
1969–1970**	Franklin L. Orth		
1970–1973	Clifford H. Buch		
1973–1977	Phillip O. Krumm		
1977–1981	Robert J. Kane		
1981–1985	William E. Simon		
1985**	John B. Kelly, Jr.		
1985–1991	Robert H. Helmick		
1991–1992	William J. Hybl		
1992–	Dr. LeRoy Walker		

Key: * = Acting President/Executive Director
       ** = Died in office

the USOC's sensitivity and commitment to having the organization reflect the diversity of American society. In addition to Walker's ascension to the presidency of the USOC, ethnic minorities and women have made progress in gaining administrative power in the body and now serve as committee chairs and members of the board.

Perhaps the largest challenge that the USOC has faced, one that affected the organization's ability to address all of the other challenges, concerns the efficiency and effectiveness of the committee itself. Responding to charges of disorganization, wasteful spending, and inadequate service to athletes, as well as the high-profile resignations and political squabbling among senior officials, the USOC sought to reform its organizational structure and operations. The management woes of the organization had brought much criticism from the press, which had attacked the USOC with such bantering as: "if there were a gold medal for bickering, the U.S. would win" and, playing on the USOC description as an "organization of organizations," referred to the body as a "disorganization of organizations." Moreover, the USOC was plagued by having too many committees with overlapping jurisdictions, too broad a mission, with dozens of organizations within its umbrella of responsibility, and high administrative and other overhead costs.

In the late 1980s the Olympic Overview Commission was formed and charged with restructuring the USOC. Though this was certainly not the first attempt to improve the administration of the U.S. Olympic movement, the two-year process of trimming administrative costs and increasing efficiency was an aggressive effort. At a 1989 house of delegates meeting, the commission made its recommendations, and the USOC's legislative committee began implementing reforms and changing the constitution and bylaws. In 1990, restructuring of the USOC eliminated the three-tier organizational structure of a house of delegates, an executive board, and an administrative committee, replacing it with a streamlined, smaller two-tier system of a board of directors and an executive committee.

Leaner and reformed, the USOC is leading the U.S. Olympic movement through a new era of Olympic-sized challenges. In keeping with the Olympic motto, "Citius, Altius, Fortius," which translated from Latin means "faster, higher, braver," or more commonly, "swifter, higher, stronger," the USOC's most important challenge will continue to be to lead the best possible U.S. team to Olympic glory.

BIBLIOGRAPHICAL ESSAY

For basic information on the role of the USOC, its mission, organizational structure, budget, and program operations, the USOC publishes an annual edition of the *United States Olympic Committee Fact Book.* Another source that provides an overview of the USOC is on videotape: Bud Greenspan and Nancy Beffa, *Sharing the Dream* (1990), a USOC production. Also, Kenneth Reich, *Making It Happen: Peter Ueberroth and the 1984 Olympics* (Santa Barbara, Calif., 1986), offers an inside look at the many aspects of organizing an Olympic event, as does the related work by Jeffrey M. Humphreys and Michael K. Plummer, *The Economic Impact on the State of Georgia of Hosting the 1996 Olympic Games* (Atlanta, 1992).

Records and official sources are available for legal, statistical, and official information on the USOC and Olympics. The *USOC Constitution and Bylaws* (1991) is available through the USOC, and information on the expenditures of the national governing bodies of Olympic sports and USOC finances in general is found in *USOC Support of NGBs* (Colorado Springs, 1991).

For those interested in a general history of the USOC and the U.S. Olympic movement, see C. Robert Paul, Jr., "Historical Background of the USOC," *U.S. Olympic Academy Conference Report* (Colorado Springs, 1987) pp. 68–75.

For a more detailed history of USOC leaders, key events in the organization's past, and efforts at improvement and reform, see Robert E. Lehr, *The American Olympic Committee, 1896–1940: From Chaos to Order* (1985); *Toward a More Effective United States Olympic Effort: Report to the United States Olympic Committee* (1965); and Allen Guttmann, *The Games Must Go On: Avery Brundage and the Olympic Movement* (New York, 1984).

The U.S. Olympic Academy annual conferences provide a forum for the discussion of themes pertaining to the Olympics. Often the USOC and issues relating to the organization are among the topics discussed. Published proceedings of the USOA sessions, in the form of scholarly papers, are a source of information on the Olympics and the USOC.

Robert P. Watson

APPENDIX C: OLYMPIC FILMS

Olympic Documentary Films

Of the more than 100 motion pictures that deal with the Olympic Games, about one-third fit under the category of documentary. More than a decade ago, film critic Andrew Sarris declared that sports movies do not work, since what is important is the outcome, not the moral. However, when it comes to the topic of Olympics films, a number of scholars have proved that dictum limited in its scope.

While feature films about the Olympic Games are mostly comedies or biographies, others use the Olympics as a showcase for displaying the talents of particular athletes, deal with a particular political agenda, or focus on such matters as what can happen to a medal winner past his or her prime or how inspirational a specific story might be. Stylistically and categorically, however, documentaries about the Olympic Games predominate. The majority of Olympic documentary films have been made in the United States. Other countries in which Olympic documentaries have been made include Great Britain, Japan, France, Germany, and Italy.

As Taylor Downing points out in *Olympia* (London, 1992), his examination of the Leni Riefenstahl film of the 1936 Summer Olympic Games, the modern Olympic movement and the era of motion pictures began at almost the same time. Although no filming seems to have been done at the Athens Games of 1896, there is brief footage of the next two Games in Paris and St. Louis, well mixed in with the world's fairs held simultaneously with the Games in each of those cities. The 1908 London Games were the subject of many newsreels, which had become common by then, and the 1912 Stockholm Games were the subject of hours of film, again of newsreel format.

Not until the Paris Olympics of 1924 was there an attempt to create a feature-length film on the Games. After producing a short two-reel film on the Chamonix Winter Games, the Rapid Film Company put together a ten-reel film, running 150 minutes, on the Summer Games. The unnamed silent film covers a wide range of events and was edited in both French- and English-titled versions.

For the 1928 Winter Games at St. Moritz, the German filmmaker Arnold Fanck (who later worked with Riefenstahl) produced *The White Stadium* (Das weisse Stadion). Although this film had the sanction of the International Olympic Committee (IOC), it was a low-budget effort, hastily edited and without character or inspiration. Oddly, no official film was made of the Summer Games that year in Amsterdam, nor was there a significant film of the Los Angeles Games of 1932, despite the proximity to Hollywood. By 1936, when Leni Riefenstahl filmed her epic account of the Berlin Games, there was little in Olympic film history for her to build upon.

Nevertheless, Riefenstahl's *Olympia* is without question the most important documentary film about the Olympic Games—indeed, perhaps the most important sports film ever made. Commissioned by Adolf Hitler as a hymn to nazism and the glories of the Aryan race, this film stands as the ultimate irony in that African-American world-record setter Jesse Owens walked away from the 1936 Berlin Games with four gold medals and all the attention.

Cooper C. Graham has written a complete accounting of this film and its author; in addition, he outlined some of *Olympia*'s more propagandistic qualities from a media perspective at a 1987 conference on the Olympic movement and the mass media. Graham notes how hosting the Olympics provides a built-in propaganda opportunity and analyzes how the Germans took advantage of this opportunity. The documentary film on the Berlin Games was intended to show the world how large, efficient, and well organized the Games were, how well the German athletes performed, and how friendly the German hosts were toward their foreign guests.

Still, *Olympia* is most often considered an aesthetic creation, artistically weaving experimental photography, camera movements, and editing techniques together with an inspirational musical score. Riefenstahl used more than 150 borrowed military troops to shoot 1.4 million feet of film. She also introduced a number of innovative cinematographic notions to heighten the dramatic impact of her work. She mounted cameras on rails to follow the sprints, placed them on horses to cover the equestrian events, and installed them in tethered balloons in an attempt to shoot overhead views. To film swimming and diving events, photographers would jump into the water with a camera to follow the action.

Running some 225 minutes, *Olympia* consists of two parts: *Fest der Volker* (Festival of the Nations) and *Fest der Schonheit* (Festival of Beauty). The film begins with a stylized view of Athens, with close-ups, overlays, zoom-ins, and

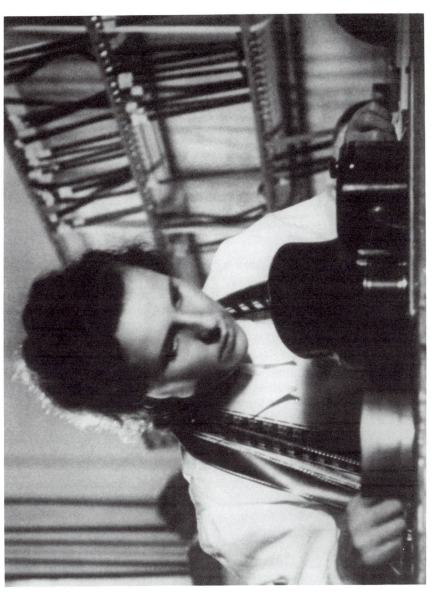

Leni Riefenstahl editing *Olympia*, her film of the 1936 Berlin Olympics. Courtesy of University of Illinois Archives, Avery Brundage Collection.

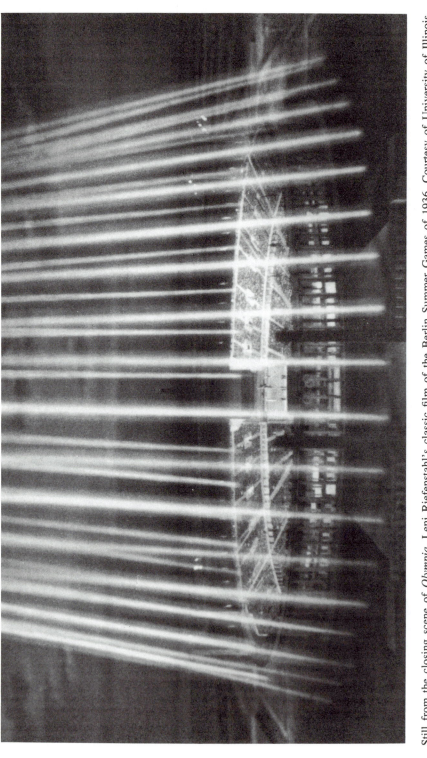

Still from the closing scene of *Olympia*, Leni Riefenstahl's classic film of the Berlin Summer Games of 1936. Courtesy of University of Illinois Archives, Avery Brundage Collection.

dramatic music to establish the grace and grandeur of the athletes, and symbolic sequences depicting the birth of the Olympic Games. Given the nominal purpose of the film, it is amazing that women in general and Jesse Owens in particular are featured as much as they are, but Leni Riefenstahl remained both the creator and the gatekeeper for what footage was taken and what footage was included in the final version.

In 1948, *King of the Olympics,* a severely edited version of *Olympia,* was released, but the original remains the standard by which all subsequent Olympic documentaries are judged. And with the exception of the 1952 Helsinki Olympics, documentaries have been produced on all subsequent Summer Games.

Olympic Games in White, a Swiss-Swedish collaboration, chronicles the 1948 Winter Olympics in St. Moritz, while *XIVth Olympiad—The Glory of Sport* contains some sixteen versions of the 1948 London Olympics. Australians sold exclusive rights to cover the 1956 Melbourne Games to the French; directed by René Lucot, *Rendez-vous à Melbourne* is the result. *The Grand Olympics,* an Italian production on the 1960 Rome Olympics, highlights the Soviet's winning most of the medals. Emphasizing limits on the human body during the 1964 Tokyo Olympics, *Tokyo Olympiad,* directed by Kon Ichikawa, is considered an artistic triumph, one of the finest photographic monuments to athleticism ever produced. *Grenoble,* also known as *13 Jours,* is also highly praised for its technical brilliance. Featuring such famous athletes as skier Jean-Claude Killy and figure skater Peggy Fleming at the 1968 Grenoble Olympics, it was codirected by Claude Lelouch and François Reichenbach.

Major events of the 1968 Mexico City Olympics are covered in *Olympics in Mexico.* The German production *Olympia-Olympia* (1972) chronicles the history of the Olympic Games from 1896. It was made to tie in with the 1972 Munich Olympics. Prepared by fifty-two Japanese photographers, the documentary *Sapporo Winter Olympics* (1972) highlights the Russian-Czechoslovakian hockey game. *Games of the XXI Olympiad Montreal* (1976), produced by the National Film Board of Canada by four directors, is notable for footage on star athletes Bruce Jenner and Nadia Comaneci.

The 1976 made-for-television movie *21 Hours at Munich* has documentary overtones, as it deals with the tragedy during the 1972 Games when eight Arab terrorists invaded the Israeli dormitory and took eleven hostages. The official film version of the Munich Games, however, is *Visions of 8,* a David L. Wolper production. *Visions of 8* consists of perspectives on the Games from eight international directors: Milos Forman of Czechoslovakia, Kon Ichikawa of Japan, Claude Lelouch of France, Juri Ozerov of the Soviet Union, Arthur Penn of the United States, Michael Pfleghar of West Germany, Mai Zetterling of Sweden, and John Schlesinger of Great Britain.

''The Beginnings,'' by Ozerov, has as its focus the 8,000 would-be champions waiting for their own individual moments of competition, each seeking his or her ''private grace.'' Sweden's Mai Zetterling, the only woman director, chose a sport she knew nothing about: weight lifting. Her reasoning for ''The Strongest'' was that she was not interested in sport for its own sake but was fascinated with the idea of obsession, which, she felt, weight lifters possessed in abundance. Arthur Penn chose pole vaulters, producing an artsy, aesthetic vision in ''The Highest.'' Because more women than ever before competed at Munich, Michael Pfleghar chose to focus on them in ''The Women.'' From photographs of women warming up to making up to competing, Pfleghar's subjects come across as very similar to their male counterparts. Using thirty cameras and 20,000 feet of film, Ichikawa zeroes in on the difference of 10 seconds in ''The Fastest.'' Milos Forman, fulfilling his lifelong dream of seeing an Olympics, tackled ''The Decathlon,'' considered the most difficult of the track and field events.

''The Losers'' were the centerpiece of Claude Lelouch's contribution. Curious to see how different people face defeat, he found similarities in both sexes in their reactions of sorrow, anger, disappointment, tears, or frustration. John Schlesinger's ''The Largest,'' which focuses on the grueling marathon, is a most appropriate ending to this Olympics documentary.

No discussion on Olympic documentary films would be complete without mention of Bud Greenspan, considered by knowledgeable people as an outstanding Olympics documentarian. Beginning his career as a sportscaster, Greenspan founded his own film company, Cappy Productions, in 1967 and has been a prolific sports filmmaker since that time.

In 1974, Greenspan began making films on specific Olympic themes or stirring moments in Olympic history. A total of twenty-two such films comprise *The Olympiad* series, released together as a video package in 1988. Among these episodes are *Great Moments at the Winter Games,* which many critics consider his greatest work; *Those Who Endured,* which profiles four winners who had suffered earlier defeats; and *The Immortals,* featuring Sonja Henie, Toni Sailer, Birger Ruud, and Billy Fiske.

Other parts of Greenspan's *The Olympiad* include: *The Australians* (1975), *The Big Ones That Got Away* (1975), *The East Europeans* (1980), *The 800 Meters* (1979), *The Fastest Men in the World* (1980), *The 1500 Meters* (1980), *The Incredible Five* (1975), *Jesse Owens Returns to Berlin* (1964), *The Magnificent Ones* (1979), *The Marathon* (1974), *The Persistent Ones* (1975), *The Rare Ones* (1979), *The Soviet Athlete* (1976), *They Didn't Have a Chance* (1979), and *Women Gold Medal Winners* (1975).

Greenspan has also produced a made-for-television film biography of track and field champion Wilma Rudolph (*Wilma,* 1977), as well as *Time Capsule: The Los Angeles Olympic Games of 1932* (1982), *America at the Olympics* (1984), *An Olympic Dream* (1988), *Time Capsule: The 1936 Berlin Olympic Games* (1990), *For the Honor of Their Country* (1991), and, most recently, *The Measure of Greatness* (1992) and *Triumph and Tragedy: The 1972 Munich Olympics* (1992).

Of all Greenspan's work, his four documentaries entitled *16 Days of Glory* deserve special mention. The first, produced in 1986, deals with the 1984 Los Angeles Olympics. It is a 5-hour documentary focusing on the drama of individual athletes, not ideological politics. Heroes may be difficult to distinguish. "Sometimes my heroes come in last," Greenspan has said (*New York Times,* November 11, 1988). *Barcelona '92* also takes on the sixteen-days theme in a 2-hour special that premiered on the Disney Channel. Appropriately, Greenspan was awarded the coveted Olympic Order in 1985 by Juan Antonio Samaranch, president of the IOC, for his contributions to the Olympic movement. Following his success with the Los Angeles Games, Greenspan has produced three subsequent Olympic documentaries for television and the home video market, each using *16 Days of Glory* as a subtitle; these treat the Seoul Games of 1988, the Barcelona Games of 1992, and the Lillehammer Winter Games of 1994.

The filmography includes a number of other notable motion pictures: *Portrait of a Champion* (1979), by Hungarian director Forenc Kosa; *XXII Olympiad: Moscow 1980* and *Oh, Sport, You Are Brave* by Juri Ozerov; Alvin Rakoff's 1984 documentary, *The First Olympics—Athens, 1896;* the IOC's film on the 1984 Winter Games, *A Turning Point: The Official Film of the XIV Winter Olympics* (1984); and two offerings on the 1988 Olympic Games: *Seoul Summer Olympics* by NBC Sports and *The Official 1988 Winter Olympic Video* on the Calgary Games.

The NBC sports department also produced the documentary *Barcelona '92 Olympic Games.* Hosted by Bob Costas, it highlights what it calls "The Great Performances behind the XXV Olympiad." *Sports Illustrated* recently opted into the video action with three documentaries from 1992: *Great Olympic Confrontations,* featuring Carl Lewis versus Ben Johnson at Seoul in 1988, Katarina Witt competing against Debi Thomas in Calgary, and the controversial U.S.A.-U.S.S.R. basketball final of 1972; *Record Breakers of the Olympic Games,* focusing on Mark Spitz, Nadia Comaneci, and Bob Beamon, among others; and *U-S-A! U-S-A! U-S-A!* a patriotic profile of outstanding U.S. Olympic athletes and teams.

Clearly the market for Olympic documentaries is growing. When the media currently have the capability of providing coverage of the Olympic Games to 3 billion of the world's 5 billion inhabitants, when Olympics triplecasting gains increasing market penetration, when video stores report ever-increasing interest in Olympic films, and when the Olympic Games are now scheduled to take place every two years, it is appropriate to assess the role of film documentaries on the Olympic Games.

BIBLIOGRAPHICAL ESSAY

The most comprehensive source on Olympic documentary films is Harvey Zucker and Lawrence Babich, eds., *Sports Films: A Complete Reference* (Jefferson, N.C., 1987), which includes a section, "Olympics and Track and Field," listing seventy-three films of which thirty-five deal in some way with the Olympic Games. Judith A. Davidson and Daryl Adler, eds. and comps., *Sport on Film and Video* (Metuchen, N.J., 1993), a publication of the North American Society for Sport History, lists eighty-one films under its

"Modern Olympics" category. Neither index, however, lists Greenspan's work, perhaps because it was made for television rather than the movie theater. Ronald Bergan, *Sports in the Movies* (New York, 1982), is a heavily illustrated narrative history of major sports films.

There is a considerable body of scholarship on Leni Riefenstahl and *Olympia*. One might start with Reifenstahl's own version of her life, first published in German as *Memoiren, 1902–1945* (Munich, 1987), and in English as *The Sieve of Time: The Memoirs of Leni Riefenstahl* (London, 1992) or *Leni Riefenstahl: A Memoir* (New York, 1993). Incredibly detailed and self-adulatory, Riefenstahl's writing is viewed skeptically by many critics but contains much information on the filming and editing of *Olympia*. Researchers should also consult Cooper Graham, *Leni Riefenstahl and Olympia* (Metuchen, N.J., 1986), probably the best secondary account; Glenn B. Infield, *Leni Riefenstahl: The Fallen Film Goddess* (New York, 1976), a popular account, but one based on archival sources; Renata Berg-Pan, *Leni Riefenstahl* (Boston, 1980), part of Twayne's Theatrical Arts Series; and Taylor Downing, *Olympia* (London, 1992), a publication of the British Film Institute, which offers a close examination of the film.

Two articles are also worth consulting. Frank Deford, "The Ghost of Berlin," *Sports Illustrated,* August 4, 1986, pp. 48–64, is a lengthy, sensitive biographical sketch that includes much on Riefenstahl's later life, and Cooper Graham, " 'Olympia' in America, 1938: Leni Riefenstahl, Kollywood, and the Kristallnacht," *Historical Journal of Film, Radio and Television* 13 (October 1993): 433ff., examines the reception Riefenstahl and *Olympia* received in the United States on the eve of World War II.

Much less has been written on other Olympic documentaries and their makers. Bud Greenspan's early work is described in his *Play It Again, Bud* (New York, 1973), which details some of his work on early parts of *The Olympiad* series. John Brant describes Greenspan's early career in "The Games According to Greenspan," *Runner's World* 19 (July 1984): 50–54. Beyond that, one must rely on newspaper articles, often with interviews or film reviews, for information about Greenspan and other prominent producers of Olympic documentaries. Happily, this situation will be resolved with the forthcoming publication of Linda K. Fuller, *Olympic Films: An Illustrated History.*

OLYMPIC DOCUMENTARY FILMS

1928   *Das Weisse Stadion* (Germany). Producer: Arnold Fanck.

1938   *Olympia* (Germany). Director: Leni Riefenstahl.

1948   *Olympic Games in White* (Switzerland-Sweden). Director: Torgny Wickman.

1948   *XIVth Olympiad—The Glory of Sport* (Great Britain). Director: Castleton Knight.

1957   *Rendez-vous à Melbourne* (France). Director: René Lucot.

1961   *The Grand Olympics* (Italy). Director: Romolo Marcellini.

1965   *Jesse Owens Returns to Berlin* (United States). Producer-director: Bud Greenspan.

1965   *Tokyo Olympiad* (Japan). Director: Kon Ichikawa.

1969   *Grenoble* (France). Directors: Claude Lelouch and François Reichenbach.

1970   *Olympics in Mexico* (Mexico). Director: Alberto Isaac.

1972   *Olympia-Olympia* (West Germany). Director: Jochen Bauer.

1972   *Sapporo Winter Olympics* (Japan). Director: Mashiro Shinoda.

1973   *Visions of 8* (United States). Directors: Milos Forman (Czechoslovakia), Kon Ichikawa (Japan), Claude Lelouch (France), Juri Ozerov (U.S.S.R.), Arthur Penn (United States), Michael Pfleghar (West Germany), John Schlesinger (Great Britain), and Mai Zetterling (Sweden).

1975   *The Big Ones That Got Away.* The Olympiad Series (United States). Director: Bud Greenspan.

1975   *The Decathlon.* The Olympiad Series (United States). Director: Bud Greenspan.

1975   *The Incredible Five.* The Olympiad Series (United States). Director: Bud Greenspan.

1975   *The Persistent Ones.* The Olympiad Series (United States). Director: Bud Greenspan.

1975   *Women Gold Medal Winners.* The Olympiad Series (United States). Director: Bud Greenspan.

1976   *Games of the XXI Olympiad Montreal* (Canada). Directors: Jean-Claude Labrecque, Jean Baudin, Marcel Carriére, and George Dufaux.

1976   *21 Hours at Munich* (United States). Director: William A. Graham.

1976   *The 800 Meters.* The Olympiad Series (United States). Director: Bud Greenspan.

1976   *The African Runners.* The Olympiad Series (United States). Director: Bud Greenspan.

1976   *The Australians.* The Olympiad Series (United States). Director: Bud Greenspan.

1976   *The East Europeans.* The Olympiad Series (United States). Director: Bud Greenspan.

1976   *An Olympic Symphony.* The Olympiad Series (United States). Director: Bud Greenspan.

1976   *The Soviet Athlete.* The Olympiad Series (United States). Director: Bud Greenspan.

1977   *White Rock* (Great Britain). Director: Tony Maylam.

1979   *Portrait of a Champion* (Hungary). Director: Ferenc Kosa.

1979   *Great Moments at the Winter Games.* The Olympiad Series (United States). Director: Bud Greenspan.

1979   *The Magnificent Ones.* The Olympiad Series (United States). Director: Bud Greenspan.

1979   *The Marathon.* The Olympiad Series (United States). Director: Bud Greenspan.

1979   *The Rare Ones.* The Olympiad Series (United States). Director: Bud Greenspan.

1979   *They Didn't Have a Chance.* The Olympiad Series (United States). Director: Bud Greenspan.

1980   *The 1500 Meters.* The Olympiad Series (United States). Director: Bud Greenspan.

1980   *The East Germans.* The Olympiad Series (United States). Director: Bud Greenspan.

1980   *The Fastest Men in the World.* The Olympiad Series (United States). Director:
       Bud Greenspan.

1980   *The Immortals.* The Olympiad Series (United States). Director: Bud Greenspan.

1980   *Those Who Endured.* The Olympiad Series (United States). Director: Bud Green-
       span.

1981   *XXII Olympiad: Moscow 1980* (U.S.S.R.). Director: Juri Ozerov.

1981   *Oh, Sport, You Are Brave* (U.S.S.R.). Directors: Juri Ozerov and Boris Rychov.

1982   *Time Capsule: The Los Angeles Olympic Games of 1932* (United States). Pro-
       ducer-director: Bud Greenspan.

1984   *America at the Olympics* (United States). Director: Bud Greenspan.

1984   *The First Olympics—Athens, 1896* (United States). Director: Alvin Rakoff.

1984   *A Turning Point: The Official Film of the XIV Winter Games* (Switzerland). Pro-
       ducer: International Olympic Committee.

1986   *16 Days of Glory* (United States). Producer-director: Bud Greenspan.

1987   *Greatest Moments in Olympic History* (United States). Producer: *Sports Illus-
       trated.*

1988   *An Olympic Dream* (United States). Director: Bud Greenspan.

1988   *Seoul Summer Olympics* (United States). Producer: NBC Sports.

1988   *The Official 1988 Winter Olympic Video* (United States). Producer: NBC Sports.

1989   *16 Days of Glory: Seoul '88* (United States). Director: Bud Greenspan.

1989   *The World to Seoul* (South Korea). Producer: Seoul Olympic Organizing Com-
       mittee.

1990   *Time Capsule: The 1936 Berlin Olympic Games* (United States). Producer-
       director: Bud Greenspan.

1991   *For the Honor of Their Country* (United States). Director: Bud Greenspan.

1992   *Barcelona '92 Olympic Games* (United States). Producer: NBC Sports.

1992   *Great Olympic Confrontations* (United States). Producer: *Sports Illustrated.*

1992   *The Measure of Greatness* (United States). Director: Bud Greenspan.

1992   *Record Breakers of the Olympic Games* (United States). Producer: *Sports Illus-
       trated.*

1992   *Triumph and Tragedy: The 1972 Munich Olympics* (United States). Director: Bud
       Greenspan.

1992   *U-S-A! U-S-A! U-S-A!* (United States). Producer: *Sports Illustrated.*

1993   *16 Days of Glory: Barcelona '92* (United States). Director: Bud Greenspan.

1994   *16 Days of Glory: Lillehammer '94* (United States). Director: Bud Greenspan.

                                                                  Linda K. Fuller

Olympic Feature Films

In terms of the athletic genre there seems little doubt that film critics hold to the view that boxing and baseball have provided sports movies with their most artistically pleasing moments. The *Pride of the Yankees* (baseball) in the World War II era and the *Rocky* quintet (boxing) in contemporary cinema are frequently described as great movies. Other critics have praised the monumental aesthetics of *The Natural* (baseball) and the brash and uncompromising muscularity of *Raging Bull* (boxing). With respect to Olympic films, the work of Leni Riefenstahl, Mashiro Shinoda, Kon Ichikawa, and Bud Greenspan has elevated the documentary feature to great heights, but very little attention has been given to the Olympic feature film. In fact, while there have been few feature films made with a significant Olympic component, some of them epitomize classic filmmaking. After ten years, *Chariots of Fire* (1981) is assuming the celebrity status of a film classic as it appears increasingly in the top choices of leading critics.

The definitive source in terms of identifying Olympic feature films is Howard Zucker and Lawrence Babich, eds., *Sports Films: A Complete Reference* (1987), which describes a number of films of varying quality that focus on the Olympics. *Jim Thorpe—All American* (aka *Man of Bronze*), released in 1951, tells the story of America's greatest track and field athlete. Instead of merely chronicling Jim Thorpe's athletic versatility, its canvas goes from his days on the Indian reservation to the loss of his Olympic gold medals because of his playing professional baseball. The casting of Burt Lancaster as Thorpe was perfect. He had begun his career as a gymnast/acrobat, and with his sculpted physique and passionate personality, he personified the athlete-as-actor folk-hero.

Three years later Allied Artists brought out *The Bob Mathias Story* (aka *The Flaming Torch*), starring Bob Mathias playing himself. Despite clever editing, with real footage from the 1948 and the 1952 Olympics, the film failed because Mathias was undistinguished as an actor, and the screenplay failed to capture the magnetism that Mathias communicated in real life.

Perhaps the most disappointing of the Olympic feature films was Twentieth Century Fox's *The Games,* released in 1970. It had all the elements for success, including a star-studded international cast (Michael Crawford, Stanley Baker, Ryan O'Neal, Jeremy Kemp, Charles Aznavour) and a screenwriter (Erich Segal) who had enjoyed enormous success with *Love Story.* The story line deals with four runners from different countries (Great Britain, United States, Czechoslovakia and Australia) as they prepare for the 1960 Rome Olympics. The result was a cinematic disaster. An absence of character development, unreal acting performances (only Crawford looked as if he was a runner), and a weak plot doomed *The Games.*

If *The Games* marked the nadir of the Olympic feature film, *Goldengirl* (1979) fared nearly as badly. Nevertheless, *Goldengirl* deserves watching because its polemical thesis calls attention to the moral and ethical conflict that is part of Olympic sport. Coaches need to be committed, and athletes must train ferociously to succeed. *Goldengirl* is the story of a female American runner who sets out to win triple sprint medals (100-, 200-, and 400-meter races) at the 1980 Olympics. Susan Anton was miscast as a muscular athlete but James Coburn, Curt Jurgens, and Robert Culp are interestingly assembled as the Machiavellian troupe determined to win at all costs.

One of the most controversial contemporary sports films was the 1982 Warner Brothers feature, *Personal Best,* a brave effort at setting out a lesbian relationship against a background of Olympic track and field athletics. Mariel Hemingway did look as if she could run quickly and sprint hard, and her relationship with Patrice Donnelly attempted to raise serious questions about issues of gender and sexuality in the competitive sports arena. Scott Glenn as the hard-driving coach strikes a familiar chord in Olympic studies. Just how far should coaches go in pushing athletes to become Olympic champions?

Lost among these titles is a delightful vignette film that too often has been labeled as trite and superficial. *Wee Geordie* (released in Great Britain as *Geordie*) is a 99-minute British Lion/Times Film Corporation comedy. It tells the story of a gamekeeper's weak son in the Scottish Highlands who finds fame and a new physique by sending off for a mail-order physical culture program. Bill Travers, in the starring role, develops into a towering Celtic giant, specializes in the hammer throw, and represents Great Britain at the 1956 Melbourne Olympics. There is a love interest with another athlete at the games (remember that at the 1956 Games, Hal Connolly, the American hammer thrower, had a celebrated romance with an East European athlete), but Travers comes home and lives happily ever after in his Scottish village. Three positive points should be stressed. The film had no pretensions; it set out only to popularize and caricature the quaintness of Scotland. The original novel by David Walker is a quintessential romance, but Walker had a fine eye for the nuances of athletic competition. Director Frank Launder used actual Highland Games settings to give a sense of credibility and reality to a variety of ''heaving'' and ''tossing'' athletic events.

The greatest of Olympic feature films is the Twentieth Century Fox release *Chariots of Fire* (1981). The story concerns the successes of an evangelical Protestant Scot, Eric Liddell, and an English Jew, Harold Abrahams, at the 1924 Paris Olympics. Abrahams won the 100-meter race, upsetting the favored Americans, and Liddell, normally a dash man, raced the 400 meters to take the gold medal. Critics speak of memorable track sequences, and researchers have a wonderful treasure trove for exploring a myriad of Olympic issues. Tom McNab, a distinguished British track and field coach and sport historian, was a consultant for the film, and his many contributions elevate it to a work of generally accurate artistry. Winner of the Academy Award for best film in 1982, *Chariots of Fire* to a great extent recreated the flavor and substance of the Abrahams and

Liddell lifestyles, the ethos of Cambridge, the aristocratic administration of British track and field, and the events of the 1924 Olympics. Although some critics bemoaned *Chariots of Fire*—Pauline Kael in the *New Yorker* thought the slow-motion running sequences artificial and staged—Roger Ebert considered *Chariots* a great film because it went beyond the story line to make important statements about human nature. Without doubt *Chariots of Fire* will continue to demand analysis and examination for many years to come.

Two years after *Chariots of Fire,* Buena Vista films released *Running Brave,* the story of Cree Indian Billy Mills who, in a magnificent final lap dash, won the 10,000 meters gold medal at the 1964 Olympics. Despite a sincere and sympathetic portrayal of Mills by Robby Benson, the film saw limited runs and quickly was sold to video markets. This is a great pity because the film focuses on important issues about sport, minority groups, and the roles of both in American society.

Much work needs to be done identifying and classifying Olympic feature films made outside the United States. Australia, a country justly acclaimed for movies such as *Gallipoli, Breaker Morant,* and *Picnic at Hanging Rock,* is also the country in which *Dawn* was produced. The fascinating story of swimmer Dawn Fraser, who won gold medals in the 100-meter freestyle at the 1956, 1960, and 1964 Olympics, sadly did not translate successfully into a film despite the selection of Bronwyn Mackay-Payne, an outstanding athlete, for the lead role. The South African film *My Way* (aka *The Winners*) appeared in 1974, with actor Joe Stewardson in the role of the 1948 Olympic marathon winner who becomes obsessed with victory. He marries and then subjects his children to draconian training philosophies. The film addresses the survival of humanitarian values in the face of an excessive commitment to sporting success. The 1977 German comedy *Ties to the Olympics* develops the scenario of a firm's winning the shoe contract for the West German Olympic team. It is intriguing to view, knowing that when the film was released, the German firms of Adidas and Puma dominated the world and Olympic market in sports shoes.

Olympic feature films have been around for a long time and have explored virtually every facet of human behavior. In 1925 the American Charles Paddock appeared in *Nine and Three-Fifths Seconds.* This sprinter, who had been upset by Harold Abrahams of Great Britain in the 1924 Olympic 100-meter final, appears as the hero who outruns a horse and chases a villain who had kidnapped his girlfriend. The 1976 Aragon movie *2076 Olympiad* was a science fiction feature that stretched the bounds of credulity even further. The year is 2076, and the Olympic Games are being televised by a cable network that specializes in erotica. Instead of athletic skills, the Games focus on sexual performance.

Other contemporary films with an Olympic flavor have been equally dismal. Olympian gymnast Kurt Thomas of the United States appeared in the 1985 martial arts movie *Gymkata,* and Dorian Harewood as Jesse Owens in the 1984 Paramount film, *The Jesse Owens Story*, looked wooden and dull. This film tried the old formula of using documentary footage of Owens racing in the 1930s.

The result was clumsy and merely highlighted the threadbare nature of a weakly constructed narrative. One feature film that frequently is overlooked is Columbia's 1977 production of *The Greatest*. It is well worth reviewing for its effort to craft a revisionist history of Muhammad Ali, who began his career as Cassius Clay, Olympic light-heavyweight champion at the Rome Olympics. More recent films include *The Cutting Edge* (1992), in which a former hockey player tries to win Olympic glory as a figure skater in pairs competition. Robin Cousins, the 1980 gold medalist in figure skating, choreographed the skating sequences. The 1993 film *Cool Runnings,* a comedy, starring John Candy, was loosely based on the experience of the Jamaican bobsled team at the 1988 Calgary Games.

The Olympic feature film, apart from the exceptional *Chariots of Fire,* does not come close to emulating the many brilliant documentaries of the Olympics. Nevertheless, the dramatic possibilities of the Olympics are legion. For example, none of the following scenarios has been tapped by modern filmmakers: the American black protest at the Mexico Olympics; the Munich massacre; the 1980 United States or 1984 Soviet Olympic boycotts; the incredible athleticism of Florence Griffith-Joyner at the Seoul Olympics; the Ben Johnson tragedy; the phenomenon of African distance runners; and the emergence of the world-breaking Chinese women. In short, the potential for Olympic feature films of the future is limitless.

BIBLIOGRAPHICAL ESSAY

An important source to begin the study of Olympic feature films is Harvey M. Zucker and Lawrence J. Babich, eds., *Sports Films: A Complete Reference* (Jefferson, N.C., 1987). Judith A. Davidson and Daryl Adler, eds., *Sport on Film and Video* (Metuchen, N.J., 1993) does not include feature films. For analyses of *Chariots of Fire,* see the British Cultural Studies and Sport issue of *Sociology of Sport Journal* 9, 2 (June 1992). On British film, consult Peter Lovesey and Tom McNab, eds., *The Guide to British Track and Field Literature, 1275–1968* (London, 1969), a valuable Olympics source inasmuch as Lovesey wrote *Goldengirl* and McNab was a consultant in the making of *Chariots of Fire.* Roger Ebert, *The Movie Home Companion—1994* (Kansas City, 1993), is typical of video guides prepared annually by movie critics, containing brief sketches of many hundreds of films.

OLYMPIC FEATURE FILMS

1925   *Nine and Three-Fifths Seconds* (United States). Director: Lloyd B. Carleton.

1928   *Olympic Hero* (United States). Director: R. William Neill.

1936   *One in a Million* (United States). Director: Sidney Lanfield.

1937   *Charlie Chan at the Olympics* (United States). Director: H. Bruce Humberstone.

1951   *Jim Thorpe—All American* (aka *Man of Bronze*) (United States). Director: Michael Curtiz.

1954 *The Bob Mathias Story* (United States). Director: Francis D. Lyon.

1955 *Wee Geordie* (Great Britain). Director: Frank Launder.

1962 *It Happened in Athens* (United States). Director: Andrew Marton.

1966 *Walk, Don't Run* (United States). Director: Charles Walkers.

1969 *Downhill Racer* (United States). Director: Michael Ritchie.

1970 *The Games* (United States). Director: Michael Winner.

1974 *My Way* (aka *The Winners*) (South Africa). Director: Joseph Brenner.

1975 *The Other Side of the Mountain* (United States). Director: Larry Peerce.

1977 *2076 Olympiad* (United States). Producer-director: James P. Martin.

1977 *The Greatest* (United States/Great Britain). Director: Tom Grier.

1977 *Ties for the Olympics* (West Germany). Director: Stefan Lukschy.

1979 *Dawn* (Australia). Director: Ken Hannam.

1979 *Goldengirl* (United States). Director: Joseph Sargent.

1979 *Ice Castles* (United States). Director: Donald Wrye.

1979 *Running* (United States). Director: Steven Hilliard Stern.

1980 *Olympiade 40* (Poland). Director: Andrzej Kotkowski.

1981 *Chariots of Fire* (Great Britain). Director: Hugh Hudson.

1982 *Personal Best* (United States). Director: Robert Towne.

1983 *Running Brave* (United States). Producer: Ira Englander.

1992 *The Cutting Edge* (United States). Director: Paul Michael Glaser.

1993 *Cool Runnings* (United States). Director: Jon Turteltaub.

Scott A.G.M. Crawford

GENERAL BIBLIOGRAPHY

This general bibliography describes major archival collections with Olympic-related holdings as well as books and articles that deal with more than one Olympics or that are topical in nature. While we have tried to be as comprehensive as possible, space does not permit the listing of every one of the hundreds of books and articles that have been published on the Olympics; we urge readers to pursue the published bibliographical guides noted here, as well as the many fine bibliographies included in the better books and articles on various aspects of the Games.

PUBLISHED BIBLIOGRAPHICAL GUIDES

Richard Mandell, a historian who has written much on the Olympic movement, published the first important article dealing with the availability of research materials for the study of the Olympics, "The Modern Olympic Games: A Bibliographical Essay," *Sportwissenschaft* 6, 1 (1976): 89–98. This article sets out the state of Olympic study in 1976, noting that most of the available material is in German and identifying two extensive bibliographies, both in German: Karl Lennartz, *Bibliographie: Geschichte der Leibesubungen* (Cologne, 1971), which lists only German-language works, and the forty-three-page bibliography in H. Lenk, *Werte, Ziele, Wirklichkeit der modernen Olympischen Spiele* (Stuttgart, 1964; expanded ed., 1972). Although Mandell is quite critical of Lenk's bibliography (and much else about the state of Olympic Games history), he does lay out the problem as a challenge to future researchers.

The lack of a thorough bibliographical guide in English was remedied by Bill Mallon in *The Olympics: A Bibliography* (New York, 1984). This very useful work lists all the Games organizing committee official reports and other publications, IOC and national Olympic committee publications, and hundreds of other publications in over thirty languages. Sections on theses and dissertations and on Olympic films are also included, but articles in academic or popular journals are not. Unfortunately, the citations are not annotated, so researchers have no clear idea of the content or quality of any book, but the citations are complete. Mallon's book is now twelve years old, so for more recent titles, researchers must rely on computerized databases, such as Infotrac, or CD-ROM publications dealing with sports.

To learn about libraries and archives with extensive Olympics holdings, a useful place to start is the *World Directory of Sport Libraries, Information and Documentation Centres* (Belconnen, Australia, 1994). The information in this book was supplied by the libraries themselves and compiled by the National Sport Information Centre, a part of the Australian Sport Commission, for the International Association for Sport Information (IASI), a group that promotes access to sport information resources around the world. The *World Directory* lists just over 100 libraries; not all have relevant Olympic materials.

ARCHIVES WITH SIGNIFICANT OLYMPIC HOLDINGS

The International Olympic Committee (IOC) library and archives is the logical place to begin. The archives, which contain material dating back to the founding of the modern Olympic movement and the IOC in the 1890s, are located at the IOC headquarters in Lausanne, Switzerland. Much of the material deals with the operations of the IOC itself over the years, and the collection is arranged topically, with sections devoted to the various Olympic Games and their organizing committees, international sport federations, national Olympic committees (NOC), IOC presidents and members, non-Olympic sport organizations, other international organizations, and non-IOC individuals. Correspondence is embargoed for fifty years and IOC minutes for ten years, although waivers may be granted to researchers who make application and have genuine need for access to these records. In general, researchers should notify the IOC well in advance of their planned visit and provide a letter of recommendation from their NOC or university. The director of research is Karel Wendl, and the archivist is Michele Veillard; they may be contacted at the Olympic Research and Studies Center, International Olympic Committee, Quai d'Ouchy 1, 1001 Lausanne, Switzerland.

The IOC also maintains an important library and museum at its Lausanne headquarters. The library, open to museum visitors, contains several thousand volumes, nearly all of which relate in some fashion to the Olympic movement. Items in the collection are accessible through a computerized catalog, and the classification system is logical and easy to learn. The museum, which reopened in new quarters in June 1993, contains extensive exhibits on both Summer and Winter Games, interactive exhibits on a variety of topics from notable Olympians to training tips, and Olympic art. A separate room in the museum accommodates several temporary exhibits each year.

The U.S. Olympic Committee (USOC), located in Colorado Springs, Colorado, maintains an archives of more limited use to researchers. The USOC Archives are an unaccessioned and unclassified collection of materials that document the history and activities of the USOC. There are no finding aids available at this time, but known strengths of the collection include minutes of the executive committee dating back to 1919; final reports issued by the organizing committees of most of the Games; periodical publications of the USOC and IOC, such as newsletters; and U.S. Olympic Academy and International Olympic Academy proceedings. In addition, the archives contain the following materials, but it is not known whether a full set is available or which issues are missing: USOC team media guides; USOC constitutions; Olympic festival programs and media guides; miscellaneous Olympic trials programs and results; and miscellaneous booklets, pamphlets, and brochures on each of the Games. Also included are the collections of Herb Weinberg, radio announcer and historian, and Harold Friermood, Olympic committee and volleyball association member.

Qualified researchers may use the archives upon approval of a completed application indicating the purpose and nature of the project, the type and quantity of materials needed, types and quantity of other resources used, and the projected time frame. The contact person is Cindy Slater, Director of Information Resources, Archives, U.S. Olympic Committee, One Olympic Plaza, Colorado Springs, Colorado 80909.

Other useful archival collections in the United States include the Amateur Athletic Foundation of Los Angeles, established after the 1984 Summer Games in that city. Its collection contains more than 5,000 printed volumes, 7,000 photographs, 600 video volumes, and the Avery Brundage Collection on microfilm. Among the most valuable documents in the collection is every official report of organizing committees of the modern Games since 1896, or, for Games for which no such report was published, the most reliable account of those Games. In addition, the collection includes other primary documents for each Games, including programs, U.S. and British Olympic committee reports, media guides, and, for the more recent Games, the multivolume U.S. television network research manuals used by announcers for background information.

The foundation archives contain a wide variety of magazines and newsletters pertinent to the Olympic movement, an ongoing Southern California Olympians oral history project, numbering some 100 transcribed interviews, and a substantial video collection, including complete U.S. television network coverage of all Games since 1988. There is no fee to use the library. Appointments are recommended, and the contact person is Wayne Wilson, Amateur Athletic Foundation of Los Angeles, 2141 West Adams Boulevard, Los Angeles, California 90018.

The University of Illinois Archives house the Avery Brundage Collection, an extensive archival record of the individual who was president of the IOC from 1952 to 1972. The papers fill 310 archive boxes, 109 scrapbooks and photograph albums, and several boxes of photographs, films, tapes, and microfilm. In addition, Brundage donated a collection of more than 1,500 books, many on the Olympics, which are kept in a special room in the Applied Life Sciences Library. Fortunately, there is an excellent published finding aid for the Brundage papers: Maynard Brichford, comp., *Avery Brundage Collection, 1908–1975* (Cologne, 1977). The Brundage Collection has been supplemented by another Olympic collection, which holds material on Games since 1972. This collection includes published material from organizing committees of Games beginning with Montreal 1976, although there is relatively little on the 1992 Summer and Winter Games. The archives also contain the Frederick J. Ruegsegger Collection. Ruegsegger was Brundage's business manager and adviser for many years, traveling with him and frequently translating for him. This collection contains letters and clippings related to Brundage as well as 24 boxes of audiotapes of IOC meetings between 1969 and 1972. The contact person is Maynard Brichford, University Archives, 19 Main Library, University of Illinois, Urbana, Illinois 61801.

A smaller but still useful collection of Olympic-related material is at the National Track and Field Hall of Fame Research Library at Butler University, Indianapolis. This collection contains about 3 cubic feet of clippings, arranged by Games, copies of the IOC *Bulletin* and *Olympic Review,* and assorted other materials, in addition to a comprehensive assortment of books on the Olympics. Contact the Rare Books and Special Collections librarian, Butler University, 4600 Sunset Avenue, Indianapolis, Indiana

46208. At the Gerald R. Ford Library, Ann Arbor, Michigan, are the records of the President's Commission on Olympic Sports, 1975–1977, which looked into the USOC and related sport organizations with respect to the manner in which U.S. athletes were being prepared for Olympic competition. A printed finding aid for these papers is available. Write to Don W. Wilson, Director, Gerald R. Ford Library, 1000 Beal Avenue, Ann Arbor, Michigan 48109.

In Canada, researchers should start at the Centre for Olympic Studies at the University of Western Ontario, London. A relatively new repository for Olympic materials, the center contains copies of the daily IOC press reviews for 1993–1994, summaries of the minutes of IOC sessions and executive board meetings, IOC academy reports, various Canadian Olympic Association reports, the official reports and other publications related to the 1976 Montreal Summer Games and the 1988 Calgary Winter Games, photocopied material from earlier Olympic Games, and the scrapbook of 1932 Canadian Olympian Alda Wilson, the fifth-place finisher in the 80-meter hurdles. In addition, the center's holdings include substantial slide collections, a microfilm copy of the Avery Brundage papers, and a number of theses and dissertations on Olympic topics as well as a representative collection of books on the Olympic movement. The center publishes *Olympika: International Journal of Olympic Studies*, which contains scholarly articles on the Games. Other Olympic material is housed in the special collections department of the university library, including a number of official reports and organizing committee publications, Canadian Olympic Association meeting minutes (1934–1949) and publications, scrapbooks and clippings from a Canadian who participated in the 1906 and 1912 Games, and a fairly extensive Olympic stamp collection. The contact person is Robert K. Barney, Director, Alumni Hall, Faculty of Kinesiology, University of Western Ontario, London, Ontario N6A 3K7, Canada.

In Germany, several sport history centers contain significant collections of Olympic-related material. The most extensive of these is the Deutsche Sporthochschule Köln, Cologne, where Olympic study is centered in the Carl-Diem-Institut. The centerpiece of this collection is the papers and letters of Diem, who was active in the German Olympic movement for well over fifty years, spanning the period from Coubertin to Brundage. Over 90,000 letters form the basis of this collection, and to these are added Diem's many publications, 10,000 sport photographs, his library of 3,000 books, and the papers of his wife, Liselot, a professor of sport methodology who was active in the German national Olympic committee and the World Women's Federation of Sport and who wrote more than 20 books. The school houses the largest general sport library in Europe, with over 100,000 books and 300 journals. Arrangements to conduct research should be made in advance. Write to Karl Lennartz, Director of Archives, Carl-Diem-Institut, Deutsche Sporthochschule Köln, Carl-Diem-Weg 6, 50933 Cologne, Germany.

The Institut fur Sport-Wissenschaften at Georg-August-Universität in Göttingen contains a library of 22,000 volumes and 300 journals but no original archival material. It has a computerized index of its own holdings, as well as those of the Carl-Diem-Institut, and it possesses a microfilm copy of the Brundage Papers. The institute's holdings in sport medicine are particularly strong. Contact the institute at Georg-August-Universität, Sprangerweg 2, 37075 Göttingen, Germany. Not too distant from Göttingen is the Lower Saxony Institute for Sport History (Niedersachsisches Institut fur Sportgeschichte), whose collection also contains a substantial number of published works (especially of German origin) about the Olympics. For more information, write Niedersachsisches Institut fur Sportgeschichte Hoya e. V., Hasseler Steinweg 2, 27318 Hoya, Germany.

Near the site of the 1972 Games in Munich is the Technische Universität, whose sport library contains 36,000 volumes and 190 journals. Although not Olympic specific, the library has an extensive section on the Olympic movement, including, of course, a great deal on the 1972 Games. Write to Ulrike Merke, Sportbibliothek, Technische Universität, Zentrale Hochschulesportanlage in Olympiapark, Connollystrasse 32, Munich, Germany.

Australia's Olympic heritage is documented in several repositories in addition to the library of the Sydney organizing committee for the 2000 Games. The National Library of Australia has four manuscript collections and twenty-five oral histories related to the Olympics, as well as pictorial files on Games from 1952 onward, more than thirty films and videos, and extensive clippings files from 1956 onward. The contact person is Nada Dobrijevic, Reference Librarian, Information Services, Australian National Library, Canberra, ACT, 2600 Australia.

Three separate centers at the Melbourne Cricket Club offer research material on the Games. The Australian Gallery of Sport and Olympic Museum has a general collection of material from the 1956 Melbourne Games; the Beaurepaire Collection, containing scrapbooks, albums, photographs, and a diary documenting that family's long involvement with the Olympic movement; and two smaller Olympic collections. Write to Judy Hanson, Collections Curator, Australian Gallery of Sport and Olympic Museum, Melbourne Cricket Club, P.O. Box 175, East Melbourne 3002, Australia. The Melbourne Cricket Club Museum has a collection of correspondence relating to the management of the 1956 Games, part of which were held at the club. Write to the Secretary, M.C.C., at the address above. Finally, the Melbourne Cricket Club Library, separate from the museum, contains about 200 Olympic-related books. More information is available from Ross Peacock, Librarian, at the same address.

Sport institutes and research centers exist in many other countries, but few of them specialize in Olympic studies. However, some may be useful to researchers: In France, L'Institut national du sport et de éducation physique, 11 avenue du Tremblay 75012 Paris, France; in Finland, the Sport Library of Finland (SUK), Stadion, Helsinki 00250, Finland; in Monaco, the archives of the International Amateur Athletic Federation, 17 rue Princesse Florestine, BP 359, MC-98007, Monaco Cedex, Monaco; in New Zealand, the library of the New Zealand Olympic and Commonwealth Games Association, P.O. Box 2251, Wellington, New Zealand; and in Spain, the Biblioteca de l'Esport, Generalitat de Catalunya, Valencia 3, 08015 Barcelona, Spain, which contains, among other material, the Juan Antonio Samaranch Collection and material from the 1992 Barcelona Games.

CD-ROM and Online Databases

Rapidly changing computer technology in the past few years has made possible the accumulation of large amounts of factual or bibliographical material accessible through CD-ROM disks or online databases. The best of these provide ready access to literally hundreds of thousands of citations of books and articles or complete Olympic records. Most are quite expensive and are available only at larger research libraries.

Among CD-ROM resources, SPORT Discus, produced by Sport Information Resource Centre, 1600 James Naismith Drive, Gloucester, Ontario, Canada K1B 5N4, is the most relevant to sport (and therefore Olympic) studies. SPORT Discus contains more than 330,000 citations, some of which are accompanied by abstracts, on scientific and practical literature of individual and team sports, primarily from English and French sources dating back to 1949. SPORT Discus corresponds to the online database SPORT.

CD-ROM Sportwissenschaft, produced by Bundesinstitüt für Sportwissenschaft, Carl-Diem-Weg 4, Cologne, Germany, includes approximately 470,000 citations, with abstracts, on international literature covering sport sciences. The resource, in German, covers books, periodicals, dissertations, and conference proceedings back to 1970 and corresponds to the online database SPOLIT.

CSIC, a Spanish CD-ROM resource, is produced by the Centro de Documentación e Informática Biomédica, Universidad de Valencia, Avda. Blasco Ibañez 17, 10 Valencia, Spain. CSIC contains more than 625,000 citations to articles in 2,300 Spanish journals. Most are scientific or technical publications, but a subset indexes social science and humanities journals back to 1975. CSIC corresponds to the online database ISOC.

The Social Science Citation Index—Compact Disc Edition, produced by the Institute for Scientific Information, 3501 Market Street, Philadelphia, Pennsylvania 19104, may also prove useful to researchers. This resource lists bibliographical data and citations from the 1,400 most important social science journals worldwide, as well as social science articles from some 3,200 natural science journals, including medical publications. It covers journals from 1986 to the present and corresponds to the Social Scisearch online database.

Finally, the Academic Index, produced by the Information Access Company (IAC), 362 Lakeside Drive, Foster City, California 94404, has more than 500,000 citations to academically oriented articles and reviews in some 400 social science, humanities, natural science, and current events journals, as well as the *New York Times*. Coverage begins with 1985 publications, and the index corresponds to an online database of the same name.

Online Databases

Online databases differ from CD-ROM resources in that they can be updated daily. They are available by subscription through their producer or, more often, through an online database vendor. Although many online databases are linked to a CD-ROM resource, others stand alone. Relevant addresses are given at the end of each description.

AGORA-SPORTS (ASPO), produced by Agence France-Presse, 13, Place de la Bourse, B.P. 20, F-75061, Paris, France, contains 210,000 news items dealing with sports and sporting events, as well as a chronology of world records. The coverage dates back to 1989, and the working language is French. It is accessible through Européenne de Données (ASPO), 164 Ter, rue d'Aguesseau, F-92100 Boulogne-Billancourt, France.

Olimpiades (OLIM), produced by the Ministerio de Cultura de España, Consejo Superior de Deportes, Martin Fierro s/n, 28040 Madrid, Spain, includes the results of more than 3,000 Winter and Summer Olympic Games events and other world championships. In Spanish, the database contains Olympic data back to 1896 and other competitions back to 1960. It is accessible through the Ministerio de Cultura.

The Olympic Factbook, produced by Gale Research Inc., 835 Penobscot Building, Detroit, Michigan 48226-4094, is a guide to all Olympic Games—their history, highlights, rules, and procedures—as well as profiles of past winners. Licensed by the U.S. Olympic Committee, it is accessible through NEXIS (Mead Data Central, Inc.), P.O. Box 933, Dayton, Ohio 45401-0933.

Because the technology is changing so quickly in this area, researchers would be well advised to consult the latest edition of Kathleen Lopez Nolan, ed., *Gale Directory of*

Databases (Detroit, 1995). This comprehensive publication appears at least twice a year and is well indexed. Information for this section of the bibliography was drawn from the January 1995 edition.

Books and Articles

There are many general histories of the modern Olympics. Most, either pictorial histories or journalistic accounts, concentrate almost exclusively on the athletic performances at the Games themselves and treat their political, social, and cultural context, if at all, in a very perfunctory manner. One notable exception is Allen Guttmann, *The Olympics: A History of the Modern Games* (Urbana, Ill., 1992). Guttmann, who has also written a biography of Avery Brundage, emphasizes the political maneuvering behind the Olympics and notes only briefly the outstanding athletic achievements. Unlike most general histories, *The Olympics* does not have a separate chapter for each Olympic Games; rather, its eleven chapters touch on disparate stages of Olympic history. The book also contains a good bibliographical essay.

Among the pictorial histories of the Olympics, the most recent of note is a *Sports Illustrated* publication, *The Olympics: A History of the Games* (New York, 1992), published after the Albertville Winter Games but before the Barcelona Summer Games of 1992. One of the earliest such histories, but still very worthwhile, is Richard Schaap, *An Illustrated History of the Olympics* (New York, 1963). Schaap, a veteran sports journalist, touches on both the highlights and the controversies of the Games in his text, and the photographs are well chosen to capture the dramatic moments of the Games. A statistical appendix is included. John Rodda and Lord Killanin, *The Olympic Games: 80 Years of People, Events, and Records* (London, 1976), written while Killanin headed the IOC, is a reliable pictorial history with more text than most other such books; Lee Benson et al., *Athens to Atlanta: 100 Years of Glory* (Salt Lake City, 1993), is the U.S. Olympic Committee's view of the Olympic Games; Nicolaos Yalouris, *The Olympic Games* (Athens, 1976), is a coffee table book covering both ancient and modern Games, with roughly equal space devoted to each. The modern Games are covered on a Games-by-Games basis. Yalouris does present some information on the fine arts competitions accompanying each Olympic Games as well, noting that competitive exhibitions were dropped after 1948 because of the mediocre quality of the work and controversies over its judging. Paul Lecia, *Sports Shots* (New York, 1937), is an older book that is all pictures. Researchers of the history of the Winter Games should not overlook Ossi Brucker, *Titel, Tranen und Triumphe: die Olympische Winterspiele von 1924–1992* (Kassel, 1992), a pictorial survey but one of the very few general histories of the Winter Games, with an informative chapter on the background and origin of those Games. Another pictorial survey is the U.S. Olympic Committee, *Chamonix to Lillehammer: The Glory of the Olympic Winter Games* (Salt Lake City, 1994), quite possibly published in conjunction with Salt Lake City's successful bid to host the 2002 Winter Games.

General histories in which text is emphasized over pictures include Bill Henry, *An Approved History of the Olympic Games* (New York, 1948), written by an individual who worked at the 1932 Los Angeles Games and for many years had close ties with the U.S. Olympic Committee; Alexander M. Weyand, *The Olympic Pageant* (New York, 1952), by a retired military officer who was a wrestler in the 1920 Games; R. D. Binfield, *The Story of the Olympic Games* (London, 1948), which is organized by event rather than by Games, as is Nicolaos Yalouris, *The Eternal Olympics* (New Rochelle, N.Y., 1979). Another general history is Hugh Harlan, *History of the Olympic Games: Ancient and Modern* (Los Angeles, 1964), which has a section on the origins of the modern Olympics. A shorter history is Xenophon L. Messinesi, *History of the Olympic Games* (New York, 1973), which also contains a chapter on the International Olympic Academy. John Lucas, a respected academic historian of the Games, has written ''The Modern Olympic Games: Fanfare and Philosophy, 1896–1972,'' *Maryland Historian* 4 (Fall 1973): 71–87, which he expanded into *The Modern Olympic Games* (Cranbury, N.J., 1980). Another important Lucas article is ''From Coubertin to Samaranch: The Unsettling Transformation of the Olympic Ideology of Athletic Amateurism,'' *Stadion* 14, 1 (1988): 65–84. Two publications that relate the ancient Games to their modern counterparts are Paul J. Wade, ''Greece and the Olympic Games,'' *Gourmet* (March 1984): 28–32, 68–76, an article without scholarly pretension, and Roland Renson et al., eds., *The Olympic Games Through the Ages: Greek Antiquity and Its Impact on Modern Sport* (Athens, 1991). This publication contains the proceedings of the Thirteenth International Congress of HISPA, held in Olympia, Greece, in May 1979.

General histories in German include Friedrich Mevert, *Olympische Spiele der Neuzeit—von Athens bis Los Angeles* (Niederhausen, Germany, 1983), a survey history; Klaus Ulrich, *Olympische Spiele* (Berlin, 1978), which touches on some of the political and ideological issues of the Games; and Manfred Blodorn, ed., *Sport und Olympische Spiele* (Reinbek, Germany, 1984), an anthology of essays on Olympic ideas and ideals, with essays on the 1936 Berlin Games, women and the Olympics, and amateurism, among others. Willi Knecht, *100 Jahre Olympische Spiele der Neuzeit, 1896–1996* (Munich, 1990), is a four-volume pictorial history honoring the centennial of the Games. It contains short essays on the Games in four languages and an abundance of outstanding illustrations with captions in six languages.

French readers may consult Gaston Meyer, *Le Phémonène Olympique: Athènes—Rome* (Paris, 1960), a general account with a separate chapter on Coubertin and appendixes that contain the IOC constitution and Olympic records. For the earliest of the modern Games, see Otto Mayer, *Retrospectives olympiques: Athènes 1896–Rome 1960* (Geneva, Switzerland, 1961), which discusses the organization and staging of the first two Games.

Olympic record books abound, as many are published by television networks or corporate sponsors prior to each Olympics, but two books devoted almost entirely to Games statistics stand out above the rest. Erich Kamper and Bill Mallon, *The Golden Book of the Olympics* (Milan, 1992), is an exhaustively complete statistical review of Olympic performance. Not content to list the medal winners in each event of each Games, Kamper and Mallon have recorded virtually every combination and permutation of Olympic records conceivable. Thus, a researcher can learn the oldest and youngest gold medal winner at each Games, the number of medals athletes from each country have won and the number of records they have set, and winners of the arts competitions, of discontinued sports, and of demonstration sports. The book contains the birth and death dates of each nation's medalists, and much more. More modest in scope but more accessible is David Wallechinsky, *The Complete Book of the Olympics* (New York, 1991), which contains the records of the first eight finishers in each Olympic event. Arranged on a sport-by-sport basis, the book also includes some commentary about most events at most Games, pointing out something unusual or remarkable about that event. The book has a brief general history of the Games, a listing of national medal totals for each Games, and four sections of action photographs.

As the Olympics have become more embroiled in international political issues, writers have risen to the bait and published books on the subject. Two books that cover the political ground of the post–World War II Olympics are Richard Espy, *The Politics of the Olympics* (Berkeley, 1979), and David B. Kanin, *Political History of the Olympic Games* (Boulder, Colo., 1981). Peter Graham and Horst Ueberhorst, eds., *The Modern Olympics* (West Point, N.Y., 1976), and Jeffrey O. Segrave and Donald Chu, eds., *The Olympics in Transition* (Champaign, Ill., 1988), are both anthologies containing articles on the Olympics; many touch on the politics of the Games. Uriel Simri and Sarah Lieberman, eds., *Sport and Politics* (Netanya, Israel, 1984), is a collection of articles that deal with such topics as the 1980 Moscow Games, the 1984 Los Angeles Games, issues related to China and South Africa, and the participation of Israel in the Asian Games. John Lucas, mentioned earlier, may have the last word with *Future of the Olympic Games* (Champaign, Ill., 1992), in which he tackles the difficult contemporary issues facing the Olympic movement: nationalism, commercialism, drugs, and the role of women.

Other important publications with a political bent include John Hoberman, *The Olympic Crisis: Sport, Politics and the Moral Order* (New Rochelle, N.Y., 1986), a study of the IOC and the Olympic movement as an international institution that has survived the twentieth century by accommodating distasteful political regimes and issues rather than resisting them, a doctrine Hoberman calls "amoral universalism," where universal participation sometimes calls for the sacrifice of moral standards. A more journalistic view of recent Olympic politics is found in Geoffrey Miller, *Behind the Olympic Rings* (Lynn, Mass., 1979). Miller, the European sports editor for the Associated Press, discusses such issues as amateurism, television, and the IOC presidencies of Brundage and Killanin. Similar themes are echoed in John Sugden, "The Power of Gold: The Course and Currency of the Political Olympics," *Physical Education Review* (Manchester, England) 4 (1981): 65–78. See also Joel Thiver, "Politics and Protest at the Olympic Games," in Benjamin Lowe, David Kanin, and Andrew Strenk, eds., *Sport and International Relations* (Champaign, Ill., 1978). One book and two articles deal specifically with the apartheid question and South Africa: Richard Lapchick, *The Politics of Race and International Sport* (Westport, Conn., 1975); March L. Krotee and Luther C. Schwick, "The Impact of Sporting Forces on South African Apartheid," *Journal of Sport and Social Issues* 3 (1979): 33–42; and Peter Hain, "The Politics of Sport and Apartheid," in Jennifer Hargreaves, ed., *Sport, Culture, and Ideology* (London, 1982).

A number of books trace the Olympic history of a particular country. Max and Reet Howell, *Aussie Gold* (Albion, Queensland, 1988), survey the long history of Australian participation in the Olympics, as do Gary Lester, *Australians at the Olympics: A Definitive History* (Melbourne, 1984), and Harry Gordon, *Australia and the Olympic Games* (St. Lucia, Queensland, 1994). Henry Roxborough, *Canada at the Olympics* (Toronto, 1963), summarizes Canadian performance at the Games from 1896 through 1960, along with some general history, and includes appendixes on Olympic literature, stamps, and symbols and Canadian medalists. A book published in conjunction with the 1988 Calgary Games, *Canada at the Olympic Winter Games: The Official Sports History and Record Book* (Edmonton, Alberta, 1987), by Wendy Bryden, traces the history of winter sports in Canada and the background of the Calgary Games. The book also includes information on Canadian athletes in the Winter Games.

For the People's Republic of China, see Rolf von der Laage, *Sport in China: Gestern und Heute* (Berlin, 1977), which surveys sport in mainland China, including developments back to 1913 and China's participation in past Olympics. The Republic of China

Olympic Committee has published *Amateur Sport in the Republic of China* (Taipei, 1984), which incudes material on Taiwan at the Olympics. Cuba's recent Olympic history is profiled in Raymond Pointu and Roger Fidani, *Cuba: Sport en Revolución* (Paris, 1975).

For Czechoslovakia, there is Jan Kotrba et al., *Czechoslovakia and Olympic Games* (Prague, 1984). Arnd Krüger has detailed Germany's long association with the Olympic movement in a two-volume work: *Deutschland und die olympische Bewegung (1918–1945)* (Berlin, 1982) and *Deutschland und die olympische Bewegung (1948–1980)* (Berlin, 1982). Krüger devotes much space to the 1936 Berlin Games but relatively little to the 1972 Munich Games. More about Germany and the Olympic movement can be learned from four biographical studies of Olympic leaders: Carl Diem's autobiography, *Ein Leben fur den Sport* (Ratingen, Germany, 1974); Arnd Krüger, *Theodor Lewald: Sportführer ins Dritte Reich* (Berlin, 1975); Eerke Hamer, *Willibald Gebhardt: der erste deutsche Treuhander des olympische Gedankens* (Cologne, 1970); and Klaus Huhn, *Der vergessene Olympier: das erstaunliche Leben des Dr. Willibald Gebhardt* (Berlin, 1992). East Germany's strong showing in recent Olympics is examined in Yuri Brokhin, *The Big Red Machine* (New York, 1978). For a survey of the postwar sporting relationship between the two Germanys, see G. A. Carr, "The Involvement of Politics in the Sporting Relationships of East and West Germany, 1945–1972," *Journal of Sport History* 7, 1 (Spring 1980): 40–51.

For Hungary, see Jenoe Boskovits, *Die Geschichte des ungarischen Sports* (Budapest, 1983), a general sport history that includes information on Hungary's participation in the Olympics. Saradindu Sanyal traces India's participation in the Games in *Olympic Games and India* (Delhi, 1970). Mexico's Olympic experience is described in Antonio Lavin, *México en los Juegos Olímpicos MCMLXVIII* (Mexico, 1968), written for the 1968 Games. Jerzy Jabrzemski, *Sport in Poland* (Warsaw, 1956), mercifully translated into English, is an older book that highlights Poland's efforts at the Olympics and includes many illustrations, as well as sections on winners and Polish women at the Games. The Romanian Olympic Committee published *Liebeserziehung und Sport in Rumanien* (n.p., n.d.) to highlight that country's role in the Olympics. South Africa's turbulent relationship with the Olympic movement is detailed in Rudolf W. J. Opperman, *Africa's First Olympians: The Story of the Olympic Movement in South Africa, 1907–1987* (Johannesburg, 1987). Several books have been published on sport in the Soviet Union. Among those that deal with the Olympics, James Riordan, *Soviet Sport: Background to the Olympics* (New York, 1980), discusses the evolution, structure, and organization of Soviet sport, its application in gymnastics and soccer, and the problems of women in sport. A separate chapter traces Soviet Olympic history. See also Riordan's article, "The USSR and the Olympic Games," *Stadion* 6 (1980): 291–314. Norman Schneidman, *The Soviet Road to Olympus* (Toronto, 1978), touches on similar themes. German readers can also consult Martinus van den Heuvel, *Rusland en de olympische Spielen* (Haarlem, 1980). Finally, Ali Ramos discusses Venezuela's Olympic experiences in *Venezuela Olímpica* (Caracas, 1980).

A substantial number of resources are available for those wishing to study the biographies of Olympians. By far the most comprehensive source is Erich Kamper, *Lexicon der 12000 Olympioniken* (Graz, Austria, 1975), published also in an English edition, *Who's Who at the Olympics*. The 1975 edition was updated to include 14,000 Olympians in a 1983 edition and updated again in a 1992 edition, with Bill Mallon as coauthor. Entries in this publication are very brief, containing just home town, birth and death dates, and a record of Olympic participation. Mallon has published a book dealing only with U.S. Olympic medalists, *Quest for Gold: The Encyclopedia of American Olympians* (New York, 1984), which has longer sketches for many subjects.

Other collective biographies are Dimiter Mishev, *Meet the Olympians* (Sofia, Bulgaria, 1964), which contains data on Olympic athletes between 1896 and 1960 and essays on early specialization and sports longevity; Lewis H. Carlson and John J. Fogarty, *Tales of Gold: An Oral History of the Summer Olympic Games Told by America's Gold Medal Winners* (Chicago, 1987), containing fifty-eight oral histories of athletes representing a variety of Olympic events between the 1912 and 1984 Games; William O. Johnson, *All That Glitters Is Not Gold: An Irreverent Look at the Olympic Games* (New York, 1972); Erich Kamper and Herbert Saucel, *Olympischen Heroen: Portraits und Anekdoten von 1896 bis Heute* (Erkrath, Germany, 1991), a collection of short essays and anecdotes of Olympic highlights and biographical sketches of sixty-four Olympic heroes; and Stan Tomlin, ed., *Olympic Odyssey: The Olympic Story as Told by the Stars Themselves from 1986 to 1956* (Croydon, England, 1956), a collection of essays on each Games from 1896 to 1952, as told by participants such as Fanny Blankers-Koen. The book includes many photographs and the program for the Melbourne Games. General books on women in the Olympics include Uriel Simri, *Women at the Olympic Games*, 2d ed. (Netanya, Israel, 1979); Adrianne Blue, *Faster, Higher, Further* (London, 1988); and relevant parts of Allen Guttmann, *Women's Sports: A History* (New York, 1991). Sheila Mitchell, "Women's Participation in the Olympic Games, 1900–1926," *Journal of Sport History* 4, 2 (Summer 1977), analyzes the relationship between the IOC and the international sport federations that led to an increase in women's events at the Olympic Games.

Olympic champions from down under are the subject of Graeme Atkinson, *Australian and New Zealand Olympians: The Stories of 100 Great Champions* (Canterbury, Victoria, 1984). Ian Buchanan provides short biographies of British winners in *British Olympians: A Hundred Years of Gold Medallists* (Enfield, England, 1991); see also Sam Mullins, *British Olympians: William Penney Brooks and the Wenlock Games* (London, 1986), a British Olympic Association publication. Bulgarian athletes are profiled in Nikolai Kolev, *Bulgaria's Olympic Champions* (Sofia, 1988). For Canadian athletes, see Frank Cosentino and Glynn Leystion, *Olympic Gold: Canada's Winners in the Summer Games* (Toronto, 1975) and *Winter Gold: Canada's Winners in the Winter Olympic Games* (Markham, Ontario, 1987). French Olympic champions are highlighted in Raymond Marcillac, *Champions olympiques* (Paris, 1967), while Hungarian winners through 1952 receive their due in Ferenc Mezo, *The Golden Book of Hungarian Olympic Champions* (Budapest, 1955). For Soviet medalists, see Valerii Shteinbakh, *638 Olympic Champions: Three Decades in the Olympic Movement* (Moscow, 1984).

Somewhat more specialized are James Page, *Black Olympian Medalists* (Englewood, Colo., 1991), which deals with African-American winners, and Michael D. Davis, *Black American Women in Olympic Track and Field* (Jefferson, N.C., 1992), which surveys African-American women's performances at various Games from 1932 to 1988 and includes biographical sketches and a short appendix on chromosome sex testing. Dennis H. Phillips, *Australian Women at the Olympic Games, 1912–1992* (Kenthurst, New South Wales, 1992), is a chronological survey of Australian women's participation in the Summer Games, based in part on interviews. An older work is K. Silberg, *The Athletic Finn: Some Reasons Why the Finns Excel in Athletics* (Hancock, Mich., 1927), which profiles the great Finnish runners Hannes Kolehmainen, Willie Ritola, Paavo Nurmi, and Albin Stenroos. See also Martti Jukola, *Athletics in Finland* (Helsinki, 1932), a profile of the

Finnish teams in the 1932 Winter and Summer Games, but which emphasizes track and field and includes a lengthy sketch of Nurmi and shorter sketches of Lauri Lehtinen, Volmari Iso-Hollo, and several other track and field athletes.

Biographies and autobiographies of individual Olympic athletes must be used with great care. Although we have tried to avoid including those that would fall into the juvenile literature category, others meant for an adult readership are frequently so highly adulatory (or self-congratulatory) that one is forced to question their factual accuracy. Nonetheless, there are those that are honest treatments of the subject's life and career and present useful insights into what it means to compete (and, often, win) at the Olympics.

In addition to the biographies mentioned in some of the bibliographies following the essays on each of the Games, the following books are a representative sampling of what is available. Most deal with the greatest of the Olympic heroes, many of whom went on to successful careers in professional sports, film, or broadcasting.

Track and field, the most popular event (for most Americans, at least) on the Summer Olympic program, has produced the largest number of biographies. Eric Liddell, the Scottish runner at the 1924 Paris Games who later went on to a missionary career in China, where he died in 1945, is the subject of D. P. Thomson, *Eric H. Liddell: Athlete and Missionary* (Barnock, Perthshire, Scotland, 1971), and Sally Magnusson, *The Flying Scotsman* (New York, 1981). Interestingly, his teammate, Harold Abrahams, who with Liddell was memorialized in the 1981 film *Chariots of Fire* and went on to a long and distinguished career in the British Olympic movement, has not been the subject of a significant biography. For Paavo Nurmi, the best distance runner of the 1920s, consult the heavily illustrated, celebratory biography by Sulo Kolkka and Helge Nygren, *Paavo Nurmi* (Helsinki, 1974).

Jesse Owens, the African American who won four gold medals at the 1936 Berlin Games, is the subject of William J. Baker's fine biography, *Jesse Owens: An American Life* (New York, 1986). Owens also published an autobiography, *Jesse: The Man Who Outran Hitler* (New York, 1983). Another runner at the Berlin Games, 1,500-meter champion Jack Lovelock of New Zealand, is the subject of two biographies: Norman Harris, *The Legend of Lovelock* (London, 1964), and Christopher Tobin, *Lovelock, New Zealand's Olympic Gold Miler* (Dunedin, N.Z., 1984). Bob Mathias, the 17-year-old decathlon winner at the 1948 London Games and later a U.S. congressman, found biographers in Jim Scott, *Bob Mathias: Champion of Champions* (n.p., 1952), and Myron Tussin, *Bob Mathias: The Life of an Olympic Champion* (New York, 1983). Mathias also played himself in a poorly received film biography. Harold and Olga Connolly, whose love affair at the 1956 Melbourne Games breached the iron curtain, told their story in *Rings of Destiny* (New York, 1968). In 1964, Bob Hayes was considered the "fastest man in the world" after his victory in the 100-meter sprint. His autobiography, *Run, Bullet, Run: The Rise, Fall, and Recovery of Bob Hayes* (New York, 1990), tells of the difficulties he faced after the Games were over. Kip Keino, the celebrated Kenyan distance runner who won medals in the 1964, 1968, and 1972 Games, is the subject of Francis Noronha, *Kipchoge of Kenya* (Nakura, Kenya, 1970). Alberto Juantorena, the Cuban middle-distance runner who won two gold medals at the 1976 Montreal Games, is made into a role model for Cuban youth in E. Montesinos, *Alberto Juantorena* (Havana, 1980).

Bruce Jenner, the telegenic 1968 decathlon winner, told his life's story in *The Olympics and Me* (Garden City, N.Y., 1980), while Frank Shorter, the marathon champion four years later at Munich, wrote his autobiography, *Olympic Gold: A Runner's Life and*

Times (Boston, 1984). Lasse Viren, the Finnish distance runner who won gold medals in the 5,000- and 10,000-meter runs in both the 1972 and 1976 Games, published an autobiography, *Lasse Viren: Olympic Champion* (Portland, Ore., 1978). The two-time decathlon winner, Daley Thompson, one of Britain's most popular sport heroes, wrote *Daley: The Last Ten Years* (London, 1986), and was the subject of Skip Rosin, *Daley Thompson: The Subject Is Winning* (London, 1983). Carl Lewis, the American athlete who dominated the sprints and long jump during the 1980s, wrote, with Jeffrey Marx, *Inside Track: My Professional Life in Amateur Track and Field* (London, 1990). For another view of Lewis, see the *New York Times Magazine,* June 17, 1984, a special issue on the 1984 Summer Games, which contains an article, "Carl Lewis: The Quest for Olympic Greatness." Lewis's great rival in the 1988 Seoul Games, Ben Johnson, is the subject of James R. Christie, *Ben Johnson: The Fastest Man on Earth* (Toronto, 1988), which was written before Johnson's drug-induced downfall.

Boxing and swimming are the other Summer Games events that have produced subjects for biographies. The best of several biographies of Muhammad Ali, who as Cassius Clay won a gold medal at the 1960 Rome Games, is probably Thomas Hauser, *Muhammad Ali: His Life and Times* (London, 1991). The Cuban boxing champion, Teofilo Stevenson, is the subject of Mariolo Cabale Ruiz, *Teofilo Stevenson, grande entre los grandes* (Havana, 1985). For swimmers, consult Narda Onyx, *Water, World and Weissmuller: A Biography* (Los Angeles, 1964), and Mark Spitz and Mickey Herkovitz, *Seven Golds: Mark Spitz' Own Story* (Garden City, N.Y., 1984). Greg Louganis, the diving champion, tells his story in *Breaking the Surface* (New York, 1995). Finally, French readers may profit from Pierre Jonqueres d'Oriola, *A Cheval sur cinq Olympiques* (Paris, 1969), a member of the French equestrian team in every Olympic Games between 1952 and 1968.

Nearly all the major biographies of Winter Games athletes focus on figure skating champions. A number of biographies have been published on Sonja Henie, gold medalist in the 1928, 1932, and 1936 Games, who later had an important film career. The most recent is Raymond Strait, *Queen of Ice, Queen of Shadow: The Unsuspected Life of Sonja Henie* (New York, 1985). Most of the later women's champions have been the subject of biographies. See Clay Moore, *She Skated into Our Hearts* (Toronto, 1948), on Barbara Ann Scott; Robert Parker, *Carol Heiss: Olympic Queen* (Garden City, N.Y., 1961); Dorothy Hamill, *Dorothy Hamill on and off the Ice* (New York, 1983); and Bernard Heimo, *Katarina Witt* (Altstatten, Germany, 1985). Men have not been so celebrated, but see Dick Button, *Dick Button on Skates* (London, 1956), and Keith Money, *John Curry* (New York, 1978). Finally, the speed skater Eric Heiden is the subject of Suzanne Munshower, *Eric Heiden: America's Olympic Golden Boy* (New York, 1980).

A few scholarly books and articles that deal with one sport at the Olympics have been published. Heiner Gillmeister, *Olympischen Tennis: Die Geschichte der olympischen tennisturniere (1896–1992)* (Augustin, Germany, 1993), describes the feud between the IOC and the Fédération internationale du lawn tennis over the use of "reamateurized" professionals in the 1920s that led to tennis being dropped from the Olympic program. In 1968, the International Skating Union published *The Olympic Games: Results in Figure Skating 1908, 1920, 1924–68; Results in Speed Skating 1924–1968* (n.p., 1968), whose title is self-explanatory. A National Rifle Association publication, Jim Crossman, *Olympic Shooting* (Washington, D.C., 1978), does much the same for that event. Jean Sonmor, *Burned by the Rock: Inside the World of Men's Championship Curling* (Toronto, 1991), deals with the history of Canadian curling but also includes information about the sport's reintroduction at the 1988 Calgary Games. Even more specialized is John D. Fair, "Olympic Weightlifting and the Introduction of Steroids: A Statistical Analysis of the World Championship Results, 1948–72," *International Journal of the History of Sport* 5, 1 (1988): 96–114, which concludes that steroids are not solely responsible for the record-breaking performances of recent years.

Still other books touch on miscellaneous aspects of the Olympic movement. Barclay F. Gordon, *Olympic Architecture: Building for the Summer Games* (New York, 1983), surveys the architecture and design utilized in Olympic venues, with separate chapters on the 1936 Games, and each of the Games from 1952 through 1980. The book is well illustrated with drawings and photographs. Giulio Andreotti, *Sport et arte* (Rome, 1960), surveys the art and architecture displayed at the 1960 Games in Rome. Takis Doxas, *Light of Olympia* (Athens, 1980), presents in several languages the poem "Light of Olympia," recited at each Games. Information on the medical side of Olympic sport may be found in A. Dirix, H. G. Knuttgen, and K. Tittel, *The Olympic Book of Sports Medicine* (Oxford, 1988).

Philatelists view the Olympic Games with special delight because many countries have issued commemorative stamps since 1896 honoring the Games. Among books that deal with Olympic stamps are Vsevolod Foorman, *Olympic Stamps* (Moscow, 1981), which treats stamps thematically rather than by Games or issuing country. An IOC publication, *Philatélique Olympique/Olympic Philately* (Barcelona, 1982?), also focuses on themes, while another IOC publication, *Postes, Philatelie et Olympisme/Post, Philately and Olympism* (Barcelona, 1984), includes a summary of stamps issued for each Games between 1896 and 1928, special Olympic postal markings, illustrated postcards and labels, as well as stamps and special postmarks commemorating IOC Congresses to 1930. Collectors may also wish to consult *Philatelie + Olympia* (Munich, 1972), published by Schwaneberger Verlag, which also publishes a stamp catalog for German collectors. This book is an anthology, with a number of illustrated articles on the various stamps and postmarks created for the 1972 Munich Games. Robert J. DuBois, *Catalog of Olympic Labels, 1894–1985* (Pottstown, Pa., 1986), deals with the stamplike commemorative labels that have been issued for most Games. Michele Menard, *Coins of the Modern Olympic Games* (Rockcliffe, Ontario, Canada, 1991), covers Olympic coins issued by host countries, often to raise funds. A projected second volume will treat coins issued by countries not hosting a Games. Mary A. Danaher, *The Commemorative Coinage of Modern Sports* (New York, 1978), focuses primarily on the many coins minted for the 1976 Montreal Games.

Journals and Organizations

A number of journals dedicated to sport studies frequently publish articles of interest to Olympic historians. Among them are the *Journal of Sport History,* the publication of the North American Society for Sport History (NASSH); *Stadion; Canadian Journal of the History of Sport; International Journal of the History of Sport;* and *Olympic Review,* the journal of the IOC. Special mention should be made of *Citius, Altus, Fortius,* the journal of the fledgling International Society of Olympic Historians (ISOH). Founded in 1991, ISOH is the only group dedicated solely to the study of Olympic history. Bill Mallon, a founder of ISOH, has compiled a list of Olympic-related dissertations and theses. For information about these or ISOH, write Mallon at 303 Sutherland Court, Durham, North Carolina 27712.

INDEX

Page numbers set in **bolface** indicate the location of the main entry.

ABOUT THE EDITORS AND CONTRIBUTORS

DONNA ADDKISON-SIMMONS, adjunct instructor of political science at Troy State, received her master's degree at Missippissi State University. She has published numerous articles and book reviews in scholarly publications. She has also been an active political consultant for many years.

MOHAMMED B. ALAM received his Ph.D. degree from Cornell University. Among his numerous publications are *India's Nuclear Policy* (1988) and *Aspects of American Government* (1994). He has taught history and political science at Midway College, Kentucky.

ANGELIKA ALTMANN is a doctoral candidate at the Geschwister-Scholl-Institut für Politische Wissenschaft der Universität München in Germany.

JOSEPH L. ARBENA is a professor of history at Clemson University. He has a Ph.D. from the University of Virginia, and has published on the aspects of sports across Latin America. His latest book is *An Annotated Bibliography of Latin American Sport* (1989). Currently, he is the editor of the *Journal of Sport History*. He believes that he is living proof that a sound mind does not require a sound body.

TIM ASHWELL teaches in the Sport Management Program at the University of Massachusetts in Amherst. A longtime sports broadcaster and journalist, he earned his Ph.D. in history at the University of Massachusetts in Amherst and studies the connections between political and popular culture in the twentieth century United States.

C. ROBERT BARNETT is a professor and chairman of the Division of Health, Physical Education and Recreation at Marshall University in Huntington, West

Virginia. He became interested in the 1904 Olympic Games when one of his students had difficulty researching the topic. He has subsequently published more than thirty articles and papers on those Games.

ROBERT K. BARNEY is a professor in the Faculty of Kinesiology at the University of Western Ontario, and is the director of the Center for Olympic Studies there. He is the editor of *Olympika*, and has written extensively on both the ancient and modern Games as well as Canadian sport, baseball, and the Turner movement.

MAYNARD BRICHFORD is university archivist at the University of Illinois in Urbana-Champaign. He prepared the finding aid for the Avery Brundage Collection and supervised its processing in the University Archives. He has presented ten papers on aspects of Brundage's career.

DOUGLAS BROWN is a doctoral student at the University of Western Ontario. His area of interest includes the Olympic Games and other large-scale events, such as the Canadian National Exhibition, within the larger cultural context of their times.

JAMES R. COATES, JR., is an energetic bundle of muscle mass. He was born in Annapolis, Maryland, and received his degrees from the University of Maryland. Presently, he is an assistant professor at North Carolina A&T State University. Married with two children, he loves listening to old soul music, dancing, lifting weights, and having fun. He's the little man with the big voice.

SCOTT A.G.M CRAWFORD is a Scottish-New Zealand professor of physical education at Eastern Illinois University where he teaches a graduate class, ''Sport, Culture and Film.'' In the summer of 1994, he received a National Endowment of the Humanities Fellowship (College Teachers) in Visual Anthropology at the University of California at Berkeley.

JOHN A. DALY is a professor at the University of South Australia and lectures on the History and Sociology of Sport and Australian History. He is the author of numerous books and articles including *Quest for Excellence* (1991). Dr. Daly has been associated with the Australian athletic team for twenty years as either head coach or manager, and he managed the national track and field team at the Barcelona Games—his fifth Olympics representing Australia. For his services to Australian sport, he was awarded the medal of the Order of Australia in 1991.

JOANNA DAVENPORT is a professor in the Health and Human Performance Department at Auburn University, Auburn, Alabama where she served as Women's Athletic Director from 1976–1985. A former member of the Education Council of the U.S. Olympic Committee (1977–1985), she has been three times an American delegate to the International Olympic Academy in Olympia, Greece, and one time to the Olympic Academy in Taiwan. A sport historian, she has written extensively on the Olympic Games and on women's sports and biography.

ERIC LESLIE DAVIES received his Ph.D. in modern European history at the State University of New York at Buffalo. His other interests include African studies, computers in history, and art history. He speaks several languages, including French, German, Russian, and some Swahili.

ROBERT DUNKELBERGER graduated from Bowling Green State University in Ohio and the University of Illinois at Urbana-Champaign. He works in the archives at the University of Illinois as an assistant archivist and conducts research on the history of college football, in addition to being a long-time fan of the Cincinnati Reds.

WILLIAM DURICK, while earning his doctorate at Penn State, worked closely with Olympic authority John Lucas and renowned sports historian Ron Smith. He has published a number of articles in scholarly journals including "The Gentlemen's Race: An Examination of the 1869 Harvard-Oxford Boat Race" in the *Journal of Sport History*. Durick teaches history at the secondary level and enjoys coaching track and football.

ASTRID ENGELBRECHT is a doctoral student in sport studies at Georg-August-Universität in Göttingen, Germany.

JOHN FEA is currently a Ph.D. candidate in history at the State University of New York at Stony Brook.

JAMEY J. FINDLING is a graduate student in philosophy at Villanova University. He spent a year studying at the University of Freiburg in Germany, is a devoted Grateful Dead fan, and the 1994 winner of the Chimay Cup.

JOHN E. FINDLING is a U.S. history professor at Indiana University Southeast. He has written and edited several books including *Historical Dictionary of World's Fairs and Expositions, 1851–1988* (1990); and with Frank W. Thackeray, *Statesmen Who Changed the World* (1993), *Events That Changed the World in the Twentieth Century* (1995), and *Events That Changed America in the Twentieth Century* (1996). When not working at his stamp store, he can usually be found combing local area flea markets in search of old license plates, or sipping perfectly made Manhattans prepared by his favorite bartender.

LINDA K. FULLER is an associate professor of communications at Worcester (MA) State College and an author or editor of more than a dozen books. She teaches sportscasting and monitors the baseball movie genre. She has published several articles on Olympic film, and is presently working on an illustrated history of Olympic films.

EDWARD S. GOLDSTEIN is a native of Denver, Colorado. He was a volunteer press aide with the Los Angeles Olympic Organizing Committee during the 1984

Summer Olympics. As a White House environmental policy aide from 1990–1993, he counts among his favorite memories meeting Kristi Yamaguchi before she won the gold medal in Albertville and became a cereal box icon.

ALLAN W. HALL is the assistant athletic director at Ashland University where he also teaches courses in the history and philosophy of physical education. Besides the Olympics, his research interests include the Akron Yankees, a minor league baseball team, and the history of women's sports at Ashland University.

DIETMAR HERZ is a lawyer and an assistant professor of the Geschwister-Scholl-Institute for Political Science at the University of Munich. He has published numerous articles and books including *Frieden durch Handel. Zur Aussenwirtschaftspolitik der Roosevelt Administration in der ersten Halfte der dreissiger Jahre* (1987).

ADAM R. HORNBUCKLE is a public historian and freelance writer living in Alexandria, Virginia. He holds a master's degree in history from the University of Tennessee and a master's degree in medical history and ethics from the University of Washington. He works for History Associates Incorporated in Rockville, Maryland.

MAX L. HOWELL is a professor in the Department of Human Movement Studies at the University of Queensland, St. Lucia, Queensland, Australia, and until her recent death, REET ANN HOWELL was an associate professor in the School of Human Movement Studies at Queensland University of Technology, Kelvin Grove, Queensland, Australia. Together the Howells published numerous articles and books on sport history, including *A History of Australian Sport* (1987) and *Aussie Gold: The Story of Australia at the Olympics* (1988).

IAN JOBLING is an associate professor in sport history and director of the Center for Physical Activity and Sport Education in the Department of Human Movement Studies at the University of Queensland, Australia. He was the inaugural chair of both the Oceania Olympic Academy in Australia and the Education Commission of the Australian Olympic Federation. He is a member of the editorial review board of *Olympika—International Journal of Olympic Studies* and the president and a member of the editorial review board of *Sporting Traditions—Journal of the Australian Society for Sports History.*

JOHN J. KENNEDY, JR., is a doctoral student in history at Temple University, focussing on the environmental history of colonial America. He has done research on the Rocky Flats nuclear weapons plant in Colorado, on Denver's attempt to secure the 1976 Winter Games, and on the USOC's procedures in selecting a site to put forward for the 1998 Winter Games.

BRUCE KIDD wanted to be a professional hockey player, until his father brought home inspiring film footage and stories from the 1952 Olympics in Helsinki (where he was the entire Canadian Broadcasting Corporation TV production team) and turned his athletic interests completely around. Kidd has followed the Olympics ever since.

MICHELE LELLOUCHE is an employee benefits attorney, with a law degree and a master's degree in history from Florida State University. When not working at becoming the next Scott Turow, she is a very amateur figure skater.

KARL LENNARTZ is the director of the Carl and Liselott Diem-Archive at the Deutsche Sporthochschule Köln in Köln (Cologne), Germany. He is the author of *Die VI. Olympischen Spiele Berlin 1916* (Cologne, 1978); *Die Geschichte des Deutschen Reichsausschusses fur Olympisches Spiele*, 3 vols. (Bonn, 1981–85), and with Walter Teutenberg, *Die Olympischen Spiele 1906 in Athens* (Kassel, 1992), as well as other books and articles on the Olympic movement.

GORDON MacDONALD is a doctoral student at the University of Western Ontario. He has done research in a number of Olympic-related topics, including the history of the Canadian Olympic Committee and the conflict over German representation in the IOC after World War II.

LARRY MALONEY attributes a life-long fascination with the Olympic movement to his quest for a master's degree in International Service from the American University. He has attended the Olympic Games in Los Angeles and Barcelona, as well as the brutally cold Games in Lillehammer. He resides in Washington, D.C.

MARTIN J. MANNING was born and raised in Boston, Massachusetts, a city which has never hosted an Olympics. He has degrees from Boston College and from Catholic University. He is presently archivist for the United States Information Agency, Washington, DC, and curator of its historical collection, which includes records of the Agency's involvement in sports exchanges. He has contributed entries to the *Dictionary of American Biography* and to the *American National Biography;* wrote the entry on the Osaka, Japan, 1970 exposition for the *Historical Dictionary of World's Fairs and Expositions, 1851–1988;* and is presently working on a book on American propaganda for Greenwood Press.

KATHY NICHOLS received her master's degree in public history from Indiana University-Purdue University in Indianapolis. She was assistant editor on a book-length project involving the editing of physics texts used in colonial America and has studied rural-urban migration in Kentucky. She bakes wedding cakes in her spare time.

RON PALENSKI is one of New Zealand's most experienced sports journalists. He has written several sports books including *The Games* (1983), an analysis of New Zealand's history in the Olympic movement. He was also one of the invited media speakers at the Centenary Congress of the International Olympic Committee in Paris in 1994.

JERRY A. PATTENGALE is associate director of the Scriptorium Center for

Christian Antiquities in Grand Haven, Michigan. He contributed to *Events That Changed America in the Twentieth Century* (1996), edited by John E. Findling and Frank W. Thackeray, and formerly taught at Azusa Pacific University, Azusa, California.

KIMBERLY D. PELLE earned degrees in journalism and political science from Indiana University Southeast. She was the assistant editor of *Historical Dictionary of World's Fairs and Expositions* (1990). When not wielding her blue editing pencil or taking her three children to endless music lessons, she seeks to build the perfect Manhattan in her job as a bartender.

CURTIS H. PETERS is professor of philosophy at Indiana University Southeast. He is the author of several articles and books on continental philosophy, most recently *Kant's Philosophy of Hope* (1994). He has directed overseas study programs in Germany and the former Soviet Union.

STEPHANIE L. PETERS is a doctoral student in Russian literature at the University of Michigan, completing a dissertation on the Russian poet, Feodor Sologub. She has studied in Germany, Russia, and Poland, and has taught German at Indiana University Southeast and the University of Michigan.

DORIS PIEROTH is an independent historian in Seattle working in Northwest regional history. A foray into Washington State aquatic history led to her book on the 1932 Olympic women, and provided her with the "unforgettable bonus of talking with eleven of those marvelous people." She received her doctorate from the University of Washington.

ROLAND RENSON was born in Sint-Truiden in occupied Belgium in 1943 and liberated one year later by the U.S. Army. He studied physical education, physical therapy, and social anthropology in Leuven. He is a professor at K. U. Leuven on the Faculty of Physical Education and Physical Therapy where he teaches sport history, comparative physical education and sociocultural aspects of sports and games. He has been president of the international sport history association (ISHPES).

JAMES RIORDAN is presently chairman of Russian Studies in the Department of Linguistic and International Studies at the University of Surrey, Guildford, England. He has traveled extensively in the Soviet Union and attended the Moscow Olympics. He is the author of several books, including *Sport and Soviet Society* (1977), *Soviet Sport* (1980), and *Sport, Politics and Communism* (1991).

SWANTJE SCHARENBERG is a scientific assistant for the Department of Sports Sciences at the University in Göttingen in Germany. During her study of sports, journalism and ethnology, she started to work as a journalist for various newspapers. She is currently coaching and judging gymnastics. She likes photography, writing, and getting in touch with people all over the world.

UTE SCHWABE is currently a fellow at Harvard University, doing research on

U.S. relations with Israel for her Ph.D. dissertation at the University of Munich. She has also studied the United Nations and published an article on model United Nations for high school and college students in *Vereinigen Nationen,* a German journal.

DONALD C. SIMMONS, JR., is an assistant professor of history and political science at Troy State University where he is currently serving as director of the University Honors Program. He is also the co-editor of *Latin America and the Caribbean in Transition* (1994). Simmons received his Ph.D. from the University of Denver.

JON W. STAUFF, assistant professor of history at St. Ambrose University, Davenport, Iowa, recently completed a dissertation on German sport and political culture during the 1920s and 1930s. He intends to conduct further research in this time period as well as extending his studies to the post–World War II era.

HORST UEBERHORST, born in Bochum, Germany, studied physical education, history, and German at Bonn after the war. His career consists of many prestigious positions, several awards, and the publication of more than twenty books concerning Germany and international problems and contemporary history. He is currently editor of a seven-volume work on the history of world sports.

RICHARD A. VOELTZ is an associate professor of history at Cameron University in Oklahoma. He is the author of *German Colonialism and the South West Africa Company* (1988), and has published articles and reviews in numerous journals, including the *Journal of Sport History.*

K. B. WAMSLEY is an assistant professor in the Faculty of Physical Education at the University of Calgary. He received his Ph.D. in 1992 from the University of Alberta. His research interests include leisure, sport, cultural activities, the state of nineteenth century Canada, hegemony, gender construction, and international sport festivals. He has published articles in *Social History* and the *Canadian Journal of History of Sport,* and has recently edited a book on research methods in sport and cultural history.

ROBERT P. WATSON teaches government at Northern Arizona University and is the author of numerous articles on topics such as environmental protection, bureaucracy, women in politics, and U.S. foreign aid. He is the co-editor of *Latin America and the Caribbean in Transition,* and is presently working on a book on human rights.

PAULA D. WELCH is professor of Excercise and Sport Sciences at the University of Florida in Gainesville. She is a sport history researcher and vice-chair of the Education Committee of the United States Olympic Committee.

WAYNE WILSON is director of Research and Library Services for the Amateur

Athletic Foundation library in Los Angeles. He received his Ph.D. in sport studies at the University of Massachusetts and has published and edited several
articles on sports culture.

DWIGHT H. ZAKUS holds a joint appointment in the Faculty of Physical
Activity Studies and the Department of Sociology and Social Studies at the
University of Regina. Other than an academic interest in the Olympic movement,
he enjoys cross-disciplinary studies in all aspects of human movement. This
supports claims of his eclectic nature and interests.